6 31

Modern Dance in America: The Bennington Years

Hanya Holm Dancers at Bennington, 1937. Left to right: Elizabeth Waters, Lucretia Wilson, Louise Kloepper. Photograph courtesy of Eve Gentry.

Modern Dance in America: The Bennington Years

Sali Ann Kriegsman

G.K. Hall & Co., 70 Lincoln Street, Boston, Massachusetts

Library of Congress Cataloging in Publication Data

Kriegsman, Sali Ann.
Modern dance in America–the Bennington years.

Bibliography: p.
Includes indexes.
1. Bennington School of the Dance–History.
2. Modern dance. I. Title.
GV1786.B38K74 793.3'2'097438 81-13332
ISBN 0-8161-8528-X AACR2

This publication is printed on permanent/durable acid-free paper.
MANUFACTURED IN THE UNITED STATES OF AMERICA

Grateful acknowledgment is made to the following for permission to quote from the materials cited:

The American Scholar. John Martin, "The Dance Completes a Cycle." Reprinted from volume 12, number 2, Spring 1943. Copyright © 1943 by the United Chapters of Phi Beta Kappa. By permission of the publishers.

Dance Magazine. Excerpts from articles and reviews in *Dance Magazine* (December 1930, June 1943), *American Dancer* (October 1935, October 1938), and *Dance* (October 1936, March 1937, July 1938, October 1938, November 1938, April 1939, October 1941). Reprinted courtesy of *Dance Magazine*.

Dance Scope. Excerpts from volume 2, number 2, © 1966 National Dance Teachers Guild, Inc., and volume 8, number 2, © 1974 American Dance Guild, Inc. Reprinted by permission of *Dance Scope*.

International Herald Tribune. Excerpts from articles and reviews 1934, 1935, 1940, 1941, 1942 in *The New York Herald Tribune*.

Modern Music. Excerpts from 1937–1942. Reprinted by permission of the League of Composers-International Society for Contemporary Music, U.S. Section, Inc.

The Nation. Excerpts from Hubert Herring, "Bennington," 6 December 1933, © 1933; Paul Love, "New Forms of the Dance," 12 June 1937, © 1937; Paul Love, "Bennington Festival," 28 August 1937, © 1937; Lincoln Kirstein, "Martha Graham at Bennington," 3 September 1938, © 1938; Sherman Conrad, "Bennington Festival," 24 August 1940 and 30 August 1941, © 1940, © 1941. All copyrights The Nation Associates.

Newsweek. Excerpt from "Dance, pantomime and music in Bennington," 22 August 1936. Copyright 1936 by Newsweek, Inc. All rights reserved. Reprinted by permission.

The New York Times. Excerpts from John Martin's columns and reviews. © 1934/35/36/37/38/39/40/41/42/53 by The New York Times Company. Reprinted by permission.

The New Yorker. Excerpts from Angelica Gibbs, "The Absolute Frontier," 27 December 1947.

Time. Excerpt from "Intellectual Dance," 26 August 1940. Reprinted by permission from *TIME, The Weekly Newsmagazine*; Copyright Time Inc. 1940.

Current Biography. Excerpt from September 1971 biography of Jean Erdman. From *Current Biography Yearbook, 1971*, copyright © 1971 by the H. W. Wilson Company.

Harper & Row. Excerpts from Ruth St. Denis, *An Unfinished Life*, 1939, and Barbara Jones, *Bennington College: The Development of an Educational Idea*, 1946.

Holt, Rinehart and Winston. Excerpts from *Martha Graham: A Biography* by Don McDonagh. © 1973 by Praeger Publishers, Inc. Reprinted by permission of Praeger Publishers, Inc., a Division of Holt, Rinehart and Winston.

Alfred A. Knopf, Inc. Excerpt from Lincoln Kirstein, Lynes Platt, and George and Martha Swope, *The New York City Ballet*, Copyright © 1973 by Alfred A. Knopf, Inc.

Random House. Excerpts from Harold Clurman, *The Fervent Years: The Story of the Group Theatre and the Thirties*. Copyright © 1945, 1957 by Harold Clurman.

Wesleyan University Press. Excerpts from Selma Jeanne Cohen, *Doris Humphrey: An Artist First*, 1972. Copyright © by Selma Jeanne Cohen. By permission of the publisher. Excerpts from Walter Sorell, *Hanya Holm, The Biography of an Artist*. Copyright © 1969 by Wesleyan University.

For Mike—at last

CONTENTS

PREFACE xi

INTRODUCTION 1

HISTORY: *Background and Themes* 5

Background to Bennington 5
The School of the Dance, 1934-1938 11
The School of the Dance at Mills College, 1939 18
The School of the Arts, 1940-1941 19
The End of the Summer Dance Program 22
Reflections on Bennington 26

CHRONOLOGY: *The Summer Sessions* 39

1934 41
1935 46
1936 53
1937 63
1938 74
1939 82
1940 93
1941 103
1942 116

CATALOG: *Bennington Premieres* 125

Sinister Resonance 127
New Dance 127
Panorama 131
With My Red Fires 139
Quest: A Choreographic Pantomime 147
Opening Dance 154
Immediate Tragedy–Dance of Dedication 154
Dance to the People 156
Ravage 156
Festive Rites 156
Danza de la Muerte 158

Façade-Esposizione Italiana 159
Opus for Three and Props 160
Trend: A Dance in Two Sections 161
Ode to Freedom 176
"Bonja Song" from *American Folk Suite* 177
Romantic Theme 177
Statement of Dissent 177
Earth Saga 178
Out of One Happening 179
Passacaglia in C minor 180
Dance of Work and Play 184
Dance Sonata 186
Opus 51 188
American Document 191
Ceremonial Dance 202
The Spirit of the Land Moves in the Blood 202
Danzas Mexicanas 202
Liberty Tree–A Set of Four Dances 204
Insubstantial Pageant–A Dance of Experience 204
Yankee Bluebritches–A Vermont Fantasy 204
El Penitente (The Penitent) 205
Letter to the World 208
In Time of Armament 216
Decade: A Biography of Modern Dance from 1930 to 1940 216
Punch and The Judy 221
Seeds of Brightness 227
Credo in Us 227
Renaissance Testimonials 227
The Transformations of Medusa 228
Ad Lib 228
"Scherzo" and "Loure" from *Suite* 230

CURRICULUM: *Courses and Faculty* 231

School of the Dance: 1934 231
School of the Dance: 1935 233
School of the Dance: 1936 234
School of the Dance: 1937 237
School of the Dance: 1938 240
School of the Dance at Mills College: 1939 242
School of the Arts, Dance Division: 1940 244
School of the Arts, Dance Division: 1941 245
Bennington College Summer Session–Dance: 1942 246

IMPRESSIONS: *A Bennington Album* 249

Looking Back: Four Points of View 249
Bessie Schönberg 250
Alwin Nikolais 252
Merce Cunningham 256
Erick Hawkins 259
Images and Voices 263
Hanya Holm, Anna Sokolow, Ben Belitt, Walter Terry, John Martin, George Beiswanger, Anna Halprin, Beatrice Seckler, Mark Ryder, May O'Donnell, Jean Erdman,

Ethel Butler, Sybil Shearer, Eve Gentry, Louise Kloepper, Esther Junger Klempner, Charles Weidman, Betty Ford, Otto Luening, Joseph Campbell
Selected Readings 277
Contemporary Exponents of the Dance, by Barbara Page 277
The Dance and Today's Needs, by George W. Beiswanger 280
New Dance, by Doris Humphrey 284
Artists and Audiences, by Charles Weidman 287
Declaration, by Doris Humphrey 287
The Future of the Dance, by Martha Graham 288
The Dance Completes a Cycle, by John Martin 288

SOURCES: 291
Archives and Special Collections 292
Research Tools 292
Written Accounts 293
Interviews 303
Visual Records (Photographs, Films, Videotapes) and Scores 305

APPENDIX A: *Brief Biographies of Bennington Figures* 315

APPENDIX B: *Background to Bennington: A Timetable* 327

APPENDIX C: *Bennington Credits* 333
Bennington Premieres, by Choreographer 333
Musical Scores Written for Dance Premieres 336
Student Compositions and Dance Projects 338
Faculty, Associate Faculty, and Courses Taught 338
Teaching Assistants 342
Guest Lecturers 343
Advisory Board and Trustee Committee 344

TITLE INDEX 345

NAME INDEX 349

PREFACE

The history of the Bennington School of the Dance is the story of an emerging American art in a time of shattered assumptions. Modern dance was in search of definition and values and was struggling to secure a base of support in a society recovering from catastrophic economic depression and headed for global war. Modern dance came of age in the Bennington years, but its rites of passage at Bennington have received scant treatment in dance histories.

This book is a documentary history of the Bennington School of the Dance, 1934-1942. It tells how and why the school was established and how it functioned, who was involved with it and what was taught there, what works were created and what was recorded and written about them. It traces the careers of artists associated with Bennington and catalogs the dances that were produced there, most of which have not survived in performance. It is both map and collective memoir compiled by interweaving contemporary records and accounts with retrospective views.

The Bennington school was by no means the whole of modern dance in America at that time, but it was a central force and influence. The Bennington enterprise can thus serve as a prism through which the configuration of modern dance in its developmental phase can be seen. This first history of Bennington is meant to serve as a resource for further studies of modern dance in America.

I first became conscious of Bennington's crucial role in modern dance history while I was associated with American Dance Theater (ADT), a modern dance repertory company that was attempting to become established as a constituent of Lincoln Center. Among ADT's goals was the restoration of "classics" of modern dance. One of the dances the company had revived had Bennington roots—Doris Humphrey's *Passacaglia in C minor*. As a corollary to the reconstruction of historic repertory, I proposed that ADT develop a *catalog raisonné* of modern dances, as there was—and is—no such tool. When ADT collapsed in 1966, the catalog project was left on the drawing board without institutional sponsorship. In the course of investigating the choreographic histories of modern dancers, I had seen the dim outline of Bennington emerge as a persistent but elusive nexus.

Like Denishawn in the twenties, Black Mountain in the fifties, and Judson in the sixties, Bennington had engendered a mystique as a fount of artistic experimentation and collaboration. The mention of Bennington prompted wistful panegyrics from those who had been there and veneration from younger dancers. I wanted to penetrate Bennington's aura to discover precisely what had occurred there and what it was that accounted for its enduring reputation. I was frustrated by the lack of available information and fearful that Bennington's true history might prove as irretrievable as the works that had been spawned there—only three dances had survived in repertory into the mid-sixties.

I suppose my curiosity was aroused by the creative ferment in the dance of the mid-sixties, and the shift away from earlier modern dance models. The old ways—some of them Bennington ways—were being challenged by a young group of mavericks. The old guard discounted these recent experiments as nothing new, pointing out that they had done and discarded such experimentation decades earlier, at Bennington. It seemed to me the right moment—while many of the principal figures were still alive—to try to reconstruct the history of those early years. There was some urgency too: Doris Humphrey, Arch Lauterer, and Louis Horst were already lost to a Bennington history, and Helen Tamiris died in 1966.

When I first began work on the Bennington period in 1967, the major published accounts of the school were those contributed by critics John Martin and Margaret Lloyd in their books *America Dancing* and *The Borzoi Book of Modern Dance*. There were as yet no biographies of Martha Graham, Doris Humphrey, Hanya Holm, Helen Tamiris, or Lester Horton (there still is none of Charles Weidman or Louis Horst), among the senior pioneers, or complete listings of their works.

When I learned that cartons of documents were housed at Bennington College, apparently untouched in the quarter-century since the project's end, I wrote to William Bales, who was in charge of the college dance program, volunteering to catalog the documents and stating that my goal was to write a chronicle of the modern dance movement at Bennington. I visited the Bennington campus in the autumn of 1967 and, with permission from President Jacob Bloustein, arranged to have the documents transferred temporarily to the Dance Collection of the New York Public Library. There, I assembled a master set of original records from material in the Bennington cartons and from sources I had uncovered within the Dance Collection and Circulating Division of the library.

The Dance Collection was the main repository of Bennington-related materials, including books, newspaper and magazine articles, manuscript and scrapbook collections, photographs, programs, audio tapes, sketches, and films. The Louis Horst Scrapbooks documented Martha Graham's work in these years. Some important material emerged from a cursory search of the Doris Humphrey Manuscript Collection which had just been deposited but was not cataloged. The New York Scrapbooks (dance and music reviews from New York newspapers) contained articles and reviews that were not found in the scrapbooks of individual dancers. *Dance Observer*, a monthly periodical devoted to modern dance that began its life the same year as the Bennington program, was an invaluable source for premieres.

The set of original documents was preserved on microfilm at the Dance Collection and a copy was provided Bennington College. I compiled a rough list of premieres and prepared to begin a series of interviews with Bennington figures. At that point, however, William Bales informed me that Martha Hill and Mary Jo Shelly, the project's original co-directors, were planning to write a history of Bennington and he proposed that I abandon my plans. Attempts to pursue my work independently failed, and I reluctantly put aside my research and preliminary chronology in 1968.

In 1976 Mary Ann Liebert, Vice President of Marcel Dekker, Inc., publishers, asked me to resume work on Bennington for Dekker's new dance book series. The commitment of a publisher seemed a key factor in assuring that the project could be completed. Several major figures in Bennington's history had died in the years since I had begun my research—among them Pauline Lawrence, José Limón, and Charles Weidman, followed in 1976 by Mary Jo Shelly. It seemed imperative to try to capture the recollections of others in the Bennington group while it was still possible. Martha Hill had not produced her book, though she stated that she intended to do so. I reasoned that even if she carried out her intentions, it seemed likely that her book would be a personal memoir, an insider's account, while mine was to be written from an outsider's perspective. Both seemed important and, indeed, complementary projects. If I passed up this opportunity and Martha Hill did not succeed in producing her book, the field would be left with neither. I agreed to resume work on my Bennington chronicle.

Ten years had given me fresh perspective and additional editorial, writing, and research experience. I began anew in 1976, surveying collections I had looked into years before that had since been augmented or cataloged. The Doris Humphrey Collection, for example, was now meticulously organized and yielded letters and manuscripts that were not accessible earlier. Bennington sources had multiplied: new collections of scrapbooks, manuscripts and photographs had come into the Dance Collection, oral history interviews with choreographers and teachers had been initiated, dances from the Bennington period had been reconstructed and filmed, biographies and dissertations had been published. All of this ground had to be explored.

The chronology that I had prepared in 1968 served as the starting point for the present book. As I discovered new sources and began interviewing Bennington participants and observers, the dimensions of the book's outline expanded.

In 1977 I revisited the Bennington College archive to study documents concerning the relationship of the school to the college (the Bennington School of the Dance and the dance department of Bennington College employed a common physical plant and some of the same faculty, but they functioned independently and with different goals). These shed light on the selection of artists and faculty, problems and tensions during the project's life, reasons for its termination, and the economics of this early model of arts patronage and support.

Interviews with Bennington figures and with observers centered on their assessment of the project's impact on their lives and careers and on Bennington's role in the ascent of the modern dance, as well as on their own specific involvement with Bennington. Their recollections and views helped fill in missing details of the Bennington profile, especially descriptive and factual information about the dances that were created.

In 1978 Martha Hill agreed to clarify a few questions of fact put to her in writing, but she declined to be interviewed or to write a statement for this book. Although the book lacks Martha Hill's present-day view of her Bennington experience, it draws substantively on the accounts that she and Mary Jo Shelly prepared following each session, and on other documents that reflect Hill's and Shelly's goals and philosophy at the time.

Martha Graham would not consent to an interview, and I was not able to study documents, photographs, and films in her possession. Some potentially important material acquired by the Dance Collection in the late 1970s could not be examined because it had not yet been cataloged, including the Charles Weidman, José Limón, and Pauline Lawrence-José Limón collections.

I regret any inadvertent omissions and sins of comission as well, and I apologize for errors that may have crept into my research. I welcome corrections and additions to this record.

In 1979 Marcel Dekker suspended its dance book series. Responsibility for publishing my manuscript was transferred to G. K. Hall in mid-1980. Some important new sources have emerged in the three years since I completed my manuscript and I have added some of these to the sources section, including a listing of oral history interviews conducted under a grant from the National Endowment for the Humanities awarded to Bennington College in 1978, after my manuscript was completed (these transcripts and tapes are closed to scholars until publication of Martha Hill's book).

The course of this project has been interrupted several times; it has been turbulent and unduly attenuated. I could not have hoped to complete it without assistance from dozens of individuals and institutions.

I am first of all deeply in the debt of dancers, choreographers, critics, historians, musicians, teachers, designers, theater people—and their relatives and heirs—who responded to my letters and calls, granted interviews, and shared their memories, scrapbooks, and ideas about Bennington with me. They are witnesses to the vitality of the Bennington experiment, and in a true sense this is their book. They are all cited individually in the pages that follow. I want especially to thank Merce Cunningham, Erick Hawkins, Alwin Nikolais, and Bessie Schönberg for allowing me to quote at length from our interviews.

I owe a special debt of gratitude to George and Barbara Beiswanger, John Martin, and Walter Terry, who not only gave fully of their writings, recollections, and views but also put me in touch with many others who could help fill in the picture. I thank all of the individuals and publications whose names are to be found in the notes and sources as contributors of quotes and excerpts to this history. Special appreciation is due John Sloper for his help in allowing me to quote from Margaret Lloyd's writings in the *Christian Science Monitor* and *The Borzoi Book of Modern Dance*, to Ralph Taylor and Louis Himber for articles and photographs from *Dance Observer*, to Rosamond Gilder for articles, excerpts, and illustrations from *Theatre Arts* and *Theatre Arts Monthly*, to Marian Van Tuyl for material from *Impulse*, and to Joseph Campbell, Edwin Denby, Jean Erdman, Maxine Cushing Gray, Hanya Holm, Eleanor King, Lincoln Kirstein, Winthrop Palmer, and Christena Schlundt for permission to quote from their published writings.

Charles Humphrey Woodford granted use of letters and manuscripts in the Doris Humphrey Collection. Henry Kurth provided designs, letters, and manuscripts from the Arch Lauterer Archives, Cleveland. Linda Mann Reed located uncataloged papers and films and contributed information about reconstructions and revivals of Charles Weidman's dances. Eleanor Lauer sent documentation of the dance program at Mills College. Muriel Topaz made material in the Dance Notation Bureau files available. Charles Reinhart and Brian Rogers opened the Connecticut College-American Dance Festival archive and files to me.

A half-dozen Bennington films are now preserved and available to researchers. Special thanks are due Ann Hutchinson Guest, who carried Zelia Raye's Bennington films across the Atlantic so that I could see them and arrange for their safe keeping. Agnes de Mille helped me locate Ralph Jester so that I could secure his Bennington documentary; it has been preserved with the able assistance of Audrey Kupferberg at the American Film Institute Archives. Betty Lynd Thompson unearthed her home movies taken at Bennington and sent them on from Oregon. Suzanne Weil at the National Endowment for the Arts helped me arrange to preserve the material, and David Parker at the Library of Congress Motion Picture Section lent expert technical assistance.

Aline Fruhauf, who created delightful caricatures and impressions of dancers of the time, made her drawings available. I regret that she did not live to see them in print again.

Ruth Alexander, Sidney Bernstein, Herbert Binzer, Thomas Bouchard, Eve Gentry, Ray Green, Ann Hutchinson Guest, Donald Hatfield, Esther Junger Klempner, Henry Kurth, Eleanor Lauer, Tina Flade Mooney, Barbara Morgan, Alwin Nikolais, Nona Schurman, Anna Sokolow, and Betty Lynd Thompson supplied rare photographs. David Thaxton helped prepare illustrative material for publication. Ethel Butler, Joan Levy, Linda Mann Reed, and Andrew Wentink helped identify dancers and establish dates.

Genevieve Oswald and her staff at the Dance Collection, New York Public Library, were immensely important—especially Barbara Goldberg Palfy and Robert Dunn in the early phase and Andrew Wentink later on.

Josef Wittman assisted me with the Bennington documents in 1967, and Alex Brown and Rebecca Stickney supplied photographs from the college files in 1978.

Diana Theodores Taplin revived my interest in the project in 1974 when we attempted, unsuccessfully, to carry it on together. Don McDonagh's use of my early compilation of Bennington documentation for his biography of Martha Graham enhanced my sense of the potential value of the project to scholars.

This book owes its genesis to Al Pischl of Dance Horizons who set me on the road to Bennington and provided advice and sympathy along the way, and to Mary Ann Liebert whose intrepid commitment and zeal made it possible for me to expand my study and complete the manuscript, against all odds. Donna Sanzone and Janice Meagher at G. K. Hall are responsible for seeing this manuscript into print—a not inconsiderable achievement considering the course of events.

Suzanne Levy devoted months of her time and boundless energy working with me in the final research and manuscript stages. I could have had no more intelligent or conscientious assistance. Deborah Stephens was a great help with proofreading.

Barbara Ribakove, Richard Lorber, and Vicki Cohn made perceptive suggestions about the manuscript. Michael Sims at G. K. Hall was clear-headed about its final form and offered a fresh prespective.

From the outset an during the most uncertain times, my husband Alan (Mike) kept his faith, understanding, and unwavering support—and my spirits—high.

INTRODUCTION

In 1934 the Bennington School of the Dance began an audacious experiment in Vermont's Green Mountains, one that brought together in common cause most of the prominent figures and viewpoints in the burgeoning young world of the modern dance.

The enterprise was designed to consolidate and propagate the new art as it was coming of age. Although the school was initially conceived as a training ground for dancers and teachers of the dance–the first center devoted wholly to the study of the modern dance–it quickly became as well a haven for the leading artists of the day; a laboratory for experienced and neophyte choreographers; a major production center that drew informed audiences and critics to programs of new works; a tryout site that made revisions possible before New York premieres; and an arena for experiment in which the sister arts of music, drama, design, and poetry were assembled in the service of the dance.

A project of this dimension had never before been attempted. To a remarkable degree, the school succeeded in its complex endeavors during nine brief summer sessions, eight of them on the Bennington College campus and one at Mills College in Oakland, California.

The school's three founders were its director, Martha Hill, who taught dance concurrently at Bennington College and New York University; its administrative director, Mary Josephine Shelly, administrator and physical education teacher at New College, an experimental school within Columbia University Teachers College; and the first president of Bennington College, Robert Devore Leigh.

Heading the first faculty of the Bennington School of the Dance were four artist-teachers of established reputation: Martha Graham, Doris Humphrey, Charles Weidman, and Hanya Holm. "The Big Four," as they were called, scaled heights of creativity in the Bennington years. At the same time they struggled with the difficulties of trying to produce dances without means, finding theaters in which to mount them, attracting audiences, and keeping their dancers together without money to pay them. There was no subsidy of any kind for the modern dance at this time– private or public.

Bennington offered a few weeks respite from these concerns. The Big Four and their dance groups were housed and fed for periods of uninterrupted creative work made more stimulating and attractive by the availability of apprentice dancers, and of designers and composers. During these brief summer residencies, a strong new modern dance repertory was brought into being.

Forty-two dances had their premieres at Bennington during the project's lifetime. Six Bennington Festivals 1935-1938; 1940, 1941) featured new works, including 16 dances composed by the Big Four: Martha Graham's *Panorama, Opening Dance, Immediate Tragedy, American Document, El Penitente, Letter to the World,* and *Punch and The Judy*; Doris Humphrey's *New Dance, With My Red Fires, Passacaglia in C minor*, and *Decade*; Charles Weidman's *Quest* and *Opus 51*; and Hanya Holm's *Trend, Dance Sonata,* and *Dance of Work and Play*.

In addition to the Big Four, the school's original faculty was composed of Louis Horst, music director for Martha Graham and pioneer teacher of dance composition; John Martin, first dance critic of the *New York Times* and champion of the modern dance; Gregory Tucker, pianist and composer on the Bennington College faculty; Bessie Schönberg, Martha Hill's student and assistant; and Hill herself. Later, the faculty was expanded to include, among others, theater designer Arch Lauterer, drama specialist Louise Martin, musicians Norman Lloyd and Franziska Boas, poet Ben Belitt, and teaching associates of the Big Four.

Original music was a prominent Bennington feature—of the 42 major premieres, only 5 used pre-composed scores. Among the composers in residence were Vivian Fine, Ray Green, Louis Horst, Hunter Johnson, Norman Lloyd, Harrison Kerr, Alex North, Robert McBride, Jerome Moross, Lionel Nowak, Harvey Pollins, Wallingford Riegger, Gregory Tucker, and Esther Williamson [Ballou].

The school also nourished new talent. In 1937 and 1938 six young choreographers—Anna Sokolow, José Limón, Esther Junger, Eleanor King, Louise Kloepper, and Marian Van Tuyl—were given Bennington fellowships to create original works during a summer's residency.

There were a few significant omissions, dancers of recognized stature (such as Agnes de Mille, Pauline Koner, Lester Horton, and, most conspicuously perhaps, Helen Tamiris) who remained outside the Bennington group. On the whole, however, the student and faculty rosters embraced not only the leading generation of modern dancers, teachers, and disciples, but also those who would succeed them.

Among the young dancers and choreographers were William Bales, George Bockman, Merce [Mercier] Cunningham, Eva Desca, Jane Dudley, Jean Erdman, Nina Fonaroff, Eleanor Frampton, Gloria Garcia, Eve Gentry [Henrietta Greenhood] Joseph Gifford [Gornbein], Harriette Ann Gray, Anna Halprin [Ann Schuman], Erick Hawkins, Ann Hutchinson, Pearl Lang [Lack], Welland Lathrop, Katherine Litz, Iris Mabry, Marjorie Mazia, Barbara Mettler, Alwin Nikolais, Harriet Roeder, Mark Ryder [Sasha Liebich], Nona Schurman, Mary-Averett Seelye, Sybil Shearer, Bernice van Gelder, Martha Wilcox, and one Elizabeth Bloomer, who later became First Lady, Mrs. Gerald R. Ford.

The student body (a total of approximately 1000 in 9 summers, from every state in the union and more than a few foreign countries) included both amateur and professional dancers. But the majority of students were themselves teachers—private studio instructors, secondary and college level teachers, heads of university physical education programs, and even a sprinkling of ballet teachers (for example, Muriel Stuart and Mary Ann Wells).

Among the prominent dance eduators enrolled as students were Ruth Alexander, Helen Alkire, Fannie Aronson, Ruth Bloomer (who later codirected the summer dance project at Connecticut College), Alma Hawkins, Delia Hussey, Truda Kaschmann, Marian Knighton [Bryan], Eleanor Lauer, Gertrude Lippincott, Virginia Moomaw, Claudia Moore, Ruth Murray, Barbara Page [Beiswanger], Esther Pease, Helen Priest [Rogers], Carmen Rooker, Virginia Tanner, Betty Lynd Thompson, Theodora Wiesner, and Mildred Wile.

The Bennington faculty, though diverse in outlook and temperament, shared the need to build a larger, more knowledgeable audience. From the Bennington crucible, the modern dance spread to every corner of America in a widening circle of influence far greater than numbers of first-hand participants would suggest. Inspired at the source, teachers who had enrolled as students at Bennington returned to their own classes infused with the experience and began to book engagements on their home campuses for Graham, Humphrey-Weidman, Holm, and others. Beginning in 1935 modern dance groups embarked on transcontinental tours, taking their Bennington repertory with them. The School of the Dance was catalyst for a network of entrepreneurial contacts, which came to be known as "the gymnasium circuit" (though curiously enough Bennington itself had no gym). The effect of centering the modern dance movement at Bennington was to decentralize the dance nationally, through the dispersion of Bennington alumni.

The project survived less than a decade, ending in the early years of World War II. But it was a harbinger of such enterprises as the Connecticut College School of the Dance and American Dance Festival (which six years later resumed where Bennington had left off), the Juilliard dance department, and dance residency programs devised by the Rockefeller Foundation and the National Endowment for the Arts.

The Bennington experiment clearly was shaped and colored by the Great Depression, a profoundly dark but resurgent period in America's history. The Bennington years were characterized by an uncommon sense of commitment and serious purpose, a passion for experimentation, and a desire for growth. Despite internal rivalries, the forces gathered at Bennington gave the modern dance movement impetus and coherence. Bennington's impact on the world of the dance was immediate and deep, and its influence was felt into the next generations.

Modern Dance in America: The Bennington Years

Background and Themes

Robert Leigh and his associates in student body and faculty are building on their Vermont hilltop an institution so boisterously uninstitutional, so forthright and radical as to leave one gasping. This in Vermont, the State where the eternal verities continue eternal, and where women are ladies; the State of Calvin Coolidge and marble. Robert Leigh left the marble out of the Bennington plan. He has seen how rigid a college can be, and he has fought rigidity in the Bennington scheme of things. If he has his way, there will be no ancient landmarks to which faltering and tearful alumnae will return fifty years hence. Nothing goes on forever at Bennington, neither students nor faculty nor trustees nor president.

Hubert Herring
The Nation
6 December 1933

Background to Bennington

The College Opens

Bennington College had been ten years in the planning when it opened on 6 September 1932 to its first class of 87 women. The college was conceived in the Jazz Age, but its proponents met with one setback after another, capped by the stock market crash of 1929, which almost scuttled the project. When the original campus site in Old Bennington was withdrawn, the Trustees gratefully accepted Mrs. Frederic B. Jennings' offer to donate 140 acres of her North Bennington farm.

Architectural plans calling for a brand-new campus of Gothic design, in tune with inflated dreams of the 1920s, had to be abandoned. "Fortunately," noted Bennington's first president, Robert Devore Leigh, "the College did not come into being at once, and both the building and educational programs came gradually to express the deeper tendencies of protest against the age of 'normalcy' and 'jazz' rather than to represent the evanescent tendencies of the period itself. The College was brought into physical being in one of the darkest years of the depression. . . . The Trustees and architects [built] honest structures fitted to the serious purpose of education, creating the atmosphere for an institution signalized by simplicity, directness, and relation to function."[1]

Louis Horst called it a model dairy farm. Existing farm buildings—barn, chicken coops, brooder—were pressed into use as classrooms, library, offices, and music and sculpture studios. (During the 1938 dance festival, the chicken coop served as hatchery for dance scores.) Gothic was supplanted by New England Colonial of the unadorned Vermont variety. White clapboard houses were set on a green quadrangle, open at its south end to Mt. Anthony, enclosed on the north by the sizable Commons Building (whose attic housed the College Theatre). The serenity and spaciousness of the countryside, the simple grace of the college's campus, and the innovative humanism of its educational plan—these elements formed the crucible in which the modern dance made its experiments in a search for common ground, integration, and clarity.

The bucolic setting provided an atmosphere in which individual learning and doing were encouraged. Bennington's physical environment recalled the rigor and rhythms of farm life, with its strong ties to family and community, its devotion to growth and production.

Bennington College campus, 1938. Photograph by Betty Lynd Thompson.

Progressive Education and the Arts

The college faculty were themselves practitioners in their fields, honoring the progressive philosophy that doing is a potent means of learning. (John Dewey was among a raft of eminent advisers in the college's planning, and William Heard Kilpatrick of Teachers College, Columbia University, was an ardent advocate.[2])

Faculty member Barbara Jones characterized Bennington as an exemplar of John Dewey's educational philosophy, one that addressed "the central problem for contemporary education: that of achieving the unity-in-diversity which modern society needs." The progressive movement espoused "a recognition of diversity." Student initiative and a creative approach to learning were emphasized, along with the belief that the way students learned was probably as important as what they learned. "An underlying unity and stability of cultural values" was assumed, "which could be reached from many different points of departure." Jones observed, however, that "the cultivation of diversity does not automatically produce enough unity for the purposes of general education."[3]

From the outset, the arts were set on an equal footing with other academic subjects in the Bennington curriculum, with dance a major component within the Arts and Music Division; a student could obtain a Bachelor of Arts degree with a concentration in dance. By 1936 dance was a separate division within the college.

According to trustee John McCullough, President Leigh's wife was influential in introducing dance into the curriculum:

> One thing she initiated . . . was Bennington College's unique "athletic program." The whole College was without one because a gym cost like old scratch. Mrs. Leigh had run across a little-known dancer—Martha Graham by name—who was virtually unknown except to people who danced. . . . Presumably Mrs. Leigh pondered, "Well, why not have the exercise classes be an art form." Which is what set Bennington into the whole dance orientation.[4]

Bennington College historian Tom Brockway reported that Robert Leigh sought Martha Graham's advice about a person to head the dance program, and Graham recommended Martha Hill.[5]

Martha Hill Is Enlisted

Martha Hill had been a member of the Martha Graham Dance Group for two years and was then teaching at New York University, which offered a graduate dance major to men and women in its School of Physical Education. Hill rejected Leigh's offer of a full-time appointment as director of dance or of physical education but agreed to teach two days a week at Bennington College while maintaining her instructorship at NYU.[6] By 1934 she was spending three days a week at Bennington College, and she continued this dual responsibility until 1951, when she left both campuses to direct the new dance program at the Juilliard School of Music.

Martha Hill's background was unusually broad. Born in East Palestine, Ohio, around 1900, she graduated from the Kellogg School of Physical Education in Battle Creek, Michigan, in 1920, taught Swedish gymnastics and ballet there (1920-1923), and then became director of dance at Kansas State Teachers College in Hays, where she staged "large and elaborate" dance festivals each spring (1923-1926).[7] She studied ballet with Vestoff-Serova, Portia Mansfield, and Kobeleff; Dalcroze Eurhythmics with Elsa Findlay and Nelly Reuschel; and dance with Anna Duncan. On her Bennington resume she listed courses and training in piano, music theory, costume and stage design, aesthetics, and art history.

Hill was in the audience at Martha Graham's debut in 1926, an event that dance educator Mary P. O'Donnell termed "probably the most important in Martha Hill's entire career." She immediately signed up at the Graham studio "for instruction in the only form of dance which compelled her to forsake the ballet. For the remainder of the year, Miss Hill was absorbed in these classes, where the seeds of Martha Graham's great art were sown."[8]

In 1927 Hill took the summer course with Margaret H'Doubler at the University of Wisconsin. H'Doubler, a pioneer in dance education at the college level, had inaugurated the first dance major at a university (in the physical education department).[9] H'Doubler's approach to dance education had enormous influence in the field, and she was a charismatic teacher. But Hill's experience with H'Doubler followed her exposure to Graham; H'Doubler had little discernible impact on her. Barbara Page, another of H'Doubler's students, who was teaching at the University of Oregon, remembered that "Martha was offered a job at Oregon in the physical education department and went out and developed the wonderful kind of dance in education that she expanded so beautifully later at New York University and Bennington."[10]

Hill taught at Oregon from 1927 to 1929, replacing one of H'Doubler's pupils who, according to Page, "wore costumes of chiffon and did things a little on the order of Duncan, all 'inspired.' And here came Martha Hill in a leotard and nothing else!"[11]

Martha Hill, 1938. Photograph by Betty Lynd Thompson.

Hill returned to New York after a summer stint at the University of Chicago and got her B.S. at Teachers College, Columbia, in 1929. She joined the Graham concert group that year, taught at the Lincoln School at Teachers College, and became an instructor at New York University in 1930. Summers, she taught dance to physical education graduate students at NYU's camp on Sebago Lake in Sloatsburg, New York.

Hill danced with the Graham group in both seasons of the Dance Repertory Theatre, a bold attempt organized by Helen Tamiris to present the leading American concert artists and their groups in a joint New York season. Martha Graham, Doris Humphrey, Charles Weidman, and Tamiris gave the first performances in January 1930; in February 1931, Agnes de Mille joined them with her partner, Warren Leonard. The project was abandoned after its second season, with bruised egos, good houses, and a mixed press. "Everybody stepped pretty generally on everybody else's toes," was how critic John Martin put it.[12] There was no one to mediate among the artists. The situation must have made an impression on Hill. Perhaps she saw a role for herself emerge out of this need.

Dance in the Period

Performance opportunities for American modern dancers in the concert field were gravely affected by the Great Depression. Foreign attractions were booked into New York theaters and on cross-country tours (La Argentina, Kreutzberg and Georgi, Shan Kar, Wigman), but the cost of a New York recital was far greater than the financial resources available to independent American artists; nor could they afford to tour without the guarantee of a sufficient audience outside New York to offset costs. (Even Ted Shawn, renowned through his years of touring with Ruth St. Denis, was forced to abort a tour of Ted Shawn and His Dancers in 1932 to cut his losses. The next year, he ventured forth again, this time with his newly formed Ensemble of Men Dancers, to prove the place of men in dance. The troupe began the first of seven national tours (1933-1940) in Burlington, Vermont. Plagued by small houses at first, they ended their eight-month circuit of 101 American cities with sufficient surplus to cover all costs and make improvements in the stage of the old barn at Jacob's Pillow.[13])

In 1930 the plight of the concert artist was dire:

> The mere act of renting a theatre, rehearsing, costuming, etcetera, indicates an obligatory outlay of close to a thousand dollars. To recoup that, the artist must fill the house, and even then, when expenses have run too high, money is lost. Add to that the difficulties imposed by the Sabbath laws forbidding dance events and you have a depressing picture all too familiar to every dance artist. . . . An answer to this is suggested by the teaming of artists: the cooperation of groups, with the consequent application to the dance world of sane business methods.[14]

Most of the first-generation American modern dancers had taken flight from Denishawn in the twenties—Martha Graham, Doris Humphrey, Charles Weidman—and also Louis Horst and Pauline Lawrence. Denishawn, which disbanded two years before the Bennington School of the Dance opened its doors, had been a breeding ground for the modern dance where, as Doris Humphrey recalled, "everything was ready and provided."[15] In that period, explained Charles Weidman in 1972, the moderns were in revolt against the exoticism of Denishawn and the predilection of ballet dancers to depict nature. The modern dance issued a manifesto. Said Weidman, "We were going to dance man and woman in American society today."[16]

Bands of devotees followed their trailblazing, but the moderns had neither the broad appeal nor the glamour of foreign imports. Nor was there any reason to suppose that a large public was eager to receive what the modern dance had to offer. While Martha Graham danced before sparse audiences, movie palaces were packing Depression audiences in to see the new talkies—Hollywood extravaganzas that barely hinted at the serious social struggles of the period. Partisan clans began to form around the leading artists, but their numbers and influence were small. Each artist fought for a chance to dance and for a share of recognition. Each held tenaciously to a vision of America dancing that was somewhat different from the others. This generation of rebels was to find sanctuary at Bennington.

In this period, dancers made numerous attempts to form groups to effect political change (the prohibition against dancing on Sundays was revoked by such action in 1932) and to divide the costs of recitals. But there was as yet no real prospect of relief in sight for the independent artist; the Federal Dance Project (1936-1939) was still several years off.[17]

Physical Education and the Modern Dance

Most American dancers eked out a living by teaching. Mary Wigman's first American tour in 1930-31 brought new competition. The New York Wigman School of the Dance opened in 1931, under Sol Hurok's wing, with Hanya Holm in charge. Physical education instructors from colleges in places as distant as Oregon made the trek to New York to take the summer course in German modern dance at the Wigman School; some of them also patronized the studios of Graham, Humphrey-Weidman, Tamiris, and others.

In April 1932 a symposium at Barnard College brought together dance teachers from several Eastern women's colleges and several concert artists and their pupils to discuss methods, aims, and principles of modern dance. Martha Hill was a participant in this first of many meetings across the country involving physical education instructors and modern dancers. Just as Hill had been inspired by seeing Graham, so other teachers were turned on to new ways of moving through direct contact with Holm, Weidman, Humphrey, Tamiris, and other modern dancers.

Modern dance found eager acceptance in physical education departments across America.[18] "The modern dance," explained dance aesthetician George Beiswanger in 1936, "puts into art form the meanings and the philosophy of life for which physical education stands. It is physical education's own dance, its own art."[19]

Other Incubators

Physical education teachers were not the only new enthusiasts for modern dance. In 1929 Japanese dancer-choreographer Michio Ito was in residence for four weeks at the Cornish School in Seattle, a pioneering school of the arts that Nellie Centennial Cornish opened in 1914.[20] With him was a company that included Pauline Koner and Georgia Graham (Martha Graham's younger sister). The following summer, Martha Graham and Louis Horst arrived to teach and perform. The Graham influence left its mark at Cornish through the work of Bonnie Bird, Merce Cunningham's first modern dance teacher.

Beginning in 1932 with Doris Humphrey, Portia Mansfield and Charlotte Perry brought a steady stream of modern dancers to teach summer sessions at their camp and school of the dance in Steamboat Springs, Colorado, a project they launched in 1914, a year before the founding of the Denishawn School. Perry-Mansfield, as it was called, was not wholly devoted to the dance; it also offered full camping activities, horseback riding, and theatrical training. Louis Horst became musical director there in 1928, the same year he began teaching a course in modern dance composition, said to be the first of its kind, at the Neighborhood Playhouse in New York.

In 1928 composer Henry Cowell joined the faculty of the New School for Social Research and sometime afterward invited Martha Graham and Doris Humphrey to give lecture-demonstrations there. They asked John Martin to organize the venture, which was to become one of the most influential educational projects in the history of the modern dance.[21]

Martin, who began writing about the dance for the *New York Times* in 1927 and in 1928 became their dance critic, had allied himself to the modern dance movement from its earliest days, and he was indefatigable in his efforts to build and educate an audience for it. In 1931 he introduced his landmark series of lecture-demonstrations at the New School, where dancers, composers, teachers, and artists discussed and demonstrated their work in open forum. The format of the lecture-demonstration forced the moderns to clarify their own thinking in order to present and defend their viewpoints to an audience eager to challenge them and to compare one artist to another. Through this device—which Martin employed to great advantage in the early thirties at numerous educational settings, including Columbia University's Institute of Arts and

Sciences—a small but influential cadre of students, teachers, artists, and concertgoers became aware of differences and affinities among the various contemporary schools of dance.

It was at the New School that John Martin became well acquainted with Martha Hill and Mary Jo Shelly.[22]

Mary Jo Shelly, 1938. Photograph by Betty Lynd Thompson.

Mary Josephine Shelly Joins Martha Hill

Like Martha Hill, Mary Josephine Shelly had graduated from the Kellogg School in Battle Creek. It had been at her suggestion that Hill was invited to teach at Oregon, where Shelly had preceded her (1924–1928). From 1929–1932 Shelly was on the faculty at Teachers College, Columbia; she then taught physical education and held an administrative position at New College, a select experimental school within the Teachers College orbit. When New College closed in 1935, she moved on to the University of Chicago, where she later became chairman of the women's physical education department. By then she had begun spending summers at Bennington as administrative director of the School of the Dance.

Inception of the School of the Dance

In Martin's introductory lecture series at the New School, he defined the modern dance as "a point of view":

> It is evident that the scheme of modern dancing is all in the direction of individualism and away from standardisation. That is why it is likely to be so confusing for the man in the street to go to dance recitals. . . . Nevertheless, there is a great similarity throughout the dance field. . . . The mistake that is made is in looking for a standard system, a code such as characterised the classic dance. The modern dance is not a system; it is a point of view. This point of view has been developing through the years, and it is by no means an isolated development. It has gone hand in hand with the development of points of view on other subjects.[23]

John Martin had brought leading practitioners of the contemporary dance into a central arena. The idea of the Bennington School of the Dance proceeded quite naturally from Martin's pioneering series. In addition to lectures, demonstrations, and discussions, the School of the Dance offered the study of several contemporary "points of view." Mary Jo Shelly emphasized the need for a unified approach to the study of the modern dance, and this approach exemplified the concept of "unity-in-diversity" that was a hallmark of the progressive education movement. Shelly described the need for the School of the Dance in this way:

> A point of view on the modern dance is at the present time a more individual matter than a matter of wide common agreement. . . . The only basis for a well-founded opinion about the modern dance, on the part of anyone who works in it, is one which includes a consideration of all of the significant contemporary lines of development. . . . The growing need for a plan by which the study of the modern dance might be made more unified and at the same time more economical of time and travel, makes appropriate the inauguration of such a center for study at Bennington College. . . . The plan has developed out of the interest of the college in modern art, and out of a belief that a point of view on the modern dance must be a comprehensive one.[24]

On 2 March 1933, at the low point of the Great Depression, Bennington trustees charged Robert Leigh with finding some way to keep the college plant functioning in the summer, in order to pay the staff and maintain the grounds and buildings as well as to bring some needed income to the college. The project would have to be entirely self-supporting. A conference of secondary school heads and teachers was convened during the summer of 1933, and its success persuaded Leigh that a summer operation was indeed feasible. Moreover, it appeared to him to be an opportunity to bring a new population into contact with the college, enhancing its prestige and making its work more widely known. The kind of project it should be soon became apparent:

> I have talked with many people about the best use of our summer plant and I am convinced that a summer school of the modern dance under the direction of our present instructor, Miss Martha Hill, would be the wisest type of summer session to develop. We happen to have as our present director of the dance one who is, I believe, the best teacher of the modern dance in the country and is quite widely recognized as one of the best at least. . . . there is practically no competing school in the East. The only other place where instruction is given is in Colorado and California. The Bennington school could, I believe, from the outset become the outstanding summer center in the modern dance in the United States. . . . There is a very real clientele for this type of instruction consisting mainly of people engaged in physical education or getting training for it who are realizing these days that the dance is a

much more important part of their training than the schools of physical education have been able to give. There is no existing school of physical education except New York University [where Martha Hill was then teaching] which has first-rate dance training—certainly Wellesley has not and I question whether Columbia has. Finally, dancing is necessarily group instruction and can be carried on economically. It is also true that at the end of the summer we could have a very attractive dance festival which would bring to the campus people from the surrounding region. [This part of the plan did not materialize until 1935.]

I have talked the plan over with Miss Hill and she is very much in favor of doing it. . . . I think that it is possible that we could secure as a sort of business manager, Miss Mary Jo Shelly, who is at the New College, Columbia. . . . Miss Hill and our present assistant, Miss Schönberg, could carry on the full-time instruction. We would have a fund for several distinguished dancers who could visit during the summer to talk about the dance and to give an exhibition of their methods. There would be the possibility of Mr. Gregory Tucker who is working splendidly with Miss Hill in the field of music and possibly Mr. and Mrs. Lauterer to give some instruction in the drama and costume and stage design background of the dance. . . .[25]

This informal two-page memo prepared in October 1933 served as the scenario for the first summer of the Bennington School of the Dance. Leigh's preliminary budget of $4000 was predicated on 100 students (at $40 tuition for the six weeks), with a charge of $125 for room and board, giving the college a 6 percent return on its investment in building and grounds. (The estimate of a minimum of 100 students was apparently later changed to 45—the figure that appears in all subsequent accounts.)

"Bennington College provided the environment," wrote Shelly in 1972, looking back. "Financial subsidy began and ended with access to the College facilities."[26]

Recruitment of Faculty

The trustees approved Leigh's proposal on 21 October, and Mary Jo Shelly and Martha Hill began to recruit the faculty:

The keynote to success would be the capture of the four acknowledged modern dance leaders of the day—Martha Graham, Hanya Holm, Doris Humphrey and Charles Weidman. These untameable pioneers were not known for lovingly cooperating with each other's work. It seemed on the face of it uncertain that the four would agree to trek to remote Vermont for little more than it would cost to get there, and then in addition bear amicably with one another's presence if they did. The exciting possibilities of the venture however were evident to these pioneers, and Martha Hill prudently scheduled the four artists to arrive and depart in sequence that first session.[27]

George Beiswanger theorized that the Big Four were "ready to accept the challenge of the Bennington project when it came, if in fact they did not actually create the occasion for that challenge by a hearty reception of the teachers of dance in their own studios, and a readiness to take their dance at every opportunity into educational circles."[28]

Martin, Horst, and Graham were caught up in the plan on the instant. Martin offered to teach for expenses only, to publicize and promote the school in his Sunday column, and to allow the school to use his name in any way it saw fit as a supporter of the project.[29]

Hanya Holm was enthusiastic, but as she had accepted an invitation to teach at California's Mills College, she offered to send an assistant to Bennington. Shelly advised Leigh that this would be acceptable in Holm's case "since she is not a concert dancer in her own right, but rather the representative of a school."[30] In fact, when the school opened, Holm was the only one of the Big Four who had not established a career in America as a dancer and a choreographer. She had, however, made a mark as a master teacher. After leaving Germany in 1931, she toured the United States, mainly on the college circuit, lecturing, teaching, and demonstrating while serving as director of the New York Wigman School. She was undoubtedly invited to Bennington because of her superb teaching skills. Moreover, she represented a major school of the modern dance—one that had been attracting Americans abroad to study. Bennington's directors shrewdly assessed her drawing power in designing the new dance center.

Hanya Holm remembered how she came to be invited to Bennington:

We all knew each other but nothing was happening. Martha Hill and Jo Shelly said, look we want to do something because we were all going in different ways. They got the brilliant idea of putting these people under one common denominator, one roof so to speak, and that's why I was invited to come, and that's why I went. The first year I almost couldn't come because I had schedule complications. But I flew from Mills just in time to teach my one week [at Bennington], and then went to Germany.[31]

Holm's recollections suggest that the policy of inviting each artist in succession was as much a matter of resolving schedule conflicts as it was of circumventing personality clashes.

Doris Humphrey, speaking for Charles Weidman as well as herself, hesitated to make a commitment immediately. She was concerned lest she and Weidman compete with their own summer course in Manhattan. (They were subsequently scheduled at Bennington for the week immediately preceding their New York summer course.) Shelly assured Humphrey that the Bennington plan would be incomplete without her and Weidman; furthermore, she informed Leigh that they had no choice but to come, as she already had verbal agreements from "all the other important persons in the concert field."[32]

Martha Graham resolved the conflict with her New York summer course by having Bonnie Bird teach classes at the Graham studio.

Tamiris was conspicuously absent from the Bennington plan. The problems associated with the Dance Repertory Theatre experience might have been one reason; differences in temperament and aesthetic approach, another. She was the only one of the leading American moderns not to have come from the Denishawn cradle. Christena Schlundt speculated that she was left out of the Bennington group because they were afraid that "she might teach bad choreography by practice" and saw a positive side to her absence. As she viewed it, "Tamiris was too much of a maverick to be happy in a rarified college atmosphere or satisfied with the esoteric artistic stratosphere which these artists inhabited."[33]

In these years, Tamiris' choreography was reviewed unfavorably in the *Dance Observer*. One critic (Mary Jo Shelly!) called her "a dancer of considerable experience whose talent lies beyond question in the category of those who dance, not of those who compose dances."[34]

Like Tamiris, Agnes de Mille had appeared in lecture-demonstration series and on concert stages alongside Graham, Humphrey, and Weidman. She was in London in the summer of 1934 and taught the 1935 summer session at Perry-Mansfield, but de Mille was never invited to Bennington. "The moderns were haughty about ballet at that time," she recalled. "I wasn't asked."[35]

The School of the Dance, 1934-1938

The School Opens

Having "captured" the Big Four, Hill and Shelly were ready to announce the school's opening. Several trustees, made wary of taking financial risks by the deepening national depression, dragged their feet, urging that the opening depend on adequate response to a preliminary announcement and to requests for support that would be made to the Carnegie Foundation or some other private agencies. But John J. Coss, professor of philosophy at Columbia University, who had recommended Leigh for the job as college president in 1928, threatened to withdraw from the advisory committee to the School of the Dance unless it went ahead, regardless of outside support. In late December 1933, Leigh agreed to take this risk.[36] Official announcement was made in the February 1934 issue of the *Bennington College Bulletin*:

The Bennington School of the Dance will be initiated during the summer of 1934 as a center for the study of the modern dance in America. Under the auspices of a college which includes all of the arts as an essential part of its curriculum, the Bennington School is designed to bring together leaders and students interested in an impartial analysis of the important contemporary trends in the dance.

The modern dance, in common with the other arts of this period, is a diversified rather than a single style. At the same time it possesses certain identifying characteristics which are common to all of its significant forms. The most advantageous plan of study is, therefore, one which reflects this diversification and, by affording comparisons, aims to reveal the essentials of modernism in the dance. The Bennington School presents contrasting approaches to technique and composition and, by giving a large place to the related aspects of the dance, such as music, undertakes an integrated analysis of the whole structure of the art. Under this plan, the student of the dance has access to the experiences necessary to the formulation of a well-founded point of view.

Since the development of the modern dance in America is affected by the many aesthetic and educational purposes which it serves, the Bennington School includes the contributions of dance artists, teachers, critics, musicians and artists in allied fields such as the theatre. The School serves all types of dance students—teachers, professional dancers, those interested in the art as amateurs and as audience. It is open to the novice as well as to the advanced student.[37]

On the basis of 5000 copies of the *Bulletin* mailed to schools and dance studios across the country, 103 students and teachers enrolled for the first session, representing 26 states, the District of Columbia, Canada, and Spain. They were 15 to 49 years of age. Sixty-eight were teachers, 35 of whom taught at colleges and universities. All were women.

The first six-week session met from 7 July to 18 August 1934. Martha Hill, Mary Jo Shelly, Gregory Tucker, and Bessie Schönberg made up the permanent staff; Martha Graham, Doris Humphrey, Charles Weidman, Hanya Holm, Louis Horst, and John Martin were visiting faculty. An advisory board chaired by Robert Leigh included, in addition to the visiting faculty, John J. Coss, professor at Columbia; Dorothy Lawton, director of the Music Library, including the Dance Collection, of the New York Public Library; and Jay B. Nash, professor of education and director of the department of physical education at New York University, who had brought Martha Hill to NYU.

The First Session

In his address at the first meeting of students and faculty, Leigh attributed the exclusion of dance in most traditional institutions of higher learning to "the survival of the medieval tradition of education [wherein] the important things in school have to do primarily with listening, . . . talking, writing and reading."[38] Where dance had infiltrated the college program, it had "come in by the back door" and had done so largely through student initiative.

Bennington College, he said, had broken with this tradition by organizing the dance as part of their Arts and Music Division. (Dance did not become a separate division until 1936.) The interrelationship of dance with the other arts was potentially productive. However, he warned, dance should not be "a handmaid to music" but must "establish its integrity." In many colleges, he noted, "we see the most dead or dying types of academic art instead of the most vital forms." He spoke against the blind acceptance of tradition and congratulated the school's community for its participation in this new project. As Leigh said,

in the times we are living in so much is dying and so much is irrelevant that to find one's interest along the lines of things that are vital and growing is of great significance. The great advantage is to be attached to something that does belong to our times and gives every indication of growth. . . . It is indisputable that the arts are going to have a bigger place in American life.

The program was divided into two parts. The first, led by the permanent staff, comprised fundamental techniques, dance composition, music for dancers, teaching methods and materials, practice, and production. The second, conducted by the visiting staff, had three intensive units: a sequential course of study with each of the visiting artists, an analysis of dance composition based on a study of pre-classic forms taught by Louis Horst, and a survey of dance history and critical theory—very likely the first course of its kind in America—taught by John Martin. "I boned up like mad at the 42nd Street library beforehand," recalled Martin, "and I was barely one step ahead of the class."[39]

Along with the course work were discussions centered around what the school's "First Annual Report" (October 1934) called "questions and topics growing out of the work of the School and those current in the contemporary dance." Recitals "to promote the education of an audience for modern dance" filled out the six-week calendar. Graham, Humphrey, and Weidman performed current repertoire, and Holm presented a demonstration of the German modern dance on a shared program with a sampling of the best student work from the session.

Hill and Shelly reported that the school's working scheme received "unanimous affirmation" from students at a final meeting of the school community.[40]

John Martin gave the project an A-plus in his Sunday column at the summer's end, unqualified endorsement from the influential critic of the *New York Times*:

It is not often that an event in the arts can safely be pointed to as a milepost of progress until time has given it perspective. . . . The idea of the school was rooted in a need that has become progressively more evident during the past five or six years, the need for an integration of the modern dance. That the Summer's experiment has provided the groundwork for such a result makes it a significant achievement. [It] has succeeded beyond the hopes of its most ardent well-wishers. . . . The final record was merely a matter of writing Q.E.D. on the prospectus. . . . Perhaps it is too soon even to whisper such names as Malvern and Salzburg and Bayreuth. At any rate, for those who have been working and praying for some American equivalent of the German dance congresses, and for those others who have almost feared to hope for a centre where the modern dance might gather all its forces, this has been a very substantial foundation. To call it a school is not to give it its full significance, for it does not direct its efforts toward merely teaching certain individuals something they did not know before but rather toward building a sounder and more vital art.[41]

The Bennington School of the Dance was soon to become a major production center and a haven for most of the country's leading modern dancers. But, as an authoritative feature article in the *Springfield* (Mass.) *Union Republican* emphasized, this was not its initial goal:

To make the school's esthetic ends clear its organizers reiterate over and over again that it does not seek to serve the dancer as such but the teacher; it does not wish to promote only one style of the modern dance; it does not concern itself, except briefly and historically, with the ballet, tap, folk, classic, romantic dances; it is a center for the study of the modern dance in America.

"What is the modern dance?". . . . The dance is movement in space and in time. It is not the theater, acting, pantomime; it is not music, the transliteration of musical values into motion . . . it is not the pictorial arts, presenting a picture or an animated sculpture; it is not literature, telling a story. So generally the modern dance proclaims itself, its sole medium is movement, its sole intention is kinesthetic, it asks to be judged only in terms of itself.[42]

1935–1938: Vintage Years

With both financial and educational success a matter of record, the trustees of the college were asked to approve the School of the Dance for the summer of 1935 and "in the interests of continuity . . . a plan for three additional sessions . . . subject to approval annually upon the basis of the outcomes of each successive session." The school's informal relationship to Bennington College was to be replaced by its establishment as "an autonomous unit or department of Bennington College with the College trustees and the President responsible for its adequate operation."[43] In October 1934, on the recommendation of the Educational Policies Committee, the Board of Trustees so voted.

"Educational enterprises of considerable significance often have very small beginnings," wrote Mary Jo Shelly in *Progressive Education* in October 1935:

The Bennington School of the Dance began in a small black notebook in the hands of Mr. Robert Leigh, President of

The Commons Building, Bennington College campus, 1938. Photograph by Betty Lynd Thompson.

Bennington College, on a snowy Vermont afternoon in November, 1933. On this occasion, Mr. Leigh, with the future director and administrative director of the school, sketched the outline of a plan which has now been realized in two sessions of the school and which has proved so right for the purposes originally set that it is likely to hold firm as the framework of a project to be continued at least through another few summers. . . . The fact that this school in two short summers has assumed so energetic a character and has had so organic and unforced a growth, generated by the synthesis of personalities and action which make up the school, is an index to a wider and deeper development taking place in American art and education. . . . It has been most propitious that the first of such experiments should have taken place under the auspices of a college committed to experimentation and one in which the arts are consistently treated as a major area of human experience. . . .

The experiences of the student in the art [of modern dance] have been either narrowly specialized along the line of one or another of the strong leaderships which are directing the course of the modern dance today; or those experiences have failed to include the many related aspects of the dance, such as music; or, most regrettably of all, the student who is often himself teaching dance to large numbers of persons for whom he is the sole guide has had access only to the most diluted and secondary version of the work of those artists who personify the modern dance in this country. The plan was, therefore, to place within reach of the many persons—teachers, young dancers, laymen—who are inevitably building the foundations for the functioning of the dance as an art and as an educative medium, a first-hand cross-section of the whole structure of the art, to do it within one enterprise and, moreover, to do it by assembling the artists themselves. . . . Those responsible for the plan entertained no illusions of securing technical mastery nor of creating dancers wholesale in this time. It was frankly a plan aimed at orientation. . . .

The danger in the plan lay in the fact that it might create little except confusion. Confusion there has doubtless been, but the predominant result has fortunately been disturbance, which emerges at a different point for the individual than does mere confusion. . . . The curriculum of the school religiously excluded the dissemination of formulae for applying the work done in it to other teaching situations. Methods as such were ignored. The adaptation and organization of material were, like individual integration, believed to be the prerogative—in fact, the obligation—of the individual. . . . The school mimeographs nothing except schedules for classes. . . . The principle of action, as against that of reaction, dictates every procedure of the curriculum. This principle is indispensable if the school is to create in the student that disturbance which evolves into a new clarification, instead of confusion which lapses into an old complacency. . . .

An enterprise which is rooted in an actual need generates its own energy and evolves a personality of its own, distinct from and larger than the sum of the personalities which make it up. [Bennington] provides strong support for the growing tendency in American education to bring the artist directly into contact with the student, especially the student who is a teacher of other students. [It is] a center where the artist both works and teaches, where art is both made and taught, and where the way of working and teaching stem entirely from the material itself.[44]

Permanence was not written into the Bennington plan. From its inception, the school proved responsive to needs and experience in a rapidly accelerating field. But while Hill and Shelly took an experimental approach to their planning, the foundations of the school remained essentially fixed. In its nine-summer history, no major choreographers were added to the original four.

From 1935 through 1937, the general program of the school was amplified incrementally. Music composition and accompaniment, stage design, and advanced workshops in choreography and experimental production were offered, and there were new opportunities for students interested in performance careers to dance with the leading artists and their groups. The majority of the student body continued to be made up of teachers rather than dancers. In 1935 the school began to serve as a laboratory for choreographers, musicians, composers, stage designers, and dancers, all of whom were engaged in creating new works. The momentum of the school's first session continued to build each succeeding summer in carefully designed blocks. Beginning in 1935 the Bennington Festivals invariably featured new compositions prepared during the session by one or more of the major artists and, in 1937 and 1938, by younger choreographers and fellows. In 1938 there was a culminating festival in which all four artists produced new works.[45] The Bennington Festivals drew capacity audiences at a site that was within reach of other summer arts centers and festivals, including the Berkshire Music Festival, which also opened in 1934, Yaddo, the Stockbridge Summer Theater, and Jacob's Pillow, which had begun offering "tea concerts" by Ted Shawn and his Ensemble of Men Dancers in 1933.

If the Bennington experiment could succeed so well in a

brief but intensive summer session, what might be accomplished over a longer period of time? In August 1936 Martha Hill drafted plans for a year-round "central school for the modern dance" to be located in New York, which would bring a number of dancers to a national facility and give them studio space and performance opportunities. It was to be a two-pronged educational project for academicians and artists. Proposals were written and revised, and requests were submitted for planning grants, but the project was never realized.[46]

The Workshop Program, 1935–1938, and the Fellowship Program, 1937–1938

Two production programs were inaugurated, the results of which were put on display for the first time in the Bennington Festivals of 1935–1938.

The Workshop Program gave each visiting artist the opportunity of having his or her own concert group in residence for six weeks, augmented by a group of apprentice students, for the purpose of composing and mounting large-scale compositions. This was one of the first forms of subsidy for choreographers and accounted for important works by Martha Graham (*Panorama*, 1935), Doris Humphrey (*With My Red Fires*, 1936), Charles Weidman (*Quest*, 1936), and Hanya Holm (*Trend*, 1937). Choreographers were given an enlarged company with which to work and virtually uninterrupted rehearsal time. Composers were brought in to write original scores. The theater was paid for, the audience solicited, and critics invited. Neither the college nor the School of the Dance exercised proprietary rights over the productions. After their Bennington premieres, decor, costumes, and music were the choreographers' to do with as they wished. In addition, apprentices selected by audition to augment the professional concert groups acquired performing experience in a professional production with one or more of America's leading modern choreographers.

The project was hampered throughout its history by the lack of an adequate theater, but stage designer Arch Lauterer adapted available space to the changing needs of the dance. In 1934 the small College Theatre in the Commons Building on campus was used for dance recitals. It was an airless attic with a deep, narrow stage and a flat floor seating about 150. It continued to serve as a recital stage, but in 1935, when large-scale productions were planned, it became clear that this facility was inadequate for performances involving as many as forty dancers at a time. A new site was found in the 500-seat capacity Vermont State Armory in the town of Bennington several miles distant. Lauterer converted the Armory into a brilliantly functional dance theater for the major festival productions from 1935 through 1938.

In 1937 the Fellowship Program was introduced "to aid directly in the training of future leaders for the modern dance."[47] Fellowships were offered by invitation to "recognized young dancers elected by the officers and Advisory Board of the School." Fellows were provided with studio space and accompanists, and their dances were given full production in the festival series. They were to work independently on new compositions for groups, subject to approval by a committee of the faculty, who acted as advisers. They were housed and fed for the session and awarded a small stipend to cover travel and other costs. "The establishment of Fellowships," reported the 1937 *Bulletin*, "extends the scope of the School to include a sharing of responsibility for the important developments of the future in the modern dance."[48]

Anna Sokolow, José Limón, and Esther Junger were the first Fellows. Junger was the only Fellow not associated with a group. Each composed and presented new group works. Limón had choreographed duets and trios, but this was his first chance to compose for a large group, as it was Junger's.

In 1938 Louise Kloepper, Eleanor King, and Marian Van Tuyl were elected Fellows. Kloepper produced three works, her first independent choreography; King and Van Tuyl each mounted new compositions.

The fellowships introduced some new choreographic blood into the Bennington family, though five of the six Fellows were progeny of the Big Four.

Other Activities in Brief, 1935–1938

Recitals, lectures, demonstrations, and discussions—not just on the dance but on far-ranging topics including the gathering world crisis—augmented the basic curriculum and production activities. Tina Flade, a Wigman pupil teaching at Mills College, and Marian Van Tuyl, an independent artist from Chicago, gave recitals in 1935 and 1936 respectively. The New Dance League, to which many students and members of concert groups belonged, gave recitals in the College Theatre in 1935 ("An Evening of Revolutionary Dance") and 1936.

Ballet at Bennington

The thirties were also a period of birth and struggle for the American ballet. There were fledgling companies in San Francisco, Chicago, and Philadelphia, and in 1934 George Balanchine and Lincoln Kirstein launched their crusade to gain a toehold on the public's love affair with imported dance attractions. The School of American Ballet, like the Bennington School of the Dance, was conceived in 1933 and gave its first public performance in 1934. The embattled worlds of modern dance and ballet crossed paths at Bennington in 1936, with enduring repercussions.

Frances Hawkins (no relation to Erick Hawkins), Martha Graham's concert manager, booked the first tour of Ballet Caravan, a group of twelve dancers from the American Ballet and its school, which set out to produce new choreography from within its ranks. Hawkins had been at Bennington the previous summer (1935) as administrative assistant, and she later returned to run its festival publicity. And so it was at Bennington in July 1936 that the world debut of Ballet Caravan took place. Many years later Lincoln Kirstein reflected on this curious circumstance:

> Our performances at Bennington were no more than open dress rehearsals, but the audiences allowed us the benefit of many doubts, and in an important sense, Modern Dance may be said to have launched Ballet Caravan.[49]

George Balanchine, who was not part of Kirstein's venture, sent the company a telegram on the occasion of its debut:

> Best wishes to the young American choreographers and ballerinas/don't be afraid of the Big Bad Wolf [John] Martin and for heavens sake don't get married/Grandpa Balachine [*sic*].[50]

Ballet Caravan returned to Bennington in 1937; Lincoln Kirstein delivered lectures on dance history both summers in conjunction with the Caravan performances. He attended the festival in 1938, and in 1940 he was named visiting lecturer.

In October 1937 the *Dance Observer*, a journal Louis Horst had founded in 1934 that was devoted entirely to the modern dance, announced that Lincoln Kirstein had joined its editorial board and would contribute "on that particular branch of dance which draws his particular support," that is, the ballet. The *Dance Observer* editorialized:

> The modern dance no longer needs the kind of defense we intended. It is no longer a stranger in a hostile country. Both as a mature and a popular art form, the modern dance needs no special nurturing. It stands well alone; walks, runs, and on occasion leaps well enough in a field that is no longer cramped into a couple of seaboard cities.[51]

Conclusions After the Fourth Summer

At the conclusion of the fourth session, Shelly and Hill pronounced the school "the outstanding single agency for promoting the growth of the dance as an art in America":

> The main area of growth . . . is in the public schools and the colleges and universities . . . directly traceable to the influence of The Bennington School of the Dance. . . . Dance in the theatre and the concert dance are beginning to spread beyond the restricted limits of the one or two metropolitan centers where an educated audience is most readily available. . . . The School has given to a new and still struggling art a center which publicly identifies it as an independent art. . . . It has maintained its collective and non-partisan character through four intensive sessions. . . . It is proposed the School be continued . . . along these three lines—integrated study of the whole art, experimental production, and audience education.[52]

Beginning in January 1935 with a tour by the Humphrey-Weidman group from Toronto to Texas, modern dance groups began large-scale cross-country tours. Tamiris toured the Midwest in 1936; that same year Hanya Holm took her newly formed group across the country and Martha Graham made her first transcontinental solo tour, following it the next year with a transcontinental tour for her group.

Dance critic George Beiswanger, writing in *Theatre Arts Monthly*, concurred that the Bennington project was "without a doubt the major factor in the growth of the continental audience":

> For over four hundred teachers of the dance it has served not only to round out that intimate association of teacher and practising artist which brought physical education and the modern dance together in the first place, but to present the dance as an integrated art movement. Through its students, the channel from professional artist to the local community and back again to the dance as an American art was direct.[53]

At the conclusion of the 1937 session, faculty and staff met to discuss future plans, among them the idea of moving the program to Mills College in California for one session. The percentage of students from each of the regions had remained more or less constant in the first four years: 50 percent from the East; 35 percent from the Midwest; 9 percent from the South; and 6 percent from the Far West. Transferring the project to another part of the country was very desirable from the point of view of reaching students in all parts of the country, but there was some hesitation about "tearing up" the enterprise from the place in which it had been so successful.[54] A final decision was not made until the spring of 1938.

In the meantime, the plan for 1938 at Bennington had been decided on: it would be the culmination of the first five years of the school. All four artists would bring their concert groups to Bennington and produce new works. (This was the first and last time that they would all be in residence simultaneously, teaching, composing, and mounting new dances.) The festival productions were to be "less extensive and more strictly experimental" than the workshop productions had been.[55] (These turned out to be Graham's *American Document*, Holm's *Dance of Work and Play* and *Dance Sonata*, Humphrey's *Passacaglia in C minor*, and Weidman's *Opus 51*.)

Conclusions After the Fifth Summer

At the end of the fifth session, with the largest enrollment (180) and festival audiences (3800 total for six performances) thus far, and with the broadest press coverage the school had ever garnered, the directors looked back at their five-year record and drew four major conclusions that they said represented "the consensus of opinion of the faculty, the student body, and the audience participating in the festival."[56] These were set forth as "a statement of position for the art as a whole and this project in particular":

> First—The contemporary American dance has come of age; and the promise for the future, seen in the mature work

of the leading artists, and in the persons and performances of the succeeding generation, including the six fellows and the members of the concert groups, is assured. The craftsmanship of the dance among laymen and semi-professional workers, as well as among the core of artists leading the field, has been sufficiently developed and consolidated to afford a permanent foundation for the continued growth of the art.

Second—A cooperative enterprise which brings together at the same time and in the same place all of the leaders of this movement is no longer an eventuality to be hoped for, but an accomplished fact.

Third—The combination of intensive teaching and professional production . . . makes it the kind of center required by a performing art which is undergoing rapid evolution and which must, therefore, intimately relate what is taught with what is produced. Because it lacks standardized content and a classic tradition, it is imperative that the whole process of the dance and not merely preparatory or intermediate phases, be included in all possible situations where study of the art is going on. The School offers to the student the opportunity to make a comprehensive and unified study of the whole contemporary American dance, adequately and authoritatively presented, in a project within the financial reach of many people. This function is being served in no other single place in the United States.

Fourth—As illustrated in the 1938 festival, the dividing lines between dance and the other theatre arts have been crossed at so many points in recent seasons that it is not only possible but inevitable that this project, with others, should utilize this tendency toward enrichment of its material and move in the direction of a center making available all of the resources of the theatre: dance, music, stage design, drama.

Although some former Bennington participants believed that the faculty was pressured into the idea of the School of the Arts, this recommendation was made forcefully by Hill and Shelly themselves. They further stipulated that if the plan could not be achieved in 1940, the school should move to another part of the country, following the Mills residency—this time "preferably the Middle West."[57]

The Sister Arts, 1935-1938: Music, Stage Design, and Costumes

During the vintage years of 1935-1938, the art of the dance reigned supreme at Bennington, flooding every conceivable space on campus and flowing onto the green lawns of the college quadrangle. Music, stage design, costumes—all were in its service, and in turn, the dance was a powerful magnet for musicians and artists.

"The dance at Bennington," said composer Otto Luening, "was to American composers what the opera house was to European composers. Musicians came to Bennington because there were opportunities for them that didn't exist in many other places."[58]

"What attracted us," said composer Norman Lloyd about himself and his wife Ruth, who were Bennington's musical mainstays, "was the feeling that you were part of a movement, that anything could be tried. There was a wonderful sense of experimentation."[59]

The School of the Dance employed accompanying musicians for every class and every performance. Much of the music in class was improvised. "This was not the kind of music-making that conservatories prepared one to do," said pianist-accompanist Ruth Lloyd.[60] The need for new music was so acute that in 1936, Louis Horst and Norman Lloyd initiated a special training course for dance composers and accompanists. Horst would select the best student dance composition from his Pre-Classic Forms or Modern Forms classes, set to music selected from among Horst's choices. The dance was shown to the student musicians without music, and they were assigned to write a score—usually overnight. The dance was then performed to each of these scores in turn. "It was a little like trying on many costumes," explained Ruth Lloyd, "to see which one really fit, made the wearer comfortable, and did something for the wearer. The effect of different scores on the same movement phrases were most instructive."[61]

Very little music written at Bennington has survived. Most of it was *Gebrauchsmusik*, or music for an occasion, written to serve the dance and not intended for an independent life. Louis Horst discussed the special properties of dance scores in 1936:

> Music for the dance cannot be judged apart from the dance for which it was written, because it is an integral part of it. Music can underscore or set off the dance, hold it in check, give it a certain boundary, for the body is the most dangerous of instruments and without the boundary of music and the authority of form, is likely to run riot in emotional expression. . . . The musical accompaniment provides aural assistance to the audience, giving emphasis to the movement either by definitely underlining the rhythms or contrasting with counter-rhythms with quiet passages of music to active passages of dance, or with energetic music against passive movement.[62]

But critic Edwin Denby perceived the dance's need for rhythmic independence. In order for it to achieve this, its music "must have a life of its own as music." As Denby said, "Seeing a dancer dance smack on his *Gebrauchsmusik* [is about as dramatic as] a man riding an electric camel."[63]

The sparse texture of the dance scores of this period followed Horst's dictum that music should be sufficiently transparent so that the dance could be seen through it. Piano and other percussion instruments provided the most usual sonorities, with woodwinds and brass added, budget permitting. (All five new works in the 1938 festival used only piano or piano and percussion.)

The composer usually would write the score after seeing the completed dance. This imposed considerable restrictions

Hanya Holm, 1937. Photograph courtesy of Herbert Binzer from Bertha Rhea Desenberg Scrapbook.

on composers. During the Bennington period, however, especially after 1938, there was some loosening of this procedure. In 1938 Hanya Holm took the unusual step of having Harrison Kerr write a score for *Dance Sonata* before she composed the dance. And Doris Humphrey shocked the resident musical community in 1938 by turning away from the "harshness, dissonance, starkness, the bare angular line" of modern music in favor of the "richness, ordered complexity, grandeur, serenity" of Johann Sebastian Bach in her *Passacaglia in C minor.*[64]

Not only did Bennington's support of contemporary composers offer those writing for the dance an important outlet, but it also served other composers whose music was performed infrequently. For example, Edgard Varèse's *Ionisation* (1931) was introduced to Bennington audiences in Hanya Holm's *Trend* in 1937. That performance also marked the first use of recorded music at the Bennington Festival. There were occasional instances of "canned" music thereafter, but live music was a Bennington fixture.

Franziska Boas' work with percussion and Louis Horst's far-ranging musical repertoire and curiosity opened up a world of new musical possibilities to choreographers. Horst, said Otto Luening, taught young choreographers a respect for music. He would not permit them to "knock the music all out of shape just because they had a great gleam in their eye about movement."[65]

Composers who wrote for the dance were regarded as second-class citizens by some members of the musical establishment. Bennington gave them a more respectable image, but even at Bennington a distinction was made between "pure composition" and composing for the dance: Norman Lloyd recalled the college music faculty's diffidence toward dance musicians.[66]

In 1934 George Beiswanger suggested that the dance composer "forget music and with an innocent mind explore anew the wide world of sound" to create a new "tonal space" for the dance. "The day may come," he forecast, "when the dancer will work out an accompaniment not with tympanist and pianist and flautist but with the free facilities of the laboratory and the sound track. He will put this accompaniment together and record it by machine and project it also by machine as is done in the motion-picture theatre today."[67]

In 1938 Beatrice Hellebrandt, who took the Music for the Dance course at Bennington in 1936 and 1937, described the current and future relationship of music and dance:

> A *new music* is being written. The impetus for its creation arose from a revolt of dancers against their dependence upon musical structure. They began to evolve their own dance forms from the stuff of movement itself. As a result, the musical accompaniment is now often written to the completed dance form, is entirely dependent upon it and subservient to it. The pendulum has swung so far that the creative musician is subjected to an artistic association which submerges his creativeness and makes of him only a skilled craftsman. Both the dancer and the musician are entitled to a modicum of individual completeness, but the contribution of each must yet remain so harmoniously related that the dance is enhanced and neither party to the union is unnecessarily restricted. . . . Dance composition has become a fairly systematized and intelligently conceived procedure in contrast with the old vague and formless reaction to some music, idea or dramatic situation. However, the consensus of opinion among those most competent to judge is that the best accompaniment for dance is yet to be achieved, although interesting experiments are in progress. The new music is largely a sound accompaniment which does not develop according to musical tradition, being confined to the form of the movement structure. It is a percussive type of accompaniment with some melodic but little harmonic development. As such it is imminently suitable to the aggressive, strong, percussive movements so characteristic of modern dance. . . . This is an age of bold experimentation in all art forms, and insofar as the dancer and musician remain alive to the stimulating potentialities of the times, both will contribute to the creation of a dance form unique in the history of this art.[68]

In the area of stage design, within the limitations of available space at Bennington, Arch Lauterer created a new "world for dance to live in" in collaborations with Martha Graham (beginning in 1935) and Hanya Holm (beginning in 1937). It was Lauterer's belief that dance and "decor" were mutually exclusive, that the "picture-box" proscenium theater was antipathetic to the three-dimensional qualities and requirements of the dance, and that painted backdrops were nothing more than wallpaper.[69] The essential purpose of design for the dance, said Lauterer, was "to show the movement."[70]

In Lauterer's view (following the path of Adolphe Appia, the pioneer stage producer who developed stage lighting techniques) light rather than painting was the primary element. His ideas about light, time, and movement lent impressive new dimension and expressive potential to the dance stage. From the Armory's inadequate stage and unraked, bare floor, Lauterer constructed a spacious multilevel performance arena. He built side "fins" through which large groups of dancers could be moved on and off the performance space, giving the dance fluidity and depth, and he placed the audience above, looking down at the dancers. In the College Theatre in 1940 and 1941, Lauterer's functional settings evolved into more intimate, detailed scenic designs, and he introduced properties. There he opened up the back of the stage with shutters, through which dancers made exits and entrances.

Lauterer's imaginative designs replaced the ubiquitous black velvet-curtained proscenium stage, but his dream of a theater plant adapted to the needs of the dance was never fulfilled at Bennington. It was not until 1976 that the college erected a modern performing arts center.

The whole look of the dance, particularly in the early Bennington period, was Spartan. There were no plush fabrics or yards of billowing silk. The modern dance was lean, trim, and hardy. It could afford nothing more elaborate than muslin skirts for the women and trousers and shirts for the men. Its methods fit its means and its purpose: movement was the primary element. "The dance costume must be in complete unity with the dance," wrote costume designer Betty Joiner in 1937. "Dance is primarily movement—not color, fabric, nor their combinations."[71]

But gradually the dance began to employ more varied theatrical resources. Slippers and shoes made their appearance at Bennington in new works in 1938—the year in which Humphrey had special sandals made for *Passacaglia in C minor*—and in 1940 Graham used slippers in *Letter to the World*. In other works dancers put on shoes, wore hats, and manipulated props. Still, when Edythe Gilfond designed costumes for *American Document* in 1938, she worked directly on the dancers' bodies, sculpting cloth to figure, in much the same way composers made music to fit the dance, shaping the sounds and phrases of the music to conform to the movement's contours.[72]

The School of the Dance at Mills College, 1939

The School Moves West

The Bennington School of the Dance spent the summer of 1939 at Mills College in Oakland, California. This session signalled a change in quality and intensity. The idea of the move can be traced back to 1936, when Rosalind Cassidy, head of the physical education department at Mills College, visited the Bennington session to see what all the excitement was about. She returned home eager to link arms with Bennington in order to build a center of comparable strength on the West Coast.[73]

Cassidy had been working for some years to make Mills the center of modern dance in the West. Dance was introduced into the Mills physical education department in 1925. In 1934 Cassidy brought Wigman-trained dancer Tina Flade to Mills to develop a dance major. Hanya Holm was guest artist during the Mills summer sessions of 1934–1936. Flade left Mills in 1938, after teaching the summer course with composer Lou Harrison, Lester Horton, and Bonnie Bird.

Following a conversation with Hanya Holm in 1937, Cassidy extended a formal invitation to Bennington to hold a summer session in Oakland in 1939. In May 1938 Mills College approved the plan to bring Bennington west for a total cost of $20,780. Originally Cassidy had proposed that Holm restage *Trend* at Mills with a new workshop group and that Graham, Humphrey, and Weidman each teach two weeks and give a demonstration at the session's end but not produce any new works. This plan was dropped after meetings between Martha Hill and Cassidy. The financial burden of mounting a festival production on top of the expense of moving faculty and staff west seemed too risky; the idea of restaging a single work already created at Bennington by an artist who was well known on the West Coast was replaced by one giving each of the four equal time for teaching and a 30-minute demonstration at the session's end. There would be no festival.

"Every little thing I do is fraught with such important consequences," wrote Doris Humphrey from Mills in 1939. "My group *must* be trained to make the best possible appearance at the demonstration with the competition between the four of us so terribly keen."[74]

"The Mills summer," recalled Bessie Schönberg, "was nothing like any of the others. We were a little like trained bears brought out there to do what it was we had been publicized to do. The overall intensity that vibrated through Bennington was missing."[75]

None of the Big Four produced a new work or gave a recital. But their teaching assistants—José Limón, Ethel Butler, Louise Kloepper, and Katherine Manning—presented a joint program that included some new compositions.

"There is a real base and a substantial population in this region for the study of the contemporary American dance," the Bennington directors concluded.[76] Half of the students at Mills came from the Far West—just as half of the students in Vermont had come from the East. Otherwise the group was surprisingly similar to the student body of the previous five summers—except for their level of dance training. The caliber was later reported by the Bennington directors to be below "the level reached in the east by 1938 because the west coast had had less development. That was one reason we went west."[77]

The Mills program was enhanced by Bennington's presence. Rosalind Cassidy announced the immediate outcome:

The question was asked continually during the summer, "What is the significance of this western session?" How can Mills best serve dance in its subsequent plans? Finally, in the last week, sitting at supper to confer on this question, Martha Hill, Mary Josephine Shelly, Martha Graham, Hanya Holm, Doris Humphrey, Charles Weidman, Esther Rosenblatt and I made a three point plan which was approved the next day by the President of Mills College and announced with the 1940 Bennington plans at the closing general meeting of the School. This is the plan:

> Mills, we hope, may serve, under a long term plan, three definite purposes in the dance field: (1) that Mills continue its summer program in dance with a long term plan for the development of a program for teachers of dance centering its emphasis on the dance in Education; (2) that Mills become a center to encourage the outstanding young dancers by giving them the opportunity to compose for and dance in concerts and production as well as the opportunity to teach; (3) that Mills each year extend to the two dancers not involved in the Bennington production an invitation to center their summer teaching on its campus.

To move at once on our plan, invitations for 1940 were extended to Louise Kloepper, José Limón and Marian Van Tuyl. Doris Humphrey and Charles Weidman were also invited to teach during the last part of this session.[78]

Conclusions After the Sixth Summer

In 1939, Hill and Shelly appraised Bennington's historic service to the art of modern dance:

The School's inauguration was innocently but nonetheless perfectly timed to coincide with a need, only then becoming conscious, for stability, consolidation, authoritativeness in a field alive with enthusiasms but beset at every turn by insecurities. Launched earlier, the forces gathered into it in 1934 would have been too scattered for cohesion. A collectivism bred of growing maturity in the art and the artists came to pass only because the time was ripe. The School unwittingly put itself in the way of a trend far larger than its own designs, took the full impact of focusing that trend for the first time, and was actually the agent for entering in the record of contemporary culture, a new phenomenon. This unsolicited function of making history accounts for the character of the six-year record.[79]

The principal goals of the school had been accomplished, they reported. The next step was of a quite different order: the making of a new American theater, with dance as a central component:

Dance is now one of the forces working to create an American theatre of a new kind and one of great social and psychological importance in present-day American culture. . . . The time has come for planned affiliation between the dance and the other performing arts. . . . The launching of the collaborative project in 1940 is properly timed and that incorporation into a center for all the performing arts will conserve what the School has accomplished and will carry it into a new and greatly enriched phase.[80]

The School of the Arts, 1940-1941

Toward a School of the Arts

The idea of a School of the Arts had been broached in 1938. In April 1939 Robert Leigh informed the faculty that the idea in principle had been approved unanimously and with real enthusiasm by the trustees.[81] The faculty could begin to plan for it, but with the understanding that new theater facilities were not assured.

The plan that was forged drew on contributions from each one of the school's directors—Martha Hill for dance, Francis Fergusson for drama, Otto Luening for music, and Arch Lauterer for theater design—all of them members of the college faculty. The motivating impulse was "not to merge the arts, but to place them side by side and so make possible the easy access from one to the other demanded in the coming American theatre."[82] In the winter of 1939 Martha Hill, Arch Lauterer, poet Ben Belitt, and Gregory Tucker collaborated on a Bennington College theater production of *The Bridge*, adapted from Hart Crane, whose success seemed a proclamation of collaborative possibilities among the arts.[83]

"The die had . . . been cast," wrote Shelly in 1941, "at Martha Hill's and my instigation, for incorporation of the School into the School of the Arts. . . . Predominant [among the reasons] was a genuine belief in the rightness of the step and a genuine enthusiasm for the animating principle of the new venture, collaboration."[84]

In March 1940 a 26-page issue of the *Bennington College Bulletin* published the first prospectus of the new School of the Arts:

Beginning with 1940, the School of the Dance with its Festival will be incorporated intact into an enterprise which, by its wider scope and fresh resources, permits not only continuance of the original plan of study and production in dance, but the development of those relationships with the other arts of the modern theatre for which the time has now so plainly come. It is appropriate that Bennington, having served the American dance in its first period as the rallying point of its forces, should now serve as a point of excursion into new alliances.[85]

The School of the Arts, 1940

The School of the Arts offered students a specialization in any one of four areas as well as the possibility of numerous crossovers.

The Dance Division retained the basic plan of the School of the Dance "intact," offering "a cross-section of the structure of the art, presenting impartially the most significant points of view and methods of work which make up the modern American dance."[86] Only one of the Big Four would be in residence in a single session producing new work, while a second taught a master course for advanced students. The remaining two were either on a leave of absence for the entire session (Mills was to extend them an invitation to teach on the West Coast) or in Vermont for very brief stays. Each of the four would be represented at Bennington by a teaching associate. As before, the Dance Division would subsidize the creation of new work, mounted during a festival of the arts.

For the first time, the producing artist—in this case Martha Graham—was relieved of teaching responsibilities and could devote herself full-time to the production of two new works: *El Penitente* and *Letter to the World*. Hanya Holm taught a master course. It was her last Bennington summer. She returned to Colorado afterward and in 1941 began a long-term association as director of the summer dance program at Colorado College.

The dance curriculum was broadened by the addition of a course in dance notation given by Helen Priest. Lincoln Kirstein was visiting lecturer for a series of talks on theatrical dancing. Most surprising, a class in ballet technique was taught by Erick Hawkins.

In 1940 Lincoln Kirstein gleefully reported that

today all the young "modern dancers" are industriously catching up on their five positions; the movement has absorbed so many traditional elements that it is scarcely any longer a distinct branch of instruction in itself.[87]

Kirstein's comments indicate that a blurring of distinctions between the modern dance and the ballet had begun by then, an erosion of boundaries that in the years since has profoundly altered both forms.

Discussing the change in attitude from earlier years, Hanya Holm explained that up to that time the modern dance had been busy clearing new trails. It had to put on blinders, she said, in order to see the road ahead. Within a few years it took off the blinders and looked around. It began to see the ballet not as foe but as useful discipline.[88] By the early 1940s not only ballet but tap (taught by William Bales) and folk and country dancing (taught by Martha Hill) were included in the Bennington curriculum.

The first Festival of the Arts was to have been held for a separate week following the six-week school session in a new theater designed by Arch Lauterer, to be erected in the town of Bennington.[89] The plan was not carried out, and the Armory was unavailable because of the war emergency.

Problems

The idea of the School of the Arts was bold and entailed the hazards of any new venture. But there were unforeseen difficulties. Mary Jo Shelly enumerated them:

We had counted on an unlimited dance population as security until we got a toe-hold among the countless competing enterprises in drama and music. That dance population shrank in half overnight. The sound of the new project, we know now, scared away many old customers and potential customers; we suddenly put our fee up $25; it was a summer of the most extensive competition we had ever had in dance, most of our competitors being our own step-children; and we had been going strong in a relatively small field for six years.[90]

As a result, stringent economy was suddenly necessary. One of the first cutbacks was the new theater. Arch Lauterer was called upon to transform the little College Theatre on campus into the festival site. He moved the proscenium and put up bleachers seating 304.

In that space the Drama Division presented *The King and the Duke*, the first stage adaptation of *Huckleberry Finn*. Hill, Tucker, Lauterer, and Fergusson collaborated in the production. Two concerts of modern music were given in the Recreation Building, directed by Otto Luening and including work by composers in residence at the school. Musicologist-harpsichordist Ralph Kirkpatrick directed two recitals of seventeenth- and eighteenth-century music.

Graham used a few male student apprentices in *Letter to the World*; *El Penitente* had a cast of three—Graham, Hawkins, and Merce Cunningham, who had joined Graham after the summer at Mills. Previously, Bennington students had made possible such large-scale works as *Panorama* and *Trend* and *With My Red Fires*. But now interest had begun to shift toward smaller theater pieces. At the same time, the student body at Bennington had also changed; there were fewer teachers enrolled and more dancers. Those who had come to Bennington for professional training expecting to dance with the masters were frustrated by the lack of sufficient performance opportunities.

The School of the Arts opened at the end of a spring during which German troops invaded Norway, Denmark, the Netherlands, and Belgium. The British had evacuated Dunkirk, and the French had just signed an armistice with Germany and Italy. American involvement in the war seemed ever closer, but the school determined to go ahead under normal planning conditions.

Robert Leigh, addressing the first School of the Arts session, stated his belief in the increasing importance of the arts in times of national emergency as reported in an article in the *Bennington Banner*:

"American wealth lies not alone in factories and fields and the defense of America is not only her armed forces for in times such as these which can only be described as revolutionary, the culture of a country is both a source of great wealth and a mighty force against the inroads of ignorance and intolerance," said Robert E. [*sic*] Leigh in his welcoming address yesterday. . . . Dr. Leigh told the students further that art is not to be regarded as an ivory tower to which one repairs in times of stress. On the contrary it is, he said, an even more necessary part of life at such a time, and it is the duty and privilege of every real artist to foster and develop national culture, just as it is the duty of the manufacturer and farmer to husband economic and agricultural resources.[91]

In October the report on the first session of the School of the Arts, presented to a committee of the trustees, contained no recommendations for a next session in view of the world emergency, the need to remove the deficit (the first the project had ever run), and the necessity of revising the 1940 plan, which clearly was not working smoothly, to achieve fuller collaboration among the arts.

Robert Leigh, first president, Bennington College. Photograph courtesy of Bennington College.

From the Dance Division's official perspective, collaboration with the other arts was seen as having been beneficial. (However, some participants felt strongly that dance had ceded its sovereignty, with adverse consequences.[92]) The summer, Hill emphasized, had freed Martha Graham from teaching to devote her time wholly to producing new works. She pointed out that with the prospect of war looming, Bennington was now more than ever responsible for keeping the art of dance alive.

Robert Leigh saw the shift away from a teacher population as undesirable. The arts, he said, could be most critically influenced through the educational system, which was where one would find the paying population that could ensure the school's enrollment and thus its future. He recommended that the school grant graduate credit in order to attract teachers and also to tie the School of the Arts more directly in with the curriculum of Bennington College. In his view, the school's most essential and logical function was the education of teachers.[93]

In March 1941 a skimpy seven-page issue of the *Bulletin* announced the second session. The school offered graduate credit leading to a Master of Arts degree, as well as professional training.[94]

But by April the school found itself on the verge of cancellation. Enrollments were substantially lower than they had been at the same time the previous year. The directors of music and drama offered to eliminate their own divisions, but their generous proposals were rejected to keep the concept of the School of the Arts intact. Grant requests were made; a few anonymous small gifts were received. John Martin and Edith Isaacs, editor of *Theatre Arts Monthly*, functioning informally as advisers, urged that the school be continued. In order to risk another session, the faculty were asked to surrender their salaries and work for room and board only. Humphrey, Weidman, and Graham agreed—on condition that they be allowed to produce festival-level work and that there be a festival.[95]

Humphrey was to have the major production. In April she wrote to her husband about her interest in playwright William Saroyan's work:

There's the man I would like to collaborate with. I tried to persuade the Bennington people to invite him to produce there this summer, but their enrollment is low, and they're scared. The academic mind closes tight against the idea of taking chances, and the prospect of going into debt for something that might be a brilliant success and increase their prestige and drawing power frightens them stiff. We had a meeting on Sunday at which they decided instead of attempting something bold to improve enrollments, that they would instead remove all guarantees of salary. This is what you get from people who are nicely fixed with comfortable salaries, and unaccustomed to danger.[96]

With the budget pared to the bone, the decision was taken to proceed with the 1941 session. In mid-May the trustees authorized the school's continuance based on a deficit not to exceed $2000. Their action was extremely pragmatic: they faced a potential loss of money equal to the deficit if the session were cancelled, and they had to consider their public image.

Even while urgently involved with the immediate problems of financial survival, all the parties concerned were aware that the school's educational, artistic, and financial policies needed review before plans beyond 1941 could be made.[97]

The School of the Arts, 1941

To everyone's amazement, the summer session drew a larger paid enrollment than had been forecast, and a highly successful box office for the festival effectively wiped out the expected deficit. Salaries were restored from surplus funds at the summer's end.

During the second and last session of the School of the Arts there were 27 performances, the most by far of any festival up to that time. The school also took an active part in the Green Mountain Festival held in Middlebury on the occasion of Vermont's Sesquicentennial. The Humphrey-Weidman Company and the Martha Graham Company each gave a concert of repertory; the Music Division presented Mozart's *The Impresario* (honoring the 150th anniversary of the composer's death); the Drama Division presented Molière's *School for Wives*, with ballet interludes choreographed by Martha Hill. Back at Bennington two weeks later, The Theater and Music Divisions took over the General Stark Theatre, a movie house in the town of Bennington that had once been used for opera and vaudeville. Through an arrangement whereby Bennington provided vaudeville interludes for movie audiences, the management of the theater provided the stage for festival presentations of Kenyon Nicholson's *The Barker*, directed by Francis Fergusson, and a double bill of *School for Wives* and *The Impresario*. The Dance Division offered a series of nine performances in the College Theatre split between Humphrey-Weidman and Graham.

For some time Humphrey had been stymied in her search for a theme for her Bennington production. "The world situation continually urges me to make some sort of comment—yet the whole thing is so vast that any statement seems silly," she wrote her mother in the spring of 1941.[98] She made her decision just before the session opened: "It's going to be a Biography of the years 1930–40 at 18th Street [their studio]. The general theme being the struggle of pioneer art in a world geared to profit. We ought to be able to do that with feeling!"[99]

The work, entitled *Decade*, was a kaleidoscopic revue of ten years of struggle and choreography. It had a spoken script plus excerpts from more than a dozen compositions. For the first time, the modern dance looked back on its history. *Decade* ended with the company gesturing toward a door at the rear of the stage, which represented Humphrey-Weidman's new home in New York, the Studio Theatre. It was Doris Humphrey's last production at the Bennington summer school.

Martha Graham reprised *El Penitente* and *Letter to the World* (both of which had been changed substantially from their first productions the previous summer) and mounted *Punch and The Judy*, a new work that also employed spoken text, in this case by Gordon Craig. Erick Hawkins, Jean Erdman, and Jane Dudley gave a joint concert preceding the festival. (Hawkins had made his solo debut at Bennington in 1940.) Composer Henry Cowell, in residence with the Music Division, conducted two recitals of contemporary music, and Ralph Kirkpatrick gave two harpsichord recitals.

As the *Dance Observer* reported, "in the summer when many another plan had to be cancelled or trimmed, Bennington managed to survive by sheer persistence and faith in its function in the American scene today."[100]

The End of the Summer Dance Program

Money and Other Numbers

The School of the Dance was a self-sustaining enterprise that ran in the black through the Depression years (it would likely have been terminated abruptly had it not) and paid the college for use of its facilities and plant.[101]

Enrollment for the six sessions of the School of the Dance (1934–1939) totalled 850 fully paid students, or about 700 different students attending one or more sessions. Of an average of 141 students each summer, about 65 percent were teachers of dance and 35 percent students. The age range was from 15 to 50, with an average age of 26.

By 1939 all 48 states and the District of Columbia had been represented in the student body, with the exception of Arkanasas. (Arkansas completed the roster in 1940.) There was a small number of students from Canada, France, England, Spain, India, and Hawaii. The largest male contingent was enrolled during Charles Weidman's special Men's Workshop in 1936 (the same summer Ted Shawn organized his School for Men at nearby Jacob's Pillow); still, there were but 11, raising the average per session to 5 for the years 1935-1939. The school enrolled its first black student, from Spellman College, in 1935.

The fee rose from $190 (including room and board) in 1934 to $255 in 1938 and dropped back to $250 for the Mills summer. With curricula expansion and festival production, the school's expenses climbed from $17,000 in 1934 to a high of $41,000 in 1938, the most ambitious of the festival years. Production costs averaged under $2000 for each festival summer from 1935-1938, exclusive of salaries. (Salaries in 1937 accounted for about $9000 out of the total budget of $32,000. Graham, Humphrey, and Weidman earned $325 each for two weeks of teaching, in addition to living expenses. Holm was paid $450 to direct the major workshop. Composer Wallingford Riegger received $75 for five weeks' work on the score for *Trend*. Accompanists for the full session earned between $75 and $125, over and above modest living expenses and room and board. The Armory rented for $25 a night; tickets to the Bennington Festival productions were one dollar.[102]) There were no advertising expenses until 1937 and 1938. Advertising costs in those years were $100 and $73, respectively.

The average expense for the six summers was $31,500. Each session ended with some surplus of income over costs (from a low of $82 in 1937 to a high of $2373 during the Mills session).

Within the School of the Arts, dance drew the largest enrollments and brought in the greatest revenues. The fully paid student enrollment in the School of the Arts for its two sessions averaged 89 (compared with 141 before that in the School of the Dance), of whom over 70 percent were dance students. Their average age—23—was slightly younger than that of the students in the School of the Dance, and there were five times as many men (32 in 1940, attributable to the number of scholarships and fellowships offered; the number dropped to 17 in 1941, reflecting attrition caused by the draft).

In 1940-41, for the first time in the school's history, the proportion of teachers to nonteachers was reversed—almost exactly. Thirty-five percent of the student body were teachers; 65 percent were not.

The fee reached its highest point in 1940 ($275) and was cut back to $250 in the hope of increasing enrollment in 1941. The proportion of faculty and staff to students soared with the expansive multiarts program to nearly double what it had previously been within the School of the Dance, resulting in a larger payroll (an average of 62 as compared with 35). Income for the two sessions remained stable at about $31,000, but expenses had increased by about 22 percent. The 1941 session ended with a deficit that equalled the unpaid costs of the college plant (around $4000).

Almost all expenses for the School of the Arts were higher than they had been for the School of the Dance, including advertising costs, which totalled $465 for the two sessions. In October 1941 the school's directors reported the following:

> On the financial side, the income base of the School is too narrow for its expanded superstructure of costs; and on the personnel side, the market for the School has shifted from teachers primarily, to primarily a younger, more professional group. How to read the two facts for the future depends upon the nature of that future. Certainly any financial plan must be curtailed even over the rock-bottom budget drawn up in the emergency of May 1941. Last summer's actualities do not serve as a safe minimum. Too many of the factors making for loss of income in 1940 and 1941 are still at work, and these are not offset by sufficiently strong new inducements to students, to allow any but very conservative expectations.[103]

The Presidential Succession

At the close of the 1941 session, Robert Leigh resigned as president of Bennington College, a move he had written into the college plan to assure fresh leadership. He was succeeded by Lewis Webster Jones, a member of the original college faculty and a professor of social studies who had served as acting president during Leigh's leave of absence in 1939.

Jones' commitment to the School of the Arts could not be expected to run as deep as Leigh's. Leigh after all had created the School of the Dance with Hill and Shelly. The school and its festivals had attracted international notice by now. It would have been impolitic of Jones to appear to be less than supportive of it or to terminate it without good cause. Simultaneously, the plan of the college was itself undergoing intensive scrutiny; changes within the college were to have important ramifications for the summer project.

Internal Disunity

In the two summers of the school's life, potentialities of collaboration among the arts were only partially realized, and there had been internal squabbles. Jones expressed concern at the disunity among various divisions of the School of the Arts, which he perceived had grown deeper after two sessions. He was also perturbed by the remote relationship between the school and the college. It was his view that the School of the Arts should be a direct extension of the Bennington College curriculum, and he urged the school's directors to tighten that link.

In the fall of 1941 meeting followed meeting, with position papers drawn up by every side. The heart of the problem was that the Dance Division had a strength relative to the other divisions in the school that gave it clear advantage and caused a serious imbalance. Dance drew most of the school's enrollment and thus accounted for most of its income. Its international prestige derived largely from its ability to attract the leading artists in its field, and these artists, who both taught and performed, demanded the highest level of production. This put the other divisions at some disadvantage. It was not necessarily desirable, for example, for the Drama Division to enlist the most prestigious actors, directors, and playwrights in order to achieve their own particular educational and artistic ends. The Dance Division contended that the Drama Division was the weak element in the scheme, and that while collaborations between dance, music, and theater design had been productive by and large, those between dance and drama had been far less successful. Hill and Shelly voiced reservations about the proficiency of the acting company and also questioned the Drama Division's aesthetic point of view, which they saw as being less innovative than that of the Dance Division.

Martha Hill argued against forcing too direct a tie between the summer school and the college. In her view, the School of the Arts had been created to serve an adult, professional population and it could and should enlarge upon the undergraduate college curriculum, not replicate it.

Francis Fergusson's view of things was quite different. The concept of the School of the Arts, he emphasized, had evolved from collaborations at the college. He argued for integrating the summer school more closely with the winter curriculum of the college. Fergusson could see that it would be difficult, if not impossible, to achieve a coequal School of the Arts so long as the Dance Division was concerned with maintaining control of the modern dance movement at Bennington, which implied the involvement of "the big dancers" and their needs for production. Bringing in stellar names in drama and music, for example, a Leopold Stokowski or a Max Reinhardt, would not necessarily enhance the school's educational or artistic values and might, he warned, cause much more serious problems.

Arch Lauterer allied himself with the Dance Division, urging separate design programs, one for drama and opera and one for dance. Otto Luening saw the collaboration as working rather well, except for the split between drama and dance. He urged continuance of the whole School of the Arts after such a successful summer and an earnest effort to resolve the major issues in dispute. This, however, would have taken more time than was available before planning the 1942 session.[104]

On 24 October 1941, the Trustee Committee resolved that

> the idea of the School of the Arts is excellent and ought not to be lost sight of; but . . . in view of the war emergency and the necessity for coordinating a long-range plan for the School with such reorganization as there may be in the College, and for reasons of economy . . . it would be wise to operate the Dance Division of the School of the Arts alone this summer.[105]

In December the United States was at war in Europe and the Far East. Nonetheless, plans were drawn up in January to

Charles Weidman and Doris Humphrey at Bennington, 1938. Photograph by Betty Lynd Thompson.

continue the School of the Dance for the coming summer, calling for Humphrey, Weidman, and Graham with their two concert groups to be in residence. In addition, Lauterer, Horst, Lloyd, Schönberg, Hawkins, and Henrietta Greenhood [Eve Gentry] (Hanya Holm's assistant) would serve as core faculty. But in March Lewis Jones informed the dance faculty of further economies in the summer plans that would make production impossible. To boot, he could offer no salaries—just food, lodging, and a small allowance for expenses.

Doris Humphrey and Charles Weidman withdrew:

> We are obliged to make every effort to meet the heavy expenses that go on in the summer for us, and could not afford to set aside six weeks which would pay living costs only. This is a very unhappy decision for us, as you must know that the opportunity to create and teach and perform at Bennington is one which we have prized highly and we consider it a major sacrifice to have to give it up, even for one season. . . . We hope that when more settled times recur, the dance center, for which Bennington is justly famous will once more be able to function as a unit.[106]

Erick Hawkins agreed to come but sent a strong letter to Jones expressing his feelings about the curtailment of the program:

> It is a great pity, I feel, that when the Berkshire Music Festival announces in the press months ahead that a large part of their series of concerts are sold out, that when the Jacob's Pillow organization under Mr. Ted Shawn is building a new theatre and announcing performances by every Tom, Dick and Harry, always including of course the exotics, the nucleus of this native American art which is already a part of history, this Bennington in the summertime, this unique germ of the dance

art which penetrates almost every college and thousands of high schools throughout the country, this thing which did not come from Russia or France or Germany or England, should announce to the world months in advance—"Sorry, we can't show you any dancing now. Not even 900 people can see new works produced. That dancing is the most successful entertainment in England during the War means nothing to us."

I know these things are a matter of dollars and cents, but I also know . . . that they are a matter of spirit, imagination and courage. . . . [Bennington] performed a job no other organization was equipped to do or had the imagination to do; and to see its momentum checked is a grievous thing to me.[107]

The future of the School of the Arts, which had already been in jeopardy, was sealed by the coming war.

The Summer of 1942

The dance program continued for one more session as part of the Bennington College Summer Session in the Arts, but this time alongside course offerings in music, graphic and the plastic arts, government, economics, and science. The dance session had one major artist in residence—Martha Graham. Assistants for Humphrey-Weidman and Hanya Holm were vestigial links to the School of the Dance. College music faculty members—Otto Luening, Robert McBride, and Gregory Tucker—worked with the dancers. There was no drama component. Graham began to prepare *Deaths and Entrances*, which was performed at Bennington College in 1943.

There was no festival, but several young choreographers performed new works. Among them were Merce Cunningham and Jean Erdman making their joint choreographic debut. Thus did the end of the Bennington period forecast new beginnings.

In the fall of 1942 Mary Jo Shelly was granted a leave of absence from Bennington College (where she had served in administrative capacities since leaving the University of Chicago in 1938) to become a lieutenant in the women's naval reserve (WAVES) in charge of physical training and drill.

In 1943 the curriculum and calendar of the college were revised, following the major survey of its plan. The winter recess was extended to a four-month off-campus term to conserve fuel in the war years. There was henceforth only a three-week break between semesters in August—insufficient time for a summer session. Though Bennington shut down its summer program, other dance projects kept going through the war years. Hanya Holm led a hugely successful ten-week summer session at Colorado College in 1943.[108] And Jacob's Pillow, which opened its new dance theater during Bennington's last summer, 1942, managed to operate throughout the war as a school and performance center.[109]

Lewis Jones recognized the importance of keeping some semblance of the college's historic connections with the modern dance. Martha Graham found Bennington's atmosphere congenial and wanted to return the following summer to plot a new composition. In June and July of 1943-1945, Graham returned to Bennington College as visiting artist for a four- to six-week residency, along with Louis Horst and members of her company, during the college's regular academic session.

On 11 July 1946 Bennington College once again served as the site for some historic dance premieres when José Limón brought his newly formed company to make its debut with two new works composed by Doris Humphrey, *The Story of Mankind* and *Lament for Ignacio Sánchez Mejías.*

Bennington to Connecticut: Six Years Later

At the war's end in 1946, Martha Hill resurrected the idea of a summer center for the modern dance. She enlisted support from Ernest Melby, dean of New York University's School of Education. When they failed to find suitable facilities in Manhattan, Hill investigated academic plants nearby. At Connecticut College for Women in New London, she found a prospective site that housed a modern 1300-seat theater—Palmer Auditorium. In December 1947 Rosemary Park, president of Connecticut College, notified Hill that the college would collaborate with New York University in a summer school of the dance in 1948.[110]

Hill lined up many former Bennington colleagues for the new venture, including Arch Lauterer, who was then at Mills:

> I respond like a fire horse to a seven alarm signal. I'm hoping so that it will all happen . . . what we were all doing [at Bennington] was really the grass roots of an American theatre art—and of course it moved and grew slowly—but when it stopped—real, true, and growing theatre stopped.[111]

The American Dance Festival modelled itself on Bennington but later veered from the original Bennington pattern in many particulars. By the time the idea was transplanted to Connecticut in 1948, both the state of the country and the situation of its leading dancers had altered dramatically. America had become a world power, and the country was adjusting to peace after a victorious but costly war. Although the economy was temporarily depressed, a boom was just around the corner.

The original Connecticut faculty roster, though studded with former Benningtonites (17 out of 20 had taught, danced, or studied at the Bennington School of the Dance), was lacking two of the Big Four—Charles Weidman and Hanya Holm.

During the six-year hiatus between the end of the Bennington project and the start of Connecticut, Doris Humphrey had quit the stage because of an arthritic hip. She was now choreographic mentor to José Limón, who had his own company. Martha Graham had, in the interim, ascended to preeminence as a performer and choreographer. (In May 1943 she ventured a historic one-week engagement on Broadway at the National Theatre; in 1947 she was "profiled" by the *New Yorker.*) Following the dissolution of the Humphrey-Weidman

Company, Charles Weidman held a small group together for a time and also worked in nightclubs and on Broadway. But Weidman did not participate in the Connecticut project in 1948. Nor did Hanya Holm (not then, and not ever), who had found a more amenable summer situation of her own in Colorado Springs. In 1948 Holm was also on the verge of a major Broadway success as choreographer of the hit show *Kiss Me, Kate.*

A form letter sent to potential donors in July 1948 by the Connecticut College Festival Committee described the first summer's plan:

> The Festival this summer will not try to begin at the point of extensive new production reached at Bennington after successive seasons of development. Production costs have doubled and prospective income has not. But it will begin with a series of concerts that are in effect a statement of the growth of the art since Bennington ended, with such new production as is possible at this time.[112]

For the festival audience of 8000 (as compared with about 13,000 in all six Bennington festivals) Martha Graham produced a bright new work, *Wilderness Stair* (*Diversion of Angels*); Doris Humphrey premiered *Corybantic* with José Limón and his company; Erick Hawkins presented *The Strangler*, and the Dudley-Maslow-Bales company performed recent works.

As a concomitant of sponsorship by NYU's School of Education, there were more formal courses in teaching methods and materials than there ever had been at Bennington. Everything was on a somewhat larger scale—the campus, the theater, the size of the orchestra (and the union fees charged)—except for student enrollment, which was sharply lower than anticipated. The school ran a deficit its first summer and struggled through its early years with low enrollments. In 1951 New York University withdrew its affiliation, and Connecticut College became sole sponsor.

Martha Hill served as chairman of the Administrative Board in 1948 and as co-director of the School of the Dance with Ruth Bloomer, who had been a student at Bennington, until 1958. She remained on the American Dance Festival Committee until 1968, ending twenty years' affiliation with a project she had pioneered at Bennington more than thirty years before.[113] Through her direction of the dance department at the Juilliard School, Martha Hill continued her behind-the-scenes role in nurturing the modern dance.

Mary Jo Shelly was a member of the Connecticut College American Dance Festival Committee in its first year but had no subsequent formal tie with the project. She left Bennington College in 1954, having worked in various administrative capacities on her return from war service in both World War II and the Korean War, to be director of public relations for the Girl Scouts of the USA. She died on 6 August 1976.

The Connecticut College School of the Dance and American Dance Festival, whose roots lay within the Bennington School of the Dance, held its 30th and last session in 1977. Citing financial and administrative difficulties with the college, the project's directors announced that the school and festival would take up residence at Duke University in Durham, North Carolina, beginning in the summer of 1978.

Reflections on Bennington

The Bennington project could have belonged to no other decade but the thirties. It was at once a time of economic, social, and political turbulence, widespread fear and disillusion, and also of uncommon energy, pluck, and vision. America, not yet a world power, was on the move in the wake of a devastating depression. The spirit of the New Deal and its promise to rebuild society along more just and progressive lines permeated all aspects of life, including the arts. (It was in this period that the federal government first began subsidizing artists through the Works Progress Administration.) Times were hard, and like others caught in them, dancers were impelled to try to work together toward goals that were impossible to achieve working alone. In the general bustle of national recovery, the insurgent modern dance took hold and spread like wildfire.

In 1935 George Beiswanger perceived a critical link between those "difficult years in which social stress evoked communal vision" and the modern dance:

> The dance has been important when it has had something of communal import to say. This fact the modern dance has instinctively sensed from the beginning. In most of its manifestations, from the early groups that gathered around Isadora Duncan to the Bennington School of the Dance, it has been a reflection of the twentieth century desire for a renewal of the collective life. It has voiced, however inadequately, the need of men to depend upon each other, the need of finding together the solution of our problems, and the need of "a common faith."[114]

Martha Graham put it this way in 1937: "Man used to dance to ally himself with the cosmic forces about him in a religious sense; man dances today in a social sense to ally himself with mankind."[115]

The Bennington school's fundamental purpose was to be a center for the study of the modern dance—a rallying point for a new American art. By bringing most of the leading figures in the field into one arena, Bennington nurtured individual careers and provided unique opportunities for creative work, collaboration, and recognition. And in sanctioning their mission—by giving psychological as well as financial

Martha Graham, 1936 or 1938.
Photograph by Sidney Bernstein.

support to the leading artists—Bennington fostered a new image of the modern dance as a cohesive movement.

Unlike the Federal Dance Project (1936-1939), Bennington proposed no social remedies; nor was its primary intention to put unemployed artists to work or to bring modern dance to "the people." The art rather than the individual artist was of paramount concern. Yet by virtue of its design and its success, Bennington coined an innovative form of arts patronage. Through Bennington, artists were subsidized and the art of the modern dance was disseminated across America.

Still, Bennington was conceived first and foremost as an educational experiment. The strategy of making a progressive college a springboard for the modern dance movement had consequences no one could have imagined. At the time, it was simply an idea born of necessity.

The school's functional unity, its sense of high purpose and conviction, emanated from a remarkable twinning of talents and personalities: Mary Jo Shelly as administrator-planner—elegant, cool, and effective, and Martha Hill as mediator-teacher-confidante—warm and cheerful, a woman of infectious determination. They were the catalysts who espoused the ideal of cooperation while keeping separate camps at arm's length. Their own personal sympathies, however, were clear: Bennington was essentially Graham territory. Doris Humphrey noted this the very first summer. "There is," she wrote, "a permanent staff of Martha's Votaries, so anyone else is at a decided disadvantage."[116] Nonetheless, Hill and Shelly earned and retained the respect and gratitude of all. They had something tangible to offer, something no one could afford to refuse. The two juggled myriad problems of scheduling, temperament, facilities, time, and money. There could be little waste, for there were no resources to squander. Plans and proposals were honed to a fine edge. Despite perpetual crises, including the prospect of cancellation based on projected deficits as small as $1500, they pursued their vision with unwavering zeal and composure.

Without Martha Graham, the project could not have succeeded; and it was Graham who gained most conspicuously from the Bennington association. Of the Big Four, she alone was in residence each summer; after the school closed in 1942, only Graham was invited by Bennington College to return as artist-in-residence for three consecutive years. During Bennington summers, she started collaborating with Arch Lauterer and met Erick Hawkins and Merce Cunningham. A new phase of her work began in 1938 with the addition of Hawkins to her previously all-female group. It was at Bennington that Graham experimented with moving sculpture (*Panorama*), the spoken word (*American Document*), properties (*El Penitente*), and poetry (*Letter to the World*).

Although Doris Humphrey was rankled by the favoritism shown Graham, dismayed by what she perceived as a lack of daring on the part of the school's administrators, and resentful of having to teach in order to compose,[117] she created some of her greatest works at Bennington. The availability of large numbers of dancers made possible the creation of dances on a symphonic scale. The competitive atmosphere Humphrey so abhorred may actually have stimulated a period of brilliant creative intensity.

Bennington brought Hanya Holm, and thus the German school, into the mainstream of American modern dance. At Bennington Holm made her East Coast debut (1936), created her first and possibly greatest composition (*Trend*, 1937), and began a fruitful collaboration with Arch Lauterer which continued later in Colorado. After 1938 Holm produced nothing new at Bennington. She ended her association in 1940, and in 1941 she became director of the summer dance program at Colorado College. There she was the central figure.

Of the Big Four, Charles Weidman composed the fewest new dances at Bennington, and it is hard to assess its influence on him.[118] Both *Quest* and *Opus 51* show traces of the ideas, conflicts, and temperaments that converged at Bennington. Unquestionably, his irrepressible, irreverent wit acted as a leavening agent in what may at times have seemed a sanctified meeting ground for evangelists. His graphic imitations of Martha and Doris and Hanya demonstrated the acuteness of his powers of observation; moreover, he was not above laughing at himself. Without Charles Weidman, Bennington would have been a female preserve. He provided a needed balance. Weidman recognized Bennington's key role in building an audience for the dance, an issue with which he was much concerned. Asked in 1965 what Bennington's chief importance had been, he replied, "I think it was propaganda for the American modern dance."[119]

No small factor in the propagation of the modern dance was the amount and kind of publicity Bennington generated. Official records of the school, and much of the critical reportage, strike one today as disarming propaganda. Annual reports and published articles paint a virtually flawless portrait of the project and its accomplishments. These accounts were, and still are, persuasive, even allowing for their inherent biases.

Many critics who wrote about Bennington were simultaneously engaged with the project as advisers, faculty, guest lecturers, or students. Partisanship in the 1930s was not only tolerated but virtually unavoidable, given the small size of the dance world. It was an era for proselytizing, a time when critics and dancers were trying to build support and understanding for a new art.

At the outset, the school enlisted the sympathies and participation of America's preeminent dance writer, John Martin. In Louis Horst they not only had an adviser, colleague, and collaborator on the permanent faculty but an influential publisher and critic to boot. Horst's monthly journal, the *Dance Observer*, devoted to "a sincere and serious consideration of the contemporary American dance," began its 30-year existence a few months before the Bennington school opened its doors.[120] Mary Jo Shelly and Martha Hill served on its editorial board, and Bennington faculty and students wrote about Bennington and about their colleagues in its pages.

George Beiswanger, who reported on Bennington for *Theatre Arts Monthly* and the *Dance Observer*, was guest lecturer during two sessions; his wife, dance educator Barbara Page, was enrolled as a student.

Not all supporters were insiders. Margaret Lloyd, dance critic of the *Christian Science Monitor*, took to Bennington with alacrity. Her classic *Borzoi Book of Modern Dance* is saturated with Bennington references and shows the influence Bennington had on her critical perceptions. But it was also Margaret Lloyd who cautioned that the project might be settling into a mold, like the town's famed pottery, and ought to consider bringing in someone new, for instance Tamiris.[121]

Walter Terry voiced reservations about Bennington's narrow focus on the modern dance to the exclusion of other dance forms (his sympathies at the time were with Denishawn and the ballet). Bennington was Terry's initiation into the modern dance; he wrote his first articles for the *Boston Herald* from Bennington in 1936 but never lectured or taught there himself. Terry chastised the moderns for being too introspective and for playing to cult audiences. He saved his harshest criticism for Martha Graham but began to warm to her work when she emerged as a theater artist. (Eventually he became one of Graham's ardent admirers.) As Terry went off to the war in July 1942, at the start of Bennington's last session, he described the change he had witnessed in the modern dance: "I have seen the modern dance make its final emergence from the strangling shrouds of cultism into the bright light of pure theater."[122]

Among other critics, many of them now little-known, only a few were sharply critical of Bennington.

Hill and Shelly succeeded in garnering wide and enthusiastic coverage because they had a good story to tell. The modern dance was new and peculiar; therefore it was automatically newsworthy (*vide* "Campus Seethes With Women Who Leap About in Odd Fashion," a 1938 article in a Midwestern newspaper[123]). The image of women (and a few men) cavorting on the grass under Vermont skies carried provocative connotations of recreation, sport, amusement, and even a smidgen of salaciousness—a perfect brew for news editors. Modern dance was good copy. An astonishing number of photo features were published in small-town newspapers. (A Lewiston, Maine, paper gave over its Sunday front entertainment pages to a local student's detailed impressions of Bennington.[124])

The Bennington years also saw an outpouring of substantive critical writing about the modern dance. Aesthetic debates were waged in public forums and in the pages of major newspapers. Because a handful of writers took the dance and its issues seriously, the public was encouraged to regard the subject in the same light. Eventually this attitude began to counteract the image of dance in the mass media as frivolous or ridiculous, though it by no means put an end to all the snickering.

Bennington gave the modern dance an aura of academic respectability and a shelter and conferred cultural and intellectual status upon it. In return, the summer dance school gave Bennington College an international reputation and enlarged its constituency and influence beyond a small, elite class of undergraduate women.

Through the Bennington model, American colleges became major ports of subsidy for the modern dance, but a price was exacted. In order to compose, a choreographer had also to teach. Teaching thus was not only a way of perpetuating a technique, approach, or style but a means of survival.

Bennington gave Martha Hill the opportunity to put into practice a deeply held belief that the dance student must learn through direct contact with the professional artist and that dance training must occur in the context of professional production. According to Hill, without such performance opportunities and experience, the education of a dancer would be deficient.[125] At Bennington, teachers learned how to teach

Louis Horst, 1938. Photograph by Betty Lynd Thompson.

dance and composition by dancing and composing themselves. (After 1935 no "methods" courses were offered.) This was a manifestation of learning by doing, the philosophy of progressive education. The dance and progressive education had strong affinities; in dance, doing is the traditional way of learning.

The School of the Dance granted no degree (although credits could be applied toward a degree elsewhere) and offered no certificate or grades. Nonetheless, because Bennington was the first coherent representation of the modern dance as a movement, it became something of a Good Housekeeping Seal for those who were affiliated with it; those who weren't felt left out. Moreover, Bennington and "the modern dance" had become synonymous, so that in a sense Bennington did promulgate a "method" or "approach"—that which was taught at Bennington. Given the school's concentrated authority and success and the geometric expansion of its influence through students, this was perhaps inevitable. Bennington's curriculum, its methods, and its approach to training and composition were widely imitated.[126]

Technique was confined to the three major schools represented within the Bennington hierarchy—Graham, Humphrey-Weidman, and Holm—and to a basic modern dance technique taught by Martha Hill and Bessie Schönberg, principally to teachers.

The curriculum was designed not only to foster greater technical proficiency but to get students to pay more attention to form and structure in their dance-making. Louis Horst introduced notions of discipline and historical model. He insisted that to dance meaningfully one first must learn the craft of choreography. Horst's theories, based on musical form, and his teaching methods were powerful correctives to amorphous self-expression. But soon, in lieu of the dances he disparagingly called "collegiate plastique,"[127] pale replicas of pre-classic and modern forms began to crop up across the landscape. Simultaneously, the techniques of the Big Four, absorbed by students during a summer's intensive orientation, were taught in turn to their students. The modern dance was, for the first time, in double jeopardy of becoming academized through repetitious formulas and diluted through the well-meaning (but not always accurate) efforts of students who came, saw, and returned to their classrooms to teach after the briefest of encounters with the Big Four.

Hanya Holm foresaw the dangers early on and lectured students at Bennington about them.[128] In 1940 Walter Terry surveyed the college dance scene and reported:

> Several of our leading American dancers have told me of the great harm done to dance and to education by those gymnasium instructors who, because of student demand for dance, have taken a few lessons in dance at the Bennington School of the Dance or from Ted Shawn and returned to their classes with a garbled mass of motor activity which tried to pass muster as educational dance.[129]

These problems of transmission were to become more serious as the interval between originators and disciples increased. Perhaps Bennington accelerated the process of dilution by precipitating a dispersion of the modern dance.

Bennington opened up a host of possibilities for students, including the chance to see and partake of a variety of dance expressions and techniques at first hand, and the challenge of choosing among them, of representing them adequately in teaching others or, alternatively, of fashioning out of the whole something new, something else. These prospects could only be handled by each student in a wholly individual way.

Bennington's approach to composition emphasized discipline, structure, form, and systematic method, but it also nurtured individual creativity. In the spirit of progressive education, Horst's and Hill's and Schönberg's students did not learn someone else's dances; they made their own—though within strictly defined formal boundaries. Hill's and Lauterer's experimental workshops offered a range of collaborative prospects for choreographers, musicians, designers, and poets.

Young dancers naturally began experimenting and working independently. Some undertook to work together (Bales, Dudley, and Maslow; Erdman and Hawkins; Cunningham and Erdman). A few broke away from their parent groups (May O'Donnell, José Limón, Anna Sokolow, Sybil Shearer).

The basic premise of the modern dance, said former Humphrey-Weidman dancer George Bockman, was "to teach you to be an individual." He explained:

> Once you became aware of what you could do, then you were expected to compose. And the minute you got into the field and got recognition, then you no longer wanted to be part of the group; you wanted to be you. It's intrinsically a self-destructive premise.[130]

The seeds of rebellion were sown during the Bennington years, but the revolution was to occur later, outside Bennington's grounds.

Modern dance was essentially the creation of individualists, artists who practiced their art despite the indifference or even antipathy of society. Although they worked side by side as participants in the Bennington experiment, the leading artists remained stubbornly independent. John Martin observed this in 1936:

> To speak of such a thing as a Bennington Group is very much like speaking of the equator, which, though it is a useful concept, actually does not exist. All the individuals who comprise this group are artists who are independently active, who are by no means of one mind in their views and practices of the dance, and who had achieved high degrees of success in their individual work long before the Bennington project drew them together. They have no formal relationship to each other beyond the fact that they have agreed to work on a joint educational enterprise for a specified number of summers, each contributing annually from two to six weeks of his time. Yet the fact of the Bennington project inevitably gives them a kind of unity in spite of themselves.[131]

The Bennington experiment was a group experiment. Yet while there was a sense of community and perhaps even "a kind of unity," Bennington did not itself give rise to communal or collective choreography. Preexisting dance groups were strengthened at Bennington by adding to their ranks students and apprentices, but Bennington itself bred no new group. In contrast to such other experiments of the period as the Federal Dance Project (1936-1939) and the Group Theatre (1931-1941), no attempt was made to subordinate the individual to the larger interests of a group creation or social cause. Even in the act of collaboration, the individual artist put his or her signature on the whole. In the works of Martha Graham involving collaborators on design, music, and costumes, the end result always had a distinctive Graham stamp. Nor did the school itself function as a collective. Control flowed downward from the upper rungs, where the artist-teacher perched, to the student minions. (Merce Cunningham alluded to the difference in this respect between Black Mountain College and Bennington in an interview quoted on p. 257.)

But the Big Four were not only individual artists and performers; they were also leaders of groups. And it was through the structure of group and leader that dance was taught at Bennington. "The dance is fundamentally a communal art," Martha Hill said in 1934. "Individual styles only emerge from working together first. Group styles are made from what each individual brings."[132]

The impact and role of the Bennington experiment itself can best be understood through the dances that were produced there. Many of them were informed with a communal vision.

In his book about the Group Theatre, Harold Clurman called the thirties "the fervent years," a period when the arts were inspired by "the humanistic tradition of the Emerson, Thoreau, Walt Whitman epoch."[133] The artist's goal was broader than "a few political-social reforms." It was nothing less than "man and his relation to the world or life itself on all the planes that the concept implies."

These concerns were the marrow of many dances that had their premieres at Bennington, especially Doris Humphrey's *New Dance* and *Passacaglia* and Hanya Holm's *Trend*, works of affirmation which employed a large canvas to explore man's relation to man, destructive and constructive forces at work in the world, and the elusive goal of harmony in human relations. In a sense these dances mirrored the Bennington experiment itself; each artist's reflection of that experience was of course individual and different, but Bennington's aspirations, the coming together of large groups of dancers in common cause, and the rivalry and competition among artists and among their groups, were woven into the fabric of the works.

In this light, Doris Humphrey's *New Dance* might speak of the Bennington experiment and her hopes for it:

> *New Dance* presents a view of the world as it might be where all members will have a functioning part within the whole; where each member will retain his individuality and at the same time be an active member of an harmonious group.[134]

These ideals and tensions can be observed in photographs and films that show dancers moving singly and *en masse*—running and leaping across the green, stretching out and reaching upward to the Vermont skies.

Dance forms were enlarged and extended at Bennington. The group, augmented by apprentices from a dozen or a dozen and a half to upward of thirty dancers, was deployed to give a sense of mass and volume. Problems between individual and society were articulated as soloist moved in relation to the group. "It is only through this large use of groups of men and women," wrote Doris Humphrey in 1936, "that the modern dance can completely do what it has always said it would do."[135]

The modern dance began to work out its destiny at Bennington. To a great extent, the works and concerns were autobiographical, even though cast in a larger social framework. Doris Humphrey and Charles Weidman made dances about their travails as individuals in society and as pioneer artists in "a world geared to profit."[136] In *Quest* Weidman was the artist in search of "conditions under which he may achieve full and free expression." The dance concluded with "a strong affirmation of his oneness with the masses of mankind" in a section entitled "Affirmation."[137]

Martha Graham's early Bennington works thrust the individual into relation with society amid a stream of history (*Panorama*, 1935; *American Document*, 1938). Later, in *El Penitente* and *Letter to the World*, events in her inner life eclipsed the outer landscape. In these new experiments, the group could be encapsulated within a single dancer, conflict could be internalized. Simultaneously, Graham sought more theatrical modes through which to express the inner landscape.

During the Bennington years, East Coast critics wrote at length about large issues, among them the imperative for the modern dance to reach beyond its followers and cults to a wider audience. While some writers harped on the need for accessibility and recommended using more theatrical means to achieve this end, others argued for dances of greater social significance, against intellectual abstraction, and for abandoning the notion of dance for dance's sake.

Although Bennington was by no means a radical outpost in a period of leftist agitation, a number of works were charged with political and social consciousness and concerned with such issues as the destruction of life and the suppression of liberty in dictatorships and the rise of fascism (Martha Graham's *Immediate Tragedy*, Anna Sokolow's *Façade-Esposizione Italiana*, José Limón's *Danza de la Muerte*); the hypocrisy of war (Charles Weidman's *Quest*), and the search for meaning in the American past (Graham's *Panorama* and *American Document*). The *Daily Worker* praised Graham's *American Document*, calling it a work "destined to appeal to masses of people." This, said the *Worker*, was "the greatest proof of a socially conscious artist."[138]

Pressures on choreographers and dancers were manifold and unrelenting. "Someone who simply wanted to dance was out of joint with these times," observed May O'Donnell.[139]

The sharp, percussive outcries of the early experiments in modern dance began to give way in the Bennington years to a more fluid, even lyrical, movement. The modern dance was evolving from the darkly austere "abstract" style of the 1920s and early 1930s to a more consciously programmatic theater dance that attempted to integrate costumes, stage design, music, spoken word, and poetry with movement. Elaborate program notes accompanied dances to explicate the choreographer's intent and help audiences "understand" the modern dance. Longer dances lasting half a program or more replaced short solo recital pieces. Large groups of dancers flooded the stage. "Except for an occasional brilliant individual," wrote Doris Humphrey in 1936, "I believe that the day of the solo dancer is over."[140]

In 1939 *Dance Observer* critic Henry Gilfond described two major trends in American dance,

> one to the people by way of contemporary materials, of the moment or its traditions; . . . the other inward back to the abstract pattern, the precious audience, and away from the people. One goes forward, the other retreats. There can be no question, at all, as to which direction spells development and progress for the art; and which does not.[141]

In 1940 John Martin looked back at Doris Humphrey's *New Dance* and pronounced it "the beginning of a new era":

> Henceforth the recital form, consisting of a succession of unrelated little compositions without theatre dimensions, was cast aside, and composers turned their attention to large forms dramatizing the conflict between the individual and his universe. . . . The dance had become a theatre form.[142]

This evolution can be traced through the Bennington repertoire. As it grew beyond its revolutionary roots and moved toward enlarged theater forms, the staunch purity of the modern dance in its earlier, experimental phase was relinquished. A trend toward eclecticism had already begun in the Bennington years. Beginning in 1938 the school's curriculum reflected détente with the ballet, tap, and folk dance. Ballet Caravan's debut in 1936 may have had little demonstrable impact on the modern contingent, but ballet had made a symbolic incursion into the inner sanctum of the modern dance. Doris Humphrey expressed concern about the stylistic mongrelization of the modern dance in 1937:

> The one indispensable quality in a work of art is a consistent point of view related to the times, and when this is lost and there is substituted for it an aptitude for putting together striking bits of this and that, there can be no integrity. I do not therefore favor the most common combination of styles, the so popular mixture of the ballet and modern techniques. . . .[143]

Support groups that formed around the Big Four were close-knit families headed by a leader or leaders of power, stature, and charismatic command. This social unit was somewhat different from the extended family structure of the world of ballet—a tradition-bound international community to which all ballet dancers feel related. The modern dance family evolved as a modern nuclear family: a self-contained, mobile, and monolithic (or, in the case of Humphrey-Weidman, duolithic) unit, operating in some desired isolation from the rest of society, and generating internal rebellion.

The fealty of a dancer to a choreographer reflected the degree of commitment necessary to sustain a life in dance. Once a dancer chose a particular choreographer and group, shopping around, taking a class here and there, or moving freely from one group to another was not easily accomplished. There were no union restrictions on hours spent rehearsing, and usually there was no pay for rehearsals or for performances. "We all danced regardless," Agnes de Mille said about those years—a time when all was asked, all given.[144]

The modern dancer of the 1930s belonged to a rare species and was not easily replaced. There was no ready means of substitution, no pool of trained talent to draw on, no videotape or score from which to learn a role. Under such circumstances, the loss of a dancer to another group was a major setback. (In a certain sense, the modern dancer of today is an interchangeable component in a modular dance society. Just as open living arrangements are supplanting the nuclear family, with a loosening of ties and commitments, so contemporary dancers now move more freely from company to company.)

The Bennington groups were hand-crafted in the technical and stylistic image of their creative leaders. The groups existed to perform the choreography of their leaders and no other. Possibly the Graham group was more autocratic than the others. Though she molded movement to her dancers' unique bodies and personalities, Graham the incomparable performer, Graham the dancer, was the primal model and source. Humphrey, Weidman, and Holm may have allowed somewhat more leeway for creative contributions from their dancers. (For example, company members choreographed their own variations in *New Dance* and the group solos in *Trend*; and Doris Humphrey helped José Limón with his composing.)

The groups were organically unified, yet, paradoxically, within each group the dancers were markedly individual. They were of different sizes, shapes, personalities, and abilities. There was no featureless, assembly-line replication. Cohesiveness was the result of intimate contact with the powerful procreative force of the choreographer, who danced with the group. (Some group members clung to the original ideas and formulas of Graham or Humphrey or Weidman or Holm, unable to perceive that the artists had opened themselves up to fresh possibilities and were ever changing. Some dancers remained frozen in a movement phase or a stage of technical evolution or choreographic invention from which their "leader" had since departed.)

Strict demarcations between groups and styles may have become blurred, however, by their mere proximity at Bennington. Although professional dancers rarely crossed over from one group to another, a new generation of students had the option of apprenticing with any or all of the Big Four.[145]

The issue of authenticity is passionately debated whenever works are revived. The imprint and impact of a dance at its birth cannot be replicated. The few dances that survive from the Bennington period have been distilled from memories of their initial configurations and recreated years afterward on different performers and sensibilities. Not only are other dancers involved, but body archetypes have altered in the intervening years.

Dancers' bodies were different in the Bennington years, partly because of diet. They were heavier, more rooted to the earth, less aerial, more in touch with nature—the pull of gravity, the violent, primal force of contraction, the weight and flow of air. The line of the body doing the movement was less essential than the uncompromising mandate of the choreography. A new work was not merely a test of the dancer's mettle but a statement about life and art, danced, as Martha Graham might say, "on the instant."

Today's modern dancers are a different breed. Ballet-trained, capable of exceptional flexibility and sleek virtuosity, with limbs long and stretched out, dancers can don or shed styles of movement like costumes. Total concentration on "the one way" of dancing in the Bennington years has been replaced by brilliant versatility. Reconstructions of the masterworks of modern dance often seem pallid because they lack the weight, dynamics, volume, and galvanic power of the original.

A faculty member wrote in 1942 that the excitement of Bennington College's first years was never again to be equalled.[146] The same was true for the School of the Dance. In retrospect, the summers of 1935-1938 seem to have been the vintage Bennington seasons. Some of the fervor of those years and the sense of high adventure derived from the happenstance that the School of Dance, itself new and experimental, was housed within an institution that was also newborn. Yet even this period of vitality was fleeting. (In 1937, when the school had completed its fourth session, some critics suggested it was in need of a blood transfusion.) Those who were there in its first phase seem to have been most deeply marked by the experience. "The pure fire was there to do something completely new, completely honest," said former Humphrey-Weidman dancer Maxine Cushing Gray.[147]

The Bennington project probably could not have sustained such intensity much longer than it actually did, for it was itself implicated in the process of change, growth, and dispersion that in many ways it had inspired.

NOTES

1. "The College and the World About Us. Extracts from Remarks of President Robert D. Leigh at the First Community Meeting of the Second Year at Bennington College, September 6, 1933," *Bennington College Bulletin* 2, no. 1 (August 1933): 6. Robert Devore Leigh was appointed president of Bennington College in January 1928. He was at the time of his appointment professor of government at Williams College and had taught at Reed, Barnard, and Columbia.
2. "Some Recollections of the Beginnings of Bennington College," *Bennington College Bulletin* 25, no. 2 (June 1957).
3. Barbara Jones, *Bennington College: The Development of an Educational Idea*. (New York: Harper & Bros., 1946), p. 118.
4. John McCullough, "Recollections on Recollecting Recollections," *Quadrille* 7, no. 1 (Fall 1972): 4-7.
5. Tom Brockway, "Dance at Bennington, 1932-41," *Quadrille* 12, no. 1 (Spring 1978): 25.
6. Ibid.
7. Mary P. O'Donnell, "Martha Hill," *Dance Observer* 3, no. 4 (April 1936): 37.
8. Ibid.
9. Margaret H'Doubler's Oral History for the American Alliance for Health, Physical Education and Recreation (AAHPER) by Mary Alice Brennan, 8 October 1972, gives 1923 as the date of the first dance major at Wisconsin and 1921 as the year in which H'Doubler first developed dance courses there. Other sources give 1917 as the year H'Doubler began teaching dance in the physical education department, and 1926 as the year the University of Wisconsin offered the first degree program in dance–a Bachelor of Science degree in physical education with a dance major.
10. Interview with Barbara Page Beiswanger.
11. Ibid.
12. John Martin, "In the Realm of the Dance," *Drama* 21, no. 6 (March 1931): 21. See also Christena L. Schlundt, *Tamiris: A Chronicle of Her Dance Career, 1927-1955* (New York: New York Public Library, 1972), pp. 14-24.
13. Ted Shawn, *One Thousand and One Night Stands* (New York: Da Capo Press, 1979), pp. 239-259. See also Christena L. Schlundt, *The Professional Appearances of Ted Shawn & His Men Dancers: A Chronology and an Index of Dances 1933-1940* (New York: New York Public Library, 1967); Schlundt, *The Professional Appearances of Ruth St. Denis & Ted Shawn: A Chronology and an Index of Dances 1906-1932* (New York: New York Public Library, 1962), pp. 73-78; and Walter Terry, *Ted Shawn: Father of American Dance* (New York: Dial Press, 1976).
14. [Paul R. Milton], "The Coxey's Army of the Concert World: A Study of the Ills and Ailments of the 'Serious' Dance Fields," *Dance Magazine* 15, no. 2 (December 1930): 10.
15. [Doris Humphrey], "Doris Humphrey Speaks. . . ," *Dance Observer* 29, no. 3 (March 1962): 38.
16. Interview with Charles Weidman in *Festival of the Dance* (film), Ted Steeg Productions, 1973.
17. Schlundt, *Tamiris*, Chapter 4, contains a succinct survey of efforts to organize dancers and cites sources for the WPA Dance Project. See also Jeanne Lunin Heymann, "Dance in the Depression: The WPA Project," *Dance Scope* 9, no. 2 (Spring/Summer 1975): 28-40.
18. Lucile Marsh, "Terpsichore Goes to College," *Dance Magazine* 18, no. 7 (June 1943): 4, gives another point of view: "Unfortunately the following year [1933] a group of New York Moderns gained political control of the board of tryouts and excluded all applicants except those that measured up to New York modernistic standards of dancing. This, along with the fact that in most colleges the physical education department handled the dance, and therefore, were more sympathetic to a gymnastic approach, gave the New York Modern Movement an edge in the college group."
19. George W. Beiswanger, "Physical Education and the Emergence of the Modern Dance," *Journal of Health and Physical Education* 7, no. 7 (September 1936): 413-16, 463, in *The Dance Experience*, ed. Myron Howard Nadel and Constance Gwen Nadel (New York: Praeger Publishers, 1970), p. 320.
20. Nellie Centennial Cornish, *Miss Aunt Nellie: The Autobiography of Nellie C. Cornish*, ed. Ellen Van Volkenburg Browne and Edward Nordhoff Beck (Seattle: University of Washington Press, 1964).
21. Selma Jeanne Cohen, *Doris Humphrey: An Artist First* (Middletown, Conn.: Wesleyan University Press, 1972), p. 96.
22. Interview with John Martin.
23. John Martin, *The Modern Dance* (Brooklyn, N.Y.: Dance Horizons, 1965), pp. 19-20.
24. Mary Jo Shelly, "A Point of View on the Modern Dance," *Sportswoman* 10, no. 8 (May 1934): 11.
25. "Memorandum on the tentative proposal for a Summer School of the Dance to be held at Bennington College during the summer of 1934," from Robert D. Leigh, 17 October 1933 [Bennington College Archive].
26. Mary Jo Shelly, "Footnote to the History of an Art," *Quadrille* 7, no. 1 (Fall 1972): 19.
27. Ibid.
28. George Beiswanger, "The New Theatre Dance," *Theatre Arts Monthly* 23, no. 1 (January 1939): 44, 47.
29. Letter from Mary Jo Shelly to Robert D. Leigh, 25 November 1933 [Bennington College Archive].
30. Ibid.
31. Interview with Hanya Holm.
32. Letter from Mary Jo Shelly to Robert D. Leigh, 8 December 1933 [Bennington College Archive].
33. Schlundt, *Tamiris*, pp. 27, 29.

34. Mary Jo Shelly, *Dance Observer* 2, no. 2 (February 1935): 17. The reasons for Tamiris' exclusion from the Bennington group remain unclear. She made her New York debut in 1927 and by 1929 had established herself as a concert soloist. In 1930 she formed the nucleus of a concert group and subsequently appeared in the same New York concert halls as Graham, Humphrey, and Weidman. Following the demise of Dance Repertory Theatre, Tamiris shared the stage with all of the leading artists in major showcase presentations. Schlundt (*Tamiris*, pp. 27–29) describes Tamiris' position in the field: she straddled the worlds of abstract modern dance and social protest dance, pleasing neither by her refusal to ally herself with any one group. Asked in 1978 why Tamiris had not been invited to Bennington, Martha Hill replied, "Tamiris was off on her own on other projects. She was beginning her musical theater career and wasn't as involved as the others in concert dance. Others have suggested that we were passing over Tamiris, but they are wrong. There was lots of dance in those days; dance was burgeoning. You couldn't have everyone. Agnes de Mille wasn't there and could have been." (Telephone conversation with Martha Hill.) According to Schlundt, Tamiris' prodigious career in the musical theater did not commence until 1943. During the Bennington years, Tamiris was active in the concert dance field, and from 1936–1939 she was heavily involved with the Federal Dance Project. A photograph taken by Donald Hatfield at Mills College in the summer of 1939 shows Tamiris in the company of Doris Humphrey; it is evidence that Tamiris once visited a Bennington session.

35. Telephone conversation with Agnes de Mille, 1977.

36. Letter from Robert D. Leigh to Mary Jo Shelly, 20 December 1933 [Bennington College Archive].

37. *Bennington College Bulletin* 2, no. 3 (February 1934): 1–2.

38. Address by Robert Leigh, 9 July 1934, as reported in *Bennington Evening Banner*, 10 July 1934, p. 1.

39. Interview with John Martin.

40. "First Annual Report of the Bennington School of the Dance," Summer 1934, in *Reports of Offjicers*, Bennington College, 2, no. 3, 1933–34 (October 1934): 3.

41. John Martin, *New York Times*, 26 August 1934.

42. "Study of Modern Dance in America Pioneering Venture," *Springfield* (Mass.) *Union Republican* Sunday Magazine, Section E, 22 July 1934. (No byline.)

43. "First Annual Report," p. 6.

44. Mary Jo Shelly, "A School of the Modern Dance," *Progressive Education* 12, no. 6 (October 1935): 417–21.

45. The title of the festival series needs clarification. The designation "American Dance Festival" was never officially used at Bennington. That title made its first and only appearance in the 1935 program for Martha Graham's workshop production, which announced a plan to hold "an American dance festival" in August 1937 to round out the workshops initiated in 1935. The 1937 festival, however, was called "Bennington Festival," as were the festivals held in 1936, 1938, 1940, and 1941. The 1935 performance series, which later was designated the first of the Bennington Festival Workshops, was titled at the time "A Series of Four Programs in the Modern Dance." To complicate matters further, the 1938 Bennington Festival called itself "The Fifth Bennington Festival Series," which would have made the first one date from 1934. That summer's performances were actually called "A Series of Four Recitals in The Modern Dance and Music." For the purposes of easy reference, the 1935 series is counted as the first of six Bennington festivals–1935, 1936, 1937, 1938, 1940, and 1941, in which new dance productions were introduced.

46. The earliest document is a draft dated 30 August 1936 in Martha Hill's hand. There are several versions of "Proposed Plan for The American School of the Dance," including 9 February 1937, revision as of 23 February 1937, 5 March 1937, and a letter from Martha Hill and Mary J. Shelly to the William C. Whitney Foundation, 30 March 1937, requesting support to organize a national center for the study of the dance [Bennington College Archive]. Hill and Shelly discussed their plan with Lincoln Kirstein. See Kirstein's intriguing account of their meeting in "Blast at Ballet," 1937, in *Three Pamphlets Collected* (Brooklyn, N.Y.: Dance Horizons, 1967), pp. 90–91. See also Ruth Bloomer, "Bennington School of the Dance–Summer 1937," *Dance Observer* 4, no. 7 (August-September 1937): 84.

47. "Fourth Annual Report of the Bennington School of the Dance," Summer 1937, in *Reports of Officers*, Bennington College, 5, no. 3, 1936–37 (August 1937): 2.

48. *Bennington College Bulletin* 5, no. 3 (February 1937): 2.

49. Lincoln Kirstein, *The New York City Ballet* (New York: Alfred A. Knopf, 1973), p. 49. See also Lincoln Kirstein, "Blast at Ballet," in *Three Pamphlets Collected*, pp. 41–42.

50. Ballet Caravan Scrapbooks, vol. 1, 1936 [Dance Collection of the New York Public Library].

51. Editorial in *Dance Observer* 4, no. 8 (October 1937): 91. Kirstein's contribution to *Dance Observer* was short-lived (October 1937–January 1938). He resigned after the *Observer* refused to print an article he had written on John Martin. See Kirstein, *Three Pamphlets Collected*, p. 73.

52. "Fourth Annual Report," p. 3.

53. George Beiswanger, "Dance in the College and on the Road," *Theatre Arts Monthly* 22, no. 7 (July 1938): 491–92. There are no reliable statistics on the growth of modern dance in American colleges and universities during the Bennington period, but three surveys conducted between 1937 and 1941 show 50 to 75 colleges offering modern dance, most under the aegis of the physical education department, in which modern dance was by far the most prevalent of all dance forms offered. The first survey was an unpublished study made in 1937–38 by the administrative office of the Bennington School of the Dance with funds from the William C. Whitney Foundation (see Mary J. Shelly, "Facts and Fancies About the Dance in Education," *Journal of Health and Physical Education* 11, no. 1 [January 1940]: 18–19, 56–57). The second was a *New York Herald Tri-*

bune Dance Department survey made in the spring of 1940 by Walter Terry (see Walter Terry, *New York Herald Tribune*, 9 June 1940 and 16 June 1940; see also Walter Terry, *Invitation to Dance* [New York: A. S. Barnes & Co., 1942], Chapter 8: "Collegiate Dance," which summarizes the *Herald Tribune* survey). The third was by Frances Davies, "A Survey of Dance in Colleges, Universities, and Teacher-Training Institutions in the United States for the Year 1941–42," New York University, 1942; this was unpublished, but see *Dance Observer* 12, no. 3 (March 1945): 27, 35, for a review.

54. Letter from Mary Jo Shelly to Rosalind Cassidy, 1 October 1937 [Bennington College Archive].
55. "Fourth Annual Report," p. 4.
56. "Fifth Annual Report of the Bennington School of the Dance," Summer 1938, in *Reports of Officers*, Bennington College, 6, no. 3 (August 1938): 6–7.
57. "Fifth Annual Report," p. 9.
58. Interview with Otto Luening.
59. Interview with Norman Lloyd.
60. Ruth Lloyd, unpublished recollections, 1977, contributed for this book.
61. Ibid.
62. Quoted in Margaret Lloyd, "Relation of Music to Movement," *Christian Science Monitor*, 3 March 1936.
63. Edwin Denby, "With the Dancers," *Modern Music* 14, no. 2 (January-February 1937), reprinted in Edwin Denby *Looking at the Dance* (New York: Popular Library, n.d.), p. 273.
64. Doris Humphrey quoted by Margaret Lloyd, *Christian Science Monitor*, 23 August 1938.
65. Interview with Otto Luening.
66. Interview with Norman Lloyd.
67. George Beiswanger, "Music for the Modern Dance," *Theatre Arts Monthly* 18, no. 3 (March 1934): 184–90.
68. Beatrice Hellebrandt, "Manual for the Study of Dance Accompaniment," mimeographed (Madison: University of Wisconsin, 1938).
69. Margaret Lloyd, "Building a World for Dance," *Christian Science Monitor*, 17 July 1943, and "Collaboration Is Multiplication," *Christian Science Monitor*, 7 August 1943. (This is a two-part article on Arch Lauterer.) See also Arch Lauterer, "Arch Lauterer on Dance in the Theatre," *Dance Observer* 12, no. 2 (February 1945): 16.
70. Arch Lauterer, "Design for the Dance," *Magazine of Art* 31, no. 3 (March 1938): 137.
71. Betty Joiner, *Costumes for the Dance* (New York: A. S. Barnes and Company, 1937), p. 3. Joiner designed costumes for several Bennington productions, including *Trend*. According to the book's jacket copy, this textbook resulted from "her contacts with the leading artists in the dance field at Bennington College during the past summers." See also Pauline Lawrence, "Costumes," *Dance Observer* 3, no. 8 (October 1936): 85, 92–93, on costumes and lighting for the modern dance.
72. Telephone conversation with Edythe Gilfond, 1977.
73. Information in this section about the Mills session is drawn from documents in the Bennington College Archive and Mills College Archive, and from correspondence with Rosalind Cassidy, Eleanor Lauer, and Marian Van Tuyl.
74. Letter from Doris Humphrey to Charles Francis Woodford, n.d., 1939 [Doris Humphrey Collection, C426]. Dance Collection of the New York Public Library. By kind permission of Charles H. Woodford.
75. Interview with Bessie Schonberg.
76. "Sixth Annual Report of the Bennington School of the Dance at Mills College," Summer 1939, in *Reports of Officers, 1938–39*, Bennington College, 7, no. 3 (August 1939): 3.
77. "Second Annual Report of the Bennington School of the Arts," Summer 1941, in *Reports of Officers, 1940–41*, Bennington College, 9, no. 3 (October 1941): 5.
78. "So Bennington Went West?" *Dance Observer* 6, no. 7 (August-September 1939): 248, 256. Doris Humphrey and Charles Weidman did not go to Mills in 1940; Louise Kloepper, José Limón, and Marian Van Tuyl did, and they worked with composers Lou Harrison, Esther Williamson, and John Cage. Ruth Murray, Eleanor Lauer, and Marian Van Tuyl (all former Bennington students) were in charge of teacher training and composition. (Van Tuyl took over the dance program at Mills College after Tina Flade left in 1938.) The Chicago School of Design, including Moholy-Nagy and Kepes, was also in residence, and there was a good deal of interaction between artists and dancers. According to Eleanor Lauer: "This 1940 summer was the follow-up of the Bennington session, which we hoped and planned would be the beginning of a continuing series of artistically productive dance summers at Mills. The war situation made it impossible to carry through the plan as originally conceived." (Letter from Eleanor Lauer to the author, 21 July 1977.)
79. "Excerpts from the Press Book of the Bennington School of the Dance. A Resume: 1934–1939" [Bennington College Archive].
80. "Sixth Annual Report," p. 4.
81. Memorandum from Robert D. Leigh, 4 April 1939 [Bennington College Archive].
82. "Preliminary Plan for the Bennington School of the Arts," 9 June 1939 [Bennington College Archive].
83. "Adventures in Cooperation," *Theatre Arts* 24, no. 7, (July 1940): 500–503.
84. "Second Annual Report of the Bennington School of the Arts," p. 6.
85. *Bennington College Bulletin* 8, no. 3 (March 1940): 2.
86. Ibid., p. 4.
87. Lincoln Kirstein, "Ballet: Record and Augury," *Theatre Arts* 24, no. 9 (September 1940): 651.
88. Interview with Hanya Holm by Billy Nichols conducted in 1965 for NET's *Four Pioneers* (phonotape) [Dance Collection of the New York Public Library].

89. *Bennington College Bulletin* (March 1940): 10–11.

90. "Second Annual Report of the Bennington School of the Arts," pp. 6–7. In "Miss Shelly at Luncheon: An Interview That Fizzled," *Bennington Banner*, 1 August 1940, Shelly told a reporter: "There is nothing to be gained from having only one center. . . . Partially as a result of our efforts, dance centers this year have been established at Stanford, Northwestern, Mills, the University of California, Colorado State Teachers College and the University of Maryland. [Doris Humphrey was in residence in Maryland in 1940.] All of them . . . follow the Bennington pattern of offering students a chance to study art themselves and then to translate it on their own initiative and if they are teachers [get] it across to their pupils in their own way. . . . To be sure, Bennington is the only place with a Festival; we have the leading artists, and resources and the greatest experience."

91. "Culture Has Real Part in U.S. Defense. Dr. Robert Leigh Stresses Its Value in Address at the Opening of School of the Arts at the College," *Bennington Banner*, 1 July 1940.

92. See, for example, the interview with Bessie Schönberg in this book, p. 251.

93. "Minutes of the School of the Arts Committee of the Trustees," 18 October 1940 [Bennington College Archive].

94. *Bennington College Bulletin* 9, no. 3 (March 1941).

95. Memorandum from Mary Jo Shelly, 20 May 1941 [Bennington College Archive].

96. Letter from Doris Humphrey to Charles Francis Woodford, 21 April 1941 [Doris Humphrey Collection, C473].

97. Memorandum from Mary Jo Shelly, 20 May 1941 [Bennington College Archive].

98. Letter from Doris Humphrey to Julia Humphrey, Good Friday, 1941 [Doris Humphrey Collection, C470].

99. Letter from Doris Humphrey to Julia Humphrey, n.d. (January-July 1941) [Doris Humphrey Collection, C470].

100. Esther Rosenblatt, "Bennington–1941," *Dance Observer* 8, no. 7 (August-September 1941): 91.

101. All information in this section is, unless otherwise attributed, from "Second Annual Report of the Bennington School of the Arts," 1941, Appendix A.

102. "Fourth Annual Report of the Bennington School of the Dance," 1937, and festival programs.

103. "Second Annual Report of the Bennington School of the Arts," p. 8.

104. Information in this section is from "Executive Committee Meeting Minutes, School of the Arts," 19 September 1941, 26 September 1941, 3 October 1941 [Bennington College Archive].

105. "Minutes of the School of the Arts Committee of the Trustees," 24 October 1941 [Bennington College Archive].

106. Letter from Doris Humphrey and Charles Weidman to Lewis Jones, 15 February 1942 [Bennington College Archive]. By kind permission of Charles H. Woodford.

107. Letter from Erick Hawkins to Lewis Jones, May 1942 [Bennington College Archive]. By kind permission of Erick Hawkins. Ted Shawn opened his new dance theater at Jacob's Pillow in the summer of 1942 with a broad-ranging dance festival. Included among the "moderns" was Helen Tamiris. (Doris Humphrey and Charles Weidman were invited to participate but turned down the offer because they expected to be working in some other part of the country since they were not to be at Bennington.) See Anthony Fay, "The Festival of '42: A History-Making Summer at Jacob's Pillow," *Dance Magazine* 50, no. 7 (July 1976): 61–65.

108. See *Dance Observer* 10, no. 8 (October 1943): 91.

109. Walter Terry, *The Dance in America* (New York: Harper & Row, 1956), pp. 73–74.

110. Letter from Martha Hill to Dean Ernest O. Melby, 22 November 1946; "Notes for conference on dance project for summer session" (memorandum from Martha Hill to Dean Melby et al., 11 December 1946); letter from Rosemary Park to Martha Hill, 3 December 1947. [American Dance Festival Archive, New London, Connecticut].

111. Letter from Arch Lauterer to Martha Hill, n.d., 1947 [American Dance Festival Archive]. By kind permission of Henry Kurth, Arch Lauterer Archives.

112. Form letter from Doug Hudelson, Martha Hill, et al., 23 July 1948 [American Dance Festival Archive].

113. Tom Borek, "The Connecticut College American Dance Festival, 1948–1972: A Fantastical Documentary," *Dance Perspectives* 50 (Summer 1972).

114. George Beiswanger, "The Dance and Today's Needs," *Theatre Arts Monthly* 19, no. 6 (June 1935): 447. Reprinted in this book, pp. 280–83.

115. Interview with Martha Graham by Leah Plotkin (transcript), "Exploring the Seven Arts," WPA Federal Radio Theatre, WQXR New York, 23 June 1937 [Research Center for the Federal Theatre Project, George Mason University].

116. Letter from Doris Humphrey to Julia Humphrey, 21 August 1934 [Doris Humphrey Collection, C353].

117. See, for example, letters from Doris Humphrey to Charles Francis Woodford, 6–8 July 1937 (one letter) and 21 April 1941 [Doris Humphrey Collection, C353, C398, and C473].

118. Charles Weidman's personal notes and manuscripts (in the Charles Weidman Collection, Dance Collection of the New York Public Library) which may reveal more about his Bennington experience, were not accessible.

119. Interview with Charles Weidman by Billy Nichols, "Four Pioneers" (phonotape), National Educational Television, 1965 [Dance Collection of the New York Public Library].

120. Editorial, *Dance Observer* 1, no. 1 (February 1934): 2.

121. Margaret Lloyd, *Christian Science Monitor*, 5 July 1938.

122. Walter Terry, "Final Criticism," *New York Herald Tribune*, 12 July 1942.

123. Winsor French, *Cleveland Press*, 29 July 1938 [Hanya Holm Scrapbooks, Dance Collection of the New York Public Library].

124. Charlotte Michaud, "Bennington with Its 'Workshop' Exciting for Those Who Would Study and Comprehend the Modern Dance," 3 and 10 October 1936. See also "Thoughts on Second Visit to Bennington School of Dance," 10 September 1938, *Lewiston* (Maine) *Journal* Illustrated Magazine Section.

125. Interview with Martha Hill by Billy Nichols, "Four Pioneers" (phonotape), National Educational Television, 1965 [Dance Collection of the New York Public Library].

126. A comparative study of the influence on training of Margaret H'Doubler at the University of Wisconsin and of Martha Hill at Bennington and NYU would be revealing.

127. Louis Horst, quoted by Bessie Schönberg, in letter to the author, 30 October 1977.

128. See Holm's admonition, reported by Marjorie Church in "The Bennington Dance Festival," *Dance Observer* 3, no. 7 (August-September 1936): 77.

129. Walter Terry, "Dance in Colleges," *New York Herald Tribune*, 16 June 1940.

130. Interview with George Bockman.

131. John Martin, *America Dancing* (Brooklyn, N.Y.: Dance Horizons, 1968), p. 175.

132. Martha Hill, quoted in "New School Series," *Dance Observer* 1, no. 6 (August-September 1934): 68.

133. Harold Clurman, *The Fervent Years: The Story of the Group Theatre and the Thirties* (New York: Hill & Wang, 1957), p. 271. By kind permission of Alfred A. Knopf, Inc.

134. Program note for *New Dance*, 1935.

135. Doris Humphrey, "New Dance" (manuscript), ca. 1936. [Doris Humphrey Collection, M25].

136. Description of *Decade* in a letter from Doris Humphrey to Julia Humphrey, undated (January-June) 1941 [Doris Humphrey Collection, C470].

137. Humphrey–Weidman souvenir program, 1938. See also notes on *Quest* (1936), p. 147.

138. Margery Dana, *Daily Worker*, 10 October 1938.

139. Interview with May O'Donnell.

140. Humphrey, "New Dance."

141. Henry Gilfond, "Summing Up," *Dance Observer* 6, no. 6 (June-July 1939): 238.

142. John Martin, "Dance Since Isadora," *Theatre Arts* 24, no. 9 (September 1940): 645.

143. Doris Humphrey, "New Trends in the Dance" (transcript), a program in the series "Exploring the Seven Arts," WPA Federal Theatre, Radio Division, WQXR New York, 7 April 1937 [Research Center for the Federal Theatre Project, George Mason University].

144. Agnes de Mille, "We All Danced Regardless," *Dance Scope* 2, no. 2 (Spring 1966): 27–32.

145. There were exceptions. For example, Jane Dudley left Hanya Holm's Wigman group and joined Martha Graham after apprenticing with Graham at Bennington, and William Bales studied and danced with each of the Big Four.

146. Barbara Jones, *Bennington College: The Development of an Educational Idea* (New York: Harper & Brothers, 1946), p. xv.

147. Telephone interview with Maxine Cushing Gray, 1977.

Bennington School of the Dance 1934 Class Photo, courtesy of Bennington College.

The Summer Sessions

In the Chronology, the reader may see in their actual sequence the major events, programs, and participants for each summer session. Information is based on the school bulletins issued before each session, annual reports prepared by the school's directors at the end of most summer sessions, and class schedules. Where possible, information was cross-checked with Bennington participants, as well as with original programs, reviews, and other published accounts. Unresolved discrepancies are noted.

Faculty, students, visiting lecturers, and guests are listed selectively. Programs are given in full, excepting a few for which neither the original published program nor a detailed account could be located, and student recitals, especially in the later years, for which highlights are given.

Works that received their premieres at Bennington are designated with an asterisk in the Chronology and are treated fully in the Catalog that follows. A sequential list and description of curricula follows the Catalog.

In general, information is rendered precisely as it appears on printed programs. However, where there were variant spellings of a person's name, a single spelling has been adopted: for example, Serge Prokofiev for Sergei Prokofieff; Katherine Manning for Katharine Manning; George Bockman for George Bochman; Letitia Ide for Laetitia Ide; Harriette Ann Gray for Harriet Ann or Harriette Anne Gray. Names that were changed professionally later are given in brackets: for example, Ann Schuman [Anna Halprin], Pearl Lack [Lang], Mercier [Merce] Cunningham, Sasha Liebich [Mark Ryder], Joseph Gornbein [Gifford], Henrietta Greenhood [Eve Gentry]. First names of composers frequently omitted on the published programs are given by the author in brackets.

An introduction describes the special character of each session and provides some perspective on it.

Abbreviations used: *chor*=choreography; *mus*=music; *danc*=dancers or danced by; *art collab*=artistic collaborator; *asst*=assistant(s); *dir*=directed by; *tech dir*=technical director; *accom*=accompanist; *prod asst*=production assistant(s); *props*=properties; *sets & light*=setting(s) and lighting design, also decor or scenery; *light*=lighting.

MODERN DANCE GAINS RATING WITH SPORTS IN GIRLS COLLEGES: ATHLETE'S AGILITY REQUIRED FOR RHYTHMIC MOVEMENTS. NEW SCHOOL OF DANCING WHICH IS ENROLLING TEACHERS AND STUDENTS FROM ALL PARTS OF U.S. WILL SOON BE OPENED AT BENNINGTON COLLEGE.

What goes on at the new school this summer will inevitably bring the modern dance out from behind the veil of confusion which has obscured it from general understanding in its infant years. Teachers and students of the dance from all parts of the country have enrolled, and when they have thrashed out their ideas in practice of what the basic standards of the modern dance are, their pupils and audiences the country over will see the dance in a clearer light. Better understanding will automatically increase its prominence. . . . Its place in physical education in women's colleges has been elevated to such a height in the last five years that in sum it has completely supplanted gymnastics as fundamental training and at all gatherings of physical education directors, it is one of the main topics of discussion. . . . A staff of instructors and administrators has been gathered together which is to the modern dance what a combination of the late lamented Knute Rockne plus Pop Warner and Chick Meehan would be to football.[1]

Janet Owen *New York Herald Tribune*

1934
First Session of the Bennington School of the Dance

7 July 1934—18 August 1934

Drawing of Martha Graham and pupils by Aline Fruhauf.

The first session was a "sampler," with each of the Big Four in residence for a week, in succession. The goal was to bring teachers and students from across America into direct contact with the leading points of view and techniques in the modern dance. In addition to teaching technique, Graham, Humphrey, and Holm led lecture-discussions on the modern dance, and Graham, Humphrey, and Weidman gave recitals of current repertoire in the 150-seat theater in the Commons Building (College Theatre). Hanya Holm demonstrated the modern German dance, sharing the stage with a showing of student work produced during the session. There was no festival; no new works were produced. The recital series was not covered by the *New York Times* or the *Dance Observer* (which had begun publishing five months before), but the *Bennington Banner* carried front-page notices.

Margaret H'Doubler was invited as guest teacher and gave a "Demonstration Dance Lesson." Martha Hill gave a course geared to teaching methods and materials—one of the few such courses offered in the project's history. Dance teacher Barbara Page, who was enrolled as a student, described the summer's classwork in detail in a major article, "Contemporary Exponents of the Dance."[2]

John Martin wrote a lengthy encomium in the *New York Times* at the session's end. The school, he concluded, had "succeeded beyond the hopes of its most ardent well-wishers . . . toward building a sounder and more vital art."[3]

Dancers at Bennington, 1934.

Dance students at Bennington, 1934.

THE SESSION IN BRIEF

Each of the Big Four was in residence for one week, in succession. The session featured comparative study of the four "leading" points of view in the modern dance through brief but intensive exposure to the techniques of the four guest artists. There was a recital series but no premieres or new productions.

FACULTY AND STAFF

Martha Graham (assistant: Dorothy Bird). Doris Humphrey (assistant: Cleo Atheneos). Charles Weidman (assistant: Gene Martel). Hanya Holm (assistant: Nancy McKnight). John Martin. Louis Horst (assistants: May O'Donnell, Dini de Remer). Gregory Tucker. Martha Hill (assistant: Bessie Schönberg). Accompanists: Jerome Moross (Humphrey). Harvey Pollins (Holm). Pauline Lawrence (Weidman). Dini de Remer (Graham and Horst). Norman and Ruth Lloyd, accompanists for the school.

STUDENTS

Total 103, ages 15–49, from 26 states, D.C., Canada, and Spain. 68 teachers (35 college or university). 32 students (24 college or university, 8 high school). Including Ruth Bloomer (teacher, University of Oregon). Evelyn Davis (Director, Evelyn Davis School, Washington, D.C.). Delia Hussey (teacher, Public Schools, Detroit). Marian Knighton (teacher, Sarah Lawrence College). Ruth Murray (teacher, Wayne University). Barbara Page (teacher, Ohio Wesleyan University). Helen Priest (student, New College, Columbia University). Sybil Shearer (student, Doris Humphrey Studio, New York). Marian Van Tuyl (dancer, teacher, University of Chicago).

LECTURES AND SPECIAL EVENTS

Lecture-discussions by Martha Graham, Doris Humphrey, Hanya Holm, John Martin. Guest teacher Margaret H'Doubler gave a "Demonstration Dance Lesson" (11 August) and showed moving pictures from the dance department at the University of Wisconsin. Norman Lloyd demonstrated and analyzed musical forms. Louis Horst led a recital-discussion of "Music from Pre-Classic to Modern," with May O'Donnell demonstrating (no program located). There were discussions on current events, physics, American painting, and modern poetry led by Bennington College faculty, and showings of sculpture, painting, and moving pictures (including some taken of the school). Maude Adams and company performed *Twelfth Night* in the College Theatre. John Martin led a concluding "Symposium on the Modern Dance."

RECITAL SERIES 20 July 1934

"A Series of Four Recitals in the Modern Dance and Music." Martha Graham, Doris Humphrey and Charles Weidman, Gregory Tucker (piano), and Hanya Holm and Students of the Bennington School of the Dance performed to a total audience of 437 in the 150-seat College Theatre in the Commons Building.

Martha Graham. Solo recital. *Chor* Martha Graham. *Accom* Louis Horst. College Theatre. No premieres. Program: ***Dance Prelude*** *mus* [Nikolai] Lopatnikov. ***Lamentation*** *mus* [Zoltan] Kodály. ***Dithyrambic*** *mus* [Aaron] Copland. ***Satyric Festival Song*** *mus* [Imre] Weisshaus.

Hanya Holm (left) with dancers, 1934.

Hanya Holm students, 1934. Photographs courtesy of Ruth Alexander.

Exstasis, Two Lyric Fragments *mus* [Lehman] Engel. ***Primitive Canticles, a. Ave, b. Salve*** *mus* [Heitor] Villa-Lobos. ***Sarabande*** from the suite ***Transitions*** *mus* Engel. ***Frenetic Rhythms, a. Wonder, b. Renunciation, c. Action*** *mus* [Wallingford] Riegger, *voice* Norman Lloyd. ***Harlequinade, a. Pessimist, b. Optimist*** *mus* [Ernst] Toch.

Review

Bennington Banner:

> Martha Graham has probably seldom danced before a more sympathetic audience. . . . The compelling force of her personality held their minds and drew them with her as for two hours, with one intermission, she danced tirelessly.[4]

27 July 1934

Doris Humphrey-Charles Weidman. *Accom* Pauline Lawrence, Vivian Fine. *Cos* Pauline Lawrence. College Theatre. No premieres. Program: ***Three Mazurkas*** *mus* [Alexander] Tansman, *danc* Humphrey, Weidman. ***Counterpoint No. 2*** *mus* [Harvey] Pollins, *danc* Humphrey. ***Memorial–To the Trivial*** *mus* [Jerome] Moross, *danc* Weidman. ***Rudepoema*** *mus* [Heitor] Villa-Lobos, *danc* Humphrey, Weidman. ***Two Ecstatic Themes, a. Circular Descent*** *mus* [Nikolai] Medtner, ***b. Pointed Ascent*** *mus* Malipiero, *danc* Humphrey. ***Kinetic Pantomime*** *mus* [Colin] McPhee, *danc* Weidman. ***Alcina Suite*** *mus* [G. F.] Handel, *chor danc* Humphrey, Weidman. (Choreographic credits are not given in the printed program.)

Review

Bennington Banner:

> The recital of Doris Humphrey and Charles Weidman last night was attended by an even more appreciative audience than the one which crowded the College Theatre one week ago. . . . Upon two occasions the dancers received calls which could only be answered with encores.[5]

3 August 1934

Gregory Tucker, pianist. College Theatre. A program of works by [Antonio] Vivaldi, [L. v.] Beethoven, [Robert] Schumann, [Manuel] de Falla, [Carlos] Chavez, and Leo Ornstein.

Review

Bennington Banner:

> The importance of music as a complement to the dance is recognized by the presentation of this recital among the other three which are strictly dance.[6]

10 August 1934

Hanya Holm and Students of the Bennington School of the Dance. College Theatre. Part I: Demonstration of Techniques from the Modern German Dance. Miss Holm and Selected Group of Students. *Asst* Nancy McKnight. *Pianist* Harvey Pollins. (No details given.) Part II: Compositions Under the Direction of Martha Hill. *Asst* Bessie Schönberg. *Accom* Norman Lloyd, Ruth

THE BENNINGTON SCHOOL OF THE DANCE
PRESENTS
A SERIES OF FOUR RECITALS
IN THE MODERN DANCE AND MUSIC

HANYA HOLM
and
STUDENTS OF
THE BENNINGTON SCHOOL OF THE DANCE

In the College Theatre
Friday, August 10, 1934
At 9:00 p. m.

PART I

DEMONSTRATION OF TECHNIQUES FROM THE MODERN GERMAN DANCE

Miss Holm and Selected Group of Students

Nancy McKnight, *Assistant*
Harvey Pollins, *Pianist*

INTERMISSION

PART II

COMPOSITIONS UNDER THE DIRECTION OF MARTHA HILL

1. Folk Song . . . . *Bartok*
   Choreography by Group
2. Three-part Canon . . . *Unaccompanied*
   Choreography by Ruth Bloomer and Ruth Murray
3. Ridicolosamente . . . . *Prokofieff*
   Choreography by Ruth Alexander and Group
4. Berceuse - Copyright 1934 . . . *Tansman*
   Choreography by Christine Dobbins, Charlotte MacEwan, Ellen Adair
5. Rondo . . . . . . *Norman Lloyd*
   Choreography by Berta Ochsner

Bessie Schönberg, *Assistant*
Norman and Ruth Lloyd, *Pianists*

PART III

COMPOSITIONS BASED ON PRE-CLASSIC FORMS UNDER THE DIRECTION OF LOUIS HORST

1. Pavane . . . . *Byrd*
   Choreography by Marian Van Tuyl
2. Rustica (Bouree) . . . . . *Fasch*
   Choreography by Marie Heghinian
3. Processional (Pavane) . . . . *Ravel*
   Choreography by Group
4. Zweispiel (Gavotte) . . . . . *Bach*
   Choreography by Berta Ochsner
5. Bouree . . . . *Fasch*
   Choreography by Betty Fleming
6. Le Roi Fait un Discours au Rythm d'une Courante . . *Chambonnieres*
   Choreography by Berta Ochsner
7. Exhibition Piece (Rigaudon) . . . *Rameau*
   Choreography by Marian Van Tuyl

May O'Donnell and Dini de Remer, *Assistants*
Louis Horst, *Pianist*

Costumes and Lighting under the direction of Jane Ogborn
Chairman of Costume Committee, Barbara Spaulding
Chairman of Lighting Committee, Alice Sherbon

Louise Kloepper and Holm dancers, 1934. Photograph courtesy of Ruth Alexander.

Lloyd. Program: ***Folk Song*** *mus* [Bela] Bartók, *danc* group. ***Three-part Canon*** (unaccompanied) *danc* Ruth Bloomer, Ruth Murray. ***Ridicolosamente*** *mus* [Serge] Prokofiev, *danc* Ruth Alexander and group. ***Berceuse–Copyright 1934*** *mus* [Alexander] Tansman, *danc* Christine Dobbins, Charlotte MacEwan, Ellen Adair. ***Rondo*** *mus* Norman Lloyd, *danc* Berta Ochsner. Part III: Compositions Based on Pre-Classic Forms Under the Direction of Louis Horst. *Asst* May O'Donnell and Dini de Remer. *Pianist* Louis Horst. Program: ***Pavane*** *mus* [William] Byrd, *danc* Marian Van Tuyl. ***Rustica*** (Bourrée) *mus* [J. F.] Fasch, *danc* Marie Heghinian. ***Processional*** (Pavane) *mus* [Maurice] Ravel. *danc* group. ***Zweispiel*** (Gavotte) *mus* [J. S.] Bach, *danc* Ochsner. ***Bourrée*** *mus* Fasch, *danc* Betty Fleming. ***Le Roi Fait un Discours, au Rythm d'une Courante*** *mus* [Jacques Champion de] Chambonnières, *danc* Ochsner. ***Exhibition Piece*** (Rigaudon) *mus* [J. P.] Rameau, *danc* Van Tuyl.

Review

Bennington Banner:

> The final recital at the Bennington School of the Dance presented last night at the College Theatre by Miss Hanya Holm and selected groups of students illustrated primarily the latitude and possibilities of group dances and yielded special attention to the modern German dance. . . . Miss Holm's demonstration of the German dance was outstanding. With a few simple explanations she proceeded to illustrate step by step in movement analysis the technique of the German dance with the assistance of a chosen group of students. Beginning with the simplest movement the group did unrelated movement analyses working toward more intricate forms until finally each movement became a significant part of the whole. [Hanya Holm did not dance herself.] Each [of the student demonstrations] was simple in form, only one or two departing from straight unison dancing, but all were patently the products of careful study and thorough preparation. Consistent with the character of the school, young in its first year, form and technique were emphasized as the groundwork for further and more ambitious compositions. . . .[7]

NOTES

1. *New York Herald Tribune*, 3 June 1934 (sports pages).
2. Barbara Page, "Contemporary Exponents of the Dance," *Journal of Health and Physical Education* 6, no. 4 (April 1935): 11–14, 60. Reprinted in this book, pp. 277–279. The author describes the structure, content, and emphasis of courses taught by Martha Hill, Martha Graham, Doris Humphrey, Charles Weidman, Hanya Holm, Louis Horst, and John Martin.
3. "The Dance: A Vermont Experiment," *New York Times*, 26 August 1934. See also the excellent front-page article in the *Springfield Union Republican* Sunday Magazine, Section E, 22 July 1934, which surveys the plan for the School of the Dance and provides background.
4. *Bennington Banner*, 21 July 1934. (Unless specified, *Bennington Banner* reviews carried no bylines.)
5. *Bennington Banner*, 28 July 1934.
6. *Bennington Banner*, 4 August 1934.
7. *Bennington Banner*, 11 August 1934.

1935
Second Session of the Bennington School of the Dance

5 July 1935—17 August 1935

Drawing of Tina Flade by Aline Fruhauf.

The teaching plan of 1934 was expanded and an innovative Workshop Program was inaugurated which resulted in the first Bennington-sponsored original production. This first of four successive Workshop Programs (1935-1938) was given to Martha Graham. Graham composed a full-length work in three sections, performed by a group of 36 made up of her concert group and 24 advanced students. *Panorama* had two performances in the Vermont State Armory before an audience of about 1000. It was Arch Lauterer's first collaboration with Graham (he created a multilevel performance space for her in the Armory); the score was Norman Lloyd's first extended dance work, and Alexander Calder designed mobiles for it in his first dance collaboration.

Graham's 1936-1937 souvenir program pronounced *Panorama* "the first full-length American ballet produced with American choreographer, composer and performers." After its Bennington debut, the work was abandoned.

The Workshop offered the first opportunity for anyone outside Graham's own group to observe her creative process firsthand and dance with her group in a professional setting. The company of 36 was the largest body Graham had ever worked with, and *Panorama* was her longest and most ambitious composition to date.

Among the Workshop students were Marian Van Tuyl, a young dancer from Chicago; Jane Dudley, a member of the New Dance Group who had been trained by Hanya Holm in New

York; and Muriel Stuart, a ballet teacher from the School of American Ballet and former soloist with Anna Pavlova's company. According to Don McDonagh, Lincoln Kirstein enrolled Stuart to find out what Graham was up to.[1] Ethel Butler recalled that sometime earlier Stuart had taught a few ballet classes at Graham's New York studio and that this had been the first ballet experience for many Graham dancers. Stuart reportedly was so distressed at their posture at the barre that she had them execute the exercises on their backs with their feet in the air.[2]

Graham had the official Bennington limelight. But before Graham's new production could be unveiled in the Armory, Doris Humphrey presented a large new work of her own, not yet completed, in the College Theatre, with herself, Charles Weidman and their company of 17 dancers. For lack of a better title, Humphrey called the work *New Dance*. It had been performed two days earlier in Burlington under the title *Dance Variations*, but the Bennington performance was its official premiere. The work, which ran about 25 minutes (its final section, "Variations and Conclusion," was added later), was immediately hailed by John Martin as a masterwork. *New Dance* was the first movement composed by Humphrey of her magnum opus *New Dance Trilogy*, which she completed the next summer at Bennington.

Wigman-trained Tina Flade, alternating for Hanya Holm, who was teaching the summer session at Mills College, made her East Coast debut in a program of solos composed by her in America. The success of her Bennington recital led to two New York appearances later that season.

Earlier in the summer, eight members of the New Dance League (recently renamed from the former Workers Dance League) who were enrolled as Bennington students presented "An Evening of Revolutionary Dance" under the school's auspices.

The public performances attracted an audience from as far away as Honolulu. "It was not foreseen that the whole project would in the short space of a year become something in the nature of a national festival," wrote John Martin.[3] The idea of a Bennington Festival was not so warmly embraced by the *Brooklyn Eagle*, which published an editorial against it on the same day:

> There are hints of Bennington's possible future as an "American Salzburg. . . ." A summer festival of theatre arts—of the drama and the dance, of music and even moving pictures—is something that the country could do with very nicely, and the only cloud on the horizon which these intimations expose to view resolves itself, on closer inspection, into a hovering group consisting of Martha Graham, Doris Humphrey, Charles Weidman and other major and minor practitioners of the "modern" dance and its allied arts. For the fact is that the modern dance is art in the raw, not even half baked, and a festival of theatre arts founded on this amorphous and inutile dough would be bound to sag grotesquely.[4]

The *Eagle*'s critic, "T. B. W.," expanded on this in a long report from Bennington:

> There is the spirit of pioneering abroad and nothing is too new or too mad to be given a fair trial. Sandy [Alexander] Calder and his "mobiles," or moving scenery, are given a place on Martha Graham's festival program this Thursday night, and almost the entire personnel of the Workers Dance Group has been accepted into the student body. Zeal piles up by its own momentum and the discharge of energy has an impact which can be felt by the most casual visitor. What is more, the majority of these enthusiasts are teachers and consequently "carriers." Thirty-five different colleges and universities, thirty-three public and private schools and classes will shortly be impregnated with the germs transmitted from this teeming source. . . .
>
> Observing it all objectively, it is impossible not to find enormous interest and stimulation in so much active devotion, even if the dance as a cause is not nearest your heart. The very best that can come of it all from the dancer's point of view is perhaps the education of a wider public for the dance—an essential element if the art is to live and dancers are to eat.

> The endless chain of pupils turned teachers in order to teach more pupils to be teachers is not quite so inspiring, although this is actually what it all amounts to in the long run. The chances of a "discovery," a great dancer being brought into the focus of a promising public career through the brief propulsion of even such an intensive six-week session, are slim. Such real genius, in any of the arts, will rise with its own yeast. Not that the school would not be good for it, in the discipline of group development, but it is not for this that it was founded. The education of the dance public, then, and the opportunity for the dance student to obtain a fair cross-section of all that is contemporary in his chosen field—these are the ends stated in the prospectus and eminently fostered in practice. "What happens afterward we don't know," admits one of the directors, "just so we have upset them, completely stirred them up—that must satisfy us. . . . As for the dancers, of whom there are too many, the rigors of the Bennington School can quickly right that situation for literally only the fit can survive. As for the dance and its position among the other stage arts, the answer is equally apparent here. If there is anything in it all, such a laboratory as Bennington provides will find and establish it. All that can be done toward the promotion and development of the art today is being done here. If it succeeds and the dance emerges triumphant, and understood at last, hugged to the bosom of a long-lost public, then we may thank such projects as this at Bennington and whatever may prove to be its logical outgrowths, such as the hoped-for American Salzburg. If on the other hand, the dance refuses to seize its opportunities and, true to the prophesies of its most ardent cynics, eventually commits suicide, thanks will again be due to Bennington for giving it the coup de grace.[5]

As if to rise up in protest against this disputation of its value, the school closed with a day-long "Forum on the Modern Dance," sponsored by "Mrs. Leonard Elmhirst's Committee" and the School of the Dance, involving the artists and the students. Its purpose was "to clarify for a modern dance audience the differences in ideology, technique and goal which actuate the leaders of the modern dance in America."[6] Among some of the strongest views put forward were these:

> The modern dance belongs to its period; it emerges as an expression of something vital in the life of the times. . . . The romantic dance arose from the need to express human values. People were wearied from repeating stereotyped forms. The modern dance emanates from a similar urge, but it aims to correct the mistakes of formlessness which characterized romantic dances. . . . There is only one school of the modern dance because there is no system. It represents a unified point of view. Whatever differences there are within the various groups representing the modern dance are personal and not fundamental. There is no standard technique from which modern dancers fear to depart. There is no such thing as a Martha Graham technique, or a Doris Humphrey technique. Techniques change continually. Each individual dancer works within a common frame of reference but on the basis of different experiences. . . . There is no pedagogy of the modern dance; the student is encouraged to participate in the experience and from this experience he or she may or may not learn how to teach others. . . . The real difficulty does not lie in the existence of different schools of the modern dance but rather in the fact that none of it is understood. The modern dancer has departed from tradition but the audiences have not. . . . The public does not know how to respond to movement; they still prefer spectacles. They were reared in an environment which denied the body; they do not recognize a noble art in the functioning of the body. . . . The

modern dance does not consist merely in the translation of what we already know into movement; its essence lies in rendering the body so aware of itself, so strong, so unafraid, and so integral with all its functions that our intuitive sense is restored and a new consciousness passes through us.[7]

THE SESSION IN BRIEF

Martha Graham directed the first of four summer Workshop Programs. The General Program was expanded with several new course offerings. The first Bennington production series was mounted (though it was not officially called a "festival").

FACULTY AND STAFF

Martha Graham, full session. Tina Flade (alternate for Hanya Holm) and Doris Humphrey and Charles Weidman, each two weeks in succession. Faculty same as in 1934 with the addition of Louise Martin, Norman Lloyd, Mary Jo Shelly, and Jane Ogborn and the deletion of Gregory Tucker. Louis Horst, musical director, Workshop concert. Arch Lauterer, designer for Workshop concert. Norman Lloyd, composer of Workshop production. Norman Lloyd, Ruth Lloyd and Alex North, school accompanists. Ruth Bloomer, photographer. Frances Hawkins, administrative assistant.

STUDENTS

Total 144, ages 16-50, from 27 states and Canada, including 83 teachers, 29 students, 23 dancers. General Program 108, including two men (one of whom was Welland Lathrop, a teacher from the Cornish School, Seattle). Workshop Program 36 (24 in addition to 12 members of Martha Graham's Dance Group), including Miriam Blecher (dancer, teacher of private classes, New York). Jane Dudley (dancer, New Dance Group). Muriel Stuart (teacher, School of American Ballet). Theodora Wiesner (teacher, University of Pennsylvania).

LECTURES, SPECIAL EVENTS, RECITALS, AND STUDENT DEMONSTRATIONS

Tina Flade, and Doris Humphrey and Charles Weidman gave lecture-discussions. Arch Lauterer talked about scenic design. There were exhibits of Mexican masks and art, Pueblo pottery, and Indian dances. George Sklar talked about "Contemporary Theatre." Ralph Steiner showed experimental films. Jacques Barzun lectured on "Culture and Revolution." George Beiswanger lectured on "The Social Implications of the Contemporary Dance." On 16 August a "Forum on the Modern Dance" with all of the principal artists, teachers, and students in residence was sponsored by "Mrs. Leonard K. Elmhirst's Committee and the School of the Dance." There were two demonstrations of Pre-Classic and Modern Forms by Louis Horst with Martha Graham's Concert Group, two student demonstrations of work at the school on 16 August (no programs located), and the following special recitals:

28 July 1935

Members of the New Dance League in "An Evening of Revolutionary Dance." Solos *Chor and danc* Anna Sokolow, Miriam Blecher, Sophie Maslow, Merle Hirsh, Jane Dudley, Lily Mehlman, Marie Marchowsky, Lil Liandre. *Accom* Alex North, Esther Williamson. Presented by the Bennington School of the Dance, College Theatre. No confirmed premieres. Program: ***Greeting*** *chor and danc* Sokolow, *mus* [V. Y.] Shebalin. ***Three Negro Poems*** *chor and danc* Blecher, poems Frank Horne, Langston Hughes. ***Themes from a Slavic People*** *chor and danc* Maslow, *mus* [Bela] Bartók. ***Affectations, a. Ennui, b. Sentimentale*** *chor and danc* Hirsh, *mus* [Alexander] Scriabin, [Maurice] Ravel. ***Dilemmas, a. Aesthete, b. Liberal*** *chor and danc* Dudley, *mus* [Arthur] Honegger, [Serge] Prokofiev. ***Fatherland, a. Persecution, b. Defiance*** *chor and danc* Mehlman, *mus* Honegger. ***Agitation*** *chor and danc* Marchowsky, *mus* [Gyorgy] Kosa. ***Woman*** from ***The Disinherited*** *chor and danc* Blecher, *mus* Parnas. ***Impressions of a Dance Hall*** *chor and danc* Sokolow, *mus* [Louis] Gruenberg. ***Forward*** *chor and danc* Maslow, *mus* [Alex] North. ***Time is Money*** *chor and danc* Dudley, *mus* S. Funaroff. ***American Sketches, One of the West, Two of the South, One of the East*** *chor and danc* Liandre, *mus* Gruenberg.

No reviews located.

10 August 1935

Julian de Gray, pianist. "A Recital of Modern Music." College Theatre. Works by J. S. Bach, Arnold Schoenberg, Igor Stravinsky, Ernesto Halffter, Francesco Malipiero, Serge Prokofiev, Maurice Ravel, and Alexander Scriabin.

16 August 1935

Final Demonstration of Student Work. No program located. In his review, Joseph Arnold Kaye published the program for "School recital of Martha Hill's class at Bennington School of the Dance" as an example of the school's "grimly theoretical approach to the dance": A. From the Space Unit: 1. Direction of Movement, 2. Direction of Focus, 3. Level, 4. Dimension. B. From the Time Unit: 1. Tempo, 2. Cumulative Rhythm, 3. Twice as fast as I. 4. Twice as fast as II. C. From the Sequential Form Unit: 1. Canon, 2. Round, 3. Theme and Variations. D. Larger Forms: 1. Dance Cycle–Sonata Form, 2. Dance of the Cycle–Sonata Form, 3. Cycle of Dance forms of the Romantic Period (March, Waltz, Mazurka), 4. Dance in Jazz Idiom, 5. Work and Play, 6. Theme and Variations, 7. American Themes.

Kaye quoted the following description of Martha Hill's course (from the Bennington College Bulletin, "Techniques of Dance Movement"):

> The material derives from a formulation of the principles, forces and factors present in all movement of the human body, and from a consideration of the content and significant form to be discovered in the medium of movement.

"The spirit at Bennington is one of extreme absorption in all sorts of problems posed as relating to the dance," Kaye continued:

> The teachers are dedicated, with a zeal amounting to consecration, to applying the clinical microscope and scalpel, in order that the eyes of the students may see the palpitating entrails of the art which peasants called dancing. . . . Research and experimentation is one thing and teaching dancing is another.[8]

"A SERIES OF FOUR PROGRAMS IN THE MODERN DANCE"

A solo recital by Tina Flade, the first appearance at Bennington of Doris Humphrey and Charles Weidman with their full concert group, a lecture by John Martin, and the Workshop production of *Panorama* by Martha Graham, performed twice.

13 July 1935

Tina Flade. Solo recital. *Chor* Tina Flade. *Accom* Ruth Hunt. *Cos* Tina Flade. College Theatre. Program: ***Dance in the Early Morning*** *mus* [Henry] Cowell. ***Paeans*** *mus* [Dane] Rudhyar. ***Obsession of the Spiral*** *mus* Crawford. ****Sinister Resonance*** *mus* Cowell. ***Two Sarabandes*** *mus* [Arcangelo] Corelli. ***Elegy*** *mus* [Alejandro] Caturla. ***Fire Cycle, a. Fire Preservation, b. Fire Torture, c. Fire Purification*** *mus* Cowell. *See Catalog.

This was the world premiere of *Sinister Resonance* and the East Coast premieres of the other works, all of them composed by Flade in America. Flade recalled her Bennington debut as "quite a triumph."[9] She especially remembered Martha Graham's reaction:

> She liked much of the program. I remember her saying to me, "Anything that has a lilt to it we have to learn laboriously while you Europeans have it in your blood." And she told me that I had the gayest legs she'd ever seen. In a certain sense I was at the opposite end of the pole from her in my dancing, but in some very generous way she appreciated what I was doing, and that made me very happy and gave me encouragement.[10]

Early Morning, Flade said, was danced to Cowell's *Aeolian Harp,* which was "played or rather plucked on the inside strings of the grand piano by the pianist, Ruth Hunt, standing up."

Reviews

Katherine Vickery, *Dance Observer*:

> It was Miss Flade's first appearance in the East in several years. . . . Her work has grown and changed so greatly that this performance was almost in the nature of a debut. Miss Flade has developed from being "the youngest dancer of Mary Wigman's first famous group" into a solo dancer of great ability and promise.[11]

John Martin, *New York Times*:

> When she danced in New York [1932 debut] she revealed not only an excellent technical background along the characteristic Wigman lines but a distinct flair for movement of an individual kind. She was gay, light, exuberant and altogether charming. But there was a lack of solidity, of substance, in her dances that made her gifts as a composer seem to lag behind her gifts as a performer.
>
> With a wisdom that is rare . . . Miss Flade took stock of herself in relation to the new country to which she had so recently come as a stranger. . . . What she needed was several years of quiet work and re-orientation. Her performance at Bennington . . . was the first opportunity to judge of the results of this period of adjustment. . . . The dancer who appeared there was recognizably the same dancer who had formerly appeared in New York but a vast transformation had taken place.
>
> Here was not only a superb performance merely from the stand-point of excellent technique and first-rate theatrical presentation, here was also the conviction of a genuinely big creative talent. . . . The program as a whole vibrated with a fine and simple emotional sincerity. Here were the solidity, the substance, that had previously been missing . . . with no loss of the distinctive buoyancy and delicacy that had been there before.[12]

27 July 1935

John Martin. Lecture, "The Ancient Art of Modern Dance."

3 August 1935

Doris Humphrey-Charles Weidman and Concert Group. *Accom* Vivian Fine, Pauline Lawrence. *Cos* Pauline Lawrence. College Theatre. Program: ***New Dance,** mus* Wallingford Riegger, *danc* Humphrey, Weidman, and group. ***Traditions,** mus* Lehman Engel, *danc* Weidman, José Limón, William Matons. ***Life of the Bee,** danc* Humphrey, Letitia Ide, and group. ***Studies in Conflict,** mus* Dane Rudhyar, *danc* Weidman, Limón, and group. ***Memorials, a. To the Trivial, b. To the Connubial, c. To the Colossal,** mus* Jerome Moross, *danc* Weidman and group. ***Alcina Suite, a. Introduction Pomposo and Allegro, b. Pantomime, c. Minuet, Musette, Minuet,** mus* [G. F.] Handel, *danc* Humphrey and Weidman. (Choreographic credits are not given in the printed program.) *See Catalog.

14 and 15 August 1935

Martha Graham and The Workshop Group. *Mus dir* Louis Horst. *Sets & light* Arch Lauterer. *Tech dir* Jane Ogborn. Vermont State Armory. Program: ***Celebration** mus* Horst, *danc* Martha Graham Dance Group. ***Sarabande*** from the suite ***Transitions** mus* Lehman Engel, *danc* Graham. ***Frontier*** from the suite ***Perspectives** mus* Horst, *danc* Graham. ***Panorama** mus* Norman Lloyd, *danc* Martha Graham and Workshop Group. *See Catalog.

Originally *Panorama* was to have its premiere on 15 August, but a second performance on 14 August was added to meet the demand for tickets.

NOTES

1. Don McDonagh, *Martha Graham* (New York: Praeger, 1973), p. 108.
2. Interview with Ethel Butler.
3. John Martin, *New York Times*, 11 August 1935.
4. *Brooklyn Eagle*, 11 August 1935.
5. T. B. W., "The Bennington School of the Dance: Another Successful Session Draws to a Close," *Brooklyn Eagle*, 11 August 1935.
6. Frederick Morton, "A Forum on the Modern Dance," *Theatre Arts Monthly* 19, no. 10 (October 1935): 794, 797–98.
7. "A Brief Summary of the Proceedings of a Forum on the Modern Dance Conducted at the Bennington School of the Dance, August 16, 1935" (unpublished) [Bennington College Archive].
8. Joseph Arnold Kaye, *American Dancer* 9, no. 1 (October 1935): 10–11.
9. Interview with Tina Flade Mooney and letter from Tina Flade Mooney to the author dated 3 September 1977.
10. Ibid.
11. Katherine Vickery, "The Summer at Bennington," *Dance Observer* 2, no. 7 (October 1935): 77.
12. John Martin, *New York Times*, 21 July 1935.

1936
Third Session of the Bennington School of the Dance

3 July 1936—15 August 1936

Drawing of composer Wallingford Riegger by Aline Fruhauf.

Doris Humphrey and Charles Weidman had charge of the double Workshop which, including their own concert groups, numbered 45 dancers—the largest company ever assembled at Bennington. Humphrey composed the last part of her *New Dance Trilogy, With My Red Fires,* a powerful, massive group work which treated the love relationship between man and woman. Despite its romantic theme—considered by some of her own dancers to be out of sync with the times—it was generally pronounced a masterwork.

With My Red Fires had its premiere alongside restagings of *New Dance* and *Theatre Piece*, programmed on two successive evenings. Bennington thus provided the first, and possibly only, opportunity to see the *Trilogy* in its entirety, albeit not in one sitting.

Charles Weidman created an ambitious 12-part, 50-minute work entitled *Quest*, which dealt with the role of the artist in society. *Quest* was also deemed a major work, though one in need of revision.

Critics embraced this extension of dance forms as a watershed in the development of the modern art. As Paul Love put it, "With these new avenues opened, the modern dance may be removed from its Sunday-evening cultism and brought into relationship with the arts and the modern world at large."[1]

Hanya Holm gave her first major concert in the East, marking her debut there as performer and choreographer. John Martin recognized her great talent for group choreography, a promise Holm fulfilled at Bennington in 1937. It was a relatively uneventful summer for Martha Graham. She made no new works, taught only two weeks, and gave two solo recitals of works composed between 1930 and 1936.

The Bennington environment was especially felicitous for Doris Humphrey. She enjoyed the beautiful surroundings and creature comforts:

> I am sitting at a window looking out on the most peaceful and bucolic scene imaginable. It's a Corot landscape with a soft meadow, animals grazing, dark trees spreading large and verdant. . . . In the house there is taste and comfort too, electric this and that, plenty of room, charming pictures and furniture. To think that after only twenty years the humble Art of the Dance has brought this home and hearth to one of its dissenters.[2]

The nine events in the Bennington Festival (now officially called a festival) were attended by about 3000 persons, including the school's community of 200 students, faculty, and staff.

Lincoln Kirstein's Ballet Caravan made its world debut at the College Theatre, and Kirstein delivered a lecture on the classic ballet, followed by a demonstration by William Dollar. A week later the New Dance League presented a second program at Bennington, with guest artist Anna Sokolow, who was dance director at the summer Institute for Arts in the Theatre on Triuna Island, Lake George.

Within the Bennington community "there were divergent and often controversial social and political points of view, a range in ability from the novice to the established artist, strong contrasts in regional and professional interests, and 34 years difference in age between the youngest and oldest student."[3] The force that held it all together was Martha Hill, who provided in her own teaching "a point of equilibrium."[4]

John Martin conducted his first seminar in dance criticism, and *Dance Observer* devoted an entire issue to Bennington, with reviews contributed by Martin's students and feature articles by other Benningtonites. Four advanced students passed muster for the first Program in Choreography. The handful of students in Louis Horst and Norman Lloyd's new Program in Music Composition for the Dance composed 17 pieces for student dances. *Dance Observer* praised "this chance for workmanlike development of ideas into dance forms, having accompaniment composed for them, and having the best of criticism on them from their first beginnings."[5]

In November Margaret Lloyd, who observed most of the session, wrote a four-part series in the *Christian Science Monitor* about Bennington's impact on the dance in America.[6]

> Whether the Bennington School of the Dance is an outgrowth of the increased interest in the dance in America or one of the chief contributing causes of that interest, is a question. In any case, it is a potent factor in the extraordinary development of the dance in this country both as art and as education. In three great strides over as many summers, Bennington has become the focal point of the modern American dance, the terminal station drawing dance-thinking people from all over the land and sending them out after a six-weeks' intensive session, to spread the new dance doctrine.[7]

To Lloyd, Bennington in 1936 seemed "alive with oppositions . . . a discussion place as well as a dancing place—a place of conflicts as well as of unified dance culture."[8]

Lloyd interviewed several students. One of the youngest, a high school junior with some previous dance training, told her:

> I went up thinking I would do as I liked—if anything went against the grain of my own conception, I'd just have nothing to do with it. But that notion soon melted away. It was all so stimulating. I began to fall in line and do the best I could even against the dictation of my own artistic consciousness.[9]

Despite efforts to attract male dancers, Charles Weidman's Men's Workshop enrolled but five students, none of whom returned to Bennington. (This same summer, Ted Shawn offered a workshop for men at Jacob's Pillow.) One of the five had recently come from Europe where he had studied with Wigman and others. Exposure to a range of American movement presented great challenges. He remarked, "This modern American technique is to the modern European technique what the atonality of a Schoenberg or Alban Berg is to the tonality of a Debussy or Ravel."[10] At Bennington he experienced "encouragement of the creative faculty that enlarges the individual's powers of projection on his own account, instead of fostering a purely technical outlook bearing a teacher's stamp."[11]

Hanya Holm foresaw danger in a superficial ingestion of numerous "methods" by students, and cautioned them that "a few weeks' experience in any method is insufficient to warrant anyone's thinking that he or she 'knows' the method in its entirety, and certainly insufficient to the point of making it unethical for any person to teach what he has learned *as* that method."[12]

Several weeks before the session began, Ted Shawn had written an article (one of a series) for the *Boston Herald* on "The Influence of Germany upon the American Dance," in which he chastised his former students for siding with the German "extreme left wing":

> For the last ten years or so, there has been each year a number of American dancers and teachers of dancing, making the journey to Germany to study with Mary Wigman and other German dancers. In 1931, I brought Margarete Wallman, who had for years been the director of the Berlin-Wigman Schule, to America to be a guest teacher at Denishawn. Following this, Hanya Holm, who had been a teacher in Mary Wigman's Dresden School, established a Wigman School in New York. . . . During the same period, we had in the concert field every season, one or more German dancers touring America. The result has been that there are thousands of young American dancers and teachers who are either teaching the German dance, or have embodied some of it in their teaching material—or who have embraced the German style in their individual and group performances. . . .
>
> The effect in America for the past ten years has been to create a tremendous controversy, and controversy is always a sign of health and growth in any art form. My own former pupils, Martha Graham, Doris Humphrey and Charles Weidman, who with Hanya Holm of the Wigman School form the large part of the faculty at Bennington College's dance department in the summer, although they have been grounded in the rich and inclusive styles which I taught them, have remained strongly on the side of the German extreme left wing—dynamism, distortion, "abstract" and "absolute" dance being preached by them, with a parallel denial of all else in the dance as having value.[13]

Virginia Mishnun wrote of another "potential source of danger" in the Bennington scheme:

> Until three years ago there was no modern dance school in America. There were private studios of the dance and organizations such as the Wigman

School where a method was sufficiently elaborated to require the services of several teachers for the various elements of the one particular method. But there was no school where different methods and opposing points of view might be studied and a thorough grounding in all the aspects of the modern dance be acquired. Such schools have long existed in the other arts. But in the dance each outstanding performer was a teacher, and each teacher had his group of pupils whose course of study consisted, for the most part, in the recapitulation of the teacher's technical method and process of artistic creation. Life within the other self-enclosed studio walls was generally ignored or disparaged. Moreover, since its outstanding exponents were concentrated in New York City, the modern dance suffered the additional narrowness of New York provincialism. Today, at last, a school exists where the young dancer can obtain a well-rounded and comprehensive view of the modern dance. . . .

The general program includes intensive work with four prominent figures in the modern dance world, Martha Graham, Doris Humphrey, Hanya Holm and Charles Weidman. In addition to this work, Martha Hill presents a course in the fundamental analysis of movement for the dance. Miss Hill occupies an unusual position in the modern dance in that she is not a performer, and has no axe to grind. She supplies a general foundation of movement without dictating to what use it is to be put. The student benefits both from Miss Hill's basic work and also from being exposed to the esthetic prejudices of four distinct personalities in the art. . . .

The great virtue of the Bennington School is at the same time a potential source of danger. What I mean to say is that the happy family life of contrasting views of the dance may become a little too happy to be productive. It is necessary in art that opposing points of view and schools of opinion clash with vigor and pride in their beliefs. There is danger in burying the hatchet too easily and too superficially because unless it is buried deep enough its edge is likely to cut the toes of both parties. Factionalism is the heart of the development of non-primitive art. It sharpens the artist, urges him to clarify the outlines of his art, to achieve convincing realization of his beliefs in art form. The presence of factions facilitates also the solution of esthetic problems. If everyone agrees offhand on a method of procedure in order to preserve a state of amicability, too many issues may be ignored. The solution arrived at may exclude vital elements. Moreover, there are any number of possible solutions that differentiates one artist from another, and makes for the variety and life of art. With factionalism absent, the modern dance is in danger of becoming merely a school of dance rather than contemporary dance, as surrealism and futurism in painting. . . . It would be a sad state of affairs if the whole modern dance were to hold hands and plunge down the fatal abyss of the one tendency, be it surrealism, dramatic dance, abstraction or what you will. Because then the modern dance would cease to exist and become merely an attitude, a vogue. That, incidentally, is what it was a few years ago when the regimented attitude of modern dancers was the purely formal, and only obscure differences in abstraction existed. Then it could truthfully be said that the modern dance was only a state of mind. . . . Some element of factionalism must always persist if an art is to be a growing organism. It is this balance of harmony and strife that creates a healthy and developing art form. On the surface, at least, Bennington seems to represent such a balance with Miss Hill's unbiased study of body movement as the point of equilibrium.[14]

THE SESSION IN BRIEF

The General Program continued. The Workshop Program was enlarged with a Women's Workshop, directed by Doris Humphrey, and a Men's Workshop, directed by Charles Weidman. A Program in Choreography for advanced students and a Program in Music Composition for the Dance were added.

FACULTY AND STAFF

Doris Humphrey and Charles Weidman, full session. Martha Graham and Hanya Holm, each two weeks in succession. Workshop Productions: Norman Lloyd, musical director. Gerard Gentile, technical director (formerly drama department, Western Reserve Univeristy). Thomas Bouchard, photographer. Wallingford Riegger, composer in residence for *With My Red Fires.*

STUDENTS

Total 166, ages 15–48, from 29 states and Canada, including 97 teachers, 40 students, 19 dancers. General Program 113. Including Elizabeth A. Bloomer (student-teacher, Calla Travis School of Dance, Grand Rapids, later Mrs. Gerald R. Ford). Truda Kaschmann (Alwin Nikolais' teacher, YWCA, Hartford). Barbara Mettler (teacher, New York). Women's Workshop 34 (24 in addition to 10 of Doris Humphrey's group). Including Eva Desca, Harriette Ann Gray, Ethel Mann, Bernice van Gelder. Men's Workshop 11 (5 in addition to 6 of Charles Weidman's group). Program in Choreography 4. Including Marian Van Tuyl, Ruth Bloomer, Fannie Aronson. Program in Music for the Dance 4.

LECTURES, SPECIAL EVENTS, RECITALS, AND STUDENT DEMONSTRATIONS

Lecture-demonstrations by Doris Humphrey, Charles Weidman, Martha Graham with concert groups, Lincoln Kirstein and members of Ballet Caravan, Irma Dombois-Bartenieff and Irma Otto-Betz on Laban Dance Script. Lecture-discussions by Hanya Holm, Thomas Bouchard. Piano recitals by Julian de Gray, Norman and Ruth Lloyd, Jean Williams, and Esther Williamson. Ballet Caravan made its world debut sponsored by the Bennington School of the Dance with four new ballets and a series of divertissements danced by a company of 12. Members of the New Dance League with Anna Sokolow, guest artist, gave a concert. The session ended with a demonstration of student work.

17 and 18 July 1936

The Ballet Caravan. *Dir* Lincoln Kirstein. *Accom* David Stimer. College Theatre. Program (17 July): ***Encounter*** (Classic ballet in one act) *chor* Lew Christensen, *mus* W. A. Mozart (The *Haffner* Serenade), *cos* after the drawings of J. G. von Schadow. ***Harlequin for President*** (Ballet-Pantomime after the Italian Popular Comedy) *chor* Eugene Loring, *mus* Domenico Scarlatti (from the Sonatas), *cos* Keith Martin. ***Divertissements:*** 1. ***Mazurka,*** *mus* [Mikhail Ivanovitch] Glinka. 2. ***Morning Greeting,*** *mus* [Franz] Schubert. 3. ***Pas de deux,*** *mus* Liebling. 4. ***Gitana,*** *mus* Torré. 5. ***Can-Can,*** *mus* Strauss. 6. ***Pas Classique,*** *mus* [Benjamin] Godard. 7. ***Rhapsody,*** *mus* [Franz] Liszt. Program (18 July): ***Promenade*** (Classic ballet in one act) *chor* William Dollar, *mus* Maurice Ravel (*Valses Nobles et Sentimentales*), *cos* after Horace Vernet. ***Pocahontas*** *chor* Lew Christensen, *mus* Elliott Carter, *cos* after the engravings of Theodore de Bry. ***Divertissements:*** 1. ***Rhapsody,*** *mus* Liszt. 2. ***Can-Can,*** *mus* Strauss. 3. ***Morning Greeting,*** *mus* Schubert. 4. ***Valse,*** *mus* [Francis] Poulenc. 5. ***Gitana,*** *mus* Torré. 6. ***Pas Classique,*** *mus* Godard. 7. ***March,*** *mus* [Serge] Prokofiev. *Danc* Ruby Asquith, Ruthanna Boris, Gisella Caccialanza, Harold Christensen, Lew Christensen, Rabana Hasburgh, Erick Hawkins, Albia Kavan, Charles Laskey, Eugene Loring, Annabelle Lyon, Hanna Moore. *Premiere.

Reviews

Lincoln Kirstein, *Blast at Ballet*:

> In six weeks we made a little repertory and gave our first performances in July 1936, at the very centre of the bitterly anti-ballet, "modern-dance" school in Bennington, Vermont. That debut was a nightmare, although the Bennington audience was a great deal more patient, tolerant and

> interested than many other people for whom we would dance when we became much better known.[15]

Ruthanna Boris, *Dance Herald*:

> At first our ideas were disjointed and vague, but gradually they connected themselves and emerged as a beautiful, possible dream—a dream of American ballet dancers dancing America!
>
> In the spring of 1936 Lincoln Kirstein founded the Caravan. [It] was a small company—only twelve members. The choreography was done by members of the company. . . . We prepared four ballets and a series of folk dance divertissements. . . . Our first step in the direction we planned to go was *Pocahontas* with music written by a young American, Elliott Carter, Jr. We had to go slowly at first, to feel our way until we saw our path clearly ahead. . . .
>
> When Bennington applauded us we felt more than ever that we were headed in the right direction, for there our audience was composed of young dancers who, though their technique was different, had been doing for a long time what we were beginning to do.[16]

Walter Terry, *Boston Herald*:

> The audience kindly overlooked the flaws in technique, and heartily applauded a talented group of young men and women for their promising efforts and sincerity of purpose. The emphasis here was on dance and performance; not on elaborate lighting effects and multi-colored settings. This seemed to suggest rather plainly that these young artists had discovered the real meaning of the word "theater."[17]

Marjorie Church, *Dance Observer*:

> The performances showed promising individual technique and style on the part of several members of the company, but the group choreography as a whole is not tightly knit, as yet—and there is room for speculation as to the choice and treatment of subject-matter. If we must have Pocahontas and Harlequin and eternal romance, for instance, a new slant on them would be refreshing. New steps don't mean a new slant. [The young dancers] seem a bit lost in eclecticism, at present, both of style and of technique. Classic ballet training and idiom are apparently at a loss when confronted with modern reality clamoring for expression. We wonder if it's necessary to try to make the twain meet?[18]

26 July 1936

Members of the New Dance League. *Pianists* Alex North, Clair Leonard, Elizabeth Gottesleben. *Percussion* Nancy McKnight. College Theatre. No confirmed premieres. Program: ***Histrionics*** *chor* Anna Sokolow, *mus* [Paul] Hindemith. ***Romantic Dances, a. Illusion, b. Désir*** *chor* Sokolow, *mus* [Alexander] Scriabin. ***Speaker*** *chor* Sokolow, *mus* [Alex] North. ***Four Little Salon Pieces, a. Début, b. Élan, c. Rêverie, d. Entr'acte*** *chor* Sokolow, *mus* [Dmitri] Shostakovitch. ***Ballad in Popular Style*** *chor* Sokolow, *mus* North. ***Hunger*** *chor* Fara Lynn, *mus* [Serge] Prokofiev. ***Well Fed*** *chor* Bill Matons, *mus* Brown. ***American Rhapsody*** *chor and danc* Matons and Edith Orcutt, *mus* Scriabin, *poem* Kenneth Fearing. ***Transition*** *chor* Eva Desca, *mus* [Elizabeth] Gottesleben.

15 August 1936

Final Demonstration of Student Compositions in Dance and Music. College Theatre. I. Dance Composition, under the direction of Martha Hill and Bessie Schönberg. Four sets of Themes and Variations, one each *chor* by Helen Knight, Fara Lynn, Truda Kaschmann, Caryl Cuddeback, with groups. *Mus* Silvine Savage, Jean Williams, Beatrice Hellebrandt, Phyllis Van Vleet, Esther Williamson. II. Pre-Classic Forms, under the direction of Louis Horst. *Chor* Ruth

New Dance, Vermont State Armory. Photograph by Sidney Bernstein.

Diamond, Karen Burt, Barbara Mettler, Florence Warwick, Marjorie Church, Van Vleet. *Mus* Lambranzi, [J. P.] Rameau, Hellebrandt, Williams, Williamson. III. Modern Forms, under the direction of Louis Horst. Studies in the Archaic, the Medieval, Impressionism, 5/8 Time, Cerebralism, Americana. *Chor* Marian Van Tuyl, Ruth Bloomer, Alice Gates, Tosia Mundstock, Isabelle Katz, Margery Schneider. *Mus* Williamson, Williams, [Maurice] Ravel, Larmanjat, Hellebrandt, Paul Nordoff, David Guion. IV. Program in Choreography and Program in Music Composition for the Dance, under the critical direction of Martha Hill, Louis Horst, and John Martin. ***Gay Promenade*** *chor* Schneider, *mus* Hellebrandt, *danc* group. ***Road to Success*** *chor* Fannie Aronson, *mus* Williamson, *danc* group. ***American Gospel Hymn: Throw Out the Life Line*** *chor* Schneider, *mus* Elizabeth Gottesleben, *danc* group. ***Piazza Sketches–From a Mid-Western Suite, Alone; Together*** *chor* and *danc* Van Tuyl, *mus* Williams. ***Zodiac*** *chor* Bloomer, *mus* Williams, *danc* group.

BENNINGTON FESTIVAL SERIES

Nine performances, beginning with a lecture by John Martin, "The American Dance," then two solo retrospective recitals by Martha Graham, Hanya Holm's first major concerts of her choreography with a group from the New York Wigman School, all in the College Theatre, and four evenings in the Armory of Workshop productions by Doris Humphrey (*With My Red Fires,* plus newly staged productions of *New Dance* and *Theatre Piece*) and Charles Weidman (*Quest*).

31 July and 1 August 1936

Martha Graham, solo recital. *Mus dir* Louis Horst. *Musicians* Ensemble of five instruments and voice. College Theatre. No premieres. Program: ***Praeludium*** *mus* Nordoff. ***Lamentation*** *mus* [Zoltan] Kodály. ***Frontier*** *mus* Louis Horst. ***Satyric Festival Song*** *mus* Imre Weisshaus. ***Imperial Gesture*** *mus* Lehman Engel. ***Sarabande*** *mus* Engel. ***Building Motif*** from the suite ***Horizons*** *mus* Horst. ***Ekstasis*** *mus* Engel. ***Act of Piety*** from the suite ***American Provincials*** *mus* Horst. ***Harlequinade, a. Pessimist, b. Optimist*** *mus* Ernst Toch.

7 and 8 August 1936

Hanya Holm and Group of The New York Wigman School of the Dance. *Accom* Harvey Pollins, Thomas McNally, piano. Elizabeth Gottesleben, percussion. *Cos* Peggy Boone. College Theatre. No premieres. Program: ***Salutation*** *mus* [Henry] Cowell *danc* group. ***In a Quiet Space*** *mus* [Franziska] Boas *danc* Holm. ***Drive*** *mus* Pollins, *danc* Holm. ***Dance in Two Parts: A Cry Rises in the Land, New Destinies*** *mus* [Wallingford] Riegger *danc* Holm and group. ***Dance Stanzas*** *mus* Jurist *danc* Holm, Melvene Ipcar, Dora Brown. ***Sarabande*** *mus* Pollins *danc* Holm. ***City Nocturne*** *mus* Riegger *danc* group. ***Four Chromatic Eccentricities*** *mus* Riegger *danc* Holm. ***Primitive Rhythm*** *mus* Lucretia Barzun *danc* Holm and group. *Danc* Louise Kloepper, Dora Brown, Margaret Dudley, Carolyn Durand, Melvene Ipcar, Nancy McKnight, Elizabeth Waters.

This program had been given at Mills College on 25 July during Holm's teaching residency. John Martin called her Bennington recital "to all intents and purposes the formal debut of

"Variations and Conclusion" from *New Dance*, Vermont State Armory. Photographs by Sidney Bernstein.

"Variations and Conclusion" from *New Dance*, Vermont State Armory. Dancers include: Joan Levy, Eva Desca, Charles Weidman, Doris Humphrey, Katherine Litz, George Bockman, Sybil Shearer, José Limón, Beatrice Seckler, William Bales, Edith Orcutt, Katherine Manning.

Miss Holm in this country and of her group in any important dance series."[19] In November 1936 Holm severed her official affiliation with Mary Wigman in light of anti-Nazi sentiment.[20] She renamed the New York Wigman School of the Dance, the Hanya Holm School of Dance and reorganized her dancers into the Hanya Holm Group. Under this name they made their American concert debut in Colorado in November 1936, in a program almost identical to the one at Bennington.

Reviews

Margaret Lloyd, *The Borzoi Book of Modern Dance*:

> When, in 1936, she first danced before the semi-private but very professional audience at Bennington, she seemed scared and inhibited, bound to small, tight planes, quite unlike the heroic Wigman scale from which her technique derives, quite unlike the large, free elasticity of her own dancers. She was probably suffering from stagefright before that stern jury of her peers. In later performances there was discernible a freer, lyrical quality of movement, a small-scaled style of her own that befitted her diminutive stature and dresden-doll appearance.[21]

John Martin, the *New York Times*:

> It is as a group choreographer that she emerges most triumphantly. . . . There are no bits of technique transferred bodily from the practice room, no combinations of isolated gestures, but a building of design in terms of sequential movement. . . . What a composer with such a rich knowledge of her material and such a flair for group composition can conceivably accomplish with a large company such as the annual Bennington "workshop" project provides, makes next Summer's festival production already a matter of great promise.[22]

12 and 14 August 1936

Doris Humphrey and Charles Weidman with their Concert Groups and Students of the Workshops of the School. Vermont State Armory. No premieres. Part I: ***Theatre Piece.*** Part II: ***New Dance.*** *Chor* Humphrey (Weidman composed ***In the Theatre*** in ***Theatre Piece*** and ***Third Theme*** in ***New Dance***). *Mus* Wallingford Riegger. *Mus dir* Norman Lloyd, *Musicians* Ruth Lloyd,

"In the Stadium" from *Theatre Piece*, Vermont State Armory. Photograph by Sidney Bernstein.

Clair Leonard, piano. H. Tafarella, clarinet. V. Peretti, trumpet. E. Armando, English horn. S. Gershek, Nancy McKnight, percussion. ***Sets*** Erika Klein, ***Cos*** Pauline Lawrence. ***Danc*** (see ***With My Red Fires*** and ***Quest*** in Catalog, pp. 139 and 147, respectively).

These two previously composed parts of Humphrey's *New Dance Trilogy* were rehearsed and restaged for performance immediately prior to the world premiere of the newest segment, *With My Red Fires*. This was the first and possibly only opportunity to see the full work, on two successive nights. So far as can be determined, the whole *Trilogy* was never performed in a single evening.

As had been done for *Panorama* the previous year, two levels of the Armory were utilized. The *Bennington Banner* reported:

> From ceiling to floor the whole front half of the Armory has been "masked" with black screens designed especially to give an impression of height through the use of vertical lines. In addition to the stage, an area 30 feet in front of it on the auditorium floor will be utilized in the recitals. Gerard Gentile, new addition to the regular faculty of Bennington College, is chiefly responsible for the creation of the set. He has been here since August 1, after leaving work with Western Reserve University and the Cleveland Playhouse.[23]

Margaret Lloyd, *Christian Science Monitor*:

> Then was armory hammered into theater, stage extended over steps to floor, a series of rectangular black wings erected on either side to hide the musicians and add extra entrance and exit places. The platinum-colored blocks of *Theatre Piece* and *New Dance* were variously dispersed over both stage and floor.[24]

13 and 15 August 1936

Doris Humphrey and Charles Weidman with their Concert Groups and Students of the Workshops of the School. Vermont State Armory. ****With My Red Fires chor*** Humphrey, *mus* Wallingford Riegger. ****Quest: A Choreographic Pantomime chor*** Weidman, *mus* Norman Lloyd, Clair Leonard. *See Catalog.

Sequence from *Theatre Piece*, Vermont State Armory. Photograph by Sidney Bernstein.

NOTES

1. Paul Love, "New Forms of the Dance," *Nation* 144, no. 24 (12 June 1937): 679–80.
2. Letter from Doris Humphrey to Charles Francis Woodford, 12 July 1936 [Doris Humphrey Collection, C390].
3. "Third Annual Report of the Bennington School of the Dance," Summer 1936, in *Reports of Officers, 1935–36,* Bennington College, 4, no. 3 (August 1936): 2.
4. Virginia Mishnun, "Bennington Festival," *Brooklyn Eagle*, 23 August 1936.
5. Marjorie Church, "The Bennington Dance Festival," *Dance Observer* 3, no. 7 (August-September 1936): 76.
6. Margaret Lloyd, *Christian Science Monitor*, 10, 17, and 24 November 1936 and 1 December 1937.
7. Margaret Lloyd, "On with the Dance," *Christian Science Monitor*, 10 November 1936.
8. Ibid.
9. Margaret Lloyd, "Student Impressions," *Christian Science Monitor*, 17 November 1936.
10. Margaret Lloyd, "The Workshop Group" (interview with Otto Ashermann), *Christian Science Monitor*, 24 November 1936.
11. Ibid.
12. Quoted in Marjorie Church, *Dance Observer* 3, no. 7 (August-September 1936): 77.
13. Ted Shawn, "Influence of Germany upon the American Dance," *Boston Herald*, 10 June 1936.
14. Virginia Mishnun, "Bennington Festival," *Brooklyn Eagle*, 23 August 1936.
15. Lincoln Kirstein, "Blast at Ballet," in *Three Pamphlets Collected* (Brooklyn, N.Y.: Dance Horizons, 1967), pp. 41–42.
16. Ruthanna Boris, "The Ballet Caravan," *Dance Herald* 1, no. 1 (October 1937): 1.
17. Walter Terry, *Boston Herald*, 23 July 1936. This was Terry's second article for the *Boston Herald;* the first was a story about the Bennington session. See his *I Was There: Selected Dance Reviews and Articles, 1936–1976*, compiled and edited by Andrew Mark Wentink (New York: Marcel Dekker, 1978), pp. 1–4.
18. Marjorie Church, "The Ballet Caravan," *Dance Observer* 3, no. 7 (August-September 1936): 78. See also Nancy Reynolds, *Repertory in Review: 40 years of the New York City Ballet* (New York: Dial Press, 1977), and Lincoln Kirstein, *The New York City Ballet* (New York: Alfred A. Knopf, 1973), p. 49.
19. John Martin, "Hanya Holm: Artist and Group Make Debut in Bennington Festival," *New York Times*, 16 August 1936.
20. Walter Sorell, *Hanya Holm: The Biography of an Artist* (Middletown, Conn.: Wesleyan University Press, 1969), p. 44.
21. Margaret Lloyd, *The Borzoi Book of Modern Dance* (New York: Alfred A. Knopf, 1949), pp. 160–61.
22. John Martin, *New York Times*, 16 August 1936.
23. *Bennington Banner*, 11 August 1936.
24. Margaret Lloyd, *Christian Science Monitor*, 8 September 1936.

1937
Fourth Session of the Bennington School of the Dance

2 July 1937—14 August 1937

"Caricature at Bennington: the puzzle being to find Louis Horst, Wallingford Riegger, Mary Jo Shelly, Frances Hawkins, Norman Lloyd, Martha Graham, Doris Humphrey, Charles Weidman, Hanya Holm, Martha Hill, John Martin."

Drawing by Betty Joiner, courtesy of Rosamond Gilder, *Theater Arts*.

The last of four Bennington Workshop projects was Hanya Holm's epic *Trend*, danced by a combined group of 33 women. It was her first major composition in America, and it became her legendary masterwork. John Martin gave *Trend* his annual award for the year's best choreography, calling it "one of the most important works of the period" in its advancement of the dance along a "new road toward an organic synthesis of the theatre arts."[1]

Its staging at the Armory exploited the potentialities of different levels, planes, and lighting dimensions which Arch Lauterer had first introduced in *Panorama* (1935). A specially composed score by Wallingford Riegger was augmented by Edgard Varèse's brief but shocking *Ionisation*, projected at ear-splitting volume over a special amplification system. This was the first use of recorded music in Bennington productions.

Martha Graham presented two new solos, one of them, *Immediate Tragedy*, a major work. Doris Humphrey and Charles Weidman made no new works but gave especially compelling performances of *New Dance* and *Theatre Piece*, restaged for the occasion. Wrote Humphrey:

> I was really pleased for once—the company was pulled together, the stage is superb—I danced as well as I ever have and the audience was most responsive. Now, however, I have a long summer to look forward to with nothing but teaching in it—a pretty barren outlook. What I would really like I'm afraid will never happen during my dancing days here . . . three performances a week. Dancing doesn't draw well enough for that in a remote spot like Bennington.[2]

Anna Sokolow, José Limón, and Esther Junger were elected from 15 nominees as the first of six Bennington Fellows. This new Fellowship Program gave each a chance to work

Hanya Holm Dancers at Bennington, 1937. Photographs and descriptions by Eve Gentry.

Louise Kloepper's Jump. "This was a very special jump that Louise created. It began in a deep second position plié, with the right arm bent and contracted in towards the body, elbow pulled downward and leftward, wrist rotated outward. Left arm contracted parallel to right, but right arm describing a lightning-like zig-zag, ending at its apex straight up to the sky. It was a brilliant action. We all learned it. But I never saw anyone approximate the dynamics of Louise's explosive action." Eve Gentry, 1 October 1977.

independently for six weeks on new group compositions, free of teaching or performing responsibilities, with living costs paid and studio space, accompanists, composers, and production facilities provided. It was the first time new choreographic blood was injected into the Bennington community, though Junger was the only one of the three outside the influence of the "Bennington Group." Limón, reported Doris Humphrey, was "completely on his own for the first time—no lessons to give, no rehearsals called for him . . . I expect he will produce something remarkable."[3]

Lincoln Kirstein's return with Ballet Caravan occasioned a first meeting between Erick Hawkins and Martha Graham. Kirstein's lecture on "The Classic Ballet," reported *Dance Observer*, interrupted "the business of lusty pioneering by an air from the past, faintly scented with nostalgia."[4]

Dance Observer asked the Fellows for their views on the ballet, and reported them as follows:

> Contrary to the general supposition, Anna Sokolow believes that training in ballet should ideally be a part of the modern dancer's education. . . . She has never studied the ballet technique. . . . Miss Sokolow sees in the future a single modern dance which will combine the technique of the ballet with the creative freedom of the present modern dance, resulting in a more effective form than has yet been achieved.[5]

> [Esther Junger] asserted that unless we are careful, the modern dance will soon become another rigid form to rebel against. . . . Now, too many people are trying to say the same thing in the same way. . . . She warns people to be wary of accepting things too readily without questioning. . . . She does not believe ballet training is important to the modern dancer, and that superimposing a general type of movement upon all varieties of physique and personality is a dangerous procedure.[6]

> [José Limón] believes the ideal and only training for men in the contemporary dance is through Charles Weidman's technique, and that the place of men in the dance . . . must be restored to its original dignity in the eyes of the world, a difficult task involving the breaking down of acquired prejudice centuries old. The ballet . . . is an alien and exotic form of dance, and while these qualities are not in themselves objectionable, he finds the ballet decayed and reactionary both artistically and ideologically and cannot concede it a place in the American scene.[7]

The Spanish Civil War had erupted the summer before, and in July it entered its bloodiest

Preparation for "Study in Falls," from Demonstration Part II Dance Studies. Hanya Holm Dancers, Elizabeth Waters (center).

phase. The impact of world affairs can be seen in the works produced at Bennington in the summer of 1937: Martha Graham's new solo, *Immediate Tragedy*, and José Limón's first group work, *Danza de la Muerte*, both inspired by the situation in Spain; Anna Sokolow's group work *Façade-Esposizione Italiana* by the rise of fascism in Italy; and Hanya Holm's *Trend* by the gathering forces of war and imminent cataclysm.

New Masses magazine saw Bennington as "more or less a pulse of whither the dance" and took the occasion to scrutinize the political concerns—and lack of them—in dances composed by leading artists and students, praising Hanya Holm, José Limón, and Anna Sokolow and criticizing Esther Junger's choice of themes as "scarcely [of] immediate interest."[8] *New Masses* noted a "discrepancy" between "the work of the school and the work of the masters" and wondered why the student work was not more socially involved. In particular, "the student demonstration . . . shows a curious and disquieting predilection for the abstract pattern which was the manner of dancing several years back." The critique continued:

> It is interesting to note that in its four years of existence, Tamiris has never put in an appearance at Bennington—whether by design or accident, her presence is decidedly missed at the school. The work here definitely leans to the cerebral both in subject matter and execution; the emotional qualities are lacking.[9]

Holm Group doing falls.

Revolving Jump preparation for "Roll-Over Fall." "The 'Roll-Over Fall,' the leit-motif of the 'Study in Falls,' was the creation of Hanya Holm and members of her company. It happened before I joined the company. I was told that it emerged in a flash of creative and physical excitement during rehearsals, while working on the 'Study in Falls.' It came out of a repeated pattern of slides, turns, elevations, contraction, and a rolling, rollicking, fall that bounced right up again to a crescendo and even more so, a series of repetitions that became intoxicating to performer and spectator alike. It was not long before other dancers, other companies, were using 'our' 'Roll-Over Fall.' Now it is seen frequently, with many variations, almost a cliche!" Eve Gentry, 1 October 1977.

An historic visit was paid by Ruth St. Denis, who attended Martha Graham's solo concert and returned as "an official Festival guest" for later performances. John Martin called her Bennington visit the "beginning of a rapprochement that has been long overdue between a great pioneer and an art movement for which she is in large part responsible. . . . Whatever she may think of the work of her recalcitrant children, it is fine to have her coming to see it and to claim her part in it."[10]

St. Denis sat in on a Graham class at Bennington, "a magnificent example of body building and strengthening but extremely ugly—and hard. . . ." she noted in her diary. In what she saw of Graham's work at Bennington, "there is no rhythmic response taught—no melodic line taught—no hands nor head" nor facial gesture.[11]

St. Denis gave her Bennington visit an important place in her autobiography. She felt during this period, that she had been "marooned on a desert island."

> It must be remembered that as the reputed dean of the American dance, a creative artist of some distinction, and, since the death of Isadora, the sole surviving instigator of this new epoch, I was suffering a complete eclipse. The intelligentsia of the dance made it appear that my offering was not only in the discard, but had been, in retrospect, largely composed of theatrical tricks. . . .
>
> Finally, I had to drop, clearly and without compromise, those personal and impersonal resentments toward the movement as a whole. But not until some years later did I go up to Bennington College, that stronghold of the modern dance. Then I found that when we face our fears they change into friendly beings who help us on our way. Mary Jo Shelley and Martha and Charles and John Martin, and countless students who had touched the life of Denishawn at some period, greeted me with friendliness, and an appreciation far beyond what my self-incrusted fears had imagined. I spent three extraordinary days watching Louis Horst in his classes, and observing Martha's strict but beneficial techniques. I had the joy of seeing one of Hanya Holm's free, lovely groups, and admired an enchanting dance of Anna Sokolow. [No doubt not the new group work but one of the earlier lyric solos on the program.] But more than anything,

Broad sweeping chassé, building toward climax. Hanya Holm (seated) and group.

> I saw the emergence out of hatred propaganda and political gloom into beautiful, although austere, concepts of American life.[12]

Composer Dane Rudhyar visited Bennington in 1937 and stayed for the full session:

> Six weeks of constant contact with this "Bennington Idea" has . . . shown to me more than ever the amazing vitality of the modern dance movement, and the hold it has on the country at large. While modern music is somnolent, after having been doped by the imported neo-classicism of defeatist Europeans, the modern dance surges on, fresh and filled with hope and ideals. I hope that through the dance music may become revivified and made a vital experience. Whether or not this can occur as long as the dancer considers it usually a necessary but secondary adjunction remains to be seen. I do not think that "music *for* the dance" as taught in Bennington is an ideal concept. I believe in "music *and* the dance"—centered by a common goal.[13]

Rudhyar also noted the larger implications of the Bennington project:

> This purpose of wide cultural dissemination of ideals and of centralization of practical means to "put over" the modern dance was evidently the central purpose of the origination of the Bennington Dance sessions. At a time when the modern dance is growing out of its initial and youthful clothes—the "dance recital"—and looking toward larger forms of presentation to a rapidly increasing public, the work accomplished in Bennington is of vast significance.[14]

In August 1937 the *Magazine of Art* published a photo feature survey entitled "Dance Captures America," which began:

> Dance has caught the imagination of America and regained a part of the heritage belonging to the mother of the arts. Throughout the land a great general audience supplants the tiny specialist following that used to center in New York. For, although New York remains America's dance capital, it is only one of a loop of cities in many a company's far-flung itinerary.[15]

John Martin attributed the survival of American dance and its extraordinary growth to a supportive audience composed not of dowagers but of young people and to the spread of dance through American colleges and universities:

> The leading native dancers have now found it possible to make tours of the country on the strength of the support which exists in the public itself, and have

Holm Group and apprentices, "Turns and Twirls."

found large and eager audiences to prove their theory sound. As an absolutely democratic art [the modern dance] has discovered a democratic audience.[16]

THE SESSION IN BRIEF

The General Program continued. Hanya Holm directed the Workshop Program, last in the series of four. Programs in Choreography and Music Composition for the Dance continued. The first Bennington fellowships were granted "to aid directly in the training of future leaders for the modern dance." Anna Sokolow, José Limón, and Esther Junger were selected from 15 nominees to be the first Bennington Fellows.

FACULTY AND STAFF

Hanya Holm, full session. Martha Graham, Doris Humphrey, and Charles Weidman, each two weeks in succession. Other principal faculty same as in 1936. Franziska Boas (percussion accompaniment). Alex North, Morris Mamorsky, Harvey Pollins (pianists-composers). Wallingford Riegger, composer in residence for *Trend*. Thomas Bouchard, photographer. Festival concerts: Gerard Gentile, technical director. Edward Glass, assistant. Norman Lloyd, musical director. Betty Joiner, costume designer, Workshop and Fellows' productions.

Holm Dancers at Bennington.

Holm Dancers doing turns.

STUDENTS

Total 159, ages 16–44, from 31 states, Canada, and Hawaii, including 97 teachers, 36 students, 12 dancers. General Program 118 (4 men). Including Jean Erdman (student, Sarah Lawrence College), Eleanor Lauer (student, University of Chicago), Gertrude Lippincott (student, University of Minnesota), Alwin Nikolais (dramatic director, Recreational Division, Hartford Park Department). Workshop Program 35 (23 women plus Hanya Holm's Concert Group of 12 women). Including Harriet Roeder (teacher, Denver), who joined the Holm group shortly afterward. Program in Choreography 4 (the four students enrolled in 1936). Program in Music for the Dance 2.

LECTURES, SPECIAL EVENTS, AND STUDENT RECITALS

Hanya Holm and Charles Weidman offered lecture-demonstrations. Doris Humphrey and Martha Graham gave lecture-discussions. Paul Love delivered a series of lectures and a seminar on dance notation. Lincoln Kirstein lectured on "The Classic Dance," with a demonstration of ballet technique by Ballet Caravan members. Francis Fergusson, chairman of Bennington College's Drama Division, lectured on "The Relationship Between the Arts of the Theatre." Arch Lauterer discussed "A Project Theatre for Bennington College." There were informal music recitals and analyses of dance music by Ruth and Norman Lloyd, Morris Mamorsky, Harvey Pollins, Esther Williamson, and Edward Glass.

Ballet Caravan paid a second visit, performing in the Armory this time. The newly organized American Dance Association, an amalgam of the New Dance League, the Dancers' Association, and the Dance Guild, sponsored an "informal dance concert" by Marian Van Tuyl and Group from Chicago and a lecture on "Why Spain Is Important to You" (the Spanish Civil War had erupted in July 1936). On 9 August the entire community of about 200 met "to discuss future plans of the School based on suggestions and criticisms of the group; and to sample opinion on a plan for a permanent central school for modern dance."[17] A Final Demonstration of Student Work ended the session.

24 July 1937

The Ballet Caravan. *Dir* Lincoln Kirstein. *Mus dir* Elliott Carter, Jr. *Accom* David Stimer. *Danc* Ruby Asquith, Ruthanna Boris, Harold Christensen, Lew Christensen, Douglas Coudy, Fred Danieli, Jane Doering, Rabana Hasburgh, Erick Hawkins, Mary Heater, Marie Jeanne, Albia Kavan, Lorna London, Eugene Loring, Marjorie Munson, Helen Stewart, Audrey White. Vermont State Armory. No premieres. Program: ***Encounter*** *chor* Lew Christensen, *mus* W. A. Mozart. ***Yankee Clipper*** *chor* Loring, *mus* Paul Bowles. ***Showpiece*** *chor* Hawkins, *mus* Robert McBride.

Showpiece, which had its premiere 15 July 1937 in Saybrook, Connecticut, was Hawkins' first ballet. Composer McBride, on the Bennington College music faculty, later wrote *Punch and The Judy* for Martha Graham (1941). Graham and Hawkins met for the first time at the Armory after this performance.[18]

Holm Dancers at Bennington.

25 July 1937

Marian Van Tuyl and Group. Presented by the American Dance Association. *Chor* Marian Van Tuyl. *Danc* Van Tuyl, Ruth Ann Heisey, Eleanor Lauer, Theodora Wiesner, Mildred Wile. *Accom* Ruth Lloyd, Margaret Lidy. College Theatre. No premieres. Program: ***Salutation*** *mus* Carlos Chavez, *danc* Van Tuyl. ***No Retreat*** *mus* Egon Wellesz, *danc* Heisey, Lauer, Wiesner, Wile, Van Tuyl. ***Americana*** *mus* Jean Williams, ***Alone*** *danc* Van Tuyl, ***Together*** *danc* Van Tuyl, ***Public Condolences*** *danc* Heisey, Lauer, Wiesner, ***Public Rejoicings*** *mus* Paul Nordoff, *danc* Van Tuyl. ***Triumphant Figure (An Archaic Dance)*** *mus* Esther Williamson, *danc* Van Tuyl. ***Epilogue to Victory*** *mus* Williams, *danc* Heisey, Lauer, Van Tuyl. ***Exhibition Piece*** *mus* Williams, *danc* Heisey, Lauer, Wiesner, Van Tuyl. ***In the Clearing (Variations on a Theme)*** *mus* Gregory Tucker, *danc* Heisey, Lauer, Wile, Van Tuyl.

The concert was reviewed by Alwin Nikolais and Naomi Lubell as a project of John Martin's Seminar in Dance Criticism, published in *Dance Observer*, August-September 1937.

14 August 1937

Final Demonstration of Student Compositions in Dance and Music. College Theatre. I. Dance Composition, under the direction of Martha Hill and Bessie Schönberg. Compositions included ***Waltz*** *chor* Truda Kaschmann and Alwin Nikolais, *mus* Yolanda Lorenz. II. Pre-Classic Forms, under the direction of Louis Horst. Compositions included ***Threnody*** (Allemande) *chor* Theodora Wiesner, *mus* Edward Glass. ***Momentum*** (Courante) and ***Americana*** (Bourrée) *chor* Nikolais, *mus* Beatrice Hellebrandt. III. Modern Forms, under the direction of Louis Horst. Compositions included ***Study in Cerebralism: Abstract*** *chor* Jean Erdman, *mus* Hellebrandt, ***Obsession*** *chor* Barbara Mettler, *mus* Ernst Toch. IV. Program in Choreography and Program in Music for the Dance, under the critical direction of Martha Hill, Louis Horst, and John Martin. ***Directions: 1. Flight*** (First section of a projected dance in three parts) *chor* Marian Van Tuyl, *mus* [Nikolai] Lopatnikov. ***First Heritage*** (five parts) *chor* Margery Schneider, *mus* Hellebrandt, *danc* Schneider and group. ***Three Dances of Judith,*** *chor* Ruth Bloomer, *mus* Ruth Lloyd, Esther Williamson, *danc* Ruth Bloomer and group.

BENNINGTON FESTIVAL SERIES

Seven performances in the Armory to a total audience of about 2000. Doris Humphrey, Charles Weidman, and Concert Groups, two performances, no premieres. Martha Graham, two solo recitals, two new works (*Opening Dance, Immediate Tragedy*). Esther Junger, José Limón, and Anna Sokolow each with new work in a shared Fellows' program (Junger and Limón presented their first group works). Two performances of Hanya Holm's Workshop production *Trend*, with a company of 33 women.

2 and 3 July 1937

Doris Humphrey, Charles Weidman, and their Concert Groups. *Mus dir* Norman Lloyd. *Musicians* Ruth Lloyd, Norman Lloyd, piano, M. Goldenberg, percussion, H. Tafarella, clarinet, V. Peretti, trumpet. *Cos* Pauline Lawrence. Vermont State Armory. No premieres. Program: ***To the Dance*** *mus* Clair Leonard, *danc* Humphrey, Weidman, and group. ***Theatre Piece*** *chor*

Holm Dancers doing leaps.

Humphrey (***In the Theatre*** *chor* Weidman), *mus* Wallingford Riegger, *danc* Humphrey, Weidman, and group. ***New Dance*** *chor* Humphrey (***Third Theme*** *chor* Weidman), *mus* Riegger, *danc* Humphrey, Weidman, and group. Members of group: Katherine Manning, Joan Levy, Ruth Sloan, Katherine Litz, Edith Orcutt, Lily Verne, Miriam Raphael, Sybil Shearer, Harriette Ann Gray, José Limón, William Bales, George Bockman, Philip Gordon, Lee Sherman.

30 and 31 July 1937

Martha Graham, solo recital. Vermont State Armory. *Mus dir* Louis Horst. *Musicians* Hugo Bergamasco, flute, V. Peretti, trumpet, H. Tafarella, clarinet, J. Youshkoff, bass clarinet, S. Gershek, drums. Program: ***Opening Dance*** *mus* Norman Lloyd. ***Lamentation*** *mus* [Zoltan] Kodály. ***Frontier*** *mus* Louis Horst. ***Satyric Festival Song*** *mus* Imre Weisshaus. ****Immediate Tragedy,*** *mus* Henry Cowell. ***Spectre 1914*** from the suite ***Chronicle*** *mus* Wallingford Riegger. ***Ekstasis*** *mus* Lehman Engel. ***Imperial Gesture*** *mus* Engel. ***Act of Piety*** from the suite ***American Provincials*** *mus* Louis Horst. ***Harlequinade*** *mus* [Ernst] Toch. *See Catalog.

12 August 1937

Esther Junger, José Limón, Anna Sokolow, Fellows of the Bennington School of the Dance, 1937. Vermont State Armory. *Mus dir* Norman Lloyd. *Sets & light* Gerard Gentile. *Asst* Edward Glass. *Cos* Betty Joiner (for the new works). Part I. Esther Junger. ****Dance to the People*** *mus* Jerome Moross, ****Ravage*** *mus* Harvey Pollins, ****Festive Rites*** *mus* Morris Mamorsky. Part II. José Limón. ****Danza de la Muerte*** *mus* Henry Clark[e], Norman Lloyd. Part III. Anna Sokolow. ***Ballad in a Popular Style*** *mus* Alex North, *danc* Sokolow. ***Speaker*** *mus* North, *danc* Sokolow.

THE BENNINGTON FESTIVAL 1937

CONCERTS IN THE MODERN DANCE

July 2, July 3 — DORIS HUMPHREY, CHARLES WEIDMAN and Concert Groups

July 30, July 31 — MARTHA GRAHAM

August 12 — ESTHER JUNGER, JOSE LIMON, ANNA SOKOLOW (Fellows of the Bennington School of the Dance)

August 13, August 14 — HANYA HOLM and Concert Group with Students of School Workshop in a New Major Composition

Address The Bennington School of the Dance, Bennington, Vermont for Concert Tickets ($1.00 each) and for enrollment in the School's courses

Advertisement for The Bennington Festival, 1937, appearing in *Dance Observer*.

Hanya Holm and her group in *Festive Rhythm*, Vermont State Armory. Photograph by Bouchard, copyright © 1978 by Thomas Bouchard.

***Façade-Esposizione Italiana** mus* North. Part IV. ***Opus for Three and Props** chor* Limón, Junger, *mus* Dmitri Shostakovitch. *See Catalog.

Each Fellow was provided with materials to compose a group work. Dancers were auditioned from the General Program, musicians and composers were engaged to write music, and costumes and the full production were specially designed. Limón and Junger created their first group compositions. Sokolow performed a new group work and two earlier solos. Limón and Junger made a closing dance for the three.

Said John Martin:

> For Miss Sokolow such an assignment was nothing of a novelty, for her work in this medium is well known and much admired. But for Miss Junger and Mr. Limón the evening was something of a new experience. That they acquitted themselves with distinction on this single occasion is perhaps not so important as that they revealed themselves as group composers who are to be reckoned with importantly in the future.[19]

13 and 14 August 1937

Hanya Holm and her Concert Group with Students of the School Workshop. Vermont State Armory. *Mus dir* Norman Lloyd. Program: ***Salutation*** *mus* Henry Cowell, *danc* Concert Group. ***City Nocturne*** *mus* Wallingford Riegger, *danc* Concert Group. ***Rhythm II*** *mus* Lucretia Wilson, *danc* Concert Group. ***Festive Rhythm*** *mus* Riegger, *danc* Hanya Holm and Concert Group. ***Prelude*** *mus* Riegger, *danc* Concert Group and Workshop Group. ****Trend*** *mus* Riegger and Edgar[d] Varèse, *danc* Concert Group and Workshop Group. *See Catalog.

According to Holm, all of the works preceding *Trend* had been performed previously, including *Prelude*, in which dancers from the Workshop Group augmented her Concert Group. However, no evidence of a prior performance of *Prelude*, with music by Riegger, was found. Barbara Page Beiswanger lists *Prelude*'s first performance at Bennington on 13 August 1937.[20]

NOTES

1. John Martin, "The Dance: On Awards," *New York Times*, 22 May 1938.
2. Letter from Doris Humphrey to Charles Francis Woodford, 6–8 July 1937 [Doris Humphrey Collection, C398].
3. Ibid.
4. Karen Burt, "Lincoln Kirstein Lecture Demonstration," *Dance Observer* 4, no. 7 (August-September 1937): 83.
5. Ruth Ann Heisey, "Anna Sokolow–Interview," *Dance Observer* 4, no. 7 (August-September 1937): 77.
6. Naomi Lubell, "Esther Junger–Interview," *Dance Observer* 4, no. 7 (August-September 1937): 77–78.
7. Naomi Lubell, "José Limón–Interview," *Dance Observer* 4, no. 7 (August-September 1937): 78. (Limón's view on ballet changed in the next decade.)
8. Owen Burke, "The Dance," *New Masses* 24, no. 10 (31 August 1937).
9. Ibid.
10. John Martin, "The Dance: New England," *New York Times*, 15 August 1937.
11. 11 August 1937 entry in the Journals of Ruth St. Denis, with kind permission of Ruth St. Denis Collection, Department of Special Collections, Research Library, University of California, Los Angeles. Excerpt courtesy of Suzanne Shelton.
12. Ruth St. Denis, *Ruth St. Denis: An Unfinished Life, An Autobiography* (New York: Harper & Brothers, 1939), pp. 330–31.
13. Dane Rudhyar, "My Bennington Experience," *Dance Observer* 4, no. 7 (August-September 1937): 75.
14. Ibid.
15. Elizabeth A. Douglas, "Dance Captures America," *Magazine of Art* 30, no. 8 (August 1937): 499–505.
16. John Martin, "The Dance–Pioneer American Art," *North American Review* 244, no. 2 (Winter 1937–1938): 248–49. See also two general surveys of Bennington in 1937: Naomi Lubell, "The Bennington School: An Educational Project in Modern Dance," *American Dancer* 10, no. 12 (October 1937): 12–13, 29, and Paul Love, "Theme and Variations," *Dance* 3, no. 1 (October 1937): 11, 30. See also Mary Jo Shelly, "Willingly to School," *Dance Observer* 4, no. 6 (June-July 1937): 63, which outlines the plan for the session, and Ruth H. Bloomer, "Bennington School of the Dance–Summer 1937," the lead article in a whole issue devoted to the session, *Dance Observer* 4, no. 7 (August-September 1937): 73–74, 83–84.
17. "Fourth Annual Report of the Bennington School of the Dance," Summer 1937, in *Reports of Officers*, Bennington College 5, no. 3 (August 1937): viii.
18. Interview with Erick Hawkins.
19. John Martin, *New York Times*, 13 August 1937.
20. Barbara Page Beiswanger, "A Selected List of Music Especially Written for Dance by Composers in America" (Master's thesis, New York University, 1945), p. 19.

1938
Fifth Session of the Bennington School of the Dance

2 July 1938—13 August 1938

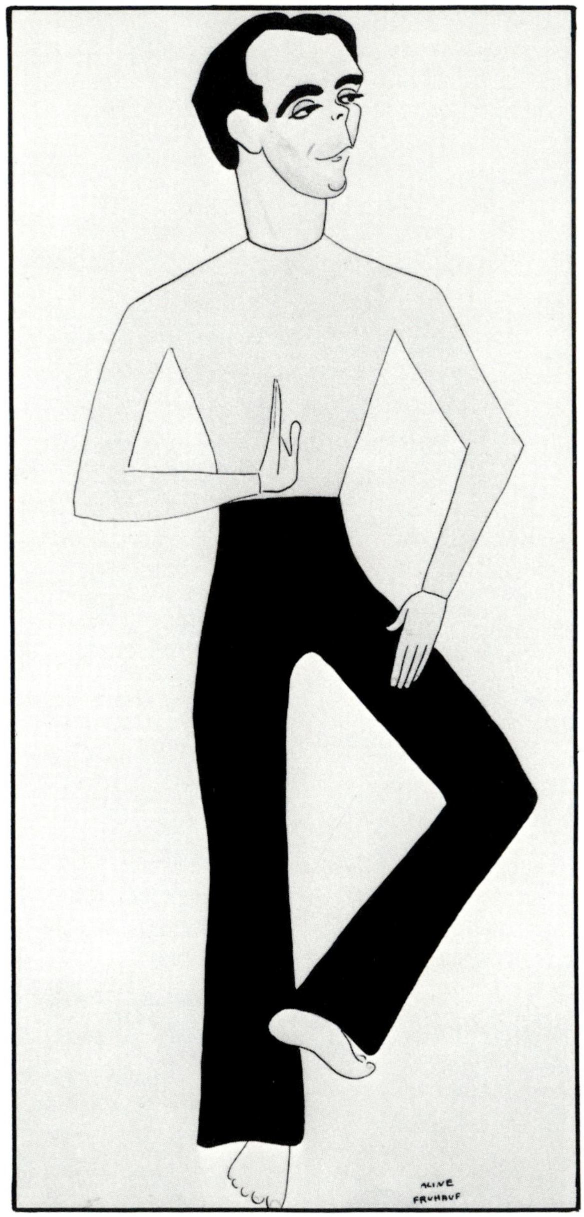

Drawing of Charles Weidman by Aline Fruhauf.

The first phase of the Bennington School of the Dance culminated with its largest, most ambitious session to date and a week-long festival. For the first time, Martha Graham, Doris Humphrey, Charles Weidman, Hanya Holm, and their concert groups were in residence for the full session. A new trio of Fellows joined them. Eleven dances had their premieres at the Bennington Festival of 1938, including *Passacaglia in C minor* (Humphrey), *American Document* (Graham), *Dance of Work and Play* and *Dance Sonata* (Holm) and *Opus 51* (Weidman). (These were Holm's and Weidman's last Bennington productions.)

"With the rounding out of a five year cycle of production at the Bennington School of the Dance," wrote George Beiswanger, "it becomes plain that the modern dance has succeeded in reaching its most important objective, the creation of an American theatre dance."[1]

When a large circus tent erected on campus by Arch Lauterer to serve as the festival site proved unsuitable, the festival was moved to the Armory in Bennington, and festival dates were advanced a week. Normally combustible temperaments and tensions were brought to the boiling point by heightened pressure to complete the new dances, schedule rehearsal space, and meet the diverse needs of four artists and their groups and three young Fellows, all living and working in close proximity.

Bennington in 1938 was described by one student as a "hotbed of modern dance."[2] And, indeed, according to Fellow Eleanor King, Bennington was divided into "seven armed camps." The Graham dancers "were forbidden to speak to other groups. . . . Cliqueishness and factionalism prevailed."[3]

Of the new works, Doris Humphrey's *Passacaglia in C minor* and Martha Graham's *American Document* were the most controversial. The first employed an already composed score for the first time at Bennington. The second introduced into the previously all-female Graham group a male ballet dancer (Erick Hawkins) and used speech extensively. Margaret Lloyd wrote later that *American Document* marked "the beginning of Martha Graham's Dance Company, the transitional step between concert and theater."[4]

Humphrey's choice of Johann Sebastian Bach was based on her need for music that would express the strivings of man toward perfection—the theme of her *Passacaglia*. Although she had used pre-existing music earlier—as had others—her decision to do so now ran against the prevailing current at Bennington, where 11 composers were in residence, working at breakneck speed to write music for the new dances. Hanya Holm also broke with modern dance "tradition" by having Harrison Kerr write his score for *Dance Sonata* before she composed the dance.

All of the new festival music was scored for piano and percussion. Other instruments were not employed, possibly because the expense would have been prohibitive during a summer in which the four major artists and their groups were in residence.

Marian Van Tuyl, Louise Kloepper, and Eleanor King completed the sextet of Bennington Fellows. Van Tuyl, from Chicago, was the first to come from outside New York. (Carmelita Maracci was elected to a fellowship but declined.)

For the first time, the session occasioned criticism from some of its staunchest advocates. Even John Martin seemed somewhat less enthusiastic than usual. Margaret Lloyd raised an eyebrow about the faculty's composition:

> I sometimes wonder if [Bennington] is not becoming such a close corporation that its seal will eventually be tantamount to a stencil. There is latent danger of a stamp being set upon its students, of stock patterns issuing from it, like the stock patterns in chinaware that can be replaced in case of breakage. There is even now a distinctly recognizable Humphrey-Weidman pattern, a Martha Graham and a Hanya Holm pattern, which in the minor dancer lacks the force and integrity of the original model. Why not call in Tamiris? Why not change leaders another year?[5]

Henry Gilfond alluded to an "amorphous quality" in many of the works of the Fellows and the major artists, and suggested that there was an "unhealthy artistic atmospheric pressure" prevalent at Bennington, but he did not elaborate.[6]

Ironically, the highest praise came from Lincoln Kirstein, former arch enemy of the "moderns," who wrote that *American Document* (which costarred his protégé, Erick Hawkins) vindicated any and all of Bennington's past failings.[7]

Compared with previous summers, political and social consciousness in the works themselves seemed to have diminished. "Social content reared its head warily," wrote Maxine Cushing, only in Lillian Shapero's *We Are the Living*, which was "complete with air raid," and in Hanya Holm's *Dance of Work and Play*. Weidman, she quipped, had received a letter from "members of the 'Society for the Clarification of Social Content'" signed by "G. O. Getter,

S. Tinker, Will Krushem and Robt. 'Red' Herring" requesting clarification of the meanings of his new work, *Opus 51*:

> At the point in the dance where certain members of your group receive dorsal propulsion ("kick in the pants" to you) it is left to the audience to decide whether it is the bloated capitalist or the downtrodden proletarian who is on the receiving end of the movement. If it is the latter, we shall have no alternative but to picket your show should you dare to produce it in New York. Meanwhile, we still hope that you are dancing the right side of the political fence. Never let it be said that *Opus 51* is unfair to organized labor.[8]

Cushing also reported that "ballet was in the air with a vengeance." She could see it infiltrate many of the technique classes. The Graham group's demonstrations showed "a considerable increase in aerial work."[9]

One of the least publicized functions of the school was as a placement bureau for teachers. Cushing further reported that "ten teaching jobs were filled through the Bennington clearing house. . . , bringing the five-year total to almost a hundred instances."

The Humphrey-Weidman group completed a major transcontinental tour before coming to Bennington. Paul Love reviewed their press books and concluded:

> The audiences did not seem to be bothered by abstraction as they had been in the past. [This] probably has more to do with the slow but inevitable shift in social values than it does with specific dance education. . . . The audiences seemed "ready" . . . for a contemporary work expressing contemporary themes in a contemporary technique.[10]

For the causes of this change in attitude, Love suggested that "a careful perusal of Arnold's *The Folklore of Capitalism* will give you more leads than will Bennington."

When Humphrey arrived at Bennington, she was greeted with criticism:

> The first thing we heard here was that yes, we had a wonderful tour but why did we want to jazz up our dances in order to be successful—because that's just what you left Denishawn for. [This] is doubtless the current opinion in the Graham camp to explain our success.[11]

At the end of the session, the directors announced that Bennington would move to Mills the following summer and that on its return to Vermont, the School of the Dance would be incorporated into a new School of the Arts.

John Martin remarked that the tremendous public response to the festival (several hundred people had to be turned away for lack of space) "must be a grave temptation to the sponsors to extend the project for an extra period of years, but it is the official feeling that it has accomplished its purpose, which is an educational as well as a theatrical one, and should not be allowed to continue merely as a functionless tradition."[12] He looked back on what he viewed as the school's most positive accomplishments:

> To treat any art educationally and keep it from becoming academic is something of an achievement in itself, but the Bennington idea has gone further and maintained a high professional standard along with its educational aims. Taking four leading artists from the concert field and working them into a scheme of activity with values for both young professional dancers and lay educators, it has made something of a revolution in . . . dance education. . . . The enrollment has touched key people in every section of the country. . . . A national overturning of opinion has been set in motion. . . .
>
> The annual festivals have provided an opportunity [for the professional artists] to compose in however experimental a form without financial worries or routine responsibilities, and to present their finished work before as fine an

> audience for modern dance as is to be found anywhere in the world. . . . Unlike many art festivals of larger dimensions and greater social and financial réclame, these have been creative events. They have not contented themselves with the mere repetition of works already more than familiar, but have carried on in new fields and toward new goals.[13]

Joseph Arnold Kaye concurred that Bennington was "a valuable laboratory. . . . Its performances have made the little town of Bennington an unique dance center, nationally known and respected." But he continued:

> This observer believes that the school could accomplish a great deal more than it already has if it could dissociate itself from those of its devotees who bring to Bennington the faddist hysterical spirit that has become in large measure characteristic of its festivals.[14]

To Margaret Lloyd "the idea of the Bennington School" appeared "bigger than its realization, its essential aim and influence more significant than actual accomplishment":

> Its chief value so far has been in opening up new paths through free experimentation in dance and its allied arts—music, stage design, lighting and costuming; in setting a national standard (which has barely averted becoming a stamp) for the American dance forms; in coloring modern American music by scores written especially for the dance—scores sometimes feeble, inconsequential, sometimes powerful, nearing the mark, but mostly useful for their experimental quality; and finally, in stirring new and more general interest in the dance and in turning out a large number of young women and a few young men who may not and need never be professional dancers, but who have learned that dance is an integrating cultural and recreational part of life.

The school, she continued, had "at last outgrown itself":

> It must expand into new and larger forms. It requires new faces. And not only in the student body.
>
> The new set-up should include new modern dance teachers and other branches of dance. Ballet, even tap-dancing, would be permissible in the trend toward theater. Music and drama critics who may be called upon to serve in their individual capacities anyway, would be helpful in expressing the laymen's response to dance.
>
> And unless the modern dance appeals directly to the layman, without cult or pretense, without artificial bogs of information to plow through, it is not fulfilling its obligations or possibilities as art.[15]

THE SESSION IN BRIEF

General Program continued, as did Programs in Choreography and Music for the Dance. Laboratory in Experimental Production replaced Advanced Dance Composition. Program in Stage Design for the Dance was added. The Workshop Program was supplanted by the Professional Program, wherein each of the four leading artists directed members of their concert groups and advanced apprentices in "less extensive and more strictly experimental" productions. Eleanor King, Louise Kloepper, and Marian Van Tuyl were Fellows in the second and last phase of the Fellowship Program.

FACULTY AND STAFF

Martha Graham, Doris Humphrey, Charles Weidman, and Hanya Holm each in residence for the full session. Permanent faculty as in 1937, with the addition of Arch Lauterer. (John and Louise Martin on leave.) Festival productions: Arch Lauterer, designer. Henry Seymour, assistant. Norman Lloyd, chairman of music for the festival. Elizabeth Beebe, Edythe Gilfond,

Betty Joiner, Pauline Lawrence, costume designers. Vivian Fine, Ray Green, Harrison Kerr, Norman Lloyd, Morris Mamorsky, Harvey Pollins, Gregory Tucker, Esther Williamson, composers. Barbara Morgan, photographer.

STUDENTS

Total 180, ages 16-41, from 34 states, Canada, and Hawaii (in the school's first five years all states but Arkansas represented), including 81 teachers, 34 dancers, 34 students. General Program 101. Including Alma Hawkins (teacher, YWCA, Minneapolis), Alwin Nikolais, Ann Schuman [Halprin] (student, Winnetka, Illinois), Betty Lynd Thompson (teacher, Oregon State College, Corvallis). Professional Program 70. Including 5 men. Professional concert group members 30, apprentices 40. Including Jean Erdman, Erick Hawkins, Helen Priest, Eleanor Frampton, Maria Maginnis, Ethel Mann, Barbara Page Beiswanger. Program in Choreography 2. Lillian Shapero, Florence Warwick. Program in Music for Dance 4. Including Ralph Gilbert, Freda D. Miller, Drusa Wilker. Program in Stage Design 3. Including Philip Stapp.

LECTURES, SPECIAL EVENTS, AND STUDENT DEMONSTRATIONS

Lectures by Curt Sachs and John Martin in the Bennington Festival Series. Other lectures by Margaret Einert, *London Dancing Times*, "Dance in England." Francis Bosworth, Federal Theatre Project, "New Horizons of the Theater," with accompanying exhibit of photographs and drawings from the project. Paul Boepple, director, Dalcroze School of Music, "Space and Time in Music." George Beiswanger, professor of philosophy, Monticello College, "Music and the Dance." Exhibits of books, photographs, costumes, and designs for the dance. Performance by Yale Puppeteers, with a puppet of Martha Graham. Demonstration lessons by each of the four leading artists with their concert and apprentice groups, and a Final Demonstration of Student Work.

17 July 1938
7 August 1938

Two concerts of music written for the dance. College Theatre. Featuring compositions produced at the Bennington Festivals by Vivian Fine, Ralph Gilbert, Ray Green, Louis Horst, Harrison Kerr, Norman Lloyd, Ruth Lloyd, Morris Mamorsky, Harvey Pollins, Wallingford Riegger, Gregory Tucker, Esther Williamson. With a lecture by Louis Horst. Also, a concert of recorded dance scores, organized by Otto Luening. New Music Quarterly Recordings, including Riegger's score for *Trend*. No programs located.

According to a press release issued by Bennington, "Rarely, if ever, here or abroad, have several composers whose compositions are almost exclusively constructed for the dance presented a joint recital of their work. This is a significant development in musical annals since the relationship of music and dance is of growing importance on the contemporary scene." (Two years earlier, on 31 January 1936, the Dance Guild and Composers' Collective had presented a forum-recital, "Music for the Dance—What Composers Think About It," at Studio 61, Carnegie Hall.[16])

Reviews

Bennington Banner:

> Should the music be able to stand alone was the subject of a lecture by Louis Horst. . . . The various composers of the School of the Dance then played their compositions preceding them with a brief discussion of the circumstances under which they wrote the dances, such as the demands placed upon them, or the values of the music in relation to the dance composition and the frequent need of revision of the music as the dance progressed.[17]

George Beiswanger, *Dance Observer*:

> No one can listen to the works presented at Bennington this summer, as one has previously listened to compositions now become dance classics, and not realize that something has happened to music, now that the composer is writing

> for the dance. Its idiom is being remade and its body suffused with new life. The dance has restored to music a kind of rhythmic vitality suppressed since the days of Haydn and Mozart. It has given music a functional reason for the use of polytonality and modern counterpoint. By bringing forth the percussive nature of dissonance, it has not only transformed the purpose of dissonance in music but has uncovered a whole new range of atmospheric, emotional and dramatic effects, effects which one simply cannot find in the main tradition even as late as Stravinsky. . . . In short . . . the modern dance is good for music. It has brought to it new life. It has given it new sustenance by supplying it a new reason for being . . . in a day when the springs of musical inspiration are threatening to run dry.[18]

13 August 1938

Final Demonstration of Student Work. College Theatre. I. Percussion Studies under the direction of Franziska Boas. Students included Alwin Nikolais. II. Elementary and Intermediate Composition and Music for the Dance, under the direction of Martha Hill, Norman Lloyd, Bessie Schönberg. Including *mus* Ruth Lloyd, Philip Stapp, Drusa Wilker, Freda Miller, Ralph Gilbert. *Chor* Eleanor Lauer and group, Delia Hussey. III. Pre-Classic Forms and Music for the Dance, under the direction of Louis Horst. *Asst* Mildred Wile. Including ***Pavane-Authentic*** *chor* Nikolais, *mus* Traditional. ***Tragic Departure*** (Allemande) *chor* Nikolais *mus* Gilbert. IV. Modern Forms and Music for the Dance, under the direction of Horst. *Asst* Wile. Including *chor* Lauer, Theodora Wiesner, Gertrude Lippincott, Truda Kaschmann. ***Studies in Americana, American Greeting*** *chor* Nikolais, *mus* Horst. V. Experimental Production and Music for the Dance, under the direction of Hill, Arch Lauterer, Norman Lloyd. Including ***Line in Space*** *chor* Lillian Shapero, *mus* Boas. ***Line and Plane*** *chor* Nikolais, *mus* Minnie Goodsitt, *sets* Lois Lord, *light* Henry Seymour, *danc* group of 7. VI. Choreography, Music for the Dance and Stage Design for the Dance, under the direction of Hill, Horst, Lauterer. ***Fixations, One, Two and Three*** *chor* Florence Warwick, *mus* [Bela] Bartók. ***Exultation*** *chor* Warwick *mus* [Henry] Cowell. ***American Scene, Two Dances of Protest: Workaday Song, Road Song*** *chor* Shapero, *mus* Miller. ***We Are the Living: Premonition, Catastrophe, Renewal-Affirmation*** *chor* Shapero, *mus* Gilbert, *sets* Stapp, *light* Ruth Bloomer, *danc* group of 13.

THE BENNINGTON FESTIVAL SERIES

4-10 August 1938

Four formal lectures (originally planned as an extensive series for publication under the auspices of the Bennington School of the Dance but never published). Curt Sachs (author, *World History of the Dance*, 1937) on "Dance and Music" and "Dance, Anthropology, History." John Martin (author, *America Dancing*, 1936 and Bennington faculty, on leave) on "Background of the American Dance" and "Isadora Duncan and the Modern Dance."

Six dance programs (three concerts, two performances each) in the Vermont State Armory 4–10 August featuring 11 new works: Doris Humphrey's *Passacaglia in C minor* (Humphrey, Weidman, and group of 23). Hanya Holm's *Dance of Work and Play* (Holm and group of 8) and *Dance Sonata* (Holm and group of 19). Charles Weidman's *Opus 51* (Weidman and group of 15). Martha Graham's *American Document* (Graham, group of 22, and actor). Fellow Eleanor King's *Ode to Freedom* (King and group of 10) and "Bonja Song" from *American Folk Suite* (trio). Louise Kloepper's solos *Romantic Theme* and *Statement of Dissent*, and *Earth Saga* (Kloepper and group of 9). Marian Van Tuyl's *Out of One Happening* (Van Tuyl and group of 9).

The festival was originally scheduled for the last week of the session. The brightly striped tent erected by Arch Lauterer on campus was used for rehearsals and festival lectures, but the major performances were moved to the Armory and rescheduled for the next-to-last week of the session.

An audience of nearly 3800 persons attended the festival from all over the United States and abroad. Several hundred persons had to be turned away. The *Bennington Banner* recorded visits by Lincoln Kirstein, Isamu Noguchi, Sheldon Cheney, Betty Horst, Anna Sokolow, Alexander North, Margaret H'Doubler, and Sai Shoki, "the Korean Pavlowa . . . on tour in the U.S. . . . The first woman to raise the dance in Korea to the station of an independent stage art."[19]

The *Banner* described Lauterer's design for the Armory:

> The Armory has undergone a metamorphosis so complete that almost the only thing left as it was originally are the steel girders near the roof. . . . The first row of seats are placed on the floor, those on the last row are nearly five feet from the floor level.
>
> The stage itself has been blocked off by flats painted in two shades of gray which is the color scheme for the stage setting. Arch Lauterer and his assistants have made of the floor at the front of the old stage a square of approximately 30 by 30 feet. . . . Down the sides near the wall are set panels opened out diagonally and pointing toward the front with spaces in between from which the performers make their entrances and exits. The sides of the gallery are faced with gray.[20]

4 and 8 August 1938

Eleanor King, Louise Kloepper, Marian Van Tuyl. Fellows of the Bennington School of the Dance, 1938. Vermont State Armory. Program: Part I. King. ***Ode to Freedom*** *mus arr* John Colman, Norman Lloyd. Part II. Kloepper. ***Romantic Theme*** *mus* Harvey Pollins. ***Statement of Dissent*** *mus* Gregory Tucker. ***Earth Saga*** *mus* Esther Williamson. Part III. Van Tuyl. ***Directions, a. Flight, b. Indecision, c. Redirection*** *mus* [Nikolai] Lopatnikov, *danc* Van Tuyl. ***Out of One Happening*** *mus* Tucker. ***In the Clearing: Variations on a Theme*** *mus* Tucker, *danc* Van Tuyl, Eleanor Lauer, Marjorie Muehl, Theodora Wiesner. Part IV. King. ***American Folk Suite, a. *Bonja Song,*** *mus arr* Williamson, ***b. Hoe-Down*** *mus* Reginald Forsythe, *danc* King, William Bales, George Bockman, Ann Schuman [Halprin], ***c. Hornpipe*** *mus* Traditional, *danc* King, Bales, Bockman, Wanda Graham, Schuman. *See Catalog.

All new works were composed during the four weeks preceding the festival. Students auditioned from the General Program for Fellows' groups. Many had had no prior performance experience. Louise Kloepper's works were her first independent compositions. The first section of Marian Van Tuyl's *Directions: Flight* had been composed during the 1937 Bennington Program in Choreography.

5 and 9 August 1938

Hanya Holm and Group. Doris Humphrey and Group. Vermont State Armory. *Mus chair* Norman Lloyd. *Sets & light* Arch Lauterer. *Asst* Edward Glass, Henry Seymour. Program: Part I. ***Passacaglia in C minor*** *chor* Humphrey, *mus* J. S. Bach. ***Dance of Work and Play*** *chor* Holm, *mus* Lloyd. Part II. ***Dance Sonata*** *chor* Holm, *mus* Harrison Kerr. ***Variations and Conclusion*** from ***New Dance*** *chor* Humphrey, *mus* Wallingford Riegger, *danc* José Limón, Beatrice Seckler, Katherine Litz, William Bales, George Bockman, Sybil L. Shearer, Humphrey, Charles Weidman, and Concert Group. *Pianists* Morris Marmorsky, Pauline Lawrence. *Percussion* Franziska Boas. *See Catalog.

Humphrey had planned to complement her new *Passacaglia* with a first Bennington performance of *Race of Life* (*mus* Vivian Fine), but José Limón could not arrive in time to rehearse for the new festival dates. As a result, Humphrey substituted the concluding section of *New Dance*. Limón arrived in time for the second performance on 9 August but did not dance in the premiere of *Passacaglia*.

6 and 10 August 1938

Charles Weidman and Group. Martha Graham and Group. Vermont State Armory. *Mus chair* Norman Lloyd. *Sets & light* Arch Lauterer. *Asst* Edward Glass, Henry Seymour. Program: Part I. Weidman. ***Opus 51*** *mus* Vivian Fine. Part II. Graham. ***American Document*** *mus* Ray Green. *See Catalog.

NOTES

1. George W. Beiswanger, "The New Theatre Dance," *Theatre Arts Monthly* 23, no. 1 (January 1939): 41–54. This is one of the key critical articles on dance in the Bennington period, in which Beiswanger examines the five premieres at the 1938 Bennington Festival, citing them as examples of the new trend toward dance theater. It is reprinted in *Theatre Arts Anthology: A Record and a Prophecy*, ed. Rosamond Gilder, Hermine Rich Isaacs, Robert M. MacGregor, and Edward Reed (New York: Theatre Arts Books, 1950), pp. 209–21. For survey articles of Bennington not specifically cited here, see also Margaret Einert, "Bennington . . July . . 1938 . . Focal Point of the American Modern Dance," *Dancing Times*, n.s. no. 336 (September 1938): 645–48, Charlotte Michaud, *"Thoughts on Second Visit to Bennington School of Dance," Lewiston* (Maine) *Journal* 10 September 1938 [Hanya Holm Scrapbooks, Dance Collection of the New York Public Library], and Patricia Shirley Allen, "Mecca for Moderns: Bennington Completes a Cycle," *American Dancer* 11, no. 8 (June 1938): 19, 49.
2. Maxine Cushing, "Bennington Commentary," *Educational Dance* 1, no. 3 (August-September 1938): 12.
3. Eleanor King, *Transformations: A Memoir, The Humphrey-Weidman Years* (Brooklyn, N.Y.: Dance Horizons, 1978), p. 259.
4. Margaret Lloyd, *The Borzoi Book of Modern Dance* (New York: Alfred A. Knopf, 1949), p. 60. Until 1941, however, the group was listed on Bennington programs as "Martha Graham and Dance Group." In 1941 its name was given as "Martha Graham and Dance Company" for the first time at Bennington.
5. Margaret Lloyd, *Christian Science Monitor*, 5 July 1938.
6. Henry Gilfond, "Bennington Festival," *Dance Observer* 5, no. 7 (August-September 1938): 100–101.
7. Lincoln Kirstein, "Martha Graham at Bennington," *Nation* 147, no. 10 (3 September 1938): 230–31.
8. Maxine Cushing, *Educational Dance* 1, no. 3 (August-September 1938): 12.
9. Ibid. Cushing reported that Martha Graham and her group had taken ballet classes the previous winter. In the October 1938 issue of *Educational Dance*, however, Graham's manager, Frances Hawkins, denied that Graham had studied ballet "last winter or any previous winter."
10. Paul Love, *Dance* 4, no. 4 (July 1938): 14.
11. Letter from Doris Humphrey to Charles Francis Woodford, 4 July 1938 (Doris Humphrey Collection, C409).
12. John Martin, *New York Times*, 14 August 1938.
13. John Martin, *New York Times*, 21 August 1938.
14. Joseph Arnold Kaye, "Fifth Bennington Festival of the Modern Dance," *Dance* 5, no. 1 (October 1938): 11, 30.
15. Margaret Lloyd, *Christian Science Monitor*, 16 August 1938.
16. Henry Gilfond, "Composers in Symposium," *Dance Observer* 3, no. 3 (March 1936): 25, 28–29, gives a full account.
17. *Bennington Banner*, 8 August 1938.
18. George W. Beiswanger, "Music at the Bennington Festival," *Dance Observer* 5, no. 7 (August-September 1938): 102–104.
19. Bernard A. Tetreault, *Bennington Banner*, 8 and 11 August 1938.
20. "Nations of the World at Dance Festival," *Bennington Banner*, 5 August 1938.

1939
Sixth Session of the Bennington School of the Dance at Mills College, Oakland, California

1 July 1939—11 August 1939

Hanya Holm's group. Drawing by Betty Joiner, courtesy of Rosamond Gilder, *Theater Arts.*

Bennington, "the recognized center for the study of modern dance in America,"[1] moved to Mills College in Oakland, California, under a plan initiated in 1937 by Rosalind Cassidy, director of the Mills College Summer Session and chairman of the Department of Physical Education. The two regions shared "a common enthusiasm for the art [of the dance] and a common energy in promoting it."[2] Benningtonites predicted that the school would be "fundamentally affected by influences belonging inherently to the West," and the result of the "exchange" would be "permanently felt in a new enrichment and strong consolidation of the whole field of the dance."[3]

The "exchange" transferred 26 Bennington faculty and staff persons west, including the Big Four; but there was no comparable contingent from the West.

The Bennington implant was effected during Mills' fourteenth summer session. The Mills sessions, unlike those at Bennington, embraced other disciplines, so that in 1939 there were programs at Mills in art and music as well as in dance. (The Budapest String Quartet and Benny Goodman were in residence.)

While the school was meeting in California, a new "half-million dollar theatre" was to be constructed on the Bennington campus, to be ready for the opening of the School of the Arts the next summer.[4] This theater failed to materialize.

The California terrain contrasted markedly with the open spaces and rolling hills of Vermont. "The whole nature of the place is denser," wrote Doris Humphrey:

> The trees grow right in the windows so there is no view and there are no long stretches of space for the eye and the spirit on the campus. California's famous eucalyptus trees, tall and shaggy, line the roads and are lovely, but for the most part it all presses in too much.[5]

The Bennington School of the Dance

announces

its sixth annual session to be held at

MILLS COLLEGE
Oakland, California

July 1 Through August 11, 1939

MARTHA HILL
Director

MARY J. SHELLY
Administrative Director

ROSALIND CASSIDY
Director of the Mills College Summer Session

For information address:

THE BENNINGTON SCHOOL OF THE DANCE
Bennington, Vermont

Advertisement in *Dance Observer.*

Ethel Butler, Martha Graham's teaching assistant, experienced a similar case of claustrophobia:

> I couldn't breathe out there. The buildings were lined with a deep red-brown wood with great beams on top of the same color, and I had the feeling the rooms were pulling in on us. Outside, the growth was so lush, the leaves gigantic. . . . I needed to get somewhere where I could see out and beyond.[6]

Tina Flade, who had left Mills after the summer of 1938, found California "too open" in a certain sense:

> The magnificent landscape at times depressed me. I couldn't handle it. It was too big—the mountains too big, the ocean too big. Bennington was smaller, more intimate. I think intensive artistic work is helped by a binding around it.[7]

The creative pitch at Mills was less intense than at Bennington, and not only because there was no festival and no major production. The student body—made up mostly of Westerners for the first time—didn't seem to have quite the drive of students in Vermont. At Bennington there was nothing to distract from the dance. Everyone lived on campus, where they ate, slept, and drank dance for six weeks. At Mills, faculty could live off-campus and take advantage of the whole San Francisco Bay region, among whose attractions that summer was the Golden Gate Exposition.

Lisser Hall, Mills College. Photograph by Donald Hatfield.

Some of the student workshop projects reflected California "themes." José Limón created a five-part solo composition, *Danzas Mexicanas*, which related to his Mexican roots. (Lester Horton's *Conquest*, produced the previous summer at Mills, provides a fascinating comparison.[8]) This work had its premiere in the only formal concert of the session, a joint recital by Limón, Ethel Butler, Louise Kloepper, and Katherine Manning, teaching assistants of the Big Four. Said a reviewer, "One had the impression of looking at a newer generation of Graham, Holm, Humphrey and Weidman, their influence was so clearly stamped" on their assistants.[9]

Margaret Lloyd had anticipated "a welcome exchange" of ideas between the widely separated East and West" and had hoped that the "somewhat egocentric Eastern seaboard would profit by a generous close-up view of [the] work" of other active dance centers. Lloyd had hoped that the experience would stimulate a flow of Western dancers East.[10]

One Westerner lured East as a result of the Bennington residency was Merce [Mercier] Cunningham, a student at the Cornish School in Seattle, who enrolled at Mills for a second summer session in 1939. When Ethel Butler taught her morning class in technique, she was astonished to find

> the most magnificent creature of a man I'd ever seen. When he started to move I couldn't believe it. I immediately got on the phone to Martha [Graham] who was in Santa Barbara and said get up here right away and grab this man before anybody else does. It was Merce of course. He was spectacular.[11]

This was Cunningham's first Bennington summer (Graham invited him to join her company that fall), and it was José Limón's last as a member of the Humphrey-Weidman Group. At Mills, Limón's new *Danzas Mexicanas* disclosed a heroic, dramatic style which was to flower in later years. (In 1940 Limón returned to Mills to teach the summer session with Louise Kloepper and Marian Van Tuyl, and left Humphrey-Weidman shortly afterward. He then joined May O'Donnell in the Pacific Northwest—she had left the Graham Group after the summer of 1938 at Bennington—and they performed together in that region for a few years. Limón later taught at Bennington College.)

Poet Ben Belitt, who had apprenticed himself informally to Hanya Holm at Bennington in 1938, codirected the experimental workshop at Mills, where he introduced as a problem the use

Charles Weidman outdoors at Mills. Frame enlargement courtesy of Linda Mann Reed.

of the spoken word—poetry and prose. Martha Hill and Arch Lauterer, said Belitt, "were very receptive to the addition of poetry to dance and very seductive in recruiting me for the Bennington summer at Mills."[12] (The workshop experiments with poetry and dance at Mills preceded Martha Graham's exploration of poetry in *Letter to the World*, composed at Bennington in 1940.)

The whole community was drawn into the making of a documentary film on the Bennington School of the Dance. *Young America Dances* took four days and a Hollywood crew of 15 to shoot. Directed by former Bennington College faculty member Ralph Jester, the script had two girls—one a tap dancer, the other a "highfalutin" modern dancer—pay a visit to the School of the Dance. Of about 17,000 feet of 35mm film, 1000 feet were edited into a ten-minute short intended for release through Paramount Pictures to movie theaters across the country. The making of a Hollywood movie was an unprecedented opportunity to expand the audience for the modern dance and to widen its base of support and appreciation. Yet everyone also realized that it could, if poorly received, jeopardize the tenuous gains the art had made in developing an audience.

Acting President Lewis Jones supported the film project but would not authorize the use of Bennington College's name. He was concerned that a negative public response to the movie might jeopardize plans for the School of the Arts. Despite good reactions at preview screenings, the film was never released.[13]

During the filming, Doris Humphrey wrote that it was "a great worry knowing that every move is frozen forever for better or for worse."[14]

Before leaving for Mills, Humphrey received a letter from Pauline Lawrence reporting Mary Jo Shelly's distress that the Big Four "and their cohorts do not co-operate and are jealous and do not function as progressive, intelligent individuals." According to Lawrence, Shelly "thought last summer a disgrace."[15] (Even Margaret Lloyd had noted in 1938 that the groups seemed "more competitive than cooperative."[16])

In 1939 there was no festival to sustain the pitch of competition, so the four artists put tremendous energy into their final demonstrations of technique. On her arrival at Mills, Humphrey found herself, "as usual,"

> in considerable disagreement with what goes on here, mostly on the score of the rigidity and frigidity of the dancing they teach. Animated geometry with a touch of acrobatics—all against my principles.[17]

Louise Kloepper at Mills. Photograph by Donald Hatfield.

Surprisingly, reviewers remarked how similar in approach the four techniques seemed in the final demonstration. "In spite of individual differences of style and method," wrote one observer, there was

> a return to the use of the melodic line in movement, more stress on mood and lyricism and less on abstraction. It seemed as if the dance had very nearly explored all possible modes and "tours de force" and had at last begun to discard them in favor of a directness and honesty of expression which is truly American.[18]

Among visitors during the session was Helen Tamiris. A photograph by Donald Hatfield shows Tamiris in the company of Doris Humphrey—possibly the only visit Tamiris ever made to the Bennington project.

The 1939 session was the last manifestation of the School of the Dance as a separate, autonomous entity. In 1940 it became the central constituent of a new School of the Arts on the Bennington campus.

THE SESSION IN BRIEF

The five Programs of Work (General, Professional, Music for the Dance, Choreography, Stage Design) were replaced by three Major Courses in Dance, Music for the Dance, and Stage Design for the Dance. There was no festival and no major production.

FACULTY AND STAFF

Twenty-six members of the Bennington School of the Dance were transported to California, with two West Coast staff members added. Faculty for the full session included poet Ben Belitt, Franziska Boas, Martha Hill, Louis Horst, Arch Lauterer, Norman Lloyd, and Bessie Schönberg with assistants Ethel Butler, Louise Kloepper, Katherine Manning. José Limón, Hortense Lieberthal, Henry Seymour, and Mildred Wile. Martha Graham, Doris Humphrey, Charles Weidman, and Hanya Holm taught the last three weeks of the session.

STUDENTS

Total 170, ages 16–48, from 29 states and five foreign countries (50 percent from the Far West, 24 percent from the Middle West, 16 percent from the East, 5 percent from the South). Major Course in Dance 153 (five men). Including Mercier [Merce] Cunningham (student, Cornish School, Seattle), Alwin Nikolais, Nona Schurman (dancer, New York), Ann Schuman [Halprin], Mary Ann Wells (Mary Ann Wells School of Dancing, Seattle). Major Course in Music 6. Including Zoe Williams. Major Course in Stage Design 5. Including Nathan [Nik] Krevitsky.

Ethel Butler with class including Mercier [Merce] Cunningham, Mills College Greek Theatre. Photograph courtesy of Eleanor Lauer, Mills College.

LECTURES, SPECIAL EVENTS, RECITALS, AND FINAL DEMONSTRATIONS

Lectures by Dr. Douglas Campbell, University of Chicago, "Thalamic Communication." Sol Babitz, Dance notation lecture, "Dance Writing." Edith Ballwebber, University of Chicago, "Methods of Teaching Social Dancing." Lloyd Shaw, author *Cowboy Dancing*, 1939, three sessions and discussion on "American Country Dancing." Lesson-demonstration by José Limón with a high school boys' dance group. Exhibits of photographs by Barbara Morgan and Victor Haveman, costumes by Betty Joiner. The Budapest String Quartet and Benny Goodman in residence at Mills during the session.

Filming of a documentary short movie, *Young America Dances*, by American Pictures, based on a day in the life of a dancer at the Bennington School of the Dance (see Sources—Films).

A concert of percussion music under the direction of John Cage. A joint concert by the four teaching associates: Ethel Butler, José Limón, Katherine Manning, and Louise Kloepper with new dances by Limón and Butler. A final demonstration of student work. The four major artists in a concluding demonstration of technique. A total audience of about 1000 (nonpaying) for these events in Lisser Hall and the college gymnasium.

27 July 1939

A Concert of Modern American Percussion Music under the direction of John Cage. Lisser Hall. *Mus* William Russell, Lou Harrison, Henry Cowell, Franziska Boas, and others. *Musicians* Xenia Cage, Mercier [Merce] Cunningham, Ralph Gilbert, Zoe Williams. No program located.

Review

Louis Horst, *Dance Observer*:

> This unique program impressed this reviewer with two significant facts. One, that the modern dance has sponsored, encouraged and utilized compositions for percussion instruments more than any other of the theatrical arts. Two, that, with the exception of Franziska Boas, most of the important experimenters and composers in this tonal realm are at present located on the west coast.[19]

4 August 1939

A Concert of Modern Dance by Ethel Butler, Louise Kloepper, José Limón, Katherine Manning. Lisser Hall. *Pianists* Ralph Gilbert, Freda Miller, Lionel Nowak. Program: ***Danza chor*** Limón, *mus* [Serge] Prokofiev, *danc* Limón. ***Romantic Theme chor*** Kloepper, *mus* Harvey Pollins, *danc* Kloepper. ****Ceremonial Dance chor*** Butler, *mus* Gilbert. ****Danzas Mexicanas chor*** Limón, *mus* Nowak. ***Statement of Dissent chor*** Kloepper, *mus* Gregory Tucker, *danc* Kloepper. ***Cancion y Danza chor*** Limón, *mus* [Federico] Mompou, *danc* Limón. ****The Spirit of the Land Moves in the Blood chor*** Butler, *mus* [Carlos] Chavez. ***Suite in B minor: a. Polonaise, b. Rondo, c. Badinerie chor*** Limón, *mus* [J. S.] Bach, *danc* Limón and Manning. *See Catalog.

Louise Kloepper's works were composed at Bennington the previous summer. The Bach *Suite in B minor* was one of Limón's earliest pieces. For the Mills production, he revived it with Katherine Manning. "Styles have changed since he composed it," wrote Doris Humphrey. "It was done in a flat mirror style . . . two-dimensional, which is something juiceless that we all outgrew five years ago. Katy [Manning] is doing [the suite] quite well, but it's a long process as all the movements have to be molded by hand."[20]

Review

Esther Pease, *Educational Dance*:

> The noticeable feature was the similarity between the dances created by these four and the compositions of their teachers. One had the impression of looking at a newer generation of Graham, Holm, Humphrey, and Weidman, their influence was so clearly stamped.[21]

11 August 1939

Final Demonstration of Student Work. Lisser Hall. Program: I. Pre-Classic and Modern Forms and Music Group, under the direction of Louis Horst. *Asst* Mildred Wile. Including ***Courante, Contagion chor*** Mercier [Merce] Cunningham, *mus* Zoe Williams. ***Sarabande, Resentment chor*** Nona Schurman, *mus* Williams. ***California Suite–(An Independent Project)*** comprising seven pieces on California themes. ***Primitive Studies,*** including ***Exorcism chor*** Ann Schuman [Halprin], *mus* Williams. Part II. Experimental Production, Advanced Composition and Music and Percussion Groups, under the direction of Ben Belitt, Franziska Boas, Martha Hill, Arch Lauterer, Norman Lloyd, Bessie Schönberg. Including ***"Never Sign a Letter Mrs." from "Etiquette" by Emily Post chor*** Hortense Lieberthal. ***"Costume," a Paragraph from "Information for Students, Bennington School of the Dance at Mills College 1939" libretto*** Mary Josephine Shelly, *mus* Lloyd. ***Nine Notations from "Thirteen Ways of Looking at a Blackbird" chor*** various, *poetry* Wallace Stevens. ***Diagonal Line chor*** Karen Burt, *mus* Freda Miller, *light* Henry Seymour, *danc* group of 11.

The problems worked out in Part II had to do with the use of space and stage properties, the voice as an element, and percussion accompaniment. Music and stage settings and lighting were mainly designed by students in the concentrated programs.

This was Ben Belitt's first formal affiliation with the School of the Dance. He introduced the use of poetry and the spoken word. Said Belitt:

> I was concerned with moving the spoken word rather than using poetry as a series of subtitles or a vague scenario that could be recited by a professional actor somewhere in the wings and used rhythmically by professional dancers. I wanted the dancer to speak and to move inside a matrix of language that mobilized the

> power of both—to see what stresses and opportunities developed in the tension of the two media, and how they might affect dance. It was the dancer herself, speaking and moving the word, that was my concern.[22]

Reviews

Oakland Tribune:

> The use of speech as well as choral, instrumental and percussive sound, stage design, lighting and costume as complementary factors in the production of modern dance is being essayed in many ways in the Experimental Production Class of the Bennington School of the Dance now in session at Mills College. According to Martha Hill, . . . it is the purpose of Experimental Production to coordinate the work of the other sections of the school as well as to give young choreographers an opportunity to work with groups in actual production of theatre dance. . . . Norman Lloyd . . . is working with a picked chorus of voices who will sing Thompson's composition from *Americana*, "Apples are God's Bottles." Choreography to this chorus will then be done by students in the class. "This reverses the usual procedure," Lloyd explained, [wherein] the musician is called upon to produce the music after the dance has been made. [However] we are also doing that, fifteen compositions having been written by the students in music already." Ben Belitt, young American poet and member of the Literature faculty at Bennington College, is working with groups of students on the use of speech—either poetry or prose—in conjunction with the dance. Among the problems to be considered: . . . What type of poetry or prose best lends itself to movement, should the speech be done by the dancer, by another person onstage or by voice offstage, etc.?[23]

Nell Silva, *People's World*:

> The most unusual section of the public demonstrations was the program devoted to experimental production. . . . After seeing this part of the program one felt that efforts were being made to relate the art dance with life and above all to make it understood and liked by the average layman. The sample of Bennington experimental work was refreshingly varied. There was a lot of geometric abstract maneuvering round red lines and black or diagonal lines on the stage. The percussion orchestra was very good. The most valuable parts of the program were [those] which used the human voice to explain or accompany the movement of the performers. Selections from the American poet Wallace Stevens were used as short dance librettos and were interestingly conceived. Even a paragraph from . . . Emily Post . . . had more life than all the rest of the program. The Emily Post, moreover, had implications of social satire. Only a beginning but the local performers and poets should absorb the stimulus and go on in their own way.[24]

11 August 1939

Final Demonstration of Techniques from the Major Course in Dance under Martha Graham, Hanya Holm, Doris Humphrey, Charles Weidman. Gymnasium. No program located.

Doris Humphrey gave her impressions of the event:

> I finished up Mills successfully I think at the cost of considerable effort. You would have been interested to see the demonstration of the four of us, each with half an hour. Martha was first with something that looked very much like *American Document*, only gayer and more lyric. No more hard angles or glum faces. They smile, they run, they skip and leap. How these gals do change—Hanya too. I must say we're the only ones who appear to have made up our minds about dancing once and for all, as to theory, movement, style, focus, everything. My group did very well and I was proud of them. For one thing they were more

Hanya Holm and Mary Jo Shelly at Mills. Photograph courtesy of Eleanor Lauer, Mills College.

accurately trained than any of the others. . . . In [Charles'] demonstration at Mills he had again the same characteristics as always—the winning charm, the irresistable humor, the messy, illogical technique, much too difficult and too long for his admiring and frantic group.[25]

Reviews

Karen Burt, *Dance Observer*:

> An unexpectedly large, enthusiastic and informal audience sat or stood on a hard gymnasium floor for very nearly three hours without intermission to witness what was probably the longest, and in Hollywood terms, the most "colossal" technical demonstration of modern dance ever held.
>
> The program was unique in that for the first time in the west all four artists were represented in the same evening and all demonstrated in varying degrees an educational approach in the use of large student groups rather than professional. . . . The emphasis [was] on performance throughout, and the range of movement varied . . . from a simple foot exercise to excerpts from the artists' own concert dances.
>
> Strangely enough, and in spite of individual differences of style and method . . . the outstanding impression . . . was that of a tendency toward similarity in a return to the use of the melodic line in movement, more stress on mood and lyricism and less on abstraction. It seemed as if the dance had very nearly explored all possible modes and "tours de force" and had at last begun to discard them in favor of a directness and honesty of expression which is truly American.[26]

Nell Silva, *People's World*:

> The Bennington summer session group takes itself very seriously as the Godmother of the modern movement in dance. . . . On Friday night, the Bennington School gave its final demonstration of the various techniques of modern dance

represented by the groups of Martha Graham, Doris Humphrey, Charles Weidman and Hanya Holm. The Graham group seemed the most strictly trained. The Humphrey group was very well disciplined and had been taught bits of choreography from the various well known dances which have been performed in the East. The performance of dances at the Mills program came as a surprise for the audience. Most interesting of these bits was the exit from *American Holiday,* in which the human voice was used as a chanting accompaniment. Hanya Holm's group seemed to have more young and previously untrained dancers. Charles Weidman with a few men dancers and [Katherine Manning] pleased the audience with the "knocking dance" from his satiric dance-drama, *Candide*. This is an amusing tour de force based on a five-beat rhythm.

It is interesting to note how all the techniques of these various leaders have merged throughout the years. But while the techniques may be similar, the individual ideas are still distinct, as evidenced in the dances composed by one or the other of the leaders.[27]

Marjorie Lucas, *Educational Dance*:

Through the clever use of groups, Miss Graham welded her cross section of the work covered by the dancers during the session into an exciting and interesting pattern which had in itself many of the elements of a dance form.

Hanya Holm gave a demonstration of a typical class lesson leading to leaps and turns, and closed her portion of the program with a short dance study for seven dancers, assisted by Louise Kloepper.

The group under Doris Humphrey followed exercises for feet and legs and single stretches of [*sic*] the floor with variations on the run and leap. A series of advanced falls was demonstrated by three talented members of the group. This

Katherine Manning at Mills.
Photograph by Donald Hatfield.

was followed by a series of connecting forms or variations in which the group was assisted by José Limón. An excerpt from *American Holiday,* danced with choral accompaniment, concluded the demonstration.

Opening his section of the demonstration with a brilliant leap study, Charles Weidman led his group through exercises for feet and legs, air work, and finally techniques leading to turns and falls. After a brief explanation of the principle of kinetic movement, which he divided into dramatic, pantomimic and emotional, Mr. Weidman presented examples of kinetic pantomime in dance form. Assisted by Katherine Manning, José Limón and Gregory MacDougall, he danced the Knocking Dance from the ballet *Candide.* The dance group then presented the "Primitive Study" from the *Dance of the Elevens.* This was followed by the "Men's Dance" from *New Dance,* in which Mr. Weidman was assisted by Mr. Limón, Gregory MacDougall, and Mercer Cunningham. . . .

The demonstration . . . brought out clearly the similarity of purpose which exists in the work of the four leading artists in the field. . . . What it may have lacked in brilliant or outstanding work on the part of the majority of the students, it made up by the very obvious sincerity and intelligent application of principle with which every dancer performed. On watching the demonstration one could only be amazed at the astonishing amount of ground covered and could feel that great impetus has been given to dance on the Pacific Coast through this experiment.[28]

NOTES

1. *Bennington College Bulletin* 7, no. 3 (February 1939): 1.
2. Ibid.
3. Ibid.
4. Maxine Cushing, "Bennington Makes Plans," *Educational Dance* 1, no. 3 (August-September 1938): 5.
5. Letter from Doris Humphrey to Charles Francis Woodford, postmarked 27 July 1939 [Doris Humphrey Collection, C426].
6. Interview with Ethel Butler.
7. Interview with Tina Flade Mooney.
8. Larry Warren, *Lester Horton: Modern Dance Pioneer* (New York: Marcel Dekker, 1977), pp. 86–88.
9. Esther E. Pease, "Young Artists in Concert at Bennington," *Educational Dance* 2, no. 3 (August-September 1939): 13.
10. Margaret Lloyd, *Christian Science Monitor*, 10 June 1939.
11. Interview with Ethel Butler.
12. Interview with Ben Belitt.
13. Telegram from Lewis Webster Jones to Mary Jo Shelly, July 1939 [Bennington College Archive]. See also Esther E. Pease, "Highlights at Bennington," *Educational Dance* 2, no. 3 (August-September 1939): 10–11.
14. Letter from Doris Humphrey to Charles Francis Woodford, 6 August 1939 [Doris Humphrey Collection, C426].
15. Letter from Pauline Lawrence to Doris Humphrey, postmarked 17 July 1939 [Doris Humphrey Collection, C433].
16. Margaret Lloyd, *Christian Science Monitor*, 16 August 1938.
17. Letter from Doris Humphrey to Charles Francis Woodford, 27 July 1939 [Doris Humphrey Collection, C426].
18. Karen Burt, "Final Demonstration of Technique," *Dance Observer* 6, no. 7 (August-September 1939): 251.
19. Louis Horst, "Modern American Percussion Music," *Dance Observer* 6, no. 7 (August-September 1939): 250.
20. Letter from Doris Humphrey to Charles Francis Woodford, postmarked 1 August 1939 [Doris Humphrey Collection, C426].
21. Pease, "Young Artists in Concert at Bennington," p. 13.
22. Interview with Ben Belitt.
23. "Thrills of a Lifetime at Mills College," *Oakland* (California) *Tribune*, 30 July 1939.
24. Nell Silva, "The Dance: World Famous Bennington School of the Dance Holds Festival at Mills College in Oakland," *People's World* (San Francisco), 16 August 1939.
25. Letter from Doris Humphrey to Charles Francis Woodford from Perry-Mansfield, 1939 (undated) [Doris Humphrey Collection, C426].
26. Karen Burt, *Dance Observer* 6, no. 7 (August-September 1939): 251.
27. Nell Silva, *People's World*, 16 August 1939.
28. Marjorie Lucas, "Final Demonstration, Bennington School of the Dance at Mills College," *Educational Dance* 2, no. 3 (August-September 1939): 12–13.

1940
First Session of the Bennington School of the Arts: Dance Division

29 June 1940—17 August 1940

Drawing of Martha Graham by Aline Fruhauf.

The Bennington School of the Arts opened its inaugural session—six weeks plus a seventh festival week—with the lowest enrollment of any prior session and lacking a proper theater in which to stage its first festival of dance, music, and drama. The Armory was unavailable and would be for the duration of the war emergency, and Bennington College had not come up with a means of realizing Arch Lauterer's designs for a new theater.

Lauterer made the best of the College Theatre on campus by enlarging the stage and erecting 304 bleacher seats. Despite his wizardry, the theater was bound to disappoint those who had hoped for enlarged facilities in keeping with the expansive ambitions of the School of the Arts. John Martin found the College Theatre wholly inadequate for professional dance and theater productions.

As in 1935 the concentration in dance was on one of the Big Four: Martha Graham and her company were sole producing artists in the Dance Division. Relieved for the first time of all teaching responsibilities, Graham mounted two new works, *El Penitente* and *Letter to the World*, which were destined to endure. In what turned out to be the last of her Bennington summers, Hanya Holm taught a master course but did not perform or produce dances. Doris Humphrey and Charles Weidman were "on leave." Erick Hawkins made his solo debut in a pre-festival concert with three new works, all having new music.

The Dance Division drew the largest enrollment, and for the first time dancers rather than teachers were in the majority. Ballet and dance notation were introduced into the curriculum. (An advertisement in the festival program for the School of American Ballet listed Martha Graham as guest instructor for its seventh season, 1940-1941; Lincoln Kirstein was guest lecturer at Bennington.) Dancers could collaborate with actors, musicians, and designers in myriad modes. The expanded arts curriculum seemed to one student "like pouring champagne into a glass long empty. . . . Dance no longer had to stand alone like the bare hull of a ship, minus all the rigging."[1]

Jean Erdman, Nina Fonaroff, Nelle Fisher, Jane Dudley, Sophie Maslow, Katherine Litz, George Bockman, and poet John Malcolm Brinnin were involved in experimental workshop projects. Composers in the Music Division wrote a slew of new scores for dance students. Even Louis Horst's Pre-Classic and Modern Forms studies had music written especially for the dance.

Most experimental of all was Martha Graham's *Letter to the World*. Later acclaimed as one of her most penetrating masterworks, *Letter* drew sharp criticism in its first Bennington presentation, which was quite different from its subsequent productions. Walter Terry thought the Bennington "try-out" had been crucial:

> Miss Graham discovered from it that the work had to be completely revised. This test production enabled her to bring a fully realized and a truly magnificent dance piece to New York audiences the following winter. From this approach alone, the Bennington system proves its worth. . . . There is the aura of creation about Bennington and an audience is eager and curious to see any new dance piece revealed in the place of its inception and its rehearsal.[2]

Among the first-time students was Ann Hutchinson, a recent graduate of the three-year course at the Jooss-Leeder Dance School in England. She had first seen Martha Graham in New York earlier that year. "Her strong technique," Hutchinson recalled, "so strange, held a fascination, and the attraction of her choreography as theatre was irresistible. I had to learn more about American Modern Dance."[3] Bennington was her introduction. Hutchinson brought to Bennington a dance background quite different from others. She explained:

> The Jooss-Leeder technique was based on Laban's theories of movement, the broad spectrum of spatial and qualitative possibilities. The emphasis was on the performance of movement. A position was usually a point to be passed through rather than held. Line of body, so important to ballet, was given little importance. Most of the technique was based on Space Harmony, a variety of swinging patterns. A sensitive performer emerged, but the training lacked repetitive, highly disciplined exercises through which the instrument itself is developed. Most students came from a ballet background, with a basic physical discipline and control and an understanding of stance and alignment.
>
> At the 1940 Bennington summer course I enrolled in Hanya Holm's Master Classes, designed supposedly for more advanced students. In fact the technical level of many participants was too low for higher level work, and despite the degree to which Hanya had developed a more personal American style, the Laban-based work had too familiar a ring and did not hold a challenge for me. I took advantage of the special individual one-week trial courses in Humphrey, Weidman and Graham technique. The Humphrey-Weidman work had a range and flavor which I found stimulating and within my scope. But it was the Graham technique which captivated me: the sheer strength of it, the defiance of gravity in the floor work as well as the falls, the discipline, the precision demanded—all so foreign to what I had previously experienced.

Ethel Butler taught the classes and her earthy amazonic quality was a tremendous contrast to the sensitive Jooss-Leeder work with its concentration on subtle distinctions in gestural pathways.

Martha Hill's and Arch Lauterer's stage production course [Experimental Production] provided another eye opener. Simple stage sets such as an arrangement of vertical poles, or a tape bisecting the stage, or a group of flats, established a choreographic challenge. Each adventurous student gathered together three to five willing bodies on whom to work out his/her ideas. These then were shown and commented on by Martha Hill and Arch Lauterer. My attempts followed the preparation-result, gathering in and expending of energy—the "waves breaking on the shore" style typical of the Laban "school." In vivid contrast were the efforts of other students. Stark staccato isolations—sequences such as step-close, pause, raise the lower arm, pause, head turn, pause, pause, step close, step close, pause—and so on, left me gaping. Was this dance? Dance was movement, and this was sparse separated movement leading to positions and stillnesses. The idea of moving architecture, of design composed of body parts, of the design in time and space made of movement fragments and the choreographic impact were new to me, not as basic possibilities, but in the style and presentation. Such non-human movement was such a complete departure from dance as I had learned to know it, could I accept it? Listening to the evaluations and discussions which followed each choreographic effort, I began to see the relation of this approach to abstract art, to cubism, the dynamics of shapes separated by stillnesses echoing the dynamics of much modern art and modern music. The sparseness, the economy, the use of motifs repeated, developed and contrasted, all revealed an approach to composition and choreography quite new to me, but recognizably valid. Experience in application of such an approach came in working in longer choreographic pieces, as for instance George Bockman's stark *Johnny Got His Gun,* a war piece on the experience of a paraplegic.

Experiments in movement to spoken poetry, one piece by John Brinnin comes to mind, provided the opportunity to see how U.S.A. modern dance handled such a form in contrast to the few attempts I had witnessed at the Jooss-Leeder School. The Bennington pieces were more abstract, less literal in movement with a finer thread connecting the action with the words.[4]

Hutchinson was impressed by the whole experience of "milling around daily with people from so many places, backgrounds, interests, drives and personalities." She observed that "in later years at Connecticut College, the summer modern dance program became much enlarged. Bennington 1940 was of a size which allowed the individual student to feel part of the whole. It was rich and varied without being overwhelming."[5]

To John Martin and Margaret Lloyd the festival seemed less exciting than in previous summers. Martin thought the move from town to campus had given the festival an academic taint. The school, he said, would have to decide whether it would be "an educational project, in which the benefits accrue chiefly to the participants," or "a professional project, in which it is the audience that is rightly the beneficiary."[6]

There was, he said, a marked disparity between the leadership level of the Dance Division and that of the Music and Drama Divisions led by college faculty: "Miss Graham is certainly entitled to associate with artists of her rank and reputation in the other arts, and the modern dance itself surely deserves more respect from its own advocates."[7] When Doris Humphrey took up her residency the following summer, Martin suggested that she should have as her colleagues artists of the caliber of a Stokowski or a Piscator.

The Drama Division's production of *The King and the Duke*, adapted for the stage from *Huckleberry Finn*, came in for a drubbing from the dance critics, though Martha Hill's dances and Gregory Tucker's score were generally admired.

To poet Ben Belitt, uneasy collaboration among the arts was inevitable, for the new school was engaged in "another kind of trailblazing." Although some faculty relationships were stormy, he credited Martha Hill with the ability to find affinities with whatever the situation concretely demanded. Belitt called Hill's collaboration with Francis Fergusson on *The King and the Duke* an extraordinary accomplishment, one of several innovative experiments among the theater arts at Bennington, both within the college and at the summer school.[8]

Reviewing the concerts of contemporary music in *Modern Music*, pianist John Kirkpatrick wrote that the most successful contribution to modern music was made by the two new dance scores of Louis Horst and Hunter Johnson.[9] "Dance," concluded Margaret Lloyd, "is still the star attraction in the festival performances and the sister arts are best served here when used in conjunction with it."[10]

John Martin allowed that it would take time to find the bedrock on which to build, as was the case with the School of the Dance in its first year. Despite misgivings about the first session, he recognized that "there is probably no other place in the world where a dancer is provided with such an opportunity for intensive creative work without a worry of any kind about eating and drinking and paying the rent."[11]

Doris Humphrey came up to see the festival and observe classes. She had just completed a teaching stint at the University of Maryland's new summer dance program, one of several new competitors to Bennington for students. Humphrey's impressions of the new Bennington setup were "mixed":

> The idea of the plan—combination of drama, music, dance, is good, but the working out of it inferior in quality. The festival itself, consisting of music programs, a drama with music and dancing and a dance program by Martha were all disappointing, and besides that the enrollment was less than ever before. [I] don't think it's just my finicky taste . . . as the critics panned it too.[12]

She was more explicit in another letter:

> The sight of the festival . . . considerably strengthened my belief in myself. At the same time it terrified me—for how shall I ever be able to carry on the modern dance alone? If this sounds egotistical to a fantastic degree, all I can say is that you should have seen it. It was thin, it was barren, it was boring. Even the critics who commonly rave were downright disappointed. I also saw some moving pictures of a good many different dancers, which depressed me further—although Charles and I were good. . . . Lincoln Kirstein gave a lecture in which he predicted doom for all of us—with a possible hope in joining an opera company. I would usually leap at his throat, but after the concerts I saw, I have an awful feeling he is right. And moreover that no opera company would have it either.[13]

Kirstein's dour predictions were related in an article in *PM's Weekly* entitled "PM Takes You to Bennington for a Dose of American Culture." The article went on to report:

> Recently the modern dance, partly through Bennington's influence, has shown signs of becoming less abstract, easier to understand, readier to cooperate with the theatre. . . . The Festival showed how the arts were moving closer to each other.[14]

The *Nation*'s critic singled out *Letter to the World* and *The King and the Duke* as successful attempts toward a new concept of "theater-poetry":

> [The School of the Arts had] set up a stage where the three arts may complement each other and combine [moving] toward that working heaven we recognize in the theater of the Greeks and the Noh play; a combination which Cocteau has named for our century, "theater-poetry. . . ." The new direction . . .

Martha Graham and group at Bennington. Photograph courtesy of *Dance Observer*.

> began to be apparent in the Dance School a few years back. With attendant fumbling, risk, and difficulties, the planners and performers have gone forward. Today they represent the advance guard of theater experimentation, in a world where the opportunities for such artistic growth become less each day.[15]

As if to confirm the rightness of the Bennington experiment, *Theatre Arts* magazine devoted its entire September 1940 issue to "American Theatre Dance," with George Beiswanger as special editor. In its pages, John Martin accounted for the "steady and consistent" growth of dance from recital to theater art. American dance was now "fully of the theatre, and ready for a theatre . . . in which to function."[16]

Lincoln Kirstein saw the revolt of the dance against the ballet at an end:

> Today all the young "modern" dancers are industriously catching up on their five positions; the movement has absorbed so many traditional elements that it is scarcely any longer a distinct branch of instruction in itself.[17]

Critics across the country described a need for the modern dance to develop new audiences. Cecil Smith said that while Chicago had a serious dance audience, "only a small segment of the populace will ever interest themselves seriously in the purer reaches of dance art." The larger American public will become acquainted with "dancing of high artistic merit" when it appears in "the totality of good popular stage entertainment."[18]

Bostonians, said Margaret Lloyd, turned "an indifferent shoulder" to the modern "expressional" dance: "It remains true that Boston audiences are still conservative, remarkably incurious as to new developments and completely apathetic to the younger experimentalists."[19]

Samuel Wilson described central Ohio audiences as "ballet rather than dance minded"; in his region there had been "no well-organized attempt . . . to develop the potential audience that exists for the modern dance."[20]

And Alfred Frankenstein succinctly summarized the plight of the dance in San Francisco:

> As elsewhere the possession of an eastern or European reputation is the first requisite for obtaining respectable support. The conventional, spectacular and well publicized goes over. The contemporary and progressive gets a lean squeeze—and the local boy makes good somewhere else.[21]

Beiswanger issued a warning that despite its surface health and vigor, the future of the dance "has never looked so dark. . . . Dance as a profession does not pay. Group after group faces the coming season with no plans and the imminent necessity of disbanding."[22] As a result, dancers were now leaving the concert stage to earn a livelihood on Broadway, in Hollywood, and in nightclubs or "in teaching positions in the hinterlands." Outside of New York and a few other cities, colleges, and universities, "dance is still in its swaddling clothes, compared with the legitimate stage." The future for dance seemed most secure when allied with the lyric theater—alongside opera, concert, and "the dance-oriented play." It could not survive for long on its own, eking out a tour here and there, struggling to book a single New York season.

A new dance theater could be created by consolidating American dance forces and linking up with "their natural theater allies." The Bennington School of the Arts in its first session had ventured toward this solution. "It is," he concluded, "the only way."[23]

Two months later, on the eve of opening her New York season with the two new Bennington works, *El Penitente* and *Letter to the World*, Martha Graham talked of a new purpose with Walter Terry:

> We must win back our audiences. We have alienated them through grimness of theme and a non-theatrical approach to our dancing. Now that we modern dancers have left our period of "long woolens" behind us, we must prove to our audiences that our theater pieces have color, warmth and entertainment value. We must convince our audiences that we belong in the American theater.[24]

THE SESSION IN BRIEF

The School of the Dance was incorporated as a division into a four-division School of the Arts. Basic plan of School of the Dance continued for a six-week session, with a final week of festival production. Additions to curriculum were Dance Notation and Ballet Technique. Hanya Holm directed a Master Course in Dance. Martha Graham and Dance Group was the resident producing company. Workshops, festival productions, and experimental work engaged faculty and students in all four divisions.[25]

FACULTY AND STAFF

School of the Arts: Mary Jo Shelly, administrative director. Martha Hill, director of dance. Francis Fergusson, director of drama. Otto Luening, director of music. Arch Lauterer, director of theater design. Dance Division: Hanya Holm (Master Course). Ethel Butler, Graham technique (Graham did not teach this session). Harriet Roeder, Katherine Manning, Claudia Moore, associates for Holm and Humphrey-Weidman (the latter on leave 1940). Also Norman Lloyd, Bessie Schönberg. New dance faculty: Erick Hawkins (Ballet Technique), Helen Priest (Dance Notation), Lincoln Kirstein, visiting lecturer. Festival productions: Martha Graham, director of dance. Louis Horst, musical director. Arch Lauterer, designer. Frances Hawkins, publicity representative.

STUDENTS

Total 119, ages 16–47 (but many more younger students), from 29 states, no foreign countries (first time), including 32 men. Three categories of students: general, apprentices, and fellows. Dance 87, drama 12, music 16, theater design 4. Of 87 dance students, only 33 were teachers, with 48 experienced student-dancers and 6 beginners. Including David Campbell, Merce Cunningham, Jean Erdman, Joseph Gornbein [Gifford], Ann Hutchinson, Katherine Litz, David Zellmer.

LECTURES, RECITALS, AND STUDENT WORK

Series of lectures on theatrical dancing with illustrative material by Lincoln Kirstein, and the following recital and workshop presentations:

13 July 1940

Erick Hawkins in a Program of Dances (solo recital). College Theatre. *Accom* Ralph Gilbert. Program: ***Liberty Tree** chor* Hawkins *mus* Gilbert. ***Insubstantial Pageant** chor* Hawkins, *mus* Lehman Engel. ***Yankee Bluebritches** chor* Hawkins, *mus* Hunter Johnson. *See Catalog.

This was Hawkins' first public showing of choreography since *Show Piece* (1937, Ballet Caravan).

6, 13, 20, and 27 July, 3 and 9 August 1940

Workshops presenting student projects in Experimental Production, Pre-Classic and Modern Forms, Advanced Composition, Advanced Rhythmic Basis Class, Compositions from the Master Course directed by Hanya Holm, two projects in drama, a discussion of lighting for dance and drama by Arch Lauterer. Projects included ***Music Montage Using Two Victrolas** chor* Katherine Litz. ***Light Plan Only** chor* George Bockman, *mus* Carl Miller. ***The Garden Is Political** chor* Molly Howe, *poem* John Brinnin. ***Lyric Jazz Study** chor* Jean Erdman, *mus* Blair Fairchild. ***Spirit Possessed*** (Air Primitive) *chor* Nina Fonaroff, *mus* [Federico] Mompou. ***Mountain Song*** (Americana) *chor* Nelle Fisher, *mus* Wendell Keeney. ***Archaic Duet** chor* Jane Dudley and Sophie Maslow, *mus* [Erik] Satie. ***The Kiss of Judas** chor* Jane Dudley, *mus* Malingreau. ***Cube** chor* Litz *mus* Beatrice MacLaughlin. ***Jazz Study to "St. Louis Blues"** chor* David Campbell, Bockman, Ethel Butler, Litz, Marjorie Mazia. ***Kentucky Hill Tune*** (Americana) *chor* Maslow, *mus* Ralph Gilbert.

BENNINGTON FESTIVAL

10–17 August 1940

Eight performances in the College Theatre (four in dance, four in drama) and four concerts in the Recreation (Fairview) Building. Audience total approximately 3000, including 1200 for dance (theater capacity 304) with two additional houses turned away. (Dance programs follow listings of music and drama events.)

The *Bennington Banner* announced the festival opening:

> The audience is as colorful and exciting as the performances they will see. Already Lincoln Kirstein, Director of Ballet Caravan, Roy Harris, No. 1 American composer whose symphony is the only American work being played this summer at the Berkshire Festival, Quincy Porter, head of the Yaddo Festival Committee, Mrs. Rita Wallace Morgenthau of The Neighborhood Playhouse have arrived.
>
> The College Theatre has been remodeled. The stage has been enlarged because of the elaborateness of the productions. A new proscenium arch and a front curtain have been installed. Arch Lauterer, head of the Theatre Design department, has used in these productions many devices new to the theatre and expert critics are of the opinion that these innovations may revolutionize the Broadway stage.[26]

10, 12, 14, and 16 August 1940

The King and the Duke: A Melodramatic Farce from "Huckleberry Finn." College Theatre. *Devised and dir* Francis Fergusson. *Dances composed and staged* Martha Hill. *Mus composed and conducted* Gregory Tucker. *Sets & light* Arch Lauterer. *Cos* Helen Bottomly. In Three Acts, a Prologue and Epilogue, with an Overture. Orchestra of 11, cast of 32, including Katherine Manning and Bessie Schönberg.

Reviews

John Martin called the production "stuffy and academic."[27] Walter Terry was more severe:

> a dramatic production that would have abashed an amateur. . . . A fake folk aura surrounded the work, which thick drawls and drooping britches only enhanced. Martha Hill's simple folk dances and Gregory Tucker's frequently attractive

Martha Graham and members of her group at Bennington. Left to right: Jane Dudley, Elizabeth Halpern, Jean Erdman, Ethel Butler, Frieda Flier, Sophie Maslow, Nina Fonaroff, Nelle Fisher. (Ann Hutchinson is in the striped dress, back to the camera behimd Graham, looking into the Commons Building.) Photograph courtesy of Ann Hutchinson Guest.

music were of little value to this erring drama with its aimless dialogue, its lame characterization, its lack of dramatic suspense and sequence and its insult to Mark Twain.[28]

John Kirkpatrick wrote that "the net result wasn't nearly as bad as has been painted."[29] and Sherman Conrad applauded the attempt:

In this Americana Fergusson has revealed a deeper "cynical fable," which is mostly suggested by the dances designed by Martha Hill and the folk tunes imitated in the music of Gregory Tucker. Static scenes interrupted by rhythmic interludes give it the jerky effect of a Broadway musical, and in this way it fails for the most part to weld drama and dance into a whole. In a few scenes, such as the lynching, it does get a fused depth of meaning and movement that nothing since "Murder in the Cathedral" has approached.[30]

Margaret Lloyd counted the dance and music as the worthiest elements of the production:

Miss Hill's incidental dances were less incidental than indispensable. They flowed throughout the action, held it together. Varying the old-time square dances dynamically, using the retard, the pause, against the animated, balancing the sinister against the gay, introducing characterizing movement as well as steps, the play became professionally a dance production. Mr. Tucker's harmonium, combined with wind, strings (including banjo), drums, and voice lent pervasive aid. . . . The spoken word . . . fared less well.[31]

11 and 16 August 1940

Contemporary Music. Fairview Recreation Building. *Dir* Otto Luening. Musicians 13. Program: *Mus* Quincy Porter, Karol Szymanowski, Charles Ives, Ernst Bacon, Mary Howe, Emerson Whithorne, Samuel Barber, Theodore Chanler, Marc Blitzstein, Paul Bowles. Also Lionel Nowak, Reba Marcus, Ann McDougle, Otto Luening, Robert McBride, composers in residence at the Bennington School of the Arts.

Review

John Kirkpatrick, *Modern Music*:

> It would gratify professional pride to be able to say that modern music came, saw and conquered at the first summer festival of the Bennington School of the Arts. Actually it betrayed the tentative uncertainty of a debutante, for the contemporary program . . . suffered from an apparent feeling of obligation to include too many different items. Fifteen composers were represented but no central work of stable dimensions. A spotty total effect was inevitable.[32]

Kirkpatrick concluded that "in every way the most valuable contribution" to modern music at the festival were the two dance scores by Louis Horst and Hunter Johnson.

14 and 17 August 1940

Seventeenth- and Eighteenth-Century Music. Fairview Recreation Building. *Dir* Ralph Kirkpatrick, harpsichord. *Musicians* 11. Program: *mus* Johannes Rosenmüller, J. C. de Mondonville, G. F. Handel, Henry Purcell, J. S. Bach.

Review

Sherman Conrad in the *Nation* called the program "somewhat irrelevant to the contemporary tone of the Festival." He suggested that "in music, as formerly in dance, Bennington finds distinction in being 'completely modern.'"[33]

11, 13, 15, and 17 August 1940

Martha Graham and Dance Group. College Theatre. *Mus dir* Louis Horst. Program: I. ***El Penitente*** (The Penitent) *chor* Graham, *mus* Horst. II. ***Every Soul Is a Circus . . : A Satire*** *chor* Graham, *mus* Paul Nordoff. *Sets & light* Arch Lauterer. *Props* Philip Stapp. *Cos* Edythe Gilfond. *Characters of the Arenic World: Empress of the Arena* Martha Graham. *Ring Master* Erick Hawkins. *Acrobat* Merce Cunningham. *Ideal Spectator* Jean Erdman. *First Arenic Performer* Nelle Fisher. *Other Arenic Performers* Sophie Maslow, Ethel Butler, Marjorie Mazia, Frieda Flier. *Action:* 1. Prologue: Empress of the Arena, 2. The Ring Master, 3. Parade, 4. Training Ring, 5. Entrance of the Spectator, 6. The Show Begins: Star Turn, 7. Garland Entry, 8. Arenic World (1) Triangle, 9. Poses and Plastiques, 10. Arenic World (2) Duet, 11. Ariel Interlude, 12. Finale.

> Every soul is a Circus
> Every mind is a tent
> Every heart is a sawdust ring
> Where the circling race is spent.
> —Vachel Lindsay

> *Program Note*: This is not the literal circus of canvas and sawdust ring but a circus of ridiculous situations and silly behaviors. In every woman there is the desire to be featured in a "star turn," as the apex of a triangle and as the beloved of a duet. In the life of every woman there is some force which, however temporarily, holds the whip hand. Throughout the circus of her life every woman is her own most appreciative spectator. In this circus of the silly woman's life, the sum total of episodes and of interludes does not add up to mature dignity but to a tragic addled confusion.

III. **Letter to the World chor* Graham, *mus* Hunter Johnson. *See Catalog.

After the first performance, the order of the program was changed, so that *El Penitente* opened, followed by *Letter to the World* and *Every Soul Is a Circus* .

NOTES

1. Dorothy Sperber, "Dance in Bennington Workshops," *Dance Observer* 7, no. 7 (August-September 1940): 103-104. For a summary of the session, see also Mary Jo Shelly, "The New Plan at Bennington," *Dance Observer* 7, no. 4 (April 1940): 48-49, and Steffi Nossen, "Bennington Festival–1940," *Educational Dance* 3, no. 3 (August-September 1940): 10-11.
2. Walter Terry, "Bennington in Action," *Dance* 10, no. 1 (October 1941): 10.
3. Ann Hutchinson Guest, "Bennington Memories–1940" (unpublished recollections contributed for this book).
4. Ibid.
5. Ibid.
6. John Martin, *New York Times*, 18 August 1940.
7. Ibid.
8. Interview with Ben Belitt.
9. John Kirkpatrick, "Bennington's Festival of the Arts," *Modern Music* 18, no. 1 (November-December 1940): 54.
10. Margaret Lloyd, "Bennington Festival, New Style," *Christian Science Monitor*, 17 August 1940.
11. John Martin, *New York Times*, 18 August 1940.
12. Letter from Doris Humphrey to Julia Humphrey, 1940 (undated) [Doris Humphrey Collection, C443].
13. Letter from Doris Humphrey to Charles Francis Woodford, 13 August 1940 [Doris Humphrey Collection, C447].
14. Henry W. Simon, *PM's Weekly*, 18 August 1940.
15. Sherman Conrad, "Bennington Festival, 1940," *Nation* 151, no. 8 (24 August 1940): 158-59.
16. John Martin, "Dance Since Isadora," *Theatre Arts* 24, no. 9 (September 1940): 648.
17. Lincoln Kirstein, "Ballet: Record and Augury," *Theatre Arts* 24, no. 9 (September 1940): 651.
18. "The Critic from Coast to Coast," *Theatre Arts* 24, no. 9 (September 1940): 660-66.
19. Ibid., pp. 666-67.
20. Ibid., pp. 667-68.
21. Ibid., pp. 668.
22. [George Beiswanger], "Dance in the Red," *Theatre Arts* 24, no. 9 (September 1940): 671-80.
23. Ibid., p. 680.
24. Quoted in Walter Terry, "The State of Dance," *New York Herald Tribune*, 15 December 1940.
25. Statistics quoted for the 1940 session are taken from "First Annual Report of the Bennington School of the Arts," Summer 1940, in *Reports of Officers, 1939-40*, Bennington College, 8, no. 5 (October 1940), which does not have the detail of prior reports for the School of the Dance; Appendix to "Second Annual Report of the Bennington School of the Arts," Summer 1941, in *Reports of Officers, 1940-41*, Bennington College, 9, no. 3 (October 1941), which contains comparative statistics for the eight summers; and memorandum from Mary Jo Shelly to Francis Fergusson, 30 September 1941, which analyzes the student population for the two sessions of the School of the Arts. Information pertaining to faculty, curricula, and general activities was taken from the *Bennington College Bulletin* 8, no. 3 (March 1940), published prior to the session. Since the focus here is the Dance Division, staffing, curricula, and activities of the Music, Drama, and Theatre Design Divisions are selectively listed. All public festival performances are listed.
26. *Bennington Banner*, 10 August 1940.
27. John Martin, *New York Times*, 12 August 1940.
28. Walter Terry, *New York Herald Tribune*, 18 August 1940.
29. John Kirkpatrick, *Modern Music* 18, no. 1 (November-December 1940): 54.
30. Sherman Conrad, *Nation* 151, no. 8 (24 August 1940): 158-59.
31. Margaret Lloyd, *Christian Science Monitor*, 17 August 1940.
32. John Kirkpatrick, *Modern Music* 18, no. 1 (November-December 1940): 54.
33. Sherman Conrad, *Nation* 151, no. 8 (24 August 1940): 158-59.

1941
Second Session of the Bennington School of the Arts: Dance Division

5 July 1941—17 August 1941

Drawing of Doris Humphrey by Aline Fruhauf.

"It may have been the war," wrote Rosalyn Krokover, "it may have been a manifestation of the growing dance consciousness of the public; or it may have been a desire to get in everything possible while gas still was available for the family auto; [but] the Dance Festival at Bennington, Vt., together with festivals of a similar nature throughout the vicinity, enjoyed the greatest popular success it has met with during the eight years of its existence."[1]

The sixth and last Bennington Festival featured premieres of Doris Humphrey's evening-length *Decade* and Martha Graham's *Punch and The Judy*, produced in the College Theatre, which was remodeled anew by Arch Lauterer. (Its capacity was reduced to 256 from 304; a total audience of about 2300 attended nine dance performances.) There were four concerts of contemporary and old music in the Carriage Barn on campus and four combined programs of opera and drama at the General Stark Theatre in Bennington. The School of the Arts also participated in the Green Mountain Festival in Middlebury, in honor of Vermont's Sesquicentennial—the first and only time the school moved out of Bennington proper.

Enrollments remained at the reduced level of 1940. Gains in the number of male students made the previous summer were wiped out by the draft. Once again dance was the main drawing card. Collaboration among the arts in major productions was about the same as in 1940: musicians from the Music Division accompanied and wrote music for the dance; Martha Hill devised dances for the drama production.

In return for producing half-hour variety shows between movie double bills at the General Stark Theatre in the town of Bennington, the Drama and Music Divisions had use of the stage for their own presentations. The addition of this excellent facility helped reduce problems of inadequate rehearsal and performance space, but its location off campus further separated the school's divisions. The General Stark, Francis Fergusson recalled, was a superior theater. "It had a well-equipped stage, excellent acoustics and sightlines. We loved it."[2]

In honor of the 150th anniversary of Mozart's death, the School of the Arts presented and English version of *The Impresario*, directed by Otto Luening. Martha Hill created the dance interludes for Molière's *School for Wives*, directed by Francis Fergusson. Players from the Vermont State Symphony augmented the ranks of the Bennington ensemble in the pit. Ralph Kirkpatrick returned as guest artist to play the harpsichord, and Henry Cowell made his first Bennington appearance, directing a program of contemporary music.

Cowell was impressed with what he saw. Music and dance, he said, were "brought together more closely here than . . . anywhere else in the country. Creative people in music and dance do as they should do always and everywhere—work hand in hand with the realization that movement needs the punctuation of music, and that music is made living through movement."[3] The immediacy of stage production was a great stimulus to young composers; the quality of work was high, and the variety and reach impressive:

> The astonishing thing is that among the students there [were] many remarkably good compositions written, both for dance productions and for musical performance alone: works for orchestra, string orchestra, trios, quartets, solo works—all of them subject to being reviewed by several instructor-composers, rather than just by one, as is customary. The students have the advantage of showing their works to several men of differing views, both in music and dance composition. . . . The student has a chance to arrive at his own point of view, rather than following the views of any one teacher. Nor is any one style of music favored. Works in pre-classic dance forms in ancient style may be found, side by side with ultra-dissonant things in contemporary idioms, and all points between are liberally represented.

But the *Nation*'s critic, who had sounded a bright note for the school's future the previous summer, reported finding a distressing quantity of "pabulum." "Not only," he said, "have the arts failed to collaborate interestingly, but the separate fields have themselves lost vitality. Only in Martha Graham and the workers around her have the school's new aims found fruition."[4]

In order to attract a larger corps of teachers, the school offered graduate credit for the first time. But the percentage of teachers, though slightly higher than in 1940, still showed dance students in the majority. "Project groups" gave all students performance experience and opportunities to compose. Technical study was further broadened by the addition of tap (taught by William Bales) and American country dancing.

The eighth session of the dance component at Bennington, wrote Mary Jo Shelly, was "designed to follow the central directions in which dance, in itself and in its relations to other arts, is moving in American education and the American theatre":

> The evolution of modern dance in this country has . . . made important, acquaintance with the elements of ballet. Tap and country dancing are coming into new uses. All of these are part of the dancer's and the dance teacher's repertoire. . . . Time was when a relatively simple series of technical exercises represented the core of modern technique. That is no longer true, and the dancer and teacher have at one and the same time a wider range to cover and many richer materials with which to work. Much the same maturing has taken place in dance form. Lyric forms, theatrical forms, forms derived from antique and pre-classic sources, dances involving a spoken text or new musical setting such as voice, the use of decor and lighting, are today open for exploration at even the simplest levels.[5]

Doris Humphrey had charge of the major production, *Decade*. Charles Weidman taught the master course and also directed the first repertory class which Shelly said marked "a whole new trend. This is the way the master works in the modern dance, like the classics in any other art such as music, are going to be made available and perpetuated."[6] Weidman taught *The Shakers* and *Lynch Town*, and students performed the works in weekly workshops.

Hanya Holm (spending her first summer in Colorado Springs) was represented by Harriet Roeder. Martha Graham produced a new work, *Punch and The Judy*, and taught. Pearl Lack [Lang], Sasha Liebich [Mark Ryder], and Marion Scott were among the newest Graham dancers in what was now billed as "Martha Graham and Dance Company." (The Humphrey-Weidman Concert Group was now called "Doris Humphrey-Charles Weidman and Dance Company.") Jean Erdman made her first major appearance outside the Graham company in a concert of works by Erick Hawkins and Jane Dudley. A program of "Dance Projects" included William Bales' first production of *Es Mujer* and Nina Fonaroff's reworked *Yankee Doodle Greets Columbus, 1492*.

The spoken word was used by Martha Graham in *Punch and The Judy* and also by Doris Humphrey in *Decade*.

Decade, Humphrey's last Bennington work, looked at the state of dance in a world geared for profit—as she and Charles Weidman had lived through it. This compendium of their past repertoire concluded with the company gesturing optimistically toward the entrance of the new Humphrey-Weidman Studio Theatre.

The Studio Theatre had opened in December 1940 on West 16th Street in New York. Doris Humphrey explained:

> Too long we have been like those children who always have to play in the neighbor's houses because they have no room to play in their own homes. For years we have strolled like Gypsies, prodigal of our dances, scattering them the length and breadth of the country. Now we think we should like to stay at home for a while, see what store of dances we have accumulated, show them to our friends, show them more than once, give the dances a chance to live for a while, at home, among friends not strangers, remember the old dances and revive them, make new ones.[7]

The perils of touring and difficulties of performing in the commercial theater had closed off the former paths. With the change at Bennington, even the prospect for a secure summer "season" was in jeopardy. The Studio Theatre served not only as a repertory theater for the Humphrey-Weidman company but as a showcase for other choreographers.

Now Martha Graham appeared to be reaching out toward a wider audience—she would tour *El Penitente*, *Punch and The Judy*, and *Letter to the World* with new success, while Doris Humphrey seemed to some to have retreated. Not only did some critics blast *Decade* for lacking the dramatic power of earlier compositions, but they took her to task for playing to a group of "insiders" familiar with the Humphrey-Weidman repertory. In an uncharacteristically harsh notice, Margaret Lloyd wrote, "This is no time for pioneers to be looking back."[8]

Humphrey was not alone in looking at where the dance had been in order to see ahead. Walter Terry described the art's current plight as "desperate":

> For more than a decade Doris Humphrey, Charles Weidman and Martha Graham have followed the course of Denishawn, bringing great and important dance to the people of the country, but bringing it without subsidy. Today they and their colleagues face a desperate situation. New York performances are so expensive that one or two a season are all that are possible. The touring field is overcrowded, making it almost impossible for any one to finish a tour with a substantial profit. Somehow American dancers seem to scrape along season after season, giving us glimpses of great dance and then rushing back to teach classes in order to raise money for further appearances. This state of affairs should not continue for long or one day the American dance might die in a studio.[9]

In John Martin's words, *Decade* was a work in which Humphrey retraced "the steps of her joint career with Charles Weidman since the day when they broke with the past and set out on an independent course."[10] But, said Martin, the real issues raised by *Decade* were

> the concentrated effort of the dancers to force themselves into the commercial world as so many little manufacturers of wares dispensable for profit. They had no market of their own, so they sought an outlet through those long-established markets which dealt in kindred goods. There were the opera, the movies, the revue, the dramatic theatre, the night club, the commercial concert field—all doing nicely, thank you, on their own, but not one of them in the least concerned with the native dance as a medium of art. Sweater girls, hoofers and, of course, Russians could all be counted on to turn a profit in the culture and amusement industries, but who ever heard of selling kinesthetic reactions?[11]

Through the last of the large-scale Bennington summers there was enmity within the ranks. Doris Humphrey's husband tried to persuade her of the futility of in-fighting, which had apparently continued unabated throughout the Bennington years:

> To hell with competition! What a waste of time and effort and between artistic groups too. . . . Among artists whose common misery is patent, one would think it could be submerged by the realization of common struggle against larger issues than personal aggrandizement in the State of Vermont.[12]

At the same time, some movement toward accommodation could be discerned. Virginia Tanner remembered hearing Pauline Lawrence predict during a run-through of *Letter to the World* that "someday all dance will be one—and the technique of each will not be so strangely different so that a well-trained dancer can do the works of today's choreographers."[13]

By 1941 the modern dance had built a strong repertory of works, many of them generated at Bennington. But how could and would these survive, as the Big Four grew older and companies disbanded? George Beiswanger saw the critical problem as one of maintaining what he termed a new American repertory, combining both modern and ballet masterworks. "Ballet," he wrote, "has the organizational base, the prestige, and the authority that go with any carrier of tradition. Dance outside its fold lacks all three, but it carries in its body the seeds of life. . . . The two need each other."[14] Beiswanger proposed either the creation of a new company that could absorb the modern repertory or the adoption of the modern dance groups by a company like the fledgling Ballet Theatre.

Doris Humphrey was open to the idea: "The proposal for a combined repertory of the ballet and the modern dance seems on the whole a very good idea."[15] Her skepticism was based not on artistic conflicts (there are none, she said, "which intelligent direction—and money—

could not cure"), but on the impossibility of securing adequate support for a new dance theater.

Lois Balcom somberly observed that dance needs in 1941 appeared to be the same as they had been in 1931. Economic conditions "have not changed in ten years and certainly the dancers' basic need for a place to work—a place with some degree of permanence and security—has not changed at all."[16]

After 1941 Bennington ceased to provide such a place for all but Martha Graham. The Humphrey-Weidman company was disbanded following Doris Humphrey's retirement in 1945. Hanya Holm had found Colorado Springs amenable to her needs, but she too was forced to disband her group in 1944. Only Martha Graham survived the war period and was able to maintain a dance company over the years.

Just after America entered the war, Margaret Lloyd surveyed Graham's career in a two-part series in the *Christian Science Monitor*. Graham, wrote Lloyd, was now at an extraordinary peak of power:

> It's a long way looking back to the stark austerities of Martha Graham's dancing in its early stages of development. Then movement told all, and movement only. The eye was not allowed to be distracted by any decorative opulence whatever. Dismal close-fitting princess gowns for the girls of the group—there was not a man in sight—moving resolutely before dark draperies. No pretty brightness, no lightness of step, the downward pull of gravitation rather than the upward spring of levitation, this was the Martha Graham dance in its experimental years. Bareness, harshness unrelieved, and mystifying rites, that's what the lay public, or those who could be enticed to a concert performance, saw.
>
> For the inner circles, the devotees, there was the affluence of freedom, the opulence of movement expressing the stripped core of feeling. And there are still some among them who lament the passing of the old, the arrival of the new Martha Graham.
>
> Now and then a streak of humor shot through the closely woven texture. Humor became satire, comment, brightness, lightness entered in, as the fabric of Miss Graham's dance grew in richness and luminosity. The inner circles widened to a larger public as the artist increasingly expanded her vision and the means of giving it shape.
>
> It's a long way looking back to the rapt mask of face, the stiffly held hands, closed fingers bent to a formal angle from the knuckles, thumbs tucked half under, the bare, tensile feet, the body movements distorted as in a dream. For now her face is alight with the feeling of the character she is playing, her fingers, once held so tightly together, separate and speak. Now the whole being dances. What began as an axial, almost static conception, and gradually extended in range, now roams free and wide, drawing constantly on the vast reservoir of movement which she reveals as inexhaustible. She wears more sumptuous, more becoming and characterizing costumes, sometimes encases her feet in slippers, and suggests scene with decor. What was once virtually a vestal group is now a supporting dance company of men and women. What once was concert, abstract and often abstruse, is now theater.
>
> For today a new Martha Graham is presenting dance as entertainment. Her current touring program consists of theater pieces. So happy a combination is the triple billing of *El Penitente, Punch and The Judy*, and *Letter to the World*, in the climactic order named, that the program stands and calls for repetition again and again. So great is her present popularity that three extra New York performances had to be arranged between touring dates, while on the road thousands turned out to cheer.[17]

The following year Lloyd wrote a profile of Arch Lauterer, a two-part article that sheds light on Lauterer's collaborations with Martha Graham:

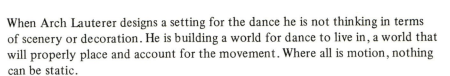

When Arch Lauterer designs a setting for the dance he is not thinking in terms of scenery or decoration. He is building a world for dance to live in, a world that will properly place and account for the movement. Where all is motion, nothing can be static.

"Each plastic form must be so designed as to live in time—the particular rhythmic and emotional time of the dance," he said in a recent interview.

Witness those wonderful black portals that formed the background for the early Bennington productions of Martha Graham's legend of Emily Dickinson, *Letter to the World*. They were an intrinsic part of the action—ominous in their openings, as for the entrance of the Ancestress, dolorous in their closing upon the departure of the Ancestress and the Lover, stern with portent during the brighter moments, as when the remembrance of party gaiety passes before them.

Even the white bench downstage, which suggests a garden seat, is a part of what is going on inside the drama. When Emily frolics innocently with the playful, spritely March, they turn the bench upside down to make a swing. The Ancestress, strict Puritan that she is, reprovingly compels Emily to help her set it right again, placing it with minute exactness just as it was before. The white bench is still when Emily is still, when Emily in her white dress sits in the white stillness of peace following resignation, when turbulence has been resolved into the serenity of joy in creative work.

A further example of the activity of this dance setting was described by the young director: "The way the outer, visual world supports the inner emotion is illustrated by the entrance of the Lover. It is seen first in the shadow cast by the wall (of portals) through which he is to enter, then, delicate as an eggshell, the breaking up of the shadow as he comes onto the stage of Emily's life, and finally, the lengthening of the shadow into an entire dark world when he is gone. What has happened emotionally through movement has been borne out by what the visual picture is saying."

Or, again, in the Graham comedy of warfare on the domestic front—*Punch and The Judy*—a cleft in the bare wall, stage left, rear, turns into a window that can be opened and through which Pegasus can enter.

"The window had to be dreamed before it could appear, before it could be opened and Pegasus could come. If the window had been painted on, defined from the beginning, and immobile, the setting would have been deprived of all that motion—mental, physical and emotional." And there would have been no visible means of ingress for the escapist-dream.

He compares the building of a dance world to architecture. "Everything must be related to the moments of life to be enacted. The relationship of the quality of the dance movement to the objects which make up its world must be considered.

"You cannot have anything on the stage not related to the dance, because dance movement itself is so alive it would make anything not belonging to it look dead. Where an object is, and what it does, its part in the unfolding of action and emotion, is more important than how it looks. Decor, the outward aspect of a setting, may be what hits the audience first, but what sinks in is the architecture as it is proven by the movement. This kind of architecture is proven only by living movement, whereas decor, in the conventional sense, exists whether the stage is alive or dead.

"Economy in the art of dance is fundamental rather than financial. It is essential to force and clarity. It is a good thing there has not been more money to spend on modern dance productions, for it might have brought a temptation to be lavish. Money does not simplify the problem."

Indeed, the problem has little to do with money. It is primarily spatial. The dance must have space to move freely in its own realm, a realm of fantasy, not fact. The problem is to make this realm practicable for the dancer, valid to the spectator, and truthful in itself. . . .

It was when Martha Graham was taking her first steps into theater that they met. He had worked on the very problem that she had come to realize was her problem, and she was trying to do what he had been hoping somebody would do. Always he had regarded scene design as something more than decoration. Always he had been searching for movement as the core. And she was looking for a world in which to place her new theater dance. It was a most felicitous meeting of minds.

Panorama was produced in the Bennington Armory. The setting, framed by screens, not on a raised platform but on the Armory floor, was made of varied levels, and these levels, Mr. Lauterer points out, were used to make a viable stage for the dance rather than to adorn it with startling scenic effects. It was a more or less tentative effort in a new direction.

The combined ideas took more tangible shape in the *American Document* of 1938, again produced in the Bennington Armory. Here the spatial problem was "to make a cool, clear, fast world, allowing for the rapid exits and entrances required by Martha's conception in the minstrel form, and giving it a third dimension by opening up the back as well as the sides" (an idea that was developed in later works).

In [1940] came *El Penitente* and the first production of *Letter to the World*, this time in the College Theater. In the tender and reverent little miracle play, many properties are used, and not one that is nonessential. These, interwoven with the action, create its world. There is no setting but that which the three dance players evoke in the imagination.

"Here," Mr. Lauterer says, "inarticulate religious feelings are articulated in a continuous flow of religious imagery."

Just as in *Letter to the World* (which was revised to its present high estate) "the poetic imagery hitherto existent only in Emily Dickinson's verse is made concrete in a continuous stream of clear-cut movement imagery within its world. Poetry, dance and architecture are blended into a single whole."[18]

"To do a theater dance production is to match function and form in every detail," Mr. Lauterer says. "The significance of objects, forms and spatial arrangements lies in the degree of resistance projected from them. This resistance, the dynamic expression of forms, sharpens the meaning, both kinesthetically and emotionally, of the dance movement."

Mr. Lauterer's ideas may be in part derived from the stagecraft of Adolphe Appia, but they are individually applied to modern dance theater. Appia began with music as the source of his inspiration, later explored the possibilities of "living light," and even later, after meeting Jaques-Dalcroze, the plastic use of the human acting or dancing body.

"The designed control of lighting planned in collaboration with the movement," Mr. Lauterer says, "helps to determine the appearance of objects and areas of space as they enter into or recede from the action, enabling them to live in time along with the dancers as they proceed from situation to situation."

Meanwhile, the music furnishes a continuous propulsion, underscoring, traveling with, or opposing the action. All is inextricably tied together.

"The world for dance must be envisaged before it can be made." The preparation is an evolution of setting, music, and so on, in pace with the development of the choreography.

In a Martha Graham work, her ideas are pretty sure to dominate. She has a voice in every department of her productions. What she does with movement tempers what Mr. Lauterer does with setting; yet he, with his plastic design and recognition of movement as the heart of theater, may influence the choreography. As ideas multiply and grow, one cannot always recall their authorship or incipient state. But movement is the keystone of the structure.

In the dance comedy, *Punch and The Judy*, "a busy world had to be created to hold the busy action. For the combination of periods and style in movement, there had to be a corresponding combination of styles and period in setting."

And that is why the focal point of the Three Fates . . . around a large globe and library chair, against a draped wall, stage right, is done in the style of a Copley painting; the entry to the unpeaceful domicile of Punch and his recalcitrant mate, with its touch of commedia dell'arte, is in Renaissance-Baroque; and the region at stage left, with the wall that turns into a window for The Judy's escapist-dream Pegasus to enter, and below it the "petrified beauty-rest mattress" for Punch to return to between adventures outside and inside the home, is Modern.

The world for dance is neither a conventional stage set nor a copy of the exterior world. It is a world having the phantasmagorial aspect of dreams. It must be veracious, not in the sense of material realism, but in that of its own inner realities. . . .[19]

THE SESSION IN BRIEF

Graduate credit was offered for the first time. The Humphrey-Weidman and Graham companies were in residence. Additions to the dance curriculum were Tap Technique and Technique of Modern Dance for Teachers. Charles Weidman taught the master course and conducted the first repertory class. The notation course, offered in 1940, was dropped.[20]

FACULTY AND STAFF

Dance Division: Martha Graham, Doris Humphrey, Charles Weidman (Ethel Butler, Claudia Moore, Maria Maginnis, associates for the three) and Harriet Roeder, associate for Hanya Holm. Festival productions: Arch Lauterer, stage designer. William Bales taught Tap Technique. Faculty included Louis Horst, Erick Hawkins, Bessie Schönberg, and Norman Lloyd.

STUDENTS

Total 126, ages 15-44 from 28 states. Including 17 men. Dance 90, drama 14, music 17, theater design 5. Among 39 teachers enrolled in the Dance Division were Virginia Tanner, Fannie Aronson, Theodora Wiesner. 51 dancers, apprentices, and members of two companies, including Pearl Lack [Lang] for her first Bennington summer and Sasha Liebich [Mark Ryder] for his. Joseph Gornbein [Gifford] and Iris Mabry.

LECTURES

No listings available. John Martin gave a series of lectures on the state of the dance.

SPECIAL PERFORMANCES

The School of the Arts participated in the Green Mountain Festival, celebrating Vermont's Sesquicentennial. The Humphrey-Weidman Company performed *Alcina Suite, Atavisms,* and *The Shakers*. Martha Graham and Dance Group performed *Every Soul Is a Circus*. The Vermont State Symphony Orchestra played for the drama and music productions and then provided accompaniment at the Bennington Festival (but not for the dance productions). There were numerous student projects and a concert by Erick Hawkins, Jane Dudley, and Jean Erdman.

Doris Humphrey and Charles Weidman at Bennington. Photograph courtesy of *Dance Observer*.

12, 19, and 26 July and 2, 9, and 16 August 1941

Weekly workshops presenting student projects. Including ***Dances with words*** *chor* Mary-Averett Seelye. ***Pentatonic Study*** *chor* Nina Fonaroff, *mus* [Lothar] Windsperger. ***Study in Dissonance*** *chor* Jane Dudley *mus* Windsperger. ***Diagonal*** *chor* Virginia Tanner, a. *mus* Betty Jean Horner, danced with set. b. *mus* Giovannina deBlasiis, danced without set, *danc* group of 8. ***The Hoofer*** (Study in 5/4) *chor* Fonaroff. ***Bird Spell*** (Air Primitive) *chor* Iris Mabry, *mus* Yolanda Lorenz. ***Fare Thee Well*** (Secular Medieval) *chor* Pearl Lack [Lang], *mus* Phyllis Cunningham. ***Religious Medieval Study*** *chor* Mabry, *mus* Lorenz. ***Composition for a Fugitive Spot*** (Cerebral) *chor* David Campbell, *mus* Maxwell Powers. ***With words*** *chor* and words Tanner. A series of dances with words, including ***The Evening*** *chor* Joseph Gornbein [Gifford], *poem* John Malcolm Brinnin. ***Patrick's Day Parade*** *dir and chor* William Bales, *mus* Harrigan and Hart, *danc* group of nine (Advanced Tap Dancing class). Humphrey-Weidman Repertory Class: ***Lynch Town*** *chor* Charles Weidman *mus* Lehman Engel, *danc* group of 18. ***The Shakers*** *chor* Doris Humphrey, *mus* Traditional, *danc* group of 15.

Nina Fonaroff's *The Hoofer* was likely a first study for her popular solo *Hoofer on a Fiver* [see 1942 Chronology]. The two Humphrey-Weidman repertory works were the only repertory works taught in Bennington summer sessions.

19 July 1941

Erick Hawkins, with Jean Erdman (assisting artist) and Jane Dudley (guest artist). College Theatre. *Pianist* Ralph Gilbert. Program: ***Trailbreaker-Kentucky** chor* Hawkins (solo), *mus* Gilbert. ***The Ballad of Molly Pitcher** chor* Dudley (solo), *mus* Earl Robinson (sung by Richard Chamberlain), *verses* Edwin Rolfe, *cos* Edythe Gilfond. ***Trickster Coyote** chor* Hawkins (solo), *mus* Henry Cowell (woodwinds played by Cowell), *mask* James W. Harker, *cos* Gilfond. ***Chaconne: The Pilgrim's Progress** chor* Hawkins (solo), *mus* Wallingford Riegger, *set* Philip Stapp. ***Yankee Bluebritches–A Green Mountain Dance** chor* Hawkins (solo), *mus* Hunter Johnson, *set & cos* Charlotte Trowbridge. ***Harmonica Breakdown** chor* Dudley (solo), *mus* Sonny Terry and Oh Red (recorded). ***In Time of Armament** chor* Hawkins, *mus* Johnson, *danc* Hawkins and Erdman. *See Catalog.

13 and 15 August 1941

A Program of Dance Projects. College Theatre. I. Directed by Louis Horst: 1. ***Fanfare** chor* Joseph Gornbein [Gifford], *mus* Carl Miller. 2. ***Dilemma** chor* Iris Mabry, *mus* [Federico] Mompou. 3. ***Three Sarabandes** mus* Ralph Gilbert, ***a. Pattern for the Imperial Procession** chor* David Campbell, ***b. Act of Faith** chor* Mabry, ***c. Sarabande** chor* Ethel Butler. II. Directed by Bessie Schönberg. ***"Mississippi Sketches" from "The River" by Pare Lorenz** chor* Bessie Schönberg, *mus* Norman Lloyd, *light* Stanton Benjamin. 1. ***"From as far west as Idaho . . . ,"*** 2. ***"And we made cotton king . . . ,"*** 3. ***"We built a hundred cities and a thousand towns,"*** *danc* group of 9, 4 singers. III. Directed by Horst: 1. ***Night Suite** chor* group, *dir* Nik Krevitsky, Fannie Aronson, Gertrude Green, *mus* Darius Milhaud. In 5 parts for 4 dancers. 2. ***Yankee Doodle Greets Columbus, 1492*** (An American Fantasy *chor* Nina Fonaroff, *mus* Horst, *danc* Fonaroff, Mabry, and 5 dancers. IV. ***Today's Stepchild** chor and dir* Harriet Roeder, *mus* Zoe Williams, *light* Octavia Frees, *danc* Carolyn Wilson, Roeder, and group of 7. V. ***Es Mujer** chor and dir* William Bales, *mus* Traditional *arr* Louis Sandi and Geronimo Baquerio Foster, recorded by Carlos Chavez, *light* Teru Osato, *danc* Osato, Bales, and group of 8.

> *Program Note:* The theme of the dance is based on the cultural tradition that a child is accepted as an adult when she is to become a bride. The title is a Mexican idiom translated "She is a Woman."

VI. ***From "The Swallow-Book" by Ernst Toller** Dir* Martha Hill, Arch Lauterer, Norman Lloyd. *Production Scheme* Lauterer, *Movement and Dance* Hill, *Music and Speech* Lloyd. *Cast* Edward Glass with group of 16. *Musicians* Lloyd, Richard Chamberlain, Ruth Ives, Ruth Lloyd.

At least two of these projects had subsequent performances: William Bales' *Es Mujer* was his first major work. It had its New York premiere on 10 March 1942 at the Studio Theatre. Margaret Lloyd noted that

> the simplicity of the work, its restrained intensity and solemn dignity, its atmosphere of primitive naivete, and the unpretentious effectiveness of its well-wrought design won it instant recognition.[21]

Lois Balcom, *Dance Observer*:

> This festival presentation of the age old rite of a young girl's preparation for marriage, a young man's choosing of his bride, and the attendance of the group upon both, has freshness and feeling, style and coherence. [The dancers] have so possessed themselves of the traditional content of the dance that they are able to present it with a sense of inner conviction instead of as an external device, which is too often the defect of a modern dancer's gesture toward primitivism.[22]

Nina Fonaroff's *Yankee Doodle Greets Columbus, 1492* was, said Balcom, distinctly improved over its "pre-Bennington presentation" (25 May 1941, Studio Theatre), and "might stand as a 'before-and-after treatment' testimonial, to the benefits of Bennington's project system."[23]

BENNINGTON FESTIVAL

3–17 August 1941

27 performances in all, 9 of them in dance. Concerts given on campus, opera and drama mounted at the General Stark Theatre (a movie house) in the town of Bennington. Five performances by Doris Humphrey-Charles Weidman and Company and four by Martha Graham and Dance Company in the College Theatre (capacity 256, total dance audience 2273).

3 and 4 August 1941

The School for Wives by Molière. *The Impresario* by [W. A.] Mozart. General Stark Theatre, Bennington, Vermont. I. ***The School for Wives*** *dir* Francis Fergusson, *mus dir* Otto Luening, *ballets chor and dir* Martha Hill, *screens* Edwin Avery Park, *English version* Emily Sweetser. *Cast* Edward Thommen, Joseph M. Dixon, Ray Malon, Shirley Stanwood, Elisabeth James, Paul Rockwell, David Crowell. *Danc* Mary-Averett Seelye, Sidney Stambaugh, Ray Malon, Joan Cheeseman, Muriel Brenner, Ita Hoxsie. With two "Ballet Interludes" and a "Dance Pantomime." II. ***The Impresario: An Operatic Squabble*** *scenario* Eric Blom, *staged* Fergusson, *mus dir* Luening, *screens* Park. *Singers* Richard Chamberlain, Ethel Luening, Ruth Ives/ Margaret Codd. *Musicians* 20-piece orchestra, including members of the Vermont State Symphony Orchestra. *Conductor* Otto Luening.

Reviews

The School for Wives

Bennington Banner:

> The ballets are done to the music . . . of Lully and Rameau. They tell the story of Pantaloon, the father of three charming daughters, Isabella, Sylvia and Fanciula, who are enamored of Amorosa, the lover. Throughout the ballets, Pantaloon is harrassed by Zani, a comic character. . . . Excellently produced, effectively lighted and brilliantly acted.[24]

The Impresario

Henry Cowell, *Dance Observer*:

> Sung superbly, acted with wit—a stage production to delight any jaded metropolitan fop as well as the less initiated.[25]

"Smith," *Variety*:

> It was presented in English for the first time in this century . . . in a performance which was probably equal to anything the Metropolitan might have done. . . . English translations by Eric Bloom [*sic*] with additional dialogue by Francis Fergusson were modern and yet perfectly attuned to the story. . . . Opera has been brought up to date so well that, if longer, it would be adequate for Broadway.[26]

9 and 16 August 1941

Ralph Kirkpatrick, Harpsichord Recital. Carriage Barn, Bennington College. *Mus* Jacques Champion de Chambonnières, J. S. Bach, Thomas Morley, Orlando Gibbons, Giles Farnaby, J. P. Rameau, Bernardo Pasquini, François Dandrieu, Allessandro Poglietti, Domenico Scarlatti.

10 and 17 August 1941

Henry Cowell, Concert of Contemporary Music. Carriage Barn, Bennington College. With Ethel Luening, Ruth Ives, sopranos. Otto Luening, flute. Lionel Nowak, piano. *Mus* Richard Franko Goldman, John Becker, Herbert Elwell, Edwin Gerschefski, Walter Piston, Lou Harrison, Louis Horst, John Alden Carpenter, John Barrows, David Van Vactor, Henry Cowell.

Cowell also reviewed the concert in *Modern Music*.[27]

10 and 11 August 1941

The Barker: A Play of Carnival Life in Three Acts, by Kenyon Nicholson. General Stark Theatre, Bennington. *Dir* Francis Fergusson, *sets* Ben Hudelson, *cos* Edward Thommen. *Cast* Joseph M. Dixon, Paul Rockwell, Ben Hudelson, Faith Richardson, Shirley Stanwood, David Crowell, Elisabeth James, Ray Malon, Will Parker, Marion C. Fergusson, Edward Thommen, Virginia Lunsford, and 14 extras. *Hawaiian Girls* Natalie Disston, Hortense Lieberthal (dancers).

THE SCHOOL FOR WIVES

by

MOLIERE

Sunday, August 3
8:30 p.m.

Monday, August 4
The General Stark Theatre

English version by .... Emily Sweetser
Directed by .... Francis Fergusson
Musical direction by .... Otto Luening
Ballets composed and directed by .... Martha Hill
Screens designed by .... Edwin Avery Park

CAST IN ORDER OF APPEARANCE

Arnolphe, alias M. de la Souche, who has ideas on educating wives .... Edward Thommen
Chrysale, his skeptical friend .... Joseph M. Dixon
Alain } Arnolphe's servants { .... Ray Malon
Georgette } .... Shirley Stanwood
Agnes, the innocent girl whom Arnolphe is trying to educate as a wife .... Elisabeth James
Horace, a young man in love with Agnes .... Paul Rockwell
Oronte, Horace's father and Arnolphe's friend .... David Crowell

MEMBERS OF THE BALLET

Pantalone .... Mary-Averett Seelye
Amoroso .... Sidney Stambaugh
Zani .... Ray Malon
Isabella .... Joan Cheeseman
Sylvia .... Muriel Brenner
Fanciulla .... Ita Hoxsie

The Scene is a street in front of a house where Arnolphe keeps Agnes

SYNOPSIS

PART I

1. Overture .... Orchestra and Ballet
   Overture from Concerto .... *Lully*
2. Acts I and II
3. Ballet Interlude .... Orchestra and Ballet
   Louré from Concerto .... *Lully*
4. Act III
5. Ballet Interlude .... Orchestra, Amoroso, Isabella, Sylvia and Fanciulla
   Acanthe et Cephise, "Chansons de nos plaisirs" .... *Rameau*
   Vocal Solo .... Reba Marcus

The curtain will be lowered between Part I and Part II

PART II

1. Overture .... Orchestra and Ballet
   Bourrée from Concerto .... *Lully*
2. Act IV
3. Dance Pantomime .... Orchestra, Ballet, Horace, Alain, Georgette and Agnes
   Marche et Passepied from Concerto .... *Lully*
4. Act V
5. Finale .... Orchestra, Ballet and Cast
   Rigaudon from Concerto .... *Lully*

Intermission: Fifteen Minutes

HENRY COWELL

Concerts of Contemporary Music

assisted by

ETHEL LUENING, *soprano*
RUTH IVES, *soprano*
OTTO LUENING, *flute*
LIONEL NOWAK, *piano*

Sunday, August 10
4:00 p.m.

Sunday, August 17
The Carriage Barn

PROGRAM

I.

Divertimento for Flute and Piano .... *Richard Franko Goldman*
Aperitif — Icy Pastorale — Tempo di Fado
Otto Luening and Lionel Nowak

II.

You and I .... *John Becker*
Ousel-Cock .... *Herbert Elwell*
Meeting at Night and Parting at Morning .... *Edwin Gerschefski*
Ruth Ives

III.

Sonata for Flute and Piano .... *Walter Piston*
Allegro moderato e grazioso — Adagio — Allegro vivace
Otto Luening and Lionel Nowak

IV.

Music for Flute and Percussion .... *Lou Harrison*
Otto Luening, Henry Cowell, Frank Wigglesworth

V.

Change (1925) Poem by Witter Bynner .... *Louis Horst*
That Soothin' Song (1926) Poem by Langston Hughes .... *John Alden Carpenter*
Song (1941) Words by the composer .... *John Barrows*
I Know a Maiden Fair (1934) Poem by Longfellow .... *David Van Vactor*
Ethel Luening

Intermission: Fifteen Minutes

VI.

Piano Works .... *Henry Cowell*
The Tides of Manaunaun
The Aeolian Harp
Exultation
Sinister Resonance
Antinomy
Fairy Answer
Whirling Dervish
The Banshee
Lilt of the Reel
Advertisement

Henry Cowell

9, 11, 13, 15, and 17 August 1941

Doris Humphrey–Charles Weidman and Company. College Theatre. Program: ***Decade: A Biography of Modern Dance from 1930 to 1940.*** *See Catalog.

10, 12, 14, and 16 August 1941

Martha Graham and Dance Company. College Theatre. Program: I. ***El Penitente*** (production credits and cast identical to its premiere in 1940 except for the addition of a mask by Noguchi). II. ***Letter to the World*** (production credits same as 1940 premiere). Characters: *One Who Dances* Martha Graham. *One Who Speaks* Jean Erdman. *Lover* Erick Hawkins. *Ancestress* Jane Dudley. *March* Merce Cunningham. *Young Girl* Ethel Butler. *Fairy Queen* Nina Fonaroff. *Two Children* Pearl Lack [Lang], Marion Scott. Madge Friedman, Harriet Garrett, Barbara Livingston, Iris Mabry, Frances Sunstein, David Campbell, David Zellmer, Sasha Liebich [Mark Ryder]. III. ****Punch and The Judy chor*** Graham, *mus* Robert McBride. *See Catalog.

This was the order on the printed program, but after the first performance the program opened with *El Penitente* and closed with *Letter to the World*. The new work, *Punch and The Judy*, was sandwiched in between.

NOTES

1. Rosalyn Krokover, "Vermont Center Is Host to Dance Devotees," *Musical Courier* 124 (September 1941): 14.
2. Interview with Francis Fergusson.
3. Henry Cowell, "Music at Bennington," *Dance Observer* 8, no. 7 (August-September 1941): 96-97.
4. Sherman Conrad, "Bennington Festival: 1941," *Nation* 153, no. 9 (30 August 1941): 186-87.
5. Mary Jo Shelly, "Eighth Summer at Bennington," *Dance Observer* 8, no. 3 (March 1941): 36-37. For other surveys of the session, see also Steffi Nossen, "Bennington Festival 1941," *Educational Dance* 4, no. 3 (August-September 1941): 12-13, and Esther Rosenblatt, "Bennington—1941," *Dance Observer* 8, no. 7 (August-September 1941): 91-92, and Walter Terry, "Bennington in Action," *Dance* 10, no. 1 (October 1941): 10-11.
6. Mary Jo Shelly, *Dance Observer* 8, no. 3 (March 1941): 37.
7. Doris Humphrey, "A Home for Humphrey-Weidman," *Dance Observer* 7, no. 9 (November 1940): 124-25.
8. Margaret Lloyd, *Christian Science Monitor*, 30 August 1941.
9. Walter Terry, *New York Herald Tribune*, 3 August 1941.
10. John Martin, *New York Times*, 4 January 1942.
11. Ibid.
12. Letter from Charles Francis Woodford to Doris Humphrey, Summer 1941 (undated) [Doris Humphrey Collection, C479]. Selma Jeanne Cohen, *Doris Humphrey: An Artist First* (Middletown, Conn.: Wesleyan University Press, 1972), p. 128, places this letter in 1934, but Andrew Mark Wentink, "The Doris Humphrey Collection: An Introduction and Guide," *Bulletin of The New York Public Library* 77, no. 1 (Autumn 1973): 80-142, places it in 1941. Woodford discusses *Decade* in this letter, and so the 1941 date is confirmed.
13. Letter from Virginia Tanner to the author, 21 December 1976.
14. George W. Beiswanger, "Dance Repertory—American Style," *Theatre Arts* 25, no. 6 (June 1941): 443-50.
15. *Theatre Arts* 25, no. 10 (October 1941): 774.
16. Lois Balcom, "It's a Trend!" *Dance Observer* 8, no. 6 (June-July 1941): 78-79.
17. Margaret Lloyd, "The New Martha Graham," part 1, *Christian Science Monitor*, 21 March 1942. (Part 2 was published 11 April 1942.)
18. Margaret Lloyd, "Building a World for Dance," part 1, *Christian Science Monitor*, 17 July 1943.
19. Margaret Lloyd, "Collaboration Is Multiplication, part 2, *Christian Science Monitor*, 7 August 1943.
20. Information about the 1941 session was taken from *Bennington College Bulletin* 9, no. 3 (March 1941); "Second Annual Report of the Bennington School of the Arts," Summer 1941, in *Reports of Officers, 1940-41*, Bennington College 9, no. 3 (October 1941); and a "Daily Schedule" listing classes and faculty. No complete report of the session was located.
21. Margaret Lloyd, *The Borzoi Book of Modern Dance* (New York: Alfred A. Knopf, 1949), p. 188.
22. Lois Balcom, "Projects at Bennington," *Dance Observer* 8, no. 7 (August-September 1941): 95. Note that the description of *Es Mujer* in *Don McDonagh's Complete Guide to Modern Dance* (New York: Popular Library, 1977), pp. 197-98, is of another work, not *Es Mujer*, probably Bales' *Sea Bourne* (1943).
23. Lois Balcom, *Dance Observer* 8, no. 7 (August-September 1941): 95.
24. *Bennington Banner*, 31 July 1941 and 4 August 1941.
25. Henry Cowell, *Dance Observer* 8, no. 7 (August-September 1941): 97.
26. Smith, *Variety*, 6 August 1941.
27. Henry Cowell, "Summer Festivals in the U.S.A.," *Modern Music* 19, no. 1 (November-December 1941): 42.

1942
Bennington College Summer Session: Dance

6 July 1942—15 August 1942

Drawing of Louis Horst by Aline Fruhauf.

"The War makes it impossible to hold the Festival at this time, but the basic plan of work remains the same," stated the *Bennington College Bulletin* which announced the first summer session of the college.[1] The arts curricula were to include "dance, music, painting, sculpture, graphic art, and architectural drawing." The dance curricula featured three basic areas—technique, composition, and music for the dance—which would be "augmented by study of the special uses to which the related materials of dance and music may be put for community and recreational purposes." The daily schedule of classes and workshops issued at the session's start listed three components of the College Summer Session: Dance, Government and Economics, Graphic and Plastic Arts. For the first time, the arts were not the only activity on the Bennington campus.

While the School of the Dance was holding its last session, "the first theater built expressly for the dance in America" opened less than 100 miles south of Bennington.[2] In July 1942 Ted Shawn produced a major festival of dance at Jacob's Pillow. Doris Humphrey and Charles Weidman were invited but declined. Helen Tamiris, who had never worked at Bennington, participated in a program devoted to the "Second Generation of American Dance."[3]

Out in Colorado, Hanya Holm, Arch Lauterer, and composer Roy Harris mounted two new productions.

Martha Graham and Company were in residence at Bennington for the summer. Graham mounted a revised production of *American Document* and also began planning a new work with composer Hunter Johnson. The score was commissioned by Bennington College. (*Deaths and Entrances* was completed during Graham's residency at the college in 1943 and had a preview performance there that summer. Graham, Louis Horst, and members of her company were invited back as artists-in-residence by Bennington College during the spring-summer college sessions of 1943–1945.)

The lack of a major production and festival in 1942 placed some of the younger choreographers in bold relief. A formal concert by Jean Erdman, Merce Cunningham, and Nina Fonaroff typified "that aspect of Bennington which provides a try-out theatre under felicitous conditions, not the least important element being the presence of a trained and critical audience, for young artists to show their works."[4]

Cunningham and Erdman made their joint choreographic debuts. John Cage's music was heard at Bennington for the first time (*Credo in Us*). Gregory Tucker composed a jazz score for *Ad Lib*, a piece which boasted improvisational elements.

Jane Dudley, Sophie Maslow, and William Bales repeated their New York debut program as a trio, adding two new sections of a jointly composed opening suite to music by Bach.

Henrietta Greenhood [Eve Gentry] and Nona Schurman composed new group works which drew on the small student body.

John Martin praised this opportunity for the younger generation of choreographers:

> Such a series as this is just exactly what the American dance field needs, for it abounds in gifted young artists who are generally so busy working in other people's companies that they have no time to do their own creative work. . . . All in all it does not look as if the handicaps of the first war Summer had cramped the Bennington dance project too much. Always a fairly plastic institution, it seems to have adapted itself to the situation with admirable results and a spirit which can only be described as spunky. Says Miss Shelly: "We are in no better shape to plan for the future than is any one else, but certainly no worse, and we are, after nine years, pretty tenacious."[5]

During the war years, the modern dance lost some of its skilled male dancers to the armed services. And dancing wives were left without benefit of their husbands' subsidy. As Nona Schurman put it, "The War swallowed up most of the ambitions of my generation. From 1942 on it was just a matter of keeping the wolf from the door."[6]

Walter Terry joined the armed forces as Bennington's last summer session opened. Before leaving for duty, he assessed "the record of American dance":

> During my seasons with the Herald Tribune I have seen the modern dance make its final emergence from the strangling shrouds of cultism into the bright light of pure theater. The grim countenances, the body-racking movements, the too abstract abstractions, the ear-rending musical accompaniments and the costumes, which always looked as if they had been borrowed from a house of detention, are all gone. In their place we have Martha Graham's eloquent revealing in dance of a great New England lady, Emily Dickinson . . . and her hilarious analysis of domestic squabblings in *Punch and the Judy*; Doris Humphrey has given us her document of American dance in *Decade* and Charles Weidman has proved the range of appeal for modern dance by carrying his *Flickers* from the concert stage to the Rainbow Room; discarding her occasional and violent editorials on the social state of man, Helen Tamiris has danced the simplest and the greatest editorial of her career in *Liberty Song*. In fact, all of the modern dancers have at last become truly modern, and not simply modernistic. After years of revolt from heritage, they have at last turned to that heritage for the richness it has

to offer. Ballet is recognized as a valid and usable technique for those moderns who wish to broaden their range of action, and the achievements of America's own Denishawn organization are beginning to appear again, this time through the productions of the moderns themselves.[7]

"The art of the radical American dance," wrote John Martin in 1943,

> is at the threshold of great achievement right now. Its cycle of experimentation is over and cannot be extended merely for expediency; its next cycle is as a magnificent and encompassing theater. . . . What the chances of survival are—who can say? [The modern dance] is now at the moment of development where with recognition practically expressed it could go ahead to unpredictable glories, and where, lacking that recognition, it may simply face a hungry death with its lap heaped with seeds ripe for the planting. By the nature of its unique virtues, it has no traditional material to hand down to keep barren periods busy until new leaders arise to illuminate it; if the present leaders disappear from the field before the seeds have germinated, there will be no future whatever.[8]

How could the modern dance retain vitality and yet continue to progress and develop? How could art and artist survive in a society that did not recognize their intrinsic worth? Could the modern dance maintain integrity in the face of the economic imperative to be self-supporting?

These and other issues were hotly debated within the pages of *Dance Observer* and other journals during the war years. They would gather force in the 1950s toward a revolutionary break from the past, a break as radical as the one made in the late 1920s and early 1930s. Already in 1944 John Cage noted the dissipation of the original creative force in the dance. Cage wrote in the *Dance Observer*:

> The strength that comes from firmly established art practices is not present in the modern dance today. Insecure, not having any clear direction, the modern dancer is willing to compromise and to accept influences from other more rooted art manners, enabling one to remark that certain dancers are either borrowing from or selling themselves to Broadway, others are learning from folk and oriental arts and many are either introducing into their work elements of the ballet, or, in an all-out effort, devoting themselves to it. Confronted with its history, its former power, its present insecurity, the realization is unavoidable that the strength the modern dance once had was not impersonal but was intimately connected with and ultimately dependent on the personalities and even the actual physical bodies of the individuals who imparted it.
>
> The techniques of the modern dance were once orthodox. It did not enter a dancer's mind that they might be altered. To add to them was the sole privilege of the originators.
>
> Intensive summer courses were the scenes of the new dispensations, reverently transmitted by the master-students. When the fanatically-followed leaders began, and when they continued, to desert their own teachings (adapting chiefly balletish movements to their own rapidly-growing-less-rigorous techniques), a general and profound insecurity fell over the modern dance.[9]

Horton Foote warned of the seductive powers of the profit system, of the corrosive influences of "Finance Capitalism," and of the lure of Hollywood and Broadway:

> I see dancers furiously in search of individual security. I do not like the places toward which they are turning. . . . Every day on the Theatrical Page we read of one more well-known dancer going to Broadway or Hollywood. It has become a mammoth exodus, a giant trend. I wonder what it will leave of the dynamic dance we have come to expect of our modern dancers. . . . Modern dance has reached a serious crisis in its development. . . .

> During those years when it was furiously forging an artistic manifesto the dance was surrounded by the impossible. Impossible to keep a group together, impossible to finance themselves, impossible to find an audience. A group was kept together, an audience found, things were financed. And out of the planning, the bitterness and the sacrifice great things were brought forth. . . . Dancers must not forget that much they fought and struggled to establish in those earlier years has now become safe. People are apt to look at the modern dance and wonder why it ever had to struggle so to be accepted. The best of the preceding years should be kept to enrich and feed the years to come. The dance will only become decadent if it continues solely to feed off the past, to continue to create in the old terms, to do only variations of the old themes.
>
> The period of revolt must be built upon, not discarded. It is time the American artist takes a mature attitude toward himself and his society. We have spent twenty years in decrying the materialism of America and its philosophy. Are we now going to try to make peace with that materialism, until we are so sickened by it that we begin once more the old cycle of revolt and criticism?[10]

THE SESSION IN BRIEF

First Bennington College Summer Session included courses in government and economics, and in graphic and plastic arts. The basic School of the Dance curriculum continued. Martha Graham and Company were in residence. Graham began working with Hunter Johnson on *Deaths and Entrances*. There was no festival and no major new production.

FACULTY AND STAFF

Martha Graham and Ethel Butler taught Graham technique. Henrietta Greenhood [Eve Gentry] and Nona Schurman taught Holm and Humphrey-Weidman technique, respectively. Additional faculty: Erick Hawkins, Martha Hill, Louis Horst, Hortense Lieberthal, Norman Lloyd. (Bessie Schönberg and Ruth Lloyd were on leave.) Music faculty included Otto Luening, Ethel Luening, Robert McBride, and Gregory Tucker.

STUDENTS

Total approximately 70, including Theodora Wiesner, Hazel Johnson. (No enrollment figures or roster located.)

SPECIAL EVENTS, RECITALS, AND WORKSHOPS

A weekly "Forum on War and the Future" included a "Forum on Arts and the War," with Martha Graham, Martha Hill, Louis Horst, Norman Lloyd, and Gregory Tucker participating. Robert McBride and Gregory Tucker gave a program of music for piano and woodwinds which included a two-piano version of *Punch and The Judy*. Weekly workshop compositions included *Authentic Pavanne* *chor* Jane Dudley, *mus* Arbeau, and *Authentic Galliarde* *chor* Ethel Butler, *danc* Martha Graham Group, *American Nostalgia* *chor* Theodora Wiesner, *mus* Drusa Wilker. Martha Graham presented a slightly revised version of *American Document* in the College Theatre (no program located). There were two formal concerts by young choreographers and a concluding program of dance projects and solos composed by associates for Holm and Humphrey-Weidman.

1 August 1942

Jean Erdman, Nina Fonaroff, and Merce Cunningham in "A Program of Dances." College Theatre. *Musicians* Helen Lanfer, piano. Nancy Calafati, Hazel Johnson, Helen Lanfer, Ray Malon, percussion. *Light* Joann Straus. *Cos* (for Erdman and Cunningham) Charlotte Trowbridge. Program: 1. ***Seeds of Brightness*** *chor* Erdman, Cunningham, *mus* Norman Lloyd. 2. ***Theodolina, Queen of the Amazons (Fantasy of a little creature): a. Theodolina, the huntress, b. Theodolina dances for joy, c. Theodolina has a thought, d. Theodolina flies through space.*** *chor and danc* Fonaroff, *mus* Louis Horst. 3. ***Credo in Us*** *chor* Erdman, Cunningham, *mus* John Cage. 4. ***Renaissance Testimonials*** *chor* Cunningham, *mus* Maxwell Powers. 5. ***Cafe***

Chantant–Five A.M. *chor and danc* Fonaroff, *mus* Larmanjat. 6. ****The Transformations of Medusa*** *chor* Erdman, *mus* Horst. 7. ***Hoofer on a Fiver*** *chor and dance* Fonaroff, *mus* Tcherepnin. 8. ****Ad Lib*** *chor* Erdman, Cunningham, *mus* Gregory Tucker. *See Catalog.

Nina Fonaroff's pieces had been performed previously (*Hoofer on a Fiver* was developed the previous summer in a Bennington workshop performance). This was Jean Erdman and Merce Cunningham's joint choreographic debut. They presented the same program on 20 October 1942 at the Humphrey-Weidman Studio Theatre, for which occasion Cunningham added a second solo.

2 August 1942

Robert McBride, woodwinds, piano. Gregory Tucker, piano. Fairview Rehearsal Room, Bennington College. Program included ***Punch and The Judy*** (two pianos) *mus* McBride: ***The Three Fates, Overture, Soliloquy of Judy, Pony Express, Pegasus, Punch. Prelude, In the Clearing*** *mus* Tucker.

9 August 1942

Martha Graham Dance Company. College Theatre. Program: ***American Document.*** No program located.

13 August 1942

Jane Dudley, Sophie Maslow, William Bales, assisted by members of Martha Graham Dance Company in a Program of Dances. College Theatre. *Pianists* Helen Lanfer, Hazel Johnson. *Light* Joann Straus, Dorothea Douglas. *Cos* Edythe Gilfond, Charlotte Trowbridge, Helen Bottomly. Program: 1. ***Suite: a. *Scherzo, b. *Loure, c. Gigue*** *chor and danc* Dudley, Maslow, Bales, *mus* [J. S.] Bach. 2. ***Two Dust Bowl Ballads: a. I Ain't Got No Home in This World Anymore, b. Dusty Old Dust*** *chor* Maslow, *mus* Woody Guthrie, 3. ***Short Story*** *chor* Dudley, *mus* Paul Creston, *danc* Dudley, Elizabeth Halpern, Pearl Lack [Lang]. 4. ***To a Green Mountain Boy*** *chor* Bales, *mus* Zoe Williams. 5. Excerpts from ***Folksay*** *chor* Maslow, words from Carl Sandburg's "The People Yes," folksongs sung by Burl Ives, *readers* David Campbell, Ray Malon, *danc* Maslow, Joan Cheeseman, Pearl Lack [Lang], Margaret Strater, David Campbell, Sasha Liebich [Mark Ryder], David Zellmer. 6. ***Black Tambourine*** *chor and danc* Bales, *mus* Williams. 7. ***Harmonica Breakdown*** *chor and danc* Dudley, *mus* Sonny Terry. *See Catalog.

The Dudley-Maslow-Bales trio had made its debut at the Studio Theatre, 10 March 1942. For the Bennington program they introduced two new parts of the opening Bach *Suite*.

14 August 1942

A Program of Dance Projects and Solos by Henrietta Greenhood [Eve Gentry], Nona Schurman, and Dance Students. College Theatre. Program: 1. ***It's a Bargain at Any Price*** (A Satire on Advertising) *chor and script* Greenhood, *mus* Betty Jean Horner, Mathilde Zwilling. *Musicians* Horner, Zwilling. *Animated radios and speaking accompaniment* Elisabeth Marvin, Ray Malon. ***Introduction: In the Private Office of Mr. Big, Business Tycoon. Episode I: Patent Medicines. Interlude–Mutual Admiration. Episode II: Beauty Aids. Interlude. Episode III: Just Open a Can. Episode IV: Four Day Diet. Finale.*** *Danc* Greenhood and group of 6. 2. ***Restless Song*** *chor* Nona Schurman, *mus* Hazel Johnson, *danc* Schurman and group of 7. 3. ***Tell Me of the Living*** *chor and danc* Schurman, *poem* Carl Sandburg, *reader* William Bales. 4. ***Four Walls Blues*** *chor and danc* Greenhood *mus* Monde Lux Lewis. 5. ***Running Laughter*** *chor and danc* Schurman, *mus* Poldowski.

It's A Bargain at Any Price was Henrietta Greenhood's [Gentry's] first professional group work in the East. She hoped to mount it in New York, but the war made that impossible. Norman Lloyd was her adviser on the project. She subsequently published the script.[11] Said Gentry:

> I felt in the face of the War that the practice of advertising was frivolous, outrageous and irresponsible. I wanted to show how the media affected the public's thinking, how it was getting people to buy and do things they didn't need and how, in spite of the War, it was continuing as though there were nothing more serious in life. It was a humorous work. I used voice and sound. In that time we got most of our advertising from the radio. I had two people with props and costumes to suggest radios.[12]

DORIS HUMPHREY AND CHARLES WEIDMAN

SUMMER COURSES: June 22 to Aug. 15 - 4 to 6 P. M. - 5 days a week
Fee for Six Weeks Course: **$75.00**
One Week: $15.00

MISS HUMPHREY AND MR. WEIDMAN WILL TEACH EXCLUSIVELY IN NEW YORK CITY THIS SUMMER

SUMMER EVENING CLASSES
for
PHYSICAL FITNESS, RECREATIONAL DANCES, BODY MECHANICS

NO PREVIOUS TRANING NECESSARY — MONDAY AND THURSDAY — 7 to 8 P. M.

FEES: $6.00 for 10 Classes — $1.00 for 1 class

108 WEST 16th STREET — NEW YORK CITY — CH. 2-9819

JUNE COURSE
Intensive Four Weeks of
Dance Techniques and Composition
June 8 through July 4, 1942

Martha Graham
Louis Horst

For information address:
Secretary - Martha Graham Studio
66 Fifth Avenue, New York, N. Y.

BENNINGTON 1942

Ninth Season — July 6 to August 15

Full curriculum of study in the American Dance

Martha Hill, Director

Martha Graham and Group

Louis Horst — Eric Hawkins
Norman Lloyd — Henrietta Greenhood
Bessie Schönberg — Nona Schurman

Summer Session includes:
THE ARTS · GOVERNMENT & ECONOMICS · SCIENCE
Forum on The War and the Future

For information address:
DIRECTOR OF ADMISSIONS, SUMMER SESSION
BENNINGTON COLLEGE, BENNINGTON, VERMONT

BARBARA METTLER
SCHOOL of RHYTHMIC MOVEMENT

Franklin, New Hampshire

SUMMER SESSION, 1942
July 6 — August 2

Recreational and
Professional Courses

MAJOR SUBJECTS
Technique of Rhythmic Body Movement, Creative Dance Expression, Sound in relation to Movement, Dance Production, Dance History, Dance Theory, Dance Pedagogy.

MINOR SUBJECTS
Dance Notation, Dance Criticism, Related Arts and Crafts, Related Sciences.

Address inquiries:
Mettler Farm, R. F. D. No. 1, Franklin, N. H.

---

hanya holm studio, new york, n. y.

summer courses 1942

june course—four weeks, june 8-july 4

late summer course—three weeks, august 24-september 12

instructor: miriam kagan (member of the hanya holm company)

hanya holm will teach personally the first part of the june course.

regular fall term starts sept. 28, 1942

215 west 11 street — new york, n. y. — wa 9-6530

Advertisement in *Dance Observer.*

Reviews

Lois Balcom, *Dance Observer*:

> The general scheme of the composition is self-evident from a glance at characters and episodes, the former including a Business Tycoon called Mr. Big, Secretaries, Advertising Man (danced by Miss Greenhood), and Radio Commentators, and the latter touching upon Patent Medicines, Beauty Aids, Four Day Diet and what not. The lines . . . were rather more hilarious than the dancing itself and gave the audience a merry time. This is not to say that the movement was not in keeping with and clearly illustrative of the script, but rather more imagination and invention were needed to give the dancing real choreographic interest. . . . The various episodes tended to take on the character of incidental dances or even pantomimic skits which is a disappointment to an audience accustomed to a more integrated type of composition.[13]

Nona Schurman recalled that Norman Lloyd had his music students watch *Restless Song* to learn how to handle theme and variation:

> The piece was strictly in the Humphrey style—musical treatment, theme and variation, no plot, no characters. (In that period, we were not supposed to be characters; we were instruments. That was part of the revolution.) It wasn't dramatic enough to please the Louis Horst contingent. The idea of the piece was to give a feeling of uprooted people, always having to move on to something new but at the same time yearning for stability. I felt variation was an ideal way of trying to say this because development, even in terms of character, was impossible for them.[14]

Lois Balcom, *Dance Observer*·

> Miss Schurman's composition was based upon a more abstract choreographic medium [than was Henrietta Greenhood's]. Simple themes, contrived from quite interesting movement, were clearly worked out and group patterns nicely handled although perhaps without startling originality in either element.[15]

Neither *It's a Bargain at Any Price* nor *Restless Song* was Performed again. The solos on the program had been composed previously.

NOTES

1. *Bennington College Bulletin* 10, no. 3 (March 1942): 10. The *Bulletin*, a "Daily Schedule" of classes, and a "Calendar of Events" are the sources for information about the 1942 session. No retrospective report giving detailed information on the session itself, its students, and its faculty was located.
2. Anthony Fay, "The Festival of '42: A History-Making Summer at Jacob's Pillow," *Dance Magazine* 50, no. 7 (July 1976): 61–65.
3. Ibid.
4. Lois Balcom, "Bennington in 1942," *Dance Observer* 9, no. 7 (August-September 1942): 87.
5. John Martin, *New York Times*, 23 August 1942.
6. Letter from Nona Schurman to the author, 26 March 1978.
7. Walter Terry, "Final Criticism," *New York Herald Tribune*, 12 July 1942.
8. John Martin, "The Dance Completes a Cycle," *American Scholar* 12, no. 2 (Spring 1943): 215. (Reprinted in this book, pp. 288–90.
9. John Cage, "Grace and Clarity," *Dance Observer* 11, no. 9 (November 1944): 108–109.
10. Horton Foote, "The Long, Long Trek," *Dance Observer* 11, no. 8 (October 1944): 98–99.
11. Eve Gentry, *It's a Bargain at Any Price* (New York: Gentry Press, 1942) [Dance Collection of the New York Public Library].
12. Interview with Eve Gentry.
13. Balcom, p. 88.
14. Letter from Nona Schurman.
15. Balcom, p. 88.

Bennington Premieres

Forty-two dances that had first performances in formal concert series and festivals at Bennington are treated in this section in detail, arranged chronologically beginning in 1935. (No new dances were presented in 1934.) Excepted are ballets performed by the Ballet Caravan in their world debut at Bennington in 1936. (For further information, consult Nancy Reynolds, *Repertory in Review: 40 Years of The New York City Ballet*, pp. 53-63.)

The Catalog documents the original Bennington productions and gives evidence of subsequent productions. Information was culled from original published programs, official school reports, reviews and articles, interviews, photographs, and films. Very few accounts from this period describe dance movement or choreographic structure, but the composite of credits, recollections, reviews, and photographs give some idea of the qualities and nature of these dances at their inception. Analyses and descriptions by other writers, using later productions and films as their basis, are cited as additional references. For a few dances, no information could be obtained beyond verifying their Bennington premiere—not even by consulting their choreographers.

Cast and Credits: Except where otherwise indicated, information is taken from published programs. Unresolved disparities with other sources are noted. The rendering of names is as described in the introduction to the Chronology (p. 39).

The following abbreviations are employed: *chor*=choreography; *mus*=composed by; *mus dir*=musical director; *chair mus*=chairman of music for the festival; *danc*=danced by or dancers; *art collab*=artistic collaborator; *asst*=assistant(s); *dir*=directed by; *tech dir*=technical director; *accom*=accompanist; *prod asst*=production assistant(s); *props*=properties; *sets & light*=setting(s) and lighting design, also decor or scenery; *light*=lighting.

New York Premieres: Dates were verified through reviews, especially in the *Dance Observer* and the *New York Times*, and program files.

Subsequent Productions: The date represents either a major revival of the work after its New York premiere, or its last-known performance. Principal source is the *Dance Observer*, checked where possible with the choreographer or dancers.

Reviews: Excerpts from a range of reviews, when available, are included. Although sometimes repetitive, they substantiate the critical reception of a work or a choreographer. Aside from their value in determining how these works were perceived initially, reviews were an important source of basic information about the dances—their length, numbers of performers, music, staging, etc. No systematic effort was made to include reviews of revivals; these are more readily available.

1935

13 July 1935

Sinister Resonance

College Theatre

Chor Tina Flade (solo). *Mus* Henry Cowell. *Accom* Ruth Hunt.

New York Premiere: 12 January 1935, Guild Theatre. No further information available.

3 August 1935

New Dance

College Theatre

Sequences from *New Dance* filmed in 1935 at Bennington. Frame enlargements courtesy of Linda Mann Reed.

Doris Humphrey and Charles Weidman.

Chor Doris Humphrey. *Mus* Wallingford Riegger (original piano score). *Cos* Pauline Lawrence. *Accom* Vivian Fine, Pauline Lawrence. *Danc* Humphrey, Charles Weidman, and Concert Group: Helen Bach, Beatrice Gerson, Ada Korvin, Katherine Litz, Joan Levy, Katherine Manning, Beatrice Seckler, Mildred Tanzer, Letitia Ide, Edith Orcutt, Sybil Shearer, George Bockman, Morris Bakst, Noel Charise, José Limón, William Matons, Jerry Brooks.

Though treated as a Bennington premiere, *New Dance* had its first public performance two days before at the University of Vermont, Burlington, under the title *Dance Variations*. (The rest of the program was the same as at Bennington. The Burlington performance program

Doris Humphrey and Charles Weidman.

"Men's Dance." Left to right: José Limón, William Matons, George Bockman.

at the NYPL shows the pencilled-in substitution of Miriam Krakovsky for Beatrice Gerson; Mildred Tanzer's name is crossed out, and Kenneth Bostock's name added.) Doris Humphrey revealed her plan "to give the concert once before coming back to Bennington on Saturday"[1] in a letter to her husband. Vivian Fine, who played the new Riegger score at Bennington, confirmed: "The Burlington performance *was* the first performance of *New Dance*. I remember it well as the dancers got lost in the complicated rhythms and Doris signalled for the curtain to come down before the finish."[2]

Humphrey completed the composition just before going to Bennington in July. According to Selma Jeanne Cohen:

> The music was commissioned from Wallingford Riegger—who never knew that Doris had choreographed some of the movement to Roy Harris's *When Johnny Comes Marching Home*, which she used as a substructure later to be removed. . . . When the entire dance was finished, Doris called on Riegger, who then wrote melodic lines that he handed over to Ruth and Norman Lloyd with the request that they "write my kind of chords for this."[3]

The Bennington program carried no descriptive program note or indication of movement demarcations. According to the *Bennington Banner*, the work was about 25 minutes long.[4] (The concluding segment, "Variations and Conclusion," was added for the New York premiere.) In later programs, Charles Weidman was credited with the choreography for the "Third Theme" (the "Men's Dance").

New Dance was the first part of a trilogy, each part approximately 40 minutes long, with music by Wallingford Riegger. *Theatre Piece* was composed next (premiere, 19 January 1936), and the last, *With My Red Fires*, was composed and had its premiere at Bennington (13 August 1936). All three parts of *New Dance Trilogy* were performed at Bennington in 1936 in the course of two successive evenings.

Doris Humphrey wrote two drafts of an essay about *New Dance* which are essential sources. One is published in her biography;[5] the other is included here. [See p. 284 in this book.]

New York Premiere: 27 October 1935, Guild Theatre. Doris Humphrey, Charles Weidman, and 13 members of the Concert Group. *Sets* Erika Klein. "Prelude," "First Theme," "Second Theme," "Third Theme" (*chor* Weidman), "Processional," "Celebration," "Variations and Conclusion."

"Women's Dance."

Beatrice Seckler, Edith Orcutt, Charles Weidman, George Bockman, José Limón, Doris Humphrey.

Program Note: "*New Dance* represents the growth of the individual in relation to his fellows in an ideal state."

Subsequent Productions: Until 1972 only the "Variations and Conclusion" movement from *New Dance* survived in performance and notation (it has received many performances in recent years and is popular with college dance groups). It was first revived on 23 August 1952 at the American Dance Festival. In 1971 Weidman began to reconstruct parts of the *Trilogy* (his desire to revive all three parts was never realized). *New Dance* was mounted at Barnard College in May 1972; both *New Dance* and *With My Red Fires* were staged at the American Dance Festival at Connecticut College in June and July 1972. (*Doris Humphrey: An Artist First* contains a fascinating account of the harrowing process of reconstructing *New Dance*.) Both versions of *New Dance* were filmed (see Sources–Films). Weidman preferred the Barnard version even though it lacked the complete Riegger score which was located in time for the American Dance Festival performance. Deborah Carr's Theatre Dance Ensemble revived *New Dance* 7 June 1980 at Emanu-El YMHA, New York, based on Charles Weidman's 1972 reconstruction, aided by George Bockman and supervised by Beatrice Seckler and Nona Schurman.

Weidman set down on paper his thoughts about the reconstruction process in 1972:

> The reconstructing of Doris Humphrey's *New Dance* has taken a great deal of time and energy. In the beginning–about a year ago–I thought by now we could have achieved both the *New Dance* and *Theatre Piece.* These two works and *With My Red Fires* constituted the *Trilogy*. All who were either in the works at the time of their creation or had seen them were extremely interested. At the start I had Louise Allen, Miriam Krakovsky, Joan Levy, Katherine Litz, Edith Orcutt, Beatrice Seckler and Ann Stern (understudy). All brought their memories which were magnificent but a little disturbing to my dancers. Each had an individual and different conception of things leaving my group not knowing exactly which way was the proper way a movement or theme should be done. For instance, Katy Litz didn't quite remember the movement of the "Processional" but strongly remembered that it was very slow.
>
> To date Wallingford Riegger's music for the "Processional" and "Celebration" (Square Dance) has been located. Stephen Morris has written music for the "First Theme" and "Second Theme" (Doris Humphrey and group). As the "Third Theme" was my percussion score, I remembered this because I have kept many of the movements as technique. As for the opening "Prelude"–spasmodic unharnessed and beautiful energy–no one including myself remembered what

we did. Maybe it was improvisational. I strongly remembered the recurring shooting in of a rattling tambourine stopping whatever we were dancing. For this Stephen Morris and I collaborated on the idea.[6]

Reviews

John Martin, *New York Times*:

> It is at present without title, and was billed simply as *New Dance*. [It is] the work of a master of composition, and one of the most exciting pieces in the modern repertoire. . . . It combines an almost primitive drive with a formal graciousness which, though it takes nothing away from its force, gives it in addition a certain poise which is altogether admirable. . . .
>
> The composition itself falls naturally into four sections. In the first Miss Humphrey and Mr. Weidman dance against the background of the group, which is brought very gradually into the movement. In the second Miss Humphrey dances with the feminine members of the group, in the third Mr. Weidman dances with the men and in the fourth the whole company joins in a kind of triumphal processional. The difference in tone of the men's section is accented not only by a divergence in the materials and the manner of treatment, but by the change from a musical to a percussive accompaniment.
>
> Transitions between the movements have been excellently handled, so that there is no chance to break the line with applause, and yet the completion of the thematic development is evident. Even more admirable is the transition from one smaller section to another within the larger subdivisions.
>
> Certainly a more authoritative piece of creation in the dance has not been seen for many a long day. It is especially significant in this time when it has become habitual to question the validity of "absolute" dance that here is a work which has the same power to stir the emotions, to kindle esthetic excitement, as is to be found in symphonic music. . . .
>
> The musical setting by Wallingford Riegger is, incidentally, by far the weakest part of the collaboration. It begins nicely but before long it has begun to meander all over the place.[7]

On the program with *New Dance* was a revival of *Life of the Bee* which Martin said seemed "curiously dated" in comparison.

At its New York premiere, *New Theatre* magazine took Humphrey to task for *New Dance*:

> The work exists on the sheer excitement of its movement. We regret to see such tremendous possibilities used for form and technique alone –with little attempt made to integrate content and idea into the form.[8]

Five years after its Bennington premiere, Martin called *New Dance* the first work to make the transition from dance as a recital art to dance as a theater art:

> It was a group composition lasting forty-five minutes [with "Variations and Conclusion"] and employing a company of men and women without specifically defined roles. It told no story but treated in abstract terms the theme of the relations of man to man in an ideal world. In character it was comparable to a symphony and brought to fruition principles of the orchestration of movement evolved many years ago with Ruth St. Denis in the first experiments at Denishawn in "music visualization."
>
> There are few works in the history of the dance that mark so definitely the beginning of a new era. Henceforth the recital form, consisting of a succession of unrelated little compositions without theatre dimensions, was cast aside, and composers turned their attention to large forms dramatizing the conflict between the individual and his universe. . . . The dance had become a theatre form.[9]

14 August 1935

Panorama

Vermont State Armory, Bennington

Chor Martha Graham. *Mus* Norman Lloyd (original score). *Mus dir* Louis Horst. *Musicians* Hugo Bergamasco (flute), H. Tafarella (clarinet), J. Youshkoff (bass clarinet), V. Peretti (trumpet), H. Denecke, Jr. (drums). *Mobiles* Alexander Calder. *Sets & light* Arch Lauterer. *Tech dir* Jane Ogborn. *Danc* Martha Graham and Workshop Group. Martha Graham Dance Group: Anita Alvarez, Bonnie Bird, Dorothy Bird, Ethel Butler, Lil Liandre, Marie Marchowsky, Sophie Maslow, Lily Mehlman, May O'Donnell, Florence Schneider, Gertrude Shurr, Anna Sokolow. Workshop dancers: Miriam Blecher, Prudence Bredt, Nadia Chilkowsky, Evelyn Davis, Jane Dudley, Nancy Funston, Alice Gates, Mildred Glassberg, Mary Anne Goldwater, Marie Heghinian, Merle Hirsh, Gussie Kirschner, Edith Langbert, Naomi Lubell, Mary Moore, Helen Priest, Pearl Satlien, Kathleen Slagle, Muriel Stuart, Maxine Trevor, Theodora Wiesner, Collin Wilsey, Marian Van Tuyl, Florence Verdon.

Program Note:

> In every country there are basic themes of thought and action. These themes are part of the national consciousness and form an inheritance that contributes to the present. *Panorama* endeavors to present three themes which are basically American. No. I. "Theme of Dedication." This theme is based on that early intensity of fanaticism with which our Puritan fathers sang their hymn of dedication of a new nation. No. II. "Imperial Theme." For this theme a southern locale was chosen since here was to be found the most striking expression of a people in bondage ridden by superstitions and strange fears. No. III. "Popular Theme." This theme is of the people and their awakening social consciousness in the contemporary scene.

The program described the Workshop production as "the result of six weeks of work with the thirty-six dancers of the Workshop Group [including] twenty-four students of the School of the Dance especially enrolled for the current session in the professional study of the modern dance." The choreography "was begun by Martha Graham on July 15. The technical work by Jane Ogborn, the composing of the music by Norman Lloyd, and the construction of the mobiles by Alexander Calder were begun the following week. The designing and execution of the setting and lighting by Arch Lauterer have been carried out in the final half of the session."

Never before had Graham worked with so many dancers or collaborators (it was her first collaboration with Lauterer, Lloyd, and Calder). She had employed stage settings twice previously—in *Integrales* (1934) huge blocks (unattributed) and in *Perspectives 1 and 2* (April 1935) Isamu Noguchi's designs for *Frontier* and *Marching Song*.

The Workshop experiment suffered from insufficient time in every respect: Lloyd composed the score at odd moments in between four or five hours of teaching each day. Graham composed her longest, largest work to date while training and rehearsing new students in addition to her own group (the 24 Workshop students were auditioned from 70 applicants), and teaching. Calder experimented with his first mobiles for the stage, and Lauterer built a multilevel dance arena for 37 dancers in the unlikely interior of the Vermont State Armory.

Music:

The 40-minute instrumental score was Lloyd's first major dance composition (he had written some short works for Elna Lillback the year before). The music was performed by Graham's New York musicians. It was Lloyd's first summer teaching (he and his wife Ruth were school accompanists in 1934).

Lloyd recalled:

> Sometime in the first week, Louis [Horst] asked me if I would be willing to

> write a work for Martha. Actually, Louis was supposed to have done it but he must have realized the time was too short. I was young and willing, if not able! In those days composers did anything. You were on the lot and you got a small salary for the summer. I was thrilled and scared to death.[10]

There were unforeseen problems. The college music faculty were suspicious of dance musicians and had put all the pianos off limits to them. "I guess they thought we were going to do something to degrade them," said Lloyd. As a consequence, he had to work on an upright in one of the dormitory living rooms between his teaching and accompanying chores. The night before the orchestra arrived, Lloyd stayed up all night copying parts. Alex North helped. The score was never recorded, and Lloyd retained no copy. "These were pre-Xerox days; there was just one copy of a score." Horst helped him surmount a problem toward the end, as he was running out of time. "I was stuck on one measure and Louis said, 'Why don't you take that measure and have oboe and clarinet play it, then flute and bassoon, alternating between them, and play it over and over.'" It was a perfect solution, he realized, because there was so much going on in the dance for the eye to take in, the ear needed something far simpler. "It was the kind of thing that Merce [Cunningham] might use now with John Cage. It was an avant-garde thing we did without knowing it."

Lloyd was given no scenario to work from. "Martha wasn't very sure what she wanted. She gave me a lot of books, sermons and such, and told me to read the source material, all of it. I learned from her how you soak up material and background, not that you ever used any of it directly." Graham showed him sections of the dance as she was making it. He would write some music for it that would then be tried with the dancers to be certain it worked. Because of time pressures, Lloyd had to write music for one of Graham's solos without ever seeing the dance. "She left it for the last and I never saw it until the curtain went up. It was all written in her notebook but she hadn't had a chance to do it. I wrote it from her counts, her phrasing. I'm sure she improvised when she got out on the stage."

Decor:

This was the first of Lauterer's eight collaborations with Graham. His design for the Armory interior was reproduced in *Theatre Arts Monthly*, with the following note:

> Mr. Lauterer says that the dancers really designed the setting and he only executed it. He explains that designing for dancers is a far more creative venture than designing a play and that the floor proportions, the stair and bleacher levels were respaced and rescaled several times to meet a dancer's bodily technique—so much freer than an actor's.[11]

The action of *Panorama* took place on two levels with a bleacher-like structure linking them. There was no curtain and a bare masking of the mechanics, so that lights, ropes, and all functional parts of the production were visible. The Workshop Group was used as a unit of 36 as well as in smaller groups and solo figures.[12]

Margaret Lloyd recalled:

> [*Panorama*] was important less for its texture or substance than for its experimentation with functional stage design. . . . The large floor space was reserved for the dancers, the spectators looking down from built-up bleachers and a balcony, a seating arrangement not without precedent in ancient times. Arch Lauterer used varied levels and screens to space the action.[13]

Mobiles:

Panorama was Alexander Calder's first theater work and the first of two collaborations with Graham. (He may have started working on the other one, *Horizons*, before *Panorama*'s premiere. *Horizons*, which was produced in 1936, employed "plastic interludes" between the four movements.) In *Panorama* Calder attempted to integrate moving sculpture into the dance in an organic way.[14] He designed white and red-and-white-striped discs which moved in countermotion with the dancers. This was one of two projected mobiles for the work; the other fizzled out on the drawing board. Ruth Lloyd recalled both:

Design by Arch Lauterer for *Panorama*, 1935, Vermont State Armory. Photo courtesy of Henry Kurth. The Arch Lauterer Archives.

> Calder had devised two mobiles for the dance. The first was a set of primary-colored discs, suspended from pulleys. Each disc was attached to a wrist of one of the five dancers. The effect was stunning, with the dipping and rising space patterns of the discs counterpointing the slow-moving, earth-bound movement of the dancers. But Calder's second mobile never worked. He had designed a huge wooden machine, jointed so that it could leap across the whole stage like a jagged bolt of lightning. Something went wrong, either in the design or in the execution of the design. The joints of the machine responded arthritically at best. This mobile never made it to the Armory.[15]

Sophie Maslow remembered it as a ruler-type apparatus which retracted and extended across the back of the stage by pressing a button. It never worked, she said, and had to be discarded.[16]

The discs were used in the first movement, "Theme of Dedication." Marian Van Tuyl remembered they were set on the small stage above and beyond the large dancing space in the Armory. "Large discs of about five or six feet in diameter were pulled across the stage so that they seemed to float."[17]

May O'Donnell recalled the difficulty dancers had manipulating the discs:

> Sandy [Alexander] Calder was up there that summer and we practiced with these discs and long ropes. Dorothy [Bird] and Bonnie [Bird] and I would manipulate them and Martha would try to have some dance movement while we'd do it. Then in the Workshop group, Muriel Stuart was there—Martha was very flattered that Muriel wanted to come up and be in her workshop because Muriel was dyed-in-the-wool ballet, but she didn't know how to use Muriel be-

> cause Muriel had never done modern movement. And so she'd have her try to shift the discs which would go up and down. We worked for hours carrying them back and forth, but the only thing she finally used her for was a series of fast chaîné turns which Muriel did well. Martha became so involved with the mobiles that she never got her piece finished.[18]

Critic Jerome Bohm described "the stage setting in irregular blocks of black and silver" as "appropriate and telling" but thought that "the discs of white and red with white stripes, suspended on ropes arbitrarily propelled kite-fashion through the air recalled the days of Dadaism."[19]

Graham remembered the mobiles being "very elementary," but added, "In those days we were all very elementary and fearful of nothing–because we had nothing to be fearful of."[20]

When Calder died in 1976, Graham reminisced about their first collaboration:

> We had no place to rehearse [with the mobiles] so we rigged them up in the open field, stretched ropes from tree to tree, and learned to manipulate them to give the illusion of the world of fantasy that Sandy wanted and which enchanted me. The field bordered a public highway and by a loud blowing of horns we became aware that we had stopped traffic and people were caught up in this fantastic world of trees and meadow and yellow flowers and Sandy and mobiles and dancers.[21]

Panorama was the only major Bennington opus that was never performed again. The dancers interviewed could not recall much about its movement. May O'Donnell remembered a series of steps that Graham used to fill time, which henceforth became known as "the Bennington triplets."[22] And Ethel Butler recalled "a lot of running in place, with everybody doing different counts in great blocks of groupings of people." The Workshop students would stay up all night memorizing that day's rhythmic patterns, and the next day Graham would change everything.[23] According to Don McDonagh, Graham "blamed the failure [of Panorama] on the visitors who came in to watch her work during rehearsals. Whether true or not, she never again permitted visitors to watch her choreographing."[24]

Subsequent Productions: None

Reviews

John Martin, *New York Times*:

> The house had been sold out more than a week . . . an additional performance was given in advance on Wednesday, and this also was packed to the doors with an audience of enthusiasts from all over the country. Both evenings were characterized by the excitement of a gala season and the quiet little town itself took on an unfamiliar air of gaiety with crowds of people in evening dress in its streets and its restaurants packed to the guards. . . . Though *Panorama* is not Miss Graham's finest work by any means, it is in many ways a notable accomplishment and marks the opening of a new field of activity for one of our most stimulating artists. This new direction is definitely toward the theatre and away from the concert hall. The action of the piece took place not only on the small stage of the armory but on a large section of the floor itself which had been arranged with great ingenuity and a fine feeling for plastic design by Arch Lauterer. How Miss Graham utilized this working space with its various levels constituted perhaps the outstanding feature of the new composition.[25]

Martin called the subject matter "epic material . . . treated in an epic vein," and added:

> In its present form, it is too long, running for something more than forty minutes, and in some places gives evidence of the haste with which it has been composed. . . . It is, on the whole, if not an intrinsically important work, a highly impressive and extremely provocative one.[26]

He elaborated in his Sunday column:

> In its present state it contains occasional extravagances of movement which do not seem to have about them the quality of inevitability which we have come to associate with Miss Graham's composition.[27]

But, he said, the piece consisted of magnificent materials, so that

> by the time Miss Graham is ready to present it in New York it should rank with her best creations. . . . Not only in the fluent handling of an unusually large group but even more in an almost uncanny instinct for dramatizing the relation of the solo figure and the group to the space at their disposal, we see new phases of Miss Graham's gifts.[28]

Martin called it "a triumph . . . from the standpoint of production" but offered the following suggestion to future Workshop directors:

> The educational aspect of the situation with its time limitation and its technical training problems interferes somewhat with the purely creative aspect. . . . It would seem to be the better part of wisdom for any dancer who undertakes the direction of the "workshop" to have his work as fully planned in advance as possible in order to forestall this inevitable conflict.[29]

In a summary of the summer's activities, Margaret Lloyd wrote:

> A quality of percussive movement, separate from the reinforcement of percussion instruments, and of vibratory movement, apart from the reedy tang of accompanying woodwind, a brilliance beyond the detonations of the brass, in Miss Graham's choreography, stir the spectator to extraordinary excitement.[30]

Jerome Bohm, *New York Herald Tribune*:

> The major contribution, both in point of artistic worth and length, was *Panorama*, the three parts of which assume symphonic proportions. . . . To the writer the choreographic symbolism seldom conveyed Miss Graham's intentions. Seldom, indeed, was the reaction an emotional one, although visually the results were frequently arresting and compelling. Miss Graham's talent to mold her human material has never been so triumphantly asserted. . . . In but six weeks' time in her hands [the Workshop dancers] have become instruments attuned to hitherto unheard-of subtleties of movement and rhythm. The welding into highly original and striking patterns has been accomplished with the intensity of a zealot. The canny juxtaposition of symmetry and asymmetry in the designs was often most effective. As an extended projection in abstract kinaesthetics, *Panorama* unquestionably is Miss Graham's greatest achievement. It is less possible to enthuse over Miss Graham's personal participation. . . . Her technical attainments were, of course, superlative. But too frequently her work seemed irrelevant and merely an interruption disturbing the continuity of the scheme.[31]

The Left press was pleased to see Graham tackling social comment in her new work but derided her naiveté and parochial concerns with American themes. (In 1977 Norman Lloyd said he felt Graham was several years ahead of them; they were soon to hold the American banner high.) Along with its political judgments, *New Theatre* magazine carried the most detailed description of the work. It praised Graham's handling of the Workshop Group, among whom, it noted, were members of the New Dance League, and hailed *Panorama* as "the first occasion when Miss Graham outspokenly, through program notes as well as theme, joined forces with those artists in America who find social comment the basis of their work."[32] (Graham had concerned herself with social themes previously, though perhaps not as explicitly or on such a large scale as in *Panorama*.)

The subject of *Panorama*, said *New Theater,*

> would faze all but the most courageous of choreographers, or the most convinced of thinkers. That Miss Graham is both is proven by her sensitive handling of so extensive a canvas within the limits of a medium which, until this time, she has arbitrarily kept free from all stage or theatrical appurtenances. Now she used these to great advantage as aid in presenting her ideas.
>
> The social comment in this work, unfortunately, does not parallel, in clarity of conception, the remarkable ability of Miss Graham to integrate comment into dance patterns at once thrilling and beautiful. *Panorama* is still no doubt in the process of crystallization, and this accounts for many weaknesses, particularly in the third section. Surely here, the most insurgent, the most rugged, the most contemporary theme of all required an ending that was powerfully heroic and unquenchable. . . . The popular theme . . . sought to remain too conscientiously within national confines. To feel, at this time, that a peoples' theme which had broad, universal implications must end on a distinctly national note is unprophetic, or else evasive. The boundaries of America have been broken through by the unity of the workers the world over; they are not arbitrarily determined by the singers of Yankee Doodle. . . . And this awakening of social consciousness should have permeated also the subject of Negro exploitation in "Imperial Theme." Not only would it have made the dance timely in view of Mussolini's impending attack on Ethiopia, but it could have been a far truer picture of the Southern locale in America in which "superstition and strange fears" [see program note] are no longer the outstanding characteristics of the Negro. . . .
>
> Despite these ideological discrepancies, . . . one can see to what great planes Miss Graham's work will reach when one realizes how far and in how short a time she has already traveled away from *Dithyrambic* and *Primitive Mysteries*. Even in *Panorama*, her first open avowal of sympathy with the growing forces of social protest, there are unforgettable characterizations. The dignified opening of "Dedication" made way for a vividly fantastic grotesquerie on hymn and prayer. And in this section also appeared some of the finest dancing of the evening; the hex dance of Anna Sokolow and Anita Alvarez. The recurrent primitive theme of the second scene and the opening phrases of "Popular Theme" were equally stirring. . . . The solo work of Miss Graham was of its usual high calibre; throughout the entire work she remains a motivating, albeit abstruse, force interpenetrating the group and moulding it. In the first scene she seems propelled by some sort of ecstatic self-communion. As the imperialist in the second she stalks through the group, wielding a red gash of handkerchief as symbol of the blood of the workers who alternately sway in ritual, or bow in tortured fear to the brazen and imperious Moloch demanding sacrifice at the altar. The solo in the third section is that of the agitator who, separate from the group—a separation which seems false—animates it to action.
>
> There is no doubt that this marks for Miss Graham the first of a series of full-length ballets dedicated to themes of contemporary importance for the American public. . . .[33]

"*Panorama*," said Katherine Vickery in *Dance Observer*, "was in effect a ballet where the choreographer, the musical director, the composer, the scenic designer and the dancers were American. This fact is not important as a piece of flag waving but it is significant."[34]

Theatre Arts Monthly called *Panorama* "clearly experimental and incomplete but vigorous, bold and beautiful in design and execution."[35]

THE BENNINGTON SCHOOL OF THE DANCE

PRESENTS

THE FINAL PROGRAM

IN A SERIES OF

FOUR PROGRAMS IN THE MODERN DANCE

MARTHA GRAHAM

and

The Workshop Group

Louis Horst, Musical Director

Setting and Lighting designed and executed by Arch Lauterer

Jane Ogborn, Technical Director

In the Vermont State Armory
South Street, Bennington, Vermont
Wednesday Evening, August 14, 1935
and
Thursday Evening, August 15, 1935
At 9:00 p. m. Eastern Daylight Time

MEMBERS OF THE WORKSHOP GROUP

MARTHA GRAHAM'S DANCE GROUP - Anita Alvarez, Bonnie Bird, Dorothy Bird, Ethel Butler, Lil Liandre, Marie Marchowsky, Sophie Maslow, Lilly Mehlman, May O'Donnell, Florence Schneider, Gertrude Shurr, Anna Sokolow.

Miriam Blecher, Prudence Bredt, Nadia Chilkovsky, Evelyn Davis, Jane Dudley, Nancy Funston, Alice Gates, Mildred Glassberg, Mary Anne Goldwater, Marie Heghinian, Merle Hirsh, Gussie Kirshner, Edith Langbert, Naomi Lubell, Mary Moore, Helen Priest, Pearl Satlien, Kathleen Slagle, Muriel Stuart, Maxine Trevor, Theodora Wiesner, Collin Wilsey, Marian Van Tuyl, Florence Verdon.

Hugo Bergamasco . . .	Flute
H. Tafarella . . .	Clarinet
J. Youshkoff . . .	Bass Clarinet
V. Peretti	Trumpet
H. Denecke, Jr. . . .	Drums

PROGRAM

1. CELEBRATION . . . *Louis Horst*
   Dance Group

2. SARABANDE . . . *Lehman Engel*
   (from suite "Transitions")
   Martha Graham

3. FRONTIER . . . . *Louis Horst*
   (from suite "Perspectives")
   Martha Graham

FIVE MINUTE INTERMISSION

4. PANORAMA . . . *Norman Lloyd*
   Martha Graham and Workshop Group

In every country there are basic themes of thought and action. These themes are part of the national consciousness and form an inheritance that contributes to the present. "Panorama" endeavors to present three themes which are basically American.

No. I. THEME OF DEDICATION. This theme is based on that early intensity of fanaticism with which our Puritan fathers sang their hymn of dedication of a new nation.

No. II. IMPERIAL THEME. For this theme a southern locale was chosen since here was to be found the most striking expression of a people in bondage ridden by superstitions and strange fears.

No. III. POPULAR THEME. This theme is of the people and their awakening social consciousness in the contemporary scene.

Music especially composed by Norman Lloyd
Mobiles by Alexander Calder

"Panorama," the first Workshop production, with Martha Graham as choreographer and solo dancer, is the result of six weeks of work with the thirty-six dancers of the Workshop Group. The Workshop Group is composed of the twelve members of Martha Graham's Dance Group and twenty-four students of the Bennington School of the Dance, especially enrolled for the current session in the professional study of the modern dance. The choreography for "Panorama" was begun by Martha Graham on July 15. The technical work by Jane Ogborn, the composing of the music by Norman Lloyd, and the construction of the mobiles by Alexander Calder were begun the following week. The designing and execution of the setting and lighting by Arch Lauterer have been carried out in the final half of the session. The music has been directed by Louis Horst. Students under the direction of Jane Ogborn have assisted in the technical work. The Workshop project is a part of the plan of the Bennington School of the Dance to be continued in future sessions under the successive directorship of dancers who are members of the faculty of the School. It is planned that the Workshop project will culminate in an American dance festival. The prospective date for the festival week is during August 1937.

NOTES

1. Letter from Doris Humphrey to Charles Francis Woodford, 31 July 1935 postmark [Doris Humphrey Collection, C374].
2. Letter from Vivian Fine to the author, 26 August 1977.
3. Selma Jeanne Cohen, *Doris Humphrey: An Artist First* (Middletown, Conn.: Wesleyan University Press, 1972), p. 136.
4. *Bennington Banner*, 5 August 1935.
5. See Cohen, *Doris Humphrey*, pp. 238–41.
6. Charles Weidman, handwritten account, ca. 1972 (unpublished). Reprinted here by permission of The Charles Weidman School of Modern Dance, Inc., Linda Mann Reed, President. Weidman's preference for the Barnard version is expressed in his letter to Herb Kummel, Dance Notation Bureau, 1 August 1972. For descriptions of *New Dance*, see also *Don McDonagh's Complete Guide to Modern Dance* (New York: Popular Library, 1977), pp. 119–21, and Margaret Lloyd, *The Borzoi Book of Modern Dance* (New York: Alfred A. Knopf, 1949), pp. 95–96, and Marcia B. Siegel, *The Shapes of Change* (Boston: Houghton Mifflin, 1979), pp. 79–89.
7. John Martin, *New York Times*, 11 August 1935.
8. Norma Roland, "The Dance Season Begins," *New Theatre* 2, no. 12 (December 1935): 26.
9. John Martin, "Dance Since Isadora," *Theatre Arts* 24, no. 9 (September 1940): 645.
10. Interview with Norman Lloyd.
11. *Theatre Arts Monthly* 19, no. 10 (October 1935): 795.
12. Letter from Mary Jo Shelly and Martha Hill to Robert D. Leigh, 24 July 1935 [Bennington College Archive].
13. Lloyd, *Borzoi*, p. 58.
14. Jean Lipman, *Calder's Universe* (New York: Viking Press, 1976), p. 174.
15. Ruth Lloyd, "The Lloyds at Bennington," 1977 (unpublished recollections contributed for this book).
16. Interview with Sophie Maslow.
17. Letter from Marian Van Tuyl to the author, 19 April 1977.
18. Interview with May O'Donnell.
19. Jerome Bohm, "Festival Ends Dance Session at Bennington," *New York Herald Tribune*, 18 August 1935.
20. Martha Graham, onstage remarks at Kennedy Center, Washington, D.C., 15 November 1976.
21. *New York Times*, 12 November 1976.
22. Interview with May O'Donnell.
23. Interview with Ethel Butler.
24. McDonagh, *Martha Graham* (New York: Praeger, 1973), pp. 110–11.
25. John Martin, *New York Times*, 16 August 1935.
26. Ibid.
27. John Martin, *New York Times*, 1 September 1935.
28. Ibid.
29. Ibid.
30. Margaret Lloyd, "Dance History in the Making," *Christian Science Monitor*, 24 August 1935.
31. Jerome Bohm, *New York Herald Tribune*, 18 August 1935.
32. Edna Ocko, "Martha Graham's 'Panorama,'" *New Theatre* 2, no. 9 (September 1935): 27.
33. Ibid.
34. Katherine Vickery, *Dance Observer* 2, no. 7 (October 1935): 77.
35. Frederick Morton, *Theatre Arts Monthly* 19, no. 10 (October 1935): 798.

1936

13 August 1936

With My Red Fires

Vermont State Armory

Chor Doris Humphrey. *Mus* Wallingford Riegger (original score). *Mus dir* Norman Lloyd. *Musicians* Ruth Lloyd, Norman Lloyd, piano. H. Tafarella, clarinet. V. Peretti, trumpet. E. Armando, English horn. S. Gershek, Nancy McKnight, percussion. *Sets & light* Gerard Gentile. *Asst* Sally Brownell. *Cos* Pauline Lawrence. *Danc* Humphrey and Charles Weidman with Concert Groups and Students of the Workshops of the School. Members of Doris Humphrey's Concert Group: Katherine Manning, Ada Korvin, Katherine Litz, Beatrice Seckler, Joan Levy, Sybil Shearer, Edith Orcutt, Miriam Krakovsky, Lily Verne, Louise Allen. Members of Charles Weidman's Concert Group: José Limón, William Matons, William Bales, Paul Leon, Philip Gordon, William Canton. Students of the School Workshops: Patricia Amster, Nanette Atchison, Anita Brady, Lillian Burgess, Betty Carper, Maxine Cushing, Eva Desca, Lois Ellfeldt, Harriette Ann Gray, Helene Hetzel, Frances Kinsky, Beatrice Lovejoy, Anne MacNaughton, Ethel Mann, Alice Marting, Frances McDonald, Eloise Moore, Jane Perry, Kaya Russell, Selma Silverman, Mary Tracht, Bernice van Gelder, Theresa Willman, Mildred Zook, Otto Ashermann, Edgar Barclift, Lynn Buchanan, William Garrett, Frederic Lane.

Part I–Ritual:

> For the Divine appearance is Brotherhood, but I am Love,
> Elevate into the Region of Brotherhood with my red fires.
>
> –*Jerusalem II,* William Blake

Hymn: Weidman, Litz, Concert Groups, and Workshop Group. ***Search and Betrothal:*** Weidman, Litz, Concert and Workshop Groups. ***Departure:*** Weidman, Litz, Concert and Workshop Groups.

Part II–Drama:

> . . . the Great Selfhood, . . .
> Having a white Dot call'd a Center, from which branches out
> A Circle in continual gyrations: this became a Heart
> From which sprang numerous branches varying their motions,
> Producing many Heads, three or seven or ten, and hands and feet
> Innumerable at will of the unfortunate contemplator
> Who becomes his food: such is the way of the Devouring Power.
>
> –*Jerusalem II*, William Blake

Summons: Burgess, Cushing. ***Coercion and Escape:*** Humphrey, Litz. ***Alarm:*** Humphrey, Workshop Group. ***Pursuit:*** Limón, Matons, Bales, Workshop Group. ***Judgment:*** Weidman, Litz, Concert and Workshop Groups. *The Characters in Part II: Choric Figures* Burgess, Cushing. *Young Woman* Litz. *Young Man* Weidman. *Matriarch* Humphrey.

Program Note: "*With My Red Fires* is the third section of the trilogy on the theme of the relationship of man to man."

With My Red Fires was performed by 45 dancers, in addition to Humphrey and Weidman (10 in Humphrey's group; 24 in the Women's Workshop; 6 in Weidman's group; 5 in the Men's Workshop). It was the largest company for any previous or subsequent Bennington production.

A festival news release described Humphrey's intentions:

> In the dance "*With My Red Fires*," Miss Humphrey is considering the central theme of brotherhood through the force of love in its romantic, possessive and destructive aspects.[1]

The work was in two parts. The release stated that the second part "also carries a quotation from Blake, 'When thought is closed in Caves then love shall show its roots in deepest Hell,'" but this quotation does not appear on the program.

According to Paul Love, Humphrey was inspired by Edward Carpenter's *Love Comes of Age*, "which clarified for her the idea of the place of romantic relationship in society. He analyzes the following four points in this order: desire, personal relationship, personal responsibility and relationship to society."[2]

The composition was conceived during the long drive up to Bennington. Humphrey had a provisional title, *Romantic Tragedy*:

> First a hymn to Aphrodite, or Priapus or Venus, anyway to the excitement, the greatness, the rapture, the pain of, frustration that is love. A voice will speak of that from a temple and the ever willing victims will respond with flutterings, stabbings, listenings, impatience, fire in the blood (I know I'm not as good as Whitman). Next the process will begin. Put the force to work, seek out the mate, rush from one to the other, buffet the rest out of the way. Yes, there are two lovers at last, the end is all but achieved, the heat and thirst quenched. But what and who is that beckoning in the window? It's a woman–old–she's beckoning to the girl lover–she's the mother–she says it's late and no time for young girls to be lugging around with unknown young men and goodness knows who he might be or what sort of a family he comes from. Come in this moment, your virtue's at stake, the world will say you're a bad girl. You won't? You will do as I say. Sew the seam, mop the floor, walk like me, talk like me, come away from the window–How can I mop the floor and sew the seam with my lover outside? I have danced in the Hymn to Priapus and I belong to my love–The old one is quiet now in the house, steal away through the window to the waiting lover. In the shadows find him, wrap him round. The old one has missed you, she's screaming now from the top of the house, the alarm is spreading, people are running, shouting, they're on the morbid scent, they gleam with virtuous hate. She's run off with a nobody? Which way? To the town, to the inn? No, here by the wall. Tear them apart, the dirty things. What shall we do, old one, marry them with a gun and giggles or run them out? See that they're well battered, punish, pinch, tear, beat, and I shall shut the door. *So–*
> let's take them over the rocks, up-down through the rocks,
> leave them at the Priapic stone. Moralists
> point the finger
> thrifty lift your eyes
> sentimental ones weep over young love's impetuosity
> Scandal mongers laugh
> And leave them[3]

Humphrey completed the *Trilogy* before reading William Blake's poetry. "I was looking for a title for 'Red Fires' when I came across the passage in *Jerusalem II*, and I immediately seized on this and its context as a word illumination for what I had been doing," she wrote to Eugene C. Howe, author of "The Modern Dance and William Blake."[4]

The idea of composing a dance on the theme of romantic love was considered retrogressive and decadent, even by some members of her own group. Walter Terry talked with Humphrey at Bennington during his first month as dance critic for the *Boston Herald*:

Doris Humphrey (upper left corner) as the Matriarch in *With My Red Fires*, Vermont State Armory. Photographs by Sidney Bernstein.

Doris Humphrey, Charles Weidman, and Katherine Litz in *With My Red Fires.*

> Doris was very upset about *With My Red Fires* and asked me what I thought. She said, "I'm being criticized by my own dancers because the theme is romance, and you know romance is taboo with modern dance." And I said, "Well if it's taboo, if anything is taboo, then modern is just as narrow as ballet with its sleeping beauties and pixies and elves, isn't it?" And she said, "Yes it is, but I can't tell you what pressure has been brought against me. My trilogy has to do with life as it is, with too much competition, fraud and everything [*Theatre Piece*] and *New Dance* which is my vision of an ideal relationship with human beings, and this is the personal theme of love which can be both creative and destructive, and this is destructive love in which creative love wins. And they think I'm getting decadent," she said, "they say I'm going back to Denishawn. But I'm an artist and I have to do it."[5]

Music: Wallingford Riegger composed the score during the Bennington session, for piano, percussion, clarinet, trumpet, and English horn. The original manuscript is on file at the Dance Notation Bureau; a full orchestral score by Riegger was obtained by the Bureau in 1974. Themes from the work were later incorporated by Riegger into an orchestral piece. For its 1972 American Dance Festival restoration, Gerald Tarack used Riegger's orchestral score to make new parts for two pianos, two percussionists, and voice.

Critical opinion of the music was mixed. John Martin praised it:

> He is not afraid to experiment with strange tonalities and by these means as well as by more orthodox methods he has succeeded in capturing the strange flavor of the choreography. It is perhaps as near as we have yet come to a truly functional dance setting.[6]

Newsweek thought that it "pleasantly suited the mood of the performance but seemed hardly worthy of the composer whose works have been presented by the New York Philharmonic and the Philadelphia Orchestra."[7] To Walter Terry, "the music sounded like a broken down organ attached in some mysterious way, to a cement mixer. . . . Either percussion alone should have been used, or else music with melody and quality on an equal plane with the theme and movements of the dance."[8] Margaret Lloyd thought Riegger had "surpassed all but the 'Variations and Conclusion' of *New Dance*."[9] She later noted "the usual Humphrey-Weidman penchant for unusual sound effects, the strings of a dismantled upright piano struck with tympani sticks in *Theatre Piece*, and the plucked strings of a grand piano in *With My Red Fires*."[10]

Costumes and Sets:

John Martin pronounced Pauline Lawrence's costumes "eminently successful": "In the suggestion of Victorianism in the Matriarch's black sleeves and enormous gray skirt, she has echoed the daring of the role itself."[11]

At the Armory, according to Margaret Lloyd, a few of the "platinum-colored blocks of *Theatre Piece* and *New Dance* were [for *Red Fires*] oddly piled right stage to suggest a house an and others formed a new level up stage."[12] She later wrote that "Arch Lauterer had a hand in the settings,"[13] but Lauterer was on leave in the summer of 1936. Lloyd recalled:

> At the State Armory, where the spectators looked down upon the dancing place, the action coursed from black screens forming wings, over the floor up on to the wide, stepped platform, and higher still to the architectual boxes as they formed house or tower.

Gerard Gentile was credited as technical director for the New York premiere at the Hippodrome. Later programs credit Humphrey and Lauterer for the sets.

New York Premiere:

15 January 1937, New York Hippodrome.

Humphrey revised *With My Red Fires* after the Bennington production. For the New York premiere, she adapted the stage as nearly as possible to the Bennington concept, with steps between the upper and lower stages and side wings. She augmented her own group with many new dancers (a total of 35) whom she had to train and rerehearse.[14]

A detailed note by Paul Love was provided for the New York program:

> This dance forms the middle section of the trilogy on the theme of the relationship of man to man. The first section, *Theatre Piece*, was concerned with the world as it is; the third section, *New Dance*, was concerned with a vision of the world as it will be, wherein each has his part within the harmonious whole. *With My Red Fires*, the second section, tells of the relationship of man to woman.
>
> HYMN TO PRIAPUS: The dance opens with a group movement of desire and the longing for completion. The action represents a primitive love-ritual.
>
> SEARCH AND BETROTHAL: Out of this group come the two lovers. Their movements weave in and out of the larger group movements.
>
> DEPARTURE: As the departing group comes in contact with the lovers, its movements seem to be magically changed. You see the group through the lovers' eyes as something new and different.
>
> DRAMA: SUMMONS: The second part of the dance introduces the Matriarch, who represents a repressive force in society. She is jealous of anyone but herself dominating the girl. She summons the two lovers. Subconsciously the girl feels the magnetic influence of the Matriarch and is drawn to her.
>
> COERCION AND ESCAPE: The girl is hypnotized by this influence and finally submerged by this psychological compulsion, disappearing into the house of the Matriarch. The loss of her lover, however, overcomes this malignant power and she returns to him and they escape.
>
> ALARM: PURSUIT: This is an affront against society. The Matriarch raises the alarm. She gathers the group, molds it to her opinion, and sends it in pursuit.
>
> JUDGMENT: The lovers are apprehended and driven out by the group. The Matriarch pronounces her judgment upon them. The group, now cold and impersonal, also pronounces judgment. The lovers are left alone, defeated. There is only a brief indication at the end that, although cursed by society, the spirit that bound them has not been destroyed.

Subsequent Productions:

The three parts of *New Dance Trilogy* were included in the repertory for the Humphrey-Weidman transcontinental tour in 1938. *With My Red Fires* was restaged for a company of about 25 for the Federal Dance Project 30 January 1939 and played a week's run at the Nora Bayes Theater in New York. It was revived on 24-26 April 1942 at the Humphrey-Weidman Studio Theatre. In 1953 Humphrey taught it to a group of Juilliard students, from a score by Eva Desca. (The Juilliard revival was notated in 1954.) She also directed a revival of portions for the American Dance Festival in 1953, and there was a performance at Juilliard on 5 May 1954. A full revival was accomplished at the American Dance Festival in 1972 and was filmed (see Sources–Films). In 1948 plans were discussed to stage *With My Red Fires* for Ballet Theatre's Metropolitan season (with Nora Kaye as the Matriarch) but this production was never undertaken.[15]

Reviews

Bennington Banner:

> The plight of the lover and the artist in this present imperfect world is successively set forth in . . . *With My Red Fires* and *Quest*. . . . The two compositions . . . are alike in that both seek to portray the troubles and stresses forced upon a sensitive individual in the modern world. Both also are built on the assumption that there can be a better world, and in the *New Dance* given the night before, that type of world was shown. . . .
>
> [In *With My Red Fires*] the first part opens with impressive lighting effects and slow orchestration to introduce the first section titled "Hymn" in which all the combined dancers come into the scene with advancing and retreating movements in harmony with the title and music. . . . The search of the young man . . . for the young woman . . . is set forth by both male and female dancers in postures symbolizing the expectancy of such an effort. This part, "Search and Betrothal," is marked by a particularly striking arrangement of the entire 40 dancers in a large oval at the conclusion of the search. The placement of large groups of the cast to form strikingly beautiful designs is in fact a feature of Miss Humphrey's work. . . . As culmination of the search, Mr. Weidman selects Miss Litz from a group of female dancers and their betrothal is signified by the dance of the whole group. Following this, the two leaders gradually withdraw from the others to a darkened part of the auditorium floor and the section of Ritual is over.
>
> The first half of *With My Red Fires* thus accomplished is given to strong and barbaric musical rhythms which indicate the elemental nature of the courtship.
>
> The dramatic second half . . . begins with the entrance of two choric figures clad in scarlet, who summon back the two lovers to the stage after their courtship. Following the section entitled "Summons," comes another, "Coercion and Escape," in which the lovers are separated by the spinster-like Miss Humphrey who bows the young woman to her own selfish will.
>
> But the two young people escape in an action which Wednesday night was largely off-stage in the wings. The high point in individual performance then comes with the dynamic dance by Miss Humphrey signifying the "Alarm" she gives of the escape. This swirling passion of fury is superb and a testimony of her greatness. It is followed by a group "Pursuit" of the young man and young woman which is scarcely on a lower plane.
>
> The lovers are finally returned and the judgment of society lashed upon them. In conclusion they overcome the wracking they have gone through and, led by two fiery choric figures, ascend the heights of the rear stage.[16]

Margaret Lloyd, *Christian Science Monitor*:

> Large use was made of the large space and large groups available, giving the effect of humanity speaking–through movement. . . . There are nuances in the movement . . . subtleties and gradations, that must be seen to be felt. Doris Humphrey's solo pantomime and duet with the daughter (a dialogue of arms), her abandon of frenzy at the lovers' escape, the strange and beautiful flash of dismembered hands from the series of wings on

the floor, the wild coursing of the groups in the pursuit, with their sudden, sharp punctuations of arrested motion, the broken woman carrying the illusion of brokenness to the last tip of visibility in her exit, are less tangible and far more forceful than words.[17]

Walter Terry, *Boston Herald*:

> *With My Red Fires* is not yet a worthy successor to Miss Humphrey's *New Dance* and *Theatre Piece*. The movement was somewhat scattered, and the focal point was tossed back and forth between Miss Humphrey, Mr. Weidman and Miss Katherine Litz. This focal point, we believe, should have been on the relationship of the three, and not on three distinct individuals.
>
> Miss Humphrey . . . created a forceful and theatrically effective character. Had she relied on her excellent pantomimic movement and less on facial contortions, Miss Humphrey's work would have come closer to the artistic demands of this dance.[18]

Joseph Arnold Kaye, *Dance*:

> The first part . . . can only be described as the finest choral composition that the modern dance has produced. . . . Never has there been such a translation of the joy of life, into terms of bodily movement. Produced on two stages, spatially ample, Miss Humphrey created patterns of processional dancing marvellously integrated and expressing a glory that can be found in a consecrated performance of Bach. . . .
>
> Part II . . . produced Miss Humphrey enacting a very melodramatic villainess, largely through pantomime. As acting, it was of a third-rate stock-company variety.[19]

Edna Ocko, *New Theatre*:

> *With My Red Fires* is a narrowing rather than an extension of its predecessors. . . . The reason for [its] being a minor work must be frankly attributed to the text. William Blake, whose obscure mystical poem, *Jerusalem II*, supplied the program notes, is scarcely the poet-prophet of the 20th century. . . . Miss Humphrey is too fine and too modern a talent to dissipate her important energies among mystics and cultists. She must continue along new paths in the modern dance, paths which she herself has blazed in *Theatre Piece* and *New Dance*.[20]

Virginia Mishnun, *Brooklyn Eagle*:

> Despite the handicap of a trite story, Miss Humphrey by the richness and imaginativeness of her choreography, creates a drama that is powerful and stirring. The dance of "Pursuit" is one of the most remarkable numbers in Miss Humphrey's repertoire, with its brilliant changes in grouping, and the sudden pauses of arrested movement in which the composition takes on a lithographic vividness.[21]

John Martin, *New York Times*:

> That the new work is equal to its predecessors in the trilogy cannot be maintained at present, for it lacks the finish which repeated performance and revision have given them. But it is potentially an extraordinary achievement and a daring one. . . . Miss Humphrey['s] conception and performance of the character are fantastic and brilliant. She becomes indeed something of a witch out of the minds of the brothers Grimm raised to a kind of cosmic malevolence.[22]

> For all her perversity and her violence, [Humphrey] remains a figure of great dignity. In her little, sharp movements there is a terrible eloquence, and as the dimensions of her action grow she becomes a colossal symbol of vengeful and self-destroying tyranny. . . . It is difficult, indeed, not to believe that in this remarkable trilogy we have seen perhaps the beginning of a new theatre. Its forms owe nothing to precedent, but have been evolved, as most of the great theatres of the world have been evolved, directly out of the elemental stuff of the dance.[23]

Doris Humphrey as the Matriarch in *With My Red Fires*. Photograph courtesy of Bennington College.

Joseph Kaye, in the *Cincinnati Enquirer* said it was "the first modern dance composition to have a realistic plot."[24]

Subsequent Reviews: Margaret Lloyd, *Christian Science Monitor*, on the New York premiere:

> The *Trilogy* is not only the greatest dance composition but the greatest artistic expression of present-day life in any form that has come out of America. . . .
>
> *With My Red Fires* . . . is a romantic interlude in this Trilogy of human brotherhood, and it cannot be discounted as lacking in sociological content merely because it is lacking in political implications. Certainly the delicate adjustments of human relationships are as close to the problem of human living as those of good government. . . .
>
> At Bennington, as I remember, with her hair drawn back into a tight psyche knot, her face lined into a permanent scowl of disapproval, she looked more the Matriarch than she did in the Hippodrome performance, with her hair flowing and the Doris Humphrey loveliness left in her face. . . .
>
> There were other changes from the Bennington production, mainly considered beneficial. To me, they left gaps rather than welding closer. Something was lacking of the first mystery and wonder.
>
> In the State Armory at Bennington, the action coursed over the floor and up on to the stage. In the first section, "Ritual," the groupings in the opening Hymn, moved with a haunting strangeness, an impending air. The meeting of the lovers and their departure was pointed up against this impending background. In the second part, "Drama," two red-robed choric figures, made awful summons. The flashing of white hands from the black wings on the floor was an incantation, an unearthly visualization of the further lines from Blake that set the mood. . . . There was breath-taking suspense in the Alarm and Pursuit; poetry in the final Judgment.
>
> At the Hippodrome, the grouping was necessarily confined to the stage, where a succession of levels was built up in mounting height. One notable improvement was the placing of the Matriarch's house nearer the center, where the action was visible from all sides. But both the Hymn and Pursuit suffered from lack of the more varied range. The choric figures did not appear. In place of the strange, sudden hands, heads and torsos in bright red flashed from the wings. There was something a little more theatrical, a little less invraisemblable about it. . . . *Red Fires* at the Hippodrome burned differently, but still with a mighty flame.[25]

John Martin, *New York Times*, on the Federal Dance Project revival:

> To see Miss Humphrey's *With My Red Fires* again is only to be convinced anew that it is one of the great works in the contemporary repertoire. . . . It is difficult to recall any other composition in which the group has been handled so remarkably, not so much with respect to design as to emotional line. . . . Miss Humphrey's performance of the Matriarch is a masterpiece. There is no other dancer who could begin to duplicate it.[26]

At the Juilliard revival in 1953, Martin reported Humphrey's opening remarks that the work's rhythms and counterpoint "were perhaps more complex than she would now employ." Said Martin, "The counterpoints may be complex but they are clear as crystal."[27]

13 August 1936

Quest: A Choreographic Pantomime

Vermont State Armory

Chor Charles Weidman. *Mus* Norman Lloyd (original score) with one section, *Transition*, by Clair Leonard. *Mus dir* Norman Lloyd. *Musicians* Ruth Lloyd, Norman Lloyd, Clair Leonard, piano. H. Tafarella, clarinet. V. Peretti, trumpet. E. Armando, English horn. S. Gershek, Nancy McKnight, percussion. *Sets & light* Gerard Gentile. *Asst* Sally Brownell. *Cos* Pauline Lawrence. *Danc* Doris Humphrey, Weidman, Concert Groups and Students of the Workshops of the School. Members of Doris Humphrey's Concert Group: Katherine Manning, Ada Korvin, Katherine Litz, Beatrice Seckler, Joan Levy, Sybil Shearer, Edith Orcutt, Miriam Krakovsky, Lily Verne, Louise Allen. Members of Charles Weidman's Concert Group: José Limón, William Matons, William Bales, Paul Leon, Philip Gordon, William Canton. Students of the School Workshops: Harriette Ann Gray, Frances Kinsky, Anne MacNaughton. Otto Ashermann, Edgar Barclift, Lynn Buchanan, William Garrett, Frederic Lane. In 12 parts: ***Prelude:*** group. ***Emergence:*** Humphrey, Weidman, group. ***Allegory:*** Humphrey, Weidman. ***Trivia (Patronage):*** Weidman, Manning, Orcutt, Seckler, Shearer, Gray. ***Transition:*** Limón, Matons, Bales, group. ***Kulturreinigung:*** Weidman, group. ***Trivia (Anthropomtery):*** Weidman, Limón, Matons, Bales, Gordon, Canton. ***Allegory:*** Humphrey, Weidman. ***Pro Patria:*** Weidman, Limón, Matons, group. ***Allegory:*** Humphrey, Weidman. ***Convergence:*** Weidman, Limón, Matons. ***Affirmation:*** Humphrey, Weidman, group.

Program Note:

> The artist, in his endeavor to find or create conditions under which he may achieve full and free expression, encounters many obstacles, in many lands. Today he struggles alone, with nothing but his inner strength to aid him. Perhaps tomorrow he will unite his forces with those of his fellows and reach his goal.

Eight Workshop students augmented the combined Concert Groups for a total of 24 dancers, in addition to Humphrey and Weidman.

According to a news release:

> Charles Weidman's new composition *Quest* is a choreographic pantomime dealing with the difficulties faced by the artist in contemporary life. The artist is depicted in tragic and comic form, as confronted with problems of social patronage, fascist culture, utopian dreams of independence, and chaotic influences of modern society. Mr. Weidman has divided his material into four major dances . . . interspersed with a number of brief episodic pantomimes.[28]

Music:

The 50-minute score by Norman Lloyd was for the same ensemble of instruments as Riegger's score for *With My Red Fires*. Lloyd retained a few sketches he made. While working on *Quest*, he was also rehearsing the musicians for the Riegger work and teaching the new composition course. Lloyd asked Clair Leonard to do the "Transition" section "because I knew I wasn't going to be able to do it in time." Lloyd recalled what it was like to work with Weidman:

> Charles was the most gifted of all in terms of inventiveness of movement. But he really improvised. Everything was always changing. People in the company never knew which version he wanted. Up until the day before dress rehearsal I don't think we'd even gone through the whole work. Nobody had any idea how long it was. Charles made new things like a sausage. He never knew exactly what he was doing in *Quest*, except for the ending, and the ending turned out to be the best part, a jazz fugue.[29]

John Martin agreed, calling the music for the final movement "the most rousing moment of a generally fine score."[30] Said Martin: "Mr. Lloyd . . . knows excellently the problems of

Quest. Charles Weidman, with José Limón and George Bockman on the floor area of the Vermont State Armory; Doris Humphrey as the Artist's Inner Self above. Photograph courtesy of Bennington College.

composing for dancing. His music is admirably simple, direct and unpretentious." Margaret Lloyd described the musical setting as "a strong, flexible frame of steel."[31]

Costumes and Sets:

Martin especially praised Pauline Lawrence's costuming both for *Quest* and *With My Red Fires*:

> She showed a delightful use of color as an element of composition. She has also managed to achieve a kind of costume which reveals the body in action instead of merely covering it up with decorative trappings. Especially successful are her costumes for the men in both works, for she has got away from that unbecoming pajamalike uniform which for some inexplicable reason got itself attached to the male dancer in the early years of the modern dance and has persisted ever since.[32]

Lloyd described the use of "white block frames . . . mounted asymetrically on either side of the stage."[33] As with *Red Fires* the action of *Quest* took place on two levels: the stage of the Armory and part of the Armory floor.

New York Premiere: 15 January 1937, New York Hippodrome. (The "Regimentation" section was performed earlier, on 26 December 1936, at Washington Irving High School by Charles Weidman and Group.) Several parts were revised and retitled. In the New York program, Weidman is assigned the character of "The Artist," Humphrey that of "The Artist's Inner Self."

Paul Love supplied the following description for the program at the New York premiere:

> The main theme of this dance-drama concerns the obstacles encountered by the artist in many lands today in his endeavor to discover or create conditions under which he may achieve full and free expression.
>
> PRELUDE: The dance opens on a shifting group like a street scene from which different kinds of people, both rich and poor, emerge and disappear.
>
> EMERGENCE: Out of this group comes the artist and his inner guiding spirit, personified by Doris Humphrey. The people are about to accept him, when the critics denounce him because his ideas are new.
>
> INTERLUDE (*Introspection*): This is his first disillusionment and he retreats into himself, communicating with that spirit which guides and controls his work. He is urged to go on.
>
> TRIVIA (*Patronage*): He decides to go to the rich and seek their patronage so that he may continue his work. He is forced to cheapen himself by having to amuse his patrons with trifles. He can endure this no longer and leaves them.
>
> REGIMENTATION: Travelling afar, he finds that there is a new force abroad in the land whereby people are molded and coerced by a dictator. He is told that it holds a glorious new future for man.
>
> KULTURREINIGUNG: The artist is invited to join so that he may partake of dictatorship's great vitalizing power. He makes an effort to do so and finds that it stultifies rather than revitalizes. The regimented group does not approve of his functioning separately and differently and turns against him.
>
> TRIVIA: (*Anthropometry*): Having given indication of being different, the artist must be measured to see if he fits the social and racial requirements of the group. During this, he first sees the violence and madness behind the dictator's methods and revolts against him.
>
> INTERLUDE (*Self-Analysis*): He communicates again with his inner spirit, finds that he has grown, and is beginning to have a firm conviction as to what should be and what should not be.
>
> PRO PATRIA: However, before he can work upon this conviction, he is caught up and coerced by war hysteria. He sees the forces that cause war showing the people pictures of war as a beautiful and glorious thing. Knowing what is behind this hypocrisy, he rebels and is cast out.
>
> INTERLUDE (*Inner Conviction*): Again he communicates with his inner spirit. On the ruined battlefield, he sees group after group in attitudes of agony and despair. His inner spirit commands him no longer to hide but to broadcast his conviction and make others see it.
>
> CONVERGENCE: The artist goes forth and calls others. He knows finally that the artist cannot live in an ivory tower, aloof from the masses of mankind. He is an integral part of the masses and must make that known.
>
> AFFIRMATION: The dance ends in a strong call to action. The artist has seen the world as it is and knows that it will no longer do to hide and pretend and ignore. The artist has his place within the whole group. The conclusion of the dance-drama is a strong affirmation of his oneness with the masses of mankind.

Subsequent Productions: *Quest* was included in the Humphrey-Weidman repertory during the company's 1938 transcontinental tour. No evidence of subsequent productions was found.

Reviews

Margaret Lloyd, *Christian Science Monitor*:

> Doris Humphrey is his [Weidman's] alter ego, the inner, guiding voice of his quest for artistic fulfillment. Her appearances with him mark intervals of allegory. Their movements match or harmonize, indicating their oneness of purpose. The artist emerges from the ordinary level of his surroundings and tests his strength. . . . In a period of transition, José Limón, William Matons and William Bales . . . and members of the men's workshop group, dance the tumult within him. They leap and whirl and fall, like so many ideas in a mind torn with conflict. A new idea comes to him, pleads for acceptance. A woman is held up before him. He is reluctant, does not grasp the full import. This passage resolves into a tranquil assertion of the thesis of men and women working co-equally together. . . .
>
> Mr. Weidman dances the role like a modern Pierrot, a bewildered, comic figure—and a great sadness underlying. He plucks the strings of laughter—and evokes a great pity. . . .
>
> War breaks out in his native land. He tries to escape it—to live only in his art. His anguished fellows beseech him to help tear out this appalling evil, through his work. Here the frieze of men dancers across the stage is stupendous in its effect.
>
> At last his conflicting ideas converge, attain unity, and in the grand group finale of affirmation the artist has not only found himself but has found the way of direct communication to the people. . . . It is all done with kinetic pantomime—with movement—which comes far closer than words.[34]

John Martin, *New York Times*:

> No previous Weidman work on anything like so large a scale has exhibited such expertness in the handling of a group, nor in the matter of content has had such substantial things to say. . . .
>
> *Quest* as a whole is much stronger in its latter half than in its earlier sections. The beginning is still a trifle confused and the middle section, from "Transition" through "Kulturreinigung" and the second "Trivia," seems susceptible of further clarification. . . . If there is any major criticism of the work, however, it is the rather extraordinary one that Weidman has given himself too little to do. The poignant, tragi-comic figure of the Artist is too often lost in the crowd; his solo bits are brief and few, and in certain small sections such as the second "Trivia," in which he is being measured, the scene belongs not to him but to the five boys who are doing the measuring. [Weidman is] one of the finest mimes of our day. Beneath a surface of clowning, that is in itself brilliant, he is able to project a comment that is frequently venomous in its satire and just as frequently colored by warmth and understanding.[35]

Bennington Banner:

> [*Quest* is] a masculine and realistic work contrasting with Miss Humphrey's by its more pronounced rhythms. . . . Much of it is made up of the delicious satire of which Weidman is master.
>
> He for instance mimics the patronage of the Grand Dames of Society and, in a ludicrous version of the Goosestep, hits the purification of the artist by a regimented program and schedule of "Kultur." The news writers and critics come in for their lambasting in a laughable pantomime in which a corps bang rhythmically on their typewriter keys, pull over the shift levers of their machines and hand out copy by the ream.[36]

Marjorie Church, *Dance Observer*:

"Pro Patria" is one of the most stirring arguments against war ever evolved, and the final dance of "Affirmation" is all that could be desired as a climax to a work of this sort, with its thrilling group rhythm, its recurrent theme like a great shout. In conception and treatment, with re-working of some parts, *Quest* is a rich achievement for Mr. Weidman and for the social potentialities of the Modern Dance.[37]

Virginia Mishnun, *Brooklyn Eagle*:

Mr. Weidman takes some well aimed cracks at critics pounding out their irrelevancies, at wealthy patronesses, at nationalism, at any number of bugaboos that beset the struggling artist. In some of these satiric episodes [his] incisive wit is at its keenest. But he has neglected his own role as the artist. The character lacks definition and functions merely as a reagent, responding to the contemporary scene. In fact the artist is almost as shadowy a figure as his allegorical lady, . . . exquisitely danced by Miss Humphrey. Their duets, composed of simple measures, provide a beautiful and restful interlude in the kaleidoscopic turbulence of the artist's life. "Convergence" and "Affirmation" resolve the composition on a positive, heroic note. There is real magnificence and grandeur in the forward movement of the final groupings. . . .

What the modern dance needs right now are a half dozen good scenario writers who can produce interesting scripts for dancers to dance to. It is the sheer choreographic inventiveness of Humphrey and Weidman that lifts their drama out of the realm of the commonplace to a level of high interest. But one would like to see what they would achieve with a story worthy of their talents.[38]

Subsequent Reviews:

Margaret Lloyd, *Christian Science Monitor*, on its New York premiere:

In the changes made for the Hippodrome performance I missed the things I had liked best at Bennington. Instead of the expected tightening was a loosening. The changes seemed to prolong some of the less desirable passages and leave more desirable passages out altogether. For example, in "Anthropometry," I liked the yardstick and the scissors, the antic pantomime by an ensemble of six men, as it was originally given. No doubt Mr. Weidman thought it too literal for he reduced it to a duo-dance with Mr. Limón that seemed much too long and not half so funny.[39]

John Martin, *America Dancing*:

In content, *Quest* is decidedly the solidest of all Weidman's compositions to date. If it contains less of his incomparable comedy, it finds him far more secure than he has ever been before in the handling of deeper matters. It is also by all odds his most successful treatment of large group movements, and the work as a whole is a new milestone in the career of this genuinely brilliant young artist. . . . His art is utterly underivative; there has been nobody in the dance before him to pattern after, and certainly there is nobody even remotely like him in the dance today.[40]

Paul Love, *Nation*:

Sections of this dance were in his [Weidman's] best satiric manner, in which he remains unequaled, but others were excessively prolix. I still feel that he is

> more at home and gets better results in the purely theatrical field. In creating for the concert stage he is not subject to the restricted time limit and the fast tempo that govern the revue. He is best in the dramatic form he has employed in *Happy Hypocrite, Bargain Counter*, and others. *Quest* was most effective in the opening sections in dance pantomime, wherein the omniscient critics and the old harridans of patrons were pilloried. The last half lost much of its impact through the sudden, unexpected shift to the symbolic.[41]

Winthrop Palmer, *Theatrical Dancing in America*:

> *Quest* was a major work. . . . Weidman expressed his belief that the artist was the true spokesman of mankind. Shawn's pre-occupation with art as religion, in the substitution of dances for the hierarchy of a priesthood, has no place at all in Weidman's philosophy. To his mind, Art as a cult and artists in ivory towers will languish or be unknown.
>
> In the performance of *Quest*, two levels are used for the action. On the lower level, the artist, played by Charles Weidman, slowly emerges from the crowd. On the upper level, his Inspiration, played by Doris Humphrey, follows his course. His first works are attacked by the critics. They disagree among themselves and the public rejects the artist. In an effort to save himself, he seeks patronage among the women, but they degrade him to the state of a gigolo. He flees from them in an interlude danced by men, and is next reincarnated in contemporary Germany, where he is classified according to racial and political ideas, only to be thrown to the dogs of war under the insignia of "Pro Patria." The allegorical figure finally emerges to inspire new "affirmations," and the crowd unites to face the future with a common purpose.
>
> This work is very similar in feeling to what Victor Hugo expresses in his ode entitled, *Le Poete*. . . . With *Quest*, Charles Weidman seems to have ended his apprenticeship. Allegory and fantasy no longer occupy him. He begins to study the life of the people around him.[42]

NOTES

1. News release, Bennington School of the Dance, 8 August 1936.
2. Paul Love, "The Adventure of Doris Humphrey," *Dance* 1, no. 6 (March 1937): 9, 30.
3. Letter from Doris Humphrey to Charles Francis Woodford, 12 July 1936 [Doris Humphrey Collection, C390].
4. Quoted in Eugene C. Howe, "The Modern Dance and William Blake," *Journal of Health and Physical Education* 9, no. 1 (January 1938): 8.
5. Interview with Walter Terry.
6. John Martin, "The Dance: A Novel Work," *New York Times*, 23 August 1936.
7. "Dance, Pantomime and Music in Bennington College's Festival," *Newsweek* 8, no. 8 (22 August 1936): 27. Copyright 1936 by Newsweek, Inc. All rights reserved. Reprinted by permission.
8. Walter Terry, "Humphrey-Weidman Workshop Group Offers New Dances at Bennington," *Boston Herald*, 18 August 1936.
9. Margaret Lloyd, "Testament of Progress," *Christian Science Monitor*, 25 August 1936.
10. Margaret Lloyd, *The Borzoi Book of Modern Dance* (New York: Alfred A. Knopf, 1949), p. 95.
11. John Martin, *New York Times*, 23 August 1936.
12. Margaret Lloyd, "Forces That Make a Festival," *Christian Science Monitor*, 8 September 1936.
13. Lloyd, *Borzoi*, p. 98.
14. Letters from Doris Humphrey to Julia Humphrey, postmarked 7 January 1937 and 17 January 1937 [Doris Humphrey Collection, C396].
15. See Selma Jeanne Cohen, *Doris Humphrey: An Artist First* (Middletown, Conn.: Wesleyan University Press, 1972), p. 191, and Charles Payne, *American Ballet Theatre* (New York: Alfred A. Knopf, 1978), p. 159. For descriptions of *With My Red Fires* see also *Don McDonagh's Complete Guide to Modern Dance* (New York: Popular Library, 1977), pp. 123–24, and Lloyd, *Borzoi*, pp. 98–100.
16. *Bennington Banner*, 14 August 1936.
17. Margaret Lloyd, *Christian Science Monitor*, 25 August 1936.
18. Walter Terry, *Boston Herald*, 18 August 1936.
19. Joseph Arnold Kaye, *Dance* 1, no. 1 (October 1936): 9.
20. Edna Ocko, "Texts for Dancers," *New Theatre* 3, no. 9 (September 1936): 19–20.
21. Virginia Mishnun, *Brooklyn Eagle*, 23 August 1936.
22. John Martin, *New York Times*, 14 August 1936.
23. John Martin, *New York Times*, 23 August 1936.
24. Joseph Kaye, *Cincinnati Enquirer*, 30 August 1936.
25. Margaret Lloyd, "The Inextinguishable 'Fires,'" *Christian Science Monitor*, 26 January 1937.
26. John Martin, "The Dance: 'Red Fires,'" *New York Times*, 5 February 1939.
27. John Martin, "The Dance: A Revival," *New York Times*, 16 May 1953.
28. News release, Bennington School of the Dance, 8 August 1936.
29. Interview with Norman Lloyd.
30. John Martin, "The Dance: A Pantomime," *New York Times*, 30 August 1936.
31. Margaret Lloyd, *Christian Science Monitor*, 25 August 1936.
32. John Martin, *New York Times*, 30 August 1936.
33. Margaret Lloyd, *Christian Science Monitor*, 8 September 1936.
34. Margaret Lloyd, *Christian Science Monitor*, 25 August 1936.
35. John Martin, *New York Times*, 30 August 1936.
36. *Bennington Banner*, 14 August 1936.
37. Marjorie Church, "The Workshop Production," *Dance Observer* 3, no. 7 (August-September 1936): 79–80.
38. *Brooklyn Eagle*, 23 August 1936.
39. *Christian Science Monitor*, 26 January 1937.
40. John Martin, *America Dancing* (Brooklyn, N.Y.: Dance Horizons, 1968), pp. 239–40.
41. Paul Love, *Nation* 144, no. 24 (12 June 1937): 679–80.
42. Winthrop Palmer, *Theatrical Dancing in America* (New York: Bernard Ackerman, 1945), pp. 80–81.

1937

30 July 1937

Opening Dance

Vermont State Armory

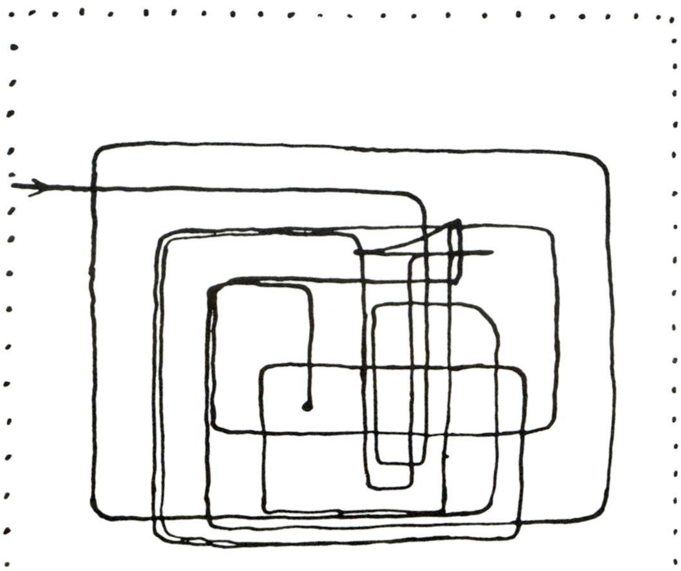

Opening Dance. Floor movement drawing by Arch Lauterer, 1937. Courtesy of Henry Kurth, The Arch Lauterer Archives.

Chor Martha Graham (solo). *Mus* Norman Lloyd (original piano score).

"Graham was at a turning point leaving the period of stark simplicity, of stripping down to essentials," Norman Lloyd recalled. "She was beginning to go into something a little more romantic and lyrical. I didn't realize it and she was inarticulate about it. I wrote it [the score] as though it were still her stark period. Later I realized I hadn't caught the thing. It wasn't successful."[1]

Subsequent Productions: As far as can be determined, *Opening Dance* was never performed again.

Reviews John Martin, *New York Times*: "The other new work is, naturally enough, less notable. [It] belongs in that most thankless category of the recital dance, something to raise the curtain with."[2]

30 July 1937

Immediate Tragedy—Dance of Dedication

Vermont State Armory

Chor Martha Graham (solo). *Mus* Henry Cowell (original score).

According to Barbara Page Beiswanger, the music was for trumpet, percussion, and piano.[3] However, Lloyd talked about oboe and clarinet.[4] Cowell wrote the score without seeing the dance, via correspondence with Graham. Norman Lloyd described the process:

> The music for *Immediate Tragedy* was written by Cowell in California, while Miss Graham composed the dance in Bennington, Vermont. Cowell knew the mood of the dance, its tempo and its meter. Not knowing how long any section of the dance was, Cowell invented a method he called "elastic form" by which his music could be matched to the dance.

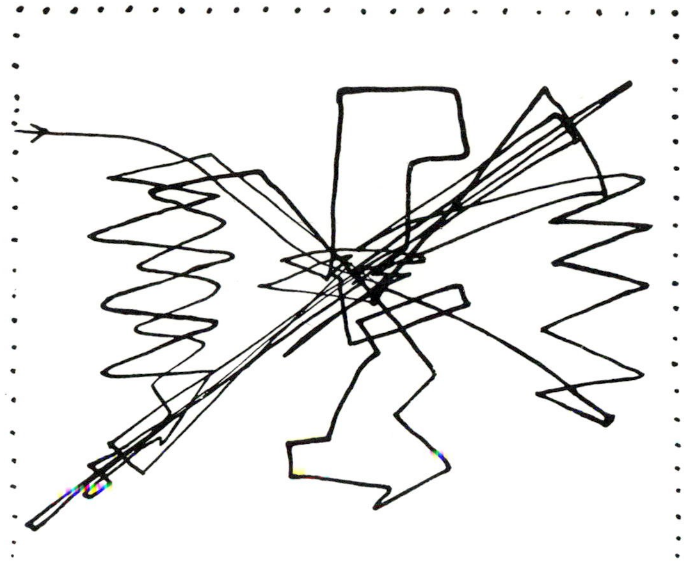

Immediate Tragedy. Floor movement drawing by Arch Lauterer, 1937. Courtesy of Henry Kurth. The Arch Lauterer Archives.

I well remember the day the music arrived at Bennington. Louis Horst and I looked at it and agreed that we had never seen anything like it. Cowell had written two basic phrases to be played by oboe and clarinet. Each phrase existed in two-measure, three-measure, eight-measure versions, and so on. All that was necessary was to fit a five-measure musical phrase to a five-measure dance phrase—or make such overlaps as were deemed necessary. The process, as I remember it, took about an hour. The total effect was complete unity—as though dancer and composer had been in the closest communication. Sombre and sparse, the music exactly matched the mood of Miss Graham's dance. *Immediate Tragedy*, and its companion piece, *Deep Song*, became two of the finest solos in the Graham repertory.[5]

Immediate Tragedy was performed at Bennington without a set, but Arch Lauterer designed a setting for it later. According to a report of an exhibit in Dance International: 1900–1937, "Arch Lauterer's sketches of the sets he designed for Martha Graham's new dance, *Immediate Tragedy*, proved to be the most elaborate settings she has used."[6]

New York Premiere: 19 December 1937, Guild Theatre.

Reviews

John Martin, *New York Times*:

> Not since the eloquent and beautiful *Frontier* . . . has she given us anything half so fine as *Immediate Tragedy*. Though its subject matter, dealing as it does with contemporary Spain, is removed half-way around the world from the early American milieu of *Frontier*, there is something that the two dances possess in common. Perhaps it is their spirit of dedication; perhaps it concerns also their simplicity of form and the transparent elements of which they are built. . . . This will be a moving dance long after the tragic situation in Spain has been brought to a conclusion, for it has completely universalized its materials. Indeed, neither its title nor its subtitle, *Dance of Dedication*, has a word to say about any specific happening or locale. It is a picture of fortitude, especially of woman's fortitude; of the acceptance of a challenge with a kind of passionate self-containment. From its emotional quality one recognizes its source rather than through any external means.

> To be sure, there is a touch of Spain in the costume, if only the merest hint; there is also an occasional bit of movement which presents the magnificent dignity of the Spanish woman as we know her through her dance. Again, Henry Cowell's deeply poignant music with its persistent phrase is couched in the measure of the sarabande. But the work communicates its meaning far less by any of these surface aids than by the innate power of evocation which belongs to Martha Graham. In this great gift she is surpassed by no other artist of our time, and *Immediate Tragedy* finds her at her best.[7]

Rose Koenig, *Dance Observer*: "The effect of this dance is indeed immediate—crying out as it does with its every movement of the tragedy that is now Spain."[8]

Lincoln Kirstein, *Dance Observer*:

> I believe [Martha Graham] to be the greatest dancer on this continent, and it is my conviction that although there is nothing in her teaching or performance alien in essence from the developed classic dance, she stands alone in her strength and catholicity. I feel that Graham's *Immediate Tragedy*, produced at the last Bennington Festival, is more interesting in intention and execution within its limitations of a solo variation, than anything in dance personality or choreography since Massine's second movement in *Choreartium* (1934).[9]

12 August 1937

Dance to the People

Vermont State Armory

Chor Esther Junger (solo). *Mus* Jerome Moross (original piano score). *Sets & light* Gerard Gentile. *Cos* Betty Joiner.

Subsequent Productions: 4 January 1941, Washington Irving High School, New York.

12 August 1937

Ravage

Vermont State Armory

Chor Esther Junger (solo). *Mus* Harvey Pollins (original piano score). *Sets & light* Gerard Gentile. *Cos* Betty Joiner.

Subsequent Productions: None documented (but see p. 157).

12 August 1937

Festive Rites

Vermont State Armory

Chor Esther Junger. *Mus* Morris Mamorsky (original piano score). *Accom* Morris Mamorsky, Harvey Pollins. *Sets & light* Gerard Gentile. *Cos* Betty Joiner. ***a. Processional, b. Betrothal, c. Recessional.*** *Danc* Esther Junger, José Limón and Group: Jean Aubry, Dorothy Barnitz, Sara Jean Cosner, Victoria Kahn, Frances Kronstadt, Eileen Logan, Margaret Ramsey, Rima Rodion, Germaine Steffes, Eva Trofimov.

Subsequent Productions: *Betrothal Dance* from *Festive Rites*, 4 January 1941, Washington Irving High School, New York.

Fellow Esther Junger and Bennington Group in *Festive Rites*, 1937. Photograph courtesy of Esther Junger Klempner.

The Bennington fellowship was especially important for Esther Junger. As an independent artist, lacking the support system of a concert group or studio, Junger had never before had the means to compose for a group. Morris Mamorsky was assigned to write music for her. His score, *Festive Rites*, won recognition on its own. In 1938 he composed *American Holiday* for Humphrey-Weidman and subsequently became head of a network radio music department. "It gave both of us a very good start," Junger recalled.[10] Although Junger got the least advanced student dancers (most, she said, preferred to work with someone they had heard of), she regarded the project as very successful. She composed simple things for the group, concentrating on the choreography for herself and José Limón. (Limón was injured during rehearsals and had to curtail his own dancing in his Fellow's piece, *Danza de la Muerte*.) According to Junger, both solos remained in her repertoire; the solo section, *Betrothal Dance*, from *Festive Rites* was performed subsequently.

Reviews

John Martin, *New York Times*, assessed her group work favorably, compared with the two solos which he found disappointing:

> Miss Junger . . . introduces a new background into the Bennington scheme. . . . *Festive Rites* proved to be a finely made and thoroughly exciting theatre work. Its movement has the admirable qualities of flow and sequence which have long

> been characteristic of her personal approach, and its composition is simple, forthright and imaginative. The work is an erotic dance in more or less primitive style. . . . Miss Junger and José Limón perform a beautifully wrought duet against the background of the group, and perform it superbly. The music . . . introduces a highly promising composer to the dance field. In this, his first work in this medium, he has hit upon an excellent scheme of rhythmic counterpoint which brings out all the values in Miss Junger's highly rhythmic choreography.[11]

Bennington Banner:

> [*Dance to the People*, a] jazz-tempo dance was lively and intense. *Ravage* [had] a spasmodic series of rather harsh movements with beats extremely accented.[12]

Henry Gilfond, *Dance Observer*:

> Esther Junger is too good technically, and has too much inventive material to be spending her energies with material of little or no meaning at all.[13]

Paul Love, *Nation*:

> Both she and Mr. Limón danced brilliantly, moving with grave gaiety through a composition that was built with the utmost clarity and simplicity. . . . It was an achievement of first rank.[14]

12 August 1937

Danza de la Muerte

Vermont State Armory

Chor José Limón. *Mus* Henry Clark [e], Norman Lloyd (original score). *Musicians* Esther Williamson, Lloyd, pianist. Robert McBride, oboe. *Sets & light* Gerard Gentile. *Cos* Betty Joiner. ***a. Sarabande for the Dead*** *mus* Clark [e]. *Danc* group. ***b. Interlude (Hoch! Viva! Ave!)*** *mus* Lloyd. *Danc* Limón, ***c. Sarabande for the Living*** *mus* Clark [e] . *Danc* group. José Limón's Group: Pauline Chellis, Gertrude Green, Molly Hecht, Emily White, Mary Elizabeth Whitney, Mildred Wile, James Lyons, Alwin Nikolais, Peter Terry, James Welch.

Program Note: "The suite of dances in *Danza de la Muerte* (Dance of Death) was motivated by the present civil war in Spain. The opening dance by the group is a tragic ritual celebrating the dead. The Interlude contains three solos which deal with the personified causes of the destruction in Spain. The closing dance by the group is one of defiance and dedication."

Limón used two sarabandes for oboe and piano written by Henry Leland Clarke (spelled Clark then). He asked Norman Lloyd to write a series of brief interludes between them. Each, said Lloyd, turned out to be about ten minutes long.[15] Alwin Nikolais was a student dancer in Limón's first group.

Limón's costume was black and he employed accessories, including a long green drape, which was used "in a striking fashion" in "Viva!"[16]

New York Premiere: November-December 1937, YMHA. Recital by the American Dance Association.

Reviews

John Martin thought Limón's solos in the middle section were "considerably less effective than the group sections . . . as in Miss Junger's case."[17] Martin continued, in the *New York Times*:

> The theme of the composition . . . deals with the war in Spain, and between the lament for the dead and the final call to action, Mr. Limon himself personifies

what he believes to be the three causes of the war. . . . In the two sarabandes there is at once evident a talent for pictorial design, and through it there flashes a certain emotional warmth. . . . The choreography is a little overwrought to match the simple phrase and the tragic dignity of Mr. Clark's music. This is perhaps one of the inevitable risks of employing music that has been written independently. Mr. Limón's invention as a composer is admirable, and it is especially noteworthy that he speaks entirely for himself with no carry-over from the personal style of Mr. Weidman.

Henry Gilfond, *Dance Observer*:

The "Interlude" . . . lacked both the vividness and the force of the group work. It was rather unfortunate that the dancer was badly hurt just two days before performance and that he was forced to mutilate his solo compositions. . . . There is a decided development in approach to subject matter for his work and a decidedly original tone in his group choreography. He is still rather much preoccupied with movement *per se*. . . .[18]

12 August 1937

Façade-Esposizione Italiana

Vermont State Armory

Chor Anna Sokolow. *Mus* Alex North (original score). *Pianists* Ruth Lloyd, North. *Sets & light* Gerard Gentile. *Cos* Betty Joiner. ***a. Belle Arti, b. Giovanezza, c. Prix Femina, d. Phantasmagoria.*** *Citizen* Anna Sokolow. *Group* Betty Bloomer [Ford], Nina Caiserman, Jean Erdman, Natalie Harris, Hortense Lieberthal, Naomi Lubell, Elizabeth Moore, Pearl Satlien, Margaret Strater, Elizabeth van Barneveld.

Program Note: "For the public gaze are shown only the finest examples of art, youth and womanhood."

Of the three Fellows, Anna Sokolow was the most experienced choreographer. Many of her early works were concerned with political and social issues. *Façade* was viewed as a companion piece to *War Is Beautiful*, composed the previous year. Among the dancers in her group was Betty Bloomer (Mrs. Gerald R. Ford), in her only Bennington performance, and Jean Erdman, dancing at Bennington for the first time.

New York Premiere: 26 February 1939, Alvin Theatre, under the auspices of *New Masses*.

Reviews

John Martin, *New York Times*:

Miss Sokolow has cast herself in the role of a citizen, who watches the exhibition of national greatness from a grandstand and on its basis defies the world. It is this central role which holds the work together, and Miss Sokolow's performance of it is magnificent for its stillness and strength. About her the group moves in a kind of surrealiste attitudinizing, and one is reminded forcibly of Massine's handling of a similar problem in the pastoral movement of *Fantastic Symphony*.

For sheer workmanship and authority Miss Sokolow has done nothing else that compares with this composition, but . . . she has not succeeded in escaping entirely the decadence of style she is denouncing, and comes perilously near to the pitfalls of the fashionable "neo-classicism." As . . . one who believes in the creation of a "proletarian" dance art, she finds herself here in a slightly anomalous situation.[19]

New Masses:

> One doesn't any longer expect student work from Sokolow—and one doesn't get it.
>
> *Façade-Esposizione Italiana* for which Alex North wrote a beautifully apt score, is a satiric comment on the irony of Italian fascist culture . . . with Anna Sokolow, the Citizen (her first appearance in her own group composition), an interested, nervous, and finally—as the whole cultural facade disintegrates like a worm-eaten pillar—accusing and protesting figure.
>
> *Façade* has less anger than *War Is Beautiful* [composed the previous year], but a more poignant human quality for all its bitterness: "Belle Arti" is crumby imitation Greek and superficial Florentine; "Giovanezza" is a hollow cartoon of athletic enthusiasm; "Prix Femina" is for the meek and bloodless "lady of kitchen"; "Phantasmagoria" has the Citizen twisted and turned till literally he walks on his head and climbs walls—backwards. The single gesture of accusation that emerges from the mess—the Citizen's hand saying, "There you have it!"—writes a dozen pages and a score of speeches.[20]

Henry Gilfond, *Dance Observer*:

> When all the cheap Fascist show, the fake art and the fake enthusiasm, falls apart of its own corruption behind her, the Citizen walks forward into the audience, with her Speaker's gesture demands recognition of what is happening, demands that the audience take cognizance of what she has said.[21]

Paul Love, *Nation*:

> The group, decadent in costume and movement, formed a moving tableau, full of biting comment and dissolute madness. Against this facade Miss Sokolow passed as a somber figure of annunciation. Motion was reduced to a minimum, yet she was able to dominate the entire dance magnificently by the sheer force of her personality.[22]

12 August 1937

Opus for Three and Props

Vermont State Armory

Chor José Limón, Esther Junger. *Mus* Dmitri Shostakovitch. *Sets & light* Gerard Gentile. *Cos* Betty Joiner. *Danc* Junger, Limón, Anna Sokolow. ***a. With Pole** chor* Limón. ***b. With Hats** chor* Junger.

Subsequent Performances: None

Reviews

Bennington Banner:

> The curtain closer was a most amusing parody on forms of dance movement in which the three young artists collaborated. . . . In each of these short skits, the artists mimicked the ballet.[23]

13 August 1937

Trend: A Dance in Two Sections

Vermont State Armory

Original production of *Trend*, Vermont State Armory. Photograph by Bouchard, copyright © 1981 by Thomas Bouchard.

Chor Hanya Holm. *Mus* Wallingford Riegger (original score). Music for ***Resurgence*** is *Ionisation* [1931] by Edgar[d] Varèse. (*Ionisation* was spelled with a z in the Bennington program; Edgard Varèse in this period had dropped the d from his name. He resumed using it after 1940.) [For the New York premiere, Holm added a final movement, ***Assurance***, with Varèse's *Octandre*.] *Mus dir* Norman Lloyd. *Musicians* Lloyd, Harvey Pollins, piano. Hugo Bergamasco, flute. H. Tafarella, oboe. J. Youshkoff, bassoon. V. Peretti, trumpet. S. Gershek, drums. Franziska Boas, Carolyn Durand, percussion. Special equipment for the reproduction of a recording of *Ionisation* by Mirko Paneyko. *Sets & light* Gerard Gentile. *Asst* Edward Glass, William H. Rudd. *Cos* Betty Joiner. *Danc* Holm and Concert Group with Members of the School Workshop. Members of Hanya Holm's Concert Group: Louise Kloepper, Lucretia Wilson, Carolyn Durand, Elizabeth Waters, Bernice van Gelder, Henrietta Greenhood [Eve Gentry], Keith Coppage, Marva Jaffay, Miriam Kagan, Ruth Ledoux, Lydia Tarnower. Students of the School Workshop: Mary Standring Adair, Helen Alkire, Mary Alice Andrews, Carol Beals, Caryl Cuddeback, Elizabeth Ann Davis, Hermine Dudley, Helen Ellis, Marianne Elser, Mary Gillette, Margaret Jewell, Helen Knight, Hildegarde Lewis, Caroline Locke, Victoria Payne,

Josephine Reddin, Harriet Roeder, Jeannette Saurborn, Dorothy Smith, Edith Vail, Florence Warwick, Martha Wilcox. I. ***Mask Motions. a. Our Daily Bread. b. Satiety. Episodes. a. The Effete*** Kloepper, soloist. ***b. Lucre Lunacy*** van Gelder, soloist. ***c. From Heaven, Ltd.*** Wilson, soloist. ***d. Lest We Remember*** Waters, soloist. ***e. He, the Great*** Greenhood [Eve Gentry], soloist. ***Cataclysm.*** II. ***The Gates Are Desolate*** Holm, soloist. ***Resurgence.***

Program Note: "*Trend* is a picture of the processes of man's survival when the usages of living have lost their meaning and he has fallen into routine patterns of conformity. Though in this direction of decadence lie only catastrophe and ultimate annihilation, there emerges out of the ordeal itself a recognition of the common purposes of men and the conscious unity of life."

Trend, for a group of 33 women, was Hanya Holm's first major composition in the United States and is considered her greatest work.

"The generally lyric character" of her earlier, smaller compositions, wrote John Martin, "afforded no hint at all of the dramatic power and the theater quality which she was to reveal in her first large work. . . . *Trend* had all the dynamic quality that is characteristic of the American dance, but it retained, also, the more subjective qualities of the German dance—its sense of space, its fluency, its unbroken relationship of movement to emotion, and at least its attitude to music, if not a full realization of it in practice. All these elements . . . brought the dance to a new realization of its theater possibilities."[24]

Holm had begun thinking about *Trend* before the start of her Bennington residency. She went to theologian Paul Tillich for advice in sorting out from among five themes a central, unifying theme for *Trend.*[25]

At the time of its New York premiere, Holm described her working processes:

> The idea of *Trend* grew upon me—it was not a sudden inspiration. The theme issued from life itself, rather than being built up as an intellectual construction. Impressions of years traveled a long path of development before they took shape as the theme of *Trend*.
>
> The vision of the theme was so far expanded, so vast, that crystallization was necessary first of all. I had to eliminate and sacrifice in order to draw things together into a logical outline, to point the conception.
>
> Then the mental image began to take shape. The motif of the whole was visionary, vital and dynamic. The form was pushed onward by timely, spatial and dynamic happenings. The visual part of the externalization resulted from experience and imagination.
>
> The character and force of the theme itself dictated the form, the volume, shape and frame of the dance. Specifically, the dance action demanded space-creating values. Planes and levels became a necessity of the composition. Ramps of various grades, as well as steps, were essential to connect the different planes: some calling forth rhythmic dynamic space action; others long sustained sweeps. Proportions of horizontal extension in relation to vertical flight were important.
>
> A large number of dancers was needed to carry out the weight of the action. This was not an arbitrary decision. It was a requirement inherent in the theme. Yet the performance of the dance action was by no means left entirely to mass movement. The theme calls for making various uses of the large group, of smaller groups and even individuals. There was a continuous change of weight, of volume, of linear and dimensional values.
>
> Themes of wider significance required more mass and architectural values in concentrated or contrapuntal relation. Such numbers were "Our Daily Bread," "Satiety," "Cataclysm," "Resurgence," and "Assurance." I must emphasize that everything was determined by organic development, rather than intellectual decision. For example, the five episodes in the opening section grew out of the whole and led back into it.

Each episode was mainly carried by a soloist. Yet each characterization had different attention demands. In one, "Lest We Remember," the soloist was self sufficient. No group movement or other factor than the values of space proportions was necessary. In another, "The Effete," the group movement was restrained, forming a sustained counterweight without action. In "From Heaven, Limited" the group was a supporting factor, and the soloist was the climactic point of the group action. In "Lucre Lunacy" the group was drawn into the soloist's activity. In the last of the episodes, "he, the Great," the group was most prominent in reacting to the soloist. In the part I took over myself, the soloist formed the sustaining transition from a dramatic climax ("Cataclysm"), through solitude, to a new development ("The Gates Are Desolate"). In this last mentioned number the same soloist carried the *leitmotif*.

The dramatic character of *Trend* demanded a departure from the usual abstract symbolic handling of dance themes. Dance action was required rather than dance abstraction. It was imperative to call for the unification of all theatrical media. Their practical use was a thematic demand rather than a decorative decision. Theatrical setting I have already touched upon. The three dimensional significance of space also demanded the architectural handling of light, as well as the rhythm and volume of color—in lights, costumes and the covering of the setting, the floor cloth and the cyclorama.[26]

After a second viewing at Bennington, John Martin described the work's action:

From the opening moment a gripping mood is created. . . . "Mask Motions" pictures a trance-like life in which men have forgotten why they live and merely go through endless repetitions of set formulas. We see first the toilers moving in droves, all exactly alike, energetic but unanimated. Happily, Miss Holm has not made them "slaves of the machine" but rather victims of that intangible mechanism which is routine living. But we are also asked to consider those lilies of the social field who neither toil nor spin and these we find equally driven, equally a herd devoid of animation.

Out of this general panorama of obsession there now grows a series of five more specific episodes, each centering about a solo figure, each presenting a particular phase of decadence, but all joining with remarkable unity, almost after the manner of the cinema's montage, into a terrible exhibition of social neurosis. This is quite the most brilliant section of the whole composition, not only for the persuasiveness of its material, but perhaps more for the keenly felt presence behind it of a healthy mind which is able to present decadence without becoming part of it.

The first of these episodes, "The Effete," is marvelously danced by Louise Kloepper, chiefly on the steps which, together with ramps at broken angles, unite the two levels of the stage. As she darts and slithers up and down in a limp but feverish futility, the group lies about the stage completely inert save for a single figure here and a pair there who sway in a lethargic counterpoint. The second episode presents the obsession of acquisitiveness for its own sake, and Bernice van Gelder performs its solo role excellently. There is next a mass movement called "From Heaven, Ltd.," in which Lucretia Wilson as a kind of composite of Sister Aimee and Father Divine leads the group to large-scale religious escapism against a musical background of slightly sour and considerably jazzed-up hymn tunes.

Out of this grows the fourth episode, chiefly a solo by Elizabeth Waters without musical accompaniment. It is called "Lest We Remember" and presents the flight into fantasy; not the whimsical fantasy of elves and sprites, but of the hashish dream and madness.

[A precis of the fifth solo, "He, the Great," is omitted in Martin's column. Margaret Lloyd describes it as "misplaced hero-worship in a deceptive political savior."[27]]

All of the forces of the decadence which had been pictured are finally climaxed in a section called "Cataclysm." Here again Miss Holm shows her surpassing sense of form. The section is in effect a compositional struggle between movement in the vertical plane and that in the horizontal. There is a highly effective use of the group in scattered formation and of parallel movement by widely separated figures.

This section is psychologically the turning point in the work. The movement which follows is called, in biblical phrase, "The Gates Are Desolate." The pattern of life has been broken, the hypnotic spell of meaningless activity has been destroyed, and for the first time the real thinking and feeling powers of men stand forth. Though the spirit of the movement is one of deepest grief, it contains also an upward note in the emergence for the first time of a warmly human tone, albeit a sorrowing one. Here Miss Holm makes her only appearance in the entire work as a solo figure uniting two groups moving in different styles. She has given herself nothing at all spectacular to do but fills admirably the simple role she has set herself.

The final section deals with the breaking up of the old mass into its essential units of force and the reassembling of these units in a more voluntary and intelligent association for joint effort.

Resurgence employs as a musical background a recorded version of Edgar Varese's "Ionization," composed entirely for percussion instruments and difficult to listen to after an evening of music in more orthodox manner. On first contact there is likely to be a feeling that the dance is overshadowed by so much volume, but on second seeing, and especially second hearing, Miss Holm's selection of this music seems more than justified.[28]

"Hanya choreographed in such a way that we in the company were often involved in creating our own action or sequence of movements," said Eve Gentry [Henrietta Greenhood], who danced in both the Bennington and New York productions.[29]

I cannot recall in what section of *Trend* this occurred, but out of the blue and in a flash of energy I did a short run, jump, turn in the air, back fall full out, an immediate backward catapult with body thrown in the air, landing face downward, stretched out, supported on hands and toes. Hanya was very excited about it and wanted many people to do it in succession. And so I taught it to those who would attempt it. I recreated the action in 1952 in my dance, *The Sea Gives Up Its Ghosts*. We each choreographed our own solos for *Trend*. Hanya would have us move, and she would select out from small phrases and movements different ideas. I wanted to do "Lucre Lunacy" or one of the other solos I had choreographed, but Hanya had selected someone else for that and wanted me to do, "he, the Great" instead because I was the smallest in the company. I was brought in standing on Carolyn Durand and Louise Kloepper's shoulders. I felt restricted because I had so little movement leeway, but experiences like that sometimes bring out something else by the very restriction. In time you find a way of making it forceful. By the time we did it in New York I had come to terms with it much more than at Bennington. For the New York performances we all had the opportunity of altering our solos somewhat, and I remember mine as being much better, much stronger as a result.[30]

When Holm worked with her group, she did not specifically discuss the philosophy of *Trend*.

> She would talk to us to try to bring something out of us. She'd say, "I want you to do such and such; I want you to enter this kind of way," and I think in trying to bring out the kind of movement she wanted, her ideas came through. Hanya never talked to us about those ideas in terms of concrete things like economics or politics. With Hanya it was a humanistic thing.
>
> *Trend* was probably the most dramatic and theatrical work Hanya ever did. I remember in I think it was the first movement, we started a series of slow deep pliés. I never moved so slowly in my life. We did these very slow pliés all the way down and all the way up, so slowly that one was hardly aware that the group was moving. I think that must have looked tremendous. It felt wonderful. Physically it was very difficult, but it grew on one, this sense of weight, endlessness, unpunctuated flow. All of *Trend* was a great individual experience as well as a great group experience. One felt the staging of it, what other people were doing on the stage. I felt a great sense of the scope of the work. When I was way downstage doing something, I felt that group way upstage who were swaying slowly from side to side. The way Hanya worked on it, the way it was choreographed, we had time to watch the various groups work as different groups, and it had a tremendous emotional impact on us. It was one of the greatest experiences of working with other people that I've ever had.[31]

Beatrice Seckler, who was with the Humphrey-Weidman group at Bennington, recalled *Trend*'s "flowing form" in which "one thing led to the next, and then to the next" in a seamless stream.[32]

Alwin Nikolais saw *Trend* during his first Bennington summer and retained an image "where the mass of dancers, just by raising one hand together, blew off the whole top of the universe."[33]

Walter Terry recalled all the exits and entrances and the feeling of depth and scale.

> It seemed like a mammoth production to us back then. Like Doris, Hanya used different levels, so it was not only the number of dancers but dancers at different levels and different depth patterns. Hanya was saying that *Trend* was the trend of the world, of mankind, of civilization, and you actually had a feeling of this passing in waves, and then it would all stop and a drama would happen, and then it would go on again. There was a sense of great size to it, both in concept and in staging.[34]

Jean Erdman wrote about its impact on her:

> Watching Hanya Holm's *Trend*, one experienced in non-objective form a revelation of the human social organism in its cycle of decline and re-creation. . . . We were carried through the drama of the dynamic principles that shape our social being, not by their representation in any particular historical or invested allegorical plot, but by seeing the rhythms of the forces themselves in conflict. The groupings of the dancers rendered them, and carried them into play. . . . One was caught in the drama of elemental forces pounding against each other. The formal pattern of the cycle of organic life was laid bare, without reference to specific event or individual catastrophe, for us to respond from the depths of our own organic being. One great Being of beings moved before us, in choral song, chanting the oracle of the everlasting Form.[35]

The sections of *Trend*, she wrote, were a "series of spiritual conformations made visible in movement-texture and formal, rhythmical relationships. The artist's choreography presented an image for our contemplation that, when understood, lifted us above our small egocentric horizon to a grandiose experience of a perspective from which came a deeper understanding of ourselves and our containing world."[36]

Music: Eve Gentry [Henrietta Greenhood], "knowing Hanya's interest in Varèse's music," introduced Holm to Varèse in New York in 1936; Gentry had met the Varèses in Santa Fe earlier that year.[37] "Hanya and Varèse met in my Eighth Street apartment for the first time. I recall how engrossed they became talking about *Ionisation* and *Octandre* and Hanya's choreographic interest in these works. Varèse took Hanya back to his apartment where she could hear these avant-garde works. So, the germ of *Trend* and its music was born."

Though Holm planned to use *Octandre* for the concluding section, "Assurance," this was not realized until the New York production. The bulk of the score for *Trend* was written especially by Wallingford Riegger, who was in residence at Bennington for five weeks. The 40-minute score is for piano, flute, oboe, bassoon, trumpet and percussion. At Bennington it was performed by an ensemble of nine musicians under Norman Lloyd's direction. A recording of Varèse's *Ionisation*, conducted by Nicolas Slonimsky, was amplified by means of special playback equipment designed by Mirko Paneyko. *Ionisation* is about five minutes long and calls for 13 musicians playing several dozen percussion instruments and two sirens. According to Norman Lloyd, the Varèse was performed in a recorded version not because Bennington lacked sufficient musical resources for a live performance but specifically "for dramatic effect."[38] "Paneyko had these tremendous loudspeakers. The idea was that *Ionisation* would come on after the Riegger score and blast you."

One section of *Trend*, the solo "Lest We Remember," was performed in silence.

Most reviewers thought the Riegger score was excellent. However, music critic Moses Smith found it on first hearing "trivial" and "too obviously derivative," though he granted it had its "forceful moments," especially in the "Cataclysm" section.[39]

Whatever the merits of the Riegger, it was no match for the iconoclasm of *Ionisation*. Composed in 1931, the work had been performed in New York but never previously in the small town of Bennington, Vermont, where the overpowering volume and battery of sounds emanating from the percussion instruments must have been shocking. "Varese's *Ionisation*," reported the *Bennington Banner* the next day, "departed entirely from melody and harmony as we know it today in conventional music. The basis of *Ionisation* seems to have been in noises of machinery such as the subway or automobile plus a peculiar quality of chemical combustion. Remarks apropos of the 'music' which obeyed the fundamental rules of subject, variation and restatement [the work is in Sonata form], were heard after the performance and they ranged from 'Chaos in a boiler factory' to 'music of the meteors.'"[40]

John Martin later asserted that *Ionisation* and *Octandre*, as previously composed works, "were completely right in color and courageous in instrumentation . . . but they inevitably imposed certain formal limitations upon the choreography."[41]

Sets: Credits for the sets and lights are confused. It is not clear why Gerard Gentile and not Arch Lauterer was credited for the Armory sets. All official documents credit Gentile as the designer of *Trend* at Bennington. However, Hanya Holm stated that Gentile executed the sets but Lauterer designed them. Gentile was technical director for the Bennington Festivals of 1936 and 1937, replacing Lauterer, who was on leave from Bennington College in that period. (Gentile was technical director and scene designer at Western Reserve University, 1931-1936, where he designed and built the Tower Theatre, Flora Stone Mather College in 1935. He returned to Cleveland in 1937.) However, Lauterer was on campus during the summer session in 1937, lectured, and made line drawings of Martha Graham's new solos in the Armory. It is clear

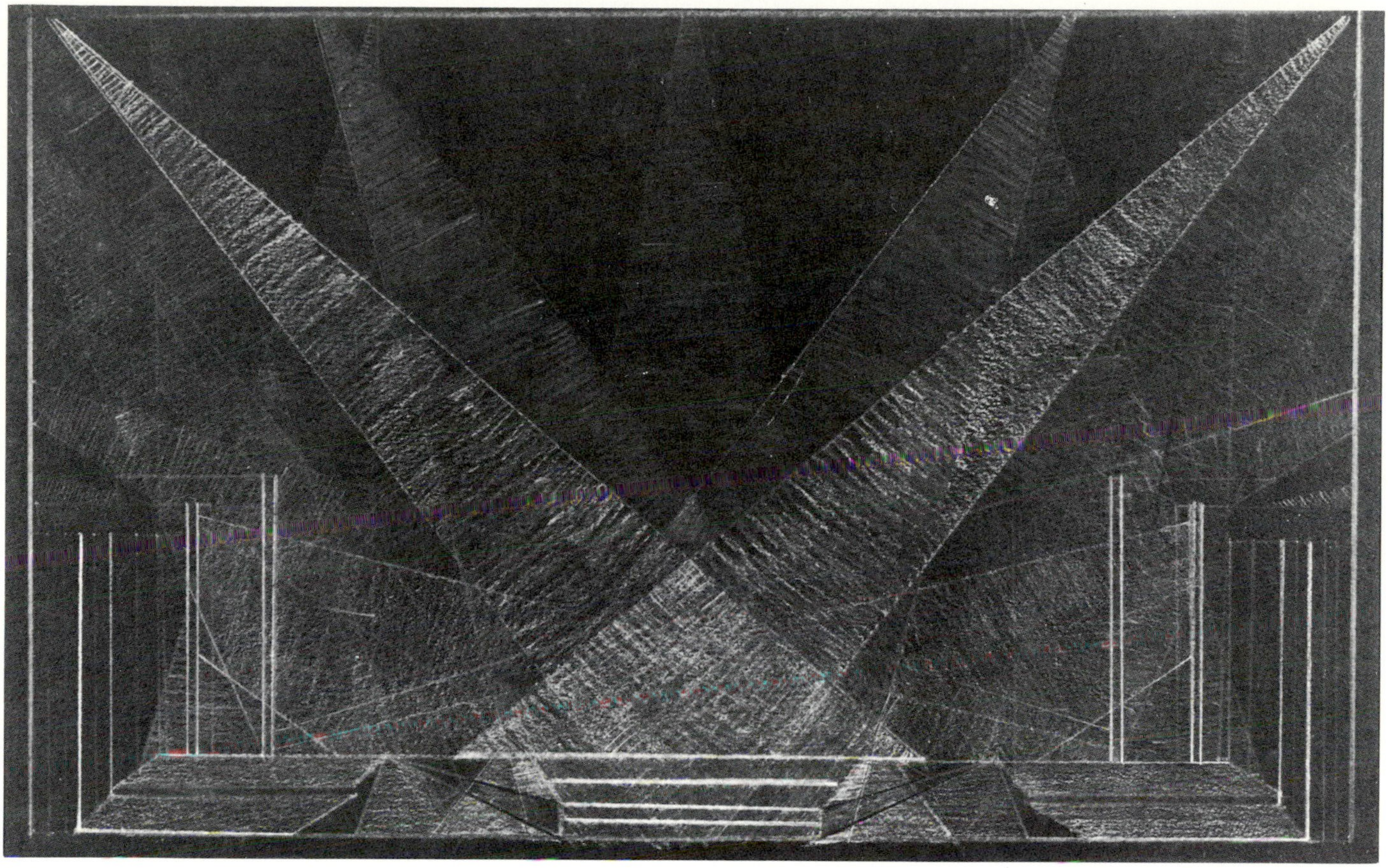

Light plan by Arch Lauterer for *Trend*. Photograph courtesy of Henry Kurth, The Arch Lauterer Archives.

that Holm collaborated with Lauterer on *Trend*; possibly these ideas were conveyed to Gentile, who then executed them at the Armory. Later biographical notes on Lauterer in the *Bennington College Bulletin* cite him as designer for the New York production of *Trend*. The New York production was more elaborately designed. Photographs taken by Thomas Bouchard at Bennington and by Barbara Morgan at the Mecca Auditorium reveal some differences. Moses Smith described the Bennington staging:

> Half of the main floor and a smallish balcony are given over to the spectators. [There were] two stages connected by ramps. The smaller one, on an upper level, was a real one, framed by a proscenium. The other was simply part of the main floor of the armory, the forward part from which the spectators were excluded.[42]

At the Mecca, all spectators were seated above; the orchestra was completely sealed off.

New York Premiere: 28 December 1937, Mecca Auditorium (later named New York City Center). This was Holm's New York debut as a dancer and choreographer. The Bennington group of 33 women (plus Holm) was reduced to 30. Featured dancers were as at Bennington, except for Keith Coppage, who replaced Bernice van Gelder in "Lucre Lunacy." Valerie Bettis, who did not dance in the Bennington production (she never attended the Bennington summer sessions), was in the augmented group at the Mecca. Holm extended her own role somewhat (though she was never a central figure) and added a concluding section, "Assurance: A World Primal Again," which according to John Martin was originally intended but not finished in time for the Bennington premiere. The music for "Assurance" was Varèse's seven-minute *Octandre* (1924) for wind ensemble, recorded specially for the Mecca performance by New Music Quarterly Recordings, under Nicolas Slonimsky's direction.

At Mecca the whole musical score (Riegger and Varèse) was played on recordings amplified through a system devised by Paneyko. Norman Lloyd conducted the original Riegger score for this recording.

Holm recalled the recording apparatus. "I went to Paneyko because he had a sound producing system that was his own—as big as anyone could have at that time. His machine had a nine-foot horn which he had backstage behind the set [at the Mecca]. In one of the side rooms, he built an enormous transformer."[43] Paneyko had been devising a variety of electrical reproduction techniques to project recorded sound into larger spaces—in and out of doors. For the Mecca production, he brought his newest, largest system.

Composer Harrison Kerr deemed the experiment "completely successful."

> Miss Holm's bold experiment with sound reproduction seems to solve the problem of adequate music for the dance. It makes available the color, sonority and rhythmic vitality of an orchestra without the use of the expensive and cumbersome symphonic ensemble. The music of a comparatively small group, so reproduced, gains sufficiently in power to become entirely adequate. Further development of this method would seem to offer limitless possibilities."[44]

Kerr's enthusiasm for the use of recordings was apparently not shared by musicians. On the day of one of the subsequent New York stagings, the recording of the Riegger was sabotaged in the sound booth, and Holm was forced to employ live musicians for that evening's performance.

Gervaise Butler, writing in *Dance Observer*, took a generally negative view of *Trend* but called the musical reproduction "an interesting device, eliminating the distraction of an orchestra or the definition of sound as coming from any one part of the stage, in other words, helping weld sound and movement into one homogeneous whole."[45]

Margaret Lloyd, who had missed the Bennington production, wrote of its realization in New York that "the score very nearly rivalled the dance in interest. . . . The special reproduction equipment . . . is considered in some circles a step in advance of music *per se* toward music as sound-effects in relation to the dance."[46] And John Martin saw it as a step toward "that goal of 'inspired sound effects' that have so long been sought for dance accompaniment."[47] "Though it will no doubt be a subject for argument in the dance field," Martin later wrote, "the result seems to justify the belief that a practical way has been opened at last to the solution of the difficult problem of replacing the obsolete piano in the accompaniment of modern dance."[48]

Arch Lauterer's name appears on the Mecca program as designer of sets and lighting. Costumes are Betty Joiner's from Bennington, in what Margaret Lloyd described as "piquant color combinations."[49] The Mecca setting she wrote was "a construction of ramps and steps of varied levels, and box-like wings with multicolored borders at either side of the stage, allowing for the unpredictable exits and entrances."

She elaborated in *The Borzoi Book of Modern Dance*:

> Arch Lauterer had built a world for dance forecasting the current vasty reaches of the Hollywood production number. It consisted of inclined planes and broken rhythms in multiple ramps and steps to join the upper and lower levels, with screens for wings and bare wall for backdrop, lighted to an eerie and chilling loneliness. The auditorium floor was cleared, the audience seated in the balconies, enhancing the sense of spatial immensity. The costumes, retained from Bennington, were along modern dance princess lines, nearly uniform, but for Hanya's long scarlet dress.[50]

At Bennington, *Trend*'s two parts were interrupted by a brief intermission. The New York program shows no such break. For the New York premiere, the program note read:

> *Trend* expresses the rhythm of our Western civilization in which social confusion overlays, but cannot eradicate, the timeless creative forces that persist beneath the surface of contemporary existence. The hectic drive of meaningless activity and strife, apathy and routine patterns of conformity, in which all the vital forces of life are debased or distorted, lead to ultimate disintegration. Out of the ordeal itself there emerges an awareness of the essential purposes of living; out of despair a renewed affirmation.

Subsequent Productions:

Trend was never again mounted in its entirety after two performances at the Mecca in 1937.

On 2 January 1938 the first two segments of Part One ("Mask Motions" and "Episodes") were performed in Dance International, 1900–1937, "An Evening of Modern Dance," at the Center Theatre, New York. On 28 January 1938 Holm and an augmented Concert Group of 30 presented Part Two ("The Gates Are Desolate," "Resurgence," and "Assurance") in a benefit "Dance for Spain" at New York's Hippodrome Theatre.[51]

Murray Louis and Alwin Nikolais danced in a revival of "Resurgence" in Colorado Springs in August 1949. For this performance Nicolas Slonimsky conducted a live performance of *Ionisation*. Nikolais recalled that one of the principal percussionists, who happened to own most of the instruments, was fired. There was no time to find others, so they improvised, using pots and pans. "It was a wild performance. Slonimsky was so excited he played it at about twice the speed it was supposed to be. It got such an ovation that he had to repeat it—more slowly this time."[52]

In 1976, Hanya Holm seemed doubtful that *Trend* was revivable.

> *Trend* used what was available—the solos were done by women. They had to behave like men because there were none. And I would have to have two stages, a lot of room. The old Mecca was absolutely even with the spectator. I closed off the orchestra and just sold the mezzanine and the gallery so you could look down, because otherwise you could only see the dancers from the waist up. I used a double stage, a platform which covered the stage, almost two stages in levels, connected with ramps and steps. On the side were ten or twelve shutters where the people came in and out rather fast. Upstage I had scrims so you could see the people in a semi-appearance before they were really visible. And a big cyclorama backdrop. That was all I had. The lighting by Arch Lauterer was superb. It couldn't be done that way anymore.[53]

In 1977 Alwin Nikolais and Murray Louis offered Holm their joint companies on which to mount a reconstruction, but the costs of the production proved too steep. The Bennington staging had cost the School of the Dance approximately $1000 (though more expense may have been involved). The New York production (1937) cost Holm about $10,000. In 1978 Holm estimated that the reconstruction in a theater large enough and having two stages with a company of 45 would entail a cost of perhaps $140,000.

Reviews

At its Bennington premiere, "an alert, intelligent, appreciative audience" included "people like Miss Graham and others associated with the school, Ruth St. Denis, Dane Rudhyar, the composer, and so forth," reported music critic Moses Smith, making his first Bennington visit. "There was nothing amateurish about the performance. The thirty-odd players had been not only drilled but had obviously been so imbued with the spirit of the movements that they seemed to be partaking of the creative process."[54]

John Martin, in his first-night review, called it "a series of sketches" rather than a finished work, but added, "nowhere else could such an important experimental production conceivably be attempted." "The work," he perceived, "is on a colossal theme, the survival of society out of a state of decadence and collapse." Holm had created "less a large group dance than a kind of heroic choric drama in which for words are substituted movement and a kind of dramatic expressionism."[55]

In his Sunday column in the *New York Times*, Martin elaborated on its "profound emotional comment" and its "intriguing concept of dance form . . . in which choreographic and dramatic values become identical. One would be tempted to pronounce the work unique in this latter regard but for the recollection that on this same stage a year ago Doris Humphrey in *With My Red Fires* built upon much the same basis." These "vastly different" compositions had one point in common: "two intuitively gifted composers have in their individual discoveries hit upon the same truth that relates the dance and the theatre in more than a superficial way."[56]

[*Trend*] emerges not as a collection of dances, but as a unified dramatic entity. Her designs appear in great sweeping dimensions, developing out of their own content, unhurried and unfaltering.

The protagonist is the group rather than the individual and personal virtuosity yields entirely to the greater powers of mass movement. The group . . . is in a continuous state of inner flux. Now a small group is posed against a larger one, now the separate figures are scattered, and one figure is employed against another. When the individual emerges, it is rather as an epitome than as a person. Dancer becomes actor in this work as in no other choreographic work that comes to mind, but he remains supremely impersonal in his emotion, a kind of symbol after the manner of the antique chorus. In the development of this approach, Miss Holm has perhaps brought the dance nearer to the substance and heart of the theatre in its fundamental sense than it has ever been brought before in our times.[57]

Margaret Lloyd spent the summer of 1937 in Europe and did not see the Bennington production of *Trend*. Writing years afterward, about its New York premiere, she admired its brilliant production but attributed its lack of impact on her to its impersonality:

> No synopsis can do justice to the musical continuity of flowing, ebbing movement, to the powerful group designs, the nuances of solo and ensemble passages, or the apt and sometimes waggish comment of Riegger's score. . . . It unfolded like a colossal panorama of diverse movement and music patterns. It was stupendous. It left me cold. I felt lost in the grim netherworld of excessive spatiality. . . . The dancers were so many forms and figures, not people.[58]

After its New York premiere, Martin wrote that the work made large demands upon its audience, but added, "Miss Holm brings to the business of composing a point of view totally different from that of any other of our major choreographers, and opens up a new vista for the production of great dance dramas."[59] He called *Trend* "a landmark in the progress of the modern dance" and singled out as a unique quality its "three-dimensional fullness:"

> The figures move not merely on a floor before a background but actually in and through the dimensions of the space enclosed. [Holm's movement also] is consciously three-dimensional, partly through its basis in the body's own potentialities and partly through its recognition that all movement must measure itself in terms of the space around it. Though it is subjected to the stylizations and distortions that all works of art demand, it maintains always the sense that there is a normal body underneath to give point to these deliberate departures from the norm.[60]

Holm's choreography, wrote Martin, demonstrated "a superb organization of material and a masterly instinct for the balancing of the values of group movement."[61]

THE BENNINGTON FESTIVAL SERIES
IN THE MODERN DANCE

The Bennington Festival Series for the season of 1937 includes seven concerts in the modern dance, of which these are the two final concerts. The Series is presented by artists who are leaders in the modern dance and members of the faculty of The Bennington School of the Dance. The first four programs in the 1937 season were: Doris Humphrey and Charles Weidman, two dance concerts with their groups; Martha Graham, two solo dance concerts; Esther Junger, Jose Limon and Anna Sokolow, one concert of solo and group dances.

The two final concerts in the Series present Hanya Holm as choreographer and dancer with her Concert Group and students of the 1937 Workshop Group of the School in two performances of TREND composed during the 1937 session of The Bennington School of the Dance and danced for the first time in these programs.

The entire composition, rehearsal and production of TREND have been carried out during the six-weeks session of The Bennington School of the Dance which opened on July 2. The dance has been composed by Hanya Holm, the music written by Wallingford Riegger, the musical direction being done by Norman Lloyd. The set by Gerard Gentile, assisted by Edward Glass, and the costumes by Betty Joiner, have been designed and executed during the School session.

The Workshop project of The Bennington School of the Dance was initiated in 1935 with the production of PANORAMA with Martha Graham as choreographer and solo dancer. In 1936 Doris Humphrey and Charles Weidman, as choreographers and solo dancers, presented "WITH MY RED FIRES" and QUEST as the Workshop concerts in the Festival Series. The School will present in 1938 a final week of concert productions by Martha Graham, Hanya Holm, Doris Humphrey and Charles Weidman, as The Bennington Festival for 1938.

The Bennington Festival Series

SUMMER 1937

THE BENNINGTON SCHOOL OF THE DANCE
Bennington, Vermont

Presents

HANYA HOLM

and her Concert Group
with Students of the School Workshop

TWO PERFORMANCES

Friday evening, August 13 and Saturday evening, August 14, 1937
In the Vermont State Armory, Bennington, Vermont
Nine o'clock Daylight Saving Time

PROGRAM

Salutation . . . *Henry Cowell*
CONCERT GROUP

City Nocturne . . *Wallingford Riegger*
CONCERT GROUP

Rhythm II . . . *Lucretia Wilson*
CONCERT GROUP

Festive Rhythm . . *Wallingford Riegger*
HANYA HOLM AND CONCERT GROUP

Prelude . . . *Wallingford Riegger*
CONCERT GROUP AND WORKSHOP GROUP

INTERMISSION — FIFTEEN MINUTES

TREND

A Dance in Two Sections
Choreography by Hanya Holm
Music by Wallingford Riegger
Music for *Resurgence* is "Ionization" by Edgar Varese
Danced by Hanya Holm, her Concert Group and students of the School Workshop
(The audience is requested to applaud only at the intermissions, not between the sections of the dance.)

I

Mask Motions
- a Our Daily Bread
- b Satiety

Episodes
- a The Effete
  Louise Kloepper, soloist
- b Lucre Lunacy
  Bernice van Gelder, soloist
- c From Heaven, Ltd.
  Lucretia Wilson, soloist
- d Lest We Remember
  Elizabeth Waters, soloist
- e He, the Great
  Henrietta Greenhood, soloist

Cataclysm

BRIEF INTERMISSION

II

The Gates are Desolate
Hanya Holm, soloist

Resurgence

TREND is a picture of the processes of man's survival when the usages of living have lost their meaning and he has fallen into routine patterns of conformity. Though in this direction of decadence lie only catastrophe and ultmate annihiliation, there emerges out of the ordeal itself a recognition of the common purposes of men and the conscious unity of life.

DANCERS OF THE GROUP

Members of Hanya Holm's Concert Group: Louise Kloepper, Lucretia Wilson, Carolyn Durand, Elizabeth Waters, Bernice van Gelder, Henrietta Greenhood, Keith Coppage, Marva Jaffay, Miriam Kagan, Ruth Ledoux, Lydia Tarnower.

Students of the School Workshop: Mary Standring Adair, Helen Alkire, Mary Alice Andrews, Carol Beals, Caryl Cuddeback, Elizabeth Ann Davis, Hermine Dudley, Helen Ellis, Marianne Elser, Mary Gillette, Margaret Jewell, Helen Knight, Hildegarde Lewis, Caroline Locke, Victoria Payne, Josephine Reddin, Harriet Roeder, Jeannette Saurborn, Dorothy Smith, Edith Vail, Florence Warwick, Martha Wilcox.

Musical Director, Norman Lloyd

Costumes for TREND by Betty Joiner

Setting and lighting for TREND designed and executed by Gerard Gentile, assisted by Edward Glass and William H. Rudd

Norman Lloyd and Harvey Pollins, piano
Hugo Bergamasco, flute
H. Tafarella, oboe
J. Youshkoff, bassoon
V. Peretti, trumpet
S. Gershek, drums
Franziska Boas and Carolyn Durand, percussion

Special equipment for the reproduction of "Ionization" by Edgar Varese is provided through the courtesy of Mirko Paneyko.

House Manager, Murray McGuire

Virginia Mishnun elaborated on Holm's compositional scheme:

> The continuity of the composition was never broken, but the soloist separated imperceptible from the group, returning to it again with equal ease and naturalness. During the solo, various sections of the group continued to dance, their movements pitched to a lower key and concentrated within a smaller area. The group maintained a constant relationship with the soloist, reflecting and answering her gestures, each member of the group expressing in her response a personal quality which yet harmonized with the general tone. The method is similar to that of the old Greek choruses, which functioned both as a living, dynamic background for the drama, and as an active agent in it. And the solo dance, set in the defining environment created by the group, gained immeasurably in sharpness of delineation and explicitness of intention. ["Cataclysm" was] a powerful section which gained consistently in strength from the poignant understatement of its opening to a climax in which falling bodies crashed to a doom made inevitable by the preceding action. [In "The Gates Are Desolate"] the group movement was direct . . . stripped of all ornament. And through this classic structure ran the vivid, lyric cry of Miss Holm's dancing.[62]

Mishnun found the rest "anti-climactic." *Resurgence* "had nothing to do with the composition which preceded it." It was "handicapped by the atrocious Varèse music against which it tried to dance, atrocious not for its modernity but for its pretentious bravura and eccentricity." The volume at which the music was played "practically demolished the dance. Nothing could be adequately expressive of the music except dismembered bodies hurled through space, careening madly through an electrically charged atmosphere. The dancers methodically contrived to recreate the rhythmic intervals at which the blasts and shrieks were emitted." Despite these reservations, Mishnun called *Trend* "a notable achievement." "It places Hanya Holm in the front rank of modern dance choreographers. She has a fine sense of theater; her entrances and exits are masterful . . . and her climaxes are brilliantly constructed. . . . The manner in which the composition is built implies recognition of the fact that dance structure need not necessarily derive from musical sources, but that it may consist, as in a drama, in the unfolding of an action through a series of rising conflicts. . . . It is this concept of the dance as a theater art, and this quality of dramatic interplay and crescendo which mark *Trend* as a significant contribution to the modern dance."[63]

Henry Gilfond in *Dance Observer* saw "a good abundance of choreographic wealth . . . unmistakably sensitive and profoundly moving commentary on a world conflict which is of especial significance to European sense and sensibility."[64] As did others, he singled out Louise Kloepper's dancing in "The Effete." In contrast to Mishnun, Gilfond praised "Resurgence" as "a compact movement in mass formations that is breathtaking in power. It emerges from the distinct unhealthy flavor of the first part of the work as a new and buoyantly optimistic sound voice." He found much of the movement lacking in motivation and rather arbitrary. But he also saw "a simplification and an exciting use of masses . . . not often employed in the concert field."[65]

Paul Love in the *Nation* found "Episodes" to be "the most integrated and cruelly biting" segment. "When further tightened and integrated, [*Trend*] should be able to sustain the excitement it arouses only in sections now. [Holm] gave a breathing quality to the stage space by her expert shuttling of line-units within the group; individual against group, two against three, four against four, in a continual forming and dissolving." *Trend* established Holm as a choreographer "on the high plane she has occupied as a teacher."[66]

New Masses analyzed *Trend* as

> built on an almost mathematical thesis-antithesis-synthesis basis. . . . Hanya Holm has taken the World War, the concept of the share of the masses of men in

> its history, the resulting emotional and physical reaction, and given us a suite of moving solo and group compositions. Her understanding of the part played by the people in the colossal imperialist calamity isn't always profoundly correct, and her technique, German (Wigmanish), doesn't always rigidly insist on necessary rather than arbitrary movement. Nevertheless, there is a deeply moving human quality in her treatment of the theme—and whatever fault may be found technically, the lack of time and the necessity for simplification (the composition had to be created and the dancers, a good many new to the Holm technique, trained within the six-weeks' period) must be taken into consideration. Whether or not it was for this reason that Hanya Holm used masses of dancers in solid mass patterns, the dancer (self-exiled from Germany) has succeeded beautifully in indicating a possible direction for better mass participation in dance composition.[67]

Subsequent Reviews:

Dance Observer's Gervaise Butler hailed the Mecca premiere as "a major production" but concluded that "it discovered for us no new idiom in the dance and realized only partially the projection of its possibilities to the audience."[68] To Butler, Holm's choreography and movement seemed oversimplified, and Lauterer's "admirable setting" was fully realized just once in "Lest We Remember," when the elaborate light score "focuses its action on the ramp at stage right and for the first time brings the set to life and integrates its great possibilities, hitherto potential, into the movement." The vastness of the Lauterer device, he added, required more than 30 dancers "to populate it properly."[69]

Composer Elliott Carter, Jr., musical director for Ballet Caravan and critic for the journal *Modern Music*, castigated the modern dance but praised *Trend*: "The insect-like machine gestures at the beginning of *Trend* and the remarkable spasmodic convulsions of isolated individuals during the 'cataclysm' . . . showed what this type of dance could be if it were freed from the personal hysteria that now surrounds it, and made more straightforward."[70]

In May 1938 John Martin bestowed on *Trend* his annual award for best choreography.

NOTES

1. Interview with Norman Lloyd.
2. John Martin, *New York Times*, 15 August 1937.
3. Barbara Page Beiswanger, "A Selected List of Music Especially Written for Dance by Composers in America," New York University, May 1943, p. 6 (unpublished).
4. Norman Lloyd, "Sound Companion for Dance," *Dance Scope* 2, no. 2 (Spring 1966): 10–12.
5. Ibid.
6. Elizabeth Douglas, "Dance International: 1900–1937," *Magazine of Art* 31, no. 1 (January 1938): 27–31, 62.
7. John Martin, *New York Times*, 15 August 1937.
8. Rose Koenig, "Martha Graham," *Dance Observer* 4, no. 7 (August–September 1937): 82.
9. Lincoln Kirstein, "Ballet: Introduction and Credo," *Dance Observer* 4, no. 8 (October 1937): 94.
10. Interview with Esther Junger Klempner.
11. John Martin, "The Dance: New Blood," *New York Times*, 29 August 1937.
12. *Bennington Banner*, 13 August 1937.
13. Henry Gilfond, "Workshops and Fellows Concerts," *Dance Observer* 4, no. 7 (August-September 1937): 79–80.
14. Paul Love, "Bennington Festival," *Nation* 145, no. 9 (28 August 1937): 226–27.
15. Interview with Norman Lloyd. This was, according to another report, the first time Limón had employed new music. See also Margaret Lloyd, *The Borzoi Book of Modern Dance* (New York: Alfred A. Knopf, 1949), p. 203.
16. *Bennington Banner*, 13 August 1937.
17. John Martin, *New York Times*, 29 August 1937.
18. Henry Gilfond, *Dance Observer* 4, no. 7 (August-September 1937): 79–80.
19. John Martin, *New York Times*, 29 August 1937.
20. Owen Burke, *New Masses* 24, no. 10 (31 August 1937): 27–30.
21. Henry Gilfond, *Dance Observer* 4, no. 7 (August-September 1937): 79–80.
22. Paul Love, *Nation* 145, no. 9 (28 August 1937): 226–27.
23. *Bennington Banner*, 13 August 1937.
24. John Martin, *Introduction to the Dance* (Brooklyn, N.Y.: Dance Horizons, 1965), p. 267.
25. Interview with Hanya Holm by Billy Nichols, "Four Pioneers" (phonotape), National Educational Television, 1965 [Dance Collection of the New York Public Library].
26. Hanya Holm, "Trend Grew upon Me," *Magazine of Art* 31, no. 3 (March 1938): 137, with photographs of the New York production by Barbara Morgan and articles by Arch Lauterer (pp. 137, 142–45) and Harrison Kerr (pp. 143, 184).
27. Lloyd, *Borzoi*, p. 163. Lloyd provides a full scenario for the work. See also *Don McDonagh's Complete Guide to Modern Dance* (New York: Popular Library, 1977), pp. 102–104.
28. John Martin, "The Dance: A Major Work," *New York Times*, 22 August 1937.
29. Letter from Eve Gentry to the author, 1 October 1977.
30. Ibid.
31. Ibid.
32. Interview with Beatrice Seckler.
33. Alwin Nikolais, *Impulse*, 1968, p. 70.
34. Interview with Walter Terry. (No reviews by Terry of the Bennington or New York productions were located.)
35. Jean Erdman, "The Dance as Non-Verbal Poetic Image," in *The Dance Has Many Faces*, Walter Sorell, ed. (New York: World Publishing Company, 1951), pp. 203–204. Originally published in *Dance Observer* 16, no. 4 (April 1949): 49.
36. Ibid.
37. Letter from Eve Gentry to the author, 7 June 1977.
38. Interview with Norman Lloyd.
39. Moses Smith, "Dance in the Modern Manner," *Boston Transcript*, 14 August 1937.
40. *Bennington Banner*, 14 August 1937.
41. Martin, *Introduction to the Dance*, p. 268.
42. Moses Smith, *Boston Transcript*, 14 August 1937.
43. Interview with Hanya Holm.
44. Harrison Kerr, "Reproduced Music for the Dance," *Magazine of Art* 31, no. 3 (March 1938): 143, 184.
45. Gervaise Butler, "Hanya Holm," *Dance Observer* 5, no.2 (February 1938): 24–25.
46. Margaret Lloyd, "Virile Is the Word for It," *Christian Science Monitor*, 4 January 1938.
47. John Martin, "New York Debut for Hanya Holm," *New York Times*, 29 December 1937.
48. John Martin, "The Dance: Hanya Holm," *New York Times*, 2 January 1938.
49. Margaret Lloyd, *Christian Science Monitor*, 4 January 1938.
50. Lloyd, *Borzoi*, p. 163.

51. Christena L. Schlundt, *Tamiris: A Chronicle of Her Dance Career, 1927-1955* (New York: New York Public Library, 1972), pp. 55-56, gives cast and credits.
52. Interview with Alwin Nikolais.
53. Interview with Hanya Holm.
54. Moses Smith, *Boston Transcript*, 14 August 1937.
55. John Martin, "Festival Dancers Appear in *Trend*," *New York Times*, 14 August 1937.
56. John Martin, *New York Times*, 22 August 1937.
57. Ibid.
58. Lloyd, *Borzoi*, p. 164.
59. John Martin, *New York Times*, 29 December 1937.
60. John Martin, *New York Times*, 2 January 1938.
61. Ibid.
62. Virginia Mishnun, "The Dance at Bennington," *Brooklyn Eagle*, 22 August 1937.
63. Ibid.
64. Henry Gilfond, *Dance Observer* 4, no. 7 (August-September 1937): 79.
65. Ibid.
66. Paul Love, *Nation* 145, no. 9 (28 August 1937): 226-27.
67. Owen Burke, *New Masses* 24, no. 10 (31 August 1937): 27-30.
68. Gervaise Butler, "Hanya Holm," *Dance Observer* 5, no. 2 (February 1938): 24-25.
69. Ibid.
70. Elliott Carter, "With the Dancers," *Modern Music* 15, no. 2 (January-February 1938): 122.

1938

4 August 1938

Ode to Freedom

Vermont State Armory

Chor Eleanor King. *Mus arr* John Colman. *Voices and percussion arr* Norman Lloyd. "The American Hero—A Sapphick Ode" by Nath. Niles, A.M. *Orig mus* Andrew Law. *Pianist* Lloyd. *Sets & light* Arch Lauterer. *Cos* Betty Joiner. *Danc* King and group: Jean Aubry, Jane Forte, Wanda Graham, Margot Harper, Gertrude Lippincott, Alice M. Mulcahy, Marian Ryder, Ann Schuman [Halprin], Mildred Rea Shaw, Mary Starks. ***a. Flight from Destruction, b. The Pillars and the Flame, c. Still Shall the Banner.***

Program Note: "*Ode to Freedom* derives its inspiration from the Yankee war hymn of the Revolution, 'The American Hero, or Bunker Hill,' written in 1775. 'This stark and splendid song . . . was sung everywhere—in camps, churches, and public meetings. . . . It summed up the hopes and fears of the rebellious colonies.'"

Eleanor King blocked out parts of *Ode* before going to Bennington. Lauterer's set was a group of poles. Joiner's costumes were black-striped red and gray wool tunics, long skirts, and cylindrical bonnets.[1]

New York Premiere: 3 November 1938, Theatre Dance Company Studio (and 1 January 1939, Kaufmann Auditorium, YMHA).

Subsequent Productions: 20 February 1943, Carleton College, with a new score for voice, harp, piano, and drum by Maricarol Hanson.[2]

Reviews

John Martin thought *Ode* "fine and convincing." It "revealed not only the effect of several years discipleship under Doris Humphrey but a marked personal gift for work in this medium."[3] It was "inclined to be obscure choreographically," but this was so with other dances "whose program is dictated by a literary antecedent."[4] Others dealt with it more harshly.

Henry Gilfond, *Dance Observer*:

> Unquestionably well and timely enough inspired, the choreography was rather muddy . . . and in no way measured up to Miss King's sharply defined anti-fascist *Icaro*. [She] has given considerably more than promise in her metropolitan appearances.[5]

He blamed her failure on "the unhealthy artistic atmospheric pressure which seems to prevail in the Bennington School."

Albertina Vitak (*American Dancer*) thought it "not very distinguished, too much use of heroically raised arms being made."[6] Joseph Arnold Kaye (*Dance*) recognized King as "a gifted artist with a strong feeling for the theatrical dance. So far she has not yet been able fully to harmonize the dance ideals which she wishes to express with the dance of spectacle and entertainment which she also desires to incorporate in her work."[7]

4 August 1938

"Bonja Song" from *American Folk Suite*

Vermont State Armory

Chor Eleanor King. *Mus arr* Esther Williamson. *Pianists* Norman Lloyd, Ruth Lloyd. *Light* Arch Lauterer. *Cos* George Bockman. *Danc* King, Wanda Graham, Mary Starks.

Program Note:

> The music for "Bonja Song" is adapted from one of the oldest burnt-cork melodies written about 1820 for the "bonja," the primitive banjo. "Hoe-Down" [the second part] is a term applied to a modern barn-dance figure. "Hornpipe" [the third part of the suite] uses two familiar old dance tunes, "Soldier's Joy" and "Young America."

"Bonja Song" had its premiere at Bennington; the other two parts of the suite ("Hoe-Down" and "Hornpipe") were enlarged from previously composed solos. George Bockman's costumes for "Bonja Song" were red polka-dotted skirts, blue bell-bottoms, and striped T-shirts. The costumes departed from "stereotyped ideas of dress for the modern dance by featuring soft slippers and straw sailor hats."[8] Eleanor King wrote that Louis Horst was "horrified" by her use of traditional tunes. "Ruling opinion in Bennington was negative," recalled King. "I was surprised at the reaction to the *Folk Suite*, considered 'unorthodox' at that purely abstract stage of modern dance."[9]

New York Premiere: 3 November 1938, Theatre Dance Company Studio.

Reviews

John Martin remarked that *Suite* "had at least one eye on the music hall."[10] Of the three parts he liked "Hornpipe" the best, but "all of them . . . though cute enough, are inconsequential and, truth to tell, inclined to be a bit inexpert."[11] Henry Gilfond found "Bonja Song" "of questionable taste,"[12] but Margaret Lloyd disagreed:

> I did not find it trivial in the least, but after an evening of watching the tryout of young wings in solemn planes and parabolas, of listening to bald areas of ineffectual music, rejoiced in its lightness and gaiety, its (in this environment almost unorthodox) steps and patterns, its music arranged from traditional sources. I relished, too, the compatible insouciance of George Bockman's dress designs.[13]

4 August 1938

Romantic Theme

Vermont State Armory

Chor Louise Kloepper (solo). *Mus* Harvey Pollins (original piano score). *Pianist* Pollins. *Light* Arch Lauterer. *Cos* Elizabeth Beebe.

4 August 1938

Statement of Dissent

Vermont State Armory

Chor Louise Kloepper (solo). *Mus* Gregory Tucker (original score). *Pianist* Tucker. *Percussion* Franziska Boas. *Light* Arch Lauterer. *Cos* Elizabeth Beebe.

4 August 1938

Earth Saga

Vermont State Armory

Louise Kloepper's group, *Earth Saga*, Vermont State Armory. Photograph by Sidney Bernstein.

Chor Louise Kloepper. *Mus* Esther Williamson (original piano score). *Pianists* Williamson, Harvey Pollins. *Light* Arch Lauterer. *Cos* Betty Joiner. ***a. The Coming** danc* group, Kloepper. ***b. The Claiming** danc* group. ***c. and d. Aftermath** danc* group, Kloepper. ***e. The Remaking** danc* Kloepper, Group: Shirley Bennett, Marjorie Browning, Mary Gillette, Winifred Gregory, Elizabeth Hayes, Hortense Lieberthal, May Mendelsohn, Joyce Palmer, Klara Sepmeier.

New York Premieres: None documented.

Earth Saga, inspired by the 1938 Pare Lorenz film *The River*, "deals with the subject of the fertility of the earth, what happens when it becomes barren, and finally the reconstruction after sterility."[14] The two solos and the group composition were Louise Kloepper's first independent choreography. She made a striking debut, not the least for her performance abilities, which were considerable.

Reviews

John Martin, *New York Times*:

> There can be no doubt that the high mark of the evening was the performance of Miss Kloepper in two solos. . . . A young dancer of remarkable gifts with an inherent beauty of movement that places her at once among the finest young artists of the day . . . she is possessed particularly of that rarest of endowments, a controlled legato. There is also an authentic creativeness about the material she employs and a complete individuality of style. As a composer she still has things to learn, though in her solos her personal performance is so engrossing that it is difficult to be analytical. In her long group work entitled *Earth Saga*, however, it is easier to see the marks of inexperience. In spite of this, hers was a brilliant debut.[15]

Martin noted "a highly distinctive style and the ability to command attention which belongs to so few young dancers" and "a sense of substance and continuity." He judged *Statement of Dissent* to be her best dance, calling it "eloquent, strong and dramatic."[16] Henry Gilfond saw in Kloepper

> a sensitivity of movement and an elegance of phrase that is second to none in the dance theatre. Much of this was evident in the most successful of her compositions, *Statement of Dissent*. . . . Her *Earth Saga* . . . was definitely of beginner's stuff, derivative and amorphous in concept as well as execution. . . . Louise Kloepper is instrumentally one of dance's most promising artists. At present, her work requires much, a more concrete thematic approach, a more pointed direction, dissent without equivocation.[17]

4 August 1938

Out of One Happening

Vermont State Armory

Chor Marian Van Tuyl. *Mus* Gregory Tucker (original piano score). *Pianists* Gregory Tucker, Margaret Lidy. *Light* Arch Lauterer. *Cos* Betty Joiner. *Danc* Van Tuyl, Group: Jeanne Hays, Lillian Lack, Eleanor Lauer, Marion Moulton, Marjorie Muehl, Polly Ann Schwartz, Marie Prahl, Theodora Wiesner, Olga Wolf.

Program Note:

> This is how it was–
> To some it was a matter of great concern
> To others no matter at all
> But in the end they went on together

Out of One Happening was "an abstract dance of continuity and progression, depicting what happens to the line of a continuous pattern when it is hit by a cataclysm from without; in other words, how different people or things react to the breaking of the pattern."[18]

New York Premiere: None documented.

Reviews

In *Out of One Happening*, wrote John Martin in the *New York Times*, Van Tuyl

> deals in a spirit of amusement with the different ways in which a group reacts to a single occurrence. Her handling of the group is deft and full of ingenuity, though . . . there is an all too general obscurity of purpose. In her solos Miss Van Tuyl exhibits a fine technical command of movement and a keen, almost too keen eye for formal matters.[19]

While he appreciated her "keen sense of design," he felt "she demands more concentration on formal matters than the average audience is equipped to give."[20]

Margaret Lloyd, *Christian Science Monitor*:

> Miss Van Tuyl, figuring largely in the field of dance in education, seems to have less to offer to dance as art.[21]

Albertina Vitak, *American Dancer*:

> Marian Van Tuyl, concert dancer from Chicago and in charge of modern classes at the University of Chicago, is the first fellow to be selected from outside New York. This might and should have meant an entirely new approach and style but in this Miss Van Tuyl was disappointing as both her style and compositions were quite conventionalized and more early Martha Graham than anything else. . . . As an individual dancer, Miss Van Tuyl has personal charm and appeal of a poetic, almost wistful sort. She moves with assured grace, with some ballet training evident, but seems not to have realized her full potentialities as yet.[22]

Henry Gilfond thought her "a dancer of considerable lyric quality, who thinks in broad human terms and who is apparently much concerned with the direction of mankind."[23] The two older works were "unclear choreographically, lending themselves to patterns of varying qualities but never to any climactic strength."

> *Out of One Happening* . . . (while the best of the Fellows' group works) falls into the same category. There are some fine folk and pre-classic moments of a more earthy tone, but the dance tends to become a series of patterns. Definite statement on definitely concrete materials . . . should aid immeasurably all three Fellows alike.[24]

5 August 1938

Passacaglia in C minor

Vermont State Armory

Passacaglia in C minor, Vermont State Armory. Photograph by Sidney Bernstein.

Chor Doris Humphrey. *Mus* J. S. Bach (Passacaglia and Fugue in C minor arr piano I. Phillippe). *Pianists* Pauline Lawrence, Morris Mamorsky. *Sets & light* Arch Lauterer. *Cos* Pauline Lawrence. *Danc* Humphrey, Charles Weidman, and Concert and Apprentice Groups. Members of Concert Group: Billy Archibald, William Bales, Mirthe Bellanca, George Bockman, Harriette Ann Gray, Frances Kinsky, Katherine Litz, Katherine Manning, Edith Orcutt, Beatrice Seckler, Sybil L. Shearer, Lee Sherman. Members of Apprentice Group: Barbara Page Beiswanger, Sara Jean Cosner, Gloria Garcia, Maria Maginnis, Ethel Mann, Claudia Moore, Pegge Oppenheimer, Ruth Parmet, Barbara Spaulding, Patricia Urner, Mildred Zook.

Doris Humphrey composed and rehearsed *Passacaglia* using the recorded Stokowski orchestral arrangement.[25] A two-piano version was employed for the Bennington premiere. The original organ score was performed with the dance subsequently, but only on rare occasions.

According to apprentice Barbara Page Beiswanger, "tremendous boxes" in the Bennington production were replaced by much smaller ones in New York. The women wore long beige and brown dresses with one arm bare and "lovely sandals that gave the foot a groomed appearance," which Humphrey had made especially for the occasion.[26] The *Bennington Banner* reported that while soft slippers and straw hats had been part of the costuming for Eleanor King's *American Folk Suite* the night before, "Miss Humphrey's dancers wore a patent leather slipper covering the instep for the first time in the Bennington festivals."[27]

There was no program note at the Bennington premiere. A festival press release issued before the performance provided background information:

> The selection of this heroic musical setting, Miss Humphrey explains, was based upon the fact that in the passacaglia—a century-old dance form—the constantly reiterated theme has the cumulative effect of an affirmation of faith and belief. Miss Humphrey points out that the treatment of the form will be contemporary and in no sense a recreation of the traditional passacaglia.

John Mueller's study guide to the 1965 film of *Passacaglia*[28] contains a number of variant program notes, the earliest of which (cited first by Selma Jeanne Cohen[29]) describes *Passacaglia* as

> an abstraction with dramatic overtones. The minor melody according to the traditional Passacaglia form, insistently repeated from beginning to end, seems to say "How can a man be saved and be content in a world of infinite despair?" And in the magnificent fugue which concludes the dance the answer seems to

mean—"Be saved by love and courage." [The dance was inspired by] the need for love, tolerance and nobility in a world given more and more to the denial of these things.

Humphrey talked with Margaret Lloyd about her ideas for *Passacaglia* immediately following the Bennington premiere. Lloyd reported:

> I went well armatured with prejudice. "What right has she," I decided in advance, "to superimpose choreography on a great musical entity, even one originating in dance form. It's as bad as Massine with Brahms's Fourth Symphony." I thoroughly did not intend to like it.
>
> But prejudiced selfhood was swept aside by inescapable magnificence. It was majestic. The fugue was overwhelming. Two pianos weren't doing the score such terrific justice, but the dancing was.
>
> Afterward, trying to rationalize my unwelcome rapture, I asked Miss Humphrey how this thing could be. "Is it," I said, "because modern movement issues from human feeling, is capable of more complexity than ballet and is therefore more adaptable to music of content?"
>
> She assented and added: "It is also because there is room in that score for emotion. I could not take a symphony for such a purpose. Let me tell you how I came to use the Passacaglia.
>
> "*New Dance*, you'll remember (these are not her exact words) ends on a note of harmonization among men, the ideal of that perfection desired and demanded by youth. Well, in maturity you come to learn that perfection is not immediately attainable, but that there is still happiness, a measure of harmony, to be found while working toward that goal. This of course I wanted to put into dance.
>
> "When the composition was in shape, I could not reconcile modern music with it. Harshness or dissonance, starkness, the bare, angular line, simply would not do. I needed richness, ordered complexity, grandeur, serenity, for my theme. And that is how I thought of the Passacaglia and fitted my composition to it.
>
> "I hope to produce it with organ accompaniment in New York."[30]

Charles Weidman, interviewed in 1965, echoed Humphrey's statement to Lloyd. *Passacaglia*, he said, followed from the unrealistically utopian "Variations and Conclusion" of *New Dance*. The world was not really as utopian as *New Dance* suggested; one must still strive toward perfection. In that sense, *Passacaglia* was really an extension of the *New Dance Trilogy*.[31] Doris Humphrey regarded it as her most mature dance, "with the finest choreography so far."[32] By comparison, she thought *With My Red Fires* "obvious and crude . . . but easy to understand—dramatic, with a plot and characters—much more what people have learned to expect from the dance."[33]

New York Premiere: 27 November 1938, Guild Theatre.

Subsequent Productions: Originally performed by a company of 23 and two soloists, *Passacaglia* was later staged for varying numbers of dancers (Doris Humphrey, José Limón, and nine dancers performed it in 1939-1940 in New York and on tour). It remained in the Humphrey-Weidman repertory until 1943.[34] A performance during an all-Bach program at the Studio Theatre, New York, in December 1942 provoked an exchange between John Martin and Doris Humphrey[35] and a defense of the use of Bach for modern dance by Norman Cazden, musical director of Humphrey-Weidman, in *Dance Observer*.[36]

In 1951 Doris Humphrey revived *Passacaglia* for students at the American Dance Festival, and she taught it to dancers at the Bellas Artes in Mexico City later that year.[37] In 1954-1955 she revived it in a Juilliard repertory class, at which time Lucy Venable, assisted by Joan Gainer, notated it (see Sources—Scores). It was given numerous performances once the score

Doris Humphrey, Charles Weidman, and Concert and Workshop Groups in *Passacaglia in C minor*, Vermont State Armory. Photograph by Sidney Bernstein.

was available, including at the American Dance Festival in 1957, 1960, and 1963, the last performance being repeated at Philharmonic Hall, Lincoln Center, by the José Limón Company in the summer of 1963. On 2 March 1965 there was a major revival directed by Lucy Venable for American Dance Theater at the New York State Theater, Lincoln Center.[38] This performance was filmed by National Educational Television as part of the program *Four Pioneers* (Sources–Films). *Passacaglia* was revived by the José Limón Dance Company on 25 September 1978 for a Doris Humphrey Celebration at Roundabout Theatre Stage One, presented by the Dance Notation Bureau.

Reviews

John Martin, *New York Times*:

> Bach . . . has never been conspicuously suitable for modern dance, and certainly becomes no more so in this work. The detail of the design, however, is rich and varied, the mark of a greatly gifted composer is upon the whole thing. [But] it does not find her at the height of her form.[39]

In his Sunday column, Martin expanded on this:

> When it finally becomes evident that this is not a case of music visualization or interpretation, it emerges as a magnificent piece of composition, elevated in tone and richly and imaginatively wrought. It contains quite the finest choreographic fugue on record. . . . The choice of such music as this is decidedly open to question and presents an obstacle to easy appreciation because it has so much entity in itself. This hurdle passed, however, it is a stirring work.[40]

Margaret Lloyd, *Christian Science Monitor*:

> Doris Humphrey's *Passacaglia* is in no sense a music visualization or interpretation of Bach's mighty work. It simply uses noble music to supplement noble movement.
>
> Pauline Lawrence's costumes in deep brown and parchment (with bronze kid sandal straps and other accessories, and soft solo yellow for Miss Humphrey), emphasizing the masculine and feminine elements in form and movement, contributed importantly to the whole. The colors were pre-eminently right for the music; the cut of the garments an assistance to the dance.[41]

Wrote Lloyd in *The Borzoi Book of Modern Dance*:

> The reiterated theme of the *Passacaglia* that becomes the subject of the "Fugue," was to her man's reiteration of faith in his ideals, despite the struggle of attaining them, the stretto passages of the "Fugue" constituted the struggle, mounting in the resolution to a majestic paean of faith. The costumes and formations were

beautifully appropriate. In graceful brown and parchment garments, shod with brown half-sandals, the dancers stood motionless in symmetrical tiers against the background screens; then with great dignity flowed into harmonious rearrangements in conformance with the music's architectonic plan. The whole movement tone was elevated, ending, with the music, on the exalted note of joy.[42]

Joseph Arnold Kaye, *Dance*:

On the same day that Doris Humphrey gave her choreographic setting to Bach's Passacaglia in C minor, Curt Sachs, the dance historian, lectured . . . on the absolute futility, and the incongruity of attempting to use a musical composition, complete in itself, for a dance. . . . Yet Miss Humphrey was highly successful with her setting. She composed a really beautiful piece, true to the contrapuntal character of its music, moving in its groupings, sometimes even inspiring in its general effect. She was so successful because . . . she is an artist who always has something to say. . . . She did not attempt to supply a literal . . . or a fancied counterpart to the music but was guided merely by the spirit underlying the Bach composition.[43]

George Beiswanger, *Dance Observer*:

Passacaglia in C minor furnished the inspiration and the *raison d'etre* for the maturest work which Doris Humphrey has so far produced. If you ask, Why Bach? the only answer is, Why not? . . . You can dance Bach if what you do is . . . a recreation of the order, the power and the dignity of Bach in terms of the simple rhythmic pulse which permeates this composition.[44]

Albertina Vitak, *American Dancer*:

[*Passacaglia* is] one of Miss Humphrey's best compositions in pure dance form. It featured choreographic patterns more than individual figures and these were often very beautiful, especially as viewed from above. Miss Humphrey was fleet and lissom swirling and turning in almost constant motion as a single contrasting design against the more static background of her group.[45]

Subsequent Reviews

Walter Terry, *Boston Herald*, reviewing the New York premiere (no reviews of his were found for the summers of 1937 or 1938):

With *Opus 51* and *Passacaglia*, the modern dance has made its strongest bid for a leading place in the theater of dance. . . . The choreography of these two new works makes use of balletic movements, pantomime, freedom of motion and a communicable joy. . . . Miss Humphrey's *Passacaglia* may suggest her "Reiteration of Faith," but its value lies in its mastery of group movement, its brilliant patterns, its flowering transitional movements and its admirable phrasing. It is a visualization of the Bach music in that it carries out in movement the quality of the music itself. Accenting it, adding the richness and color of visual pattern to the simple beauty of the audible one. It is theatrical, for it has sweep and suspense, serenity and exultation, and it is stimulating to the senses.[46]

John Martin, reviewing a restoration of *Passacaglia* at the Humphrey-Weidman Studio Theatre in 1941, called it "one of the outstanding works in the modern repertoire." The revival was an excellent one:

Like all other good revivals of important compositions [it] reveals ever-fresh values in both choreography and emotional substance. Though her form is a large one with many complexities, Miss Humphrey has managed to make its design so transparent and its form so unified that its heroic theme of human faith and dignity emerges luminously and with grandeur.[47]

5 August 1938

Dance of Work and Play

Vermont State Armory

Chor Hanya Holm. *Mus* Norman Lloyd (original score). *Musicians* Norman Lloyd, Ruth Lloyd, piano. Franziska Boas, percussion. *Sets & light* Arch Lauterer. *Cos* Elizabeth Beebe. *Danc* Holm and Concert Group: Keith Coppage, Carolyn Durand, Henrietta Greenhood [Eve Gentry], Miriam Kagan, Caroline Locke, Harriet Roeder, Marva Spelman, Elizabeth Waters. ***Origin** danc* Holm, group. ***The Empty Handed** danc* Holm, group. ***The Driven** danc* Holm, group. ***The Solitary** danc* Holm, group. ***The Communal** danc* Holm, group. ***Synthesis** danc* Holm, group.

A festival press release described the work as

> a lyric suite in six scenes dealing with the theme of work and play from youth to maturity. In spite of the subject of this dance, Miss Holm emphasizes the fact that it will contain no social comment but will be a statement of the relationship of work to life under varying conditions and during different stages of human development.

Said Holm:

> I wanted to investigate where the difference was between work and play. It was broken down to communal and personal experiences. . . . I used some compositional devices which interested me very much. For instance, in one of the communal scenes I placed three figures between audience and dancers, and used them as space design, so to speak, instead of props. The audience had to look past these three figures standing there like dark silhouettes, in no way emotionally connected with the dancers moving in bright light. These figures were set pieces, limitations to the eye, and had the characteristics of dancers utterly dehumanized.[48]

Holm introduced each of six themes, which were then developed by her group. Walter Sorell described the action:

> First, Hanya presented "The Empty-Handed," who have nothing to give and who receive nothing for their sterile work. Then there were those "Driven," who moved with frenzied gestures through their dry and tedious labors. The mechanical, chained movements as well as their rigidity bespoke our mechanized civilization. The pillars formed by three figures in the foreground were a dramatic and novel use of space design. Also, there was the "Solitary," who tried to find a solution on his own. Then the dance rose to an exciting and joyous climax in "Communal" and "Synthesis," when all moved together in a single strong line toward an ultimate goal. The ending seemed to be a symphony of motion with many falls in perfect unison.[49]

Margaret Lloyd wrote that "Hanya's solo statements introduced and concluded a theme worked out by the group in a combination of free movement and miming."[50]

When Norman Lloyd arrived to see the dance ahead of time, he recalled, "Hanya handed me a score in which she had rhythmically notated the movement of every dancer. It was like looking at an orchestral score."[51]

New York Premiere: 19 January 1939, Guild Theatre.

Hanya Holm in *Dance of Work and Play*, Bennington College, 1938.
Photograph copyright by Barbara Morgan.

Reviews

George Beiswanger, *Dance Observer*:

> Norman Lloyd added to his list of craftsmanly compositions for the dance a major work. . . . It is difficult to write of this composition except in superlatives. One has to go back to the music of Wallingford Riegger or Louis Horst to find comparable examples of compositions which evoke so truly the exact emotional quality of the dance, and which at the same time bring to the dance added qualities and meanings. The sheer facility in the two-piano medium is astonishing; idiosyncratic melodies dot the score; polytonality is used with freedom and authority; percussion and the tone-color of the piano blend without antagonism or blurring; and the whole composition rests upon a structure that is for the most part as soundly logical as it is eloquent.[52]

John Martin, *New York Times*:

> Miss Holm's *Dance of Work and Play* is wrought with fine clarity and shows once again her unfailing ability to create mood. . . . The whole is blended into a beautiful fluidity of form.[53]

Albertina Vitak, *American Dancer*:

> In this work Miss Holm achieves a truly admirable balance between large and small movement. Intense in mood, the theme is not always immediately clear and the work is slightly long but the action is as precisely executed as clock work, with an active intelligence manifest throughout. . . . In her solo passages, Miss Holm manages to make simple pacing impressively dramatic.[54]

Margaret Lloyd, *Christian Science Monitor*:

> Hanya Holm's *Dance of Work and Play* . . . hit the heart and reached the understanding without program notes and only a hasty glance at subtitles. It was organic, eloquent—design irradiated by idea. Miss Holm [danced] with a new openness and freedom.[55]

Henry Gilfond, *Dance Observer*:

> *Dance of Work and Play*, for which Norman Lloyd has written some of his best dance music, is . . . a plea . . . for a recapturing of what was once the joyousness of work. Mood rather than opinion is the essence of the dance, an impressionistic work that would reveal the essence of the different stages represented by the different titles of the sections of the choreography. But the fundamental forces underlying the various phases of the work are not considered and the dance resultingly floats away from whatever base it might rest on. . . . What might have proven a most profound work . . . disappears in essentially thinned observation, judgment and presentation.[56]

5 August 1938

Dance Sonata

Vermont State Armory

Chor Hanya Holm. *Mus* Harrison Kerr (original score). *Musicians* Harvey Pollins, Yolanda Lorenz, piano. Franziska Boas, percussion. *Sets & light* Arch Lauterer. *Cos* Elizabeth Beebe. *Danc* Hanya Holm and Concert and Apprentice Groups. Concert Group: Keith Coppage, Carolyn Durand, Henrietta Greenhood [Eve Gentry], Miriam Kagan, Caroline Locke, Harriet Roeder, Marva Spelman, Elizabeth Waters. Apprentice Group: Mary Adair, Katherine Bollard, Mary Frances Cave, Elsie C. Earle, Saralee Harris, Katherine Imig, Beatrice B. Lovejoy, Carlotte Orlov, Hildegard L. Spreen, Claire I. Weigt, Martha Wilcox. ***I. Maestoso*** *danc* group. ***II. Grazioso*** *danc* Holm, group. ***III. Andante Moderato*** *danc* group. ***IV. Allegro Vivace*** *danc* group.

A festival press release announced:

> Miss Holm's second composition is to be a dance sonata stressing spatial form. The music . . . by Harrison Kerr, is being composed before the dance itself, although Mr. Kerr is preparing his work specifically for Miss Holm's choreographic use. Since this is a reversal of the usual procedure it is in itself an interesting experiment.

Margaret Lloyd explained:

> The idea was . . . to do with motor phrases what the composer does with musical phrases, to compose a sonata in movement. The movement was not to interpret the music; it was to have its own logical development.[57]

New York Premiere: 19 February 1939, Guild Theatre.

Reviews

George Beiswanger, *Dance Observer*:

> Harrison Kerr's *Dance Sonata* is a neat solution of a problem not often put to the contemporary composer for the dance, although it belongs to the solid tradition of the Diaghileff school. What he was given to start with was the idea of a sonata in four movements, the mood which each movement was to articulate, and certain suggestions as to the larger blocks of form in which each movement was to be composed. . . . The result is a work liberally informed with the qualities of dance, and yet quite interesting in itself and, as might be expected, unusually well-knit in form. Given such collaboration between dancer and composer as to idea and basic rhythms, it is easy to see that the nice result is not a matter of happy accident; one may even guess that the choreography has gained something from having its form pre-determined, although the danger that the dance will not come up to the music has not been altogether escaped in this case. . . . Kerr's sonata is solid and attractive, a thoughtful piece of work in which there does not seem to be a measure which violates the essential spirit of the dance.[58]

John Martin, *New York Times*:

> Its four movements are . . . distinguished by perfect transparency of form, though the composition as a whole has not the same depth and substance as the *Dance of Work and Play.*[59]

Margaret Lloyd, in the *Christian Science Monitor*, said, "*Dance Sonata*, stressing spatial form . . . was not to me so successful [as *Dance of Work and Play*]."[60] But later she added that "on the whole it was an excellent example of absolute dance, affecting as pure dance and pure music can be."[61]

Joseph Arnold Kaye, in *Dance*, considered it to be "an interesting and a very laudable excursion into the idea-less dance . . . but it came out rather dull."[62] However, Albertina Vitak, in *American Dancer*, was enthusiastic about the work:

> Even more so in her second new work, *Dance Sonata*, she shows a mastery of large masses of movement.
>
> *Dance Sonata* is rather symphonic in form, using several steps in a variety of ever-changing ways, much as the theme in some symphonic works recurs again and again yet never in exactly the same way. The many entrances and exits are very skillfully contrived, making a panorama of constantly moving figures. . . . Miss Holm's dancers had more force and discipline than the other groups. . . . Miss Holm's solo in the second movement . . . with her fluttering, lilting little steps, really bird-like in speed, was true dancing.[63]

6 August 1938

Opus 51

Vermont State Armory

Charles Weidman and group in *Opus 51*, Vermont State Armory. Photograph by Sidney Bernstein.

Chor Charles Weidman. ***Mus*** Vivian Fine (original score). ***Musicians*** Fine, piano. Franziska Boas, percussion. ***Sets & light*** Arch Lauterer. ***Cos*** Pauline Lawrence. ***Danc*** Weidman and Concert and Apprentice Groups. Concert Group: Billy Archibald, William Bales, Mirthe Bellanca, George Bockman, Harriette Ann Gray, Katherine Litz, Beatrice Seckler, Lee Sherman. Apprentice Group: Pauline Chellis, Maxine Cushing, Eleanor Frampton, Molly Hecht, Maxine Munt, Dorothy Ross, Anne D. Stern. ***Opening Dance danc*** Weidman, group. ***March danc*** Weidman, Men of group. ***Comedia danc*** group. ***Solo danc*** Weidman. ***Duet danc*** Gray, Seckler. ***Spectacle danc*** Weidman, group.

Doris Humphrey suggested the title before seeing the dance: "Charles is doing a suite, called at my suggestion Opus 51 (about the number of this one since Denishawn)," she wrote.[64]

Weidman danced the solo figure in a three-part suite, without story, comprising three different kinds of movement:

> the first a gracious and grave processional ["Opening Dance"], the second a humorous sequence of kinetic pantomime for group ["Comedia"], and the last a swift-moving, technically difficult dance subtitled "Spectacle."[65]

The middle movement, "Comedia," was an experiment by Weidman to put into group form the kinetic pantomime that he had created in a solo for himself of that name in 1934.[66] In the solo version, he said, he had "juggled, reversed and distorted cause and effect, impulse and reaction [so] that a kaleidoscopic effect was created without once resorting to any literary representation."[67]

The festival press release introduced *Opus 51* as "a departure from the dramatic style of work which has interested this dancer recently." The first part was to be in "pure dance form," the second would "make use of kinetic pantomime adapted to group use," and the third "will emphasize the spectacular in dance, employing brilliant adagio work by the men in the company."

Music:

Composer Vivian Fine had recently written *Race of Life* for Doris Humphrey, Humphrey's first adventure in whimsy. In contrast to *Race of Life*, said Fine, *Opus 51* had neither story nor definite characters:

> *Opus 51*, lacking story or characters, was almost pure comedy, if there is such a thing. In it Weidman achieved a kind of collage. No attempt was made to create situations leading to a comic "point." Instead, we were shown unrelated actions strung together, the ultimate expression of the absurd. Comedy makes the every-

> day seem absurd by taking it seriously; leading us close to disaster, and then saying: "but it's not real!" Weidman, using illogical sequences of action, succeeded in making us laugh by treating these sequences as seriously as if they were the normal course of events. In this re-arrangement of reality, we sensed that reality was perhaps just another arrangement, and we enjoyed the upsetting of the proper order of things.
>
> The music . . . was written after the dance was composed, although not after the entire work was finished. I would write a section as each new part of the dance was completed. In composing for choreography there is the problem of developing a musical structure and continuity. I was able to do this by not composing for individual movements or patterns, but by sensing the impulse that moved the dancer.[68]

Maxine Cushing was delighted by Fine's melodious music:

> Vivian Fine dared to bring melodic line back into the dance accompaniment picture in her lively score for Charles Weidman's mad success; the Mazurka for his solo even came to be whistled.[69]

But George Beiswanger had reservations:

> Vivan Fine has written a score whose surface fairly scintillates. . . . For the most part, the music happily catches the mood of sheer virtuosity which animates Charles Weidman's composition, and has some electrifying moments. Her danger is a set of mannerisms, too dependent on Mendelssohn and the overture school, and too closely tied to the note patterns of the dance movement to which she is writing. This danger is pretty well concealed in the larger sections of the composition, but it comes out all too clearly when the dance requires, as in the opening section, a more organic underlying structure, or when, as in Weidman's solo, it demands a more thoughtful mood.[70]

New York Premiere: 27 November 1938, Guild Theatre.

Subsequent Productions: *Opus 51* was not given again in entirety until 8 February 1941, when it was revived at the Humphrey-Weidman Studio Theatre.[71] Charles Weidman revived the "Comedia" section in 1970 and "Opening Dance" in 1971 (for performances at state hospitals). "Opening Dance" was performed 4 May 1972 in New York at the YM-YWHA in a program entitled "Weidman Back at the Y."

Charles Weidman in *Opus 51*, Vermont State Armory. Photograph by Sidney Bernstein.

Reviews

There was a wide range of critical reaction to Weidman's "plotless" work and to his comedic jabs which "had the modern dance thumbing its nose at almost everything and everybody, including itself."[72] George Beiswanger admired Weidman's success "in penetrating gesture to its core; he has got at the essense of the ways in which men move."[73] And John Martin thought *Opus 51* "quite the finest work he has ever done."[74] Said Martin: "Never before has Weidman succeeded in putting his distinctive comedy gifts into such admirably terse and clean-cut form."[75]

Martin's initial reaction was that the work marked "the full consummation of a unique talent":

> It is a completely impudent piece of pure nonsense in which the dance is subjected to every known indignity. . . . It is an abstraction in that it has no program. But it is . . . devastatingly specific in the manner in which it thumbs its nose at practically everything. Weidman is a kind of ringmaster in a mad circus-like show embracing everything from vaudeville and campfire stunts to choreographic surrealism. Couched in that characteristic Weidman style that has come to be known as "kinetic pantomime," it carries on its ridiculous foolishness for a full half hour without an instant's pall.[76]

Margaret Lloyd added these further details:

> The concert and apprentice groups had draped themselves over, in and around the boxes which lately have become Mr. Weidman's preferential decor. I sensed vaguely in surrealistic touches—circus, gymnasium, tragedy, ballet—numberless fleeting what-nots of suggestion whirling past in abrupt transitions from strong to soft movement, in quips and quirks of fingers, scratching, fluttering, and feet finding themselves in impossible situations.[77]

She later elaborated on the work and described the range of audience reaction to it:

> The Bennington audience, which had come from all over the nation and beyond, included two of Grant Wood's Daughters of the American Revolution. Their faces remained fixed throughout, just as he had painted them. . . . The work began with deceptive formality but soon burst into the maddest, merriest prank of all the Weidman years. Expanding the idea of Kinetic Pantomime, it tossed about queer, disconnected oddments of motion or gesture that almost told you something and then darted off on another tangent—with a few private jokes on the side. . . .
>
> He kept the audience on the jump and in a state of risibles. Anything went. That is, anything within his own experience. There was hoeing and weeding at the farm, sewing costumes, stumbling over an obstacle that wasn't there, taking a shower, sweeping a floor, and a bit of hair-pulling that could have been anybody's quarrel but wasn't. Flashes of camp meeting, circus, gymnasium stunts, acrobatics, were jumbled in with the personal touches. But the dance was quicker than the eye. . . . Charles with his quips of fingers and quirks of toes, was of course the chief figure, though the groups, both concert and workshop, dressed in shades of green, mingled actively in the phantasmagoria. The *première* audience . . . devoured every morsel with glee. In New York and on tour *Opus 51* became a matter of heated controversy. To some it was arrant nonsense, signifying nothing. To others it was a brilliant kidding of everything but the kitchen sink, and maybe that, too.[78]

Henry Gilfond, *Dance Observer*:

> There was a bit of datedness about the satire . . . timely enough before 1929, when the principal occupation of the artist was to pull the leg of his smug audience. Today, however, except perhaps in Bennington, the audience is far

> from smug. One doesn't stick one's tongue out at a contemporary audience; one stirs it—and by satire, if that is the artist's medium. Charles Weidman, than whom there is no greater satirist in the dance field, who is veritably the Charlie Chaplin of the dance, can do, has done, and undoubtedly will do satires of considerably more eloquence than *Opus 51*.[79]

Albertina Vitak, *American Dancer*:

> In naming his new work *Opus* 51 . . . Mr. Weidman was apparently having his little joke. . . . True, it had an opening section which was serious enough but it was also very bad, with poor lines of the arms and body and slovenly performance of the steps. . . . The audience enjoyed it immensely but there was also an undercurrent of puzzlement on the part of these serious students of the modern dance. I, too, was puzzled at Mr. Weidman's choice of time and place to do just this composition, in spite of my oft reiterated statement that comedy is undeniably his forte.[80]

Joseph Arnold Kaye, *Dance*:

> Weidman is the best pantomimic dancer that we have in this country. . . . The fault with *Opus 51* is that there are too many stock notions and too much that can be readily anticipated.[81]

Subsequent Reviews:

Walter Terry, in the *Boston Herald*, reviewed the New York premiere:

> *Opus 51* offers the improvisational form of the Commedia dell'Arte, and the freedom of this form gives the choreographer a chance to make use of sudden contrasts in movement and in mood. . . . Movement and gesture are used in such a way and in such unusual sequences that they appear fresh and new. *Opus 51* gives us a kaleidoscopic view of man dancing, marching, cleaning house, bathing, loafing, and exhibiting himself for popular acclaim. . . . *Opus 51* is frolicking satire.[82]

Grant Code did not see its original production but wrote about its revival in *Dance Observer* in 1941:

> There is a serious undercurrent in *Opus 51*. Weidman [presents] a world that starts out in a very solemn, beautiful, intelligent and orderly way to accomplish something quite grand and then suddenly and completely goes mad. The moment when he first starts with terror, at the sight of a moving hand that has gone off on a little meaningless performance of its own, is a really brilliant and thrilling transition, more tragic than comic.[83]

Code remarked on the brilliance of Weidman's choreography, comic effect, and technique. "The work is even more brilliant in texture than I had imagined, but it is also perhaps a little less impressive in substance than it was intended to be, than I had hoped to find it."[84]

6 August 1938

American Document

Vermont State Armory

Chor Martha Graham. *Mus* Ray Green (original score). *Mus dir* Louis Horst. *Asst Pianist* Ralph Gilbert. *Cos* Edythe Gilfond. *Sets & light* Arch Lauterer. *Asst* Edward Glass, Henry Seymour. *Prod Asst* Sophie Maslow. *Danc* Graham and Graham Group and Bennington Group. Graham Group: Anita Alvarez, Thelma Babitz, Ethel Butler, Jane Dudley, Nine Fonaroff, Natalie Harris, Marie Marchowsky, Sophie Maslow, Marjorie G. Mazia, May O'Donnell, Gertrude Shurr. Bennington Group: Muriel V. Brenner, Jean Marion Erdman, Erick Hawkins, Virginia Hall

Martha Graham in *American Document* (Puritan Episode–"Song of Songs" Duet, Erick Hawkins and Martha Graham). Photograph copyright by Barbara Morgan.

Johnson, Jane Lee Perry, Helen Priest, Kaya Russell, Elaine Scanlon, Margaret Strater, Claire Strauss, Eleanor Struppa. *Characters: The Actor as Interlocutor* Houseley Stevens, Jr. *The End Figures* Alvarez, Babitz. *The Chorus* Graham Group led by O'Donnell, Bennington Group. *The Principals*: Hawkins, Graham. The Dance Procedure: ***Entrance–Walk Around. Part I. Declaration. Part II. Indian Episode: Native Figure*** *danc* Graham. ***Lament for the Land*** *danc* Graham Group, led by O'Donnell. ***Part III. Puritan Episode*** *danc* Hawkins, Graham. ***Part IV. Emancipation Episode: Group Dance. Duet*** *danc* Hawkins, Graham. ***Part V. The After Piece: Cross Fire–Cakewalk. 1938*** *danc* Dudley, Maslow, O'Donnell, Hawkins. ***Declaration. Finale and Exit–Walk Around.***

Program Note:

> The form of the piece is patterned freely after an American Minstrel Show.
>
> This is a Documentary Dance.
> "Our documents are our legends–our poignantly
> near history, our folk tales."

The libretto of *American Document* was published in *Theatre Arts* magazine in 1942, giving the text and general movement directions. According to *Theatre Arts*, Graham was inspired by hearing "vicious and terrifying words . . . from the Axis countries" on the radio. She realized "that our own country–our democracy–has words, too, with power to hearten men and move them to action."[85]

Graham's documentary sources were The Declaration of Independence, Lincoln's Gettysburg Address, The Emancipation Proclamation, Lincoln's Second Inaugural Address, the Song of Songs, the words and writings of Red Jacket of the Senecas, Thomas Paine, John Wise, Jonathan Edwards, and Francis Fergusson. Fergusson assisted Graham with the libretto. (Later performances included references to contemporary events, such as the Scottsboro case.)

Barbara Morgan's book *Martha Graham* includes 14 photographs of *American Document*.[86] A film fragment shows Graham, Hawkins, and Houseley Stevens, Jr., in rehearsal at the Armory in 1938 (see Sources–Films). Don McDonagh's Graham biography contains additional background. To McDonagh, *American Document* was

> the forerunner of a whole line of dramatically based dances that for many became the hallmark of Graham's style of theater. . . . After the summer of 1938, some of the austerity that kept the public at arm's length began to disappear, and . . . she began to modify her technique away from the percussive line [of] the previous decade. . . . She also began to script her works in a new way. From this point on, she would have an elaborate scenario prepared to give to designers and composers.[87]

When Graham revived *Document* in 1944 it was "hailed for the valid reason that its magnificent group choreography is in a style which has been disappearing from [her] more recent compositions."[88]

A festival press release issued before the 1938 premiere announced:

> For the first time in her career, Miss Graham will use a male dancer [Erick Hawkins] in one of her own works, and also for the first time, will utilize speech, the phrases of which are to be drawn from classic American documents and spoken by an actor who will be used as a character in the dramatic sequence. Miss Graham points out that speech, as she will use it, has no relationship to accompaniment, but is, on the contrary, a definite extension of idea used to augment and clarify the meaning of the composition.
>
> Erick Hawkins . . . a regular member of the Ballet Caravan . . . is a soloist and choreographer in his own right, and is probably the first member of a ballet company to have participated in a modern dance production. He will return to the Ballet Caravan in the autumn.

Hawkins was listed in the program as a member of the Apprentice Group, appearing courtesy of Lincoln Kirstein. He was enrolled as a student. Graham had met him at Bennington the summer before, after seeing his ballet *Show Piece*. They met again in New York that winter. In the spring, Hawkins began a new ballet based on the theme of the Minotaur. He was having difficulty with it and asked Lincoln Kirstein to lend him the money to study with Graham at Bennington. Kirstein agreed, and Hawkins discovered when he phoned the Graham studio that he could enroll first in the June course Graham was giving in New York. There, after classes, he watched Graham rehearse the choral dances (which he recalled being the most beautiful parts) for *American Document* in preparation for the Bennington production. Hawkins said he first learned that Graham would use him in the production when she announced to the group, "Erick and I will come in here."[89]

Jean Erdman, who had joined the Graham group earlier that year, also danced as a member of the Apprentice Group (the previous summer she had danced in Anna Sokolow's fellowship group):

> When I began to dance with the Graham group I had to learn something like five dances in ten days—quite an initiation. Martha's first technique was very frontal and square in these dances. In *American Document* she began developing spiral movement. . . . She began to evolve new techniques which have gone even more into spirals now in the studio work.[90]

For Ethel Butler, Graham's use of words was extraordinary:

> They heightened the dramatic quality of the dance. In Martha's Indian solo, she used Indian names such as Allegheny, Monongahela, Saskatchewan . . . they were just kind of floating words . . . they floated out. It was very, very beautiful.[91]

Music: *American Document* was the last of the works Graham composed before the music was written. The score exists in manuscript but, to Ray Green's knowledge, was never recorded:

> I'd written quite a lot of the music before going up to Bennington. I took counts by sequences. I'd watch rehearsals when she was ready and make notes of general things, then go away and dream up some music that would suit that episode. I remember Martha was quite taken with what I did for the *Emancipation* section. It was basically a spiritual feeling but I put it into a different harmonic and textural setting. I used percussion and also made the piano a percussive instrument. There were many changes in the choreography before the work was finally produced on stage. I wrote a piece which had originally been projected for an African solo where I used a theme of an African folksong as a take-off point, with a percussion background while the piano played my version of this African theme. But the African solo was changed into a kind of "labor on the march" or something like that, a totally different idea, and I had written the piece as a *tour de force* of percussion with this other thing in mind.[92]

George Beiswanger wrote that Green's setting was possibly the most functional of all the new music:

> In spots the work is nothing more than piano percussion tinged with a fervent color of the particular emotion evoked by the dance at that particular point. Again, as in the "Emancipation" section, it becomes one of the *dramatis personae*, evoking by its presence and challenge the group response. Still again, there are themes which embody meanings of the dance as surely as do the movement patterns themselves. The music is not of the sort to stand by itself, and that is all the more to its credit in this case, since its sole function is unobtrusively and yet with surety of touch to underline the purposes of the dance.[93]

Composer David Diamond said of it:

> Ray Green's score . . . is musically satisfying, sincere and transparent. Most music for the dance, I am convinced, is padded and over-complicated; it is governed by isolated patterns of movement. Green is one of the few composers for the dance who . . . knows how to adapt a flexible musical phrase to an extended phrase of movement. The style . . . is refreshing in its simplicity and candor. Too much emphasis on only one or two tonalities throughout creates a monotony which is further heightened by a stubborn pedal device; there is also

Martha Graham's *American Document* (Declaration Episode–Erick Hawkins, May O'Donnell, and group). Photograph copyright by Barbara Morgan.

> a lack of flow in the bass, no real movement; only accompanying figures, pedals and ostinati which produce a sameness of texture. Composers for the dance are bound to the piano keyboard, and they seldom allow the left side of the piano to function; it is perpetually playing accompaniments for the right. A more contrapuntal idiom would have enhanced the beauty of the music. Mr. Green's music . . . nevertheless breathes honesty.[94]

Costumes: Edythe Gilfond, wife of *Dance Observer* critic Henry Gilfond, had begun making costumes for Graham the year before. (Up until that time, Graham had done all of her own costumes.) Ethel Butler recalled innumerable costume changes. "The very first thing we thought of was how were we ever going to make the costume changes. Every episode was different. We were underdressing and overdressing throughout much of the piece."[95]

New York Premiere: 9 October 1938, Carnegie Hall, sponsored by *New Masses.*

Subsequent Productions: *American Document* was taken on transcontinental tours in 1939 and 1940. It was revived twice in 1944, on 25 March at the Central High School of Needle Trades and on 7-14 May at the National Theatre during a week-long retrospective of Graham's works dating from 1930.

Erick Hawkins and Martha Graham in an episode from *American Document*, Vermont State Armory. Photograph by Sidney Bernstein.

Reviews

George Beiswanger asserted that *American Document* solved "the most difficult problem of the theatre dance. Within the framework of the minstrel show it creates the most profoundly moving and completely satisfying dramatic dance which the writer has ever witnessed."[96]

Lincoln Kirstein surpassed even his paean to Graham's *Immediate Tragedy* (1937), calling *American Document* "in itself ample justification for everything else the Bennington School may or may not have done in the last five years." Wrote Kirstein:

> The subject matter . . . is our time, our place, our dangers, and our chances of survival. It is the most important extended dance creation by a living American, and if there has been another in any other time more important, there is no record of it. . . .
>
> *American Document* is conceived on the basic skeletal structure of a minstrel show. It opens and closes with a parade of participants, using gestures borrowed from minstrel strut and cake-walk. Its episodes are linked by drum rolls and fanfares of acrobatic movement. Its solo numbers are projected against a choral background. It utilized Ray Green's coherent musical score of a spare consistency. It employed a male voice as oracle, comment, and interlocutor declaiming statements from classic American papers. Its episodes commenced with an introductory duet, a preamble for a grave circus, a kind of annunciatory dominant chord of motion from which the rest of the symphony was to be amplified. There followed an Indians' lament for the spirit of the land they had lost, then a statement of Puritan fury and tenderness, an elegy of the emancipated Negro slaves, and a finale of contemporary self-accusation, a praise of our rights, and a challenge to our own powers to persist as democracy.
>
> The whole piece was so nobly framed, so flawlessly executed, that every other work, new or old, offered at the Bennington Festival seemed by comparison puerile, unprofessional, or academic. Graham's work had the sober, frank sincerity of a Thanksgiving hymn heard in the open air. Its surface finish resembled some useful Shaker wood-turning. Its exalted plasticity of formal movement was as proud and objective as a New Bedford whaler's figurehead. The Puritan duet, with Graham in severe white, her partner naked except for white shorts and a dark coat of tan, had as antiphonal Jonathan Edwards's terrible words on fornication and damnation spoken against parallels from the Song of Songs. The tenseness of its emotion, the extreme projection of restrained physicality, rendered the adolescent elements in the audience uncomfortable. Its solemn purity was hard for the shy-eyed of all ages to take. It is so serious that it can only touch those who have the courage to look at it. Happily, most of the audience were too occupied in experiencing it to be frightened of its feeling. . . .

> The use of the voice, the dominance of the ideas back of its creation, the quality of Graham's idiosyncratic gesture formulating just what she meant to say, were all miraculous. Graham in her Indian solo was a monument for which the vanishing American has waited three centuries, built from native folk gesture and ritual movement. In the end, in a plain bright red dress, with her dancing balance of suavity and abruptness, her somber levity and steady stops, she seemed an incarnate question of everything we fear and hope for in our daily lives.
>
> Her own dance group, clothed in simply cut clothes of clean transparent colors, made their first entrance like a troupe of erect peacocks driving a chariot. They were ably augmented by the group of lay and professional students from the Bennington School of the Dance. Miss Graham's partner was Erick Hawkins. His strong, solid, angry human dancing provided a splendid support, a positive male presence. Since he had ballet training, he was unacceptable to some of the "modern" dance purists, who were too prejudiced to look at him with clean eyes. Graham's use of a dancer trained in another classicism showed that elasticity which makes her unique in an experimental field. Hawkins, in the questions voiced at the end of the piece, stood and walked like a workman's best idea of himself as a dancer. Nor shall I forget for a long time the presence of the interlocutor, Houseley Stevens, Jr., or his beautiful manly voice and arresting appearance, so open and yet so decently serious. . . . Arch Lauterer's distinguished setting was memorably used. At the words "Declaration 1776," four doors at the back suddenly were flung wide open and four blue-clad dancers appeared like visual trumpets.[97]

John Martin, *New York Times*:

> [Graham's *American Document* was] substantially a new treatment of the same theme that occupied her in *Panorama*. . . . Its form, however, is totally new and highly experimental. . . . It is extremely effective, with a fine, free, objective clarity about it.
>
> [It] is strongest in its opening and closing movements and distinctly weak in its "Puritan Episode," from which in its present shape it never completely recovers. . . . This is as successful a combination of speech and movement as any that has yet been made, partly no doubt because the lines themselves are the very essence of Miss Graham's personal style and rhythm.[98]

Joseph Arnold Kaye, in *Dance*, thought it was uneven. Yet, he continued,

> there were sections so extraordinarily fine that at moments it seemed as though everything else done in the modern dance were pigmy by comparison. . . . For the first time she committed herself definitely to a literal and realistic scenario. And for the first time she made marked changes in her technique, leaning in the direction of more lyric or, specifically speaking, more rounded movements. . . . For the modern dance [*American Document*] is an experiment of immeasurable significance. For Miss Graham personally it is revolutionary. . . .
>
> ["Puritan Episode"] has beauty and power such as the modern dance has heretofore not known. . . . The protagonists are two lovers and they are alternately drawn to each other by passion and parted by the taboos and inhibitions of their society. Quotations from the Biblical Song of Songs are woven into the dialog of the Interlocutor in leit-motif fashion.
>
> This section has a symphonic range and quality that may be found in a Wagnerian music drama. It is so clear in intent, and what it has to say is said so magnificently that the audience automatically shed the indiscriminate partisanship typical of a Bennington audience and sat so hushed and tense that a rustle of a program was an offense. . . .

> The introduction of Erick Hawkins . . . was not so startling as expected. The role for him was beautifully conceived and he danced it with a strength and unmaudlin tenderness unusual for an artist brought to the modern dance from the ballet.[99]

Albertina Vitak, *American Dancer*:

> In her several quite lovely scenes with Erick Hawkins . . . she was a glowing woman instead of an abstraction of one. . . . Tall, handsome Mr. Hawkins made a good foil for Miss Graham but was at times unyielding in mood and movement. . . . Her appearance, costumed first in strong lavender, again in black, or scarlet, or white, [was] startling and dramatic.[100]

Margaret Lloyd, in the *Christian Science Monitor*, was less than enthusiastic:

> Martha Graham's . . . bizarre *American Document* [was] full of surprise, daring and, for me, disappointment. [The] script prepared by Miss Graham, assisted by Francis Fergusson of the College Drama Department . . . stated the case so clearly that much of the subsequent dance movement was unnecessary.
>
> Miss Graham, buoyant and gay, entered her first duet with Erick Hawkins, apprentice pupil from the Ballet Caravan. . . . Charming to see her in this infrequent mood. It looked like more fun ahead. But no. Mr. Stevens, Jr. began to get serious. America! And what it means to be an American! A fine theme. A stirring theme. He quoted from the Declaration of Independence. Lovely words that needed no eludication. . . .
>
> The "Puritan Episode," a duet preluded by stern lines from Jonathan Edwards against tender passages from the Song of Songs, administered a new kind of shock . . . not so much for its eroticism as for its lack of taste. . . . Miss Graham's incandescent *Ekstasis* bears witness to her ability to handle the human love theme with reserve and inward grace.[101]

Subsequent Reviews: Later Lloyd wrote:

> *Immediate Tragedy* was a sweeping indictment . . . of the torch that set the world aflame. . . . She turned from world-suffering to find comfort in the American ideal, to affirm that ideal in *American Document*. . . . Martha looked to America, as the world looked, for strength and leadership. But not with astigmatic eyes.
>
> *American Document* is set in a nebulous framework of the old-time minstrel show, part and parcel of American entertainment traditions, without being very much like one. It is not in blackface, it does not go in for "darky" or other popular comedy. It is . . . a dance documentary, and its score, by Ray Green, has the color and disjointed continuity of film music.
>
> The work was revised and considerably tightened up before its first New York showing in Carnegie Hall in October and was taken on the third transcontinental tour in 1939. Its devout patriotism won the country. It was easily understood, therefore easily appreciated, for this was one Graham work that was not a Graham mystery. It was almost too explicit. The stripped, clean, poetic words said all there was to say, so that the movement phrases served chiefly as illustrations.[102]

Walter Terry first saw it in New York:

> In the midst of Martha Graham's *American Document* at New York's Carnegie Hall, we said to ourself: "This has gone on long enough!" For more than ten years modern dancers have experimented. They have done some fine things and they have added zest and strength to the dance. But their goal has been a dance that is truly American, and in this they have failed. . . . They have won a goodly

> portion of their successes through the vividness of their personalities. When they are gone little will remain but a vast series of body exercises, for they will have bequeathed no tradition of theatrical entertainment, no lucid medium for the presentation of contemporary ideas, no style about which people might say, "This is our very own—this is American." . . . If *American Document* is the way Miss Graham sees America—bloodless, characterless, humorless—we have a right to feel insulted.[103]

Terry suggested that Martha Graham consult Ruth St. Denis and Ted Shawn "for some good sound advice." To this, Frances Hawkins took angry exception, and Terry responded to her letter with a somewhat softer stance toward *Document*:

> The work is neither abstract nor representational but a confusion of the two approaches. It was a great idea, an idea that should be danced. Miss Graham's conception of this dance reflection of America was richer, more ambitious than that of any other artist, but she failed in the actual choreographic projection of the idea. . . . Will her dance experiments pass the laboratory state and enter the realm of the theater?[104]

Edwin Denby gave *Document* a brief paragraph in early 1939:

> I see Miss Graham's sincerity, her fine technic, her intensity. But I am troubled by the monotony of equal thrusts, the unrelaxed determination. There is something too constantly solemn, too unhumorous, too stiff about it; something sectarian.[105]

Although Denby became interested in Martha Graham's work in the 1940s, he regarded a revival of *American Document* in 1944 as "a complete failure" in its "present form":

> Originally it seemed at least to conceal some sting of protest and to present our history as much for its disgraces as for its strength. At present it seems intended merely as smug glorification. It is monotonous as dancing and in sentiment varies from hollow solemnity to mawkish sentimentalism. The opening of Miss Graham's Indian solo and one sentence quoted from Jonathan Edwards are the only thirty seconds of interest; the rest seems as insincere as those patriotic full-page advertisements in color in the slick paper magazines.
>
> Miss Graham's intentions were to make the movement open, plain and buoyant [but it] turns out to be inelastic, it strikes poses and it pounds downward.[106]

But Lois Balcom in *Dance Observer* celebrated its return to the repertoire and called attention to its magnificent group choreography as a rediscovered asset:

> Abstract in mode and complex in design, [it] has had to give way in the more recent *Letter, Circus, Punch* and *Deaths and Entrances*, to the requirements of a wholly different theatre concept. . . . The tremendous crescendo of "Emancipation Episode"—with its nostalgic reminiscence of *Celebration*, the poignance of "Lament for the Land," the gathering pulse of "Declaration," the tincture of impudence spicing the elegance of the "Walk Around,"—all these take us back to an earlier, and uniquely modern, "modern dance." Yet they are as fresh as tomorrow.[107]

NOTES

1. Eleanor King, *Transformations: A Memoir, The Humphrey-Weidman Years* (Brooklyn, N.Y.: Dance Horizons, 1978), p. 261.
2. *Dance Observer* 10, no. 4 (April 1943): 46.
3. John Martin, *New York Times*, 14 August 1938.
4. John Martin, *New York Times*, 5 August 1938.
5. Henry Gilfond, "Bennington Festival," *Dance Observer* 5, no. 7 (August-September 1938): 100.
6. Albertina Vitak, *American Dancer* 11, no. 12 (October 1938): 13.
7. Joseph Arnold Kaye, *Dance* 5, no. 1 (October 1938): 11.
8. *Bennington Banner*, 5 August 1938.
9. King, *Transformations*, p. 261, 263.
10. John Martin, *New York Times*, 14 August 1938.
11. John Martin, *New York Times*, 5 August 1938.
12. Henry Gilfond, *Dance Observer* 5, no. 7 (August-September 1938): 100.
13. Margaret Lloyd, "Bennington Afterglow," *Christian Science Monitor*, 30 August 1938.
14. Bennington Festival press release, quoted by John Martin, *New York Times*, 24 July 1938.
15. John Martin, *New York Times*, 5 August 1938.
16. John Martin, *New York Times*, 14 August 1938.
17. Henry Gilfond, *Dance Observer* 5, no. 7 (August-September 1938): 100.
18. Bennington Festival press release, quoted by John Martin, *New York Times*, 24 July 1938.
19. John Martin, *New York Times*, 5 August 1938.
20. John Martin, *New York Times*, 14 August 1938.
21. Margaret Lloyd, *Christian Science Monitor*, 30 August 1938.
22. Albertina Vitak, *American Dancer* 11, no. 12 (October 1938): 13.
23. Henry Gilfond, *Dance Observer* 5, no. 7 (August-September 1938): 100.
24. Ibid.
25. Interview with Barbara Page Beiswanger.
26. Ibid.
27. Bernard A. Tetreault, "Modern Dance Wins Acclaim of Audience," *Bennington Banner*, 6 August 1938.
28. John Mueller, *Films on Ballet and Modern Dance: Notes and a Directory* (New York: American Dance Guild, 1974), pp. 23–43.
29. Selma Jeanne Cohen, *Doris Humphrey: An Artist First* (Middletown, Conn.: Wesleyan University Press, 1972), p. 149.
30. Margaret Lloyd, "Bennington Impressions," *Christian Science Monitor*, 23 August 1938.
31. Interview with Charles Weidman by Billy Nichols, "Four Pioneers" (phonotape), National Educational Television, 1965 [Dance Collection of the New York Public Library].
32. A letter from Doris Humphrey to Humphrey-Weidman dancers, "Thoughts at the Finish of the Tour," quoted in Ernestine Stodelle, *The Dance Technique of Doris Humphrey and Its Creative Potential* (Princeton, N.J.: Princeton Book Company, 1978), pp. 262–63.
33. Ibid.
34. Mueller, *Films on Ballet*, p. 27.
35. Cohen, *Doris Humphrey*, pp. 254–56.
36. Norman Cazden, "On Dancing to Bach," *Dance Observer* 10, no. 3 (March 1943): 31–32.
37. Cohen, *Doris Humphrey*, p. 202.
38. Lucy Venable, "Passacaglia 1938–1965: The Art of Remaking a Dance," *Dance Scope* 1, no. 2 (Spring 1965): 6–14. For descriptions of *Passacaglia*, see also *Don McDonagh's Complete Guide to Modern Dance* (New York: Popular Library, 1977), pp. 124–26, Marcia B. Siegel, *The Shapes of Change* (Boston: Houghton Mifflin, 1979), pp. 89–98, and Mueller, *Films*, pp. 23–43. See also George W. Beiswanger, "The New Theatre Dance," *Theatre Arts Monthly* 23, no. 1 (January 1939): 49–50.
39. John Martin, *New York Times*, 6 August 1938.
40. John Martin, *New York Times*, 14 August 1938.
41. Margaret Lloyd, *Christian Science Monitor*, 30 August 1938.
42. Margaret Lloyd, *The Borzoi Book of Modern Dance* (New York: Alfred A. Knopf, 1949), pp. 108–109.
43. Joseph Arnold Kaye, "Bennington Festival Addenda," *Dance* 5, no. 2 (November 1938): 13.
44. George W. Beiswanger, *Dance Observer* 5, no. 7 (August-September 1938): 103.
45. Albertina Vitak, *American Dancer* 11, no. 12 (October 1938): 13.
46. Walter Terry, *Boston Herald*, 28 November 1938.
47. John Martin, "Audience Cheers Miss Humphrey," *New York Times*, 13 January 1941.
48. Quoted by Walter Sorell in *Hanya Holm: The Biography of an Artist* (Middletown, Conn.: Wesleyan University Press, 1969), p. 81.
49. Ibid., p. 80.
50. Lloyd, *Borzoi*, p. 165.
51. Alice Teirstein, "Dance and Music: Interviews at the Keyboard," *Dance Scope* 8, no. 2 (Spring/Summer 1974): 19.
52. George W. Beiswanger, *Dance Observer* 5, no. 7 (August-September 1938): 103.

53. John Martin, *New York Times*, 6 August 1938.
54. Albertina Vitak, *American Dancer* 11, no. 12 (October 1938): 13.
55. Margaret Lloyd, *Christian Science Monitor*, 30 August 1938.
56. Henry Gilfond, *Dance Observer* 5, no. 7 (August-September 1938): 101. See also George W. Beiswanger, "The New Theatre Dance," *Theatre Arts Monthly* 23, no. 1 (January 1939): 50–51.
57. Lloyd, *Borzoi*, p. 165.
58. George W. Beiswanger, *Dance Observer* 5, no. 7 (August-September 1938): 103.
59. John Martin, *New York Times*, 14 August 1938.
60. Margaret Lloyd, *Christian Science Monitor*, 30 August 1938.
61. Lloyd, *Borzoi*, p. 165.
62. Joseph Arnold Kaye, *Dance* 5, no. 1 (October 1938): 11.
63. Albertina Vitak, *American Dancer* 11, no. 12 (October 1938): 13, 39. See also Beiswanger, "The New Theatre Dance," pp. 50–51.
64. Letter from Doris Humphrey to Charles Francis Woodford, 1938 (undated) [Doris Humphrey Collection, C409].
65. Press release, Humphrey–Weidman Company (undated).
66. Interview with Weidman by Nichols, "Four Pioneers."
67. Charles Weidman, "Random Remarks," in *The Dance Has Many Faces*, ed. Walter Sorell, 2nd ed. (New York: Columbia University Press, 1966), p. 54. See also "Visiting Charles," an interview by Elinor Rogosin in *Eddy* 6 (Spring 1975): 3–15. And see *Don McDonagh's Complete Guide to Modern Dance*, pp. 142–44.
68. Vivian Fine, "Composer/Choreographer," *Dance Perspectives* 16 (1963): 8–11.
69. Maxine Cushing, "Bennington Commentary," *Educational Dance* 1, no. 3 (August-September 1938): 12.
70. George Beiswanger, *Dance Observer* 5, no. 7 (August-September 1938): 103.
71. John Martin, *New York Times*, 9 February 1941.
72. Henry Gilfond, *Dance Observer* 5, no. 7 (August-September 1938): 101.
73. Beiswanger, "The New Theatre Dance," pp. 41–54; pp. 47–49 are especially important.
74. John Martin, *New York Times*, 7 August 1938.
75. John Martin, *New York Times*, 14 August 1938.
76. John Martin, *New York Times*, 7 August 1938.
77. Margaret Lloyd, *Christian Science Monitor*, 23 August 1938.
78. Lloyd, *Borzoi*, pp. 109–10.
79. Henry Gilfond, *Dance Observer* 5, no. 7 (August-September 1938): 101.
80. Albertina Vitak, *American Dancer* 11, no. 12 (October 1938): 39.
81. Joseph Arnold Kaye, *Dance* 5, no. 2 (November 1938): 13.
82. Walter Terry, *Boston Herald*, 28 November 1938.
83. Grant Code, *Dance Observer* 8, no. 4 (April 1941): 56.
84. Ibid.
85. Dance Libretto, "*American Document* by Martha Graham, with Four Scenes from the Dance," *Theatre Arts* 26, no. 9 (September 1942): 565–74.
86. Barbara Morgan, *Martha Graham: Sixteen Dances in Photographs* (New York: Duell, Sloan & Pearce, 1941).
87. Don McDonagh, *Martha Graham* (New York: Praeger, 1973), pp. 137–38.
88. Lois Balcom, *Dance Observer* 11, no. 6 (June-July 1944): 63.
89. Interview with Erick Hawkins.
90. Interview with Jean Erdman.
91. Interview with Ethel Butler.
92. Interview with Ray Green.
93. George W. Beiswanger, *Dance Observer* 5, no. 7 (August-September 1938): 102.
94. David Diamond, "With the Dancers," *Modern Music* 17, no. 2 (January-February 1940): 118–19.
95. Interview with Ethel Butler.
96. Beiswanger, "The New Theatre Dance," especially pp. 53–54.
97. Lincoln Kirstein, "Martha Graham at Bennington," *Nation* 147, no. 10 (3 September 1938): 230–31.
98. John Martin, *New York Times*, 7 August 1938.
99. Joseph Arnold Kaye, *Dance* 5, no. 1 (October 1938): 11.
100. Albertina Vitak, *American Dancer* 11, no. 12 (October 1938): 39.
101. Margaret Lloyd, *Christian Science Monitor*, 23 August 1938.
102. Lloyd, *Borzoi*, pp. 60–62.
103. Walter Terry, *Boston Herald*, 16 October 1938.
104. Walter Terry, *Boston Herald*, 30 October 1938.
105. Edwin Denby, "With the Dancers," *Modern Music* 16, no. 2 (January-February 1939): 130.
106. Edwin Denby, "Sweet and Sour Americana," *New York Herald Tribune*, 12 May 1944.
107. Lois Balcom, *Dance Observer* 11, no. 4 (April 1944): 45.

1939

4 August 1939

Ceremonial Dance

Lisser Hall, Mills College

Chor Ethel Butler (solo). *Mus* Ralph Gilbert (original score).

4 August 1939

The Spirit of the Land Moves in the Blood

Lisser Hall, Mills College

Chor Ethel Butler (solo). *Mus* [Carlos] Chavez.

No information was available on these two works, and there is no evidence of subsequent productions.

Reviews

Elizabeth Goode, *Dance Observer*:

> Ethel Butler's *The Spirit of the Land* . . . had the same vital pulse that great poetry has. . . . *Ceremonial Dance* . . . possessed formality of a rigid Spanish quality.[1]

Esther Pease, *Educational Dance*:

> The first, *Ceremonial Dance*, [was] reminiscent of the Graham *Sarabande*, done with characteristic aloofness and assurance. The second, *The Spirit of the Land* . . . (title from a line in Archibald MacLeish's *The Land of the Free*), bore resemblance to *American Document*, principally because of thematic material. Both were excellently performed, well-costumed and choreographically satisfying. Miss Butler's admirable technique and intelligent understanding of dance medium should be reason enough for her to pursue a more individualized path.[2]

4 August 1939

Danzas Mexicanas

Lisser Hall, Mills College

Chor José Limón (solo). *Mus* Lionel Nowak (original piano score). ***a. Indio, b. Conquistadore, c. Peon, d. Caballero, e. Revolucionario.***

Doris Humphrey wrote:

> José has bitten off a huge chunk of his native land to exhibit—portraits of five kinds of Mexicans—the Indian, the Spanish invader, the peon, the landowner and the Revolutionary. He's really very curious about his dances. He always scorns the dancers he knows for wanting to be dramatic—but he invariably goes for it himself. Now this is not a natural talent with him. Consequently Charles and I try to help when he is obviously looking stunning but not saying anything. One of the dances is excellent—really a remarkable piece of work for one not to the manner born.[3]

Danzas Mexicanas was approximately 25 minutes long. Margaret Lloyd reported that Thomas Bouchard had begun filming the work at Mills in 1939 in black and white and that in 1947 he "was still hoping to get it finished."[4]

New York Premiere: 6 January 1940, Washington Irving High School. (Unconfirmed prior performance 28-30 December 1939, Humphrey-Weidman Studio Theatre.)

Subsequent Productions: 13 January 1946, YM-YWHA, New York.

Reviews

Alfred Frankenstein, *San Francisco Chronicle*:

> The most important feature of the evening was the first performance of an amazing suite of dances on Mexican historical themes by Limón. . . . He has the face and body of an heroic Mayan idol, and he has endless resources both of choreographic power and dramatic expression. He does not, like many modern dancers, scorn the value of the immediately intelligible dramatic gesture. His dances exposed five stages of Mexican life—the Indian, the Conquistador, the peon, the caballero and the modern revolutionary. It seemed to me, on a first view, that he rang the bell most successfully in the first and fourth of these phases. The Indian movement conveyed very poignantly the sense of natural folk life, and the caballero movement was motivated by a fine aristocratic scorn for its fine aristocratic subject with, perhaps, an echo or two of Weidman's own *Happy Hypocrite*. But the whole work rings true, and not the least of its virtues is the splendidly sympathetic music by Lionel Nowak.[5]

Elizabeth Goode, *Dance Observer*:

> The *Danzas Mexicanas* . . . stood out for their beautiful staging, tense emotion, and dramatic quality. [In the "Caballero"] Mr. Limón . . . with gray tights and purple "tails" . . . gave the impression of a long beetle with a stuffed chest. Here he contrasted the minute movements of his hands with an occasional broad sweeping movement of his powerful body. It is interesting to note that when José Limón's floor pattern is practically stationary, his dances appear more space defining than when his floor pattern covers the stage.[6]

NOTES

1. Elizabeth Goode, *Dance Observer* 6, no. 7 (August-September 1939): 250.
2. Esther E. Pease, "Young Artists in Concert at Bennington," *Educational Dance* 2, no. 3 (August-September 1939): 13.
3. Letter from Doris Humphrey to Charles Francis Woodford, postmarked 1 August 1939 [Doris Humphrey Collection, C426].
4. Margaret Lloyd, *The Borzoi Book of Modern Dance* (New York: Alfred A. Knopf, 1949), p. 351.
5. Alfred Frankenstein, *San Francisco Chronicle*, 5 August 1939.
6. Goode, *Dance Observer*, p. 250. See also Lloyd, *Borzoi*, pp. 203-204.

1940

13 July 1940

Liberty Tree—A Set of Four Dances

College Theatre

Chor Erick Hawkins (solo). *Mus* Ralph Gilbert (original piano score). *Sets* Carlos Dyer. *Cos* Edythe Gilfond. ***1. Patriot–Massachusetts, 2. Trail Breaker–Kentucky, 3. Free Stater–Kansas, 4. Nomad Harvester–California.***

New York Premiere: 20 April 1941, YMHA.

13 July 1940

Insubstantial Pageant—A Dance of Experience

College Theatre

Chor Erick Hawkins (solo). *Mus* Lehman Engel (original piano score). *Sets* Carlos Dyer.

13 July 1940

Yankee Bluebritches—A Vermont Fantasy

College Theatre

Chor Erick Hawkins (solo). *Mus* Hunter Johnson (original piano score). *Sets* Charlotte Trowbridge.

Program Note: "I wasn't brought up in the woods to be scared by owls."—Old Proverb.

New York Premiere: 20 April 1941, YMHA.

Hawkins commissioned music for these solos, a practice he steadfastly maintained afterward. *Liberty Tree* and *Yankee Bluebritches* were performed frequently after their New York premieres. No evidence of subsequent performances of *Insubstantial Pageant* was found.

Reviews

No reviews in *Dance Observer*, the *New York Times*, the *Christian Science Monitor*, or the *Boston Herald* were located.

The *Bennington Banner* reported the debut as follows:

> An audience that crowded the Bennington College theatre to capacity . . . enthusiastically welcomed Erick Hawkins in his first performance as a solo dancer. . . . He brings to the concert stage a masculine force and strength that the dance in this country needs.[1]

The *Banner* praised Hawkins' "splendid physique . . . over six feet tall and built like an athlete." His timing and precision demonstrated "the excellence of his ballet training" and "the scope of his dancing [showed] the breadth and feeling he has gained from his association with Martha Graham."

Liberty Tree was "a sincere and warm expression of a man's realization of his heritage." *Insubstantial Pageant* was "a dance of experience, of man in the doorways of life." *Yankee Bluebritches* "with its salty humor and amusing fantasy showed that Mr. Hawkins could be witty and engaging without being whimsical." Hunter Johnson's music for *Yankee Bluebritches* included "variations on Yankee Doodle." Carlos Dyer's sets "suggested the background and content of the dance without hiding the movement of the dancer."[2]

When Hawkins presented *Liberty Tree* and *Yankee Bluebritches* in New York, Robert Sabin wrote:

> The four studies in Americana called *Liberty Tree* need shortening, but they are authentic, virile and convincing in mood. It was very refreshing to see a male dancer dance like a man, and Mr. Hawkins suggested the sturdy patriotism of revolutionary days and the venturesome courage of the pioneers without losing the thread of his design.[3]

11 August 1940

El Penitente (The Penitent)

College Theatre

Chor Martha Graham. *Mus* Louis Horst (original score for piano, flute, piccolo, clarinet, violin, and small drum). *Musicians* Horst, Otto Luening, Robert McBride, Theodore Russell.[4] *Sets & light* Arch Lauterer. *Cos* Edythe Gilfond. *Masque and Death Cart* Mary Grant. *Characters: Penitent* Erick Hawkins. *Christ Figure* Merce Cunningham. *Mary Figure: Virgin, Magdalen, Mother* Martha Graham. 1. Entrance of Performers, 2. Flagellation of Penitent, 3. Vision of Penitent: The Virgin Pleads, The Christ Blesses, 4. Death Cart: The death cart is the symbol for sin, 5. Seduction: The Magdalen seduces the Penitent, 6. The Fall of Man, 7. The Christ condemns, 8. The Penitent bears the cross on his back, 9. The Crucifixion—the penitent atones and wins salvation, 10. The Festival Dance.

Program Note:

> The Penitentes are a sect that believe in purification from sin through severe penance. Even today, in both Old and New Mexico, they practice their ancient rites including the crucifixion. This dance bears no factual relationship to these practices but is done rather as a story told after the manner of the old minstrels. The three figures enter, assume their characters and perform as a group of players acting in a Mystery Play. The action is divided by a return to the entrance theme. The Festival Dance at the end is a version of a popular dance of celebration with no ritualistic content as in the preceding scenes.

El Penitente was choreographed by Graham before the start of the Bennington session, but this was its first production.[5]

Music: The music was the last of 11 scores Louis Horst wrote for Martha Graham and the only one composed before the dance. Horst regarded it as one of his most successful efforts, "not as music that stands by itself, but as music that was right for the dances it accompanied."[6] It exemplified Horst's credo that "a good score should have the transparency of primitive music so you can look through it and see the dance."[7] According to the piano score published in 1960, Horst's orchestrated version called for flute (piccolo), oboe, clarinet, bassoon, violin, cello, and a primitive type of Indian drum "with a high, dry tone."[8]

Sets and Costumes: Costumes and decor for the Bennington production were "homespun," recalled Merce Cunningham; the properties looked like "things someone in the village might have made."[9] The properties went through innumerable alterations over the years, beginning with the New York premiere, for which Isamu Noguchi designed a ritual mask worn by the Christ figure. According to Don McDonagh, Graham felt "Cunningham had too young a face for the role of Christ."[10] For the 1947 revival, the production was redesigned by Noguchi. Margaret Lloyd preferred "Arch Lauterer's original roughhewn concepts of the players' paraphernalia," as did

Merce Cunningham.[11] Lloyd described some of the changes in decor over the years:

> The Christ Figure first wore what looked like a crown of thorns and a papal robe. In Barbara Morgan's priceless book of photographs, he wears a sunburst headdress of Mongolian effect. And I have seen him in a triangular mask that boxed in the face, in line, perhaps, with the tradition that the face of the Christ should not be shown upon the stage.[12]

Writing about the Bennington production and Lauterer's original setting, Lloyd said:

> There is no setting but that which the three dance players evoke in imagination . . . Many properties are used, and not one that is non-essential. These, interwoven with the action, create [the work's] world.[13]

Erick Hawkins said, "the most beautiful performance we ever did of *El Penitente*" occurred in the dining room at Bennington the night before the first performance. "Just Merce, Martha and me. After that we started to work on costumes, but I suspect that was the first pure crystallization of it after Martha had composed it."[14] *El Penitente* was, he thought, well suited to him. "That archaic feeling was native to me."

The 1960 piano score gives the following description of the dance:

> The figures enter in a procession. The Penitent beats himself with a rope to drive the evil from his body. Falling unconscious he dreams of forgiveness. The Virgin pleads for him and The Christ comes forward to bless them. Again the figures march about the stage, and the second part of the dance begins—the act of penance. The Penitent pulls a Death Cart, the symbol of sin. He relives the Fall of Man, the act of original sin, as the Magdalen dances seductively before him. Jumping between them, The Christ interrupts their Love Duet, condemning them with majestic leaps. With the help of the sorrowful Mother kneeling at his side, the Penitent takes up the cross on his back. Re-enacting the crucifixion he atones and wins salvation from The Christ. In another processional march the figures doff their ceremonial garments and conclude with a dance of celebration. . . .
>
> The figures assume their characters by simple costume changes or the donning of a mask, usually in full view of the audience.
>
> The performers enter carrying the props they will use in various ways throughout the dance. The Penitent's rope becomes a whip and later a harness for the Death Cart. Mary carries a hoop covered with light blue cloth, a cerise flower, and a black veil to portray her three respective roles. The Christ holds a cross from which are suspended two curtains of cloth. The cross serves as a banner for the processions and, when set up at the back of the stage, a screen from which The Christ watches the action.[15]

New York Premiere: 20 January 1941, Mansfield Theatre.

Subsequent Productions: 28 February 1947, Ziegfeld Theatre, New York, with John Butler as the Christ Figure, Pearl Lang as the three Marys (the first time another dancer had taken a Graham role), and Hawkins.

16 August 1964, Louis Horst Memorial Program, American Dance Festival, New London. Reconstructed with assistance from Pearl Lang, Erick Hawkins, and Robert Cohan. Cast: David Wood, Marnie Thomas, Gene McDonald. This production was filmed by Dwight Godwin (see Sources—Films).

2 September 1969, London Contemporary Dance Theatre debut performance in London, with Noemi Lapzeson, Robert Cohan, and William Louther.

17 June 1970, 92nd Street YM-YWHA, New York. Bertram Ross and Company, with Bertram Ross, Mary Hinkson, and Richard Kuch.

17 May 1977, Lunt-Fontanne Theatre, New York. Rudolph Nureyev made his debut in the role of the Flagellant, with Pearl Lang and Peter Sparling.

Reviews

John Martin, *New York Times*:

> Of the two new works, *El Penitente* is very much the better. [It] has a simple tenderness that is irresistible. . . . It is the first time in a number of years that Miss Graham has turned to the Southwest for her material but in doing so she has proved that it is still full of rich meaning and inspiration for her.[16]

In his Sunday column he elaborated:

> [It] abandons what is generally accepted as dancing and choreography [and] achieves its end beautifully with an exaggeratedly simple pantomime. [Graham] projects a deep sweetness through the surface of a deliberate naïveté of style. Erick Hawkins as the Penitent finds himself overmastered at times by the demands of such a style and his simplicity becomes a trifle arch. In the main, however, he is excellent. Merce Cunningham plays the "Christ Figure" just exactly as it should be played, and Miss Graham has fitted his tall, plain youthfulness with admirable movement. Here she has had first-rate collaboration from both her musician and her stage designer. Louis Horst, who advocates "eye music" but writes "ear music" has provided a rich and lovely score, and Mr. Lauterer has given the stage a fine spaciousness and a sense of sun.[17]

Water Terry, *New York Herald Tribune*:

> The dancers had the characteristics of religious figurines, their movements were highly stylized as if they had performed these rites until spontaneity and improvisation had long since departed, and the episodes themselves were stories from the Bible retold in the simple and reverent terms of Christian primitives. *El Penitente* had the charm of a folk dance, the reverent beauty of a religious dance and the dramatic and vivid qualities of a Martha Graham choreography at its very best.[18]

Margaret Lloyd, *Christian Science Monitor*:

> It seems quite finished in form, makes quite clear its intention, and is vibrantly achieved—a high-colored theatrical picture—in the line of *Primitive Mysteries*, but without that great work's subtlety or incandescence.[19]

Elizabeth McCausland, *Dance Observer*:

> Martha Graham's choreographic intention . . . is plain: to ally the dance with the theater, or rather perhaps to reunite two arts historically always allied. . . . The tradition [of the Mexican mystery plays] to which Graham has gone back in this dance, supplies the idiom of *El Penitente*. . . . Deliberately naïve passages (like costume changes in full view of the audience—used by Graham to enhance dramatic effect) derive also from the same tradition. . . . Generally, gesture in *El Penitente* is mannered and stiff, as in some of the Christos and Virgins photographed by Paul Strand in Mexican churches.[20]

Sherman Conrad, *Nation*:

> [*El Penitente*] is so simple that some of its significance eludes one; it is a dance that will deepen with the repeated seeing that its humble beauty deserves. The massive agility and Aztec mask that Erick Hawkins has brought to Miss Graham's group find here their most effective use thus far.[21]

Subsequent Reviews:

Ernestine Stodelle, some years later, in *Dance Observer*:

> Like cameos, each character emerged with chiseled clarity. . . . Yet for all its formality of gesture pertinent to the set form of the Mexican-Spanish mystery

> plays, the dance had passages of seemingly improvised movements of genuine feeling.[22]

Margaret Lloyd, in *The Borzoi Book of Modern Dance*, described the mood of the dance as "rapt and tender as a prayer":

> The trio makes its processional entrance . . . as three strolling players. They carry their properties, and publicly affix the fragments of costume that will transform them into the characters of the miracle. This they solemnly enact, and when it is over, burst into a joyous festival dance that sets the miracle apart, and unites the players with the imaginary audience of naïve people who have witnessed it.[23]

At its New York presentation in the spring of 1941, John Martin took note of the fine performances. Erick Hawkins, he said, had lost the "self-consciousness that attached to his use of Miss Graham's extreme simplifications of style in the first presentation of the work."[24] While he now saw *El Penitente* as a "less important" work than *Letter to the World*, he nonetheless admired Graham's evocation of something "truer than authenticity." Wrote Martin:

> From the merging of peasant magic with the transcendental mysteries of the church there issues a curious quality of medievalism, as if the Middle Ages were not a period in history but a state of mind.[25]

Edwin Denby described *El Penitente* and *Letter to the World* as two works "full of poetry." *El Penitente* had the effect on him of "a tender and subtle love poem, a real love held sweetly nearly in suspense by a remote terror. It was as though Miss Graham had used the Spanish-Indian farmers' expression of religious faith as a metaphor for her own faith in the strangeness love can have."[26]

11 August 1940

Letter to the World

College Theatre

Chor Martha Graham. *Art collab* Arch Lauterer. *Mus* Hunter Johnson (original piano score). *Pianist* Louis Horst. *Sets & light* Lauterer. *Asst* Elizabeth Reitell. *Cos* Edythe Gilfond. *Shoes* Herbert. *Assistance* Charles Meredith. *Characters in the Real World*: *The One in White* Margaret Meredith. *Two Children* Nina Fonaroff, Marjorie Mazia. *Characters in the World of Imagination*: *The One in Red* Martha Graham. *The Lover* Erick Hawkins. *The Ancestress* Jane Dudley. *March* Merce Cunningham. *The Happy Child* Nelle Fisher. *Boy with the Birds* George Hall. Sophie Maslow, Ethel Butler, Jean Erdman, Frieda Flier, Elizabeth Halpern, David Campbell, David Zellmer. *Action*: 1. "Because I see New Englandly": a. "Life is a Spell," b. Party Scene. 2. "The Postponeless Creature": a. Ancestress, b. "Gay Ghastly Holiday." 3. "The Little Tippler": a. Tippler, b. "Dear March, come in," c. The Happy Child, d. The Picnic. 4. "Leaf at love turned back": a. "Blue sea, wilt welcome me?" b. "I have elected one," c. "Wild Nights," d. "There came a day at summer's full." 5. "This Was a Poet."

Program Note:

> *Letter to the World*, using as its title a line from a poem of Emily Dickinson's, is built on the tradition, and not the facts, of her life. Her poems do not deal with incidents of time but with the timeless things of nature and of the heart. The spoken lines are from these poems.
>
> All of us live partly in the view of the real world and partly in a secret world of our imagination—a place created and peopled by our hopes and fears. *The One in White* and *The Children* are the actual figures of the period. *The One in Red* is the impulsive hidden self of *The One in White* who, to the outer world is calm and cool, but who in her imagination wears a crimson excitement. *The*

Letter to the World. Photograph courtesy of *Dance Observer*.

Lover is the symbol of her gesture toward happiness. *The Ancestress* is the embodiment of her background, puritan, awesome but beautiful. The Ancestress is also the symbol of the death-fear constantly in her mind. *March, The Boy with the Birds, The Happy Child* are images of her childhood. The girls in the "Little Tippler" scene are extensions of herself in the age of play and fantasy. In "Wild Nights" they are her girlhood on the verge of the love experience. At the end of the piece she fulfills her destiny and becomes before the world, the poet.

Angelica Gibbs' 1947 *New Yorker* profile of Martha Graham gives this account:

Miss Graham began planning *Letter to the World* several months before she went up to Bennington for the 1940 summer school. After reading all the Dickinson poems, George Whicher's biography called *This Was a Poet*, and several other works on the subject, she decided on a piece in which she would dance Miss Dickinson's tumultuous inner life and someone else would enact the prim, everyday Emily and recite snatches of her verse. . . . When she had selected the bits of poetry she wanted to use, she forwarded them, along with a few notes about what she had in mind, to her composer at the time, Hunter Johnson, who was then in the South. With no more than this skimpy material to go on, Johnson sat down and produced a tentative score, which somehow or other turned out to be just what was wanted, and later, at Bennington, Miss Graham delightedly worked out the dances to go with it. "Neither of us knew exactly where, in the total scheme, the bits of poetry would fit," Johnson later wrote to a friend. "Up to this time, Martha had always done the choreography first, and the poor composer had fitted in the music as best he could. I couldn't do it that way, or at least I didn't want to attempt to. After we arrived at Bennington and really started working, everything seemed to fall into place, and the piece was finished within six weeks."[27]

Erick Hawkins recommended Hunter Johnson to Graham; Johnson had written a score for Hawkins (*Yankee Bluebritches*), which had had its premiere at Bennington the month before *Letter.*[28] Louis Horst played the piano score at the premiere; it was later arranged for two pianos. In the early 1950s Johnson arranged a suite from *Letter* for small orchestra.[29]

Many years later Graham revealed the source for one of the most powerful characters in *Letter*, the Ancestress:

> *Letter to the World* came out of the poems of Emily Dickinson, but also of my family's New England background. The figure of the Ancestress is the figure of my grandmother who, for me as a child, was very beautiful and very unapproachable and very frightening. She was so beautiful because her face was utterly still. She always wore black. She became two things–the mother, the cradler of me, and the figure which is Death.[30]

Graham spoke also of the work's initial failure at Bennington:

> Sometimes a dance takes two years, two years of brooding, of thinking. You put it away, you forget about it. It comes back. It was that way with *Letter to the World*. It was a failure the first time, and John Martin wrote quite acidulously that it had better be left to sleep in the Vermont Hills.[31]

The Bennington production, wrote Margaret Lloyd, "was stamped by certain critics as a letter not worth mailing."[32]

Graham reworked the piece that fall, and it had its New York premiere in January 1941. John Martin wrote that it was a pleasure to eat his words, but he thought it could benefit from still further revision. Graham dutifully obliged, reported Angelica Gibbs, with a third and final version in April of that year.[33] In June, Martin gave *Letter* his award for the finest dance composition of the year.

Walter Terry recalled "substantial changes in the matter of choreographic core" following its Bennington premiere.[34] "Both John [Martin] and I hated it at Bennington," he said. Graham told Terry some months afterward that she realized just before going on stage at Bennington that "it was all wrong, that she had done it backwards." Said Terry:

> She had choreographed everyone else's dance and then threaded her part through it, but she then realized that Emily Dickinson was the center, that everything that happens is in her mind, in her dreams. She said to me, "Everything I've done before this has come out of my body and been extended into that of my dancers." But that was not how she had worked on *Letter*. So what she did was to start over with her own part and see that everything, all of what the group did, emanated from her last movement statement. She didn't need to change a lot of the steps *per se.*[35]

It made "all the difference in the world," said Terry. The Bennington production had been "like doing variations on a theme–without a theme." Terry saw *Letter* as the point when Graham "began reverting to the Denishawn trend, not in technique but in concept–towards dance as theater and away from Isadora as dance as concert."[36] Accordingly, said Terry, *Letter* was one of the key compositions that made people think of Graham not as a recitalist but as a theater artist.

Jean Erdman replaced Margaret Meredith in the wholly new part of the alter ego (One Who Speaks) for the New York premiere. Graham revised the role of the speaking Emily so that it would be more fully integrated with the choreography. Erdman recalled:

> In the original Bennington production, the actress was in period costume with blonde curls and a Southern accent. I learned something important about staging from that experience. She sat without moving and she began to speak. The word catches. Here Martha was dancing herself to a frenzy but all you'd notice was

> this lovely woman in white with curls just sitting there. I realized then the power of words and stillness; it was a different dynamic and it made the other look forced. Martha realized she didn't want to do it that way so she made the whole thing over.[37]

Sets and Costumes:

Graham asked Lauterer to redesign the set for the New York premiere and to make it lighter and more portable so that it could be toured. Said Erdman:

> The original Bennington set was fabulous. The stage had a wall on pivots and it would open and turn around, on a rotary. The wall would open and Erick would appear. All the fantasy figures like the Ancestress came through the wall. And then the sides, the wings were made on the same kind of louver thing so that when the situation emotionally was closed in, they would close in, and when it was open, they would open out. It wasn't so much a little set piece as it was a changing environment. It emphasized the emotional dynamic of the inner life; in a way it reflected the inner dynamic of the piece.[38]

Lauterer's drawings of the Bennington set were later published in *Impulse.*[39] Some of his ideas about the production are contained in a two-part interview with Margaret Lloyd in the *Christian Science Monitor* (reprinted in this book, pp. 108–109).[40]

The realism of the costumes surprised Ann Hutchinson:

> The costumes contained yards of cloth to maneuver—but in Martha's case, cloth with which, through twist, turn and arc of leg, to make dramatic effect. There was something of the Spaniard, the Flamenco in Martha in her taut, steely movement and use of length of skirt and props. She was indeed a great admirer of Carmen Amaya. The group wore soft ballet slippers thereby revealing a weakness not apparent in bare feet—the limited ability to point the foot, particularly in jumps. In certain instances Graham intentionally choreographed jumps with relaxed feet for expressive and stylistic effect for a primitive figure, but the elegance of the costumes in *Letter* demanded an elegance of footwork too.[41]

According to Mark Ryder, who joined the Graham company in the autumn of 1940, the original dance was 75 minutes long; Graham then cut it to 55 minutes. She deleted the part of the "Boy with the Birds," which George Hall had performed at Bennington. "She couldn't find anyone to do what he could do. He was an actor of some stature," Ryder explained.[42]

In an article on the interaction of poetry and dance, Jean Erdman cited *Letter*, "since it employs, and actually absorbs into the image, a text of rhythmically spoken words:

> The work both does and does not render a story. Every dancer has a specific identity. No use is made of an anonymous chorus; rather, each character is symbolic and meaningful in itself, like a figure appearing to the mind in a visionary moment of self-recollection. The story of a life, through the story of a soul's recollection of its own destiny, reveals the story of the Artist's fate; and this the audience experiences as not different from the story of any soul's life-realization, only greater in intensity than most.[43]

New York Premiere: 20 January 1941, Mansfield Theatre.

Subsequent Productions: 7 April 1941, Guild Theatre (second revision). 14 April 1953, Alvin Theatre, New York, Martha Graham with Pearl Lang in Jean Erdman's role, Jane Dudley, John Butler, and Robert Cohan. 3 October 1970, Brooklyn Academy of Music, with Pearl Lang, Jean Erdman, and Jane Dudley.

Reviews

The Bennington production was roundly criticized, but John Martin, Walter Terry, and other critics revised their opinions of the work in its altered form at the time of its New York premiere.

John Martin, in his first *New York Times* review:

> *Letter to the World*, though quite evidently a work of love, fails for the very reasons that *El Penitente* succeeds. Instead of making an obscure subject simple, it makes a simple one obscure by elaboration and indirection. . . . It takes for granted a considerable knowledge of both the poet and her works, and against this background attempts in a way to vivify the conflict between the inner and the outer woman. Actually, the outer woman is far clearer than the inner, for she has the incomparable advantage of being able to speak the felicitous phrases of Emily Dickinson herself. Bits of poems . . . read charmingly by Margaret Meredith . . . make the long passages of movement that are designed to illuminate them seem heavy and completely unnecessary. Miss Graham has given herself comparatively little to do and has allowed her conception to overshadow her. . . . The score . . . is persistent and dissonant and utterly un-Dickinsonian.[44]

In his Sunday column:

> The dancing seems perilously near to being superfluous. In her composition, Miss Graham has virtually eschewed choreography and dancing and provided what amounts to mise en scène in its place. It does not build dramatically through its length of nearly an hour, nor does it have any inherent compositional unity of form. It is rather a series of small episodes from the poet's life which taken in sum conspire to make her the poet. The line of continuity is therefore literary rather than choreographic, and not until the final moment (quite the most effective bit in the whole work) does Miss Graham, alone on the stage, bring the threads together. This she does by her inner power. . . . She has almost buried herself under the idea of the production, and since she is a far greater personal artist than she is a composer, this is a mistake. The score belongs in the category of what has rightly been called "eye music." . . . Its thin, persistent cacaphonies beat on the ear distressingly. Not even the gifted Arch Lauterer has been of much aid this time, for his setting is barren and choppy. If Miss Graham is well advised, she will leave *Letter to the World* to slumber in the Vermont foothills.[45]

Time magazine:

> Choreographer Graham divided her ballet in half, gave the Dr. Jekyll half to a pleasant domestic-looking chorine who recited excerpts from Emily Dickinson's hard-bitten verse. The frustrated poetic, aspiring, cockeyed half she reserved for herself, danced it with a bevy of bouncing males that would have driven prim Poetess Dickinson to a sanatorium. When she was through, her intellectual audience broke into sobs and cheers.[46]

Walter Terry, in his first *New York Herald Tribune* review:

> [*Letter to the World*] has a long way to travel before it becomes an important theater piece.[47]

In his Sunday column:

> Miss Graham's projection of [the] hidden self had less color and fire than the outer aspects of the lady in question. . . . None of [the] fantastic elements seemed to have any contact with the living, speaking character of Emily Dickinson. I am convinced of the validity of this form which fuses word and tone and movement into a theater form, and I am also convinced that thorough revision can make a success of [it]. I feel that constant contact must be maintained between the outer form of the character and the imagining self, that Graham must exaggerate through movement and mime the hidden emotions of the char-

acter so that we are always aware of the contrast between surface control and subsurface abandonment to the senses, [and] that all of Miss Graham's amazingly high leg extensions (beautiful as they are) be eliminated unless they have an actual bearing upon the characterization.[48]

Margaret Lloyd, *Christian Science Monitor*:

There is psychological import in Arch Lauterer's unfolding doors, the basis of his scenic theme for [*Letter to the World*] which makes the stage design a decidedly active factor in the production. . . . Mr. Lauterer's manifold-ing doors open into the vistas of Emily's thought. Now the large central double-doors are the walls of a white house, now black with premonitions of "The Postponeless Creature," represented by the tall and magnificent Jane Dudley, who as the Ancestress of Puritan tradition manages also to suggest Emily's preoccupation with the dark vision of death. [*Letter*] is a difficult piece at best. . . . It is a dance of intimation, like Emily's poems, elusive, evanescent, and in its present state, and on one viewing, not yet completely satisfying.[49]

Elizabeth McCausland, *Dance Observer*:

How shall the dance, medium of bodily motion in space, pair itself with the abstract and fleshless medium of the word? . . . The solution Graham arrived at was to organize the action of the dance into sections comparable to the act-scene divisions of the theater. Stage action was accelerated by the sets and lighting of Arch Lauterer, whose revolving flats were in themselves a form of dance. [*Letter*] represents a turning point in Graham's evolution, at least from the purely formal point of view. More and more, one feels, her arena will be the theater.[50]

Sherman Conrad, *Nation*:

The work lacks almost all dramatic structure; it is thematic, rather. Its achievement is that the words—so rightly spoken by Margaret Meredith—and the consequent movement flow in one line; they both seem to come from an antecedent buoyancy on which the inner and the outer lives alike ride.[51]

John Kirkpatrick, *Modern Music*:

In a way, one might question her choice, for this score, of Hunter Johnson, a Southern gentleman whose music is full of the rich sadness and potential emotional explosiveness of the South, and who could hardly be counted on to "think New Englandly." . . . On the whole the music was a joy—a bright polka for the garden party, a saucy scherzo, a lovely fluid waltz, eloquent commentaries on Lowell Mason's *Fountain* hymn.[52]

Subsequent Reviews:

Irving Kolodin, *New York Sun*, on the New York premiere:

Miss Graham has evolved what might be reasonably described as the first authentically American ballet. . . . If *Our Town* was a landmark for the American stage, *Letter to the World* is equally one for its dance.[53]

Edwin Denby, *Modern Music*, on the New York premiere:

The continuity of a lyric line, the contrast of dynamics (the sense that a gesture is not always a thrust but often a caress), both of these are a new development in Miss Graham's way of composing; as is also the use of different kinds of projection (the sense that she dances at times more publicly for the audience, at times more privately for herself). From many points of view *Letter to the World*, no matter how uneven it appears at first sight, is a moving and noble work one cannot praise too highly.[54]

John Martin, *New York Times*, on the New York premiere:

> Much of the work as originally exhibited has actually been abandoned and even more of it will necessarily be before it can be considered a finished job. Nevertheless Miss Graham's faith in her basic purpose and in her method of approach to it has been completely vindicated in the second version. . . . *Letter to the World* marks no new phase but rather the deepening and broadening of foundations already laid. Without loss of vigor or experimental curiosity, it exhibits a maturity, a sweetness, a lucidity that have not hitherto been present to any such extent.[55]

Martin attempted to classify the form, but concluded that it was "purely and characteristically Martha Graham's—fragmentary, intuitive, pragmatic." He recommended that further cuts be made, especially in the group passages:

> Miss Graham has outdistanced her own technique as she has advanced into deeper territory, and there it stands, when the group performs it, declaring baldly that it has become not only familiar but frequently arbitrary and ineffectual. In her superb personal performance everything—technical vocabulary, movement, compositional patterns—is transfigured, but no such transformation can be expected from an ensemble.[56]

Six months later, Martin gave *Letter* his annual award for the finest dance composition:

> It is not only the greatest achievement thus far in the career of one of the most distinguished artists of our time, but it opens up new territory for the dance that must inevitably affect the field at large. For a number of years there have been attempts to combine the spoken word with movement, and some of them have been distinctly interesting, but none has succeeded so perfectly in making the two elements mutually contributory.[57]

NOTES

1. *Bennington Banner*, 15 July 1940.
2. Ibid.
3. Robert Sabin, *Dance Observer* 8, no. 5 (May 1941): 66.
4. No music credits are given on the program itself. This information was taken from Eleanor Shannon, "The 1940 Bennington Season," *Dance Observer* 7, no. 7 (August-September 1940): 96.
5. See John Martin, *New York Times*, 18 August 1940.
6. Esther E. Pease, "Epilogue—A Conversation with Louis Horst," *Impulse*, 1965, p. 4.
7. "Louis Horst Considers the Question," *Impulse*, 1954, p. 6. See also "Composer/Choreographer," *Dance Perspectives* 16 (1963): 6.
8. *El Penitente*, piano score, Orchesis Publications, 1960 [Music Division, Library of Congress, and Dance Notation Bureau, which also has a tape].
9. Interview with Merce Cunningham.
10. Don McDonagh, *Martha Graham* (New York: Praeger, 1973), p. 148.
11. Margaret Lloyd, *The Borzoi Book of Modern Dance* (New York: Alfred A. Knopf, 1949), p. 66; interview with Merce Cunningham.
12. Lloyd, *Borzoi*, p. 65. Lloyd's reference to Morgan is Barbara Morgan, *Martha Graham: Sixteen Dances in Photographs* (New York: Duell, Sloan & Pearce, 1941; rev. ed. Dobbs Ferry, N.Y.: Morgan and Morgan, 1980).
13. Margaret Lloyd, "Building a World for Dance," *Christian Science Monitor*, 17 July 1943. (Reprinted in this book, pp. 108-110.)
14. Interview with Erick Hawkins.
15. *El Penitente*, piano score. Notes by Daniel Jahn. Orchesis Publications, 1960.
16. John Martin, *New York Times*, 12 August 1940.
17. John Martin, *New York Times*, 18 August 1940.

18. Walter Terry, *New York Herald Tribune*, 18 August 1940.
19. Margaret Lloyd, *Christian Science Monitor*, 17 August 1940.
20. Elizabeth McCausland, "*El Penitente* as Mystery Play," *Dance Observer* 7, no. 7 (August-September 1940): 98.
21. Sherman Conrad, *Nation* 151, no. 8 (24 August 1940): 158.
22. Ernestine Stodelle, "Midstream: The Second Decade of Modern Dance, Martha Graham," *Dance Observer* 29, no. 5 (May 1962): 70.
23. Lloyd, *Borzoi*, pp. 64–65.
24. John Martin, "Belated Justice to Martha Graham's *El Penitente*," *New York Times*, 13 April 1941.
25. Ibid.
26. Edwin Denby, "With the Dancers," *Modern Music* 18, no. 3 (March-April 1941): 195–97. Reprinted in Edwin Denby, *Looking at the Dance* (New York: Popular Library, n.d.), pp. 273–74.
27. Angelica Gibbs, "The Absolute Frontier," *New Yorker* 23, no. 45 (27 December 1947): 35.
28. Interview with Erick Hawkins.
29. Hunter Johnson, *Letter to the World*, Suite for Orchestra, Galaxy Music Corporation [Music Division, Library of Congress].
30. "Martha Graham Speaks," *Dance Observer* 30, no. 4 (April 1963): 53–55.
31. Ibid.
32. Lloyd, *Borzoi*, p. 64.
33. Gibbs, *New Yorker*, p. 36.
34. Interview with Walter Terry.
35. Ibid.
36. Ibid.
37. Interview with Jean Erdman.
38. Ibid.
39. "Arch Lauterer–Poet in the Theatre," *Impulse*, 1959, p. 50.
40. Lloyd, "Building a World for Dance."
41. Ann Hutchinson Guest, "Bennington Memories–1940" (unpublished recollections contributed for this book).
42. Interview with Mark Ryder.
43. Jean Erdman, "The Dance as Non-Verbal Poetic Image," in *The Dance Has Many Faces*, ed. Walter Sorell (New York: World Publishing Company, 1951), pp. 210–12. For other descriptions of *Letter to the World*, see Lloyd, *Borzoi*, pp. 66–68, and *Don McDonagh's Complete Guide to Modern Dance* (New York: Popular Library, 1977), pp. 79–81, and Marcia B. Siegel, *The Shapes of Change* (Boston: Houghton Mifflin, 1979), pp. 177–83.
44. John Martin, *New York Times*, 12 August 1940.
45. John Martin, *New York Times*, 18 August 1940.
46. "Intellectual Dance," *Time* 36, no. 9 (26 August 1940): 32.
47. Walter Terry, *New York Herald Tribune*, 13 August 1940.
48. Walter Terry, *New York Herald Tribune*, 18 August 1940.
49. Margaret Lloyd, *Christian Science Monitor*, 17 August 1940.
50. Elizabeth McCausland, "Martha Graham and *Letter to the World*," *Dance Observer* 7, no. 7 (August-September 1940): 97.
51. Sherman Conrad, *Nation* 151, no. 8 (24 August 1940): 158–59.
52. John Kirkpatrick, *Modern Music* 18, no. 1 (November-December 1940): 54.
53. Irving Kolodin, *New York Sun*, 21 January 1941.
54. Edwin Denby, "With the Dancers," *Modern Music* 18, no. 3 (March-April 1941): 196–97. Reprinted in Denby, *Looking at the Dance*, p. 275.
55. John Martin, *New York Times*, 26 January 1941.
56. Ibid.
57. John Martin, *New York Times*, 1 June 1941.

1941

19 July 1941

In Time of Armament

College Theatre

Chor Erick Hawkins. *Mus* Hunter Johnson (original piano score). *Pianists* Ralph Gilbert, Harry Cumpson. *Danc* Hawkins and Jean Erdman.

In Time of Armament, the only new work on Erick Hawkins' program with Jane Dudley, was taken from "The Five-Fold Mesh" by Ben Belitt (1938). Because the score was for two pianos, Hawkins recalled, it was difficult to tour.[1] This was Erdman's first major public appearance outside the Graham company. She recalled that Pearl Lang [Pearl Lack then] made her costume. "It was a very romantic duet," said Erdman, quite unlike anything she had done with Martha Graham.[2] No detailed reviews of this performance were located or evidence of a New York premiere.

9 August 1941

Decade: A Biography of Modern Dance from 1930 to 1940

College Theatre

Chor Doris Humphrey (with scenes by Charles Weidman). *Mus dir and pianist* Lionel Nowak. *Mus score and orchestrations arr* Lionel Nowak. All music by Aaron Copland was from *Music for the Theatre. Musicians* Maxwell Powers, asst pianist. Norman Lloyd, percussion. Otto Luening, flute. Edward James, trumpet. Bernard Kadinoff, violin. *Script* Alex Kahn. *Sets & light* Arch Lauterer. *Cos* Pauline Lawrence. *Danc* Humphrey, Weidman and Company: Beatrice Seckler, Katherine Litz, Maria Maginnis, Nona Schurman, Gloria Garcia, Molly Davenport, Claudia Moore, Charles Hamilton, Allen Waine. Apprentices: Ruth Parmet, Ida Reese, Patricia Balz, Jeanne Thompson, Joseph Gornbein [Gifford], Evans Davis. *Mr. Business* Evans Davis. *Voice of Mr. Business* Edward Glass. ***Part I: Vision of a New Life*** *mus* Copland (Prologue), *danc* Humphrey, Weidman, and Company. ***The Path to Realization: Scene 1. Dialogue*** *mus* Nowak, *danc* Mr. Business, Humphrey, Weidman. ***Scene 2. Moving In*** *mus* Nowak, *danc* Humphrey, Weidman, and Company. ***Scene 3. Gigue*** from ***The First Partita*** *mus* [J. S.] Bach, *danc* Humphrey. ***Scene 4. New Ideas*** *mus* Nowak, Lloyd, *danc* Humphrey, Weidman, and Company. ***Scene 5. Submerged Cathedral*** *chor* Weidman, *mus* [Claude] Debussy, *danc* Weidman. ***Scene 6. Dialogue*** *danc* Mr. Business, Humphrey, Weidman, Seckler, Maginnis. ***Scene 7. Air for the G String*** *mus* Bach, *danc* Litz, Garcia, Schurman, Parmet, Balz. ***Scene 8. Etude, Opus 8, no. 12*** *chor* Weidman, *mus* [Alexander] Scriabin, *danc* Humphrey, Weidman. ***Scene 9. Dialogue*** *danc* Mr. Business, Humphrey, Weidman. ***Scene 10. Air Gai (In Rehearsal)*** *chor* Weidman *mus* [C. W.] Gluck (from *Iphigenia*), *danc* Humphrey, Weidman, Seckler, Hamilton, and Company. ***Scene 11. Air Gai (In the Opera House)*** *mus* Gluck (from *Iphigenia*), *danc* Humphrey, Weidman, Seckler, Litz, Maginnis, Schurman, Davenport, Parmet, Hamilton. ***Scene 12. Dialogue*** *danc* Mr. Business, Humphrey, Weidman. ***Scene 13. Return to the Studio*** *mus* Copland, *danc* Humphrey, Weidman. ***Part II. The Path to Realization (continued), Curtain Music*** Copland. ***Scene 1. Before the Concert (In the Studio)*** *mus* percussion, *danc* Company. ***Scene 2. Dress Rehearsal (In the Studio): a. Circular Descent*** *mus* [Nikolai] Medtner, *danc* Humphrey, ***b. Kinetic Pantomime*** *chor* Weidman, *mus* Colin McPhee, *danc* Weidman, ***c. Water Study*** *danc* Company, ***d. Ringside*** *chor* Weidman, *mus* Winthrop Sargent, *danc* Weidman, Hamilton, Waine. ***Scene 3. Departure for the Theatre (Four hours pass)*** *mus* Nowak (*Fugue after a theme of Copland*).

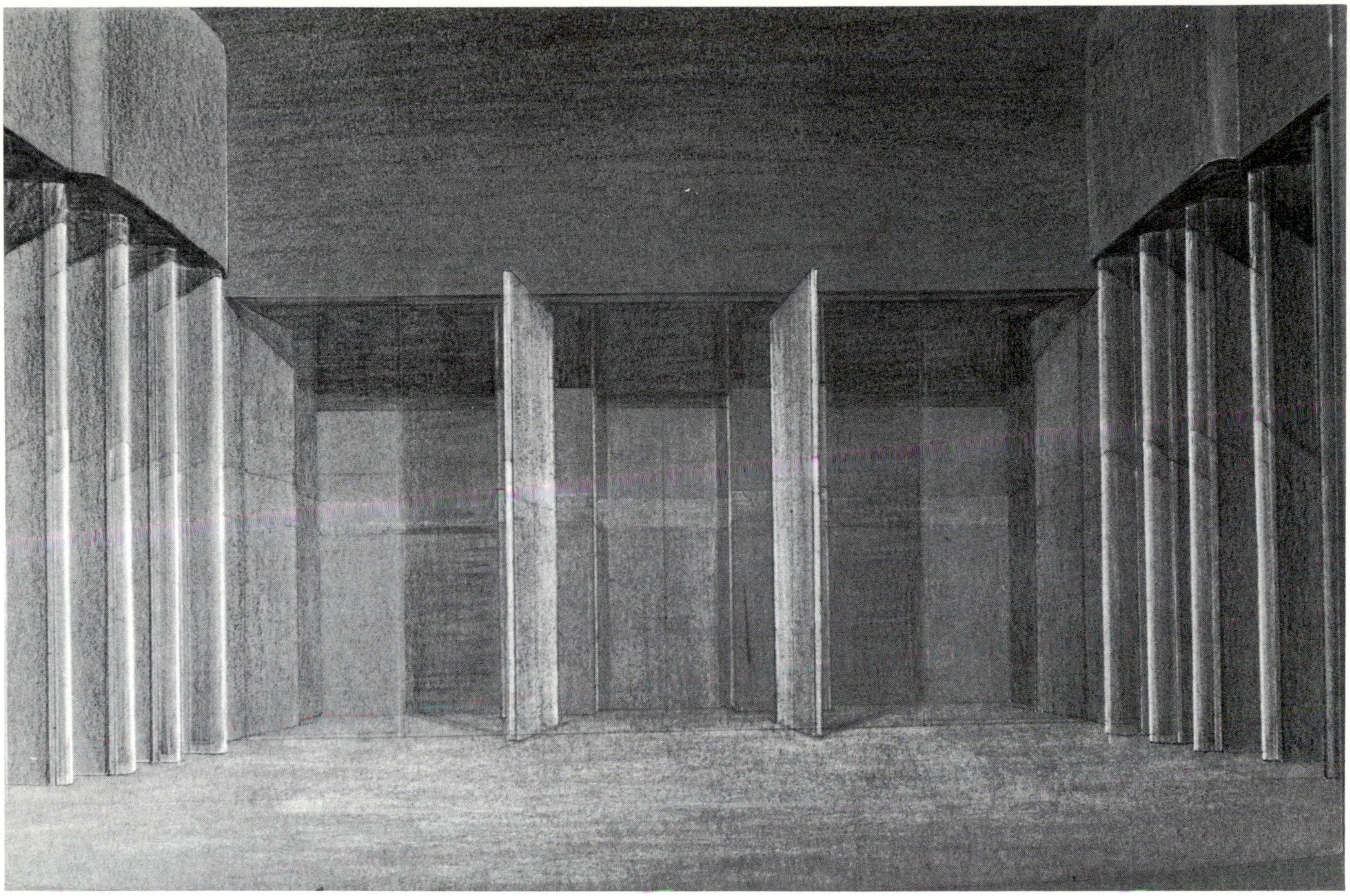

Decade: "Part I: Vision of a New Life." Designed by Arch Lauterer, Bennington College Theatre. Photograph courtesy of Henry Kurth, The Arch Lauterer Archives.

Scene 4. Return to the Studio and Dialogue *danc* Humphrey, Weidman, Mr. Business. ***Scene 5. Montage Scene in the Theatre: a. Shakers*** *mus* voice, accordion, drum, *danc* Seckler, Litz, Schurman, Hamilton, Waine, ***b. With My Red Fires (Pursuit)*** *mus* Wallingford Riegger, *danc* Humphrey as The Matriarch, and Company, ***c. Opus 51 (Interlude)*** *chor* Weidman, *mus* Vivian Fine, *danc* Weidman, Seckler, Litz, ***d. Theatre Piece (The Race)*** *mus* Riegger, *danc* Humphrey, Hamilton, and Company, ***e. The Happy Hypocrite (In the Forest)*** *chor* Weidman, *mus* Herbert Elwell, *danc* Weidman, a man with the mask of a saint, and Litz, a country girl, ***f. New Dance (Celebration)*** *mus* Riegger, *danc* Humphrey, Weidman, and Company. ***Scene 6. Departure toward a New Vision*** *mus* Copland, *danc* Humphrey, Weidman, Mr. Business, and Company.

Doris Humphrey had unsuccessfully tried to induce the School of the Arts to invite William Saroyan to collaborate with her. She experienced weeks of "torture" trying to decide on a theme. "The world situation continually urges me to make some sort of comment—yet the whole thing is so vast that any statement seems silly," she wrote.[3] At last she settled on "a Biography of the years 1930-40 at 18th Street [the old Humphrey-Weidman studio]. The general theme being the struggle of pioneer art in a world geared to profit. We ought to be able to do that with feeling!"[4] *Decade* was a full evening work approximately two hours long.

The artists' struggle against odds personified by the character "Mr. Business" was chronicled through 16 extracts from the Humphrey-Weidman repertoire. (According to Nona Schurman, *Decade* contained the first revival of *Air for the G String*. In preparation, the cast viewed the 1934 Westinghouse film in the old movie house in Bennington.[5] A draft of the script by Alex Kahn calls for a "Mr. Manager" instead of "Mr. Business," who appears in various guises.[6] Mr. Business was mimed by apprentice Evans Davis, as Edward Glass read the text into an off-stage microphone. Margaret Lloyd described the work's concluding narrative:

Decade, Bennington College Theatre. Designed by Arch Lauterer. "This scene presents the backstage view of their early recitals." Photograph courtesy of Henry Kurth, The Arch Lauterer Archives.

> After disappointments in the commercial theater come the first transcontinental tour, invitation to become part of the Bennington Festivals, and finally the founding of the new studio theater they established last fall. The group, now a dance company, performs "Celebration" from *New Dance*, an apotheosis of their departure toward the new vision—a repertory theater of dance.[7]

Lloyd also described Lauterer's setting for *Decade*:

> Indicative props are used sparingly in a stage bare except for the permanent wings of vitaglass, a mixture of cellophane and wire screening that has the metallic gleam of modernity. . . . Upstage the central doors unfold—to disclose the impressive first entry of the artists—to suggest dressing rooms at the opera—to mount a scene. The curtain is made of dimming lights.[8]

Lionel Nowak, musical director of the Humphrey-Weidman Company, arranged all of the music for a small ensemble. Sound effects and recordings were also employed. Said Nowak:

> *Decade* was changed a good deal after Bennington. Doris had trouble with it all the way along. The thing just never jelled, never quite came off, never quite reached a particular climax. It lacked the dramatic form which her other dances had. She just tried to do something in *Decade* that maybe cannot be done. But it was kind of a wonderful failure![9]

New York Premiere: 26 December 1941, Studio Theater.

The number of extracts from the repertoire was cut back. The first part concluded on an "up" note and the ending was strengthened. The text was made more dramatic and the whole work was tightened up. *Decade* was a highlight of the next season at the Studio Theater but, as far as can be determined, was not revived in full after 1942.

Reviews

Decade was poorly received at Bennington, except by Walter Terry. Its retrospective theme, episodic form, and pirating of pieces of the repertory were roundly criticized. Martin suggested that instead of bringing *Decade* to New York, Humphrey might do better to restore several works in full to the repertory. Terry thought that a general tightening and revision could work wonders. Humphrey's biographer cited *Decade* as "a unique instance of failure of control," a work that "remained subjective and became sentimental."[10] Though Margaret Lloyd was very hard on it initially, eight years later she looked back with regret to its loss from the repertory:

> It was disappointing to some of us at the time because it went over old ground instead of breaking into new, and because some of the works quoted could not adequately be handled. But now that it is no more than an intaglio in memory it has become as cherishable as an heirloom.[11]

At the time of its New York premiere, John Martin noted values in it beyond the autobiography of two dancers. He saw its conclusion as having "both philosophical and practical importance for the native American dance art." *Decade*, he wrote, "states basically the whole problem of the art regardless of individual careers":

> Reduced to a word, this point is simply that art is not a commodity; as the late Franklin Giddings said of it, it is a "phase of the social mind." "We are so much in the habit of thinking of (the arts) in terms of art products," he wrote, "that we forget that the arts themselves are groups of ideas and acquisitions of skill that exist only in the minds, muscles and nerves of living men."[12]

Margaret Lloyd, writing in the *Christian Science Monitor*, had deemed it at its premiere

> a whole that is less great than any one of its more important parts. [It is] not quite big enough for the times, or for the artist alive in and to the times. . . . This story of Doris and Charles in Dance Land, or From Loft to Studio Theater, is all very amusing, very stirring, very endearing to . . . the audiences who fill the little College Theater and the Studio Theater in New York. But these artists of America cannot so shut themselves in. The new studio is not a dead-end but another beginning, a center, not a periphery. This is no time for settling down in comparative security doing studio pieces. This is no time for pioneers to be looking back.[13]

John Martin, *New York Times*, in his first review:

> Miss Humphrey, always alert to new concepts of form, has this time found novelty, paradoxically enough, by turning back to old things. . . . It is an extremely interesting idea. . . . Yet in practice it does not quite come off. . . . It is doubtful if a dozen people in the entire festival audience have seen all the individual dances here quoted and are consequently able to reconstruct in their minds the particular period out of which each of them was born. Without . . . a constantly shifting general background certain dances in the earlier years of the decade seem merely "corny." . . . Reminiscence is justified when it is productive of a warmer sympathy with what has gone before, a better understanding of what is going on at the moment, or even simple nostalgia; but *Decade* somehow manages to miss all these goals. It is too synoptic, too scant in dramatic line, too goal-less.[14]

At its New York premiere, Martin wrote:

> Since its Bennington premiere, Miss Humphrey has done wonders with the composition, pulling it together generally and in particular giving its second half dramatic unity and punch. Where it was originally inclined to whine a bit about its hard luck and to end on a downward note, now it meets its obstacles man-

fully and with humor and in its final phrases rejoices in its emancipation from the ominous "Mr. Business," who has been plaguing it throughout. . . . Miss Humphrey has turned what was pretty close to a failure last summer into a success.[15]

Walter Terry, *New York Herald Tribune*, at its premiere:

> [*Decade* was] conceived as a dramatic document, projected through the spoken word, mimed movement, pure dance and excerpts from the Humphrey-Weidman repertoire. . . . The second act is not as well knit as the first, and the final dance . . . does not yet have sufficient force and clarity, but otherwise *Decade* is an exciting biography torn from the printed page and given body and motion in dance.[16]

Terry, in his Sunday column:

> [*Decade*] finds Miss Humphrey in a reflective mood looking back over ten years of achievement, failure, hope and determination. . . . [It also] deals with a desperate situation: the plight of the American dancers who have fought their battles without financial help from any one and who face the future with no backing to aid them in the carrying out of their plans. [Humphrey] turns in the most brilliant performance I have ever seen her give . . . radiant, beautiful and strong in her characterization. . . . The episode from *With My Red Fires* had little meaning removed from its context, for the glaring, evil matriarch in full pursuit gave the uninitiated no clew as to the reasons for glaring or pursuing. [These passages out of context] weaken *Decade* [but] they in no way shroud the intrinsic greatness of the work which should be fully revealed when revisions have been made. . . . The final statement should be potent: a determined renewal of faith; a cynical and embittered outline for the future; or complete bewilderment and resignation as if to say, "Where do we go from here?" . . . *Decade* is a great personal document and a great document of American dance.[17]

Sherman Conrad, *Nation*:

> The dancers have indulged in a great deal of bathetic self-dramatization. Every artist struggles with Mr. Business, but the struggle is precisely that, a business one. [The artist's] central combat is with his medium and his creative demon; and only there lie the real pity and drama of his situation.[18]

Robert Sabin, *Dance Observer*, at its premiere:

> [*Decade*] offers a graphic picture of the enormous strides which [Humphrey-Weidman] have made. It opens with the eclectic romanticism which grew out of Denishawn choreography and as it progresses one can see the growth of a stronger, more unified and expressive technique. How amazing, and how embarrassing it is to go back ten years and see what our dancers had to get through! The sentimental style of musical "interpretation," the faded theatricalism of the type of dancing which was almost universally prevalent only ten years ago seem very remote today, but they had to be faced and exorcised by every modern dancer. . . . We are today reaping the fruits of a long and often painful period of development in the contemporary dance. [The script] has more than one blemish of taste. . . . A straight series of dances without the framework of a sentimentalized life story would have been much more appealing. . . . The excerpt "Pursuit" from Miss Humphrey's *With My Red Fires* . . . was something compelling, something which stirred the blood and satisfied the mind. . . . But [*Decade*] merely marks time. It is neither a straight historical record nor a new contribution and the necessary pruning and cutting of some of Miss Humphrey's and Mr. Weid-

man's finest achievements leaves them in a state which can mean little to one who has not seen the dances in their original form.[19]

Lois Balcom, *Dance Observer*, on its popularity during the 1942 Studio Theater season:

> The slight revisions made between its Bennington and New York presentations have served to sharpen the dramatic theme as contrasted with the more purely reminiscent episodes in which dances from the earlier repertoire are revived in very nearly their original form. . . . Chief interest in re-seeing *Decade* a few months after its premiere lies in the realization that it is not solely nor even primarily an interesting experiment in repertory but is rather a genuinely dramatic evening of theatre dance in which, through a procession of dances which may or may not hold for portions of the audience the added interest of familiarity and revival, together with various devices which constitute their framework, a story is compactly and excitingly told.[20]

10 August 1941

Punch and The Judy

College Theatre

Chor Martha Graham. *Art Collab* Arch Lauterer. *Mus* Robert McBride (original piano score). *Pianist* Louis Horst. *Sets & light* Lauterer. *Cos* Charlotte Trowbridge. *Shoes* Herbert. *Danc* Graham and Company: Erick Hawkins, Merce Cunningham, Ethel Butler, Jane Dudley, Jean Erdman, Nina Fonaroff, David Campbell, Sasha Liebich [Mark Ryder], David Zellmer. Apprentices: Madge Friedman, Harriet Garrett, Pearl Lack [Lang], Barbara Livingston, Iris Mabry, Marion Scott, Frances Sunstein. *Characters: Punch* Hawkins. *The Judy* Graham. *Three Fates* Erdman, Dudley, Butler. *Pegasus* Cunningham. *Child* Fonaroff. *Pretty Polly* Lack [Lang]. *Three Heroes: The Soldier* Campbell, *The Scout* Zellmer, *The Pony Express Rider* Liebich [Mark Ryder]. *Action:* Overture. Prologue: The Fates set the stage. First Dilemma: The Judy soliloquizes–Punch shows off–The Child enters–Trouble starts. Interlude: Pegasus enters–The Flight to Dream. Second Dilemma: The family gathers–Pretty Polly enters–Punch seduces–The Judy rages–The Heroes exalt–The Judy despairs. Interlude: Pegasus enters–The Flight to Dream. Third Dilemma: The Justice is blindfolded–Punch triumphs–The Heroes march–The Fates intervene–Punch falls–The Judy intervenes–Punch brags again–The Judy chooses–The Fates direct, da capo.

Program Note:

> *Punch and The Judy* concerns man and woman. The text is squabble and scuffle. The Three Fates are any three women who direct the lives of others. The Three Heroes are the idealists. Pegasus is that force which enables us to imagine or to escape or to realize.

A preliminary scenario[21] describes the work as a tragi-comedy: "It is essentially a serious piece, although there are absurdities and comic happenings as there are in life."[22] The tragedy here comes from "the contrast between serious and the absurd." The core was Gorden Craig's "ironic" statement, "The quarrel, it seems, is the very basis of life. The great text for drama. . . . squabble and scuffle."

Punch and Judy is "the original pattern in theatre of the quarrel. . . . The conflict is between the dream and the actuality. . . . The piece is built around three dilemmas common to all of us: the problem of the home, the problem of the 'other woman,' the problem of the political bandwagon."

"When a dilemma becomes impossible, The Judy becomes her dream with Pegasus as her agent." The Fates "bring her back into the realm of everyday. The piece ends with The Judy a part and yet not part of anything. The real thing for her is the dream."[23]

Graham wished it to finish "lightly." "When we hit the bottom of things we often find a laugh there. It is that quality of the laugh that makes mankind immortal. . . . It is a laugh that comes as a result of knowing everything and still refusing to be taken by despair. That is why I wanted the piece to have a brilliance and absurdity." At the same time, Graham wanted at the end an emotional quality of the Judy's dream—"the element that there is a power in dream to make a world."[24]

Music: Robert McBride (composer of Erick Hawkins' *Show Piece*, 1937, for Ballet Caravan, and on the Bennington College music faculty) completed the 30-minute piano score before leaving for South America. Henry Cowell noted that the score showed "the effect of haste." Said Cowell: "Although it fits the remarkable dance technically, it is too slight in musical content to be interesting as a composition."[25] John Martin found McBride's score "fresh and spontaneous,"[26] Walter Terry appreciated its tunefulness,[27] Robert Sabin called it "bright and ingenious,"[28] but Robert Horan later described it as "bouncing and sometimes vulgar."[29]

"Dances from Martha Graham's Punch and The Judy Score" for orchestra, signed by McBride in March 1943, contains six parts: The Three Fates, Overture, Soliloquy of Judy, Pony Express, Pegasus, Punch.[30]

Decor: Working with Arch Lauterer was especially satisfying to Graham. "I am so happy about Bennington this summer," she wrote him in September, "I feel that you and I have learned to work together and we are in the beginning."[31] But it was in fact the beginning of the end of their collaborations. Just as *Letter* had to be redesigned to take on tour, so Graham had to ask Lauterer to remake his setting for *Punch* after its New York premiere before taking it to Philadelphia. A sketch of one of the sets is shown in *Impulse.*[32] Margaret Lloyd described it:

> A library chair and large globe at stage right, a narrow doorway behind them, a stretch of black and white linoleum, a couch, chimney piece, and window (or curtain of clouds) upstage—all the comforts of home in harlequinade—and all taking a strenuous part in the action.[33]

Lloyd's summary of the action shows how the setting was used by Graham. The work begins with the Three Fates

> clustered like maiden aunts or village gossips in elegant long gowns, around the library globe. Miss Erdman, book in hand, reads aloud from time to time what prove to be sardonic comments on the action from Gordon Craig's "Tom Fool." Punch reclines peacefully on the couch. The Judy daydreams at her fantastic window-piece. She casts a baleful glance at her sleeping spouse and with a flick of the wrist expresses her opinion of him. With the entrance of the child, a brat who has to be coaxed and scolded, rocked and spanked, the first round of the fighting starts. The Judy, bored with domesticity, seeks refuge in an interlude with Pegasus, a figment of romance whose means of ingress and egress is the dream window.[34]

Lauterer wrote about the evolution of his setting:

> Both ballet and modern dance-drama have their roots in the traditional theatre of the masque and the opera. The distinction in their scenic practice is that the ballet was born on the stage in the midst of decor, i.e., "decorative and ornamental painting" of the 19th Century, while modern dance was born in the dance studios and cautiously progressed to the stage of this century which is predominate in the use of light rather than paint. Today, we see the ballet utilizing the successful experiments—the young tradition—of modern dance. This is an example of the evolution of an art expression.
>
> The production of *Punch and the Judy* is a case in point. Here the stage images were so numerous in change through the use of light, both in the design-

ing of the stage space and scenic shapes and in the operation of the lighting during the dance-drama, that no single drawing can give anything but the faintest indication of the appearance of the stage. In such dance-drama, we see Adolphe Appia's dream partially realized; here all time media are joined in the creation of a single expression. The time of the speech, of the movements, and of the lighting are all essential parts of the scene in time.

The speech in this dance-drama was limited to The Fates. These were interpreted as Victorianally sentimental, and they moralized loudly and angrily on the battle between Punch and his wife, Judy. The words were akin to a fanfare announcing the immediate event; then they melodramatically forecast consequences. The speeches were delivered in a harsh and vicious tone fitting to the *action* of the dance-drama which is "to annihilate; to reduce opponent to nothing."

Since the battle of the sexes as personified in Punch and Judy has been waged since the Renaissance, the stage scene is designed so as to appear as a composite image of many periods. Hence, the home of the posing Victorian Fates with its photographer's screenlike background is framed by the profile of a Renaissance column in front and by a modern construction at the upstage end.

The dance movements of the drama's *action* require a broad band of space across the front of the stage area with two penetrations of deep space into the upstage area. One of the deep penetrations is permanent in space—the inclined hall which pierces the static, painted screen of the Fates. The other is made visible in time through change. The blank wall of the stage left side is semi-transparent so that when lights are increased in intensity behind this section, it becomes a shuttered French window. When the window is opened, it discloses a great mass of clouds painted in the late Renaissance style. These clouds when rolled apart reveal vistas of illusive space. The narrow expanse of floor at the base of the back wall and up through the hall is also changed in time. Judy, in one of her moments of rage at being continually deserted by Punch, whisks the black silk covering from these areas in a single movement. They then appear sharply patterned in black and white checks as in a parqueted floor of the Renaissance; the checks prove to be ironically fitting to the movement of Judy's giddy husband, Punch, on his return home.[35]

Graham created first roles for Pearl Lack [Lang] and Sasha Liebich [Mark Ryder]. Said Ryder:

Punch and The Judy re-explored some of the things Martha Graham did in *Every Soul*. . . *Punch* bought its laughs. But it was the first time Graham had five male characters; she had never peopled a stage with men before. She used Merce's balletic qualities to get a sense of flight as inspiration [as Pegasus]. Merce had a fantastic lightness with no plié. He managed to seem as though he were skimming the ground. It was never effortful.[36]

The work was a hit with audiences across the country. It toured with two other Bennington productions—*El Penitente* and *Letter to the World*. Robert Horan commented that this programming of *Punch* "allow[ed] an audience, built up to a considerable tension in the other works, to relax, laugh and free the attention."[37]

New York Premiere: 28 December 1941, Concert Theatre.

Subsequent Productions: 26 December 1943, 46th Street Theatre; 9 January 1944, 46th Street Theatre; May 1944, National Theatre; 21 January-2 February 1946, Plymouth Theatre, 17-29 February 1948, Maxine Elliott Theatre.

Reviews

The set by Arch Lauterer and costumes by Charlotte Trowbridge were generally praised, as were the performances by Jean Erdman (who read the text), Erick Hawkins, and Graham herself. Hawkins, it was said, gave the best performance of his career as Punch. He had "let himself go," dispensing with "the remote and highly stylized quality which usually marks his work."[38] Graham as The Judy was "woman in her most perverse, ridiculous, petty, unreasonable, irritable, and irritating, determined, yet withal lovable aspects."[39] *Punch and The Judy* was "the hit of this season," a "sparkling domestic comedy composed of the dissonances of family life."[40]

From Robert Horan's perspective in 1947, it seemed "the least interesting of Graham's recent compositions." He termed it "a satire without irony . . . a kind of farce, ribald and broad, without being really witty."[41] Constrained by its "narrative pattern" to the prolific use of "pantomimic gesture," Horan said, "it falls cleanly into the arena of pure theater." Horan complained that its "original pattern" had been distorted by performances that now were "cluttered with innuendo and downstage grimacing."

Edwin Denby found its tone puzzling on a first viewing in New York and returned to see if he "got it," but its "pointless folly" left "a bitter taste." It was, he concluded, a "serious and interesting" work, "easy to watch and hard to take."[42]

"As far as content goes," wrote John Martin in his first-night review from Bennington, it "is not to be classed as a major work [but] it is in its own vein another triumph for its creator. [Graham] has managed with wonderful intuition to keep the spirit of rough and ready banter below its polished and sophisticated surface."[43]

Martin found it uneven in quality, strongest in its earliest sections, but nonetheless imaginative and delightful comedy. And he thought it utterly charming:

> In these days, that is a serious accusation to make against a work of art, for like whimsy and fantasy, charm in the arts has acquired reprehensible connotations. . . . "The Judy" and her compact little world have all three of these suspect qualities . . . without trace of Winnie-the-Pooh. [The Judy] is all wives, at the same time brow-beaten and hen-pecking, with their family problems and their romantic dreams of escape. She weeps and rages . . . over her faithless braggart of a husband, but between brawls she draws aside her casement and indulges in a secret gallop through the clouds with Pegasus. . . . From time to time one of [the Three Fates–Jean Erdman] reads from a little book a pungent paragraph . . . written by Gordon Craig. . . . And it is their vigorous rhythms and cadences that set the flavor of the whole action. Miss Graham has captured their quality as sensitively as she captured the subtle colors of Emily Dickinson. [Arch Lauterer's setting contrasts] Victorian smugness with the freedom of the Comedia dell'Arte, its combination of plush and antimacassar with the vistas and perspectives of the early Italian masters. . . . He has achieved an extraordinary visual beauty [and] he has designed a stage which ranks with the finest work that has been seen in the field of the dance. . . . Miss Graham has another success on her hands, not world-shaking in content but gay and alive on the surface and rich and full in texture.[44]

Walter Terry declared Lauterer's setting "the best theatrical presentation that modern dance has shown to date":[45]

> Those who remember the stark days of modern dance staging will be glad to hear that the Charlotte Trowbridge costumes are richly colorful, the decor of Arch Lauterer smart and inventive, the Robert McBride score tuneful. . . . Miss Graham has given herself a broad range of dance action from the furious steps and steel-spined defiance of her squabble scenes to the lovely lyric passages that wing her away with Pegasus. [Erick Hawkins has been given] movements that thoroughly describe Punch's rampant masculinity, his head-of-the-family stance, his boyish bounce when he catches the eye of a pretty girl. Merce Cunningham is

> as light and as air-conscious as Pegasus should be, his movements as softly designed as the dream-world from which he comes. . . . Graham has produced a theater dance that can be understood and enjoyed by any one, no matter how nebulous his dance education may be, for her movements are as articulate as the spoken word—at moments as lyric as poetry and at others as pungent as your favorite cuss word.[46]

Rosalyn Krokover, *Musical Courier*:

> Graham again shows her supreme talent for welding movement with the spoken line. Her timing is so perfect that one never feels the intrusion of one art upon the other.[47]

Sherman Conrad in the *Nation* wrote that the program [*Letter to the World, El Penitente,* and *Punch and The Judy*] revealed

> why she is the most progressive of American theater artists; why she reaches an ever larger audience; why her work takes rank with the most profound modern art. *Punch and The Judy* resembles in style *Every Soul Is a Circus* but it is more sophisticated and wider in reference. . . . Erick Hawkins, having found at last a way to laugh at himself, is really funny. Graham creates the Judy with a Chaplin classicism, the inane bitchery of Bea Lillie.[48]

NOTES

1. Interview with Erick Hawkins.
2. Interview with Jean Erdman.
3. Letter from Doris Humphrey to Julia Humphrey, Good Friday 1941 [Doris Humphrey Collection, C470].
4. Letter from Doris Humphrey to Julia Humphrey, January-June 1941 (undated) [Doris Humphrey Collection, C470].
5. Letter from Nona Schurman to the author, 26 March 1978.
6. Alex Kahn, "Nine dramatic dialogues" (unpublished) [Doris Humphrey Collection, M152].
7. Margaret Lloyd, *Christian Science Monitor*, 30 August 1941. See also Margaret Lloyd, *The Borzoi Book of Modern Dance* (New York: Alfred A. Knopf, 1949), pp. 115–17.
8. Margaret Lloyd, *Christian Science Monitor*, 30 August 1941.
9. Interview with Lionel Nowak.
10. Selma Jeanne Cohen, *Doris Humphrey: An Artist First* (Middletown, Conn.: Wesleyan University Press, 1972), pp. 228–29.
11. Lloyd, *Borzoi*, pp. 115–17.
12. John Martin, *New York Times*, 4 January 1942.
13. Margaret Lloyd, *Christian Science Monitor*, 30 August 1941.
14. John Martin, *New York Times*, 17 August 1941.
15. John Martin, *New York Times*, 27 December 1941.
16. Walter Terry, *New York Herald Tribune*, 11 August 1941.
17. Walter Terry, *New York Herald Tribune*, 17 August 1941.
18. Sherman Conrad, *Nation* 153, no. 9 (30 August 1941).
19. Robert Sabin, "Doris Humphrey's *Decade*," *Dance Observer* 8, no. 7 (August-September 1941): 93.
20. Lois Balcom, *Dance Observer* 9, no. 4 (April 1942): 50–51.
21. "Punch and The Judy" scenario (unpublished) [Arch Lauterer Archives].
22. Ibid.
23. Ibid.
24. Ibid.
25. Henry Cowell, *Modern Music* 19, no. 1 (November-December 1941): 42.
26. John Martin, *New York Times*, 11 August 1941.
27. Walter Terry, *New York Herald Tribune*, 24 August 1941.
28. Robert Sabin, "Martha Graham's *Punch and The Judy*," *Dance Observer* 8, no. 7 (August-September 1941): 94–95.
29. Robert Horan, "The Recent Theater of Martha Graham," *Chronicles of The American Dance*, ed. Paul Magriel (New York: Da Capo Press, 1978), p. 240.
30. There is a later version, "Dances from Martha Graham's Punch and The Judy Score" (for orchestra) dated 14 June 1955. Both versions, Music Division, Library of Congress.
31. Quoted in Don McDonagh, *Martha Graham* (New York: Praeger, 1973), p. 155.
32. "Arch Lauterer: Poet in the Theatre," *Impulse*, 1959, p. 49.
33. Lloyd, *Borzoi*, p. 69. See also Lloyd, "Building a World for Dance" and "Collaboration Is Multiplication," parts of which are reprinted in this book, pp. 108–110.
34. Lloyd, *Borzoi*, pp. 69–70.
35. Arch Lauterer, "Punch and The Judy," in *Form and Action*, 1955-1956 (unpublished). By permission from the Arch Lauterer Archives.
36. Interview with Mark Ryder.
37. Horan, p. 240.
38. Walter Terry, *New York Herald Tribune*, 12 August 1941.
39. Margaret Lloyd, "The New Martha Graham," part 1, *Christian Science Monitor*, 21 March 1942.
40. Ibid.
41. Horan, p. 240.
42. Edwin Denby, *Modern Music* 19, no. 3 (March-April 1942): 200–201. Reprinted in Edwin Denby, *Looking at the Dance* (New York: Popular Library, n.d.), pp. 275–78.
43. John Martin, *New York Times*, 11 August 1941.
44. John Martin, *New York Times*, 24 August 1941.
45. Walter Terry, *New York Herald Tribune*, 12 August 1941.
46. Walter Terry, *New York Herald Tribune*, 24 August 1941.
47. Rosalyn Krokover, "Vermont Center Is Host to Dance Devotees," *Musical Courier* 124 (September 1941): 15.
48. Sherman Conrad, *Nation* 153, no. 9 (30 August 1941): 186.

1942

1 August 1942

Seeds of Brightness

College Theatre

Chor and danc Jean Erdman, Merce Cunningham. *Mus* Norman Lloyd (original score). *Light* Joann Straus. *Cos* Charlotte Trowbridge.

New York Premiere: 20 October 1942, Studio Theatre.

1 August 1942

Credo in Us

College Theatre

Chor and danc Jean Erdman, Merce Cunningham. *Mus* John Cage (original score for percussion quartet, including piano). *Musicians* Nancy Calafati, Hazel Johnson, Helen Lanfer, Ray Malon. *Light* Joann Straus. *Cos* Charlotte Trowbridge.

Program Note: "A dramatic playlet for two Characters: Husband—Shadow; Wife—Ghoul's Rage. Place: Westward Ho! Time: Three Generations."

> They are happied husband and wifed. They have harmonious postures. They facade their frappant ways across a sacred spot.
> Ah, but what! This breakage of pattern. And he on-and-ons—is he only machine?—with her unreality. But soon breakage too.
> So he searched for the Glory that was Greeley's, and she wondered after. It killed time.
> Ghoulish, however, digging back, this thing in her broke through to ancestral gold; and he was stampeded after. But that was no elixir.
> Boiling both and retching, now finally with fruitful efforts; a caraway! "Ah, such eyes."
> But still a zombie.

Music: In the C. F. Peters' catalog, John Cage's score, *Credo in Us*, 12 minutes, is described as "a suite of satirical character composed within the phraseology of the dance by Merce Cunningham and Jean Erdman for which it was written. The instruments used are muted gongs, tin cans, tom-toms, an electric buzzer, piano and radio or phonograph."[1]

New York Premiere: 20 October 1942, Studio Theatre.

1 August 1942

Renaissance Testimonials

College Theatre

Chor Merce Cunningham (solo). *Mus* Maxwell Powers (original score). *Light* Joann Straus. *Cos* Charlotte Trowbridge. ***Profession, Confession.***

New York Premiere: 20 October 1942, Studio Theatre.

1 August 1942

The Transformations of Medusa

College Theatre

Chor Jean Erdman (solo). *Mus* Louis Horst (original piano score). *Pianist* Louis Horst. *Light* Joann Straus. *Cos* Charlotte Trowbridge. ***Maid of the Secret Isle, Lady of the Wild Things, Queen of Gorgons.***

One part of *The Transformations of Medusa* was performed in 1941 (see notes for *Ad Lib*).

New York Premiere: 20 October 1942, Studio Theatre.

Subsequent Productions: Numerous performances recorded in *Dance Observer*, through 1961.

1 August 1942

Ad Lib

College Theatre

Chor and danc Jean Erdman, Merce Cunningham. *Mus* Gregory Tucker (original piano score). *Pianist* Tucker. *Light* Joann Straus. *Cos* Charlotte Trowbridge.

New York Premiere: 20 October 1942, Studio Theatre.

This was the joint choreographic debut of Jean Erdman and Merce Cunningham. The program was repeated in New York that fall.

Said Erdman:

> Merce and I gave our first performance together of our own work that summer. It was John Cage's idea that we do a concert together. He and my husband, Joe Campbell, were eager to have us get out from under Martha's [Graham] thumb because they wanted us to do our own creative work. So at their prodding we started.
>
> We had three beautiful ideas. *Seeds of Brightness* was an opening dance, a nice little number. I think Louis [Horst] thought it was too lyric. *Ad Lib* was in the jazz idiom. We decided with John [Cage] on the structure—that's the way you always proceeded with John. I was to have the blues theme and Merce was to have the fast theme. We each worked on our themes, and then the structure was laid out, and just as in a jazz composition, you have the improvisation. I made up my movement, he made up his, and we agreed on where we'd be. Talk about the new dance—that was what we were doing. The idea that you could do things differently was a great shock up there.

> We said the script for *Credo in Us* was a translation from the French surrealist magazine, *Minotaur*. However, it was truly written by Merce. It was a satire on suburban marriage. We were right at the age of breaking away from our families, getting into the art world, leaving it all behind. John [Cage] made a wonderful score with tin cans, a piano with tacks in it, a radio, a door buzzer—things like that. The radio was turned on and off, and the audience kept saying, "Shh, shh." We went through the alienation motif between a couple. The dance was full of Graham contractions, but it was a breakthrough in terms of using a script, speaking while we danced, and the use of a radio—things that now are taken for granted. Anyway, we got started.[2]

In *Ad Lib*, recalled Cunningham, "we each had certain kinds of movements which we knew individually and/or together but which we were then free to use in different ways. So that it would in a sense have had an improvisatory quality about it."[3]

John Cage wrote new music for *Ad Lib* in 1943. *Credo in Us* was later retitled *A Suburban Idyll.*[4] The score is published and has been recorded.

Jean Erdman had presented one section of *The Transformations of Medusa—Gorgonian*—at Bennett College on 27 November 1941 on a program with Erick Hawkins. (She did a second solo there entitled *Seeds of Brightness*, to music by Ravel). The first part of *Transformations*, she said, was inspired by "the Louis Horst archaic form."[5] Medusa was a beautiful priestess in Greek myth who was turned into a Gorgon. Erdman began to develop the work "while imitating the angular, highly stylized positions of figures on ancient Greek bas-reliefs. . . . She has since pointed to the evolution of that work to show how a choreographer should never depend on personal style but rather create for each new dance a unique style of movement intrinsic to its subject."[6]

Reviews

Dance Observer:

> *Seeds of Brightness* would probably be just another "opening dance" were it not for its sparkle and intriguing title. [*Credo in Us* was] a venture into the realm of surrealism. . . . The dance was well performed. . . . The general plan and theme were sufficiently original and interesting to make some needed revision very worth while. The experiment of correlating words and dancing could not be in better hands. . . . Their last duo, *Ad Lib*, with Gregory Tucker playing his own musical score, was witty and amusing. [Cunningham's *Renaissance Testimonials* were] typical portrayals of the religieux of that period.
>
> [Jean Erdman's] finest achievement was *The Transformations of Medusa*. [She] is a dancer to be reckoned with in the future, for she has something interesting to say and a refreshing and convincing style with which to say it.[7]

At their New York appearance, George Beiswanger, writing in *Dance Observer*, reported:

> All three dancers made easy, even instinctive, use of the vocabulary of movement and intricate syntax in which they have been schooled. They played with ideas and themes and forms and theatre accoutrements and aids that would have terrified young dancers ten years ago.[8]

13 August 1942

"Scherzo" and "Loure" from *Suite*

College Theatre

Chor and danc Jane Dudley, Sophie Maslow, William Bales. *Mus* J. S. Bach. *Pianist* Helen Lanfer.

The trio enlarged this opening suite by adding these two new movements.

New York Premiere: 28 November 1942, Central High School of Needle Trades.

Subsequent Productions: 27-30 December 1945, New York Times Hall.

Reviews

Margaret Lloyd reported that *Suite* was performed in ballet shoes,

> with turned out thighs and semi-courtly demeanor. It was not strict ballet, but a free adaptation, though it had enough of precision and formality to make it a courteous dance of greeting. It was not aristocratic classicism, but rather returned ballet to the people, whence much of its inspiration had come.[9]

"The difficulties posed by dancing to Bach," wrote the *Dance Observer* critic,

> have been argued interminably. In this instance even the die-hards must surely be won over for the artists have so 'danced into the corners' as to achieve a thoroughly satisfying handling of their material. They have found a dry, reticent style, especially in the "Loure," which gives the period atmosphere to movements which are not intended to be strictly classic, and this is a legitimate approach for the modern dancer to make to classic measures.[10]

NOTES

1. John Cage, *John Cage* (New York: Henmar Press, 1962), p. 35.
2. Interview with Jean Erdman.
3. Interview with Merce Cunningham.
4. See "A Chronology compiled by David Vaughan," in "Time to Walk in Space," *Dance Perspectives* 34 (Summer 1968): 55.
5. Interview with Jean Erdman.
6. "Jean Erdman," in *Current Biography*, September 1971, pp. 14–17.
7. Karen Wolfe, "Two Bennington Reviews," *Dance Observer* 9, no. 7 (August-September 1942): 88–89.
8. George W. Beiswanger, *Dance Observer* 9, no. 9 (November 1942): 120–21.
9. Margaret Lloyd, *The Borzoi Book of Modern Dance* (New York: Alfred A. Knopf, 1949), p. 191.
10. G. W., *Dance Observer* 9, no. 7 (August-September 1942): 89.

Courses and Faculty

Curricula listings, descriptions and faculty 1934–1939 are from *Bennington College Bulletins* and post-facto annual reports. Those for the Dance Division, School of the Arts, 1940 and 1941, and for the dance component in 1942 are from *Bennington College Bulletins* and daily schedules of classes issued prior to the sessions. No post-facto reports for the summers of 1940–1942 were available. A list of faculty and courses taught is contained in the appendix.

* = the first time program or course is offered. Description follows, including faculty. Course levels (beginner, intermediate, etc.) are not included, unless they are part of the course title.
Assoc = Associate
Asst = Assistant
Acc = Accompanist

School of the Dance: 1934

***Modern Dance**

Intensive study of the technique of the artists, representative of their points of view and constituting as a whole a comparative study of individual styles in the art.

Martha Graham (July 16-20)
Asst: Dorothy Bird
Acc: Dini de Remer

Charles Weidman (July 23-27)
Asst: Gene Martel
Acc: Pauline Lawrence, Jerome Moross

Doris Humphrey (July 30-August 3)
Asst: Cleo Atheneos
Acc: Jerome Moross

Hanya Holm (August 6-10)
Asst: Nancy McKnight
Acc: Harvey Pollins

***Dance Composition**

A study of dance composition from the standpoint of sequential form and group design in space; a single compositional factor or a combination of factors such as direction, level, tempo, dynamics, and the like; dance content, theme, or idea.

Martha Hill
Asst: Bessie Schönberg
Acc: Ruth Lloyd, Norman Lloyd

***Fundamental Techniques**

A basic study of fundamental techniques of movement for the dance analyzed into its force, space, and time aspects; the elements of form and meaning in movement for the dance.

Martha Hill
Asst: Bessie Schönberg
Acc: Ruth Lloyd, Norman Lloyd

***Teaching Methods and Materials**

Group discussion, panel discussion, and lecture based on the interests of the group including study of dance movement; form and meaning in dance; accompaniment for the dance; teaching methods; terminology; systems of dance notation.

Martha Hill

Two studies were produced by students: (1) Historical Chart of the Dance and Related Arts; (2) Percussion Accompaniment for the Dance.

***Music Related to Movement**

Historical and critical analysis of the pre-classic forms of music and dance; dance composition based on pre-classic forms including the pavane, sarabande, gavotte, rigaudon, bouree, allemande, gigue, minuet, galliard, and chaconne.

Louis Horst
Asst: May O'Donnell
Acc: Dini de Remer

***Music for Dancers**

Analysis of the rhythmic structure of music with melodic and harmonic elements; construction of movement sequences based on musical elements.

Gregory Tucker

***Dance History and Criticism**

Lecture, discussion, readings in dance history, aesthetics, and critical theory.

John Martin

***Production**

Lecture, discussion, and laboratory in terminology and equipment of the stage; scene construction and painting; physical and electrical laws for lighting; equipment for lighting; lighting and composition; makeup; color theory; costume design.

Jane Ogborn

***Practice**

Practice in techniques.

Bessie Schönberg

School of the Dance: 1935

I. THE GENERAL PROGRAM

Modern Dance

[Martha Graham, in residence for the full six weeks, taught this course as well as directing the first Workshop Program (see below). Tina Flade was an alternate for Hanya Holm, who taught the summer session at Mills College. Graham taught the full session; the others taught two weeks each. Practice sessions were directed by Bessie Schönberg, Gertrude Shurr, Nancy McKnight, Letitia Ide, and José Limón.]

Martha Graham (full session)
Asst: Bonnie Bird, Dorothy Bird, Gertrude Shurr
Acc: Dini de Remer

Tina Flade (July 8–20)
Asst: Nancy McKnight
Acc: Ruth Hunt

Doris Humphrey (July 22–August 3)
Asst: Letitia Ide
Acc: Pauline Lawrence

Charles Weidman (August 5–17)
Asst: José Limón
Acc: Jerome Moross

Dance Composition

(Introductory and Advanced)

Martha Hill
Asst: Bessie Schönberg
Acc: Ruth Lloyd, Norman Lloyd, Alex North

Techniques of Dance Movement

Martha Hill, Bessie Schönberg
Acc: Norman Lloyd, Ruth Lloyd

***The Dance in Education**

A series of sessions directed at teachers comprising Nature and Function of Dance (Martha Hill and Mary Jo Shelly); Percussion Accompaniment for the Dance (Tina Flade); Analysis of Movement for the Dance (Hill); Costuming for the Dance (Pauline Lawrence); General Aspects of Method (Shelly); Method in Teaching Dance (Hill); and panel discussion about dance clubs and symposia.

Martha Hill, Mary Jo Shelly

***Special Studies in the Dance**

[No students enrolled for this course.]

Martha Hill, Mary Jo Shelly

Composition in Dance Form

Pre-Classic Forms

Louis Horst
Asst: May O'Donnell, Anna Sokolow
Acc: Ruth Lloyd, Alex North

***Composition in Dance Form: Modern Forms**

Critical analysis of modern forms; practice in dance composition based on modern forms.

Louis Horst
Asst: Anna Sokolow
Acc: Alex North

***Elements of Music**

Study of music notation, rhythm, melody, and harmony as these relate to the dance. Analysis of musical form; practice in building rhythmic studies.

Norman Lloyd

Dance History and Criticism

John Martin

***Basis of Dramatic Movement**

Study of dramatic movement through a series of exercises designed to enable the student to discern his resources in personal experiences and to develop a technique for utilizing this material in dance or dramatic form.

Louise Martin

Stagecraft for Dancers

Jane Ogborn

*II. THE WORKSHOP PROGRAM[a]

Technique

Martha Graham
Asst: Bonnie Bird, Dorothy Bird, Gertrude Shurr
Acc: Dini de Remer

Choreography

Rehearsals and production of *Panorama.*

Martha Graham

---

[a]Students enrolled in the Workshop Program took Composition in Dance Form and Dance History and Criticism.

School of the Dance: 1936

I. THE GENERAL PROGRAM

Modern Dance

[Doris Humphrey and Charles Weidman were in residence for the full six weeks, teaching four weeks each in the General Program; Martha Graham and Hanya Holm each taught two weeks.]

Doris Humphrey (weeks 1-4)
Asst: Joan Levy, Katherine Manning, Sybil Shearer
Acc: Pauline Lawrence

Charles Weidman (weeks 1-4)
Asst: José Limón, William Matons

Louis Horst casts a critical eye from the piano during his class "Composition in Pre-Classic Forms," 1936. Photograph courtesy of Bennington College.

Martha Graham (July 20–August 1)
Asst: Dorothy Bird
Acc: Dini de Remer

Hanya Holm (August 3–15)
Asst: Nancy McKnight
Acc: Harvey Pollins

Techniques of Dance Movement

Martha Hill, Bessie Schönberg
Asst: Marjorie Church
Acc: Ruth Lloyd, Jean Williams, Esther Williamson

Dance Composition

(Introductory, Intermediate, and Advanced)

Martha Hill, Bessie Schönberg
Acc: Ruth Lloyd, Jean Williams, Esther Williamson

Elements of Music

Norman Lloyd

Composition in Dance Form: Pre-Classic Forms

Louis Horst
Asst: May O'Donnell
Acc: Dini de Remer, asst. Jean Williams, Esther Williamson

Composition in Dance Form: Modern Forms — *Louis Horst*
Asst: May O'Donnell
Acc: Ruth Lloyd, asst. Jean Williams, Esther Williamson

Basis of Dramatic Movement — *Louise Martin*

Stagecraft for Dancers — *Sally Brownell*

Dance History and Criticism — *John Martin*

***Seminar in Dance Criticism** — Advanced study and discussion in history of dance and criticism of the modern style, including practical experience in writing criticism of productions in the school series of programs. [Student reviews were published in *Dance Observer*.]

John Martin

***Percussion Accompaniment for the Dance** — A study of the principles and technique of percussion accompaniment for the dance.

Nancy McKnight

*II. THE WORKSHOP PROGRAM

***WOMEN'S WORKSHOP** — Director, Doris Humphrey

TECHNIQUE — *Doris Humphrey*
Asst: Joan Levy, Katherine Manning, Sybil Shearer
Acc: Pauline Lawrence

CHOREOGRAPHY — *Doris Humphrey*
Acc: Ruth Lloyd, Norman Lloyd, Pauline Lawrence, asst. Nancy McKnight (percussion)
Composer: Wallingford Riegger

With My Red Fires

***MEN'S WORKSHOP** — Director, Charles Weidman

TECHNIQUE — *Charles Weidman*
Asst: José Limón, William Matons

CHOREOGRAPHY — *Charles Weidman*
Acc: Norman Lloyd, Clair Leonard
Composer: Norman Lloyd

Quest

*III. PROGRAM IN CHOREOGRAPHY

Co-Directors: Martha Hill, Louis Horst
Committee on Auditions: Martha Hill, Louis Horst, John Martin

Work in independent composition for advanced students [10 enrolled; 4 qualified to take the program]. Each student completed and presented two full-length compositions.

***IV. PROGRAM IN MUSIC COMPOSITION FOR THE DANCE**

Director: Louis Horst

Practical experience in writing music for dance composed by students in the Program in Choreography and in Dance Composition and Composition in Dance Form courses. [10 students enrolled; 4 qualified to take the program].

***Music Accompaniment**

Study of the theory and practice of keyboard improvisation and the selection and reading of music for class accompaniment.

Norman Lloyd

***Music Composition**

Study of the principles of form and style in composition; laboratory problems of writing music in various styles and forms.

Louis Horst

School of the Dance: 1937

I. THE GENERAL PROGRAM

Modern Dance

[Hanya Holm in residence the full session, teaching four weeks in the General Program. Doris Humphrey, Charles Weidman, and Martha Graham each taught two weeks, one after the other. Holm directed the Workshop (see below)].

Hanya Holm (weeks 1-4)
Asst: Louis Kloepper, Elizabeth Waters, Lucretia Wilson
Acc: Harvey Pollins

Doris Humphrey (July 2-17)
Asst: Edith Orcutt
Acc: Pauline Lawrence

Charles Weidman (July 19-31)
Asst: George Bockman
Acc: Pauline Lawrence, Yolanda Lorenz

Martha Graham (July 30-August14)
Asst: Dorothy Bird
Acc: Dini de Remer

Dance Composition

(Introductory, Intermediate, and Advanced)

Martha Hill, Bessie Schönberg
Acc: Ruth Lloyd, Esther Williamson, Morris Mamorsky

Techniques of Dance Movement

Martha Hill, Bessie Schönberg
Asst: Hortense Lieberthal
Acc: Ruth Lloyd, Esther Williamson

Franziska Boas percussion class. Photograph courtesy of Herbert Binzer from Bertha Rhea Desenberg Scrapbook.

Composition in Dance Form: Pre-Classic Forms	*Louis Horst* Asst: Mildred Wile Acc: Dini de Remer, Ruth Lloyd
Composition in Dance Form: Modern Forms	*Louis Horst* Asst: Mildred Wile Acc: Morris Mamorsky, asst. Ruth Lloyd
Elements of Music	*Norman Lloyd*
Percussion Accompaniment	*Franziska Boas*
Dramatic Basis of Movement	*Louise Martin*
Dance History and Criticism	*John Martin*
Seminar in Dance Criticism	*John Martin*
***Laboratory in Composition**	Under the critical supervision of Martha Hill, Louis Horst, John Martin. This was held in conjunction with the three Fellows—Esther Junger, José Limón, Anna Sokolow—for students enrolled in the Program in Choreography. Acc: Morris Mamorsky, Esther Williamson, Ruth Lloyd, Margaret Lidy. Group compositions were given public performance August 12.

II. THE WORKSHOP PROGRAM

Director: Hanya Holm
Asst: Louise Kloepper, Elizabeth Waters, Lucretia Wilson

Louise Martin's class: "Dramatic Basis of Movement," 1937. Photograph courtesy of Bennington College.

TECHNIQUES AND CHOREOGRAPHY

Hanya Holm

Acc: Harvey Pollins (piano), Franziska Boas and Carolyn Durand (percussion)
Composer: Wallingford Riegger
Musical Director for the Performances: Norman Lloyd

Trend

III. PROGRAM IN CHOREOGRAPHY

Co-Directors: Martha Hill, Louis Horst
Committee on Auditions: Martha Hill, Louis Horst, John Martin

IV. PROGRAM IN MUSIC FOR THE DANCE

Director: Louis Horst

Music Accompaniment

Norman Lloyd

Music Composition

Louis Horst

School of the Dance: 1938

The General Program, Program in Choreography and Program in Music for the Dance continued; the Workshop Program (having completed three cycles involving each of the major artists) was replaced by the Professional Program, which involved student work with each of the four major artists. A Laboratory in Experimental Production replaced the course in Advanced Dance Composition in the General Program; a separate Program in Stage Design was added.

I. THE GENERAL PROGRAM

Modern Dance

[Each of the four taught five weeks; students were grouped so that they took two weeks with each of the four.]

Martha Graham
Asst: Ethel Butler, May O'Donnell
Acc: Dini de Remer

Hanya Holm
Asst: Elizabeth Waters, Carolyn Durand
Acc: Harvey Pollins

Doris Humphrey
Asst: Katherine Manning, Sybil Shearer, Edith Orcutt
Acc: Pauline Lawrence, Morris Mamorsky

Charles Weidman
Asst: William Bales, George Bockman, Lee Sherman
Acc: Margaret Lidy

Techniques of Dance Movement

Martha Hill, Bessie Schönberg
Asst: Hortense Lieberthal
Acc: Ruth Lloyd, Esther Williamson

Dance Composition

(Introductory and Intermediate)

Martha Hill (Intermediate), *Bessie Schönberg* (Introductory)
Acc: Ruth Lloyd and students in Program in Music for the Dance

Composition in Dance Form: Pre-Classic Forms

Mildred Wile (Introductory)
Acc: Dini de Remer

Louis Horst (Intermediate)
Asst: Mildred Wile
Acc: Dini de Remer, Ruth Lloyd, Esther Williamson

Composition in Dance Form: Modern Forms

Louis Horst
Asst: Mildred Wile
Acc: Ruth Lloyd

Laboratory in Composition

Supervised by Martha Hill, Louis Horst

Choreographers: Eleanor King, Louise Kloepper, Marian Van Tuyl (all Fellows), plus students from Program in Choreography
Acc: Drusa Wilker, Esther Williamson, Margaret Lidy
Composers: Norman Lloyd, Esther Williamson, Gregory Tucker, Harvey Pollins

[Group compositions given public performance on Fellows' program August 4 and 8].

Elements of Music — *Norman Lloyd*

Percussion Accompaniment — *Franziska Boas*

***Experimental Production**

A study of the relationships of dance composition and stage design. Experiments in composing and staging dances. Projects designed to discover methods for integrating dance with its spatial setting.

Martha Hill, Arch Lauterer
Asst: Edward Glass, Henry Seymour
Composers: Students in Program in Music for the Dance and in Percussion Accompaniment.

*II. THE PROFESSIONAL PROGRAM

Graham, Holm, Humphrey, and Weidman each directed a separate professional unit of no more than twelve students who, together with members of the choreographer's concert group, performed in new festival productions.

Martha Graham: American Document
Asst: Ethel Butler, May O'Donnell
Composer: Ray Green
Acc: Ralph Gilbert

Hanya Holm: Dance Sonata
Asst: Carolyn Durand, Elizabeth Waters
Composer: Norman Lloyd, Harrison Kerr
Acc: Harvey Pollins

Doris Humphrey: Passacaglia
Asst: Katherine Manning, Sybil Shearer, Edith Orcutt
Acc: Morris Mamorsky

Charles Weidman: Opus 51
Asst: William Bales, George Bockman, Lee Sherman
Composer: Vivian Fine
Acc: Morris Mamorsky, Yolanda Lorenz

III. PROGRAM IN CHOREOGRAPHY

Co-Directors: Martha Hill, Louis Horst
Committee on Auditions: Martha Hill, Louis Horst

IV. PROGRAM IN MUSIC FOR THE DANCE

Director: Louis Horst

Music Accompaniment — *Norman Lloyd*

Music Composition — *Louis Horst*

*V. PROGRAM IN STAGE DESIGN FOR THE DANCE

Director: Arch Lauterer
Asst: Edward Glass, Henry Seymour

Observation and analysis of selected types of dance composition in progress in the school. Lab work in the course in Experimental Production and assigned work in designing and constructing sets for the festival and staging the festival concerts.

School of the Dance at Mills College: 1939

The five separate programs of 1938 replaced by three major courses. For the first time, a student was able to study intensively with one major teacher and also take two weeks each with the other three major artists in residence.

***Major Course In Dance**

A study of professional technique. Four sections, under Martha Graham, Hanya Holm, Doris Humphrey, Charles Weidman. The course began with three weeks taught by the associate; the major artist taught the last three weeks. Students worked with one artist for six weeks.

Martha Graham
Assoc: Ethel Butler
Acc: Ralph Gilbert

Hanya Holm
Assoc: Louise Kloepper
Acc: Freda Miller

Doris Humphrey
Assoc: Katherine Manning
Acc: Lionel Nowak

Charles Weidman
Assoc: José Limón
Acc: Pauline Lawrence

***Major Course in Music for the Dance**

Problems of the musician working in collaboration with the dancer or teacher.

Louis Horst, Norman Lloyd, Franziska Boas

***Major Course in Stage Design for the Dance**

The place of dance in the theater and the role of the designer in relation to it.

Arch Lauterer
Asst: Henry Seymour

***Survey Course in Dance**

Students studying intensively with one artist in the Major Course in Dance had the opportunity to study for two weeks each with the others. Personnel same as in the Major Course in Dance.

Techniques of Dance Movement

Martha Hill, Bessie Schönberg
Asst: Hortense Lieberthal
Acc: Esther Williamson, Ruth Lloyd

Ethel Butler teaching Graham technique at Mills College, 1939. Photograph by Donald Hatfield.

Dance Composition

Martha Hill, Bessie Schönberg
Asst: Hortense Lieberthal
Acc: Esther Williamson, Ruth Lloyd

Composition of Pre-Classic and Modern Forms

Louis Horst
Asst: Mildred Wile

Percussion Accompaniment

Franziska Boas

***Rhythmic Basis of Dance**

A study of the rhythmic structure of movement, music notation and terminology, and music form and analysis as these relate to dance.

Norman Lloyd

***Experimental Production**

A study of the relationships among dance movement, speech, music, and stage design through a series of experiments in choreography and design.

Arch Lauterer, Martha Hill, Ben Belitt, Norman Lloyd, Bessie Schönberg.
Asst: Henry Seymour, Hortense Lieberthal

School of the Arts, Dance Division: 1940

Three new courses added to an array of classes and workshops, some of them open to students in the three other divisions: Music, Drama, and Theatre Design.

Dance Technique	Students select one of four major techniques for intensive study, taught by artists' associates. Martha Graham Assoc: Ethel Butler Hanya Holm Assoc: Harriet Roeder Doris Humphrey Assoc: Katherine Manning Charles Weidman Assoc: Claudia Moore
Survey of Dance Technique	Each of the four above instead of or in addition to concentrated study in one technique. Faculty same as above. Two weeks in each.
***Master Course in Dance**	For a small number of advanced students. *Hanya Holm*
***Ballet Technique**	Ballet technique to be studied as the foundation for certain areas of movement belonging in the complete range of the modern American style. *Erick Hawkins*
***Dance Notation**	Movement notation applied to professional dance, to the teaching of dance, and to movement in drama. Past and present systems of notation are briefly summarized, and concentrated work given in Laban dance script. *Helen Priest*
Technique of Movement	*Bessie Schönberg*
Dance Composition	*Martha Hill, Bessie Schönberg*
Pre-Classic and Modern Forms	*Louis Horst, Mildred Wile*
Rhythmic Basis of Dance	*Norman Lloyd*
Accompaniment for the Dance, Music Composition for the Dance	In association with Music Division. *Louis Horst, Norman Lloyd*
Experimental Production	Experiments relating dance composition to design, music, and speech. *Martha Hill, Arch Lauterer, Norman Lloyd*
***Dance Workshop**	Collaborations with students in other divisions.
***Courses in Other Divisions**	Of special interest to dance students: Acting, Makeup (Drama Division); Choral Singing, American Song Literature, Seminar in 17th and 18th Century Music (Music Division); Theatre Design.

School of the Arts, Dance Division: 1941

Technique	Martha Graham Technique *Martha Graham* (Advanced) *Ethel Butler* (Introductory) Hanya Holm Technique *Harriet Roeder* (Advanced and Introductory) Humphrey-Weidman Technique *Claudia Moore, Maria Maginnis* (Introductory)
***Humphrey-Weidman Master Course**	Advanced students. *Charles Weidman, with Doris Humphrey collaborating.*
***Humphrey-Weidman Repertory**	Students worked on *Lynch Town* and *The Shakers*. [This was the first repertory class at Bennington.] *Charles Weidman, Doris Humphrey, and Assistants*
***Tap Technique**	*William Bales* (Introductory and Advanced)
Ballet for Modern Dancers	*Erick Hawkins*
Pre-Classic and Modern Forms	*Louis Horst*
Fundamentals of Dance Composition	*Bessie Schönberg*
Dance Composition	*Martha Hill* (Advanced)
***Technique of Modern Dance for Teachers**	*Bessie Schönberg*
Rhythmic Basis of Movement	*Norman Lloyd*
Experimental Production	*Martha Hill, Arch Lauterer, Norman Lloyd*
Composition for Dance	*Louis Horst* [offered in conjunction with Music Division]
Dance Accompaniment	*Norman Lloyd* [offered in conjunction with Music Division]
	Courses offered in other divisions for dance students:
Improvisation and Speech for Dancers	*Marion Fergusson, Mary-Averett Seelye*
Makeup	*Edward Thommen*

Bennington College Summer Session—Dance: 1942

A full curriculum in the American dance continuing the plan developed through the Bennington School of the Dance and the Bennington School of the Arts.

Curriculum continues in technique, composition, and music for the dance, augmented by study of the special uses to which the related materials of dance and music may be put for community and recreational purposes.

Modern Dance

Martha Graham Technique
Martha Graham (Advanced)
Ethel Butler (Introductory)

Hanya Holm Technique
Henrietta Greenhood [*Eve Gentry*] (Introductory and Advanced)

Humphrey-Weidman Technique
Nona Schurman (Introductory and Advanced)

Techniques of Modern Dance

Hortense Lieberthal[a]

Ballet Technique

Erick Hawkins

Dance Composition

Hortense Lieberthal,[a] *Martha Hill*

Pre-Classic and Modern Forms

Louis Horst

Rhythmic Basis of Dance

Norman Lloyd

Music Accompaniment

Norman Lloyd

Music Composition

Louis Horst

***Dance and Music Recreation**

Materials and techniques for the use of music and dancing as recreational activities, including folk dancing with particular emphasis on American dance forms, squares, rounds and contras, group singing, and the use of simple musical instruments.

Martha Hill, Norman Lloyd

***American Country Dancing**

Informal sessions for dancing American square, round, and contra dances, to be held in the evening.

Martha Hill

---

[a]Bessie Schönberg, scheduled to teach these courses, was on sick leave.

Charles Weidman and Doris Humphrey walking on campus, 1938. Photograph copyright by Barbara Morgan.

A Bennington Album

Looking Back: Four Points of View is drawn from a series of taped interviews conducted by the author. The transcripts were edited into first-person narratives focusing on responses to two questions: what was Bennington's impact on your life and career, and what do you think Bennington's significance was?

Bessie Schönberg was interviewed by telephone, 15 October 1977. Alwin Nikolais was interviewed in Washington, D.C., 16 March 1977 and again 4 April 1977 in New York. Merce Cunningham was interviewed in New York 20 April 1977. Erick Hawkins was interviewed in Washington, D.C., 13 August 1976. Sources quoted in the introduction to the Nikolais interview include "Nik: A Documentary," Marcia B. Siegel, editor, *Dance Perspectives* 48 (Winter 1971): 11, and *Impulse*, 1968, p. 70.

Quotations in *Images and Voices* are from interviews by the author, with these exceptions: Charles Weidman, interview with Billy Nichols, 1965, for NET's *Four Pioneers*; Anna Halprin, letter to author, 25 February 1977; Joseph Campbell, "Betwixt the Cup and the Lip," *Dance Observer*, March 1944; Betty Ford, Remarks at the Dedication of the Bennington College Arts Center, 22 May 1976, honoring Martha Hill.

Sources for *Selected Readings* are given on p. 290.

Looking Back: Four Points of View

Alwin Nikolais, Merce Cunningham, and Erick Hawkins were among the students at Bennington just beginning careers in dance. The three went on to break new ground and to form their own dance groups after the Second World War. Inevitably, Bennington affected each of them in different ways, not only because they filtered the experience through their own distinctive esthetic sensibilities, but also because Bennington itself varied in pitch during the course of their residencies—periods that, though they overlapped, were not identical.

Bessie Schönberg, one of America's most respected and beloved dance educators, was a member of the Bennington summer dance faculty for the longest period. Through her perspective of a life spent teaching the dance, the full dimension of Bennington's meaning emerges.

Bessie Schönberg

Bennington, 1934-1942

Bessie Schönberg was born in Hanover, Germany, grew up in Dresden and first studied modern dance with Martha Hill at the University of Oregon in Eugene (1927-1928), where she was a fine arts major. She came East with Hill to enroll in the Martha Graham School and was a member of the Martha Graham Group between 1929 and 1931. A leg injury ended her performing career. Hill invited her to be her assistant at Bennington College, and Schönberg was part-time instructor in dance in 1933-1934 and 1934-1935. While teaching, she also completed her bachelor's degree at Bennington College. She was a member of the permanent faculty of the Bennington School of the Dance from 1934 through 1942 but was absent one summer (1942) because of emergency surgery. Schönberg translated into English Curt Sachs' World History of the Dance *(1937) and brought him to Bennington in the summer of 1938 as guest lecturer. That year, Schönberg began teaching at Sarah Lawrence College, and in 1956 she was named Director of Theater and Dance. She taught and directed the dance program there until her retirement in 1975.*

Bessie Schönberg in front of the Commons Building, Bennington College, 1938. Photograph by Betty Lynd Thompson.

The summers at Bennington were of the deepest importance to the life of modern dance in America. It still seems to me today a phenomenal period. For those "junior" members of the group like myself, they were some of the best years of our lives professionally. Practically no one who went on to do important work in the dance did not pass through Bennington. The younger people, like Alwin Nikolais, José Limón, Sybil Shearer, Merce Cunningham, were on the threshold of their professional lives. At Bennington they may have become more themselves, more certain of what they were all about. Twenty years later they reigned among the most important people in the dance.

Robert Leigh prepared himself for his presidency at Bennington by becoming acquainted with the arts. He spent a whole year in New York going to museums, exhibits, concerts, dance programs, and theater. He was an extraordinary man, and he had many excellent ideas. One of them was to take a walk one Sunday morning to talk with Martha Hill, who was living on campus [and teaching part-time at the college]. She was washing her hair. When Leigh got halfway up the stairs he saw that Martha Hill had a very wet head of hair, he stayed right there on the staircase and the conversation was something like: "We should do something in the summers here, and I was wondering if there was anything in the dance that you could think of." And Hill did.

Bessie Schönberg at Bennington, 1934 or 1935. Photograph courtesy of Ruth Alexander.

What Martha Hill did together with Mary Jo Shelly, which must never be forgotten, was to have had the courage to ask Martha Graham, Doris Humphrey, Charles Weidman, and Hanya Holm to be in residence in one small place at a time when they were something of artistic competitors. I was a member of Martha Graham's group [1929-1931] and became friendly with people in Doris' company and Charles' company. That kind of going over the line was rather taboo in New York then; there was quite a bit of hostility. But there was peace at Bennington.

In those times the artists were young and unsure in a way, but very ardent. They had first to figure out what they were about before they could be generous, let us say, about others. If you are a pioneer—and these people were—you are narrow to a degree. Narrow in a very important way. You stick deeply to what you are doing. You don't really have time to do anything else. And yet there was a certain generosity that is very often overlooked. The Ballet Caravan had its first performance at Bennington. This was unheard of. The ballet! Most of the dance students of that time wouldn't have anything to do with it.

For those six weeks in the summers, Bennington gave the individual artist the security of working on a new piece, the security of performance, costumes, lighting, a professional setting, a calm—such calm as artists working on new pieces can have. The countryside was soothing, it was away from the city, and everyone was fed. It may seem mundane today, but I'm sure that this was very important.

The great pieces of these years would probably not have come into being in quite the way in which they did were it not for Bennington. We were just emerging from the Depression and everybody was poor, but poorest were the dancers. Martha Graham had a camel's hair coat and saddle shoes and a little blue cap which she wore all through the winter, and, as Mary Jo Shelly used to say, "always looked like she didn't have a nickel for the subway fare"—which was probably very nearly true.

Each Bennington summer was a total experience, complete in itself. There were peaks and near disasters and human problems, of course. A terrific impetus had to be taken to begin again each summer. There was always so much "iffishness" as to money. Our first contracts were something like, "If we have X number of students, we will pay you X number of dollars; if we have this many less, only half of this will be paid; if we have that many less, we'll have you for room and board."

What kept the Bennington School going was dedication, commitment, a sheer foolhardiness and a glorious kind of adventure. If there had been more money, perhaps the productions could have been done more stylishly or more elaborately—I think dreams are made of a different stuff than unbleached muslin—but then what was on the side of this very poverty was that it was a very stark period of modern dance. The artistic product was whittled down to a "divine simplicity," as Martha Graham might say—and you couldn't dress that in silks and satins.

The Mills summer was nothing like any of the others. We were a little like trained bears brought out there to do what it was we had been publicized to do. It was a teaching summer, without a festival, and so the overall intensity that vibrated through Bennington was missing. In the last summers, the stalwarts of the School of the Dance felt the end ahead, sensed the project was doomed, and we were very sad about it. The Bennington School of the Arts killed the Bennington School of the Dance. I think that while Mary Jo Shelly and Martha Hill did not oppose taking the step, it was not necessarily one they wanted to take, but they saw the handwriting on the wall. The School of the Dance had become a nucleus, a core of something very united and strong. I think there was a certain amount of envy and jealousy in the college over the fact that some part of the college's reputation rested on a summer dance project. While the dance program grew gradually from year to year in intensity, dimension, weight, and value, the School of the Arts didn't have adequate seasoning time, and too much was tried too quickly.

The festival was the climax of the artists' work, but the thing that buttressed every summer was the school and the students. A good sector of the student body were teachers who used their summers to learn what to do with dance in their own teaching. Louis Horst had cryptic things to say about them, but they were devoted students and very probably the backbone of the summers, though not always the most ravishing dancers. They took his Pre-Classic Dance Forms with tears and pain, and then went back and taught them to others! There's no question that the Bennington curriculum enriched dance teaching within physical education curricula across America. But I think very few autonomous dance departments grew out of it. Those were started by prophets like Martha Hill, Marian Knighton Bryan, and Margaret H'Doubler, and then later by younger dancers who went into teaching.

My own views on dance widened with every summer. I was deeply sympathetic to the fact that Bennington was not the school of one person, but a center for the great in the dance with very diverse points of view and ideas. If anything, it made my thinking grow wider and wider. I felt if one has anything to do with dance education, it must encompass all dance.

The dance composition course I taught there stemmed from my work with Martha Hill. Arch Lauterer also had a great influence on me in terms of space, energy, light, dimensions. Gradually I evolved tools of choreography that could be presented as separate entities to young students, which eventually would give them a vocabulary from which to make a dance. Over the years it has become a canon of mine to say that you cannot teach anybody to make a dance. You can hand them the salt, pepper, rosemary, and other ingredients, but the cooking was to be done very personally, very individually. Teachers, I think, had better stay out of it and only be a watchful eye, adviser, and encouraging critic.

Martha Hill and Mary Jo Shelly brought together an extraordinary group of people—for example, Louis Horst, who was responsible for a new consciousness about contemporary music for the dance. In the Bennington years everyone was persuaded that music had to be as live as the dance. And I think most of us from that period have continued to adhere to working with live music, against all the odds of cost. It certainly has been a very important part of my own life.

Arch Lauterer had remarkable ideas for theater design which he used for the modern dance, and I think if he were still alive he would be very "today" in his doing and thinking. He was a magician not only in the way in which he used his eyes and could produce, but in the ways he affected the artists with whom he worked. He was indispensable for the festivals.

The atmosphere was one of tremendous seriousness. I don't know that we knew at the time how serious we all were, because we were having such a good time. The war years were destructive to the dance, but I think all of the artists must have been more secure about where they were going and what they were doing because of the Bennington summers. Bennington gave them a period of solidity, of experience, from which they drew the kind of strength they manifested in the next years as they struggled in their own studios.

Alwin Nikolais

Bennington, 1937-1939

Alwin Nikolais dates the conscious beginnings of his "total theater concept" to 1950 or so, "though the seeds of it began much earlier."

Bennington was a singularly crucial stage in the evolution toward that concept. He was a student there at the crest of the Bennington period, and the sheer density of the experience left a deep impression. This was Nikolais' first concentrated exposure to the modern dance. In 1937, when he came to Bennington, he was Director for the Hartford Parks Marionette Theatre, and in 1938 and 1939 he taught dance at a private studio and at the Hart Foundation.

At Bennington, Nikolais sampled everything he possibly could. "I came with raw nerve edges," he has written, "and with a cavity that only the bulldozing process of Bennington, at that time, could fill."

From Louis Horst he acquired his "basic beginning discipline" and developed "expressional qualities"; Franziska Boas introduced him to the possibilities of sound; Louise Martin set him on a path that led to his work in abstract expressionism; and from Arch Lauterer he learned to explore the kinetic properties and possibilities of light.

*Nikolais created some of his first pure dance compositions in Louis Horst's Pre-Classic Forms and Modern Forms classes (*American Greetings, *with music by Horst, was later performed by him in Hartford). He made a group work,* Line and Plane *(1938), in the Experimental Workshop directed by Martha Hill and Arch Lauterer.*

Except for dancing in José Limón's Danza de la Muerte *(1937), Nikolais performed only in student demonstrations at Bennington.*

He took classes with all four major artists; after the war he decided to work exclusively with Hanya Holm. Performances by the four artists had more impact on him than their classwork, perhaps because he had already subconsciously determined to make dances—to be a composer rather than a performer.

What impressed him in Trend, *for example, was Holm's skill at making small gestures done by masses of people explosive and telling. "A mass of dancers," he wrote in 1968, "just by raising one hand together, blew off the whole top of the universe."*

Martha Graham's solos remain etched in his memory, especially Frontier, *performed on several occasions at Bennington, which seemed to him "a space vision filled with enormous power. The design and concept of the use of space was extraordinary." He saw in Graham's solo "that a woman could be a goddess in space, manipulating that mystical substance—and I couldn't help but feel that I wanted to manipulate space; I wanted to explore it, and shape it into my own vision."*

And in New Dance, *José Limón appeared to him a "luminous central sun around which the dynamic happening of figures shook every molecule of your life."*

Student Alwin Nikolais attends John Martin's course in Dance History and Criticism, 1937. Photograph courtesy of Bennington College.

I don't believe I had any intention at that time of being a professional dancer. I had had one year of study with Truda Kaschmann, and she was going to Bennington. I knew nothing about Bennington, but I went along with her. I'd heard of all of these people, of course, but I'd never seen any of them. I'd seen Wigman earlier, and I thought this was something extraordinary. Even as a young man I understood it perfectly. I knew exactly what it was all about and I was deeply affected by it. It's what got me studying with Truda, which in turn led me to Bennington.

There's something about a time in the arts when it is on fire and it is the most dramatic moment. You could have gone to Bennington and studied, let's say, belly dancing, and come out with an aesthetic set of pores that you never had before. Somehow it hasn't happened since then, no matter how much they've tried to duplicate the experience. I suppose it's because Martha and Doris, Charles and Hanya, each had arrived at creative pinnacles, and Bennington gave them a marvelous opportunity to work under dynamic stress and pressure, which made for great festivals for the modern dance. In my opinion there has never been anything like the Bennington Festivals since.

I had the choice of either working with a single artist the entire six weeks or choosing a smorgasbord. I took the smorgasbord. My day's schedule began with an hour and a half of general modern dance technique, usually taught by Martha Hill or Bessie Schönberg. It didn't resemble any of the other techniques, though both of them were pretty well schooled in the Graham idiom. Then there was an experimental production workshop handled mainly by Arch Lauterer and Martha Hill. I recall particularly the freshness of the whole thing, the stimulation of new thinking that was going on through Martha Hill and Arch. They were then introducing—especially Arch—theater in the round. Not necessarily environmental theater, but they were getting away from total stage concepts.

I'll never forget Arch once set up a lighting situation, and he said, "Watch this." So we watched and watched. And he said, "Now what did you see?" Well, we didn't see anything, really, because our minds were not prepared to see what he saw, which was the trajectory of the light. "What you should have seen," he said, "was that when the dancer came into the light, the trajectory made it seem as if she were going slower, but because the other end was straighter down, she seemed to be going out of it very fast. Consequently," he said, "you've increased the kinetics of that particular moment." I always go back to that, because it enabled me to look with a keener vision.

I also took a course with Louise Martin, John Martin's wife. What she tried to do was to take literal gesture created à la Stanislavsky or Boleslavsky and restructure it into abstraction. I learned a lot from her about that process, and I think that led me a great deal toward my work in abstract expressionism.

I took John Martin's course in history and criticism. He's a very droll but very direct-thinking man, and I believe he was as important to that era of dance as Martha Graham was, because he gave verbalization to the time. We went through the whole exercise of reviewing the student performances. You had to hand your review in to John one hour after the curtain fell, and the next day in class—there were only seven or eight of us—we'd go over them.

Then, of course, I took the work with Louis. Louis was a horror. He didn't like men, so he tried to weed them out rather quickly. I remember one of the dances I first did was an *Earth Primitive* [a study in Modern Forms], and I just wore a pair of trunks. And he said, "Well, you look like Tarzan, but you solved the problem!" He was caustic, terse, and you had to learn to take it—which I don't necessarily believe in—but on the other hand, if you survived Louis—and I did survive Louis—you found a lot of aesthetic answers to dance. I really got my basic beginning discipline through him, as well as expressional qualities of dance. And I was very good at the work. Louis would choose out of the 16 to 18 students the best dance, and then he had a similar class for music, so that person would do the dance for the music class, and the best piece written by the composer would then be coupled with the dancer, and there would be an exhibition of it at one of the weekly demonstrations. I remember doing many of those things.

Louis, Arch, John Martin, and Louise Martin: they were the ones, I think, who managed for some reason and in some peculiar way to make you rise above your narcissism and ego and devote yourself to the art. Most of the influence and stimulation of Bennington for me came from these people, not so much from the dancers themselves, except in their own choreography, in what you saw them do.

Louis would often bring to his composition classes the new things that were happening, particularly with Martha. I remember the first year, Martha didn't move. She was standing on one foot. The idea in class was that you did not move unless the movement was functional in terms of your statement. We didn't dare make a gesture unless it was a "significant" one. I learned a lot of my craft from him in that particular sense. I remember having to do a courante—a running dance—and I thought, "Oh my God, you're not supposed to move. How am I going to do a courante without moving?" But I proceeded to do just that, without leaving the one spot on the floor. And Louis used to tell his students for years afterward, "Well, I remember Alwin once doing a courante, and he did it on one foot and you'd swear he was running." The next year, Louis got awfully tired of us not moving, and he said, "Why aren't you people moving? You've got some technique; why don't you use it? It's boring standing still all the time." So things changed that way from year to year.

The year Anna and José had fellowships, I auditioned for José and got into his piece [*Danza de la Muerte*, 1937]. It was my first big-time performance and the only time I danced at Bennington other than in student performances—excepting once at Mills, when Merce and I both danced for Martha for that film they were making [*Young America Dances*; see Sources—Films].

José's work was an abstract piece. Of course in those days we thought we were abstract, but we did assume roles as an actor assumes a role and surrounded that with abstract movements. The modern dancers were very seldom literal in their gesture, even though as figures we were much more "real" than the ballet figure which was the archetypal figure. In the Bennington period the men did not wear tights—I don't think I owned a pair of tights. You wore pants and shirts, and the girls wore skirts. We weren't kings and queens or fantastic creatures. We were common man.

I studied percussion with Franziska Boas, Franz Boas' daughter. She was a terrible and wonderful teacher because she never said a word, just put you among those instruments. But I learned to work with sound, although I was a musician earlier, so I had already studied some composition. But this was the first time I had studied percussion formally.

Then I would go to my other technique class, which was Graham or Humphrey or Weidman or Holm. Throughout the summer you could take two weeks of each. It was wonderfully confusing. Charles used to say, "In Martha's class you stand with the hip back; in Hanya's you stand with the hip forward. I advocate a combination of the two," and he would do a bump. I arrived during Martha's "divine awkward" stage. The shoulders were set forward, one foot ahead of the other, no turn-out, the pelvis tipped backward. Some of her solos were very square, two-dimensional.

I personally carry on the fervor of the early period of dance, when unique gesture was the thing. This is what you were taught by Louis, by Hanya, by Martha. Martha changed her gesture from one year to the next. After her new piece was performed, some of the gestures in the work were taken into the classwork. Not with Hanya. Hanya taught a specific technique, a basic technique which she still uses.

I favored Hanya's teaching. When you got out of her class you felt you had learned something tangible, something you could grasp. It wasn't only the German analysis—it was more. It was motional stuff, much of which I then went on from because I had new thoughts about time and space. But I never had to forget what Hanya taught me. All I had to do was to expand and go on.

I'm not sure I saw what Doris or Hanya or Martha or Charles wanted me to see, but what I saw was the beginning of what I probably finally did do. Interestingly, more so from Doris' and Hanya's work, because they were working very abstractly at the time. Later on, as Doris could no longer dance herself, her works became more literal, less abstract. Martha, of course, was the great performing artist. You didn't come away with visions of choreography so much as with the impact of an extraordinary dancer. She *was* the choreography. It was inseparable. That was not so true of Doris, and it was certainly not true of Hanya.

Bennington's influence flew out all over the country then and afterward. Louis' influence in particular was startling. Everyone who took a course with him went back, and soon pavanes, galliards, gigues, and medieval things were everywhere. In a way that was devastating. But on the other hand it was the gymnasium circuit that supported the whole touring thing. We could never have toured if it hadn't been for these people.

The feeling of the two summers I spent at Bennington was so strongly embedded in my own happiness and being that when it moved out to Mills it seemed sort of like leaving home. It wasn't quite the same somehow. Right after that I did my first cross-country tour with a small group called Dancers En Route. Then I was drafted, so I lost out on the last Bennington years. After the war I was frantic to get back into shape. I went to Martha, to Doris, to Hanya, and then I realized that I was on too many different diets, and I'd better choose one. I'd always thought Hanya was a great teacher. Not that the others weren't in their way, but for sheer knowledge of the craft I went to Hanya. I told her I thought I was being foolish taking a bit of each. She knew. I said I've decided to work with you, and from then on Hanya really took me over.

After a couple of years in the modern dance I felt not so much that it was necessarily finished but that I wanted to get at a new way and things which I thought were more important to the moment, to the present time. I tried to redefine, go back to basis, but I didn't know what basis was because I was never taught. Working with Hanya brought me closer. I think Merce came to it, too, but a major difference between us is that I went into decentralization, which was a step beyond, I think, in the sense that I was not concerned about the figurative presence of the dancer but the dancer simply as completely released from that into the next phase: a freer instrument of motion rather than a dancing emoting figure.

For me, the beauty of Bennington was that I came out greatly fired by the art. Because of its time and the merging of these tremendous powers of creativity, there was a force which penetrated the dance, and you became saturated with it, so that you came out devoted toward an art, not toward yourself.

I wonder if this could happen today. I'm not sure it could. Things are very fragmented now. At Bennington, everyone was zeroed in together, and even though there were different points of view, there were fewer to contend with. There were clashes, but they were very dynamic ones, not little, piddling, bone-picking ones. They were big, healthy fights about major principles.

Merce Cunningham

Bennington, 1939-1942

Merce [Mercier] Cunningham enrolled at the Bennington School of the Dance at Mills College in 1939, and it was there that Martha Graham first saw him and invited him to join her company. Cunningham had been at Mills the previous summer, when Lester Horton had been in residence. A pupil of Bonnie Bird at the Cornish School, Cunningham was in Seattle at the time. (Bird attended the Bennington School of the Dance at Mills College in 1939.)

At Mills, Cunningham took Louis Horst's Pre-Classic Dance Forms and performed a courante to music by Zoe Williams in the student demonstration at summer's end. He took Graham technique with Ethel Butler and Martha Graham, studied with Charles Weidman (students could concentrate in one method and sample the others), and danced with Weidman and José Limón in a demonstration performance of the "Men's Dance" from New Dance. *He also played percussion in a concert organized by John Cage.*

Cunningham spent his first summer at Bennington, Vermont, in 1940 as a member of the Martha Graham Dance Group and returned in 1941 and 1942. At Bennington he created the roles of March in Letter to the World, *The Christ Figure in* El Penitente *(1940), and Pegasus in* Punch and The Judy *(1941), and made his professional choreographic debut there in a joint concert with Jean Erdman and Nina Fonaroff in 1942, for which he composed* Renaissance Testimonials, *a solo, and three pieces cochoreographed and danced with Jean Erdman—*Seeds of Brightness, Ad Lib, *and* Credo in Us, *the last with a score by John Cage.*

Shortly after he arrived in New York, Cunningham began to study ballet at the School of American Ballet and taught his technique there after leaving the Martha Graham Company in 1945. Cunningham spent the summers of 1948, 1952, and 1953 at Black Mountain College in North Carolina—a period that coincided with his creative leap into new, uncharted territory and a radical departure from the Bennington concept of modern dance. In 1953, the Cunningham Dance Company was born.

Searching his memories of early dancing days at Mills and Bennington, Cunningham recalled Graham's invitation to him at Mills:

Graham asked me to be in her company. I was planning to come to New York anyway, and this was a good excuse to take to my parents. I simply said, "This is what I want to do. I'm going." I had always wanted to be in the theater. I'd studied dancing at the Cornish School and then at Mills those two summers, so I thought I'd just go to New York and see what I could. No school in New York that I was aware of then came close to Cornish, not in the kind of curriculum or allowance for what you could do. Nellie Cornish's spirit bore it all up, her energy and her interest in everything. She would almost never say no to something she thought was interesting, if it was at all possible to do. John Cage wanted to have a percussion orchestra, and she said, "Oh, I know where there are some percussion instruments." Just immediately, immediately. . . .

It was harder to be a dancer then than now in many ways, harder to find places to be trained. You could never make a livelihood because you earned no money from dancing, and so you had to earn it some other way. Every now and then you did a program. You did it by commitment, if you stayed with it, because it's a hard life—whether you're paid or not!

I enjoyed the summers at Bennington, the experience of being out of New York, going up there with the Graham company and all that implied, the fact that we were working but were in the country. It was a warm kind of experience. Louis used to say that Bennington was like a model dairy farm. I loved the outdoors. There was a beautiful green expanse with houses on the sides and then the main building, and you looked out across the hills. The working conditions weren't that easy, I suppose, but since it was my first experience, I wouldn't have thought of that. The studios weren't the best, the theater was very small, the stage terribly narrow.

It was a pleasant place for a young dancer, and it was also a working summer, some place you could go and do your dancing. You practiced, took classes, worked on a piece. The fact that there were performances of a new piece that Martha was working on made the summer a strong one in a way that, say, if you simply go away and teach or study is not quite the same. The performances enlarged the summer experience.

Bennington was drastically important for all the modern dance companies because it gave the choreographers a chance—as summer residencies have done for me—to have a company available to work with, which at that time was so difficult through the year.

Connecticut was bigger, there were more students, the whole thing was amplified. It became more of an enterprise. Black Mountain was an extraordinarily different atmosphere. It was a gathering of people, many with very different ideas. It was a place of exchange back and forth between people who were, so to speak, teachers and those who were students. There wasn't a single idea—whereas Bennington was a place where some one single person was giving out to all the students.

The prevalent idea [in the Bennington period] about dance structure was taken from musical structure. The Horst idea dealt with what he called Pre-Classic Forms and another course entitled Modern Forms—which weren't really forms; they were styles more than anything else. You had to learn the Pre-Classic Forms because those were the forms on which dancing was made. But my experience with Cage led me to the idea that musical structure *per se* was not necessarily what was involved, but that time was involved, so that you could use a time structure between the dance and the music. Louis' ideas didn't seem to me to be necessary. I didn't find them pertinent, although I admired him.

Mercier [Merce] Cunningham and Dorothy Weston at Mills College, 1939. Photograph courtesy of Eleanor Lauer, Mills College.

I have this impression of Louis: a large man sitting at the piano—from which he saw everything, while playing. He would look as though he were asleep, but he saw everything. I was impressed with the devotion he had to dance. It was part of his life in a big way, and he went on year after year teaching those classes, being involved in dance. Astonishing.

The use of music from the past always struck me as strange in all the modern dancers, particularly in the Humphrey world. For me, the most interesting thing about contemporary art of any kind is that it deals with contemporary things, and I always wanted in my work right from the start—even before Cage—to deal with the contemporary art that was around me and not to rely on something out of the past which gives someone something to hold on to. I had the feeling that we were in a different kind of world or getting into a different kind of world, which we certainly have, where you didn't have those things to hold on to. You could have them as ideas, but I didn't think it was interesting as a way to be involved in contemporary thinking. The Horst ideas I found simply to be nineteenth-century. I could see why he did it—he introduced many young dancers to the ideas of structure—but from my point of view the person who has dealt with those structures in a more interesting way is Balanchine. His ideas about those uses of structure were far more flexible than, say, what Doris Humphrey did or what the other modern dancers were doing. As for me, I thought there should be something else.

I liked Arch Lauterer very much, but I didn't always understand him. I did when he made something, but I had difficulty when he talked about it. Though I remember a lecture he gave at Bennington where he demonstrated something by walking around, and instead of saying you think in feet and inches he said you think in terms of human beings moving around. I thought that was impressive. I didn't think the sets always worked out, because some of his ideas got in the way, but the ideas about space on the stage were brilliant.

Martha was extraordinary to watch as a dancer, very beautiful. But soon something about the work and the technique began not to interest me. I was fascinated by her, not only by her way of dancing but, in her own dancing, by her way of putting things together, of phrasing. I didn't particularly like the choreographic things that I was involved with; those are the only Graham works I really know or even remember. I stayed on for several years, but I was beginning to work myself, and I had a little bit of ballet at the School of American Ballet during that period. I don't know how Martha felt about my working myself. It never came up, as I remember. But as far as studying ballet, I think she introduced me, or at least sent me, to Lincoln [Kirstein], to the school. I remember Lincoln said, "What do you want to study ballet for?" and I said, "Well, I like dancing, and I don't see any basic difference from one to the other." Essentially dancing is dancing. It can be good or bad, or it can interest you or not.

At the Cornish School I had had mostly Martha Graham's work. Bonnie Bird was a very good teacher, strict and clear, and I'm sure that the original work was clearly given and strong enough so that one had something to go on. One of the great problems with young dancers now or ever is that if they don't get the right thing in the beginning long enough for it to take hold, they're sunk. They don't have the strength.

It's hard to remember more specific things about Bennington. Those early pieces that I made are all gone now. I heard John's score for *Credo in Us* not long ago, and it brought nothing of the dance back at all. As for the dances of Graham's I was in, my memories of them are few, too. You see, I became involved in another world, not just with my own dancers but this other art world which was entirely separate from that, so that my work before that seems somewhat like high school. I don't mean to belittle it because it was an important part of my life. Still, the ideas I have been involved with since were—have been—very different.

Erick Hawkins

Bennington, 1938, 1940-1942

Erick Hawkins' first summer at Bennington, 1938, with Martha Graham. Photograph by Betty Lynd Thompson.

Erick Hawkins and Martha Graham danced together for the first time as The Principals in American Document *(1938); Hawkins was listed as an apprentice, appearing through the courtesy of Lincoln Kirstein and the Ballet Caravan. In 1940 he returned to Bennington as a member of the Martha Graham Dance Group where he created the roles of The Penitent in* El Penitente *and The Lover in* Letter to the World. *Earlier that summer, he had made his choreographic debut in the modern mode in a solo recital.* Liberty Tree, Insubstantial Pageant, *and* Yankee Bluebritches *employed original scores by Ralph Gilbert, Lehman Engel, and Hunter Johnson—a practice he has maintained in the years since.*

In 1941, Hawkins created the role of Punch to Graham's Judy in Punch and The Judy *and gave a second Bennington recital, this time with Jane Dudley and Jean Erdman, which included a new work for himself and Erdman entitled* In Time of Armament, *with music by Hunter Johnson. In 1940-1942, Hawkins was listed as Bennington faculty, teaching ballet technique.*

Hawkins first performed at Bennington in July 1936 as a member of the fledgling Ballet Caravan, on the occasion of its world debut. His roles included Hercules in William Dollar's Promenade. *Hawkins had begun his career at the School of American Ballet, where he had the opportunity of observing George Balanchine.*

No one ever watched Balanchine the way I did. I would see him do some things and tears would come to my eyes. I watched him line up those girls in *Serenade*. I don't know how much of an idea he had when he started, but I saw him feel his way into that. I sat at every rehearsal, and I even started to make a form of notation. I wanted to understand it by recording it in some manner. I hadn't done any choreography myself because I could hardly stand on two legs, but I knew I was going to be a choreographer. That's what I wanted. I was just rarin' to go. I remember saying to Lincoln [Kirstein], "We'll live on beans if you'll just let us find a way to do some performances." Within a week he called Lew Christensen and Eugene Loring and me together, and we just started to do.

[Ballet Caravan returned to Bennington the following summer, this time with Hawkins' first choreography, *Show Piece*, which had a commissioned score by Robert McBride. McBride was the first of several composers employed by Hawkins who later wrote music for Graham. It was at Bennington in 1937 that Graham saw Hawkins for the first time. She went backstage to meet him. Graham visited Hawkins backstage a second time when *Show Piece* was performed with symphony orchestra in New York. The following spring (1938), Hawkins began composing a ballet on the theme of the Minotaur. Kirstein was pressing him to finish it in three weeks.] I was just beginning to feel my way, and I said, "Lincoln, I want to go up and study with Martha Graham this summer. Would you lend me the money?" And he did. I happened to call the Graham studio the day before their June course began. I enrolled right away and asked to watch rehearsals.

There were no chairs, because no one was ever allowed to watch. So I sat in a corner while she'd rehearse after classes in the afternoon. One day she said, "Erick and I will come in here." And that was the first she said she was going to use me. She had used no man in all those years.

She had been working on the choral dances for *American Document* before I came down to the studio. It was the last of the dances she composed before the music was written. The beauty of the work was in the choral dances, I think.

That first summer at Bennington was very happy. Hanya was there, and Doris, and Charles. We performed in the Armory, and Arch made a very nice set with fins so that you could slide in and out at whatever entrances you wanted. I was in seventh heaven because Martha gave me a lot of dancing to do. I was sort of a special character, I suppose. I had the best suntan I've ever had in my life. The costume for me was shorts and a little jacket, and I didn't have to put any body makeup on. I have the feeling that was the first time—except for Ted Shawn—that anybody in modern dance ever did anything without a shirt on.

I was very euphoric. The first duet, called "African Duet," was made for me, and she gave me a solo at the end. Martha had a beautiful solo called the "Indian Solo." And I think the "Puritan Duet" was probably very good too. She had an ending where she used a lot of people, and that was one reason the intensity of it didn't quite work. Every once in a while you'll find some people who'll say they danced with Martha Graham back then, but she had difficulty getting them to do a skip across a stage.

The most important aspect of Bennington was being around Martha, learning from her; that was a terrific privilege. If I didn't learn anything else from her, I learned courage. Martha believes that one's life is for art, and I believe art is for one's life, and that's where we differ.

[Hawkins taught ballet technique at Bennington in the summers of 1940, 1941, and 1942. Pauline Lawrence played piano for him] Mary Jo and Martha Hill asked me, just to be nice to me. It was a dumb idea, just as when Martha [Graham] has ballet class in her studio now, because it was an obscuring of the issues.

I can remember how long it took me to get over some of the bad habits [from ballet]. I can recall how gently Martha tried to coax me to come back to something more integral. And she was right.

Bennington was Martha Hill's vision. I got mad at her when she strayed from that vision. She didn't hang on to it come hell or high water. She betrayed modern dance when she brought ballet into Juilliard. If you say that the virtue is *there* [in ballet] you're not going to get the respect *here* [in modern]. Eventually the ballet will go kaput, like Gothic architecture. It has to. You can't have eclecticism and have power. That's why Connecticut [American Dance Festival] is going downhill. It's going down the drain like a gurgle out of your bath, because there's no vision.

Bennington was the beginning of a Golden Age. In 1940 we did *Letter to the World* and *Penitente*. Of course *Penitente* was right up my alley. That archaic feeling was native to me, and I remember the most beautiful performance we ever did of it was the night before the first performance in the dining room at Bennington. Just Merce, Martha, and me. After that we started to work on costumes, but I suspect that night was the first pure crystallization of it after Martha composed it. Louis wrote the score first, and then Martha composed the dance.

That was about when I got going. I was now doing Martha's movement. I was learning and I was freeing myself. I was inventing. Ralph Gilbert came up to study music for the dance with Louis. I did the first solo concert up there of a piece called *Liberty Tree*, and it was a beautiful thing for me to have the opportunity to have the music written for me. There's a great sadness that that whole tradition of writing for the dance has dropped away. Even Louis dropped it long before the end.

From the very beginning I knew that if we were going to have a first-rate art it had to come out of our own blood, sweat, and tears. I could have used some Mexican music or African music or the Gagaku or anything and gotten a lot of exotic excitement—but that's not us. That's using someone else's vitality.

The way Martha Hill and Mary Jo got it going up there, that was real imagination, and whatever they had to do to persuade the people at Bennington to make it possible and give them money, that was marvelous. The people who went to Bennington lived on nothing. I don't know how, really. Mary Jo was very clearheaded about the business side. They made a place for those people they thought were going to turn out to be good artists. Martha Hill once said, "After all, I really started this for Martha Graham." I remember Hanya's *Dance Sonata*, and Louise Kloepper did one of the most beautiful solos, called *Statement of Dissent*. I can almost do a couple of the movements from it today. And didn't Doris do *Passacaglia* up there? And a revival of *New Dance*. It was a first-rate production.

If Bennington meant something it was in terms of philosophical ideas, not just a bunch of miscellaneous actions. It was going to relate to a direction of American art. Bennington was going into a whole new vision of what the dance could be in America. It was when America was being itself. It wasn't trying to copy some other, outer forms. The inner spirit was what was going to make a new art; the principle of just being one's self. It was such fresh passion. And the technique was very valid. Today, everyone thinks you can have some other vitality.

How to hang on to that pure vision is really quite a problem of human existence, whether it's political or whatever—how to hang on and be lucky enough to survive. If you really carried through one notion of what Bennington was, if you asked me why Bennington was so beautiful, I would say because of pure vision.

Mary Jo Shelly and Martha Hill, 1937. Photograph courtesy of Herbert Binzer from Bertha Rhea Desenberg Scrapbook.

Wigman-trained Tina Flade in her solo *Elegy*, performed at Bennington, 1935. Photograph courtesy of Tina Flade Mooney.

Images and Voices

Hanya Holm and group at Bennington, 1936 or 1937. Photograph courtesy of Bennington College.

HANYA HOLM

Choreographer, dancer, teacher. Bennington faculty, 1934, 1936–1939, 1940.

Hanya Holm with friends at Bennington, 1938. Photograph by Betty Lynd Thompson.

Bennington was a marvelous, relaxing atmosphere where you could be quiet inside. It was a privilege to be taken care of. You didn't have to wonder where do I get the money to pay my people tomorrow, or can I ask them for their participation, and what can I give them for an equivalent. All was provided. The bodies were there, and the worries were taken away.

Bennington brought together for the first time four people who were pioneers in their field and who were trying to develop the modern trend beyond a fad. It gave the whole modern dance movement a concentrated push. This was the beginning, and everything was embryonic. Now the dance has roots; then we had just about slithering feet. Bennington gave the dance a body.

Those were pioneering years; those times had a different feeling and texture. The people all did it for the love of it and nothing else. . . . There was nothing else.

ANNA SOKOLOW

Martha Graham Group. Choreographer. Assistant to Louis Horst, 1935, 1936. Bennington Fellow, 1937.

The fellowship was a big honor. The piece I made was a group dance on the theme of Mussolini [*Façade-Esposizione Italiana*], something I had thought about a lot but never had the chance to do. *Façade* was my statement about what was happening in Italy at that time, the Italian Fascists.

In that period I was finding my way to express what I felt about life. And what I felt about life had a very deep relation to the social times. It came out of the fact that I was born with the feeling that I would never forget my roots. Never. And the marvelous thing was that I was encouraged. At Bennington I was never told you can't do this or that. I was told you could do anything you want. Nobody censored you there. You could do what you pleased. The fellowship gave me the strength to go on and to do what I believed in.

The tremendous interest in modern dance was like discovering new artists in music or painting or literature. It was never a question in those days of being popular, but rather important. You felt you were part of something that was beginning to take form and shape and be recognized for the deep value it had for always.

Anna Sokolow in *Case History No.__*, ca. 1936. Photograph courtesy of Anna Sokolow.

Anna Sokolow, Bennington Fellow 1937. Photograph courtesy of Herbert Binzer from Bertha Rhea Desenberg Scrapbook.

Norman Lloyd, 1938. Photograph by Betty Lynd Thompson.

BEN BELITT

Observer, 1938. Bennington faculty, 1939.

The first modern dance I ever laid eyes on was the premiere of Anna Sokolow in Saratoga Springs in, I believe, the summer of 1936. I felt as though the top of my head had come off, or that I had seen a new color. It was an utterly unprecedented experience for me.

My contact with Martha Hill and Arch Lauterer at Bennington College was the lucky accident of my shift of focus from journalism to teaching in the spring of '38. They were very receptive to the addition of poetry to dance, and very seductive in recruiting me for the Bennington summer at Mills. I had an instantaneous sense that somehow dance was to representational movement as poetry was to prose—that the dynamics of immediacy—an open sensibility in which all was lyrically possible—those qualities that are innate to the poetry I prefer—were part of the dynamics of dance. The speeds and volatility of dance made it instantly attractive and intelligible to me. For me it was a "poetics" for dancers which had just come of age.

I am bound to say that the dance influenced my writing, gave it a new abandonment. I felt a great affinity with it; I felt at home with it. I was concerned with moving the spoken word rather than using poetry as a series of subtitles or a vague scenario that could be recited by a professional actor somewhere in the wings and used rhythmically by professional dancers. I wanted the dancer to speak and to move inside a matrix of language that mobilized the power of both—to see what stresses and opportunities developed in the tension of the two media and how they might affect dance. It was the dancer herself, speaking and moving the word, that was my concern.

I think all of the dancers thrived on the Bennington summers; it was the channel they had for bringing New York to Bennington, Vermont, and for the systematic extension of their permanent repertory. There were never any half-measures or any condescension in the relation of artist-teachers to student-dancers: *all* worked with equal intensity. The disciplines of intensive teaching and intensive composition were equally important to Martha, to Doris and Charles, to Hanya. No one was spared; nothing was foreshortened. I attended the technique classes of all—as an observer, of course—but Arch Lauterer, with his penchant for Bauhaus and the Germanic, had alerted me to the choreography of Hanya Holm during that first summer [1938]. At that time, Martha [Graham] remained rather remote to me. *American Document* was a revelation in its pioneering synthesis of speech and dance, but that kind of forensic and patriotic use of declamatory prose was not precisely to the point of my interests as an apprentice to the danced poem. I was interested in *penetrating* the time and texture of the danced word, moving *inside* of it, finding out what a verbal or choreographic phrase might lead to, and then how movement could extend the energy of the language in a functional union of the two. Later, I was stunned and delighted by *Letter to the World*, by Martha's instantaneous mastery of the two media, her penetration into the heart of an unprecedented genre. I came to believe that the collected works of almost any poet could constitute a kind of scenario—precisely as Martha invented (with Emily Dickinson's life and work) a dance-drama for the Complete Emily Dickinson; but no one took me up on that. It was one of the many breakthroughs made at Bennington which no one—with certain startling and spectacular exceptions (Valerie Bettis, Doris Humphrey, Arch Lauterer at Bennington and Mills College)—has pursued since.

WALTER TERRY

Dance critic, Boston Herald, *1936-1939;* New York Herald Tribune, *1939-1942.*

Bennington brought together—except for Tamiris—all of the leading moderns and their separate theories within the framework of modern dance and therefore exposed pupils in the Bennington center to several approaches to modern dance which they would not have gotten by going to an individual studio. People did not studio-hop in New York then. They didn't dare, and they didn't have the money. But up there if you were a Graham acolyte you might discover that Doris had something to say (or vice versa), which you would never find out in New York. So it expanded, even within the sacred circle, the students' awareness of the potential range of modern dance.

In a way Bennington was like the Politbureau. If you weren't at Bennington—"The Bennington Group" in quotes—you weren't in modern dance. You were on the fringe.

Bennington gave modern dance a national prestige, especially in intellectual circles. Because Bennington was a center harbored by an educational institution, a "citadel of learning," it gave modern dance a dignity it didn't have as a theatrical enterprise or a concert enterprise or a cult—which it was. Bennington helped to take modern dance out of the category of cult and put it into a respectable form of theatrical activity.

Major works of art were done under college auspices—something that could not have been afforded even in the least expensive little halls in New York. I think in a way, as a nurturing ground for modern dance, Bennington was more important than New York itself at a crucial time when modern dance could have died as a cult. Instead, it became a movement.

JOHN MARTIN

Dance critic, New York Times, *1927-1962. Bennington faculty, 1934-1937. Lecturer, 1938, 1941.*

John Martin, 1938. Photograph by Betty Lynd Thompson.

I think the most significant thing about Bennington was the idea of the festival. It was a daring thing to do. Bennington was a most inaccessible place, and the Armory was wonderful —completely wrong and therefore completely right. My great hope for it was that it would be kind of an American Salzburg, but of course people would come to Salzburg even if there wasn't a festival. For the people who came up there it was contact for the first time with all the creative figures in the dance field. The natives didn't come near it, of course.

I don't think Bennington made or broke anyone, but I think it was in a sense crucial. It brought the whole modern dance together in the public mind and in the dancers' minds. They became part of an entity instead of just separate people cutting each other's throats—which they continued to do, but it was a different throat cutting.

Martha and Mary Jo were remarkably teamed. Jo was not a dancer; Martha was. Jo was a fighter, a very good executive with a brilliant mind. She grasped things instantly, and then did them. Martha was more on the arts side—but no slouch! And they had fine support. Robert Leigh was a wonderful man. It couldn't have happened without him and Jo and Martha. That's why it hasn't happened since.

The spirit of Bennington was not transferred to the spirit of Connecticut. At Bennington you had the feeling that here it is at last; we can all work together without coalescing. You could keep your individual identity. The thing really ended in 1938. When they came back [from Mills] after 1939, it was all completely different.

I think Bennington fulfilled itself as well as was possible at that time. It was a very noble, notable experiment.

GEORGE BEISWANGER

Dance writer-editor, Theatre Arts. *Lecturer, Bennington, 1935, 1938.*

What was most remarkable about Bennington was the sheer experimentation that went on there. What I saw in 1935, and again in 1938, was a return to basic movement, pure movement. I remember how astonished I was that in Martha Graham's classes the pianist wasn't playing music of any sort, just making certain thumps or chords in the bass which picked up the emphatic point of the rhythm. The philosophy then was that every dance ought to be composed and then music composed to it. So that there was the same emphasis on primary values—independent, autonomous dance—as we saw later on in the avant-garde. Experimentation went on there in all the classes at a time when nothing was yet set.

Bennington assembled together apparently warring styles, and although they continued to war among each other, an outsider like myself was not so much impressed by the divergencies as the unities. That, in turn, produced a kind of collaboration, not just within dance itself but within the arts. Twenty years later they spoke of multi-media, but the essence of multi-media was being practiced at Bennington.

There was a unity also in the closeness between dancers and audience, the strength of an art-making community which included the audience. So it worked out as a kind of hothouse strategy. The art was being made, performed, listened to, looked at, and judged all at once. And the critics were forced to see new dance.

Bennington was highly conscious of itself as revolutionary. You knew then that you were doing something new and different, that you were making a basic cultural difference in the art itself.

ANNA HALPRIN [Ann Schuman]

Student, Bennington, 1938, 1939.

I have only one strong recollection of my Bennington days—going from Martha's class and doing contractions and releases, to Doris' class and doing fall and recovery, to Hanya's and stretching out into space. I have strong recollections because I felt each dancer was such a strong personality, and each took a strong position of their point of view. There was no interaction or correlation. As a 17-year-old, this was most amusing and confusing. I liked Louis' class because I could use my own imagination and create something for myself, even though it went through such a strict form.

The classes were big. I was lost in the crowd, which was all right and also dehumanizing for me. I went several years, and the impact was strong. The styles were powerful statements of each individual dance leader, and at some point I felt that I had to choose. I went the Humphrey-Weidman way. I liked the gravity play. I also became rigid within patterns and styles of movement as a result. My models were personalities and their points of view. Eventually I had to rid myself of these preconceptions and start all over again searching for fundamentals and natural movement.

We seldom interacted with each other. Our focus was on the teacher, and we were set up like mannequins in space and danced in the form of a military flank. And yet the movements were exciting, daring, and physically exhilarating. It was all so new, fresh, and revolutionary. The place was alive and vital with the energy of our leaders. The dance concerts given by our leaders were amazing and wonderful events.

At the time I did not have any other models, and it was enough to just spend all day dancing. I loved it!

Doris Humphrey and members of her group, Bennington, 1938. Photograph by Betty Lynd Thompson.

Guest Lecturer Margaret H'Doubler, 1938. Photograph by Betty Lynd Thompson.

BEATRICE SECKLER

Humphrey-Weidman Group.
Bennington, 1935, 1936, 1938, 1941.

It's hard to think of Bennington as separate from the experience of being with Humphrey-Weidman. It was because of them that I developed as many facets as I did as a dancer. Working with two choreographers who worked differently, two different approaches in a way, was very good for a dancer's development.

Bennington was the period when great works were done. I think probably they would have been done without Bennington, but Bennington may have made it easier, allowed choreographers to work with great concentration, which would have been difficult in New York.

The thirties was a time of worker unrest, and dancers, too, were demanding support. To some extent dancers identified with the working class, with the laborers, so we began to try to make it possible for dancers to make a living at dance. I remember not getting paid at all in those days, or getting maybe ten dollars for a performance. Bennington wasn't something that was isolated from everything else. It really grew out of the development of the modern dance, the ferment going on. It was part of the whole upsurge. It pulled it all together and perhaps even was the peak of the whole movement. And I suppose it established a certain kind of respect for the dance.

MARK RYDER [Sasha Liebich]

Martha Graham Group. Bennington, 1941, 1942.

Bennington was a place where the society acknowledged the value of your activity. That didn't happen anywhere else. Not even in New York—not in the general society. Bennington was a little world unto itself, a very nice ivory tower where everything was viewed in relation to the arts.

I've often wondered why at Bennington there was such tremendous creative output. Perhaps the modern dance was so much smaller at the time that it drew a much more dedicated and talented group of artists. I think dedication and talent go together. If you look at the names of the people who were there, it's a *Who's Who* of modern dance history. Almost everybody who was anybody was there at one time. That speaks well for the management. Today, there's no one place that could encompass that amount of activity and talent.
Of course, there were tensions. It was so many Montagues and Capulets. That was the height of the difference.

The Deweyan educational philosophy of involving people in the process as part of educating them to be able to do things was fundamental to dance. There's a Chinese proverb: "I hear and I forget; I see and I remember; I do and I understand." Well, at Bennington there was enormous provision for doing. If you wanted to get involved in something, there was a way to do it at whatever level you were capable of.

Dance does very well in the Deweyan mode because you learn by doing. It's what you do in class. Someone says, "Do this," and you do it. Other educational modes demand something more provable, something more verbal, written examinations, what they call "academic rigor." That would quash what is essential in dance. In stressing freedom, of course, some of the progressive educational people may lose discipline, but when you have a group of working professionals, all of whom are at the top of their form, this is not an issue.

The group that was attracted to Bennington was the group that was going to be influential. It was like a cadre that was trained in a certain way and then spread out across the country. Of course, dance was an activity whose time had come, so they had a place to go, so to speak. . . . The Bennington Cadre!

Louis Horst with Gertrude Shurr (left) and May O'Donnell. Photograph courtesy of Ray Green.

MAY O'DONNELL

Martha Graham Group. Assistant to Louis Horst, 1934–1936. Assistant to Martha Graham, 1938.

Bennington broadened my viewpoint. We'd see the technical demonstrations of some of the others up there. Of course we were pretty much bound together in our own little niche, protecting it because the others were protecting theirs. But you got to know people across the country, and you got the feeling that there was a concern and enthusiasm for modern dance all across the country, not just in New York. And out of these friendships and contacts it was possible to project the modern dance in a way that I think would not have been, or would have taken much longer, were it not for Bennington.

JEAN ERDMAN

Student, 1937, 1940, 1941. Martha Graham Apprentice Group, 1938. Choreographic debut with Merce Cunningham, 1942.

Bennington introduced me to the whole realm of the art of the dance, the indigenous American art. Bennington was the nugget of what was happening in dance then, and seeing it made me realize what was possible in dance and shifted my emphasis from acting to dance, because I was so excited about the creative possibilities.

The idea of modern dance is creative rather than imitative; it fosters revolution and reaction. With Louis Horst's teaching of composition and the Graham company's lecture-demonstrations with him, you began to get a creative thing going.

I realized that a dancer could work. You didn't have to wait for an author or a director or anything, and you did not have to be just an interpretive artist, but you could really create.

Martha Graham, 1938. Photograph by Betty Lynd Thompson.

Martha Graham, 1937. Photograph courtesy of Herbert Binzer from Bertha Rhea Desenberg Scrapbook.

ETHEL BUTLER

Martha Graham Group. Bennington, 1935. Assistant to Martha Graham, 1938. Associate, 1939–1942.

It's hard for me to separate Bennington out as an experience from the whole experience of being with the Graham company and being totally involved in teaching and dancing. I guess there was a more relaxed feeling at Bennington because I didn't have to struggle for a living. I was fed and housed, and we could work without the hassle of worrying about those things. That was terribly important then. Probably without Bennington, Martha [Graham] would have done nothing summers. She'd have gone home to Santa Barbara.

I doubt very much that beginners got very much out of Bennington except the general excitement that was engendered in the place—unless they had a strong sense of what movement should be. People who had dealt with their bodies before, who knew what the human body was capable of and had some sense of what was valuable and what was not, got a great deal out of it.

This was a very, very concentrated period, in which you slept dance, you ate dance, you drank dance. I have the feeling there isn't that same dedication now. My complete concern was what I was doing with my body, and the Graham company. We dedicated our whole lives to the Graham company, and when you are that dedicated you find strength where you don't think it's possible to find it.

I suppose it was easier being a woman, because you got taken out to dinner occasionally, so you ate a good meal every now and then. But I can remember days and days not having enough to eat, and weeks when I had nothing but a bowl of soup in a cafeteria, and that would be the meal of the day. But you never thought about it really. It never occurred to you to think that anyone lived differently.

SYBIL SHEARER

Humphrey-Weidman Group. Bennington, 1935–1938.

I had a chance to see, to meet, and to know everyone and their different points of view. All the important people were there. At that particular time, I think it was probably the most interesting place to be in dance, and I found it very stimulating to be where people were creating.

After I had established myself with these great artists, after I had stopped working with them as part of their companies, then I felt I had to go somewhere else to create, somewhere where I could put my roots down. I've always said you can't grow roots in solid rock, and New York is built on rock. I've been able to create the way I felt, but I have gone in a quite different direction from any of these other artists.

Sybil Shearer at Bennington.
Photograph by Sidney Bernstein.

Nona Schurman in *Running Laughter*, 1942. Photograph by Gerda Peterich, courtesy of Nona Schurman.

EVE GENTRY [HENRIETTA GREENHOOD]

Hanya Holm Group. Bennington, 1937, 1938. Associate Faculty and Guest Choreographer, 1942.

Bennington was an experience that could never be duplicated or repeated. I think it grew out of the need and the surge of the times. We were all different then; our values were different. This was a selfless devotion that doesn't exist anymore, except in isolated instances. We danced for nothing. We never asked if we would be paid. If Hanya asked us to come at two o'clock in the morning to rehearse, we would. We would do anything she asked. At that time, dance had no status economically or in any way. We had no rules, no pattern to follow. We didn't know of any other company, of how they functioned, whether we should or shouldn't be paid, how long we should work, how long we should rehearse. We had nothing to go by. So we just gave. The kind of devotion we had was the complete giving, a selfless giving, so that we got back something that you cannot get in quite the same way. All of us felt the investment Hanya made in us, and that we had made an investment too.

There were a lot of ways in which we were taken advantage of, and I expect that was so in the other companies. I don't believe in that. I feel people can be just as devoted without that. But somehow or other because dancers have a greater choice today of whom they are going to work and study with, they don't feel the kind of devotion we did. They feel that if they don't get just what they want from one person, they can go to another, or they can go to two or three at the same time. I think we could bear the hardships because we were doing something that gave us such joy and elation, such purpose in life. We didn't have time to get disgruntled. We were steady. We wouldn't think at that time of going to another studio to take lessons. It just wouldn't occur to us. I think we worked in greater depth. Today, the tendency is to skim off the top and not ever become involved. That made a big difference in the kind of people we were.

Hanya worked in a way that was very stimulating to creative people. We did a lot of the choreography ourselves. Hanya would say, for instance, "I want you to rush in from here, and when you get to this point I want you to fall," and we did it; or "I want you to come in turning in a bewildered way," and we did it. It was only in certain things that she gave us specific movements in group action, where all the people were doing the same thing, where she said exactly so. Even then, sometimes she would say, "I would like this kind of a movement," and we would all improvise it and she would choose one of ours and say, "there, like that." We felt we were choreographing, partly choreographing the dance, so we felt much more involved than when someone says to do this precisely so. That doesn't mean that Hanya wasn't precise about what she wanted. She knew what she wanted. One of the great things about working with Hanya was her ability to see people in space and to have people do something to that space and to relate to one another and to move groups of people.

Bennington was my first experience working in a dance community. While I worked with great intensity at Hanya's studio in New York, working in a community was a new experience. It opened up a whole new world. Those intensely rich summers meant a great deal to me. It was a growing up period, not only for modern dance, but for me, and I am sure for many others involved. A time of revelations!

LOUISE KLOEPPER

Hanya Holm Group. Bennington Fellow, 1938.

When you consider the state of the country in the Depression, and yet this modern dance kept growing and growing, and people performed, and sometimes you wondered how. Perhaps the time, with its grief and protest, was ripe for it. It just had so much vitality that nothing could stop it.

Esther Junger and José Limón rehearsing for their Fellow's Concert, 1937, on the green at Bennington. Photograph courtesy of Bennington College.

ESTHER JUNGER KLEMPNER

Solo recitalist. Bennington Fellow, 1937.

For the first time I was able to work as freely as I wanted, have music when I wanted, have music especially composed. The Bennington fellowship was a turning point for me. It got me started choreographing for groups.

Erick Hawkins, Doris Humphrey, Charles Weidman, Martha Graham, and Louis Horst at Bennington, 1941. Photograph courtesy of *Dance Observer.*

CHARLES WEIDMAN

Choreographer, dancer, teacher. Bennington faculty, 1934-1939, 1941.

One achieves things in association with places and with people. We achieved wonderful things in association with Bennington—as with Denishawn.

BETTY FORD [ELIZABETH BLOOMER]

Student, Bennington, 1936, 1937.

I remember being barefoot most of the time and wearing a leotard from dawn to dusk. Between classes we bounced around the green and tried to pick up as much grass as possible with our toes. That exercise was one of Martha Graham's orders. After the first few days our muscles were so sore we went up and down the stairs on our bottoms. We breathed, we ate, we slept—nothing but dance.

When I came in 1936 I had been studying dance for ten years. I already knew I wanted to be a dancer, but Bennington opened the doors for the much too brief years I spent in New York with Martha Graham. I felt I had been born to dance, as I think most of the students did. It was our whole life, and Bennington and Martha Hill helped focus our intense commitment.

Elizabeth Bloomer (Betty Ford) in Martha Hill's class at Bennington.

OTTO LUENING

Composer, Bennington College Music Faculty. Director of Music, Bennington School of the Arts, 1940, 1941.

In those days we were much more resourceful and much more modest. We worked with a small group of musicians which Louis recruited from New York. It was for reasons of economy that the group was so small, but that made it all very practical. We didn't have any tapes to use in those days. Bob McBride and I played in some of the pieces [e.g., *El Penitente*] because there wasn't enough money that summer to bring the musicians up from New York.

Louis and I got on very well. We both had a very broad background; we were pit musicians and had played in vaudeville. Louis and I agreed that we should not let people knock the music all out of shape just because they had a great gleam in their eye about movement. Louis wasn't a composer's composer; he hadn't composed the way the rest of us had, but he was an intelligent and a solid musician who devoted his talent to the dance.

The dancers didn't have any money, and they worked like dogs. Either they had to do it themselves or it didn't get done, and it was always a challenge how to outwit the fact that tuition wasn't sufficient to make the thing go. But they did it anyhow. They don't do things that way anymore. I guess dancers do, more than other artists, even now. In the old days, we cut the production to fit the size of the cloth, and then if you ran a deficit you felt quite righteous that you'd done the best you could.

Composers came because there was an opportunity there that didn't exist in many places. I suggested to Esther Williamson, one of my first composition students, that she should get involved with the dance, do everything she could, improvise, compose for it, accompany, because there weren't any opera houses in America where you could get fluency doing a lot of things, but with the dance this was possible. She did this first as a student, then on the faculty. A composer could get involved with the whole area of dance, and this was different from abstract music-making.

We had an enormous amount going on and very little to work with. Sometimes we had too little. You'd get really blocked by having four walls when you needed eight. It could get you down. You had a chance to collaborate with your colleagues if you were so inclined—in fact you had to, because otherwise nothing would happen.

There was a feeling that it could have been so much more.

JOSEPH CAMPBELL

Author, The Hero With a Thousand Faces, The Masks of God, *etc. Visiting writer.*

My first glimpse of the world of the Modern Dance was at a technique demonstration at the Bennington Summer School. Perhaps it was the suddenness of it all—but it seemed to me I was beholding a revelation of the Mankind of the Future. With an affirmation that came throbbing from a zone of inexhaustible life-abundance, those young students made visible, through the form and sweep of the human body, something of the potency of the pulsation of the blood, and the all-generating throb of time. The dead weight of circumstance, the accidents of the hour and the place, the imperfections of the flesh which condemn the majority of us to lumber along like beavers on the ground, dropped away, and there was Man, unshelled and glorious, in the full agony of life. The spirit was transported beyond the reach of words. Movement, meaning, and feeling were identical; verbalization would have been inane. I was beholding bodies hurled about by the volcano fires of the throbbing abyss out of which we all have popped—out of which the worlds have popped, out of which have popped the spinning demons of the atom and the galaxies of the night. I tell you, it was something. It was immense.

Wallingford Riegger, composer of *Trend*, 1937. Photograph courtesy of Herbert Binzer from Bertha Rhea Desenberg Scrapbook.

Doris Humphrey with Charles Woodford, Jr., at Bennington, 1938. Photograph by Betty Lynd Thompson.

Guest lecturer Curt Sachs, 1938. Photograph by Betty Lynd Thompson.

José Limón, Bennington Fellow 1937. Photograph courtesy of Alwin Nikolais.

Louise and John Martin with José Limón, 1938. Photograph by Betty Lynd Thompson.

Selected Readings
Contemporary Exponents of the Dance

Barbara Page

The school of the modern dance which was inaugurated at Bennington College during the summer of 1934 marks the beginning of a new era in the field of dance here in America. For the first time an endeavor was made to establish a center where important contemporary trends of the modern dance could be given analytic study and investigation. Rather than selecting some one type of modern dance, the curriculum provided an opportunity to study and to evaluate the work of five of the outstanding leaders in the field. The time spent with each artist was short, yet from even this brief contact certain deep-seated values emerged. Although each artist had a distinctly original approach to movement, a carefully formulated and individual philosophy of dance, there were certain identifying principles underlying the work of each.

All agreed that the dance should be approached as an art, rather than as a system of body-building exercises, or as a form of recreation. Dance which can be placed in the category of the arts gains its integrity only from an embodiment of certain fundamental principles common to all art. It must be a sincere expression of the creator's own convictions; it must be a concretion of the meanings and values which arise out of one's own time and experience. Another important issue lies in the organic or functional relationship between form and content. These two elements are inseparable except for the purpose of analysis. There is no one absolute or true criterion, yet each particular dance must possess a definite form. This form, however, is always to be conditioned by the purpose in hand and comes into existence as an emergent factor. The result is then a continuous and functional interplay between these two elements, form and content. The last point common to all the artists was the emphasis placed upon movement. The essence of the modern dance is not in the plot, the music, the costumes, the color and lighting effects, or the steps; although each of these elements at some time in the history of the dance has been given the dominant rôle. In the contemporary dance, movement stripped of all its accessories is the vital factor. The type of movement is dynamic and transitional in quality; it is concerned with the attribute of "becomingness" rather than with finality. A distinction is made between the use of natural and distorted movement. Distortion is used, not in the sense of the grotesque, but rather to mean exaggeration or intensification. Natural movement as used in the ordinary routine of living does not, in itself, supply the background out of which dance as an art can be created. A natural movement must be clarified, given direction and purpose, perhaps exaggerated to the point of extreme distortion, before it can be successfylly projected as an integral part of a dance composition.

Martha Hill at Bennington. Photograph through the courtesy of the American Dance Festival.

Before entering upon a discussion of the various artist's contributions, it is fitting to turn for a moment to the people who conceived, planned, and established the school. The three individuals responsible for its existence are Miss Martha Hill, the dance director, Miss Mary Jo Shelly, the administrative head, and Dr. Robert D. Leigh, President of Bennington College, the collaborator who made it possible to bring the project into actuality. Miss Hill and Miss Shelly, particularly during the past five years, have been prominent leaders in the educational field of the contemporary dance. Much of the present clarification and penetrating articulation of the principles and problems involved in the modern dance is due to their pervasive influence.

What were the outstanding contributions of each of the artists? It is appropriate that the specific significance of the work of Miss Martha Hill be discussed first. From a broad, extensive study of many types of dance, from experience in both the educational and concert field, Miss Hill has gradually evolved and crystallized an explicit and original approach to movement and to composition. Her techniques encompass a wide range of possibilities and are based upon the classification of movement which she and Miss Shelly had worked out together. The first premise concerns movement; its logical beginnings is in the torso. The analysis rests upon a scientific application of force. The chief concern is focused on the manner in which the movement is initiated and the resulting sequential changes which take place throughout the body. The method is distinctly creative. An attempt is made to give the student an understanding of the basic laws of physics and kinesiology in terms of their relation to the human body, to present an analysis of rhythmic, temporal, and spatial possibilities, and then to guide the student into an individual discovery of techniques.

The approach of Miss Hill to composition is also based upon creative procedures. In this aspect of her work she displays the rare combination of keen, scientific analysis coupled with artistic power. A thorough ground work in the elements of composition is presented, in the attempt to develop, first of all, skillful craftsmanship. Although great emphasis is placed upon structural principles, in particular upon the understanding and appreciation of rhythmic and musical form, yet the stress is never to the point of enslaving the composition. Perhaps more than any other one person, unless it may be Louis Horst, she is responsible for a new vision in the choice of music for the dance; for the less frequent anachronisms between music and dance, and for the more seldom appearance of the ruthless butchering of musical compositions by the dancer.

The first visiting artist was Miss Martha Graham. Great art, she feels, is an expression of a particular social order. To appreciate or to create it presupposes an understanding of the vital forces out of which the art emerges. To illustrate, a monarchic system of government will tend to develop a formal style. The Imperial Russian Ballet is a classic example. A republic, on the contrary, will have no one, set form in its art; instead it will be characterized by the struggle, the insurgence, the conflict, and the experimentations of its people. Our specific problem is to articulate and to understand the vital forces of contemporary life here in America, and then to find the quality of movement which is typically American. Miss Graham contrasts two types of dance: the one as an escape and loss of self, the other as an awareness and discovery of the self. The dance of Miss Graham is conceived out of the conviction that the essence of dance is "an integrative force, an inner concentration which creates energy." This point of reference stands in antithesis to the belief that dance arises out of an "excess of feeling which must find release."[1]

Her technique, then, in harmony with the temper and tempo of our contemporary life, is largely built upon a percussive type of movement, upon a beat or pulse and the subsequent changes throughout the body. She is concerned first of all with creating an awareness of the self; then later on, the use of space is introduced. She feels it is a dissipation of energy to attempt to cover space until one has first gained a sense of freedom through control of the self. The dancer must be trained to "purify" movement; a discipline of the most rigorous type is therefore necessary.

Perhaps, since the work of the next two artists, Miss Doris Humphrey and Mr. Charles Weidman, is so closely associated, it will be wise to consider their contributions together. Their theory of movement is built upon an organic basis. Movement is defined as the arc between two deaths: the points of polarity being the death of motionlessness, or stasis, at one extreme, and the death of destruction, or loss of balance, at the other. There are three distinct parts in all movement, the thrust or the effort of initiation, the suspension or moment of tension, and the period of recovery or relaxation. Rhythm can be approached from two aspects, the step pattern, and the breath or fall and recovery pattern.

The unique contribution of Miss Humphrey lies in the field of composition. Since this artist is particularly concerned with the inner meaning of movement techniques, she presented several short, concise compositional units which clearly incorporated her creative principles. Dance as an art, she maintains, possesses these three factors: rhythm, design, and quality or dynamics. Although all of these elements are always present, the purpose at hand determines which is to have the dominant rôle in a specific composition. The art principles which serve as guide posts through the compositional maze are reduced to three essentials: unison, succession, and opposition.

The creative process itself she described as an individual experience; one which must remain so until dance scores are more accessible. The first step in the creation of a dance is to think of all the natural movements which pertain to the theme chosen. Take, for instance, one phrase and develop all its possibilities. This point was illustrated by describing the creation of the well-known composition *The Shakers*. A square was chosen as the first design in space since this particular figure could be used to denote a restricted point-of-view. Variations in direction, forward, backward, sideward, around, and the diagonal, were all introduced. A distorted walk or a "waddle" became the principal movement pattern. Varying rhythms and changes in dynamics were added; and here in a nutshell was the composition. The second step in the creative process has to do with selectivity. What are the essential aspects? All else must be eliminated so that the final form is revealed stripped of any extraneous material. The third step, or the final problem, is one of projection. How can the form and meaning be vividly and clearly communicated? Only through a development of the "theatrical sense," through a wide experimentation in the theater itself, through painstaking criticism and careful analysis, can the tricks of artistic showmanship, so necessary to the success of the public performance, be revealed.

In conclusion, Miss Humphrey made a pertinent comment upon the dance of today. The modern dance, she feels, has a tendency to become too aggressive, too militant, where formerly it was too soft. To counteract this tendency she made a strong plea for the curved line to receive an emphasis comparable to that bestowed upon the straight line and the angle.

The specific contribution of Mr. Weidman's technique lies in his emphasis upon the qualities of strength and coordination. He enlarges and intensifies the range of the vocabulary. His locomotor work is strongly rhythmic and virile. In the realm of composition his emphasis is placed upon two elements, design and characterization. His foundations of design are very similar to those of Miss Humphrey. His particular approach to characterization is a functional one; any character portrayal is always an integral rather than an extraneous factor. He stresses the rhythmic and play elements rather than the serious or austere, in the experimentation with movement.

Miss Hanya Holm was chiefly concerned with an approach to movement. Outstanding characteristics were the meticulous attention to detail, the organic development of her progressions in movement, and the sound fundamental principles of physics upon which her work is based. Her students were directed by a vital personality into a rich experience of movement in which the elements of expansive, rhythmic freedom and exhilaration were dominant factors. Exhilaration is used not in the sense of a sentimental emphasis upon the "joy of moving," but rather as indicative of an emergent quality, something which "happens" to the individual during the course of the carefully evolved lesson. Perhaps it is not even a conscious objective of Miss Holm, but anyone able to hear the spontaneous remarks of the participants at the end of a lesson will

[1]The author is indebted for the articulation of this distinction to Martha Hill, *Symposium on Modernism in the Arts: The Dance*, p. 4.

testify to the presence of a valuable psychological adjunct. In contrast to the keen objectification and universality of the work of Miss Graham, in contrast to the delightful emphasis upon design and rhythmic play in the work of Miss Humphrey and Mr. Weidman, this particular type of dance seems to place the emphasis upon the integration of the individual in relation to art, upon the fuller realization of the self as a suitable agent through which universal forces can be released.

The course of Mr. Louis Horst in "Music Related to Movement" provided the rare opportunity for research and critical evaluation of the preclassic music and dance suites under the guidance of a noted and authoritative personality. Mr. Horst, more than any other one person, has revealed to the dance world the wealth of knowledge and appreciation of *form* to be obtained from a close scrutiny of these old suites. It is indeed fortunate that this dynamic musical genius has focused his interests and critical faculties on the development of the contemporary dance.

The term *inevitability* was the corner stone around which all his criticisms were built. In antithesis to the popular belief, his structural principles were firmly based in logic. The creator has a multiplicity of choice in regard to his first premise, but when that is once chosen certain "inevitable" results must follow. To quote one of his remarks on dance structure: "a duet, for example, must be so created that the movements are all essential for two people; so that away from each other the dance would have no meaning." His emphasis upon precise and authoritative movements, his sensitivity for design and occult balance in the use of space, and his profound musical appreciation all contributed a clarity, an order, and a breadth of vision for dance composition.

Mr. John Martin, the dance critic of the *New York Times*, in his course in "Dance History and Criticism," pointed out some of the flagrant shortcomings of the dancer. Of all artists, the dancer knows least about his own art, to say nothing of the other arts. Probably due to the fact that the instrument of the dance is the human body, a dance artist is very apt to rely upon personal charm or technical skill for success rather than upon a broad, well-disciplined craftsmanship as a necessary foundation.

An outstanding need in the dance field, he further stated, is the development of the dance audience. One manner of meeting this problem would be the adoption of an adequate dance script. Then it would be possible for dance groups throughout the country to study and to present the compositions of the great artists. First, it would be necessary to recognize that not all people who study dance have marked creative ability. The contribution of such students could then be focused upon the appreciation and understanding of the art. An analogy was drawn with the field of music. All students who study piano, or voice, or cello, etc., do not have the talent to compose or to be great concert performers, yet they can become leaders in the development of a more vital and appreciative musical audience.

Another point stressed had to do with the transitional periods of the colossal figures in the dance and the need for permanently retaining the representative compositions. To illustrate, Martha Graham, so far in the development of her art, has passed through three distinct stages: the first, a period in which she was strongly influenced by the dance of the American Indian; the second, the dithyrambic; and the present one, the moving toward a new type of classicism, a transition in which the artist is dealing more completely in terms of universal symbols. If audiences could be guided through these different developmental periods of a great artist, by skilled groups throughout the country learning the compositions representing the various phases, a new and clarified appreciation of the dance and of the individual artist would undoubtedly result. The dance film could also be of help. Perhaps its greatest value, however, lies in the opportunity it offers for the analysis of structural principles rather than in the dissemination of knowledge and appreciation among the laity.

Four cardinal enemies of the dance were indicated. The first is music; the dance is apt to lean too heavily upon its accompaniment. Dance should be able to stand alone; the accompaniment should provide only the frame or the setting. Another pernicious force at work in the field of dance is the literary mind. If an idea can be presented more adequately in another medium it should not be danced. Many social groups have been attempting to dance slogans. The result has been at times unfortunate. While all great art is in a sense propaganda, ideational content must transcend the realm of the literal to be effective in the dance. Self-expression, in the sense of undisciplined emotionalism, is also in disrepute. The self is important only as the agent through which the universal is expressed. The last of the four sins concerns beauty. To limit the dance to the beautiful is to shackle it, to place it within a narrow boundary rather than to allow it the full range of the aesthetic types. At times throughout the history of art certain restrictions have been imposed. Renaissance art was largely limited to religious subjects; Tolstoy attempted to force art to serve a moral purpose; various schools of thought have revered beauty as the high criterion. But why should art encompass only certain specified phases of human experience? A more vital, dynamic art will result if the artist is free to express the valid emotions of the time in which he lives.

This interesting and important dance experiment opens up many questions for the conduct of future dance projects. Will the original purpose best be served by continuing to give a cross-section of the contemporary dance, or will it be more effective to place greater concentration upon fewer types of work? Should the curriculum be enlarged to include such courses as "Aesthetics," and a "Study of Dance Scripts"? These questions and many more challenge those leaders of the modern dance who are imbued with artistic sensitivity and who are contributing breadth of vision and vitality to progress in this field.

The Dance and Today's Needs

George W. Beiswanger

Is there any deeper significance in the contemporary dance than a casual marshaling of new interests round an art which during the nineteenth century was largely confined to matters of relatively minor concern? The question is an important one.[1] Arts come and go. Many times they persist without contributing much to the society which continues to support them. That can be said, for instance, of the ballet during the greater part of the last century. Some people found enough satisfaction in its pursuit to give it a lifetime of devoted service. Many others enjoyed it as a means of amusement and recreation. But the ballet did not exhibit the signs of growth, its roots were not planted in the richer soils of the life of its day, and it accumulated no cultural surplus. There was little if anything to hand on to the coming generations except a set of techniques and the tradition of the art-form itself.

In contrast, one thinks of the painting of the fifteenth and sixteenth-century Italy, the drama of Elizabethan England, and the music of the classical and romantic schools. These arts occupied strategic positions in the cultural complex of their respective eras. Each one seized upon the basic values and gave them ardent and illuminating expression. It is to these arts that we turn when we want to find out what was deeply important for the men of those times.

The kind of significance possessed by the contemporary dance can be read in part by enumerating the particular impulses of our day which are finding in the dance a natural means of expression. If these needs are urgent, then the dance is, or ought to be, a major art.

I

The impulses which have generated the modern dance may be thought of as gathering around four contemporary wants.

Humanizing the Machine

There is the need to humanize the mechanical environment. We live in a world of machines. We not only have to operate them, but we have to operate with them. As Lewis Mumford points out in *Technics and Civilization*, it has been necessary for men to adapt and even to reshape the natural patterns of human activity in accordance with the imperious mechanical servants which he has created. All of this means that the modern man is inescapably beset by the problems of a mechanized way of living. He wants to know what the values are which may be extracted from it. He needs an art which, accepting movement as its medium, may show him how to compel the machine to administer to his deeper wants.

Here is reason enough for the increasing preoccupation of the dance with motion, with the techniques, the analysis, and the expressive value of body movement. No one acquainted with the discussions that go on in dance circles can help but reflect upon the thoroughness with which the study of body mechanics is being pursued. Even the terms used—impetus, acceleration, tension and release, sequential flow, dynamic line, pendular, axial, propulsive, metakinesis, and so forth—echo the conceptual framework of a mechanical world. Dynamics, the use and control of the spatio-temporal environment abstractly considered, the emphasis placed upon energetics, and consequently the very type of movement used, with its stress upon strength and its eschewal of beauty—suggest the analogy. The body is felt as a living dynamo, from the generating centre of which, in the torso, energy is propelled outward into explosive designs, compelling because of their power and their inevitability. The principle upon which there is unanimous accord—that the medium of the dance is movement as such—is essentially a bringing into emotional consciousness of that abstract concept of motion upon which the modern utilization of natural forces is built.

This is not to say that the modern dance is crudely machine-inspired, deriving its subject matter from mechanics and its symbols from an imitation of turbines and locomotives. We have already had the apotheosis of mechanized movement in the ballet. What the ballet did was to make of the body a machine. It became a cast-iron block from which the appendages were operated as if by means of a system of pulleys and levers. The esthetic aim of the ballet was the same as the utilitarian aim of nineteenth-century machinery—the greatest possible victory over the law of gravitation. To achieve this, the dancer was dehumanized: the face had to be held expressionless, and the body was submitted to a regime almost as rigid and monotonous and depersonalizing as that under which the factory worker toiled.[2]

The modern dance is a protest against this, a revolt against the mechanization of life which the ballet accepted and glorified. In its early romantic phase, the renewed dance sought refuge in the expression of personal feelings or in the idealized dances of primitive and ancient times. But as this resort proved less and less satisfactory, it turned increasingly to movement

[1] For much that has gone into the making of this article the writer wishes to acknowledge his indebtedness to two of his colleagues at Ohio Wesleyan University, Miss Barbara Page, professor of creative dance, and Dr. Laurence M. Sears, professor of philosophy. It has been in a series of discussions extending over a period of time that the interpretations presented here have developed. The responsibility of formulating them, however, in the particular shape which they have taken, is the writer's own.

[2] See the chapter in *Nijinsky* which describes ballet training in the Moscow School.

itself, to the body's natural modes of locomotion. The underlying urgency is apparent. Against the mechanical forces of modern life this new dance asserts the power of the body to move from within under its own impulse and for its own ends.

More than that, it suggests a new way of looking at machines. They are after all but extensions of the body. They are the products of human skill operating upon nature to create a new but not necessarily inhuman environment. And the rhythms which they demand of those who operate them are organic and can be made to function expressively. The dance by its cultivation of the values of dynamic movement is disclosing the good that is inherent in the machine. It is one of the arts by which men may learn to assimilate the mechanical to the natural and to control the material instruments of living.

What Is the Good Life?

What these ends shall be is another question and one for which there is no clear answer in the present cultural pattern. A world dominated by injustice, exploitation and war, a civilization daily moving toward lower standards of living, a devitalized culture in which the imaginative and creative capacities of men are unemployed and there is failure to achieve even animal satisfactions, can hardly be expected to know what the good life is. But it can be challenged to face the facts without smugness or hypocrisy. It is at this point that the modern dance is rendering important service. It expresses with complete honesty the spiritual impoverishment of contemporary life. It voices our anger at a culture which fails to supply the loyalties that give life meaning. It articulates our yearning for that which will feed the deeper wants. Its stridency and despair, its distortions and primitive supplications, its lamentations and satiric revulsions, and its hunger for ecstasy indicate how desperately we need something that will make life worth living.

And while it hardly knows what that something is, the modern dance has known from the beginning in what direction to turn. The renewal of the dance started with an awareness of the living organism (the "live creature," as Dewey calls it), its functions and its needs. This was the insight which led Isadora Duncan to slough off generations of traditional accretions and to return to the source out of which the dance originally sprang. Beneath all the confusion in her thinking one senses a natural and essentially right impulse. In the midst of a disorganized culture, reflected all too clearly in her own inability to order life around goals that could compel and discipline her powers, she turned to the body. It was here that the fresh start must be made. Just as Frank Lloyd Wright, looking out upon a stupidly industrialized world, went back to architectural fundamentals—the need for shelter and the possibilities of the natural environment—so Duncan turned to the demand of her being for satisfaction and to the fulfilment which she found in rhythmic movement. It is significant that both minds operated at the same time, in the same land, with the same needs at heart, to reach essentially the same conclusion. The business of art, and of civilization itself, is to administer to human wants—for shelter and significance, for home and a meaningful life.

The modern dance has not outgrown that. It still holds to the basic belief that men are animals, capable of free physical enjoyment. If the dance has functioned largely as an escape, it is at least an escape in the right direction. What the good life is will have to be found by taking this road.

The Personal Pattern

In a confused world, a world that does not know what it wants or what it ought to seek, there is no need more imperative than that of achieving some personal pattern of life. By what method can the centrifugal elements that constitute the contemporary man be held together long enough for him to move toward some desired goal?

What impresses one about the modern dance in this connection is the fact that it is not only deeply concerned with the problem but that it seems to find an answer in the method by which it creates its art. The ardent cultivation of technique which it stresses is more than an interest in form for its own sake. It signifies the endeavor to master the body by means of controls that are intelligently grounded. The distaste for loose "emoting," the vigorous rejection of self-expression as a legitimate end of art, the demand for complete self-awareness in an impersonal and objective sense, the consequent emphasis upon a mastery of the science of movement, with the exploration of complicated rhythms and designs, and the study of the achievement of the pre-classic forms of the dance—all these interests are essential phases of the pursuit of an ideal. In the dance there is to be such a complete organization of the human capacities of movement that the dancer will make of herself a perfectly controlled and free instrument for the creation of genuinely vital art.

The most important fact about this method of attaining artistic integrity is that it is not conceived in purely personal or in purely disciplinary terms. The modern dance rejects formalism as well as self-expressionism, for a more organic approach. The principles of design and the techniques of composition are not imposed upon the life of feeling by some external process of logic, nor are they subservient to caprice. They are generated out of movement itself as the means by which its natural meanings are to be brought to light and its natural values realized. The integrity which results is that of a dance *sui generis*. If the modern dance differs from its romantic parent in emphasizing the necessity of knowing what it is about, it holds with the romantic dance and against all ossified classicisms that techniques are but ways in which the live creature gets done what it most wants to do.

These techniques are shaped and reshaped in experience itself—at the points where inner impulse meets outer conditions and a practical adjustment is made. The essence of the dance is no longer located in culminating moments of static beauty but in "transitional movement," in the on-goingness of articulated action. The modern dance does not hold that art is what the individual can extract and salvage from the flux of things. Art is activity, is life itself, intensified, clarified and given meaning. Its values are generated in the flux. Change, which men have feared and from which they have fled to perfection, has become for the dance (as well as for the other modern arts) the opportunity to create a more continuous and sustained experience of that which is good. Man "perches"[3]—to use James' expressive word—only to gain insight, power, and control for further "flights." The dance is but a segment of life. It does not begin with itself nor end there. Its meanings are continuous with and intrinsic to the larger frame of experience from which it has been taken, and it offers to that larger life not merely an ideal but a mode of living.[4]

In effect, then, the modern dance is trying to see not what it can save from chaos, but what it can do with chaos. If life is disorganized and confused, it is not because it is basically that way, but because men have not explored its hidden capacities for order. Movement is implicitly alive with rhythm, proportion, measure, harmony, unity, and meaning. The modern dance is helping to make these values available for organized living through its mastery of body techniques. By the very nature of its approach to the problem of art-creation, it becomes an exemplification of the art of life which alone can save men from their present distress.

Modes of Associate Living

The debacle of the individualistic or atomistic way of living, and the urgent necessity of finding communal solutions for our problems, has made imperative an art that will help men to learn the modes of associative living. Such an art the dance is. More than any other art it is inconceivable apart from persons working together in a group. During the centuries in which the artist, working for the most part alone, created those masterpieces of the human spirit which, as Joseph Wood Krutch suggests, constitute the sole basis for judging western civilization "a success," the dance lay dormant, chiefly because it could not flourish under an individualistic ideal. So impossible was it under such conditions for the dance to place itself at the center of life that we hardly know what the dances of the last two or three centuries actually meant in terms of human values to those who danced them, although our information about rhythms and step patterns and accompanying music is quite full. All that one can say is that when the creative energies are forced within narrowly individual channels, the dance can function only as a form of folk recreation or else as a luxury art.

It is no secret that the dance has had more significance than this in other forms of culture. We hardly know what kind of dancing the primitives did or the early Greeks. But we do know what they danced: the crises of birth and death, of famine and war; the round of the seasons and the periods of human growth; the myths, legends, morality, faiths and religion of the group. The dance has been important when it has had something of communal import to say. This fact the modern dance has instinctively sensed from the beginning. In most of its manifestations, from the early groups that gathered around Isadora Duncan to the Bennington School of the Dance, it has been a reflection of the twentieth century desire for a renewal of the collective life. It has voiced, however inadequately, the need of men to depend upon each other, the need of finding together the solution of our problems, and the need of "a common faith."

One can, I think, say even more. The modern dance is itself a study of social relationships. It tries to explore what happens when two or three or five or a dozen people work or play together in terms of common interests and purposes. Unlike the ballet, where the number of dancers on the stage is, strictly speaking, immaterial, since each is a duplication of a standard pattern, the character of each dancer and the quality of relationship between the dancers in a group and between the dancers and the audience are matters of real concern. The process of sharing enters genuinely into the creative act, and the product is inexplicable in purely individual terms. In method and aim, then, the modern dance is related to the collective needs of our day. One suspects that it can do much to generate the power and to project the patterns by which these needs are to be met. It is at least of significance that the individuals and groups most concerned with the creation of a vital community life and a renewed state are going to the dance for vision, courage and strengthening of purpose, and that the modern dance feels most clear about its own purposes and goals when dancing for such people.

II

It may seem strange that an art with so much to say should find itself at the present moment in a state of confusion, with conflicting movements and philosophies, with no clear idea about itself, its purpose and program, and with an urgent sense of the need for some synthesis which will give it direction and a goal. The reason for this confusion is, however, not difficult to locate. Needs furnish the occasions for art and much of its substance as well. But they are not sufficient in themselves to make art. Needs are too obvious on the one hand and on the other hand too vague. To say that the dance must explore the potentialities of its own medium, must articulate the values inherent to the human body, must master the tumult of feelings, and must relate itself to the social scene is, after all, to speak in truisms, and to offer no guidance.

The dance cannot live on such generalities. If it tries to do so, one of two fates is inevitable. It can go the way of romantic art. Romanticism begins by affirming the passional needs—for satisfaction, for freedom, and for a more natural and sustaining group life. But because it fails to devise the techniques by which yearnings are translated into specific wants and ideals are transformed into plans for creating the good life, it is forced to turn in upon itself, to feed emotion with emotion (a self-devouring process), and finally to dissolve into sentiment and futility.

[3]It is perhaps superfluous to explain that this word is not used in its ballet connotation.

[4]The dependence of the above upon Dewey's *Experience and Nature* and *Arts as Experience*, and Edman's *The World, the Arts and the Artist*, is, I take it, obvious.

This is a road, the danger of which the modern dance recognizes, although there is Ted Shawn to evidence how attractive it seems in comparison with the task of facing real problems. But the modern dance seems less aware of the danger which lies in another direction. Its strong scientific and technical interests may commit the art to the business of exploiting its medium as such. That in fact is the answer which some are giving to the need of a common point around which the dancers of all schools may rally: Recognize that the dance as a movement art can admit and welcome anything that is technically possible. Reconcile conflicting theories by acknowledging the expressional potentialities of any type of movement. Bring together the divergent schools by pooling the resources of the medium, even those of rejected traditions, in a public treasury of dance language and technique.

No principle could be more persuasive theoretically, or less vital as a matter of actual practice. Granted its truth, what drive is there towards a meaningful synthesis in the mere admission that any movement has possibilities? The trouble is that a synthesis of this sort fails to take into consideration the radical nature of the issues out of which conflicting types of art arise. The qualities which distinguish, say, the Gothic from the Baroque, the Victorian from the International Style, or the ballet from the modern dance, are not primarily matters of the medium at all. They are matters of meaning. The styles say different and basically contradictory things about human values and the meaning of life.

If the modern dance is to find itself as a major art, it will probably have to decide what its philosophy is, or articulate more clearly the beliefs which are implicit in its peculiar qualities as a twentieth century art-form. The synthesis which is awaited, if it comes at all, must grow out of a common store of shared meanings that touch upon the important issues of today. In short, the dance faces the problem of subject matter. With the most expressive of all mediums at hand and with a freedom in its use that makes almost any attainment possible, the dance can and will occupy a place as a major art only to the extent to which it finds something to say that is deeply significant.

In making such a statement, one obviously pronounces dogmatically upon an issue that is highly controversial. But the issue is controversial largely because our thinking upon it has been confused. The belief is widely held that the modern dance owes the freedom and creative power which it possesses to its rejection of the representative function of art, a function which debased and devitalized the ballet. This view does not stand up under close analysis. As has recently been pointed out in the pages of this magazine, the nineteenth century ballet consisted of interludes of highly stylized and abstract dancing placed between sections of pantomime upon which the burden of whatever representation there was really fell. The ballet ossified not because it was burdened with a message but because it wasn't. As the meanings which originally gave it vitality staled and lost their appositeness, the significance of these meanings faded and became merely "literary." The movements and postures, which in the beginning had embodied important things, came to say almost nothing at all in themselves. It was at that point that the ballet ceased to have subject-matter, and it was also at that point that it ceased to be an important art.

This is what Fokine and Diaghileff dimly sensed, once they had felt the impress and caught some of the significance of Isadora Duncan's revolution in the dance. What they tried to do for the ballet was to restore its expressional function and to give it back to a general audience. But by the beginning of the twentieth century the traditional themes had become barren and the formalized patterns could not easily assimilate the materials of contemporary life. The moral of their effort can be read in tragic terms in the life of Nijinsky, whose career was one burning search for something significant to say and someone to say it to. What he needed was a subject-matter that was rich, human and meaningful enough to match the magnanimity of his genius. All that was given to him by the society in which he and his art moved was a distorted view of sex, a yearning for the white light of "Truth," and a tennis game. Nothing to dance and nobody to dance for—those are the words written over his living grave.

The question, then, is not whether the dance shall dispense with subject-matter, for to do that is death. The question is how extensive and rich, or how narrow and poor, the meanings shall be which it finds to present. If the dance, as perhaps no other art, is sensitive to present needs, if indeed its rebirth is a result of the urgency of these needs, the answer seems almost inevitable. It is difficult to see how in the long run it can escape the larger themes. How far the dance can go in expressing the meaning of toil, exploitation, injustice, frustration and the hungers that go unsatisfied, or project the patterns by which the good life and the beloved community are to be built, is not a question for the layman to answer. If the dancer participates actively as an intelligent and socially-minded person, thinking things through and choosing sides as one's values dictate, that would seem to be enough.

The danger to art is not going to come from allowing its sanctuary to be invaded by these realities. The danger is rather that an evasion of issues will leave art with nothing to say. If the dance is looking for that which will straighten out its confusions and open the way to an organic and vital synthesis, it can do nothing better than confront itself with its own most serious and impelling urges. This means a closer and more conscious entanglement with the problems that face contemporary men: personal, social, economic, cultural, and ultimately spiritual. Those who are immersed in the struggle for a new world may be wrong in some of the methods by which they would commandeer the abilities of the artist for specific programs and ends, but they are not wrong in their conviction that important art comes only from men and women who possess values and beliefs and who have the ability to make choices in their art whose consequences do not stop short of group life and social implications.

New Dance

Doris Humphrey

As far back as I can remember, group activity has always fascinated me. My early impressions of games are not connected with the participants so much as with the audience—the surge and mass-uplifting and the concerted cry. I remember also the wheel and sweep of birds in flight, the endless counterpoint of people walking on the streets, and once a battalion of ventilators across the roofs, whose helmets turned rhythmically with the wind as from one enemy to another.

From whatever source came this liking for the interplay of units moving together, I know that it gave added point to my conviction that it is only the group composed of individuals which can say anything significant or stirring about contemporary life. Comment on our times through group dancing has always been my sole aim, even though the work I do today may seem quite different from what I did when I gave my first recital in New York apart from the Denishawn company.

The aim had to wait until I was able to build a new technique. I feel that the old technique was foreign in every way to the world we live in and must be discarded. Therefore the early dances had to be confined to experiments with form and movement. For me this consisted of rediscovering and reapplying the natural laws of movement to group composition. The ballet group had been based on the social scene of which it was a part. The leading dancer was either King or Queen, the next important dancers served as all the ranks of nobility, and the *corps de ballet* was just as unimportant as the "rest of the people" were at that time.

When the modern dancers began to work, that social scene had changed radically. There were leaders, to be sure, but the group, which corresponded with the *corps de ballet*, grew in increasing importance until now group action is far more important than solo action. Even my earliest dances stressed the group and used the individual entirely in relationship to that group. This was really a difference between a democracy and an empire and obviously required a complete reorientation. New forms had to be discovered which could express concerted action and replace the solo system of the ballet.

It is only within the past two seasons that I have been able to take that form and use it in its largest sense. Dances on the recital stage were considered long ballets if they occupied ten or twelve minutes; the usual dance was about five minutes long. But the new trilogy I have composed, which includes *Theatre Piece, With My Red Fires*, and *New Dance*, requires an evening and a half for presentation, unless I had occasion to do it as a *Mourning Becomes Electra*, beginning in the early evening. In these three dances I have been able to take the forms I had been experimenting with and mold them together in the same way as a symphony. Since I was primarily interested in commenting on social experience, the purely abstract form would not do. I combined it with drama. These are no longer recital dances; they are theatre dances.

I had an accumulation of things to be said which could no longer be confined within the limits of a short dance. There was the whole competitive modern world in upheaval; it must be expressed and commented upon and it was too large a theme for fragments and episodes. Whether it was my personal life within this world or my sense of technical sureness that impelled me into these three dances is difficult to say. I believe it was both. In almost the entire dance world I had seen nothing but negation. Anyone could tell you what was wrong but no one seemed to say what was right. It was with this mental conflict that I approached *New Dance* first, determined to open up to the best of my ability the world as it could be and should be: a modern brotherhood of man. I would not offer nostrums and I could not offer a detailed answer. It was not time for that, but it was time to affirm the fact that there is a brotherhood of man and that the individual has his place within that group.

When I had stated this in *New Dance*, I could return to the theme of life as it is: in business, in sport, in the theater, and in personal relationships. This I did in *Theatre Piece*. When I had finished these two, the first in symphonic form, the second in dramatic form, there was still one element missing to round out the picture. These two had treated of social relationships and there still remained the theme of love, of the relationship of man to woman. This too is a universal theme, even though the modern cynic is inclined to scoff at it. This I treated in *With My Red Fires*.

It is easier to describe this more-encompassing form in a specific case than in theory. Let me describe *New Dance* briefly. It was, of course, the dramatic idea that dictated the form throughout the dance. It was generally, to be a dance of affirmation, progressing from disorganization to organization. The group was to be at first an audience. To suggest this, I used an arrangement of blocks in the corners of the stage, upon which they stood as though at an arena, unconvinced but interested. Within this arena, Charles Weidman and I opened the dance. When we had stated our themes, it was necessary for me to draw the women into my orbit and for Mr. Weidman to draw the men into his. This was a partial integration but could not be completed until the two groups had been fused. When this had been done, there was a combined group dance of celebration. This was a group integration but I was not satisfied to leave it at that point. The group, though fused, was still composed of individuals, and the last section of the dance was devoted to an expression of their personal themes in relationship to the group. Naturally, since all members were participating, there was no longer any necessity for an arena; there was no audience. For this last section, then, and the only place in the dance where the action was momentarily broken, the blocks were moved into a pyramid in the center of the stage to focus the action and stress this unity.

Doris Humphrey at Bennington.
Photograph by Sidney Bernstein.

In the "Prelude," since I wished to convey a sense of incompletion, I chose the Broken Form, by which I mean an unfolding continual change, with contrast but very little repetition. (This is the same form that Mr. Weidman and I used in *Rudepoema,* where a movement was done several times and then discarded, giving way to a new one.) By this means I was able to present the main themes of the whole composition, which were later elaborated in "First Theme," "Second Theme," and "Third Theme;" fused in "Processional" and "Celebration"; and re-expressed by members of the group in "Variations and Conclusion."

The movements used in the "Prelude" were by no means spontaneous. I had a very clear reason for them. Since the main direction was to move from the simple to the complex, from an individual to a group integration, I consciously eliminated any free use of the hands, arms, head, and torso, and concentrated on feet and leg themes, which were the first to be used in the primitive dance and the folk dance. The conscious use of the other members of the body was a sophisticated development at a much later time. Therefore, until the group integration had been achieved, the feet and leg themes seemed more correct and expressive.

These were developed in the following three sections, called "First Theme," "Second Theme," and "Third Theme," through the two essential movements of the body: the change of weight and the breath-rhythm. Each of these three had to have a loose form, broken, unbalanced, not symmetrical, and must have an inconclusive ending, since each was a fragment of a whole. In the sequence of dramatic idea, no conclusion was reached until "Processional" and "Celebration." Each part merged into the other, therefore, in form as well as idea.

For these, of course, the Broken Form would no longer do. Those themes which had been stated were to be conveyed to a group, and a group never accepts immediately en masse. It must be swayed and inveigled and molded; it both refuses and accepts. For the "First Theme," then, I used the Cumulative Form by which only gradually by accretion the whole group comes to perform the theme.

"Processional" uses the Cumulative Form once more and in movement brings the themes to a head; in dramatic idea brings the whole group to an integrated whole. I chose a slow tempo for this because it gives a sense of greater control and, theatrically, is obviously in sharp contrast to the preceding sections. It was here, too, that I used symmetry for the first time as the best way to express cohesion and completion.

The groups have now fused and break into a "Celebration," which is built in fugue form, joyous in character. The fugue was eminently suitable to express a harmonious chorus wherein no member was more important than another. It is a short theme and goes directly into a square dance, which is again consciously symmetrical. I could have used several symmetrical forms here, but chose the square dance because at a moment of climax, forward movement is the most powerful. Other forms do not have that direct impact.

Having thus unified the men's group and the women's group, one more section was necessary. Too many people are content to achieve a mass-movement and then stop. To me it is too cold a regimentation. I wished to insist that there is also an individual life within that group life. The dancers here work in a line in a whirling-star pattern around the central pyramid. I could have allowed the two lines to remain in one place to form a path for the new dancers who now come in and perform briefly their own personal themes. However, by having this line whirl and by having the new dancers enter from different directions, monotony was avoided and a greater space and excitement was achieved. In this "Variations and Conclusion," I used the Repetitional Form where the group performs the same movement over and over. The brief solos were in Broken Form against the *basso sostenuto* of the group.

Fusion of various forms within a single work can, I believe, broaden the field of the modern dance and give it a new life and a new potency. Solo dances flow out of the group and back into it again without break, and the most important part is always the group. Except for an occasional brilliant individual, I believe that the day of the solo dancer is over. It is only through this large use of groups of men and women that the modern dance can completely do what it has always said it would do.

New Dance and the other two works which I have not described are no longer a series of episodes strung along in a row. They are a cohesive form in the way that a symphony is and need neither music nor story as crutches to support them. Both *Theatre Piece* and *With My Red Fires* treat more specific details in dramatic form, even to the degree of having roles, but they are always stated in movement, not in acting as we know it in the theatre today.

I like to think of this as a new form of theatre using all the materials that belong to the theatre. Three acts of words spoken from various divans and chairs seem too often sterile. "Actions speak louder than words" may be a trite phrase in its present usage, but nevertheless it has the approval of modern psychology, indeed of all modern thought. The purpose of the modern dancer is to shape and form that movement into vital drama.

Artists and Audiences

Charles Weidman

"Modern"—what does this word mean? The dictionary defines it as "pertaining to the present time," but it is not enough to be merely existing in the contemporary world. Active life demands that we be mentally and emotionally aware of the world's continual change and realize the constant progressions and retrogressions.

The artist who attempts to escape the present either by delving into the past or the future is running away from his "center of being." But it is not enough for the artist alone to assume his responsibilities as mentor and preceptor. His audience also must do so, especially in the case of an artistic form which concerns the theater.

The concert dance lives only while it is being presented. It cannot be referred to later in files or books. Therefore, both the stage and the auditorium have equal importance. Those who sit in the "house" must also be of today. They also must be conscious of and sensitive to their age, for only then will the dance-work come alive and project its full meaning and value as the artist wished.

Modernism in the dance requires that we, both artist and audience, be not blind to the life that surrounds us nor shut ourselves off from it into fantasy and romance. It demands that we be part of it and merge with it. It calls upon us as artists to become mouthpieces for its expression; to cease being static and self-satisfied; to be ready each year to say new things and to say them in new ways; to keep our mode of expression fresh and vital; and to remove the dance from pleasant entertainment that lulls us into vague nostalgia, to a strong living art that touches us powerfully as we are today.

Charles Weidman at Bennington, 1936 or 1938. Photograph by Sidney Bernstein.

Declaration

Doris Humphrey

My dance is an art concerned with human values. It upholds only those which make for harmony and opposes all forces inimical to those values. In part its movement may be used for decoration, entertainment, emotional release or technical display, but primarily it is composed as an expression of American life as I see it today.

This new dance of action comes inevitably from the people who had to subdue a continent, to make a thousand paths through forest and plain, to conquer the mountains and eventually to raise up towers of steel and glass. The American dance is born of this new world, new life and new vigor.

I believe that the dancer belongs to his time and place and that he can only express that which passes through or close to his experience. The one indispensable quality in a work of art is a consistent point of view related to the times, and when this is lost and there is substituted for it an aptitude for putting together bits of this and that drawn from extraneous material and dead methods, there can be no integrity.

Since my dance is concerned with immediate human values, my basic technique lies in the natural movements of the body. One cannot express contemporary life without humanizing movement, as distinguished from the dehumanization of the ballet. The modern dancer must come down from the points to the bare foot in order to establish his human relation to gravity and reality.

I wish my dance to reflect some experience of my own in relationship to the outside world; to be based on reality illumined by imagination; to be organic rather than synthetic; to call forth a definite reaction from my audience; and to make its contribution toward the drama of life.

The Future of the Dance

Martha Graham

The future of the dance lies not alone in the hands of the dancer; it is equally in the hands of the public. No real artist is ahead of his time—he *is* his time—but the public is sometimes unwilling to desert nostalgic memories of an earlier day and face the present as the artist must.

Dance cannot exist in the vacuum of the studio. It is not an ivory-towered art. It is one of the arts of communication. Real "theatre" is that moment of contact between performer and audience. It is the spark which electrifies the performance into life. It cannot take place, no matter how brilliant the action behind the footlights, unless the audience is also alive.

I have repeatedly insisted that the so-called "modern dance" is not a contemporary phenomenon. Always there has been some dancer who was dissatisfied with the existing forms, some dancer for whom the traditional style became too sterile and who broke it open.

When the ways of us who have been classed as "radical moderns" become, through often-repeated usage, too tight and too narrow, when they have lost their fresh contact with life and have fallen into barrenness, some dancer will break them to create new patterns and we will, in turn, be the denied traditionalists.

In this constant reorientation, and revaluation, in this repeated returning to original sources lies not only the future but the power of the dance.

I do not mean by this, for one single instant, that technique can ever be denied. Technique is the craft which underlies the art. Many excellent craftsmen are not great dancers, but *every* great dancer is an excellent craftsman. It does not matter in which school of technique a dancer is trained, the essential thing is that he *be* trained. It is not the techniques which become worn and stale. Use preserves technique and keeps it constantly fresh. It is the content of the traditional dance, the style of it, which, after a time, builds walls around it. These walls are what, from time to time, must be knocked down, but technique always stands.

The future of the dance lies—as the great past of the dance lay—in the continuance of the line of dancers who, trained and skilled, are not afraid to bring fresh values to their work; and it lies in the growing number of audiences who are willing to trade their nostalgic memories of the dance of the past for the stimulation of an art form that is, as they are, alive in the present.

The Dance Completes a Cycle

John Martin

With the war always in the foreground, it is dangerous to prognosticate, but the new tendencies in the field of the ballet are distinctly healthy and heartening for the future. If it seemed curious back in 1909 for the great art of Fokine and his colleagues to come out of the supposed barbarism of unconsidered Russia, it will seem equally so that the art of the next period of the ballet's greatness bids fair to stem from stolid Britain and commercial America. That, however, is exactly what is happening before our eyes.

It is possible to take three particular choreographers as indicative of what lies immediately ahead, not because they are the only ones but because, first, they have scored notable successes and are consequently, in these early stages of a new period, influential even beyond their specific accomplishments; and second, their directions are manifestly those of the times. They are the English Antony Tudor and the two Americans, Agnes de Mille and Eugene Loring.

Of the three, Tudor—naturally enough, since he is European—is most within the tradition, for all that he violates it at every turn. He is the next logical step beyond Fokine in the progression of periodic revolts within the ballet by which it has grown. It is always the same revolt, to be sure, directed against the meaninglessness which accumulates from overrefinement, overformalization, overclassicism; and its end is always a return toward function, though with varying and, indeed, increasingly vital manifestations in each epoch. With Noverre in the 18th century the keynote of the reform was imitation of nature, with Fokine it was expression, with Tudor it is evocation—all developments of the same theme in accordance with the emphases of the times.

More than anybody who has gone before him, Tudor deals in character and individual psychology; his treatment, however, departs altogether from any naturalistic representationalism that that might suggest and aims rather at the creation of sharp images of experience. His technical basis is the traditional academic ballet but his vocabulary distorts and denies this basis in order to shape it to the presentation of heightened emotional states and conflicts. In his searching of state and conflicts he is merciless; never before has the ballet had so much of human intensity about it.

Miss de Mille's return to function is entirely unfettered by any relation to the direct line of ballet development. She cuts across it with complete independence, strongly influenced by the self-contained logic of the radical American modern dance. The academic technique forms part of her classroom practice but on stage she either repudiates it entirely or employs it for period purposes. She turns her back wholeheartedly on the spurious elegance of tradition and creates people who are of the earth, racy and colloquial. Some of the artists of the Ballet Russe have pronounced her vulgar, and if that word is returned to its true meaning, that is what she is, and with the deliberateness of artistic conviction. More than any other choreographer in the field she is aware of folk art and impulse, and most of the time it is possible to trace in her compositions some grounding in the actual materials of simple peoples, contemporary or otherwise. Her work accordingly manages to be hearty even when its undercurrents are poignant and its forms subtle.

Loring is as markedly American in texture as Miss de Mille though his work does not lean toward the genre style as hers does. It is much more interested in form and in the evocation of overtones out of ordinary American life. *Billy the Kid*, the first American ballet of real stature to be created, captures in essence an entire epoch by the simplest and most suggestive of means; and *City Portrait* and *Prairie* do something of the same thing for different milieus. Like Miss de Mille, he is first of all an actor-dancer, and like her he falls easily into the spoken word when his dramatic action seems to lead in that direction. His compositions, however, are never in the form of straightforward dramatic narrative; his most interesting innovation in this department of activity is the use of a kind of montage which bears a much closer relation to the cinema than to anything in the background of the ballet. Partly because of the necessary tendency toward formalization which his poetic point of view entails, and partly because he still lacks full command of movement in its basic aspects, he resorts to the standard academic vocabulary too frequently for the good of his quite unacademic approach. At his best, however, his movement is a kind of stylization of natural gesture, evolving ultimately out of the actor's art.

With due allowance for the marked personal differences in these three methods, a unity emerges very clearly. The new ballet is altogether a theater art, turning its back on "pure" design, neoclassicism, and the specialized cult of balletomania. Spectacle as such is a dead issue; music and décor are functional parts of the collaboration and neither of them is allowed to run away with the situation. The world of stereotyped 19th century fantasy with its elves and pixies is gone, and along with it that more lugubrious world peopled by Fate, Love, and Death in person. There is too much substantial humor in the new ballet to face these hangovers with a straight face. Humor, indeed, is a striking characteristic of the new field, whether it expresses itself in broad farce, high comedy, satire, burlesque, or merely a sense of balance in dealing with matters of tragic or introspective import. This new ballet world is above all a human world; imaginative and idealistic, if you will, but related to actuality. All of which constitutes a revolution inherently no less startling than Fokine's, for the ballet, the most artificial of the arts, has turned at last in the direction of reality. It is not reality, to be sure, in the sense of literalness and naturalism, but in the poet's sense of penetration to the core of experience. Nor, indeed, has the goal been reached, but the direction of the new cycle is definitely established.

In the development of this aim it is impossible to overemphasize the influence of the radical American dance, which came into being some forty years ago with Isadora Duncan and has fought and bled through two generations for just such a function for the dance art. Certainly the least of its concerns at any time has been its possible influence upon the ballet, which it has held in healthy contempt for the superficiality of its preoccupations; but it is ironic that some of its own ideas at secondhand have been able to attract financial subsidy within the frame of the ballet and hence to find voice for themselves, when its firsthand and unquestionably superior presentations of them have failed to do so.

This is to be accounted for quite simply, not on any basis of comparative merit but rather of comparative tact. The so-called modern dance is unavoidably tactless by its very nature just as science is tactless, for it is seeking truths and is unable to compromise even to win that patronage without which the very search cannot be carried on. Thus the art, in order to make progress, has had to disprove the impossibility of lifting itself by its own bootstraps. Its lifting muscles are overdeveloped and its bootstraps frayed, but it has done a notable job of the impossible. Given a fair hearing before a qualified jury, able to discriminate between art and pedantics on the one hand, and between social and "society" values on the other, the so-called modern dance would in all likelihood be found the most significant art manifestation of our times, its only serious competitor being that musical development known loosely as jazz.

Its great significance lies in its isolation for the first time in history of the basic substance of all dance, the same in all times, climes, and cultures, and the laws which govern its production and control. This substance is movement evolved directly out of subjective experience instead of postures, attitudes, and gestures objectively determined to conform to preconceived designs and purposes. Movement thus emotionally stimulated proves to be stimulating in turn to the emotion of the spectator, who, if he will allow himself to do so, becomes in fact a vicarious participant in it. This, in a word, is the basis of the modern dance. It achieves its results not by representation or symbol but by direct kinesthetic contact; it aims at the nerves, so to speak, rather than at the senses or the intellect.

Obviously in its early stages it is an extremely lyric art, the simple outpouring of personal feeling; and it was thus that Isadora Duncan practiced it, producing the most profound reaction throughout the artistic world by the unprecedented power and depth of her evocations. Her art had nothing in it of the theater, as she was the first to admit, and the history of the modern dance since her early revelations has accordingly been the steady building upon her principles of a dance art that is of the theater. The processes involved in this evolution are of staggering proportions, for all the subsidiary arts of this theater must stem from its main root which is creative movement. Its music is essentially the song of the dancer, based on his breath phrase and blood pulse, even though it must be transferred to other instruments than his voice as he dances; the setting of the stage must be merely the visual definition of the space through which he moves, a pointing up of its areas and levels. Obviously its musical composers cannot be symphonists long dead nor its designers easel painters however fashionable; all its collaborators must be deeply dance-minded.

Through unbelievable effort and personal heroism these results have at last been, if not materialized as richly as adequate financing would make possible, at least admirably realized both in principle and in detail. In Doris Humphrey's great *New Dance* trilogy, in Martha Graham's *Letter to the World*, in Hanya Holm's *Trend*, a new world of the dance has been opened. It is also a new world of the theater, the freest, most genuinely theatrical theater anywhere to be found, and a blessed relief from what generally passes for theater but is really nothing more than a set of condensed novels read aloud by charming people in tasteful replicas of drawing-rooms.

But as yet this mightily potential art has not been allowed to enter the promised land of financial security, where alone its true values can be realized in material shape. It must content itself with high ideals and cheese-cloth costumes, piano accompaniments and a large and passionate public of young people who believe with all their hearts but are helplessly impecunious.

We have insisted for so long that the dance is a luxurious, effeminate, and fancy diversion, shutting our eyes stubbornly to the more serious phases of its growth, that we are not without a certain consistency when at the first sign of crisis we abandon it as one of the more expendable forms of trivia. This is more consistent, however, than wise, for during the past twenty years it has proved itself in the fields of both art and education; it has substantiated to an amazing degree its claim to being the closest of all arts to basic human experience, as well as the most potent of media in the realm of pedagogy for the integration of mental, physical, and emotional life.

What the chances of survival are for the present highly advanced manifestation of the art, who can say? It is now at the moment of development where with recognition practically expressed it could go ahead to unpredictable glories, and where, lacking that recognition, it may simply face a hungry death with its lap heaped with seeds ripe for the planting. By the nature of its unique virtues, it has no traditional material to hand down to keep barren periods busy until new leaders arise to illuminate it; if the present leaders disappear from the field before the seeds have germinated, there will be no future whatever.

To be sure, there can be no such thing as extermination for an art that rises out of natural drives so long as those drives themselves exist; but no more, indeed, can the forces of fascism destroy the ultimate achievement of political and economic freedom, even under the inconceivable circumstances of a victory by Hitler over their present manifestations. There is cold comfort in contemplating these ultimates. All that can be said with certainty is that the art of the radical American dance is at the threshold of great achievement right now. Its cycle of experimentation is over and cannot be extended merely for expediency; its next cycle is as a magnificent and encompassing theater, nearer to the deep-seated drives of the people out of whom it grows than any theater has been since the theater of Dionysus. If the war does not last too long—.

Sources for Selected Readings

Barbara Page, "Contemporary Exponents of the Dance," *Journal of Health and Physical Education* 6, no. 4 (April 1935): 11-14, 60. George W. Beiswanger, "The Dance and Today's Needs," *Theatre Arts Monthly* 19, no. 6 (June 1935): 439-50. Doris Humphrey, "New Dance," ca. 1936. Doris Humphrey Collection, Dance Collection of the New York Public Library [M25]. This draft appears to be a variant of the manuscript published in Selma Jeanne Cohen, *Doris Humphrey: An Artist First*, (Middletown, Conn.: Wesleyan University Press, 1972), pp. 238-41. It differs in important respects from that version, especially in delineating Humphrey's ideas about the individual in relation to the group. Charles Weidman, "Artists and Audiences," Humphrey-Weidman souvenir program, ca. 1938. Doris Humphrey, "Declaration," Humphrey-Weidman souvenir program, ca. 1938. Martha Graham, "The Future of the Dance," *Dance* 6, no. 4 (April 1939): 9. John Martin, "The Dance Completes a Cycle," *American Scholar* 12, no. 2 (Spring 1943): 205-15.

SOURCES

The principal sources identified and explored for this project are enumerated—both those that relate directly to the Bennington project and others that provide background and context. Sources relating to the social, political, economic, or broader artistic climate of the period are not included. Special locations of materials are given in brackets.

Archives and Special Collections: The central repositories of Bennington documents and the kinds of materials found there are described. Individual documents are cited in the notes to each chapter, and in the Bibliography which follows. Programs for nearly every public and student performance at the Bennington summer school, along with most of the official reports and school bulletins gathered from several quarters by the author, are preserved on microfilm (see "Bennington College Documents," pp. 293–94).

Research Tools: Key research aids and study guides for this area of dance research are listed.

Newspapers and Magazines: Periodicals and newspapers consulted are listed. Individual newspaper articles are not listed separately in the Bibliography but are referenced in notes to each chapter.

Selective Bibliography: The bibliography is in two parts. First are those books, periodical articles, and unpublished manuscripts that constitute a selective core for the Bennington project. Second are books, articles, and unpublished materials that bear more generally on the Bennington project but also include associated phenomena, including surveys of other dance projects, individual biographies, and background to dance in America during the period. A half dozen sources published after completion of this study are also included.

Interviews: Persons interviewed by the author for this study are listed, and other important interview sources are identified.

Visual Records and Scores: The range and quality of photographs available for study are indicated, along with profiles of the two outstanding dance photographers of the period, Thomas Bouchard and Barbara Morgan. Films and videotapes of Bennington figures and works are catalogued. Notation scores for Bennington premiere works are listed.

A list of abbreviations used in this section follows.

List of Abbreviations

AD	*American Dancer*
BCA	Bennington College Archive
BCB	*Bennington College Bulletin*
BCL	Bennington College Library
BR	*Ballet Review*
DM	*Dance Magazine*
DN	*Dance News*
DO	*Dance Observer*
DP	*Dance Perspectives*
DS	*Dance Scope*
DT	*Dancing Times*
ED	*Educational Dance*
JHPE	*Journal of Health and Physical Education*
JHPER	*Journal of Health, Physical Education and Recreation*
LC	Library of Congress
MM	*Modern Music*
NYPL	Dance Collection of the New York Public Library
TA	*Theatre Arts*
TAM	*Theatre Arts Monthly*

Archives and Special Collections

American Dance Festival Archive and Files. New London, Conn., 1977; Durham, N.C., 1978 (Duke Univ.). Scrapbooks, official reports, documents, programs, photographs, and films.

Bennington College Archive. Bennington, Vt. (see under "Bennington College Documents . . .").

Bennington College Library. Bennington, Vt.

Dance Notation Bureau. New York. Scores, photographs, audiotapes, and materials pertaining to reconstructions of Bennington choreography.

The Arch Lauterer Archives. Case Western Reserve University, Cleveland, Ohio. Sketches, correspondence, manuscript and other materials.

Library of Congress. Washington, D.C. Books, periodicals, newspapers, microform dissertations. Music Division: scores, journals, reference works. Motion Picture Section: films.

Mills College Archives. Oakland, Calif. Programs, bulletins, photographs, and historical data on the development of the dance program at Mills.

National Dance Association Archives. Reston, Virginia. American Alliance for Health, Physical Education and Recreation. Oral History project transcripts. Periodicals and reports of the Association; materials on the history of dance in higher education.

New York Public Library. Circulating Dance Library, Library and Museum of the Performing Arts, Lincoln Center, New York (first floor). Periodicals, books, pamphlets, clippings, program and photograph files.

New York Public Library. Dance Collection. Library and Museum of the Performing Arts, Lincoln Center, New York (third floor).

A wide range of materials. Among the most critical sources to Bennington are: The Doris Humphrey Collection, Humphrey-Weidman Scrapbooks and Collection, Hanya Holm Scrapbooks, Louis Horst Scrapbooks, New York Scrapbooks (containing New York newspaper reviews and articles, arranged chronologically), Walter Terry Scrapbooks (collected criticism, not complete), dissertation lists and copies of theses and dissertations, oral histories, phonotapes of interviews, films and videotapes, photographs (under various choreographers), files of clippings, programs, and documents (under individual dancers, choreographers, works, and institutions), periodicals, drawings, and sketches.

Research Center for the Federal Theatre Project. George Mason University. Fairfax, Va. The largest collection of materials on the Federal Theatre Project, owned by the Library of Congress, on permanent loan at George Mason University. Cataloging completed in 1978. Includes posters, production notebooks, photographs, scripts, interviews, set and costume designs, research materials, etc., pertaining to the Federal Dance Project, 1936-1939.

Research Tools

The major specialized reference tools and finding aids for dance research in this period include the following sources for the Bennington years:

New York Public Library. *Dictionary Catalog of the Dance Collection*. Boston: G. K. Hall & Co., 1974. 10 vols. (works catalogued prior to 1 October 1973).

This is the master reference guide for dance research, though it pertains only to holdings at the Dance Collection of the Performing Arts Research Center of the New York Public Library. Multi-media materials are indexed by subject, title, and author. These include for each person, work, or subject: photographs and films, notated scores, phonotapes of interviews, prints and drawings, books, magazine and newspaper articles, files of clippings and programs, scrapbooks, published photographs, and manuscript materials. Annual supplements are issued:

_____. *Bibliographic Guide to Dance: 1975*. First Supplement, 2 vols., 1976 (includes additions to September 1975).

_____. *Bibliographic Guide to Dance: 1976*. Second Supplement, 2 vols., 1977 (materials catalogued 1 September 1975-31 August 1976).

_____. *Bibliographic Guide to Dance: 1977*. Third Supplement, 1 vol., 1978 (materials catalogued 1 September 1976-31 August 1977).

_____. *Bibliographic Guide to Dance: 1978*. Fourth Supplement, 1 vol., 1979 (materials catalogued 1 September 1977-31 August 1978).

_____. *Bibliographic Guide to Dance: 1979*. Fifth Supplement, 2 vols., 1980 (materials catalogued 1 September 1978-31 August 1979).

Wentink, Andrew Mark. "The Doris Humphrey Collection: An Introduction and Guide." *Bulletin of the New York Public Library* 77, no. 1 (Autumn 1973): 80-142. An extraordinary guide to an extraordinary manuscript collection, including a chronology of Doris Humphrey's life and career through her correspondence, a complete catalog of the collection's contents, and a subject index.

Committee on Research in Dance (CORD). *Research in Dance: Problems and Possibilities*. The Proceedings of the Preliminary Conference on Research in Dance, May 26-28, 1967. Edited by Richard Bull. New York: CORD, 1968. An excellent introductory guide for the dance researcher describing the state of the field. Especially useful are Rowe, Patricia A. "Research in Dance in Colleges and Universities in the United States, 1907-1967; and Moore, Lillian. "How Does the Researcher Get the Facts?"

The American Alliance (formerly Association) for Health, Physical Education and Recreation (AAHPER) has published several important guides to masters' theses and doctoral dissertations in dance:

AAHPER. *Compilation of Dance Research 1901-1964*. Edited by Esther E. Pease. Washington, D.C.: AAHPER, 1964.

_____. *Research in Dance I, A Supplement to the Compilation of Dance Research 1901-1963.* Introduction by Fannie Helen Melcer. Washington, D.C.: AAHPER, 1968.

_____. *Research in Dance II*. Compiled by Charlette Irey. Washington, D.C.: AAHPER, 1973. (See especially "Themes for Dance Research," compiled by Fannie Helen Melcer and Genevieve Oswald, pp. 52-95, which lists lacunae in the field.)

Goode, Elizabeth. "Dance Research Completed in the Colleges and Universities of the United States of America." Master's thesis, New York University, 1946 [NYPL].

Research Committee, National Section on Dance. "Dance Research and Theses Completed, in Process with Research Needed." Woman's College, University of North Carolina, Greensboro, North Carolina, 1955 [NYPL].

AAHPER. *Aesthetics for Dancers: A Selected Annotated Bibliography*. Compiled and annotated by Mary H. Kaprelian. Washington, D.C.: AAHPER, 1976.

Belknap, S. Yancey. *Guide to Dance Periodicals*. Gainesville: University of Florida Press, 1959-1970. 10 volumes, covering 1931-1962.

Guthman, Louise. "20 Years of Dance Observer: Index 1934-1953." Master's thesis, New York University, 1954 [NYPL, Louis Horst Collection].

Lackas, Genevieve. "A Selected List of Articles on Dance Subjects from Periodicals Covering the Period Between 1937-42." Master's thesis, New York University, 1942 [NYPL].

Magriel, Paul David. *A Bibliography of Dancing*. New York: H. W. Wilson Co., 1936. Fourth Cumulated Supplement 1936-1940, H. W. Wilson Co., 1941.

Shirley, Wayne D., comp. *Modern Music, Published by the League of Composers, 1924-1946: An Analytic Index*. Ed. William and Carolyn Lichtenwanger. New York: AMS Press, 1976 [LC Music Division].

Wimmer, Shirley. "A Selected Bibliography of Dance." Master's thesis, New York University, 1946 [NYPL].

Written Accounts

BENNINGTON COLLEGE DOCUMENTS, PUBLICATIONS, SCRAPBOOKS, ETC.

Most of the key documents, programs, and rosters are available on microfilm (see Kriegsman, Sali Ann, below). The *Bennington College Bulletins* contain announcements of the summer sessions, giving courses, faculty, a roster of students, and a description of the program. *Annual Reports* prepared post facto by the directors of the school are available in *Reports of Officers*. These are detailed descriptions of each session, including calendars of events, curricula descriptions, faculty, staff and student rosters, statistical breakdowns, finances, and recommendations. *Quadrille*, a quarterly publication of the Office of Development, published a number of pertinent articles which are cited by author in the bibliography. Two scrapbook collections of newspaper and magazine clippings are invaluable. Among other materials not specifically cited below are press releases, course schedules, student rosters, proposals, memoranda, correspondence, and committee minutes referred to in the main text.

Bennington College Bulletin [BCA]

The Bennington School of the Dance, 1934-1938, Vols. 2-6.
The Bennington School of the Dance at Mills College, 1939, Vol. 7.
The Bennington School of the Arts, 1940-1941, Vols. 8-9.
Bennington College Summer Session: The Arts, 1942, Vol. 10.

Reports of Officers [BCA]

First to Fifth Annual Reports of the Bennington School of the Dance; Martha Hill, Director, Mary Jo Shelly, Administrative Director. Summers 1934-1938, Vols. 2-6.
Sixth Annual Report of the Bennington School of the Dance at Mills College. Summer 1939, Vol. 7.
First and Second Annual Reports of the Bennington School of the Arts. Summers 1940-1941, Vols. 8-9.

Quadrille (1966-) [BCL]

July 1969; Fall 1972; Fall 1975; Summer 1976; Spring 1978. [See Bibliography under authors and periodical title.]

Kriegsman, Sali Ann. "Bulletins, annual reports and programs of the Bennington School of the Dance and School of the Arts, Bennington, Vt., 1934-42." Various pieces. Microfilm. Assembled for the Dance Collection of the New York Public Library and Bennington College by Sali Ann Kriegsman, 1968 [BCA and NYPL].

Bennington School of the Dance "Scrapbooks" [BCA].

"Excerpts from the Press Book of the Bennington School of the Dance, A Resume, 1934-1939," n.d. [BCA].

McCullough, Edith van Benthuysen. "Bennington College: Clippings." 30 vols., 1923-1957. Newspaper and magazine articles relating to the history of Bennington College with some material on the summer dance program [BCL].

"An Historical Chart of the Dance and Related Fields." Compiled by a committee of students under the direction of Martha Hill at the Bennington School of the Dance, 1934 (a research study conducted during the school's first session) [BCA and NYPL].

NEWSPAPERS AND MAGAZINES

Newspapers: Principal Sources

Bennington Banner, Bennington, Vermont
Boston Herald (Ted Shawn, Walter Terry)
Brooklyn Eagle (Virginia Mishnun)
Christian Science Monitor (Margaret Lloyd)
New York Herald Tribune (Jerome Bohm, Walter Terry, Edwin Denby)
New York Times (John Martin)

Newspapers: Others Consulted

Baltimore Sun
Boston Transcript
Burlington (Vt.) *Free Press & Times*
Cincinnati Enquirer
Cleveland Press
Columbus (Ohio) *Dispatch*
Daily Worker
Lewiston (Maine) *Journal*
New York Sun
Oakland Tribune
PM's Weekly
People's World (San Francisco)
San Francisco Chronicle
Springfield (Mass.) *Union-Republican*
Variety

Magazines and Journals: Principal Sources

American Dancer
Dance, 1936–1942
Dance Magazine
Dance Observer, 1934–1964
Dance Perspectives
Dance Scope
Educational Dance, 1938–1942
Impulse, 1951–1970 (annual)
Journal of Health and Physical Education; Journal of Health, Physical Education and Recreation
Nation
New Masses, 1937
New Theatre, 1934–1937
Theatre Arts; Theatre Arts Monthly

Magazines and Journals: Others Consulted

American Scholar
Arts in Society
Ballet Review
Connecticut College Alumnae News
Dance Digest
Dance Events, 1932–1933
Dance Herald, 1937–1938
Dance Index
Dance News
Dancing Times
Drama
Eddy
Focus on Dance

Harper's Magazine
Life
Literary Digest
Look
Mademoiselle
Magazine of Art
Modern Music
Musical America
Musical Courier
New Republic
New Yorker
Newsweek
North American Review
Panpipes
Progressive Education
Quadrille (Bennington College)
Scholastic Coach
Sportswoman
Time
Vogue
Yankee

BIBLIOGRAPHY

Major References to Bennington

Books

Cohen, Selma Jeanne. *Doris Humphrey: An Artist First*. Middletown, Conn.: Wesleyan University Press, 1972, 1978.

Jones, Barbara. *Bennington College: The Development of an Educational Idea*. New York: Harper & Bros., 1946.

King, Eleanor. *Transformations: A Memoir. The Humphrey-Weidman Years*. Brooklyn: Dance Horizons, 1978.

Lloyd, Margaret. *The Borzoi Book of Modern Dance*. New York: Alfred A. Knopf, 1949; Brooklyn: Dance Horizons, 1970.

McDonagh, Don. *Martha Graham: A Biography*. New York: Praeger Publishers, 1973; Popular Library, 1975.

Martin, John. *America Dancing*. New York: Dodge Publishing Company, 1936; Brooklyn: Dance Horizons, 1968.

Morgan, Barbara. *Martha Graham: Sixteen Dances in Photographs*. New York: Duell, Sloan & Pearce, 1941. Rev. ed., Dobbs Ferry, New York: Morgan & Morgan, 1980.

Mueller, John. *Films on Ballet and Modern Dance: Notes and a Directory*. New York: American Dance Guild, September 1974. (Descriptive analysis of a television film on the Bennington project, "Four Pioneers.")

Schlundt, Christena L. *Tamiris: A Chronicle of Her Dance Career, 1927-1955*. New York: The New York Public Library, 1972.

Sorell, Walter. *Hanya Holm: The Biography of an Artist*. Middletown, Conn.: Wesleyan University Press, 1969.

Trowbridge, Charlotte. *Dance Drawings of Martha Graham*. New York: The Dance Observer, 1945.

Magazine Articles and Unpublished Works

Allen, Patricia Shirley. "Mecca for Moderns: Bennington Completes a Cycle." *AD* 11, no. 8 (June 1938): 19, 49.

Anderson, Jack. "Project for the 'Farthest-Out' College." *DM* 43, no. 2 (February 1969): 45-46, 72, 74. (Interview with William Bales and background on Bennington.)

Balcom, Lois. "Bennington in 1942." *DO* 9, no. 7 (August-September 1942): 87-88.

Beiswanger, George W. "Dance in the College and on the Road." *TAM* 22, no. 7 (July 1938): 488-93.

_____. "Music at the Bennington Festival." *DO* 5, no. 7 (August-September 1938): 102-104.

_____. "The New Theatre Dance." *TAM* 23, no. 1 (January 1939): 41-54. Republished in *Theatre Arts Anthology: A Record and a Prophecy*. Ed. Rosamond Gilder, Hermine Rich Isaacs, Robert M. MacGregor, Edward Reed. New York: Theatre Arts Books, 1950, pp. 209-21.

Belitt, Ben. "Arch Lauterer: A Science of Radiances." *Quadrille* 7, no. 1 (Fall 1972): 29-32. See also *Impulse*, 1959, "Arch Lauterer—Poet in the Theatre," pp. 10-13.

_____. "Words for Dancers, Perhaps." *Bennington Review* 7 (April 1980): 2-17.

Bloomer, Ruth H. "Bennington School of the Dance—Summer 1937." *DO* 4, no. 7 (August-September 1937): 73-74, 83-84.

_____. "Four Summers at Bennington." *DO* 4, no. 7 (August-September 1937): 76, 84.

Brockway, Thomas. "Notes from the Year One." *Quadrille* 7, no. 1 (Fall 1972): 7-9.

_____. "Music at Bennington, 1932-41." *Quadrille* 10, no. 1 (Fall 1975): 45-52.

_____. "Dance at Bennington 1932-41." *Quadrille* 12, no. 1 (Spring 1978): 25-37.

Burke, Owen. "The Dance," *New Masses* 24, no. 10 (31 August 1937).

Cassidy, Rosalind. "So Bennington Went West?" *DO* 6, no. 7 (August-September 1939): 248.

Church, Marjorie. "The Bennington Dance Festival." *DO* 3, no. 7 (August-September 1936): 73, 77.

Conrad, Sherman. "Bennington Festival, 1940." *Nation* 151, no. 8 (24 August 1940): 158-59.

____. "Bennington Festival, 1941." *Nation* 153, no. 9 (30 August 1941): 186-87.

Cowell, Henry. "Music at Bennington." *DO* 8, no. 7 (August-September 1941): 96-97.

Cushing, Maxine. "Bennington Commentary: Sidelights on the Fifth Session." *ED* 1, no. 3 (August-September 1938): 12-13.

____. "The Bennington Record: July 2-August 13, 1938, A Factual Survey." *DO* 5, no. 7 (August-September 1938): 104-105.

Dance Observer. "1940: Bennington Plans." Editorial. 6, no. 7 (August-September 1939): 247.

Einert, Margaret. "Bennington . . July . . 1938: Focal Point of The American Modern Dance." *DT*, n.s., no. 336 (September 1938): 645-48.

Fergusson, Francis. "The Idea of a Theater—1935-47." *Quadrille* 7, no. 1 (Fall 1972): 33-36.

Gilfond, Henry. "Bennington Festival." *DO* 5, no. 7 (August-September 1938): 100-102.

[Graham, Martha.] "Dance Libretto: American Document, by Martha Graham, with Four Scenes from the Dance." *TA* 26, no. 9 (September 1942): 565-74.

Guest, Ann Hutchinson. "Bennington Memories—1940," 1978. Unpublished recollections contributed for this book.

Heisey, Ruth Ann. "Anna Sokolow—Interview." *DO* 4, no. 7 (August-September 1937): 77.

Herring, Hubert. "Bennington." *Nation* 137, no. 3570 (6 December 1933): 651-52.

____. "Education at Bennington." *Harper's Magazine* 181 (September 1940): 408-17.

Hill, Martha. "A New American Dance Center." *Scholastic Coach* 4, no. 1 (September 1934).

Holm, Hanya. "Trend Grew Upon Me." *Magazine of Art* 31, no. 3 (March 1938): 137.

Humphrey, Doris. "New Dance." Typed manuscript, ca. 1936. The Doris Humphrey Collection [M25], *NYPL*. Published in this book, pp. 284-86. This differs from the one published in Selma Jeanne Cohen, *Doris Humphrey: An Artist First*, pp. 238-41, republished in *Dance as a Theatre Art*, ed. Selma Jeanne Cohen. New York: Harper & Row, 1974, pp. 144-48.

Joiner, Betty. "A Portfolio of Dancers and Dancing." *TAM* 21, no. 1 (January 1937): 67-74.

Kirkpatrick, John. "Bennington's Festival of the Arts." *MM* 18, no. 1 (November-December 1940): 52-54.

Kirstein, Lincoln. "Martha Graham at Bennington." *Nation* 147, no. 10 (3 September 1938): 230-31.

Kriegsman, Sali Ann. "The Bennington School of the Dance, 1934 to 1942. A Chronology." Unpublished manuscript, 1968. 40 pp.

Lauterer, Arch. "A Theatre for Bennington: Notes on a Project By the Designer." *TAM* 19, no. 12 (December 1935): 929-35.

____. "Design for the Dance." *Magazine of Art* 31: 3 (March 1938): 137-43.

____. "Form and Action: Punch and The Judy." Unpublished manuscript, ca. 1955-1956. [The Arch Lauterer Archives. Also, NYPL.]

[Lauterer, Arch]. "Arch Lauterer—Poet in the Theatre." *Impulse*, 1959. (An entire issue is devoted to Lauterer.)

[Leigh, Robert D.]. "The College and the World About Us." *BCB* 2, no. 1 (August 1933): 3-11.

Lloyd, Norman. "Henry Cowell: A Dancer's Musician." *DS* 2, no. 2 (Spring 1966): 10-12.

Lloyd, Ruth. "Music for the Dance." *DO* 6, no. 7 (August-September 1939): 249, 254.

____. "The Lloyds at Bennington," 1977. Unpublished recollections, contributed for this book.

Love, Paul. "Bennington Festival." *Nation* 145, no. 9 (28 August 1937): 226-27.

Lubell, Naomi. "Esther Junger—Interview." *DO* 4, no. 7 August-September 1937): 77-78.

____. "José Limón—Interview." *DO* 4, no. 7 (August-September 1937): 78.

____. "The Bennington School: An Educational Project in Modern Dance." *AD* 10, no. 2 (October 1937): 12-13, 29.

[Luening, Otto.] "The Arts at Bennington: Music Division. An Interview with Otto Luening." *Quadrille* 10, no. 1 (Fall 1975): 23-28.

McCullough, Edith van Benthuysen, and McCullough, Hall Park. "Some Recollections of the Beginnings of Bennington College." *BCB* 25, no. 2 (June 1957): 13-68.

McCullough, John. "Recollections on Recollecting Recollections." *Quadrille* 7, no. 1 (Fall 1972): 4-7.

McDonagh, Don. "Revolution in Connecticut." *BR* 4, no. 1 (1971): 58-63.

Martin, John. "Days of Divine Indiscipline." Photographs by Thomas Bouchard. *DP* 12 (Autumn 1961).

Moore, Claudia. "An Historical Survey of Selected Dance Repertories and Festivals in the United States Since 1920." Master's thesis, New York University, 1942 [NYPL].

Morton, Frederick. "A Forum on The Modern Dance." *TAM* 19, no. 10 (October 1935): 794, 797-98.

Nikolais, Alwin. Untitled reflections on his Bennington summers. *Impulse*, 1968, pp. 69-73.

Ocko, Edna. "Martha Graham's 'Panorama.'" *New Theatre* 2, no. 9 (September 1935): 27.

_____. "Texts for Dancers." *New Theatre* 3, no. 9 (September 1936): 19-20.

O'Donnell, Mary P. "Martha Hill." *DO* 3, no. 4 (April 1936): 37, 44.

Page, Barbara. "Contemporary Exponents of the Dance." *JHPE* 6, no. 4 (April 1935): 11-14, 60. Reprinted in this book, pp. 277-79.

Pease, Esther E. "Highlights at Bennington." *ED* 2, no. 3 (August-September 1939): 10-11.

Quadrille. "The Bennington College Summer School of the Dance." 3, no. 4 (July 1969) (illustrated).

Quadrille. "Contemporary Dance: An Interview with Judith Dunn, Josef Wittman, Jack Moore and Martha Wittman." 10, no. 1 (Fall 1975): 12-15.

Rosenblatt, Esther. "Bennington—1941." *DO* 8, no. 7 (August-September 1941): 91-92.

Rudhyar, Dane. "My Bennington Experience." *DO* 4, no. 7 (August-September 1937): 75.

Shannon, Eleanor. "The 1940 Bennington Season." *DO* 7, no. 7 (August-September 1940): 96, 105.

Shelly, Mary Jo. "A Point of View on the Modern Dance." *Sportswoman* 10, no. 8 (May 1934): 11, 21.

_____. "A School of the Modern Dance." *Progressive Education* 12, no. 6 (October 1935): 417-21.

_____. "Willingly to School." *DO* 4, no. 6 (June-July 1937): 63.

_____. "The Fourth Year at Bennington," *Dance Herald* 1, no. 1 (October 1937): 3.

_____. "Facts and Fancies about the Dance in Education." *JHPE* 11, no. 1 (January 1940): 18-19, 56-57.

_____. "The New Plan at Bennington." *DO* 7, no. 4 (April 1940): 48-49.

_____. "Eighth Summer at Bennington." *DO* 8, no. 3 (March 1941): 36-37.

_____. "Bennington—1942." *DO* 9, no. 4 (April 1942): 53.

_____. "View from a Pentagon Window." *Impulse*, 1953, 5-6.

_____. "Footnote to the History of an Art." *Quadrille* 7, no. 1 (Fall 1972): 19-23.

Stodelle, Ernestine. "College or Career for Dancers? Bennington's Answer." *DM* 38, no. 9 (September 1964): 40-45.

Teirstein, Alice. "Dance and Music: Interviews at the Keyboard." *DS* 8, no. 2 (Spring/Summer 1974): 18-31.

Terry. Walter. "This Story Began in 1934." American Dance Festival Souvenir Program, June-August 1972, 25th Anniversary [American Dance Festival Archive].

Venable, Lucy. "Passacaglia 1938-1965: The Art of Remaking a Dance." *DS* 1, no. 2 (Spring 1965): 6-14.

Vickery, Katherine. "The Summer at Bennington." *DO* 2, no. 7 (October 1935): 77.

Wilson, Julia Anne. "Louise Kloepper." *DO* 5, no. 3 (March 1938): 41.

_____. "Bennington Fellows Interviewed: Eleanor King, Marian Van Tuyl." *DO* 5, no. 3 (April 1938): 57.

Background to Bennington

Books

Amberg, George. *Ballet in America, The Emergence of an American Art*. New York: Duell, Sloan and Pearce, 1949. (Background on ballet.)

Armitage, Merle, ed. *Martha Graham*. Los Angeles: Armitage, 1937. Brooklyn: Dance Horizons, 1966. New York: Da Capo Press, 1978.

Clurman, Harold. *The Fervent Years: The Story of The Group Theatre and the Thirties*. New York: Hill and Wang, 1957.

Cohen, Selma Jeanne, ed. *The Modern Dance: Seven Statements of Belief*. Middletown, Conn.: Wesleyan University Press, 1966.

Cornish, Nellie Centennial. *Miss Aunt Nellie: The Autobiography of Nellie C. Cornish*. Ed. Ellen Van Volkenburg Browne and Edward Nordhoff Beck. Foreword by Nancy Wilson Ross. Seattle: University of Washington Press, 1964. (A personal account of the Cornish School by its founder.)

Crowley, Alice Lewisohn. *The Neighborhood Playhouse: Leaves from a Theatre Scrapbook*. New York: Theatre Arts Books, 1959.

Dance Magazine. *25 Years of American Dance*. Ed. Doris Hering. New York: R. Orthwine, 1951, 1954. (Includes a history of *Dance Magazine* in its various manifestations, along with references to Bennington figures.)

de Mille, Agnes. *Dance to the Piper*. Boston: Little, Brown and Company, 1952. (See especially the chapter on Louis Horst and Martha Graham.)

Duberman, Martin. *Black Mountain: An Exploration in Community*. New York: E. P. Dutton, Inc., 1972. (A history through official documents and interviews.)

Flanagan, Hallie. *Arena*. New York: Duell, Sloan and Pearce, 1940. (History of the WPA Federal Theatre Project.)

Hawkins, Alma. *Modern Dance in Higher Education*. New York: Teachers College, Columbia University Press, 1954. (First chapter outlines the history of dance in education from 1900 to 1945. Includes a useful bibliography.)

H'Doubler, Margaret. *The Dance and Its Place in Education*. New York: Harcourt, Brace and Company, 1925.

_____. *Dance: A Creative Art Experience*. New York: Appleton Century Crofts, Inc., 1940. (Includes a useful annotated bibliography.)

Horst, Louis. *Pre-Classic Dance Forms*. New York: The Dance Observer, 1937; Brooklyn: Dance Horizons, 1969, 1972 (2nd printing).

_____, and Russell, Carroll. *Modern Dance Forms in Relation to the Other Modern Arts*. San Francisco: Impulse Publications, 1961; Brooklyn: Dance Horizons, 1967.

Howard, Ruth E., ed. *Dancer's Almanac and Who's Who . . . 1940–New York*. (Biographies of dancers.)

Humphrey, Doris. *The Art of Making Dances*. Ed. Barbara Pollack. New York: Rinehart, 1959; Evergreen Books (Grove Press), 1962.

Joiner, Betty. *Costumes for the Dance*. New York: A. S. Barnes, 1937. (Joiner designed costumes for Bennington productions.)

Kendall, Elizabeth. *Where She Danced*. New York: Alfred A. Knopf, 1979. (Origins of modern dance from Duncan to Graham.)

Kirstein, Lincoln. *Three Pamphlets Collected: Blast at Ballet* New York: 1937; Brooklyn: Dance Horizons, 1967. (References to the modern dance and to Bennington.)

_____. *The New York City Ballet*. New York: Alfred A. Knopf, 1973. (References to Ballet Caravan at Bennington.)

Kraus, Richard. *History of The Dance in Art and Education*. Englewood Cliffs, N.J.: Prentice-Hall, Inc., 1969.

Leabo, Karl, ed. *Martha Graham*. New York: Theatre Arts Books, 1961. (Chronology by Horst and Robert Sabin 1926–1961 and an essay by Sabin.)

Love, Paul. *Modern Dance Terminology*. New York: Kamin Dance Publishers, 1953.

McDonagh, Don. *The Rise and Fall and Rise of Modern Dance*. New York: Outerbridge & Dienstfrey, 1970.

_____. *Complete Guide to Modern Dance*. New York: Doubleday, 1976. (Includes a "Chronology of Significant Dates and Events in Modern Dance Development.") Paperback edition under title *Don McDonagh's Complete Guide to Modern Dance*. New York: Popular Library, 1977.

Martin, John. *The Modern Dance*. New York: A. S. Barnes, 1935; Brooklyn: Dance Horizons, 1965. (Text of four lectures delivered at The New School for Social Research in New York in 1931–1932. A seminal book.)

_____. *Introduction to the Dance*. New York: W. W. Norton, 1939; Brooklyn: Dance Horizons, 1965.

_____. *The Dance*. New York: Tudor Publishing Company, 1946.

Mathews, Jane DeHart. *The Federal Theatre 1935–1939: Plays, Relief, and Politics*. Princeton, N.J.: Princeton University Press, 1967.

Mazo, Joseph. *Prime Movers: The Makers of Modern Dance in America*. New York: William Morrow and Company, 1977. (Useful bibliography and many references to Bennington.)

Moore, Lillian. *Artists of the Dance*. New York: Thomas Y. Crowell, 1938; Brooklyn: Dance Horizons, 1969. (For chapters on Doris Humphrey and Charles Weidman, and Martha Graham.)

Nadel, Myron Howard, and Nadel, Constance Gwen, eds. *The Dance Experience*. New York: Praeger Publishers, 1970. (A collection of essays.)

Palmer, Winthrop. *Theatrical Dancing in America*. New York: Bernard Ackerman, 1945; 2nd Edition, A. S. Barnes, 1978.

Payne, Charles. *American Ballet Theatre*. New York: Alfred A. Knopf, 1978. (Historical development of Ballet Theatre.)

Radir, Ruth Anderson. *Modern Dance for the Youth of America*. New York: A. S. Barnes, 1944.

Reis, Claire. *Composers in America: Biographical Sketches of Living Composers with a Record of Their Works, 1912–1937*. New York: Macmillan, 1938; 1947 revised and enlarged. (Information about American composers active in the dance field.)

Reynolds, Nancy. *Repertory in Review: 40 Years of The New York City Ballet*. New York: The Dial Press, 1977. (For Ballet Caravan repertoire, but beyond it as a model for a documentary approach to dance history.)

Rogers, Frederick Rand, ed. *Dance: A Basic Educational Technique*. New York: Macmillan, 1941. (Essays by Martha Graham, Doris Humphrey and Hanya Holm, among others, on their theoretical and technical viewpoints.)

Rothschild, B. de. *La Danse artistique aux U.S.A. Tendances modernes*. Paris: Editions Elzévir, 1949. (Includes a brief description of the Bennington project and photographs.)

Ruyter, Nancy Lee Chalfa. *Reformers and Visionaries: The Americanization of the Art of Dance*. New York: Dance Horizons, 1979. (The early dance educators, progressive education, and the enhancement of dance's status as an art in America.)

St. Denis, Ruth. *Ruth St. Denis, An Unfinished Life: An Autobiography*. New York: Harper & Brothers, 1939; Brooklyn: Dance Horizons, 1969. (Includes St. Denis' impressions of Bennington.)

Schlundt, Christena L. *The Professional Appearances of Ruth St. Denis & Ted Shawn: A Chronology and an Index of Dances 1906–1932*. New York: New York Public Library, 1962.

_____. *The Professional Appearances of Ted Shawn & His Men Dancers: A Chronology and an Index of Dances 1933–1940*. New York: New York Public Library, 1967.

Selden, Elizabeth. *The Dancer's Quest: Essays on the Aesthetic of the Contemporary Dance*. Berkeley: University of California Press, 1935. (Essays on dance in America and Germany.)

Shawn, Ted. *One Thousand and One Night Stands*. New York: Doubleday, 1960; Da Capo Press, 1979.

Sherman, Jane. *Soaring: The Diary and Letters of a Denishawn Dancer in the Far East, 1925–1926*. Middletown, Conn.: Wesleyan University Press, 1976.

_____. *The Drama of Denishawn Dance*. Middletown, Conn.: Wesleyan University Press, 1979.

Siegel, Marcia B. *The Shapes of Change: Images of American Dance*. Boston: Houghton Mifflin, 1979. (Includes detailed analyses of Doris Humphrey's *New Dance* and *Passacaglia* and Martha Graham's *Letter to the World*.)

Stewart, Virginia, comp. *Modern Dance*. New York: E. Weyhe, 1935; republished Brooklyn: Dance Horizons, 1970, as Stewart, Virginia, and Armitage, Merle. *The Modern Dance*, with a new forward by John Martin. (Essays on Graham, Humphrey and Weidman, among others.)

Stodelle, Ernestine. *The First Frontier: The Story of Louis Horst and The American Dance*. Cheshire, Conn.: Ernestine Stodelle, 1964. (With a chronology by A. J. Pischl and photographs by Barbara Morgan.)

_____. *The Dance Technique of Doris Humphrey and Its Creative Potential*. Princeton, N.J.: Princeton Book Co., 1978.

Terry, Walter. *Invitation to Dance*. New York: A. S. Barnes & Co., 1942. (Chapter 8: Collegiate Dance.)

_____. *The Dance in America*. New York: Harper & Row, 1956.

_____. *Frontiers of Dance: The Life of Martha Graham*. New York: Thomas Y. Crowell, 1975.

_____. *Ted Shawn: Father of American Dance*. New York: The Dial Press, 1976.

_____. *I Was There: Selected Dance Reviews and Articles—1936–1976*. Comp. and ed. Andrew Wentink. New York: Marcel Dekker, Inc., 1978. (A collection of Terry's criticism dating from 1936. Chapter 1: "Some Beginnings at Bennington.")

Thompson, Betty Lynd. *Fundamentals of Rhythm and Dance*. New York: A. S. Barnes & Co., 1933. (Thompson studied with Margaret H'Doubler and at Bennington.)

Warren, Larry. *Lester Horton: Modern Dance Pioneer*. New York: Marcel Dekker, Inc., 1977.

Magazine Articles and Unpublished Works

Balcom, Lois. "Joseph Mann and His 18-Year Dance Series at Washington Irving." *DO* 9, no. 7 (August-September 1942): 94–95.

Betts, Anne. "An Historical Study of the New Dance Group of New York City." Master's thesis, New York University, 1945 [NYPL].

Borek, Tom. "The Connecticut College American Dance Festival 1948–1972: A Fantastical Documentary." *DP* 50 (Summer 1972).

Beiswanger, Barbara Page. "A Selected List of Music Especially Written for Dance by Composers in America." Master's thesis, New York University, May 1943. (Courtesy of the author. A survey of composers, choreographers and works for the Bennington period.)

_____. "National Section on Dance: Its First Ten Years." *JHPER* 31, no. 5 (May-June 1960): 23-26. Republished in *Selected Articles on Dance II, 1958-1967*. Washington, D.C.: AAHPER, n.d. (See also: Barbara Page.)

Beiswanger, George. "Music for the Modern Dance." *TAM* 18, no. 3 (March 1934): 184-90. (An excellent and prophetic survey of the state of the art.)

_____. "The Dance and Today's Needs." *TAM* 19, no. 6 (June 1935): 439-50. Reprinted in this book, pp. 280-83.

_____. "Physical Education and the Emergence of the Modern Dance." *JHPE* 7, no. 7 (September 1936): 413-16, 463. Republished in *The Dance Experience*, ed. Myron Howard Nadel and Constance Gwen Nadel. New York: Praeger Publishers, 1970, pp. 319-26.

_____. "The Stage for the Modern Dance." *TAM* 23, no. 3 (March 1939): 219-23.

[Beiswanger, George W.] "The Tributary Theatre." *TA* 23, no. 11 (November 1939): 833-37. (On the college dance movement.)

Beiswanger, George. "The American Audience and Dance." *TA* 24, no. 9 (September 1940): 627-38.

[Beiswanger, George.] "Dance in the Red." *TA* 24, no. 9 (September 1940): 671-80.

Beiswanger, George. "Dance Repertory–American Style." *TA* 25, no. 6 (June 1941): 443-50.

Bloomer, Ruth. "Summer School of the Dance." *JHPER* 20, no. 1 (January 1949): 15-16, 58-61. (Report on the first session of the New London project.)

Cage, John. "Grace and Clarity." *DO* 11, no. 9 (November 1944): 108-109.

Code, Grant. "Dance Theatre of the WPA: A Record of National Achievement." *DO* in five parts: 6, no. 8 (October 1939): 264-65, 274; 6, no. 9 (November 1939): 280-81, 290; 6, no. 10 (December 1939): 302; 7, no. 3 (March 1940): 34-35; 7, no. 6 (June-July 1940): 86.

Coleman, Martha. "On the Teaching of Choreography: 1. Interview with Louis Horst." *DO* 16, no. 9 (November 1949): 128-30.

Dalbotton, Ted. "The Teaching of Louis Horst." *DS* 8, no. 1 (Fall/Winter 1973-1974): 26-40. (Descriptions of Horst's courses with reference to music written at Bennington for them.)

Dance Perspectives. "Composer/Choreographer." 16 (1963). (Includes a listing of scores written for the dance by composers Henry Cowell, Vivian Fine, Norman Lloyd, Louis Horst, and John Cage, and discussions of their collaborations with choreographers.)

Davies, Frances. "A Survey of Dance in Colleges, Universities, and Teacher-Training Institutions in the United States for the Year 1941-42." Master's thesis, New York University, 1942 [NYPL].

de Mille, Agnes. "We All Danced Regardless." *DS* 2, no. 2 (Spring 1966): 27-32.

Douglas, Elizabeth A. "Dance Captures America." *Magazine of Art* 30, no. 8 (August 1937): 499-505.

English, Cornelia. "How One 'Y' Did It." *DM* 17, no. 12 (December 1943): 7, 30 (Report of the 92nd Street YMHA dance program.)

Enos, Sondra Forsyth. "The Wisconsin Dance Idea: 1917-1970." *DM* 44, no. 11 (November 1970): 24-27, 72-73. (A survey and history of the dance program.)

Erdman, Jean. "The Dance as Non-Verbal Poetic Image," in *The Dance Has Many Faces*. 1st Edition. Ed. Walter Sorell. Cleveland and New York: World Publishing Company, 1951, pp. 197-212. (This essay appeared under a similar title in *Dance Observer*: Jean Erdman, "The Dance as Non-Verbal Poetical Image–I." *DO*, April 1949, pp. 48-49; Part II, *DO*, May 1949, pp. 64-66.)

Evan, Blanche. "From a Dancer's Notebook." Part 1. *New Theatre* 2, no. 3 (March 1936): 16-17, 28-29. (Report on Hanya Holm's course at the New York Wigman School.) Part 2. *New Theatre* 2, no. 4 (April 1936): 31, 44-45. (Report on Martha Graham's intensive summer course, 1935, in New York.) [NYPL Theater Collection].

Fay, Anthony. "The Festival of '42: A History-making Summer at Jacob's Pillow." *DM* 50, no. 7 (July 1976): 61-65.

Foote, Horton. "The Long, Long Trek." *DO* 11, no. 8 (October 1944): 98-99.

Ford, Arthur. "Educational Dance Produces a Critic: An Interview with Walter Terry." *ED* 3, no. 4 (October 1940): 3-5.

Friedman, Edna A. "American Opinions on Dance and Dancing from 1840 to 1940." Master's thesis, New York University, 1940 [NYPL].

Gibbs, Angelica. "The Absolute Frontier" (Martha Graham). *New Yorker* 23, no. 45 (27 December 1947): 28-37.

Graham, Martha. "The Future of the Dance." *Dance* 6, no. 4 (April 1939): 9. (Reprinted in this book, p. 288).

_____. "A Modern Dancer's Primer for Action." In Rogers, Frederick Rand. *Dance: A Basic Educational Technique.* New York: Macmillan, 1941, pp. 178-87. Republished in *Dance as a Theatre Art*, ed. Selma Jeanne Cohen. New York: Harper & Row, 1974, pp. 135-43.

[Graham, Martha]. "Martha Graham Speaks." *DO* 30, no. 4 (April 1963): 53-55.

Graham, Rockwell J. "Who Are Our Dance Critics?" *DM* 16, no. 3 (July 1931): 12, 55. (A survey of critics in the major American cities.)

Hellebrandt, Beatrice. "Manual for the Study of Dance Accompaniment." Mimeograph pamphlet. Madison: University of Wisconsin, Department of Physical Education, 1938. (A discussion of the status of the relationship between music and dance by a former Bennington student).

Hering, Doris. "While There Is Youth." *DM* 19, no. 1 (January 1945): 10-11, 22. (About the New Dance Group.)

Heymann, Jeanne Lunin. "Dance in the Depression: The WPA Project." *DS* 9, no. 2 (Spring/Summer 1975): 28-40.

Hill, Martha. "An Analysis of Accompaniment for the Dance." In *Dancing in the Elementary Schools*. The Committees on Dancing of the American Physical Education Association for the Years 1931 and 1932. New York: A. S. Barnes and Company, 1933, pp. 85-105.

Holm, Hanya. "Dance on the Campus: Athletics or Art?" *Dance* 1, no. 5 (February 1937): 11, 27.

_____. "The Attainment of Conscious, Controlled Movement." In Rogers, Frederick Rand. *Dance: A Basic Educational Technique.* New York: Macmillan, 1941, pp. 298-303.

Horan, Robert. "The Recent Theater of Martha Graham," in *Chronicles of The American Dance*, ed. Paul Magriel. New York: Henry Holt and Company, 1948; Da Capo Press, 1978. (Discussion of *Punch and The Judy.*)

[Horst, Louis]. "Louis Horst Considers the Question." *Impulse*, 1954, pp. 1-6.

Howe, Eugene C. "The Modern Dance and William Blake." *JHPE* 9, no. 1 (January 1938): 6-9, 60. (An analysis of Doris Humphrey's *With My Red Fires* in relation to Blake.)

Humphrey, Doris. "Declaration." Humphrey-Weidman program book, ca. 1938. (Reprinted in this book, p. 287.)

_____. "A Home for Humphrey-Weidman." *DO* 7, no. 9 (November 1940): 124-25.

_____. "My Approach to the Modern Dance." In Rogers, Frederick Rand. *Dance: A Basic Educational Technique.* New York: Macmillan, 1941, pp. 188-92.

_____. [A reply to George Beiswanger on the need for an American dance repertory.] *TA* 25, no. 10 (October 1941): 774.

_____. "America's Modern Dance." *TA* 34, no. 9 (September 1950): 48-50. Republished in *The Dance Experience*, ed. Nadel and Nadel. New York: Praeger Publishers, 1970, pp. 105-108.

[Humphrey, Doris]. "Doris Humphrey Speaks." *DO* 29, no. 3 (March 1962): 37-40. (Transcript of a talk in November 1956.)

Kirstein, Lincoln. "Ballet: Introduction and Credo." *DO* 4, no. 8 (October 1937): 94.

_____. "Ballet: Record and Augury." *TA* 24, no. 9 (September 1940): 651-59.

Kriegsman, Sali Ann. "Interview with a Modern Maverick: Pauline Koner." *DS* 13, no. 4 (Summer 1979): 36-53.

Kulynitch, Mary. "Louis Horst, A Historical Study of His Contributions to Modern Dance Choreography." Master's thesis, New York University, 1950 [NYPL].

Lippincott, Gertrude. "Will Modern Dance Become a Legend?" *DM* 21:11 (November 1947): 24-27, 40.

_____. "A Quiet Genius Himself—Louis Horst." *Focus on Dance V: Composition*, ed. Miriam Gray. Washington, D.C.: AAHPER, 1969, pp. 3-6.

_____. "Out of Old Contexts, Into New: The Schools and the New Dance." *DS* 4, no. 2 (Spring 1970): 26-38.

Lloyd, Norman. "American Composers Write for the Dance." *Pan Pipes*, December 1950, pp. 101-104. Reprinted in *DO* 18, no. 9 (November 1951): 132-34.

Love, Paul. "New Forms of the Dance." *Nation* 144, no. 24 (12 June 1937): 679-80 (Refers to *New Dance* and *Quest*. See also letter from Owen Burke, 31 July 1937, pp. 139-40.)

_____. "Theme and Variations." *Dance* 4, no. 4 (July 1938): 14. (About Humphrey-Weidman transcontinental tour and reception across the country to the modern dance.)

McDonagh, Don. "A Conversation with Gertrude Shurr." *BR* 4, no. 5 (1973): 3-20.

Manasevit, Shirley D. "A Last Interview with Charles Weidman." *DS* 10, no. 1 (Fall/Winter 1975-1976): 32-50.

Marsh, Lucile. "Criticizing the Critics." *AD* 7, no. 4 (January 1934): 10, 19. (Traces the beginnings of dance criticism in New York and describes the critic's responsibilities.)

Martin, John. "Toward a Dance Library." *TA* 18, no. 4 (May 1934): 361-72. (Martin's survey of the literature.)

_____. "The Dance—Pioneer American Art." *North American Review* 244, no. 2 (Winter 1937-1938: 231-50. (A major survey article.)

_____. "Dance Since Isadora." *TA* 24, no. 9 (September 1940): 639-48.

_____. "The Dance Completes a Cycle." *American Scholar* 12, no. 2 (Spring 1943): 205-15. (A survey of the history and status of the art at the beginning of the Second World War.) Reprinted in this book, pp. 288-90.

[Milton, Paul R.] "The Coxey's Army of the Concert World: A Study of the Ills and Ailments of the 'Serious' Dance Fields." *DM* 15, no. 2 (December 1930): 10, 52-53.

Murray, Ruth Lovell. "The Scene: In School and College." *Focus on Dance V: Composition*, ed. Miriam Gray. Washington, D.C.: AAHPER, 1969, pp. 24-26.

[National Dance Congress]. "Proceedings of the First National Dance Congress, 1936." (A collection of reports and essays dealing with the political, economic and artistic concerns of the Congress participants.) [NYPL].

Nikolais, Alwin. "The New Dimension of Dance." *Impulse*, 1958, pp. 43-46.

O'Brien, Dorothy Adelle. "Theoretical Foundation of Dance in American Higher Education, 1885-1932." Ph.D. dissertation, University of Southern California, 1966. (A study of the pioneers in American dance training at colleges; with a bibliography.) [LC microfilm].

Page, Barbara. "Music for the Dance." *TAM* 24, no. 9 (September 1940): 683-84.

Pease, Esther. "Louis Horst: His Theories on Modern Dance Composition." Ph.D. dissertation, University of Michigan, 1953. [Typescript available at NYPL; microfilm at LC.]

Riegger, Wallingford. "I Compose for the Modern Dance." *Dance* 3, no. 2 (November 1937): 12.

Rogers, Helen Priest. "Films for Notation." *DM* 39, no. 9 (September 1965): 55-57. (Describes Rogers' first experience making movies of the dance at the Bennington School, and her work at Connecticut College filming repertory.)

Rogosin, Elinor. "Visiting Charles: An Interview with Charles Weidman." *Eddy* 6, no. 6 (Spring 1975): 3-15.

Rosen, Lillie F. "The What of the Y." *Eddy* 6, no. 6 (Spring 1975): 22-28. (A report of the 92nd Street YM-YWHA during William Kolodney's years and after.)

Rubinstein, Lucille. "An Historical Study of Dance in Education in the United States in the First Quarter of the Twentieth Century." Master's thesis, New York University, 1940 [NYPL].

Rudhyar, Dane. "Modern Dance Group at the Cross-Road." Part I. *DO* 2, no. 8 (November 1935): 85, 92-93; Part II. *DO* 2, no. 9 (December 1935): 97, 103-104.

Sabin, Robert. "Louis Horst and Modern Dance in America." Four-part series in *DM* 27, nos. 1-4. Part 1: January 1953, pp. 21-22; Part 2: February 1953, pp. 23-24; Part 3: March 1953, p. 31; Part 4. April 1953, pp. 38-40.

Shawn, Ted. "How Beautiful Upon the Mountain. A History of Jacob's Pillow," ca. 1943. [Souvenir book.]

_____. "Remember: Jacob's Pillow Was a Stone: Some Rocky Reminiscences." *DM* 44, no. 7 (July 1970): 49-61.

Sherman, Jane. "Doris and Charles and Pauline Fifty Years Ago." *DM* 52, no. 10 (October 1978): 56-62.

Smith, Cecil; Lloyd, Margaret; Wilson, Samuel T., and Frankenstein, Alfred. "The Critic from Coast to Coast." *TA* 24, no. 9 (September 1940): 660-68.

Smith, Cecil. "Festival of American Dance at New London Includes Strong Group Composition by Martha Graham." *Musical America*, September 1948, pp. 7, 23.

Sorell, Walter. "Hanya Holm: A Vital Force." *DM* 31, no. 1 (January 1957): 22-27, 86-87, 89.

_____. "Weidman Returns to Lexington 'Y,' May 4." *DN* 57, no. 9 (May 1972): 1-2.

Spiesman, Mildred. "Creative Dance in American Life and Education." Doctor of Education project, Teachers College, Columbia University, 1949. [Available only at Teachers College.]

_____. "American Pioneers in Educational Creative Dance." A five-part series in *DM* 24, no. 11 (November 1950); 25, nos. 2, 6, 7, 9 (February, June, July, and September 1951).

_____. "Dance Education Pioneers: Colby, Larson, H'Doubler." *JHPER* 31, no. 1 (January 1960): 25-27. Republished in *Selected Articles on Dance II 1958-1967*. Washington, D.C.: AAHPER, n.d.

Terry, Walter. "The Sorry State of Dance Education." *ED* 3, no. 6 (December 1940): 6-7.

Theatre Arts. "Theatre Dance in America." Issue ed. George W. Beiswanger. 24, no. 9 (September 1940). (See individual articles by Beiswanger, Martin, Kirstein, and Smith.)

Von Qualen, Lillian. "A Quarter-Century of Dance in the Rockies." *DO* 6, no. 6 (June-July 1939): 233, 242. (Background on Perry-Mansfield.)

_____. "The Saga of Steamboat Springs." *Dance* 10, no. 9 (January 1942): 14, 23. (Background on Perry-Mansfield.)

_____. "March of Dance at Perry-Mansfield." *DO* 9, no. 5 (May 1942): 63-64.

Weidman, Charles. "Artists and Audiences." Humphrey-Weidman program book, ca. 1938. Reprinted in this book, p. 287.

Wenig, Adele. "'Imports and Exports,' 1700-1940." *Impulse*, 1963-1964, pp. 16-28. (Survey and listing of touring groups to and from America. Bibliography.)

Wolfson, Bernice J. "The Use of Words with Dance: A Brief History of the Use of Words with Movement and Dance and a Statement of Principles for Such Use in Modern Dance with a Compilation of Materials. . . ." Master's thesis, New York University, 1947 [NYPL].

Wynne, David W. "Three Years with Charles Weidman." *DP* 60 (Winter 1974).

Interviews

INTERVIEWS CONDUCTED BY THE AUTHOR

All interviews were conducted in the period 1976-1978. The nature of the subject's involvement with Bennington is in brackets, followed by the interview date.

Barbara Page Beiswanger, teacher [student] 15 May 1977.
George W. Beiswanger, teacher, critic [lecturer] 15 May 1977.
Ben Belitt, poet, Bennington College faculty [faculty] by telephone 25 May 1977.
George Bockman, dancer, Humphrey-Weidman Group [Teaching Assistant, student, dancer, choreographer] 3 April 1977.
Ethel Butler, dancer, Martha Graham Group [Teaching Assistant, Teaching Associate, dancer, choreographer] 14 February 1977.
Merce Cunningham, dancer, Martha Graham Group [student, dancer, choreographer] 20 April 1977.
Jean Erdman, dancer, Martha Graham Group [student, dancer, choreographer] 1 February 1977.
Francis Fergusson, Drama department, Bennington College [Director of Drama, School of the Arts] by telephone 23 May 1977.
Vivian Fine, composer, Bennington College faculty [Composer in Residence, 1938] 27 April 1977.
Tina Flade [Mooney], dancer, Mills College faculty [Alternate for Hanya Holm, 1935] by telephone 31 July 1977.
Eve Gentry [Henrietta Greenhood], dancer, Hanya Holm Group [dancer, faculty] by telephone 24 September 1977.
Harriette Ann Gray, dancer, Humphrey-Weidman Group [student] 9 April 1977.
Ray Green, composer [Composer in Residence, 1938] 1 February 1977.
Erick Hawkins, dancer, choreographer [dancer, Ballet Caravan, Martha Graham Group; student, choreographer, faculty] 13 August 1976.
Hanya Holm, choreographer [faculty] 30 November 1976.
Esther Junger [Klempner], dancer, choreographer [Bennington Fellow, 1937] by telephone 6 July 1977.
Louise Kloepper, dancer, Hanya Holm Group [Bennington Fellow, 1938; faculty, dancer] by telephone 23 May 1977.
Pauline Koner, dancer. 1 April 1948.
Norman Lloyd, composer [accompanist, composer, faculty] 13 July 1977.
Ruth Lloyd, pianist [accompanist] 13 July 1977.
Otto Luening, composer, Bennington College faculty [Director of Music, School of the Arts] 22 April 1977.
John Martin, critic [faculty, lecturer] 23 January 1977.
Sophie Maslow, dancer, Martha Graham Group [dancer] 25 January 1977.
Barbara Morgan, photographer [photographer, 1938] 10 March 1978.
Alwin Nikolais, choreographer [student] 16 March and 4 April 1977.
Lionel Nowak, composer, Bennington College faculty [composer, musical director Humphrey-Weidman] 27 April 1977.
May O'Donnell, dancer, Martha Graham Group [Assistant to Louis Horst, Teaching Assistant, student] 1 February 1977.
Linda Mann Reed [Ethel Mann], dancer, Humphrey-Weidman Concert Group [student] 3 April 1977.
Elizabeth Ruskay [Fraenkel], dance therapist [student] 27 January 1977.
Mark Ryder [Sasha Liebich], dancer, Martha Graham Group [student, dancer] 26 May 1977.
Bessie Schönberg, teacher [faculty] by telephone 15 October 1977.
Beatrice Seckler, dancer, Humphrey-Weidman Group [dancer] 27 January 1977.
Sybil Shearer, dancer, Humphrey-Weidman Group [student, Teaching Assistant] by telephone 9 April 1977.
Anna Sokolow, dancer, Martha Graham Group, choreographer [Assistant to Louis Horst, Bennington Fellow, 1937, dancer] 10 March 1978.
Walter Terry, critic. 28 January 1977.
Betty Lynd Thompson, teacher [student] by telephone 13 August 1977.

The following individuals clarified specific areas and/or contributed recollections of Bennington:

Ruth Alexander, teacher [student].
Sidney Bernstein [photographer].
Thomas Brockway, historian, Bennington College faculty.
Rosalind Cassidy, Chairman, Department of Physical Education, Mills College [Director, Mills College Summer Session, 1939].
Maxine Cushing Gray, dancer, Humphrey-Weidman Group [student, critic].
Agnes de Mille, choreographer.
Jane Dudley, dancer, Bennington College faculty [student; dancer. Martha Graham Group].
Carolyn Durand [Brooks] [dancer, Hanya Holm Group].
Edythe Gilfond, costume designer, Martha Graham Group.
Henry Gilfond, critic.
Ann Hutchinson Guest, co-founder, Dance Notation Bureau [student].
Anna Halprin [Schuman], dancer [student].
Donald Hatfield, photographer.
Martha Hill, Director, Dance Program, Juilliard School [Director, Bennington School of the Dance].
Ralph Jester, artist, filmmaker [Producer "Young America Dances"].
Henry Kurth, Director, Arch Lauterer Archives.
Pearl Lang [Lack], dancer, Martha Graham Group [student].
Eleanor Lauer, teacher [student, dancer].
Joan Levy, dancer, Humphrey-Weidman Concert Group [dancer].
Miriam Bleamaster Lidster, teacher [student].
Gertrude Lippincott, dancer-teacher [student].
Murray Louis, dancer, choreographer.
Ruth Murray, teacher [student].
Daniel Nagrin, choreographer, dancer.
Carroll Russell, collaborator with Louis Horst [student].
Nona Schurman, dancer, Humphrey-Weidman Group [faculty].
Henry Seymour, Bennington College faculty [Assistant to Arch Lauterer].
Virginia Tanner, dance educator [student].
Marian Van Tuyl, dancer educator [student, dancer, choreographer].

OTHER INTERVIEW SOURCES

1977 Oral History Program, Dance Division, American Association for Health, Physical Education and Recreation, Washington, D.C.

Alma Hawkins, interviewed by Christena L. Schlundt, 14 July 1971
Margaret H'Doubler, interviewed by Mary Alice Brennan, 8 October 1972
Ruth Lovell Murray, interviewed by Kathryn G. Ellis, 6 July 1971
Helen Priest Rogers, interviewed by E. Vickery Hubbard, 20 February 1972
Barbara Page Beiswanger, interviewed by Theodora Wiesner, 10 February 1975

Interviews by Billy Nichols for National Educational Television (WNET), "Four Pioneers" 1965 Phonotapes [NYPL].

Martha Hill
Hanya Holm
Charles Weidman

Oral History Project,
New York Public Library Dance Collection

The following interviews had been completed by May 1978. With the exception of Anna Sokolow, these sources were not accessible. Some had not yet been transcribed; other transcripts had not been cleared or were closed. The oral history with Anna Sokolow was utilized for background, with her kind permission.

William Bales
Ethel Butler
Jane Dudley
Nina Fonaroff
Hanya Holm
Pauline Koner
Pearl Lang
Sophie Maslow
Bessie Schönberg
Marion Scott
Anna Sokolow

Oral History Program, Columbia University

Interviews conducted by Theresa Bowers, November 1978–December 1979. As of December 1980, all materials were closed pending completion of a book by Bennington College. These interviews were initiated after completion of the author's study, under a grant from the National Endowment for the Humanities to Bennington College. In addition to those listed below, approximately one dozen persons were interviewed, but permissions were pending for inclusion in the series. (Information was obtained by the author from Elizabeth Mason, Columbia University Oral History Program, by telephone, 13 November 1980.)

Emily S. Alford	Eve Gentry	Kathleen Slagle Partlon
Fannie Aronson	Lucien Hanks	Bernice van Gelder Peterson
Martha Voice Bartos	Louise Allen Haviland	Helen Priest Rogers
Jeanne Beaman	Polly Hertz	Claudia Moore Reade
Ben Belitt	Martha Hill	Mary Schlivek
George Bockman	Faith Reyher Jackson	Mary-Averett Seelye
Thomas Brockway	Hazel Johnson	Gertrude Shurr
Elizabeth Burtner	Louise Kloepper	Philip Stapp
Ethel Butler	Welland Lathrop	Natalie Disston Terrell
Marian V. T. Campbell	Esther Rosenblatt Landa	Dorothy Bird Villard
Dorothy McWilliams Cousins	Eleanor Lauer	Betty Walburg
Robert Coburn	Ruth and Norman Lloyd	Elizabeth Waters
Hermine Santhoff Davidson	Otto Luening	Elizabeth Wertheimer
Vita Ginsburg Deming	Claire Strauss Miller	Natalie Harris Wheatley
Jean Erdman	Tina Flade Mooney	Mary Elizabeth Whitney
Francis Fergusson	Barbara Morgan	Theodora Wiesner
Vivian Fine	Ruth Murray	Robert Woodworth
Catherine Osgood Foster	Alwin Nikolais	Martha Wilcox
Elizabeth Ruskay Fraenkel	Lionel Nowak	Hortense Lieberthal Zera

Visual Records (Photographs, Films, Videotapes) and Scores

PHOTOGRAPHS

Most of the photographs in this book have not previously been published. Virtually all of the production photos were taken during rehearsal or actual performance at Bennington. It is instructive to compare these with photographs of subsequent productions or with studio photographs. Aside from some snapshots and a class photograph, very little photographic documentation of the 1934 and 1935 sessions was found. The summers of 1936-1939 are comparatively well documented, but the last years, 1940-1942, are not.

Sidney Bernstein, whose wife, Joan Levy, was a member of the Humphrey-Weidman Group, took photographs at Bennington in 1936-1938; Donald Hatfield, whose wife, Ruth Sanders Hatfield, was enrolled at Mills in 1939, shot the Bennington-Mills contingent. Eve Gentry's series of snapshots of the Hanya Holm Group in 1937 may be compared with those taken by Ruth Alexander two summers earlier. (Note that the movement looks less angular in 1937.) Betty Lynd Thompson's and Bertha Rhea Desenberg's candid shots of Bennington figures humanize the enterprise and show its no-frills life style.

The relative dearth of visual sources may be due partly to the scarcity and expense of cameras in those years, but also, as Nona Schurman points out, to the compelling drive at Bennington "to do new things . . . not to record the old."[1]

More photographs were found of Doris Humphrey, Charles Weidman, and Hanya Holm than of Martha Graham, possibly because Graham exercised tight control over conditions under which photographs were permitted to be taken and shown.

In most of the photographs that do exist of Humphrey-Weidman, notes Nona Schurman, the essence of their dance eluded the camera's fixed eye. Said Schurman:

> The point in Humphrey-Weidman is not the pose but the movement: Fall and Recovery, remember, "the arc between two deaths." The choreography is in the movement not in the position. That is why there are so few good pictures of this style of dance. It is the *movement* and its relationship to its space and time that *is* the dance—not the beginning and ending positions of the body instrument, as with Martha [Graham] and Ballet.[2]

During three summers (1936-1938), the School of the Dance employed two of America's finest dance photographers as "official photographers"—Thomas Bouchard and Barbara Morgan. Some of their extraordinary photographs can be studied at the Dance Collection of the New York Public Library, but most of their Bennington photographs remain inaccessible. Many negatives have never been printed. (Only four of Morgan's photographs and two of Bouchard's could be acquired for this book.)

Morgan considers her Bennington photographs purely experimental and not of professional calibre (see below). Nonetheless, they have value to dance historians because they show the dances at Bennington in their unfinished, experimental states. Bouchard and Morgan's Bennington photographs reveal the raw power of these dances, the original impulse behind them, and the force of their birth.

Comparing Morgan's later work, made under her artistic control, with that of Bouchard, one sees distinctions between them. See, for example, Bouchard's photograph of José Limón in *Danzas Mexicanas* shot at Mills in 1939 (*DP* no. 12) and Barbara Morgan's photograph made in 1944 (*Barbara Morgan*). The sweat and strain of creation are in Bouchard's; Morgan's shows us pure form and physical beauty. Or study Bouchard's photograph of Doris Humphrey as the Matriarch (*DP* no. 12) in a frenzy, propelled backward by her destructive power, and the beautifully composed studies Barbara Morgan made two years later (*Barbara Morgan*).

John Martin wrote about Bouchard: "Being touched himself with madness, he recognized and perpetuated the madness of the artists in their state of possession and of the art itself."[3] Bouchard often came upon the dancers unexpectedly. He eavesdropped with his camera. The dancers seem unconscious of the camera's eye. Many of his photographs were taken out of doors. The dancers appear to be in their natural element in the daylight, unbounded by four walls of studio or theater. The dances look unstaged, unfinished, raw, dynamic. The motion is sometimes blurred, the light dim (indoors). Costumes are unpressed, hems are unraveled, feet are dirty and bandaged, perspiration flows on dancers' bodies. Bouchard embraces all with his lens and does not censor. He does not prettify, tidy up, or manipulate dancer or environment. He has captured the dancer in a sacred moment, in the private act of dancing. One *feels* the co-mingling of striving, exhaustion, pain, and ecstasy in the dancer. The power of Bouchard's photographs is as much kinetic as visual.

In Morgan's later photographs, those made under her artistic control, the movement and the moment are already there—distilled from what Bouchard retains. Morgan seizes upon the realization rather than the attempt.

Bouchard's dancers fly out of the frame, impelled this way and that by the dance; he does not try to contain them in the compositional proscenium of the photograph. In a Bouchard photograph, the viewer completes the movement. One senses where the movement is going, and why. In a Morgan, one sees where the movement came from as well as where it is going. It is complete, perfect, enframed. Morgan captures the rhythm and poetry of specific gesture in light and shadow by a process of "previsioning." It is an elegant and vital distillation of an essentially visual moment. Her photographs have an aesthetic life apart from their subject, and a refinement not found in Bouchard's work. Morgan's dancers need the proscenium. The act of dancing, which seems private in Bouchard's photographs, is public in Morgan's, directed toward an audience.

Morgan and Bouchard have left a rich resource for dance historians, if only their work were more widely available.

Thomas Bouchard (Bennington, 1936, 1937, 1939)

Thomas Bouchard is listed as "official photographer" in the summers of 1936 and 1937; in 1939 he traveled to Mills in an unofficial capacity and shot photographs and film.

Bouchard, born about 1896 in France, began taking photographs at the age of fourteen in Paris and shortly afterwards emigrated to Houston, Texas, where he worked as a newspaper photographer. He made photographs in Hollywood during the silent film era and returned to Paris in 1926. He moved to New York in 1932 to work with Condé Nast but soon became restless. He had seen Isadora Duncan in San Francisco when he was a young man. In New York, Edgard Varèse took him to meet Martha Graham. His interest in the dance was fired by its dynamism. He was searching for intensity and dynamic beauty in his photographic work, and found the modern dance a natural subject.[4]

Margaret Lloyd described Bouchard's working methods at Bennington in 1936:

> A huntsman of mobility, his method is to stalk classes, stalk rehearsals, find his mark and shoot—sometimes after deliberation, at performances, sometimes, having chosen his sequences, at a special repetition of them. Thus he has made a record of the school's classwork and productions of 1936. Mounted on a tall ladder, careless of any hazard, I saw him at 1:30 of the morning following the final presentations of . . . *With My Red Fires* and *Quest*—absorbed in catching the fleeting flame of these great works. . . . Fugitive moments—the minutia of movement—are ensnared in his camera and held in the finished photograph, a visualization of the elusive and the intangible bound to perpetual life.[5]

The main published sources of Thomas Bouchard's photographs during the Bennington period are: John Martin, "Days of Divine Indiscipline," *DP* (Autumn 1961); John Martin, *America Dancing*. (New York: Dodge Publishing Company, 1936; Brooklyn: Dance Horizons, 1968). "Thomas Bouchard," *US Camera* 2 (February 1939): 14–17 includes biographical information and a few Bennington photographs.

Barbara Morgan (Bennington, 1938)

Barbara Morgan spent two weeks at Bennington in 1938 and took more than a hundred photographs of Festival productions in rehearsal and performance, as well as informal shots of the Bennington community. Most have never been published; many have never been printed from the original negatives. Though listed as "Official Photographer," Morgan considers her work at Bennington "exploratory and experimental, like that of the dancers":

> When I photograph seriously I do not do it in performance because I have to be able to essentialize and do the illumination I feel is right for that specific instant, not just the flow on the stage. I wasn't able at Bennington to set up the lights the way I would have wanted to, or to work the way I needed because they were rehearsing or experimenting themselves and I couldn't interrupt. I don't consider that the work I did there was up to my own standards. I absorbed, I studied, but I didn't seriously photograph. Bennington was an opportunity to see dances launched which later became more perfected, and in this free-wheeling atmosphere I got the sense of the moods of the students. The only photographs I ever did in performance aside from these were of *Trend* [the previous winter at the Mecca], which I shot from my seat.[6]

Morgan's Bennington work is an important resource because it shows the dances in their original rough-hewn states and may be compared to polished versions which Morgan photographed later on.

Morgan's preferred working method (which she employed in preparing *Martha Graham, Sixteen Dances in Photographs*) was to attend Graham's classes "in order to get the inside feeling, not just the external presentation." She learned from observing Graham's corrections what her intentions were. She then attended rehearsals and performances in various settings to see the different "emanations" in different-sized spaces. After repeated viewings, Morgan retained images of key gestures which she then isolated and "essentialized" in her photographs. In 1940 she said:

> Previsualization is the first essential of dance photography. The ecstatic gesture happens swiftly, and is gone. Unless the photographer previsions, in order to fuse dance action, light and space expression simultaneously, there can be no significant dance picture."[7]

As an art student at UCLA (1919–1923) Morgan felt the need to understand the moving human body (she was bored with the static artist's model). She studied the dance for two years with Bertha Wardell, a pupil of Isadora, in order to explore the "inner feeling" about dance and movement, and she then used dance in her course in abstract design at UCLA.

In the 1920s Morgan spent summers in the American Southwest, where she observed the rituals of the Hopi, Zuni, and Navajo. "That was the awakening of my whole feeling for dance. To me it was far more than entertainment, far more than an ego trip. It was the unifying inner force of the whole tribe."[8] Several years later, seeing Graham's *Primitive Mysteries* in New York, she was struck "by the Indian connection." She mentioned this to Julien and Marian Bryan (he was a photographer and filmmaker; she started the dance program at Sarah Lawrence and knew Graham). Bryan invited Morgan along to take still photographs while he filmed a solo of Graham in rehearsal. At this first meeting, Morgan told Graham about her feeling at seeing *Primitive Mysteries*. She proposed a book, and Graham agreed. The book was completed in 1941. Of the 16 dances, 4 had had Bennington premieres: *American Document, El Penitente, Letter to the World*, and *Punch and The Judy*. All of the photographs in the book were of productions after Bennington.

These are the main published sources of Barbara Morgan's photographs of Bennington works: Barbara Morgan, *Martha Graham, Sixteen Dances in Photographs* (New York: Duell, Sloan and Pearce, 1941); First Revised Edition (Dobbs Ferry: Morgan & Morgan, 1980). *Barbara Morgan* (Hastings-on-Hudson, N.Y.: Morgan & Morgan, 1972) includes photographs of *El Penitente, American Document, Letter to the World, With My Red Fires, Passacaglia, Mexican Suite (Danzas Mexicanas), Trend.* Has a substantial bibliography and lists institutions which hold Morgan prints. *Limited Edition Portfolio of Dance Photographs by Barbara Morgan* (Morgan & Morgan, 1977). Of ten images, there are two of *Letter to the World*, and one apiece of *El Penitente, Mexican Suite*, and *Passacaglia*. See also Barbara Confino, "Barbara Morgan: Photographing Energy and Motion," *Saturday Review* 7 (October 1972): 62–66.

NOTES

1. Letter from Nona Schurman, 26 March 1978.
2. Ibid.
3. John Martin, "Days of Divine Indiscipline," *DP* 12 (Autumn 1961).
4. Biographical information taken from "Thomas Bouchard," *US Camera* 2 (February 1939): 14–17.
5. Margaret Lloyd, "Pictures of Motion," *CSM*, 22 December 1936.
6. Interview with Barbara Morgan.
7. Barbara Morgan, "Photographing the Dance," *Graphic Graflex Photography* (New York: Morgan & Lester, 1st ed., 1940), pp. 230–39; cited in *Barbara Morgan* (Hastings-on-Hudson, N.Y.: Morgan & Morgan, 1972), p. 9.
8. Interview with Barbara Morgan.

FILMS AND VIDEOTAPES

The legacy of film from the Bennington years is meager. Precisely how many films have survived or were made cannot be determined. Sources remain obscure, secretive, or closed to the researcher. A few films that are known to exist are embargoed, for example Julien Bryan's documentary of Martha Graham, *Frontier* (1937), which shows Graham dancing at the peak of her performance career in one of her most enduring solos. Others, reported to have been made, have not surfaced. (For example, Margaret Lloyd writes in *The Borzoi Book of Modern Dance* that Thomas Bouchard filmed Limón's *Danzas Mexicanas* in 1939.)

Six movies made at Bennington were recovered by the author in the course of research for this project, and they are newly available to researchers. Two had been in storage for nearly forty years since Betty Lynd Thompson, a Bennington student (1938-1940) and head of the dance program at Oregon State College, made them. One of these contains rare color footage of Doris Humphrey, Charles Weidman, and José Limón. The other shows some of Louis Horst's compositions in modern forms, composed and performed by members of the Martha Graham Group in 1940—typical studies worked out during the summer session. (This latter, along with a superlative film made by Julien Bryan in 1937, *Steps in the Street* from *Chronicle* [which is not available], show an impulse, style, and movement concern strikingly different from that of today's Graham-trained dancers.) It is likely that Martha Graham is better documented than this filmography reveals; the Graham organization reportedly has a great deal of film that is off-limits to researchers.

Miriam Lidster's color home movies of the 1940 session have been deposited in the Dance Collection, NYPL.

Two Bennington films were rescued, courtesy of Ann Hutchinson Guest who obtained them from Zelia Raye. In 1939 Raye, a dance teacher associated with the Imperial Society of Teachers of Dancing in England, took the summer course at Mills and made two home movies, one in color, the other in black and white, which were later shown to students abroad but have not been available in America. Bennington artists, faculty, and students appear in informal scenes and there are movement sequences from a Humphrey-Weidman class. Thomas Bouchard is seen photographing José Limón and Charles Weidman.

There is virtually no film of Hanya Holm during this period of her career. Pauline Nelson's dance filmography lists a five-minute portion, "Resurgence," from Holm's *Trend*, but no leads to its whereabouts have surfaced. The lack of film compounds history's loss, since none of Holm's choreography from this period has survived in performance. A brief glimpse of Holm dancing can be seen in *Young America Dances*, 1939, a quasi-documentary Hollywood short that was located and preserved in 1978. This was the only professional film made of the Bennington School. It is important not only because it records such figures as Holm, Martha Graham, Doris Humphrey, Charles Weidman, Martha Hill, Ben Belitt, Norman Lloyd, Arch Lauterer, Louise Kloepper, and two young students—Alwin Nikolais and Merce Cunningham—but for what it reveals about the way modern dance had to be "packaged" for mass consumption. The 1939 Bennington session in California is more fully documented on film than any other. Perhaps the presence of a professional film crew provoked the rash of home movies taken of that session.

These films are both charming and important. They bring the period to life in a way no written records can. Fragments of movement give substance to the dances and the dancers one has read about but never seen. In most instances, they are all one has to go on. Not one complete original Bennington production is known to exist on film. Shards of *Passacaglia, New Dance, Panorama, American Document, El Penitente, Letter to the World,* and *Danzas Mexicanas* survive—a phrase here, a passage there—evocative, elusive. A few revivals have been filmed but not all of these are accessible: *With My Red Fires, New Dance,* and *Passacaglia* are; *El Penitente* and *Letter to the World* are not.

This listing concentrates on films made at or about Bennington and the technique, choreography, or teaching of the major figures. A few films that provide background or record performances of special interest are also included.

Contemporary film guides and catalogs were used to locate current sources. Equally helpful were out-of-print catalogs, filmographies, back issues of periodicals, and unpublished studies citing films which have since vanished. The most important of these were: George Amberg, "A Catalog of Dance Films," *Dance Index* 4, no. 5 (May 1945); Susan Braun, "Catalog of Dance Films," Dance Films Association, 1974; *Dance Magazine*, "1965 Directory of Dance Films," September 1965; Mary Jane Hungerford, "Dancing in Commercial Motion Pictures," Ph.D. dissertation, Columbia University, November 1946 (with an excellent bibliography); John Mueller, "Films on Ballet and Modern Dance," American Dance Guild, September 1974 and Addenda; Pauline Nelson, "Dance Filmography: A Guide to Motion Pictures of the Dance," Master's project, New York University, 1941 [NYPL]; New York Public Library, *Dictionary Catalog of the Dance Collection* (Boston: G. K. Hall & Co., 1974), 10 vols. and annual supplements.

Three important recent guides are: John Mueller, *Dance Film Directory: An Annotated and Evaluative Guide to Films on Ballet and Modern Dance* (Princeton, N.J.: Princeton Book Company, 1979); David L. Parker and Esther Siegel, *Guide to Dance Films* (Detroit: Gale Research Company, 1978); Dance Films Association, *Dance and Mime: Film and Videotape Catalog* (2nd edition of *Catalog of Dance Films*), compiled by Susan Braun and Jessie Kitching (New York: Dance Films Association, 1980).

Betty Lynd Thompson, Ann Hutchinson Guest, Ralph Jester, Zelia Raye, Miriam Lidster, Linda Mann Reed, Sam Bryan; John Mueller of the University of Rochester Dance Film Archive; Genevieve Oswald and Madeleine Nichols of the Dance Collection, New York Public Library; David Parker at the Library of Congress Motion Picture Section; Audrey Kupferberg of the American Film Institute; and Suzanne Weil of the National Endowment for the Arts were of critical help in locating, retrieving, identifying, and preserving these materials.

The location of study prints is given in brackets. Most films must be reserved by appointment; a few are closed to researchers or require special permission. The archives are:

ADF	American Dance Festival Archive Duke University Durham, North Carolina 27708 New York address: 1860 Broadway New York, New York 10023
LC	Library of Congress Motion Picture Section Washington, D.C. 20540
NA	National Archives Washington, D.C. 20408
NYPL	New York Public Library at Lincoln Center Dance Collection 111 Amsterdam Avenue New York, New York 10023

Verifiable sources for the sale or rental of prints are given; consult current film guides and individual distributors for prices and availability.

DFA	Dance Films Association, Inc. 250 West 57th Street New York, New York 10019
Illinois	University of Illinois Visual Aids Service Champaign, Illinois 61820
Indiana	Indiana University Audio-Visual Center Bloomington, Indiana 47401
NARS	National Archives and Record Services Audio-Visual Archives Washington, D.C. 20408
Rochester	University of Rochester Dance Film Archive Rochester, New York 14627

General Films Made At or About the Bennington School of the Dance and Associated Background

Martha Hill and Students at NYU Summer Camp. 1930–1933 (?). 16mm, b/w, silent, 10 min.

Martha Hill and New York University physical education graduate students practice a vigorous, propulsive series of movement studies on the shores of Sebago Lake, Sloatsburg, New York. The footage shows Hill's work with students immediately before the beginning of the Bennington summer project in 1934. [ADF, NYPL]

Bennington School of the Dance: Techniques by Students of the School. 1934. 16mm, b/w, silent.

Martha Hill demonstrates with a group of Bennington students on the green. Some sequences were used in the NET program "Four Pioneers." [ADF, NYPL]

The Bennington School of the Dance. 1938 at Bennington, Vermont; 1939 at Bennington-Mills, Oakland, California, Betty Lynd Thompson. 16mm, color, silent, 14 min. (16 fps. 358 ft.).

José Limón and five dancers perform movements from Charles Weidman's classroom studies at Mills. Charles Weidman and Doris Humphrey in duet sequences from *New Dance* at Mills; Humphrey-Weidman dancers at Bennington in part of "Variations and Conclusion" from *New Dance*; Doris Humphrey in solo fragment at Bennington; Harriette Ann Gray and William Bales at Bennington; Bonnie Bird demonstrating Graham movement at Mills.

Shot by Betty Lynd Thompson, faculty, Oregon State College Physical Education Department (a Bennington student, 1938–1940), and available for rental in 1941.

Preserved in 1977 and donated by Betty Lynd Thompson to the Library of Congress and the New York Public Library, Dance Collection. [NYPL, LC]

The Bennington School of the Dance at Mills College. 1939, Zelia Raye. 16mm, color, silent, app. 12 min.

Informal shots of Charles Weidman, Doris Humphrey, Martha Graham, Franziska Boas, Martha Hill, Mary Jo Shelly, Norman and Ruth Lloyd, José Limón, Louise Kloepper, Pauline Lawrence, Merce Cunningham, and other Bennington faculty and students at Mills, 1939. Some dance sequences taken during a Humphrey-Weidman class are similar to those in the film Betty Lynd Thompson made the same summer.

Preserved in 1977, courtesy of Ann Hutchinson Guest and Zelia Raye, by NYPL. [NYPL]

The Bennington School of the Dance at Mills College. 1939, Zelia Raye. 16mm, b/w, silent, app. 2 min.

Sequences taken in the Mills amphitheater of José Limón being photographed by Thomas Bouchard in parts of *Danzas Mexicanas*; Charles Weidman in a lunge movement, being photographed by Bouchard; Weidman demonstrating movement to José Limón on the amphitheater steps; Doris Humphrey walking across the stage in long white coat carrying drum; solo female dancer doing Humphrey movements; trio of girls doing falls and spiral sequence from Humphrey technique. The brief film ends with a shot of Katherine Manning seated on the steps holding a drum.

Preserved in 1978, courtesy of Ann Hutchinson Guest and Zelia Raye, by NYPL. [NYPL]

Young America Dances. 1939. Presented by Look Magazine and Ampix Productions. Intended for release through Paramount Pictures. Originally 35mm, b/w, sound, 10 min. (app. 1000 ft.). 16mm, b/w, sound, 10 min. (382 ft.). Ralph Jester, Producer-director, American Pictures, Inc., Culver City, California.

A documentary short intended for theatrical release through Paramount Pictures. This was the only professional film made of the Bennington School of the Dance. It was shot entirely during the 1939 session, Mills College, Oakland, California. The film was previewed in New York and California (1939-1940) but never achieved theatrical distribution. Bennington College withheld its imprimatur; there is no mention of Bennington College or the Bennington School of the Dance.

Producer-director Ralph Jester taught art at Bennington College when it first opened (1932-1933) and later worked in the art department at Paramount under Cecil B. De Mille. He took a 15-member crew to Mills College, where they filmed four days of classes and demonstrations led by the Big Four, as well as performances by José Limón, Louise Kloepper, and Ethel Butler and student work (a total of 17,000 feet, of which 1000 were used). A scripted story has two young women, one a tap dancer and the other interested in "serious" dance, visit the Mills campus, where they experience the rigors and variety of modern dance. The film was touted as the first of its kind to deal with American modern dance, and it was intended to generate publicity for the dancers and the art. The final cut contains a powerful performance by Louise Kloepper of her 1938 solo, *Statement of Dissent* (not complete), and a sample of student work, Hortense Lieberthal's *Never Sign a Letter Mrs.*, based on Emily Post prose. There is some very rare but frustratingly brief footage of Hanya Holm dancing, and similar fragments of Martha Graham, Doris Humphrey, and Charles Weidman. Martha Hill, Ben Belitt, Norman Lloyd, and Arch Lauterer are seen working with students. A Graham technique class includes Merce Cunningham (his first Bennington summer) and Alwin Nikolais (his last). Conspicuous among those left on the cutting-room floor are Louis Horst and José Limón. Gregory Tucker's music for *Statement of Dissent* was replaced with a less modern-sounding score by a Hollywood composer, who scored most of the rest of the film as well. The narration, music, and focus suggest the kinds of compromises involved in presenting the modern dance to a moviegoing audience. The producer tried "not to be so modern as to drive Joe Doaks out of the theater."

Preserved in 1978, courtesy of Ralph Jester, by the American Film Institute.

[LC, The American Film Institute Collection]

Bennington School of the Arts. 1940, Miriam Bleamaster Lidster. 8mm, color, silent.

Katherine Manning, Claudia Moore, George Bockman, and Harriet Roeder at Bennington School of the Arts, 1940.

[NYPL]

Bennington, 1941. Excerpts of performances filmed by Ann Barzel in the College Theatre, including

1. *El Penitente.* Cunningham, Hawkins, and Graham.
2. *Letter to the World.* Hawkins, Cunningham, Erdman.

Preserved by the National Endowment for the Arts, 1977.

[NYPL, LC]

Dance: Four Pioneers [Part Two of ***USA Dance***]. 1965, WNET-TV, National Educational Television. 16mm, b/w, sound, 29 min. (1080 ft.). Jac Venza, Producer; Virginia Kassel, Assoc. Producer, Charles S. Dubin, Director; Bo Goldman, Writer. Audio interviews by Billy Nichols.

An introduction in documentary form to the Bennington years. Film clips include portions from the Bennington footage listed above. Barbara Morgan's photographs illustrate productions. The first half deals with Bennington and includes a brief look inside the Vermont State Armory. The film concludes with a complete performance of Humphrey's *Passacaglia and Fugue in C minor* by American Dance Theater, 1965 (see *Passacaglia* below for details of that production). John Mueller's notes are an invaluable guide to this film (see "Films on Ballet and Modern Dance," 1974).

Sale and Rental: Indiana. Rental: DFA, Rochester.

[NYPL]

Festival of the Dance, 1973. Ted Steeg Productions, 16mm, color, sound, 60 min.

A documentary on the reconstruction of works by Doris Humphrey (*New Dance, With My Red Fires*), Charles Weidman (*Flickers*), and José Limón (*Emperor Jones*) by a special repertory company assembled for the American Dance Festival, Connecticut College, in 1972. Charles Weidman and José Limón reminisce about the early days of modern dance. Outtakes of parts of *New Dance* and *With My Red Fires* are included.

Sale and Rental: Rochester. [ADF, NYPL]

Films of Martha Graham

Graham, Techniques of. Ca. 1935. 16mm, b/w, silent, shot out of doors at Bennington. Demonstrated by Dorothy Bird and Bonnie Bird.

Demonstration of technique. A group of Bennington students or members of the Martha Graham Group dance on the green. Footage was used in *Four Pioneers*. [ADF, NYPL]

Compositions in Modern Forms by Martha Graham Dance Group under the Direction of Louis Horst. 1940, Betty Lynd Thompson. 16mm, b/w, silent, app. 288 ft.

Nina Fonaroff, Jane Dudley, Sophie Maslow, with Ethel Butler, Nelle Fisher, Frieda Flier, Elizabeth Halpern. Includes *Archaic Duet, The Wrestlers, Air Primitive, Impressionism, Medieval Dance: The Kiss of Judas*. These dances were presented in student workshops at Bennington in 1940. The film was available for rental from Betty Lynd Thompson, Oregon State College, in 1941.

Preserved in 1977, courtesy of Betty Lynd Thompson, by NYPL. [NYPL]

American Document (1938). 1939 touring production. Auditorium Theater, Chicago. Filmed excerpt by Ann Barzel.

Also excerpts from *Frontier, American Lyric,* and *Chronicle,* 1938 and *Every Soul Is a Circus*, 1940.

Preserved by the National Endowment for the Arts, 1977. [NYPL, LC]

Selections from Panorama (1935) ***and American Document*** (1938). Bennington School of the Dance. 16mm, b/w, silent, app. 15 min.

Sequences from *Panorama* were filmed inside the Vermont State Armory in 1935, with the large Bennington Workshop Group in costume, including members of the Martha Graham Group. Jane Dudley and Ethel Butler can be clearly identified, and Martha Graham appears in several brief movements.

Sequences from *American Document* show up more clearly in rehearsal inside the Armory. Erick Hawkins and Martha Graham rehearse a duet; Houseley Stevens, Jr., the Interlocutor, moves in and out of the sequences. This is Hawkins' first appearance with the Graham group. [ADF, NYPL]

Chronicle: Steps in the Street (1937). 1937, Julien Bryan. 16mm, b/w, silent.

A segment from the suite *Chronicle* is performed by the Graham group during the year of its premiere. The film shows the choreography and dancers from several camera perspectives. This section of *Chronicle* was not performed at Bennington. During the 1937 summer session, Martha Graham performed a solo from the suite, titled *Spectre 1914*.

El Penitente (1940). 1964, Dwight Godwin. 16mm, b/w, sound, 19 min. (684 ft.). A Connecticut College School of the Dance Archive film. Choreography reconstructed by Martha Graham. Music: Louis Horst; Settings: Isamu Noguchi. Danced by: David Wood (Penitent), Marnie Thomas (Mary figure), Gene McDonald (Christ figure). Revived for the Louis Horst Memorial Program, 16 August 1964. [ADF, NYPL]

El Penitente (1940). 1941, Ann Barzel. 16mm, b/w, silent.

Very brief fragment, shot in the College Theatre at Bennington, with Graham, Hawkins, and Cunningham. Also *Letter to the World*.

Preserved by the National Endowment for the Arts, 1977. [NYPL, LC]

Frontier (1935). 1937, Julien Bryan and Jules Bucher. 16mm, b/w, silent.

An important record of Martha Graham in her solo from the suite *Perspectives*, two years after its première, with the original Noguchi set. The dance is shown from several camera perspectives. Though *Frontier* was not a Bennington premiere, Graham performed it in recitals at Bennington in 1935, 1936, and 1937.

Lamentation (1930). 1943, Simon and Herta Moselsio and the Harmon Foundation. 16mm, sound, color, 10 min. (360 ft.)

The title reads: "A Motion Picture Study of Martha Graham from her Dance, Lamentation." Many separate takes were edited together for this film.

Graham performed *Lamentation* in 1934 and again in 1937 at Bennington. This film was made the summer after the end of the Bennington project. Simon Moselsio was a sculptor on the faculty of Bennington College. Louis Horst is shown playing the score. The film opens with Graham sitting under a tree on the Bennington campus, consulting a musical score. John Martin introduces the work.

Sale: NARS; rental: Illinois, DFA. [NYPL, NA]

Letter to the World (1940). 1941, Ann Barzel. 16mm, b/w, silent.

A brief fragment, shot in the College Theatre at Bennington, with Erdman, Hawkins, and Cunningham. Also *El Penitente*.

Preserved by the National Endowment for the Arts, 1977. [NYPL, LC]

Letter to the World (1940). 16mm, b/w, sound, 57 min. (2053 ft.). Filmed in rehearsal 5 December 1973 for the Jerome Robbins Film Archive, NYPL, by Compton-Ardolino Films, Inc. Music: Hunter Johnson; Pianists: Stanley Sussman, Lewis Stewart; Sets: Arch Lauterer; Costumes after designs by Edythe Gilfond. Performed by members of the Martha Graham Dance Company.

Pearl Lang (One Who Dances), Jean Erdman (One Who Speaks), William Carter (Lover), Armgard von Bardeleben (Ancestress), David Hatch Walker (March), Phyllis Gutelius (Fairy Queen), Takako Asakawa (Young Girl), Judith Hogan and Yuriko Kimura (Two Children), with Lucinda Mitchell, Peter Sparling, Mario Delano, Holly Cavrell, Bonnie Oda, Eric Newton, and Tim Wengerd. [NYPL closed]

Films of Doris Humphrey and Charles Weidman

Doris Humphrey. Ca. 1935 and 1938. 16mm, b/w, silent, 21 min. (498 ft.).

"Doris Humphrey is seen dancing alone, with members of her group, including José Limón, and in informal shots with her son." [NYPL Catalog].

Sequences from "Variations and Conclusion" from *New Dance*, and *Passacaglia* were filmed at Bennington out of doors. In *New Dance*, José Limón, Edith Orcutt, Gloria Garcia, Sybil Shearer, and Katherine Manning have been identified. Sequences from *Passacaglia* may have been filmed while Humphrey was still working on it. Dancers include Humphrey, Limón (who was not in the original production), Claudia Moore, Ethel Mann. [Viewed with Linda Mann Reed (Ethel Mann), who danced the premiere of *Passacaglia*.] [NYPL]

The Modern Dance: Humphrey Technique. 1935 or 1936, Pictorial Films. 16mm, b/w, silent, 11½ min. (280 ft.).

Five exercises selected from Doris Humphrey's technique performed by members of her concert group: Beatrice Seckler, Katherine Manning, Letitia Ide, Edith Orcutt, and Katherine Litz. Filmed indoors, probably not at Bennington, but shows Humphrey technique from that period. [NYPL]

Charles Weidman and Doris Humphrey. 1935-1936(?), 1939, Helen Knight at Bennington, Vermont, and Bennington-Mills. 16mm, b/w, silent, 5 min.

Includes excerpt from *New Dance* out of doors at Bennington, Vermont, 1935 or 1936, with Letitia Ide, Katherine Manning, Katherine Litz, Beatrice Seckler, Doris Humphrey, Sybil Shearer, Joan Levy, Edith Orcutt, George Bockman, José Limón, Charles Weidman, and Bill Matons. Parts of the "Women's Dance," "Men's Dance," "Processional." Also Charles Weidman at Mills, 1939 in movements from *On My Mother's Side* and "Mazurka" from *Opus 51*; José Limón in movements from *Danzas Mexicanas*, 1939. [Viewed with Linda Mann Reed (Ethel Mann), former member of Humphrey-Weidman Company.] Note: In 1973 Charles Weidman viewed this film and described its content on tape in the form of a narration [NYPL phonotape]. [NYPL]

Perry-Mansfield Celebrities (1930-1950). Portia Mansfield. 16mm, color, silent, 48 min. (1162 ft.).

Includes shots of Louis Horst. Doris Humphrey performs a solo variation from *Passacaglia* in yellow costume. José Limón performs a solo. Also Charles Weidman and Harriette Ann Gray. Later footage shows Hanya Holm and Valerie Bettis. [NYPL]

New Dance (1935). 1938 production. Brief extract filmed by Ann Barzel, Auditorium Theater, Chicago. (Also, *To the Dance, Race of Life,* and *The Shakers*: excerpts.)

Preserved by the National Endowment for the Arts, 1977. [NYPL, LC]

New Dance (1935). 1972, Amram Nowak Associates. 16mm, b/w, sound, 23 min. (833 ft.).

This is a reconstruction by Charles Weidman, performed by members of the Charles Weidman Dance Theatre Company on 11 May 1972 at Barnard College, New York, prior to the revival at the American Dance Festival the same year.

At the time of this reconstruction, only two sections of the Riegger score could be located ("Processional" and "Celebration"). Charles Weidman engaged Stephen Morris to compose new music for the "First Theme" and "Second Theme"; the "Third Theme" was originally a percussion score by Weidman, which he restored. The opening "Prelude" was completely lost and had to be newly composed by Morris and Weidman.

Choreography: Doris Humphrey ("First Theme," "Second Theme," "Processional," "Celebration") and Charles Weidman ("Prelude" and "Third Theme"). "Variations and Conclusion" was not included in this reconstruction. Music: Wallingford Riegger, with additional music newly composed by Stephen Morris.

Dancers: Janet Towner and Robert Kosinski, with Barry Barychko, Selby Beebe, Robert Ghigliotty, Myra Hushansky, Joey Kramer, Donna Mondanaro, Margaret O'Sullivan, Paul Wilson, and Janice Wodynski.

[NYPL, Jerome Robbins Film Archive]

New Dance (1935). 1978, Ted Steeg Productions. 16mm, color, sound, 30 min.

There are two films, one made with a single fixed camera at some distance (record film) and the other edited from several camera angles. Filmed 30 June 1972 at the American Dance Festival, New London, Connecticut. The American Dance Festival Repertory Company, with Linda Tarnay and Peter Woodin, principal soloists.

This production was under the supervision of Charles Weidman with assistance from Edith Orcutt and Beatrice Seckler and includes "Variations and Conclusion," omitted in the Barnard version (May 1972), which was reconstructed from Labanotation by Jennifer Muller and Christine Clark. The Riegger score, which had not been found in time for the Barnard reconstruction, is used in this production. One piano, four-hands and percussion. Charles Weidman choreographed the "Prelude" and "Third Theme" (Men's Dance) and also provided the rhythms for the "Third Theme," which Musical Director Gerald Tarack then scored for percussion instruments.

Sale and rental (record film): Rochester. [NYPL]

Variations and Conclusion of New Dance (1935). 1972, Ted Steeg Productions. 16mm, color, sound, 7 min. Record film.

A single, fixed-camera record of the last movement of *New Dance*, excerpted from the 1972 Ted Steeg film. The American Dance Festival Repertory Company.

Sale and rental: Rochester.

New Dance: Variations and Conclusion (1935). 1959. 16mm, color, silent, app. 6 min. (179 ft.).

Reconstructed from Labanotation by Ann Hutchinson. Performed by the Senior Modern Dance Group, School of Performing Arts, New York City. [NYPL]

New Dance: Variations and Conclusion (1935). 1960. 16mm, color, silent, 9 min. (253 ft.). School of Performing Arts, New York City.

Reconstructed from Labanotation by Ann Hutchinson. [NYPL]

New Dance: Variations and Conclusion (1935). 1963, Dwight Godwin, Juilliard School. Juilliard Dance Ensemble. Direction: Ruth Currier; Artistic Collaborator: José Limón. 16mm, b/w, sound, 7 min. (265 ft.).

An onstage rehearsal, July 1963, with Jennifer Muller. [NYPL, Martha Hill Collection]

New Dance: Variations and Conclusion (1935). 1967. 16mm, color, sound. 8 min. (279 ft.). Senior modern dance students (group of 10), School of Performing Arts, New York City.

Reconstructed from Labanotation and film by Jennifer Muller. [NYPL]

Opus 51: Opening Dance (1938). 1972, Gardner Compton, Ltd., for the Jerome Robbins Film Archive, NYPL. Filmed 23 May 1972 at the 92nd Street YM-YWHA. 16mm, b/w, sound, 7 min.

Performed under Charles Weidman's supervision by members of Charles Weidman's Theatre Dance Company: Selby Beebe, Myra Hushansky, Margaret O'Sullivan, Janet Towner, Janice Wodynski. [NYPL, Jerome Robbins Film Archive]

Passacaglia and Fugue in C minor (1938). 1957, Helen Priest Rogers, Connecticut College, American Dance Festival, Palmer Auditorium, New London, Connecticut. 16mm, b/w, silent (shot at sound speed), 13 min. (468 ft.).

Danced by members of Doris Humphrey's repertory class in a revival at Connecticut College in August 1957. Soloists: Lola Huth, Glen Tetley. Costumes, sets, and performance lighting. [Note: This is not the same performance that was recorded in Labanotation, although it is similar to it.] [NYPL]

Passacaglia and Fugue in C minor (1938). 1965. Second half of WNET-TV, National Educational Television program "Dance: Four Pioneers," 16mm, b/w, sound.

Performed by the American Dance Theater, Lincoln Center, 1965. Staged by Lucy Venable, with soloists Lola Huth and Chester Wolenski. Organist: Richard Grant. Company members: (original performance by ADT, 2 March 1965, New York State Theater) Janet Aaron, Margaret Beals, Carolyn Dyer, Phyllis Gutelius, Sharon Kinney, Kathryn Posin, Sara Rudner, Nancy Stevens, Judith Willis, Manuel Alum, Glenn Brooks, Raymond Cook, Haruki Fujimoto, Heinz Poll. [See John Mueller, "Films on Ballet and Modern Dance," 1964, for a detailed analysis of the work, as performed in this version.]

Sale and rental: Indiana; rental: Rochester. [NYPL]

Passacaglia and Fugue in C minor (1938). 1969. Videotape, Reel 2, b/w, sound. Students, Dance Department, School of Performing Arts, New York City. Staged by Jennifer Muller. [NYPL]

Passacaglia and Fugue in C minor (1938). 1972, Dwight Godwin. 16mm, color, sound, 15 min. (548 ft.).

Performed May 1972 at the Juilliard School by the Juilliard Dance Ensemble, directed by José Limón. [NYPL]

With My Red Fires (1936). 1978, Ted Steeg Productions. 16mm, color, sound, 30 min. Filmed 28 July 1972, American Dance Festival, New London, Connecticut.

There are two films of the same performance: a "record" film with a single fixed camera, and a "performance" film edited from several camera angles.

The work was staged by Christine Clark from the Labanotation score. Ruth Currier, Artistic Director. An original score for small orchestra in Wallingford Riegger's hand was arranged by Gerald Tarack for two pianos, two percussionists, and voice and recorded for use in this performance. American Dance Festival Repertory Company with Nina Watt and Raymond Johnson, The Lovers; Marc Stevens, The Herald; Dalienne Majors, The Matriarch.

Sale and rental (both versions): Rochester. [NYPL]

LABANOTATION SCORES OF WORKS PREMIERED AT BENNINGTON

TITLE	NOTATOR AND DATE	LOCATION
New Dance ch/Doris Humphrey m/Wallingford Riegger	Notation of the 1980 reconstruction by Deborah Carr's Theatre Dance Ensemble in progress 1980	DNB
New Dance: Variations and Conclusion ch/Doris Humphrey m/Wallingford Riegger	Els Grelinger, Ann Hutchinson, 1949	DNB, OSU
*Passacaglia and Fugue in C minor** ch/Doris Humphrey m/J. S. Bach	Lucy Venable, assisted by Joan Gainer. As reconstructed at Juilliard by Doris Humphrey, 1954-1955.	DNB, OSU
With My Red Fires ch/Doris Humphrey m/Wallingford Riegger	Els Grelinger, Lucy Venable, Rena Gluck, Karen Kanner, and Muriel Topaz, under supervision of Lucy Venable. As learned and performed at Juilliard under Doris Humphrey's supervision, 1954. New version by Muriel Topaz, 1965	DNB, OSU
El Penitente ch/Martha Graham m/Louis Horst	Muriel Topaz. score incomplete (1976)	DNB

*At Bennington the work was titled *Passacaglia in C minor*.

DNB = Dance Notation Bureau
OSU = Ohio State University

Information verified by Dr. Mary Jane Warner, Kirkland College and Muriel Topaz, Director of Labanotation, Dance Notation Bureau.

APPENDIX A

Brief Biographies of Bennington Figures

Included are choreographers and composers whose works had their premieres at Bennington (summers 1934-1942) and major faculty, staff, and critics. Emphasis is on their activity and background prior to the Bennington years, and briefly on the nature of their later work. Further details about their Bennington activities are in the book's main text. Sources were standard biographical references, interviews, clippings, chronologies, program books, etc. Every effort was made to verify data (birthdates are especially unreliable). These sketches indicate the trajectory of individual careers in relation to the Bennington experience. The reader should refer to bibliographies and standard sources for fuller biographical information. For biographies of other persons associated with Bennington (e.g., Alwin Nikolais, Barbara Morgan, Thomas Bouchard), consult the index.

William Bales

Born 1910, Pittsburgh. University of Pittsburgh, Carnegie Institute of Technology. Studied Dalcroze Eurhythmics, folk dancing, ballet. Dance director, Irene Kaufman Settlement, Pittsburgh, 1931-1935. Martha Hill encouraged Bales to audition for a scholarship with Charles Weidman. Member, Humphrey-Weidman Concert Group, 1936-1940. Faculty assistant, Bennington College, 1940. (Bales later took charge of the dance department. He left in 1966 to set up a dance program at the new State University of New York-Purchase campus.) Bales performed with the Humphrey-Weidman dancers at Bennington, summers 1936-1938, 1941. Assisted Weidman there in 1938; taught tap 1941. His first major choreographic essay, *Es Mujer*, was produced in a Bennington summer workshop, 1941. Soon afterward he was guest artist with Hanya Holm and studied technique with Martha Graham and ballet. In 1943, Bales formed a trio with Sophie Maslow and Jane Dudley which toured the United States until the early 1950s. Bales directed a summer dance program at Connecticut College in 1947, the year before the inauguration of the American Dance Festival.

George W. Beiswanger

Born 1902, Baltimore. Carthage College; Hamma Divinity School; Ph.D., State University of Iowa, 1928. Philosophy faculty: Wittenberg College, 1923-1925; Ohio Wesleyan University, 1928-1935; Monticello College, 1935-1939; Women's College, Georgia, 1944-1963; Chairman, Division of Fine Arts, 1950-1963; Georgia State University, 1963-1969, Emeritus Professor of Philosophy, 1969- . Assistant Editor and Dance Critic, *Theatre Arts*, 1939-1944. Contributing Critic *Dance Observer*. Dance Critic, *Atlanta Journal*, 1967-1972.

Ben Belitt

Poet. Born 1911, New York City. University of Virginia faculty, 1932-1936. Assistant Literary Editor, *Nation*, 1936-1937. Shelley Memorial Award in Poetry, 1936. Author, *The Five Fold Mesh*, 1938. Bennington College literature faculty, 1938- . Belitt's first experience with the modern dance was a recital by Anna Sokolow around 1936. He participated informally in the Bennington summer session, 1938, as an observer and worked especially with Hanya Holm. Belitt codirected an experimental workshop at Bennington-Mills, 1939, and was on the faculty of the Connecticut College School of the Dance, 1948-1949. He has written poems for dancers. (Martha Graham's *Diversion of Angels* was originally titled *Wilderness Stair*, from a Belitt poem.)

Franziska Boas

Daughter of anthropologist Franz Boas. Studied with Bird Larson. Attended Barnard College. Studied with Hanya Holm and was her percussionist for six years. Directed the Boas School, New York. In 1944 opened a summer school at Bolton Landing, Lake George, which featured improvisation, composition, and percussion. Head of dance, Bryn Mawr College. Established a dance major at Shorter College, Rome, Georgia. Faculty, Halprin-Lathrop School, San Francisco. Author, *The Function of Dance in Human Society*, 1944.

Ethel Butler

Ethel Butler first saw Martha Graham at the Neighborhood Playhouse and left high school in Brooklyn to study on a two-year Playhouse scholarship. She joined the Graham group in 1933 and was one of Graham's principal teaching assistants and confidants during the next decade. Butler began to choreograph in these years, and in 1943-1944 she moved to Washington, D.C., to teach and choreograph independently. From 1946 to 1978 Butler had her own Washington studio, where she taught and choreographed and directed a company. Her students include Paul Taylor, Dan Wagoner, Lillo Way, and Kenneth Rinker. Faculty, University of Maryland, 1978–

John Cage

Born 1912, Los Angeles. Piano study with Richard Bulig, composition with Adolph Weiss, Henry Cowell, Arnold Schoenberg. Organized percussion groups on the West Coast beginning about 1936. Faculty, Cornish School, Seattle, 1937-1939 (composer-accompanist for Bonnie Bird), where he first met Merce Cunningham. In 1938 Cage wrote *Bacchanale* for dancer Syvilla Fort at Cornish, employing a new invention of his, the "prepared" piano. Composer, Mills College summer session, 1939, while the Bennington dance school was on campus (Cage presented a program of percussion music). In 1941 he accompanied for Katherine Manning's dance classes in Chicago and in 1942 he moved to New York and wrote *Credo in Us* for Merce Cunningham and Jean Erdman, which they performed at Bennington that summer. Cage and Cuningham began to tour in the mid-1940s and Cage became musical director of the Cunningham Dance Company. They worked together at Black Mountain College (1948, 1952, 1953). *Theater Piece* (Black Mountain, 1952) is known as the first "happening."

Henry [Leland] Clark[e]

Born 1907, Dover, New Hampshire. Composer, choral conductor. Studied piano with Ruth Olive Roberts, viola with Bertha L. Nichols. Harvard University (Ph.D., 1947). Composition with Nadia Boulanger, Gustav Holst, Hans Weisse,se, and Otto Luening. Assistant, Music Division, New York Public Library, 1932-1936. Teaching assistant, music, Bennington College, 1936-1938. Faculty, Westminster Choir College, Vassar College, University of Washington, Seattle. Has written for chorus, orchestra, band, opera.

Henry Cowell

Born 1897, Menlo Park, California. Died 1965. Debut (composer-pianist) 1912, San Francisco. Cowell was a major innovator and prolific composer whose output was exceeded only by the variety of his musical writing. He was a devout champion of modern music (founder, *New Music Quarterly*, 1927) and worked with numerous dancers and choreographers. In 1928 Cowell was the first American composer invited to the Soviet Union. Faculty, New School of Social Research, 1928-1963. He began working with dancers as early as 1923 and his music was performed by such choreographers as Doris Humphrey, Charles Weidman, Martha Graham, Tina Flade, Hanya Holm, Bonnie Bird, Erick Hawkins, Gertrude Lippincott, and Jean Erdman. His 1937 score for Martha Graham (*Immediate Tragedy*) was composed in California in "elastic" form, and fitted to the dance at Bennington. In 1941 Cowell visited the Bennington School of the Arts and conducted a recital of contemporary music in the last Bennington Festival.

Mercier [Merce] Cunningham

Born 1919, Centralia, Washington. Began dance training at twelve with Mrs. J. R. Barrett. Studied tap, folk, ballroom. Wanted to be an actor. At Cornish School, Seattle (1937-1939), he first met John Cage and studied with Bonnie Bird. Cunningham attended the 1938 summer dance session at Mills College and danced in Lester Horton's *Conquest*. In 1939 he returned, with Cage and Bird, to enroll in the Bennington session. He studied composition with Louis Horst and took class with Charles Weidman and Ethel Butler (Graham technique). At Mills, Graham invited Cunningham to join her group in New York. He made his debut in December 1939 in *Every Soul Is a Circus* and danced major roles with the company until 1945 (including the Christ Figure in *El Penitente*, the Revivalist in *Appalachian Spring*, and March in *Letter to the World*). Cunningham was with the Graham troupe at Bennington in 1940 and 1941 and in 1942 he made his choreographic debut there with Jean Erdman in a program they repeated at the Humphrey-Weidman Studio Theatre in New York. He made his solo debut in 1944 while still with the Graham company and during this period studied ballet at the School of American Ballet. Cunningham was commissioned by Lincoln Kirstein to choreograph *The Seasons* (music by Cage, designs by Noguchi) for Ballet Society, forerunner of the New York City Ballet, 1947, and taught modern technique at the School of American Ballet. He and John Cage performed on tour in the 1940s and early 1950s. They first visited Black Mountain College in 1948 and returned in 1952 and 1953. The Cunningham Dance Company as an entity dates from 1953. In 1959 Cunningham opened his first New York studio.

Jane Dudley

Born 1912, New York. Studied with Hanya Holm at the New York Wigman School, 1931-1935. Joined the New Dance Group 1934 and began choreographing at that time. Apprenticed with Martha Graham in the Bennington Workshop, 1935 (*Panorama*), and joined the Graham group in 1936, remaining with it for about a decade. Dudley created the role of the Ancestress in *Letter to the World*. She continued to compose while in the Graham group (*Harmonica Breakdown*, 1940); toured as a solo recitalist and taught, and in 1942 formed a trio with Sophie Maslow and William Bales which toured the United States. Dudley retired from dancing in 1954 (but danced in the 1970 revival of *Letter to the World*). Faculty, New Dance Group Studio, Bennington College, 1966, London School of Contemporary Dance, 1971.

A. Lehman Engel

Born 1910, Jackson, Mississippi. Cincinnati Conservatory, 1926-1929; Juilliard, 1930-1934. Composer, conductor. Studied composition with Rubin Goldmark and Roger Sessions. Wrote his first Broadway show in 1934. Composed more than a dozen dance scores in the 1930-1940 period, including *Ceremonials, Ekstasis, Sarabande, Transitions,* and *Imperial Gesture* (Martha Graham); *Traditions* and *Atavisms* (Charles Weidman) and *Insubstantial Pageant* (Erick Hawkins). Also wrote for Edwin Strawbridge, Tashimira, Gene Martel, Gluck-Sandor, Felicia Sorel, and others. Composed extensively for television, films, radio, theater, and Broadway. Author *This Bright Day*, 1956 (autobiography).

Jean Erdman

Born ca. 1917, Honolulu, Hawaii. Studied native Hawaiian dance, Isadora Duncan technique. She first encountered Martha Graham and Bonnie Bird at Sarah Lawrence College, 1934-1937, where she studied dance under the tutelage of Marion Knighton. Erdman was an apprentice dancer in Anna Sokolow's Bennington Fellow's group, 1937. On her return from a world travel tour in May 1938, she married writer-scholar Joseph Campbell and immediately joined the Graham group. At Bennington Erdman danced in *American Document, Letter to the World,* and *Punch and The Judy.* She made her choreographic debut there in 1942 on a joint program with Merce Cunningham (*Transformations of Medusa*). In 1943 Erdman left the Graham company and soon afterward established her own performance group. In the late 1940s she studied at the School of American Ballet and opened her dance school in New York in 1948. She has taught widely at universities and in 1966 created a dance theater program at New York University's School of the Arts (1966-1972). Her most famous work, *The Coach with the Six Insides* (1962), is based on *Finnegans Wake*. She is director of the Theater of the Open Eye, New York.

Francis Fergusson

Born 1904, Albuquerque. Harvard University, 1921-1923; Rhodes Scholar, Oxford University, 1926. Associate Director, American Laboratory Theatre, New York, 1926-1930. Drama Critic, *Bookman*, 1930-1932. Lecturer, New School for Social Research, 1932-1934. Fergusson taught literature, drama, and theater arts at Bennington College, 1934-1947. Director of Drama, Bennington School of the Arts, 1940-1941. Left Bennington in 1948 to direct the Princeton Seminars in Literary Criticism. Later taught at Rutgers, Indiana, and Princeton. Author, *The Idea of a Theater*, 1949.

Vivian Fine

Born 1913, Chicago. Studied composition with Ruth Crawford Seeger, Roger Sessions; piano with Djane Lavoie-Herz, Abby Whiteside. American Conservatory, Chicago, 1925-1931; Dalcroze School, New York, 1935-1936. Pianist, composer. Began composing at age twelve and was encouraged by many of the leading composers of the day. To support herself in New York, Fine accompanied for Gluck-Sandor. Pianist for Tina Flade's New York debut recital. Pianist and musical director, Humphrey-Weidman Group (performed the premieres of *New Dance* and *Passacaglia*). Her first dance score was *The Race of Life* (Humphrey, 1938); then *Opus 51* (Weidman), *Tragic Exodus*, and *They Too Are Exiles* (Holm). In 1960 she wrote *Alcestis* (Graham) and in 1964 *My Son, My Enemy* (Limón). Faculty, New York University, Juilliard, Connecticut College School of the Dance (1963-1964), Bennington College music faculty, 1964-

Tina Flade [Mooney]

Born Dresden. Was headed for a career as concert pianist but, after seeing Mary Wigman perform in Dresden, enrolled in the Wigman School at age fifteen. Seven months later Wigman invited Flade to join her group, whose dancers included Hanya

Holm, Palucca, and Yvonne Georgi. She began making her first dances after several years of touring and work in German theaters and opera houses, and gave her first recital in Dresden. Eve Le Gallienne invited her to dance in America and she made her New York debut in 1932. She spent the next two years teaching in New York (not in association with the New York Wigman School) and becoming acquainted with America. In 1933-1934 she taught summer courses at Norma Gould's studio in Los Angeles and gave some recitals. Rosalind Cassidy invited Flade to develop a dance major at Mills College in 1934. While at Mills Flade toured many cities under the aegis of the Mills alumni club, as a solo recitalist. Her Bennington recital in 1935 was followed by concerts in New York, Chicago, and Washington, D.C. Flade remained at Mills through the summer of 1938, then married Professor Ross L. Mooney, left Mills and her career in dance, and moved to Ohio. In later years Flade resumed her first interest in advanced piano study.

Ralph Gilbert

Composer and accompanist, Cornish School, Seattle, 1938. Student, Bennington School of the Dance, 1938. Accompanist for Martha Graham, 1939. Composed for Lillian Shapero, Welland Lathrop, Ethel Butler, Sophie Maslow, Nina Fonaroff, Erick Hawkins, and Iris Mabry.

Martha Graham

Born 1894, Allegheny, Pennsylvania. Grew up in Santa Barbara, California. First studied dance in Los Angeles after high school. In 1916 studied with Ruth St. Denis. Taught at Denishawn and toured with St. Denis, 1916-1923. Came East and danced for two seasons in the Greenwich Village Follies and taught at the Eastman School of Dance and Dramatic Action, Rochester. New York concert debut, 1926 (Martha Graham and Trio). Opened her first studio in 1927. Enlarged her women's group in 1929. By the time she joined the faculty at Bennington in 1934, Graham had composed more than 100 dances, among them *Lamentation, Primitive Mysteries,* and *Celebration*. She also danced the lead in the American premiere of Igor Stravinsky's *Le Sacre du Printemps*, staged by Leonide Massine, 1930; performed at the opening of Radio City Music Hall (1932) and staged movement for Katharine Cornell's *Lucrece*, 1932-1933. She received the first Guggenheim for choreography in 1932 (and a second in 1943). During this period, she taught at Sarah Lawrence College, Columbia, and New York universities and the Neighborhood Playhouse. Graham was on the permanent faculty of the Bennington summer school (1934-1942) and was special visiting artist at Bennington College, 1943-1945. She married Erick Hawkins in 1948 (she introduced him into her group at Bennington in 1938). In 1969 Graham retired as dancer but continued as company director, choreographer, and head of the Martha Graham School of Contemporary Dance. Of the Big Four, she alone has sustained both a school and a company while continuing to compose. In 1978 the Martha Graham Dance Company gave a week's season at the Metropolitan Opera House, New York—a first for modern dance.

Ray Green

Born 1909, Cavendish, Missouri. Studied composition with Albert Elkus and Ernst Bloch. San Francisco Conservatory, 1927-1933; University of California, Berkeley, 1933-1935. Fellowship in Europe, 1935-1937. Faculty, University of California, 1937-1938. Supervisor and director, Northern California Federal Music Project Chorus, 1939-1941. Married May O'Donnell and went to San Francisco with O'Donnell and Gertrude Shurr after the Bennington session, 1938, to open the San Francisco Dance Theatre. Began composing for O'Donnell in 1937 and wrote numerous scores for her and her company, including *Suspension* (1943). Wrote *American Document* for Martha Graham, 1938. Commissioned to write music for the official opening of the World's Fair, New York, 1938. Music Director, May O'Donnell Dance Company, 1940-.

Erick Hawkins

Born 1909, Trinidad, Colorado. Graduate, Harvard University (major: Greek Civilization). Saw Harald Kreutzberg and Yvonne Georgi dance; studied with Kreutzberg in Salzburg one summer. Studied at the School of American Ballet, 1935-1937, and was a member of American Ballet, 1935-1937, and dancer-choreographer, Ballet Caravan, 1936-1939. Danced in the premieres of such ballets as *Filling Station* with Ballet Caravan and choreographed his first ballet, *Show Piece* (1937), with a commissioned score by Robert McBride. Began study with Martha Graham in June 1938 and was immediately invited to dance with her as guest artist. He was the first male to dance with the Martha Graham Group (*American Document*, 1938). At Bennington Hawkins danced in the premieres of *El Penitente, Letter to the World,* and *Punch and The Judy* and gave his first solo recital in 1940. He taught ballet at Bennington in the summers of 1940-1942. Hawkins remained with the Graham company until 1951 (he and Graham were married in 1948 and divorced a few years later), creating major roles in such ballets as *Appalachian Spring* (The Husbandman) and *Night Journey* (Oedipus). He danced Curley in Agnes de Mille's *Oklahoma!* In 1951 Hawkins left Graham to direct his own company and to develop his own dance aesthetic and training. Hawkins works exclusively with contemporary music.

Martha Hill [Davies]

Born ca. 1900, East Palestine, Ohio. Graduate, Kellogg School of Physical Education, Battle Creek, Michigan, 1920. Taught Swedish gymnastics and ballet there, 1920-1923. Director of dance, Kansas State Teachers College, 1923-1926. Studied ballet with Vestoff-Serova, Portia Mansfield, and Kobeleff; Dalcroze Eurhythmics with Elsa Findlay and Nelly Reuschel, dance with Anna Duncan. In 1926 saw Martha Graham in New York and enrolled at the Martha Graham studio. Studied with Margaret H'Doubler, University of Wisconsin, summer 1927. B.S., Columbia University, 1929; M.A., New York University, 1941. Faculty, University of Oregon, 1927-1929; Lincoln School, Teachers College, Columbia University, 1929-1930. Member, Martha Graham Dance Group, 1929-1931. Faculty, New York University School of Education, Department of Physical Education, 1930-1951 (directed their summer camp at Sloatsburg, New York, in the early 1930s). Bennington College faculty, 1932-1951. Founder, co-director, Bennington School of the Dance, School of the Arts, 1934-1942. Faculty, University of Southern California, summer 1946. Founder, co-director, New York University-Connecticut College School of the Dance, 1948 (on the board until 1968). Director, Dance Division, Juilliard School, 1951- . (Married Thurston Davies, 1952.)

Hanya Holm

Born ca. 1898, Worms-am-Rhine, Germany [née Johanna Eckert]. Studied music, Frankfurt-am-Main, then attended the Dalcroze School at Frankfurt and Hellerau, where she earned her diploma and taught. Married artist Reinhold Martin Kuntze; divorced. Son, Klaus Holm. Holm saw Mary Wigman in one of her early recitals (1921) and began studying with her. After a year, she was appointed assistant instructor and toured with the original Wigman group in Europe. She was co-founder and chief instructor at the Wigman Central Institute, Dresden, for about ten years. She also spent two summers at Ommen, Holland, as dance director. Holm performed in the Mary Wigman-Albert Talhoff *Das Totenmal*, an antiwar memorial which had its premiere in Munich, 1930. Wigman chose Holm to direct the New York Wigman School of Dance, following Wigman's successful American tour. Holm opened the school in 1931 and, in 1936, changed its name to the Hanya Holm School of Dance. She began her American concert career that year, with a small concert group. During her first years in America, Holm devoted herself exclusively to teaching in New York and across the country, including three summers at Mills College. She was a founding member of the Bennington School of the Dance (on faculty 1934, 1936-1940). In 1941 she began a life-long directorship of the summer dance sessions at Colorado College. She disbanded her concert group in the mid-1940s (her active concert career spanned the period 1936-1944 and saw the creation of such works as *Trend, Tragic Exodus, Metropolitan Daily,* and *The Golden Fleece*). She then found great success as a choreographer in the musical theater (*Kiss Me, Kate, My Fair Lady*, etc.) The Hanya Holm studio closed in 1967 but Holm continued teaching in New York (at Juilliard and the Nikolais and Louis studios) and Colorado. Among Holm's former students are Alwin Nikolais, Don Redlich, Valerie Bettis, and Glen Tetley.

Louis Horst

Born 1884, Kansas City, Missouri. Died 1964. Horst was regarded as the patron saint of the modern dance. He was a widely influential teacher of several generations of aspiring choreographers, sage counsel to virtually all of the professional concert dancers of his day, and composer. Studied violin and piano and was playing ragtime and popular music professionally at age eighteen. In 1904 he began playing in San Francisco cafes and was a pit musician in movie theaters, vaudeville, burlesque, and weddings for the next decade. Studied composition with Boris Levenson, Max Persin, Wallingford Riegger. Musical director for Ruth St. Denis, Ted Shawn, and the Denishawn School, 1915-1925. Left Denishawn to study musical composition with Richard Stohr in Vienna, 1925. Accompanied Tamiris, Agnes de Mille, Ruth Page, Anna Sokolow, Doris Humphrey and Charles Weidman, Jean Borlin, Harald Kreutzberg, Michio Ito, Edwin Strawbridge, Martha Graham, and many others, 1925-1932. Music director, Perry-Mansfield camp, summers 1928-1933. Accompanist and musical director, Martha Graham and group, 1926-1948. Founding faculty, Bennington School of the Dance, 1934-1942. Visiting artist, Bennington College, 1943-1945. Taught at Columbia University, Barnard College, Sarah Lawrence, the Neighborhood Playhouse (where he first developed his courses in preclassic forms). In 1929-1930, Horst wrote a monthly column, "The Music Mart," for *Dance Magazine*. Editor-founder, the *Dance Observer*, 1934-1964. Author, *Pre-Classic Dance Forms*, 1937; *Modern Dance Forms in Relation to Other Modern Arts* (with Carroll Russell), 1961. Horst inaugurated a course in music composition for the dance at the Bennington School of the Dance. After the war he was on the faculties of the Connecticut College School of the Dance and the Juilliard School dance department. Horst composed more than thirty dance scores, including music for Ted Shawn, Ruth St. Denis, Ruth Page, Doris Humphrey, Pearl Lang, Nina Fonaroff, Jean Erdman, Agnes de Mille, Yuriko, Gertrude Lippincott. He wrote eleven scores for Graham, among them *Primitive Mysteries, Frontier,* and *El Penitente.*

Doris Humphrey

Born 1895, Oak Park, Illinois. Died 1958. Studied dancing with Mary Wood Hinman (folk, gymnastics) and ballet with Madame Josephine Hatlanek, Andreas Pavley, and Serge Oukrainsky. In 1917 Humphrey entered the Denishawn School in Los Angeles and joined the company in 1918. At Denishawn she created numerous dances, some of them in collaboration with Ruth St. Denis (e.g., *Soaring, Sonata Pathetique*). From the time she, Charles Weidman, and Pauline Lawrence left Denishawn in 1928 to the opening of the Bennington summer school in 1934, Humphrey composed about fifty dances, including the solo suite *Two Ecstatic Themes* and such major group works as *Water Study, Life of the Bee, Drama of Motion, La Valse, The Shakers,* and *Dances of Women.* Humphrey and Weidman opened their school in New York in 1928 and the first Humphrey-Weidman dance group made its debut that year. From 1930 to 1933 Humphrey choreographed for opera and theater (*Lysistrata* and *Die Glückliche Hand*, 1930; *Run Little Chillun!* and *The School for Husbands*, 1933). She married Charles Francis Woodford in 1932 and their son, Charles Humphrey Woodford, was born the summer before Bennington opened. In 1932 Humphrey was the first modern dancer to teach at Perry-Mansfield in Colorado. She spent the summers of 1934-1939 and 1941 on the Bennington faculty. She and Charles Weidman were active in the Federal Dance Project (1936-1939). Forced to retire from a performing career because of arthritis in 1944, she and Weidman went separate ways and the Humphrey-Weidman dancers were disbanded. From then until her death in 1958, Doris Humphrey was active as choreographer and teacher (she was on the faculties of the Connecticut College School of the Dance and Juilliard) and was artistic director of the José Limón Dance Company. Her book on choreography. *The Art of Making Dances*, was published posthumously in 1959.

Hunter Johnson

Born 1906, Benson, North Carolina. University of North Carolina, Eastman School of Music. Studied piano with Sandor Vas, composition with Bernard Rogers and Alfred Casella. Prix de Rome, 1933. Chairman, University of Michigan Department of Composition, 1929-1933. Faculty, University of Manitoba, Cornell, University of Illinois, University of Texas. His Symphony No. 1 was composed in 1931. Dance scores include *Yankee Bluebritches* and *In Time of Armament* (Erick Hawkins) and *Letter to the World* and *Deaths and Entrances* (Martha Graham), all Bennington premieres, 1940-1943.

Esther Junger [Klempner]

Born New York City. Saw Isadora Duncan dance and studied with Bird Larson at the Neighborhood Playhouse. In tribute to Larson (who died suddenly), Junger choreographed a solo, *Go Down Death*, to James Weldon Johnson's poem, *God's Trumpets*, 1929. Junger made her New York debut in November 1930. She regarded herself as a self-taught, independent soloist. Though she danced in New York recitals throughout the 1930s, Junger never toured outside New York. She was a featured dancer with Gluck-Sandor in *Petrouchka* and *El Amor Brujo*, Radio City Music Hall and Dance International, and had a successful career as choreographer and featured dancer in such shows as *Life Begins at 8:40, Parade, 'Tis of Thee* and *Dark of the Moon*. Her Bennington fellowship (1937) gave her assurance to choreograph for groups and she later staged dances for Ringling Bros. Barnum & Bailey Circus, Billy Rose's Diamond Horseshoe Show, and a variety of television specials. She staged and choreographed *Willie the Weeper* for Ballet Ballads in Los Angeles. Junger was the only Bennington Fellow who did not come from one of the seedbeds of the Big Four. In 1977 she was living in retirement in Santa Monica, California.

Harrison Kerr

Born 1897, Cleveland. Studied privately with James Hotchkiss Rogers, Cleveland, 1913-1920. American Conservatory at Fontainebleau, 1921; composition with Nadia Boulanger, piano with Isidor Phillip and Camille Decreus. Director of Music, Chase School, Brooklyn, 1923-1935. Founder and editor, *Trend* (bimonthly magazine of the arts), 1932-1935. Faculty, University of Oklahoma, 1949-1968. Scores include symphonies, chamber music, piano, opera. Composed *Dance Sonata* for Hanya Holm, Bennington, 1938.

Eleanor King

Born 1906, Middletown, Pennsylvania. Studied ballet after seeing Pavlova, then briefly attended the Theatre Guild School. First trained with Charles Weidman and Doris Humphrey at Denishawn School, New York, and was one of the original members of their dance group (1928-1935). King, José Limón, Letitia Ide, and Ernestine Henoch [Stodelle] formed the Little Group in 1931 to present their choreography. King appeared in Leonide Massine's *Le Sacre du Printemps*, 1930, and in review and theater productions including Doris Humphrey's *Orestes* and Charles Weidman's *Candide*. By 1938, when she was made a Bennington fellow, King had been choreographing for some years and had produced *Icaro*, a major group work, at the Brooklyn Museum. At the time of her Bennington fellowship, King was a member of the Theatre Dance Company, New York. In the late 1940s she moved to Seattle, where she formed her own Dance Repertory Company (1943) and was on the faculty of the University of Arkansas before moving to Santa Fe, where she currently resides. Author, *Transformations: A Memoir, The Humphrey-Weidman Years*, 1978 (autobiography).

Louise Kloepper

Born Washington, D.C., grew up in Tacoma, Washington. Studied ballet with Mary Ann Wells, Seattle. Saw Mary Wigman on tour and decided to study with her in Germany. Completed the three-year course in two years (1929-1930) and was the first American to receive the diploma from the Mary Wigman School in Dresden. In 1931 she returned to Washington state to open her own studio, and in 1932 Hanya Holm invited her to assist her at the New York Wigman School, following Fe

Alf. Kloepper worked as teaching associate and soloist with Holm from 1932 to 1942. Except for some solos in Holm's dances and an early duet with Jane Dudley, the Bennington fellowship in 1938 was Louise Kloepper's first crack at choreography. Kloepper was at Bennington with Holm summers 1936-1939 and accompanied her to Colorado College for the summer sessions, 1941 and 1942. Hailed as a dancer of exceptional beauty, Kloepper left the concert field in 1942 to honor her parents' wish that she complete a college degree. She progressed at the University of Wisconsin from student to graduate teaching assistant to faculty and, finally, to chairman of the dance program. During her tenure at Wisconsin, the program expanded from a single concentration in teacher-training to additional concentrations in choreography and performance.

Arch Lauterer

Born 1904. Died 1957. Attended Chagrin Falls High School, Cleveland. Scenic director, Cleveland Playhouse, 1926-1932. Taught stagecraft and scenic design, Western Reserve University and Cleveland College, 1930-1933; Traphagan School, New York, 1932-1933. In 1931 Lauterer designed the permanent architectural stage for Western Reserve University. Technical director, Chautauqua Repertory Players, 1931-1932 (summers). Bennington College art and drama faculty, 1933-1942 (on leave 1936-1937 to study European theater architecture). Faculty, Bennington School of the Dance, 1938-1939; director of theatre design, School of the Arts, 1940-1941. Collaboration with Martha Graham began at Bennington in 1935 with *Panorama* and continued with *American Document, Letter to the World, El Penitente, Punch and The Judy,* and *Deaths and Entrances*. He designed the sets and lighting for Hanya Holm's New York production of *Trend*, 1937, and collaborated with Holm and Roy Harris on *Namesake* in Colorado, summer 1942. At Bennington in 1941 he designed the stage for Doris Humphrey's *Decade*. His collaborations with Holm also included *The Golden Fleece* and *Tragic Exodus* and, in 1944 at Perry-Mansfield, Lauterer designed *Four Walls* with Merce Cunningham. The Museum of Modern Art mounted an exhibit of his stage architecture and lighting designs in 1946. Director of theatre arts, Sarah Lawrence College, 1942-1943. Fellowship, Western Reserve University, 1944. Professor of speech and drama, Mills College, 1946-1957. In 1948 Lauterer was production director for the first American Dance Festival, New London, Connecticut.

Pauline Lawrence

Born 1900, Los Angeles. Died 1971. Pianist, accompanist, Hollywood High School. Lawrence joined Denishawn in 1917 where she both danced and was rehearsal pianist and left there in 1928 with Doris Humphrey and Charles Weidman. From 1928 Lawrence managed the affairs of the Humphrey-Weidman concert groups and the school. She was musical director, costume and lighting designer, and general factotum, and she arranged and booked their tours. In Bennington summer sessions she played piano for all of Humphrey's classes and for many of the major premieres. Lawrence and José Limón were married in 1941. She designed costumes and carried out many of the functions of company manager for the José Limón Company.

Robert Devore Leigh

Born 1890, Nelson, Nebraska. Died 1961. Raised in Seattle, studied at Bowdoin, Columbia University (Ph.D., 1927), Colgate (LL.D., 1933). Also at Harvard University and the New School for Social Research. Board of the New School for Social Research, 1919-1920. Faculty, Reed College, Columbia, Barnard. A. Barton Hepburn Professor of Government, Williams College, 1922-1928. Advisory Board, Progressive Education Association, 1932. Bennington College President, 1928-1941 (at age thirty-seven, Leigh was one of the youngest college presidents in the United States). He was responsible for recruiting faculty, developing the initial college plan, and fundraising. (On leave of absence 1939-1940.) After Bennington, Leigh had an active career in government (he was director of the Foreign Broadcasting Intelligence Service, Federal Communications Commission, during the war), research, administration, and teaching. Leigh was a co-founder of the Bennington School of the Dance, 1934. Author, *Group Leadership*, 1936.

Clair Leonard

Born 1901, Newton, Massachusetts. Harvard University. Elkan Naumburg, and Paine fellowships. Studied composition with Nadia Boulanger. Associate professor of music, Vassar College. Chief interest, choral music. Composed for orchestra, chamber players, chorus, and the stage.

José Limón

Born 1908, Culiacan, Sinaloa, Mexico. Died 1972. Grew up in the American Southwest, attended one year of college in Los Angeles, then studied painting in New York. Saw Kreutzberg and Georgi perform and decided to become a dancer. Studied with Humphrey-Weidman and joined their group in 1930. Between 1930 and the year of his Bennington fellowship (1937), Limón composed more than a dozen dances—solos, duets, and trios—and formed the Little Group with Letitia Ide, Eleanor King, and Ernestine Henoch [Stodelle]. *Danza de la Muerte* (1937, Bennington) was Limón's first major work for a large group. During the 1930s Limón also danced in Broadway shows and staged the dances for *Roberta* and *I'd Rather Be Right*. At Bennington (1935-1939) he danced the premieres of *New Dance, With My Red Fires,* and *Quest* and choreographed an extended solo, *Danzas Mexicanas* (1939). After leaving

Humphrey-Weidman in 1940, Limon taught the summer course at Mills College and joined forces with May O'Donnell in California. In 1942 he danced with Mary Ellen Moylan in George Balanchine's *Rosalinda* (*Die Fledermaus*). At the end of World War II he formed a trio with Beatrice Seckler and Dorothy Bird and also studied ballet with Nennette Charisse. In 1946 Doris Humphrey aided him in establishing his own company and was artistic advisor and choreographer for the José Limón Dance Company until her death. Limón created his most famous work, *The Moor's Pavane*, for the second American Dance Festival, 1949, and became the leading figure there in the 1950s and 1960s. He was also on the Juilliard dance department faculty. His company continued to perform after his death, making it the first modern dance company to survive its creator.

Margaret Lloyd

Born South Braintree, Massachusetts, ca. 1888. Died 1960. Began writing about experimental film, theater, and dance for the *Christian Science Monitor* ca. 1930-1932. Husband, Leslie A. Sloper, was *Monitor* music and drama editor (died 1949). In 1936 Lloyd became dance critic of the *Monitor*. Her writing spanned the other arts, but she was most passionate about the dance and covered the New York dance scene as well as Boston and New England. She spent considerable time at the Bennington summer sessions. Lloyd studied modern dance with Pauline Chellis and ballet with Hazel Boone in the Boston area. She wrote fiction and children's stories under a pen name. Her last dance review was published in the *Monitor* on the day of her death, 2 March 1960. Lloyd's chronicle of American modern dance, *The Borzoi Book of Modern Dance*, published in 1949, remains an essential reference.

Norman Lloyd

Born Pottsville, Pennsylvania, 1909. Died 1980. New York University (B.S., 1932, M.S., 1936); theory and composition with Bertha Bailey and Vincent Jones. Studied piano with Abby Whiteside, composition with Aaron Copland. Began playing piano for Martha Hill's modern dance classes at New York University in the early 1930s. In the Bennington period Lloyd and his wife, Ruth, accompanied most of the concert dancers in recital and played for all sorts of classes (modern, folk, tap) and for stage shows and cabarets. Composed and accompanied for dancer Elna Lillback, New York. Employed in 1934 as accompanist (with Ruth Lloyd) by the Bennington School of the Dance. Began teaching the next summer, taking over Gregory Tucker's course "Music for Dancers," which he adapted to his own ideas, stressing rhythms and deemphasizing Dalcroze Eurythmics. Lloyd conducted and played many of the premieres at Bennington and accompanied for most of the classes and workshops (1935-1942). He worked closely with Louis Horst to develop new composers for the dance and to train dancers in music. In 1935 Lloyd wrote his first major dance score, *Panorama*, for Martha Graham. He created more music for the dance at Bennington than any other composer. After Bennington, Lloyd wrote *Inquest, Lament for Ignacio Sánchez Mejías*, and *Invention* for Doris Humphrey; *La Malinche, Dialogues*, and *Performance* (*Variation 9*) for Limón. He was instructor, Ernest Williams Band School, 1935-1937; lecturer New York University, 1936-1945. Lloyd was on the faculty of the Juilliard School of Music, 1949-1963, and later was dean of Oberlin's Music Conservatory and director of the Arts Program, Rockefeller Foundation. In addition to teaching, composing (for film and other forms), conducting, and doing administrative work, Lloyd wrote and compiled songbooks, textbooks, and encyclopedias, some of them in collaboration with his wife.

Ruth Lloyd

Ruth Lloyd began accompanying Martha Hill's tap dance methods class in the physical education department at New York University while she was an undergraduate music education major (1930). Though never herself on the faculty of the Bennington summer school, she accompanied practically every class and workshop and played for many of the premieres (1934-1941). After a few summers she became Louis Horst's senior accompanist at Bennington. Marian Knighton, who attended the 1934 session as a student, invited the Lloyds to play for dance classes at Sarah Lawrence and to teach. Ruth Lloyd remained on the faculty at Sarah Lawrence for many years, and worked closely with Bessie Schönberg. She also taught at New York University.

Otto Luening

Born 1900, Milwaukee, Wisconsin. Royal Academy of Music, Munich (1914-1917); Municipal Conservatory and University of Zurich, Switzerland (1917-1920). Studied with Ferruccio Busoni and Philipp Jarnach. Flutist and conductor in Europe. Conducted first all-American opera performance, Chicago, 1922. Director, Chicago Musical Art Studio, 1922-1925. Executive director, Opera Department, Eastman House School of Music, 1925-1928. Conducted Rochester American Opera Company and others. Faculty, University of Arizona, 1932-1934. Luening replaced Kurt Schindler, first director of the Bennington College music department, in the fall of 1934. He was an established composer at the time of his Bennington College appointment and had written in a great variety of formats, including an opera, *Evangeline*, with his own libretto, and *The Soundless Song*, for voice, instruments, dancers, and lights (1924). In 1940 and 1941 Luening was director of music, Bennington School of the Arts. He played flute in the premiere of *El Penitente* and collaborated with the Drama and Dance Divisions but did not himself write music for the dance during the summer sessions. (In 1956 Luening composed

Theater Piece No. 2 for Doris Humphrey.) He was a pioneer in tape and electronic music and an avid collaborator with other artists and composers. After leaving Bennington College in 1944 he taught at Barnard (1944-1947) and Columbia University, where in 1959 he co-directed the Columbia-Princeton Electronic Music Center with Milton Babbitt and Vladimir Ussachevsky. His musical output numbers more than 275 works.

Robert G. McBride

Born 1911, Tucson, Arizona. University of Arizona, 1928-1935; studied composition with Otto Luening. Played clarinet, saxophone, and piano in dance bands; oboe in the Tucson Symphony. Music faculty, Bennington College (1935-1946), University of Arizona, 1957- . Toured South America as clarinetist in a chamber group, 1941. Composer-performer, New York (1946-1957). Composed for orchestra, band, chorus, chamber groups, stage, and film. Dance scores include *Show Piece* (Erick Hawkins, Ballet Caravan, 1937) and *Punch and The Judy* (Martha Graham, 1941).

Morris Mamorsky

Born 1910, Ansonia, Connecticut. Yale University School of Music, 1937. Music director, Humphrey-Weidman Dance Group, 1937-1938. Concerto for Piano and Orchestra won the Paderewski Fund Prize, 1939. Staff composer-conductor, National Broadcasting Company, 1939. Dance scores include *Festive Rites* (Esther Junger, 1937) and *American Holiday* (Doris Humphrey, 1938).

John Joseph Martin

Born 1893, Louisville, Kentucky. Attended Louisville public schools, then worked as an actor, 1912-1915, and joined the Chicago Little Theater, 1915-1917. He was editor for the *Dramatic Mirror*, New York, 1919-1922, and executive secretary of Richard Boleslavsky's Lab Theatre, 1924-1926. He and his wife, Louise (who also taught at Bennington), were working to establish a theater group modeled on the Moscow Art Theatre. He began writing dance criticism for the *New York Times* in 1927 (retiring in 1962 from the post of dance editor-critic) just when Martha Graham, Helen Tamiris, Doris Humphrey, and Charles Weidman were launching independent concert careers. Martin became an ardent advocate of the modern dance and led numerous lecture-discussion series in educational settings, beginning with the famous project he inaugurated at the New School for Social Research (1931-1940). Taught history, criticism, and composition at Bennington (1934-1937). His first book on the dance, based on those lectures, *The Modern Dance*, was published in 1933. *America Dancing* followed in 1936, then *Introduction to the Dance* in 1939, with several others in later years. His most recent book, *Ruth Page: An Intimate Biography*, was issued in 1977. (He wrote numerous plays in addition to his dance writing.)

Louise Martin

Died 1957. Graduated from the University of Chicago and was a member of the Chicago Little Theater under Maurice Brown. She was interested in dance and in marionettes and taught "Basis of Dramatic Movement" to dancers at the Bennington Summer School of the Dance, 1935-1937. In 1938, she coached members of the Humphrey-Weidman Concert Group.

Sophie Maslow

Born New York. Studied with Blanche Talmud, Neighborhood Playhouse School of the Theatre, Grand Street. Danced in Irene Lewisohn's orchestral dramas. Went directly into Martha Graham's Concert Group in 1931 and made her choreographic debut around 1934. She continued to compose while dancing with the Graham group until 1942, and had a group of her own beginning in these years. Faculty, New Dance Group Studio. In 1942 Maslow formed a trio with William Bales and Jane Dudley. Her *Dust Bowl Ballads* (1941) and *Folksay* (1942) are major works from the Bennington years. Two movements from the trio's *Suite*, to music by J. S. Bach, had their premiere at Bennington the last summer session, 1942. Maslow continued to choreograph for various groups (*Folksay* and *The Village I Knew* are among her most important works), and to direct her own dance company in New York. She has worked on a number of revivals of the Graham repertory.

Jerome Moross

Born 1913, Brooklyn. New York University, 1929-1932 (major, Music Education). Juilliard, 1931-1932. Composer, pianist, orchestrator. Composer for the ballet, opera, and film, including dance scores for *American Pattern* (1937), *Frankie and Johnny* (1938), *Guns and Castanets* (1939) for Ruth Page and Bentley Stone; *American Saga: Johnny Inkslinger* (1934) and *Memorials* (1935) for Charles Weidman.

Alex North

Born 1910, Chester, Pennsylvania. Studied composition with Bernard Wagenaar, Juilliard (1929-1932); Anton Veprik, Moscow Conservatory (1933-1934); privately with Aaron Copland and Ernst Toch (1935-1939); piano with George Boyle. Wrote many dance scores in the 1930s including *Speaker, Ballad in Popular Style, War Is Beautiful, Slaughter of the Innocents* for Anna Sokolow; *American Lyric* for Martha Graham; *The Golden Fleece* for Hanya Holm. Music director, Anna Sokolow dance group. Later ballet scores included *A Streetcar Named Desire* (Valerie Bettis, 1957), *Mal de siècle* (Rosella Hightower, James Starbuck, 1958). North went on to a major career as a motion picture composer. His film scores include *A Streetcar Named Desire, Death of a Salesman, Viva Zapata,* and *Who's Afraid of Virginia Woolf?*

Lionel Nowak

Born 1911, Cleveland, Ohio. Studied counterpoint with Quincy Porter, harmony with Roger Sessions, composition with Herbert Elwell. Cleveland Institute of Music (M.Mus., 1933). Composed and played for Eleanor Frampton. Studied piano with Beryl Rubinstein and Edwin Fisher. Concert pianist, conductor, composer, teacher. Pianist and composer, Humphrey-Weidman Dance Group, 1938-1942. In this period he wrote *Danzas Mexicanas* (José Limón), *On My Mother's Side* and *Flickers* (Charles Weidman), *The Green Land* (Doris Humphrey). Other dance scores included *A House Divided* (Weidman, 1943) and *The Story of Mankind* (Humphrey, 1945). Taught at Fenn College, 1932-1938; Converse College, 1942-1946; Syracuse University, 1946-1948. Bennington College music faculty since 1948. Compositions include piano and chamber works and songs.

Harvey Pollins

Born Pleasantville, Pennsylvania. Music director, Hanya Holm dance studio, 1938. Composer-pianist. (No further biographical information located.) Dance scores include *Pleasures of Counterpoint No. 2* (Humphrey, 1934), *Sarabande* (Holm, 1936), *Ravage* (Junger, 1937), and *Romantic Theme* (Kloepper, 1938).

Maxwell Powers

Born 1911, Cleveland, Ohio. Died 1977. Studied Cleveland Institute of Music (1936, 1940). Faculty, Greenwich House Music School, New York, 1945-1976 (executive director). Composed *Renaissance Testimonials* (Merce Cunningham, 1942). Other works include chamber music, two piano concertos, and a symphonic poem.

Wallingford Riegger

Born Albany, Georgia, 1885. Died 1961. Institute of Musical Art, 1907 (cello). Studied composition with Goetchius, counterpoint at the Berlin Hochschule. In Germany, Riegger conducted orchestras and opera. Faculty, Drake University, Iowa (1918-1922), Ithaca Conservatory (1926-1928). Riegger's first score for the dance was *Bacchanale* (Martha Graham, 1930). Between 1933 and 1941 he composed almost entirely for the dance. In this period he worked with Graham (*Frenetic Rhythms, Evocation, Chronicle*), Humphrey (*New Dance, Theatre Piece, With My Red Fires*), Weidman (*Candide*, WPA, 1937), Tamiris (*Trojan Incident*), Sokolow (*Case History No.__*), Holm (*The Cry, Chromatic Eccentricities, City Nocturne, Dance in Three Parts, Festive Rhythms, Prelude, Trend*), Jane Dudley (*Song for Soviet Youth Day*), Saida Gerrard (*Machine Ballet*), and Hawkins (*The Pilgrim's Progress*).

Bessie Schönberg

Born Hannover, Germany. Grew up in Dresden. Studied at the Dalcroze School, Hellerau bei Dresden. She studied the history of art and music at the Technische Hochshule, Dresden, and art and crafts with Margarite Muhlhausen. In 1925 Schönberg came to America and attended the University of Oregon (1925-1929) as a fine arts major. There she studied modern dance with Martha Hill. She came to New York, studied with Martha Graham at the Neighborhood Playhouse studios, and danced with the Graham group (1929-1931). She also danced in Irene Lewisohn's productions, 1930-1931. Schönberg taught at the University of Oregon, summer 1928, and at the summer school and camp of the Henry Street Settlement, 1930. She was physical director for women at International House, 1932. Schönberg completed her undergraduate degree at Bennington College while teaching as a part-time instructor in dance (Martha Hill's assistant), 1933-1935. She was on the faculty of the Bennington School of the Dance, 1934-1939, and School of the Arts, 1940-1941, missing the last session because of an appendectomy. In 1937 her translation of Curt Sachs' *World History of the Dance* was published. At Bennington summers Schönberg taught modern dance technique and composition and led experimental workshops. In 1938 she began teaching at Sarah Lawrence College and in 1956 was named Director of theater and dance, retiring from that post in 1975. Schönberg also taught at the Juilliard School and the Connecticut College School of the Dance.

Mary Josephine Shelly

Born 1902, Grand Rapids, Michigan. Died 1976. A.B., University of Oregon, 1926; M.A., Teachers College, Columbia University, 1929. Taught at schools in Grand Rapids, 1922-1923, and Battle Creek, 1923-1924. Faculty, University of Oregon, 1924-1928; Teachers College, Columbia University, 1929-1932; New College, Columbia University, 1932-1933; University of Chicago, 1935-1938. Shelly was co-founder and administrative director of the Bennington School of the Dance, 1934-1939, and School of the Arts, 1940-1941. She joined the staff of Bennington College in 1938 as educational assistant to President Leigh and faculty in drama and the arts. She left in 1942 to serve as lieutenant commander, Women's Naval Reserve, and was in the WAVES and the demobilization program until 1946, at which time she returned to the college, serving as director of admissions. In 1951 she left again to become the second director of women in the Air Force, returning in 1953 as director of student personnel. She resigned in 1954 to direct activities at the Girl Scouts of America, retiring from that post approximately 1966.

Anna Sokolow

Born 1910, Hartford, Connecticut. Grew up on New York's Lower East Side. Studied with Elsa Pohl, Bird Larson, Blanche Talmud, Martha Graham, and Louis Horst at the Neighborhood Playhouse. Sokolow was Horst's first assistant at the Playhouse. From 1930–1938 she danced with Martha Graham's group and simultaneously began to compose independently. Her earliest group works date from about 1933 (*Anti-War Cycle*), when she directed a dance unit of the Workers Dance League. In the summer of 1934 she made a tour of the Soviet Union with composer Alex North and danced for Russian audiences. The next summer was spent at Bennington with Graham's group, where she assisted Horst and danced in a joint solo recital under the aegis of the New Dance League. In 1936 she performed several solos in a program of "Revolutionary Dance" at Bennington and directed the dance component of a summer arts project sponsored by Yaddo on Triuna Island, Lake George. (*Dance Observer* records her formal debut appearance in New York earlier that year.) She was a Bennington Fellow, 1937. In 1938 she left the Graham company and was invited by Carlos Merida of the Mexican Ministry of Culture to bring her group to Mexico. In 1939 she began an association with the Mexican dance community that endured almost a decade. There she founded the first Mexican modern dance company. Her first major choreography for the theater was *Sing for your Supper*, Federal Theatre Project. Sokolow has been among the most prolific and versatile modern choreographers. She has worked with various groups of her own and also with innumerable companies—ballet, folk, modern, and theater—throughout the world.

Walter Terry

Born 1913, Brooklyn. Raised in New Canaan, Connecticut. Majored in music and drama, University of North Carolina, 1931-1934. Studied dance with Phoebe Barr, former member of Ted Shawn's touring dancers. College roommate was Foster Fitz-Simmons, also formerly with Ted Shawn. Performed in Barr's Men's Group. Studied further with Miriam Winslow, Charles Weidman, Malvine Ipcar (Hanya Holm studio), and also took Graham technique. Taught dance to mill workers in Durham, North Carolina. Theater critic, University of North Carolina *Daily Tar Heel*, 1933-1935. In 1936 Ted Shawn recommended that the *Boston Herald* engage Terry to write about dance in New England that summer. He was dance critic for the *Herald*, 1936-1939, writing his first pieces from the Bennington summer school; then for the *New York Herald Tribune*, 1939-1942. While serving overseas during the war, Edwin Denby filled his position at the *Tribune*. Terry returned to his former post in 1945 (to 1966) and later became dance critic for the *Saturday Review of Literature*. Terry has written thirty dance books. In 1978, *I Was There*, a collection of his dance criticism, including some of his first reviews written about Bennington, was published. Terry's career as dance critic spans more than forty years.

Gregory Tucker

Born 1908, New Philadelphia, Pennsylvania. Died 1971. Philadelphia Conservatory of Music, piano study with Leo Ornstein and Edward Steurmann. Composition with Reginald Owen Morris, Rosario Scalero, Curtis Institute. Soloist, Philadelphia Orchestra. Concert tour, South America, 1927. Taught privately in New York and Greenwich, Connecticut, 1928-1933. Bennington College music faculty, 1933-1947. Studied composition with Hanns Eisler and Wallingford Riegger. Professor, Music Department, MIT, 1947-1971. Wrote dance scores for Marian Van Tuyl (*Out of One Happening* and *In the Clearing*), Hanya Holm (*Metropolitan Daily*), Merce Cunningham and Jean Erdman (*Ad Lib*); later for Dudley-Maslow-Bales (*As Poor Richard Says*), Erick Hawkins (*His Best Gal*) and William Bales (*Sea Bourne*). He also wrote scores for Bennington College theater productions of *The Bridge, Electra,* and *The People, Yes*, and for the Bennington School of the Arts production *The King and the Duke*. Tucker was on the original 1934 faculty of the Bennington School of the Dance and taught "Music for Dancers," which was largely based on Dalcroze Eurythmics.

Marian Van Tuyl

Born Wacousta, Michigan. Early training included Dalcroze and some ballet. Saw Isadora Duncan perform. Van Tuyl later studied with Martha Graham and Louis Horst. After graduating with a major in dance from the University of Michigan in 1928, Van Tuyl directed dance at the University of Chicago. She began dancing professionally in 1932 and formed a small concert group in 1936 which toured the Middle West (she brought the group to Bennington for a recital in 1936; Van Tuyl was enrolled as a student summers 1934-1937). She was a Bennington Fellow in 1938, the only one of six Fellows from outside the New York area. Said Margaret Lloyd: "Her appointment serves as a spiking reminder that New York is not the whole of America—even in the dance." Following Tina Flade's departure in 1938, Van Tuyl taught dance at Mills College. Under her chairmanship in 1941, dance was established as an independent department within the Division of Fine Arts. In the 1950s and 1960s Van Tuyl served as editor of *Impulse*, an annual dance journal.

Charles Weidman

Born 1901, Lincoln, Nebraska. Died 1975. Studied with Eleanor Frampton in Lincoln (Frampton subsequently studied and then taught Humphrey-Weidman technique and enrolled as a student at Bennington summers). Weidman took ballet with Theodore Kosloff and entered the Denishawn School in

Los Angeles about 1920. He was immediately pressed into service as a substitute partner for Martha Graham in *Xochitl*, on tour. At Denishawn, Weidman met Doris Humphrey (who was his teacher) and Pauline Lawrence. He danced many solo roles (including Crapshooter in *Danse Americaine*) and also taught. Humphrey, Weidman, and Lawrence broke with Denishawn in 1928, opened their own studio in New York, formed a concert group, and made their debuts. The Humphrey-Weidman Group was the only modern company, following the Denishawn Dancers, which included men and women. In the years before Bennington opened, Weidman worked in the musical and legitimate theater, opera ballet, and concert dance. His first major work, *The Happy Hypocrite* (1931, Dance Repertory Theatre), was followed by a group of "abstract" dances, including *Gymnopedies* (Satie), *Dance of Sport* and *Dance of Work* (Cowell), and *Studies in Conflict* (to silence). He and Doris Humphrey contributed concert dances to the revue *Americana* (1932) and in 1933 Weidman choreographed the popular Broadway musical *As Thousands Cheer*. In this same period he made his first experiment with *Candide*, which he later reworked with great success for the Federal Dance Project. In August 1933 Doris Humphrey, Charles Weidman, and their group played to an audience of 8,000 at New York's Lewisohn Stadium, and in April 1934 they introduced a number of new pieces in what reportedly was their first major concert series appearance in two years (Guild Theatre). Among the new works were Weidman's important solo, *Kinetic Pantomime*, and his cycle, *Memorials*. Weidman was on the Bennington summer faculty 1934–1939 and 1941. Following Doris Humphrey's retirement from the stage in the mid-1940s, Weidman formed his own group, Theatre Dance Company (he had had a men's group which performed occasionally before that time). In 1947 he was awarded a Guggenheim and created *Fables for Our Time*, which played on Broadway. Weidman began collaborating with sculptor Mikhail Santaro in the early 1960s and established the Expression of Two Arts Theatre in New York. He continued to choreograph until his death in 1975. In 1972 and 1973 Weidman revived portions of *Opus 51* and *New Dance*.

Esther Williamson [Ballou]

Born 1915, Elmira, New York. Died 1973. Pianist, composer, educator. Graduate, Bennington College (music), 1937. Accompanist-composer, Bennington School of the Dance, 1937. Fellow in Music, Mills College, 1938. At Mills in 1939, she composed dances for Louise Kloepper and José Limón. Studied composition with Otto Luening and Wallingford Riegger. M.A., Juilliard; studied with Bernard Wagenaar. MacDowell Fellow. Faculty, Juilliard, 1943–1950; associate professor, American University, 1959–1973. Began composing by improvising for dance students. She wrote music for many of the student dances at the Bennington summer session. Her dance scores include *Merely a Beginning* (George Bockman, 1937), *Earth Saga* (Louise Kloepper, 1938), and *War Lyrics* (José Limón, 1940). In 1963 she became the first woman composer to have a premiere at the White House.

APPENDIX B

Background to Bennington: A Timetable

A chronology of significant events leading up to, surrounding, and following directly from the Bennington project, prepared from published chronologies and original research.

1911 Barnard Greek Games commence (Barnard College, New York).

1914 Nellie Centennial Cornish establishes the Cornish School, a school of the arts, in Seattle, Washington.
Bird Larson organizes dance program at Barnard College.
Charlotte Perry and Portia Mansfield open a dance school at Lake Eldora, Colorado (Rocky Mountain Dancing Camp).

1915 The Ruth St. Denis School of Dancing and its Related Arts opens in Los Angeles (Denishawn).
The Neighborhood Playhouse opens its theater on Grand Street, New York (closed 1927).
The Perry-Mansfield Camps and School of the Theatre Arts moves to Steamboat Springs, Colorado.

1916 Diaghilev's Ballets Russes makes its first U.S. tour.

1917–1918 Margaret H'Doubler initiates a dance course at the University of Wisconsin and forms Orchesis dance group.
Gertrude Colby teachers the first classes in "natural dance" at Columbia University Teachers College.

1922 Isadora Duncan performs in United States for the last time.

1923 Martha Graham leaves Denishawn.
Ballets Suédois (1920–1925) tours America.

1925 Joseph Mann inaugurates a "Students Dance Recital Series" at the Washington Irving High School, New York (later the Central High School of Needle Trades).
Lucile Marsh named dance critic of the *New York World.*
Ruth Page choreographs *The Flapper and the Quarterback.*

1926 University of Wisconsin offers first degree program in dance (Bachelor of Science, Physical Education Department).
Martha Graham makes her New York debut and forms first concrete group.

1927 Tamiris makes her New York debut.
Mary Watkins is appointed dance critic of the *New York Herald Tribune*; John Martin begins writing dance criticism for the *New York Times*.
Death of Isadora.

1928 Doris Humphrey and Charles Weidman leave Denishawn, make New York debuts, and form a concert group.
The Neighborhood Playhouse School of the Theatre opens, with Graham and Horst leading the dance department. Horst teaches first course in "Pre-Classic Dance Forms" and becomes musical director at Perry-Mansfield.
Tamiris premieres *Negro Spirituals*.

1929 Atlanta Civic Ballet is founded by Dorothy Alexander.
Death of Diaghilev.

1930 Dance Repertory Theatre gives first series in New York (Tamiris, Graham, Humphrey, Weidman, Horst).
Mary Wigman makes first U.S. tour.
Pauline Koner makes New York solo debut.
Anna Sokolow joins Graham group.
José Limón joins Humphrey--Weidman.
Graham and Horst teach at the Cornish School.
Graham dances the lead in the American premiere of *Le Sacre du Printemps*, Philadelphia.

1931 The New School for Social Research begins series of lecture-demonstrations organized by John Martin (ends 1938).
The New York Wigman School opens, with Hanya Holm as director.
Eleanor Frampton creates a modern dance department at the Cleveland Institute of Music.
Graham premieres *Primitive Mysteries*. Humphrey presents *The Shakers*. Dance Repertory Theatre's second series includes de Mille.
Death of Pavlova.
Denishawn Dancers make last tour.

1932 **Bennington College opens, offering a Bachelor of Arts degree, with a concentration in dance.**
Lester Horton forms his first company in Los Angeles.
Martha Graham is awarded the first Guggenheim Fellowship for choreography.
The New Dance Group is organized.
Doris Humphrey introduces modern dance at Perry-Mansfield.
The governor of New York signs the law permitting dance recitals in theaters Sunday evenings.

1933 Ted Shawn forms all-male company, "Ted Shawn and His Ensemble of Men Dancers" (1933-1940), which performs at Friday "teas," Jacob's Pillow.
Ballet Russe de Monte Carlo gives first American season.
George Balanchine arrives in the United States.
Black Mountain College opens in North Carolina.
Virginia Stewart organizes the first annual summer tour to the Wigman Central School of the Dance, Dresden, for Americans.
Kurt Jooss Ballet gives first American season.
Hanya Holm teaches at Perry-Mansfield.

1934 **The Bennington School of the Dance opens, July.**
Louis Horst founds the *Dance Observer* (1934–1964), a journal devoted to the modern dance.
School of American Ballet opens and gives debut performances in White Plains and Hartford.
Ruth Page is named director of Chicago Grand Opera Ballet.
Mills College holds its first summer dance session, with Hanya Holm as guest artist (1934–1936).
Agnes de Mille spends the summer in London.
Ted Shawn gives series of ten lecture-demonstrations at Jacob's Pillow.
Fokine's *Les Sylphides* and *Scheherazade* draw record turnaway crowds at Lewisohn Stadium, New York.
Pauline Koner is invited by the Soviet Union to teach, perform, and tour.

1935 **Martha Graham directs first workshop at Bennington School of the Dance, premieres *Panorama*.**
William Kolodney inaugurates a dance recital program at the 92nd Street YMHA, New York; John Martin chairs a symposium with Graham, Holm, Humphrey, and Weidman.
The New School for Social Research begins a series of modern dance recitals.
Humphrey–Weidman Concert Group makes its first cross-country tour, Toronto to Texas.
Federal Theatre Project formed by the WPA.
Littlefield Ballet is founded by Catherine Littlefield in Philadelphia.
American Ballet, directed by George Balanchine, is named resident company, Metropolitan Opera.
Agnes de Mille, José Limón, and Louise Kloepper teach at Perry-Mansfield.

1936 **Doris Humphrey completes *New Dance Trilogy* at Bennington (*With My Red Fires*); Charles Weidman creates *Quest*. Ballet Caravan makes its world debut. Walter Terry writes his first dance reviews from Bennington.**
Bennington College graduates first three dance majors.
First National Dance Congress, New York.
Ted Shawn expands Jacob's Pillow activities with a School of the Dance for Men.
Brooklyn Museum dance center opens (1936–1939), directed by Grant Code.
Eleanor King, Paul Love, Max Otto, and Hans Wiener teacher at Perry-Mansfield.
Tamiris tours the Midwest.
Hanya Holm dissolves association with Wigman; forms first company after making American debut as choreographer and dancer at Mills and Bennington.

1937 **Hanya Holm premieres *Trend* at Bennington. Anna Sokolow, José Limón, and Esther Junger are first Bennington Fellows.**
Dance International, 1900–1937, held at Rockefeller Center, New York.
Tamiris' *How Long, Brethren?* and Weidman's *Candide* produced by Federal Dance Theatre, run for 42 performances, SRO.
Anna Sokolow makes Broadway concert debut.
American Dance Association is formed.
Doris Humphrey teaches at Perry-Mansfield.
Martha Graham is invited by Eleanor Roosevelt to dance at the White House.
The Mordkin Ballet, forerunner of Ballet Theatre, opens.
San Franciso Ballet is founded by Willam Christensen.
Martha Graham and Group make first large-scale tour across United States and into Canada.
Federal Arts Bill, H.R. 8239, is proposed.

1938 **Graham, Humphrey, Weidman, and Holm create major new works at the Bennington Festival. Louise Kloepper, Eleanor King, and Marian Van Tuyl are Bennington Fellows.**
Hanya Holm and Group make their first transcontinental tour.
Arch Lauterer teaches at the Holm studio, New York.
Jacob's Pillow offers series of ten lecture-demonstrations and School of the Dance for Men and Women.

Mills Summer Session includes Tina Flade, Lou Harrison, Bonnie Bird, and Lester Horton, who premieres *Conquest*.
Anna Sokolow leaves Graham group.
Erick Hawkins joins Graham group.
Gertrude Shurr and May O'Donnell, in association with Ray Green, musical director, open the San Francisco Dance Theatre.
Doris Humphrey, Paul Love teach at Perry-Mansfield.
Ruth St. Denis is named director of Adelphi College dance department.
Ballet Caravan premieres Eugene Loring's *Billy the Kid*.
Ruth Page and Bentley Stone create *Frankie and Johnny* for Federal Theatre Project.

1939 **Bennington School of the Dance holds its session at Mills College.**
Martha Graham and Group tour *American Document*.
Weidman, Limón, and Humphrey teach at Perry-Mansfield after the Mills session.
Merce Cunningham joins the Graham group.
Federal Dance Project ends.
Last season of Jacob's Pillow School of the Dance and Lecture-Demonstrations.
Pauline Koner gives her first New York concert in four years.
Anna Sokolow begins an association with the Mexican Ministry of Fine Arts.
NBC televises Hanya Holm's *Metropolitan Daily*.

1940 **Bennington School of the Arts begins first session. Graham premieres *El Penitente* and *Letter to the World*. Erick Hawkins in solo recital debut.**
Ted Shawn disbands his dance group.
Ballet Theatre (later American Ballet Theatre) makes its debut at the Centre Theatre, Radio City, New York.
José Limón leaves Humphrey-Weidman; joins May O'Donnell in the Pacific Northwest.
Bonnie Bird and John Cage announce formation of an "American Dance Theatre" in Seattle, "to meet the growing need for a theatre concerned with experimental productions in the youngest of the vital American arts."
Harriette Ann Gray, Elizabeth Waters, Mildred Zook, and Eleanor King at Perry-Mansfield.
Dance Archives, Museum of Modern Art, is founded in New York. Paul Magriel, librarian.
Humphrey-Weidman Studio Theatre, 108 West 16th Street, opens.
Dance Notation Bureau is founded in New York.
Tamiris re-forms her company after demise of Federal Dance Project.

1941 **Bennington School of the Arts completes its second session. Humphrey presents *Decade*; Graham premieres *Punch and The Judy*.**
Hanya Holm directs the first summer dance program at Colorado College, with Louise Kloepper and a group of five dancers in residence.
Ballet Theatre makes first transcontinental tour.
Jacob's Pillow presents gala festival of nine programs.
Erick Hawkins, Sybil Shearer, and Valerie Bettis make independent solo debuts in New York.

1942 **Bennington School of the Dance holds last summer session. Graham, Horst, and company in residence. Holm and Humphrey send assistants. Merce Cunningham and Jean Erdman make joint choreographic debut.**
Hanya Holm at Colorado Springs with Roy Harris and Arch Lauterer.
Jacob's Pillow Dance Theater opens. Festival of American Dance includes Elizabeth Waters, Sybil Shearer, Helen Tamiris. Faculty includes Margaret H'Doubler.

Dudley-Maslow-Bales make debut as trio.
Agnes de Mille's *Rodeo* premieres with Ballet Russe de Monte Carlo.
Death of Fokine.

1943 **Martha Graham and Company in residence at Bennington College, preview *Deaths and Entrances*. (Graham returns with Horst to Bennington College in early summer 1944, 1945.)**
Sarah Lawrence College holds first summer session in the arts, dance, and music, with Bessie Schönberg, Norman Lloyd, and William Schuman, faculty.
Lester Horton makes first visit to New York.
José Limón is drafted.
Agnes de Mille choreographs *Oklahoma*.

1944 Doris Humphrey performs for the last time, 26 May, in *Inquest*, Swarthmore College.
Merce Cunningham and Arch Lauterer at Perry-Mansfield.

1945 Charles Weidman forms his own company and school at the Studio Theatre.
Humphrey, Weidman, and Marion Scott begin teaching modern dance at the 92nd Street YMHA, New York.
Eleanor King and Arch Lauterer at Perry-Mansfield.

1946 **José Limón Company debuts at Bennington College, with two new works by Doris Humphrey. Humphrey becomes artistic director.**
Ballet Society is formed, George Balanchine, artistic director.
Tamiris choreographs *Annie Get Your Gun.*

1948 Connecticut College–New York University School of the Dance and American Dance Festival begin first summer in New London, Connecticut.
Hanya Holm choreographs *Kiss Me, Kate*.
New York City Ballet (formerly Ballet Society) becomes resident company, New York City Center.

1951 The Juilliard School of Music announces the establishment of a dance program. Martha Hill is chairman. Hill leaves Bennington and NYU faculties.

1954 Margaret H'Doubler retires from University of Wisconsin.

1955 Juilliard Dance Theater is formed, with Doris Humphrey as director.

1957 Death of Arch Lauterer.

1958 Death of Doris Humphrey.

1961 Death of Robert Devore Leigh.

1964 Death of Louis Horst.

1965 American Dance Theater, a modern dance repertory company, is created with José Limón as artistic director, but dissolves in 1966.

1971 Death of Pauline Lawrence.

1972 Death of José Limón.

1975 Death of Charles Weidman.

1976 Death of Mary Josephine Shelly.

1977 American Dance Festival holds 30th and last summer session at Connecticut College.

1978 First session of American Dance Festival is held at Duke University, Durham, North Carolina.

APPENDIX C

Bennington Credits

Bennington Premieres, by Choreographer

Dances choreographed by members of the Bennington School of the Dance that had their premieres in the Bennington Festivals and concert series. Information taken from programs, verified by reviews and interviews. Semi-professional projects and student workshop productions are not included. Consult the Chronology (especially 1941 and 1942) for these.

*Title	=	Bennington Festival performance
CT	=	College Theatre (Bennington College campus)
A	=	Vermont State Armory (Bennington, Vermont)
LH	=	Lisser Hall (Mills College, Oakland, California)
m	=	Music
c	=	Costumes
l	=	Lighting
s	=	Sets

CHOREOGRAPHER	TITLE	CREDITS	DANCED BY	WHERE AND WHEN
Ethel Butler	*Ceremonial Dance*	m/Ralph Gilbert	EB/solo	LH/4 Aug 1939
	The Spirit of the Land Moves in the Blood	m/Carlos Chavez	EB/solo	LH/4 Aug 1939
Merce Cunningham	*Renaissance Testimonials*	m/Maxwell Powers c/Charlotte Trowbridge l/Joann Straus	MC/solo	CT/1 Aug 1942
(and Jean Erdman)	*Ad Lib*	m/Gregory Tucker c/Charlotte Trowbridge l/Joann Straus	MC & JE	CT/1 Aug 1942
(and Jean Erdman)	*Credo in Us*	m/John Cage c/Charlotte Trowbridge l/Joann Straus	MC & JE	CT/1 Aug 1942

CHOREOGRAPHER	TITLE	CREDITS	DANCED BY	WHERE AND WHEN
(and Jean Erdman	*Seeds of Brightness*	m/Norman Lloyd c/Charlotte Trowbridge l/Joann Straus	MC & JE	CT/1 Aug 1942
Jane Dudley, William Bales, Sophie Maslow	*Scherzo* and *Loure* from *Suite*	m/J. S. Bach	JD, WB, SM	CT/13 Aug 1942
Jean Erdman (see also Merce Cunningham)	*The Transformations of Medusa*[a]	m/Louis Horst c/Charlotte Trowbridge l/Joann Straus	JE/solo	CT/1 Aug 1942
Tina Flade	*Sinister Resonance*	m/Henry Cowell	TF/solo	CT/13 July 1935
Martha Graham	**Panorama*	m/Norman Lloyd s&l/Arch Lauterer mobile/Alexander Calder	MG + Workshop Group of 36 (12 of MG Group; 24 Apprentices)	A/14 Aug 1935
	**Opening Dance*	m/Norman Lloyd	MG/solo	A/30 July 1937
	**Immediate Tragedy*	m/Henry Cowell	MG/solo	A/30 July 1937
	**American Document*	m/Ray Green c/Edythe Gilfond s&l/Arch Lauterer	MG + 23 (11 of MG Concert Group; 11 of Bennington Group; actor)	A/6 Aug 1938
	**El Penitente*	m/Louis Horst s&l/Arch Lauterer c/Edythe Gilfond Props/Mary Grant	MG, Erick Hawkins, Merce Cunningham	CT/11 Aug 1940
	**Letter to the World*	m/Hunter Johnson s&l/Arch Lauterer c/Edythe Gilfond artistic collaborator/ Arch Lauterer	MG + 15 (14 in Dance Group; actress)	CT/11 Aug 1940
	**Punch and The Judy*	m/Robert McBride s&l/Arch Lauterer c/Charlotte Trowbridge artistic collaborator/ Arch Lauterer	MG + 16 (Company, 9; Apprentices, 7)	CT/10 Aug 1941
Erick Hawkins	*Insubstantial Pageant*	m/Lehman Engel s/Carlos Dyer	EH/solo	CT/13 July 1940
	Liberty Tree	m/Ralph Gilbert s/Carlos Dyer c/Edythe Gilfond	EH/solo	CT/13 July 1940
	Yankee Bluebritches	m/Hunter Johnson s/Charlotte Trowbridge	EH/solo	CT/13 July 1940
	In Time of Armament	m/Hunter Johnson	EH & Jean Erdman	CT/19 July 1941

[a]One movement composed in 1941.

CHOREOGRAPHER	TITLE	CREDITS	DANCED BY	WHERE AND WHEN
Hanya Holm	**Trend*	m/Wallingford Riegger, Edgar[d] Varèse s&l/Gerard Gentile c/Betty Joiner	HH + 33 (11 in Concert Group; 22 in Workshop Group)	A/13 Aug 1937
	**Dance of Work and Play*	m/Norman Lloyd s&l/Arch Lauterer c/Elizabeth Beebe	HH + Concert Group (8)	A/5 Aug 1938
	**Dance Sonata*	m/Harrison Kerr s&l/Arch Lauterer c/Elizabeth Beebe	HH + 19 (8 in Concert Group; 11 in Apprentice Group)	A/5 Aug 1938
Doris Humphrey	*New Dance*[b]	m/Wallingford Riegger c/Pauline Lawrence	DH, Charles Weidman and Concert Group (17)	CT/3 Aug 1935
	**With My Red Fires*	m/Wallingford Riegger s&l/Gerard Gentile c/Pauline Lawrence	DH, CW, and 45 (16 in Concert Groups; 29 in Workshop Groups)	A/13 Aug 1936
	**Passacaglia in C minor*	m/J. S. Bach s&l/Arch Lauterer c/Pauline Lawrence	DH, CW, and 23 (12 in Concert Group; 11 in Apprentice Group)	A/5 Aug 1938
	**Decade*	m/arr. Lionel Nowak s&l/Arch Lauterer c/ Pauline Lawrence script/Alex Kahn	DH, CW, and 15 dancers, 1 actor (9 in H–W Company; 6 Apprentices)	CT/9 Aug 1941
Esther Junger	**Dance to the People*	m/Jerome Moross s&l/Gerard Gentile c/Betty Joiner	EJ/solo	A/12 Aug 1937
	**Festive Rites*	m/Morris Mamorsky s&l/Gerard Gentile c/Betty Joiner	EJ, José Limón + Group of 10	A/12 Aug 1937
	**Opus for Three and Props* b) *With Hats*	m/Dmitri Shostakovitch s&l/Gerard Gentile c/Betty Joiner	EJ, JL, Anna Sokolow	A/12 Aug 1937
	**Ravage*	m/Harvey Pollins s&l/Gerard Gentile c/Betty Joiner	EJ/solo	A/12 Aug 1937
Eleanor King	**Bonja Song* from *American Folk Suite*	m/arr. Esther Williamson l/Arch Lauterer c/George Bockman	EK, Wanda Graham, Mary Starks	A/4 Aug 1938

[b]*New Dance* had a prior public performance, 1 August 1935, University of Vermont, Burlington, under the title "Dance Variations."

CHOREOGRAPHER	TITLE	CREDITS	DANCED BY	WHERE AND WHEN
Eleanor King	**Ode to Freedom*	m/arr. John Colman & Norman Lloyd s&l/Arch Lauterer c/Betty Joiner	EK + Group of 10	A/4 Aug 1938
Louise Kloepper	**Earth Saga*	m/Esther Williamson l/Arch Lauterer c/Betty Joiner	LK + Group of 9	A/4 Aug 1938
	**Romantic Theme*	m/Harvey Pollins l/Arch Lauterer c/Elizabeth Beebe	LK/solo	A/4 Aug 1938
	**Statement of Dissent*	m/Gregory Tucker l/Arch Lauterer c/Elizabeth Beebe	LK/solo	A/4 Aug 1938
José Limón	**Danza de la Muerte*	m/Henry L. Clark[e], Norman Lloyd s&l/Gerard Gentile c/Betty Joiner	JL + Group of 10	A/12 Aug 1937
	**Opus for Three and Props* a) *With Pole*	m/Dmitri Shostakovitch s&l/Gerard Gentile c/Betty Joiner	JL, Junger, Anna Sokolow	A/12 Aug 1937
	Danzas Mexicanas	m/Lionel Nowak	JL/solo	LH/4 Aug 1939
Anna Sokolow	**Façade-Esposizione Italiana*	m/Alex North s&l/Gerard Gentile c/Betty Joiner	AS + Group of 10	A/12 Aug 1937
Marian Van Tuyl	**Out of One Happening*	m/Gregory Tucker l/Arch Lauterer c/Betty Joiner	MVT + Group of 9	A/4 Aug 1938
Charles Weidman	**Quest*	m/Norman Lloyd and Clair Leonard s&l/Gerard Gentile c/Pauline Lawrence	DH, CW, and 24 (16 in Concert Groups; 8 in Workshop Group)	A/13 Aug 1936
	**Opus 51*	m/Vivian Fine s&l/Arch Lauterer c/Pauline Lawrence	CW + 15 (8 in Concert Group; 7 in Apprentice Group)	A/6 Aug 1938

Musical Scores Written for Dance Premieres

Arr. = not an original score but an arrangement from other music, sometimes with original components.

COMPOSER/CHOREOGRAPHER	COMPOSITION	YEAR
John Cage/Cunningham and Erdman	*Credo in Us*	1942
Henry Clark[e]/Limón	*Danza de la Muerte*	1937
John Colman/King	*Ode to Freedom* [Arr.]	1938
Henry Cowell/Graham	*Immediate Tragedy*	1937

COMPOSER/CHOREOGRAPHER	COMPOSITION	YEAR
Lehman Engel/Hawkins	*Insubstantial Pageant*	1940
Vivian Fine/Weidman	*Opus 51*	1938
Ralph Gilbert/Butler	*Ceremonial Dance*	1939
Ralph Gilbert/Hawkins	*Liberty Tree*	1940
Ray Green/Graham	*American Document*	1938
Louis Horst/Graham	*El Penitente*	1940
Louis Horst/Erdman	*Transformations of Medusa*	1942[a]
Hunter Johnson/Graham	*Letter to the World*	1940
Hunter Johnson/Hawkins	*Yankee Bluebritches*	1940
Hunter Johnson/Hawkins	*In Time of Armament*	1941
Harrison Kerr/Holm	*Dance Sonata*	1938
Clair Leonard/Weidman	*Transition* from *Quest*	1936
Norman Lloyd/Graham	*Panorama*	1935
Norman Lloyd/Weidman	*Quest*	1936
Norman Lloyd/Limón	*Danza de la Muerta (Hoch! Ave! Viva!)*	1937
Norman Lloyd/Graham	*Opening Dance*	1937
Norman Lloyd/King	*Ode to Freedom* [Arr.]	1938
Norman Lloyd/Holm	*Dance of Work and Play*	1938
Norman Lloyd/Cunningham and Erdman	*Seeds of Brightness*	1942
Robert McBride/Graham	*Punch and The Judy*	1941
Morris Mamorsky/Junger	*Festive Rites*	1937
Jerome Moross/Junger	*Dance to the People*	1937
Alex North/Sokolow	*Façade-Esposizione Italiana*	1937
Lionel Nowak/Limón	*Danzas Mexicanas*	1939
Lionel Nowak/Humphrey	*Decade* [Arr.]	1941
Harvey Pollins/Junger	*Ravage*	1937
Harvey Pollins/Kloepper	*Romantic Theme*	1938
Maxwell Powers/Cunningham	*Renaissance Testimonials*	1942
Wallingford Riegger/Humphrey	*New Dance*	1935
Wallingford Riegger/Humphrey	*With My Red Fires*	1936
Wallingford Riegger/Holm	*Trend*	1937
Gregory Tucker/Van Tuyl	*Out of One Happening*	1938
Gregory Tucker/Kloepper	*Statement of Dissent*	1938
Gregory Tucker/Cunningham and Erdman	*Ad Lib*	1942
Esther Williamson [Ballou]/King	*Bonja Song* from *American Folk Suite* [Arr.]	1938
Esther Williamson [Ballou]/Kloepper	*Earth Saga*	1938

[a]One movement composed in 1941.

Student Compositions and Dance Projects

A selective listing of students whose work was presented in informal demonstrations at the Bennington School of the Dance, 1934-1942, and of dance projects presented at the school in 1941 and 1942. The first summer of the student's work is given; consult the Chronology for additional presentations.

Pre-Classic Dance Forms Under Louis Horst: Ethel Butler (1942), Mercier [Merce] Cunningham (1939), Jane Dudley (1942), Barbara Mettler (1936), Alwin Nikolais (1937), Nona Schurman (1939), Marian Van Tuyl (1934), Theodora Wiesner (1937).

Modern Forms Under Louis Horst: Ruth Bloomer (1936), Jane Dudley (1940), Jean Erdman (1937), Nelle Fisher (1940), Nina Fonaroff (1940), Pearl Lack [Lang] (1941), Eleanor Lauer (1937), Gertrude Lippincott (1938), Iris Mabry (1941), Sophie Maslow (1940), Barbara Mettler (1937), Alwin Nikolais (1938), Ann Schuman [Halprin] (1939), Marian Van Tuyl (1936), Theodora Wiesner (1938).

Composition Under Martha Hill and Bessie Schönberg: Ruth Bloomer (1934), Delia Hussey (1938), Eleanor Lauer (1937), Ruth Murray (1934), Alwin Nikolais (1937), Ann Schuman [Halprin] (1938), Mary-Averett Seelye (1941), Virginia Tanner (1941).

Experimental Production With Martha Hill, Arch Lauterer, Norman Lloyd: George Bockman (1940), Delia Hussey (1938), Nik Krevitsky (1941), Gertrude Lippincott (1938), Katherine Litz (1940), Alwin Nikolais (1938), Esther Pease (1939), Helen Priest (1939), Nona Schurman (1939), Lillian Shapero (1938), Philip Stapp (1938), Virginia Tanner (1940), Theodora Wiesner (1938).

Dance Projects, 1941 William Bales, *Es Mujer*. Ethel Butler, *Sarabande*. David Campbell, *Pattern for the Imperial Procession*. Nina Fonaroff, *Yankee Doodle Greets Columbus, 1492*. Joseph Gornbein [Gifford], *Fanfare*. Martha Hill, Arch Lauterer, Norman Lloyd, *The Swallow-Book*. Iris Mabry, *Act of Faith, Dilemma*. Harriet Roeder, *Today's Stepchild*. Bessie Schönberg, *Mississippi Sketches*.

Dance Projects, 1942 Henrietta Greenhood [Eve Gentry], *It's a Bargain at Any Price*. Nona Schurman, *Restless Song*.

Faculty, Associate Faculty, and Courses Taught, 1934-1942

INSTRUCTOR	COURSE	SUMMERS
William Bales	Tap Technique	1941
Ben Belitt	Experimental Production (with Hill, Lauterer, Lloyd, Schönberg)	1939
Franziska Boas	Percussion Accompaniment	1937–1939
	Major Course in Music for the Dance (with Horst and Lloyd)	1939
Sally Brownell	Stagecraft for Dancers	1936
Ethel Butler (Associate)	Martha Graham Technique	1939–1942
Tina Flade	Modern Dance Technique	1935

INSTRUCTOR	**COURSE**	**SUMMERS**
Martha Graham	Director, Workshop Program	1935
	Director, Professional Program	1938
	Modern Dance Technique	1934–1939, 1941, 1942
Henrietta Greenhood [Eve Gentry] (Associate)	Hanya Holm Technique	1942
Erick Hawkins	Ballet Technique	1940, 1942
	Ballet for Modern Dancers	1941
Martha Hill	Fundamental Techniques	1934
	Techniques of Dance Movement	1935–1939
	Dance Composition	1934–1942
	Teaching Methods and Materials	1934
	The Dance in Education (with Shelly)	1935
	Laboratory in Composition	
	(with Horst and Martin)	1937
	(with Horst)	1938
	Co-Director, Program in Choreography (with Horst)	1936–1938
	Experimental Production	
	(with Lauterer)	1938
	(with Lauterer, Belitt, Lloyd, Schönberg)	1939
	(with Lauterer and Lloyd)	1940, 1941
	Dance and Music Recreation (with Lloyd)	1942
	American Country Dancing	1942
Hanya Holm	Director, Workshop Program	1937
	Director, Professional Program	1938
	Modern Dance Technique	1934, 1936–1939
	Master Course in Dance	1940
Louis Horst	Music Related to Movement	1934
	Composition in Dance Forms: Pre-Classic Forms	1935–1938
	Composition in Dance Forms: Modern Forms	1935–1938
	Composition in Dance Forms: Pre-Classic and Modern	1939–1942
	Director, Program in Music for the Dance	1936–1938
	Music Composition	1936–1938, 1940 1942
	Laboratory in Composition	
	(with Hill and Martin)	1937
	(with Hill)	1938
	Co-Director, Program in Choreography (with Hill)	1936–1938
	Major Course in Music for the Dance (with Lloyd and Boas)	1939
	Composition for Dance	1941

INSTRUCTOR	COURSE	SUMMERS
Doris Humphrey	Director, Women's Workshop	1936
	Director, Professional Program	1938
	Modern Dance Technique	1934–1939
	Master Course in Dance (with Weidman)	1941
	Humphrey-Weidman Repertory (with Weidman)	1941
Louise Kloepper (Associate)	Hanya Holm Technique	1939
Arch Lauterer	Director, Program in Stage Design for the Dance	1938
	Experimental Production	
	(with Hill)	1938
	(with Hill, Belitt, Lloyd, Schönberg)	1939
	(with Hill and Lloyd)	1940, 1941
	Major Course in Stage Design	1939
	Theatre Design	1940
José Limón (Associate)	Charles Weidman Technique	1939
Norman Lloyd	Elements of Music	1935–1938
	Rhythmic Basis of Dance	1939, 1940, 1942
	Rhythmic Basis of Movement	1941
	Music Accompaniment	1936–1938, 1942
	Major Course in Music for the Dance (with Boas and Horst)	1939
	Dance Accompaniment	1941
	Dance and Music Recreation (with Hill)	1942
	Experimental Production	
	(with Lauterer, Hill, Belitt, Schönberg)	1939
	(with Lauterer and Hill)	1940, 1941
	Accompaniment for the Dance	1940
Nancy McKnight	Percussion Accompaniment for the Dance	1936
Maria Maginnis (Associate)	Humphrey-Weidman Technique (with Moore)	1941
Katherine Manning (Associate)	Doris Humphrey Technique	1939, 1940
John Martin	Dance History and Criticism	1934–1937
	Seminar in Dance Criticism	1936, 1937
	Laboratory in Composition (with Hill and Horst)	1937
Louise Martin	Basis of Dramatic Movement	1935, 1936
	Dramatic Basis of Movement	1937
Claudia Moore (Associate)	Humphrey-Weidman Technique	1940, 1941
Jane Ogborn	Production	1934
	Stagecraft for Dancers	1935

INSTRUCTOR	COURSE	SUMMERS
Helen Priest	Dance Notation	1940
Harriet Roeder (Associate)	Hanya Holm Technique	1940, 1941
Bessie Schönberg	Dance Composition	1934–1940
	Practice (in technique)	1934
	Techniques of Dance Movement	1935–1940
	Experimental Production (with Hill, Belitt, Lloyd, Lauterer)	1939
	Technique of Modern Dance for Teachers	1941
	Fundamentals of Dance Composition	1941
Nona Schurman	Humphrey–Weidman Technique	1942
Mary Jo Shelly	The Dance in Education (with Hill)	1935
Gregory Tucker	Music for Dancers	1934
Charles Weidman	Director, Men's Workshop	1936
	Director, Professional Program	1938
	Modern Dance Technique	1934–1939
	Master Course in Dance	1941
	Humphrey–Weidman Repertory (with Humphrey)	1941
Mildred Wile	Composition in Dance Forms: Pre-Classic Forms	1938
	Pre-Classic and Modern Forms	1940

Teaching Assistants (1934-1940*)

[MG=Martha Graham; DH = Doris Humphrey; CW = Charles Weidman; LH = Louis Horst; MH = Martha Hill; AL = Arch Lauterer; BS = Bessie Schönberg]

Cleo Atheneos [DH] 1934
William Bales [CW] 1938
Bonnie Bird [MG] 1935
Dorothy Bird [MG] 1934-1937
George Bockman [CW] 1937, 1938
Ethel Butler [MG] 1938
Marjorie Church [MH, BS] 1936
Carolyn Durand [HH] 1938
Edward Glass [AL] 1938
Letitia Ide [DH] 1935
Louise Kloepper [HH] 1937
Joan Levy [DH] 1936
Hortense Lieberthal [MH, BS] 1937-1939; [substitute for Schönberg] 1942
José Limón [CW] 1935, 1936
Nancy McKnight [HH] 1934; [Tina Flade] 1935; [HH] 1936
Katherine Manning [DH] 1936, 1938
Gene Martel [CW] 1934
William Matons [CW] 1936
May O'Donnell [LH] 1934-1936; [MG] 1938
Edith Orcutt [DH] 1937, 1938
Bessie Schönberg [MH] 1934, 1935
Henry Seymour [AL] 1938, 1939
Sybil Shearer [DH] 1936, 1938
Lee Sherman [CW] 1938
Gertrude Shurr [MG] 1935
Anna Sokolow [LH] 1935
Elizabeth Waters [HH] 1937, 1938
Mildred Wile [LH] 1937-1939
Lucretia Wilson [HH] 1937

*No information for 1941 and 1942 available.

Guest Lecturers

A representative listing of guest lecturers and guest teachers at Bennington, 1934–1942. (Sources: "Annual Reports," *Bulletins*, and the *Dance Observer*.)

Sol Babitz, Dance notation lecture, "Dance Writing," 1939.

Edith Ballwebber, University of Chicago, "Methods of Teaching Social Dancing," 1939.

Jacques Barzun, "Culture and Revolution," 1935.

George Beiswanger, "The Social Implications of the Contemporary Dance," 1935; "Music and Dance," 1938.

Paul Boepple, Director, Dalcroze School of Music, "Space and Time in Music," 1938.

Francis Bosworth, Federal Theatre Project, "New Horizons of the Theater," 1938.

Dr. Douglas Campbell, University of Chicago, "Thalamic Communication," 1939.

Irma Dombois-Bartenieff and Irma Otto-Betz, Series on Laban Dance Script, 1936.

Margaret Einert, *London Dancing Times*, "Dance in England," 1938.

Francis Fergusson, "The Relationship between the Arts of the Theatre," 1937.

Margaret H'Doubler, University of Wisconsin, Demonstration Dance Lesson, 1934.

Lincoln Kirstein, "History and Development of the Ballet," 1936; "The Classic Dance," 1937; Lecture Series on Theatrical Dancing, 1940.

Paul Love, Series on Dance Notation, 1937.

John Martin, "The American Dance," 1936; "Background of the American Dance" and "Isadora Duncan and the Modern Dance," 1938; Lecture-review on Dance Today, 1941.

Curt Sachs, author, *World History of the Dance* (1937), "Dance and Music" and "Dance, Anthropology, History," 1938.

Lloyd Shaw, author, *Cowboy Dancing* (1939), three sessions and discussion on "American Country Dancing," 1939.

George Sklar, "Trends in the Contemporary Theatre," 1935.

Ralph Steiner, Experimental Film, 1935.

Advisory Board and Trustee Committee

Advisory Board to the Bennington School of the Dance 1934-1939

John J. Coss, 1934, 1935
Martha Graham, 1934-1939
Hanya Holm, 1934-1939
Louis Horst, 1934-1939
Doris Humphrey, 1934-1939
Dorothy Lawton, 1934, 1935
Robert D. Leigh, 1934-1939
Norman Lloyd, 1938, 1939
John Martin, 1934-1939
Jay B. Nash, 1934, 1935
Gregory Tucker, 1935
Charles Weidman, 1934-1939

Trustee Committee of Bennington College for the Bennington School of the Dance (1935-1939) and School of the Arts (1940-1941)

Frederick Lewis Allen, 1940, 1941
Mabel Warren Bradley (Mrs. J. Gardner), 1938-1941
John J. Coss, 1935-1939
Elizabeth Jennings Franklin (Mrs. George S.), 1940, 1941
Charles Harold Gray, 1935
Frances Coleman Holden (Mrs. Arthur J.), 1935-1937
Mary Carlisle Howe (Mrs. Walter Bruce), 1939-1941
Edna Morse Jackson (Mrs. Percy), 1935-1938
Robert D. Leigh, 1935-1939
Margaret S. Lewisohn (Mrs. Samuel A.), 1940, 1941
Nathalie Swan (Mrs. Joseph R.), 1941
Isabelle Baker Woolley (Mrs. Clarence M.), 1940, 1941

TITLE INDEX

Included in this index are dance and stage productions cited in the text and appendixes. Page numbers in boldface denote major entries for Bennington productions.

A

Act of Faith, 112, 338
Ad Lib, 120, **228–29**, 256, 325, 333, 337
Affectations, 49
Agitation, 49
Air for the G String, 217
Air Primitive, 311. See also *Spirit Possessed.*
Alcestis, 317
Alcina Suite, 43, 51, 110
Americana (Humphrey–Weidman), 326
Americana (Nikolais), 70
Americana (Van Tuyl), 70. See also *Piazza Sketches*
American Document, 1, 15, 18, 27, 30, 74, 75, 79, 80, 89, 109, 117, 119, 120, **191–99**, 202, 259, 260, 265, 307, 308, 311, 317, 318, 320, 330, 334, 337; photos, 192, 195, 196
American Folk Suite, 79, 80, **177**, 180, 335
American Gospel Hymn: Throw Out the Life Line, 59
American Greetings, 252. See also *Studies in Americana, American Greeting*
American Holiday, 91, 92, 157, 323
American Lyric, 311, 323
American Nostalgia, 119
American Pattern, 323
American Provincials, 59, 71
American Rhapsody, 58
American Saga: Johnny Inkslinger, 323
American Scene, Two Dances of Protest: Workaday Song, Road Song, 79
American Sketches, One of the West, Two of the South, One of the East, 49
Amor Brujo, El, 320
Annie Get Your Gun, 331
Appalachian Spring, 316, 318
Anti-War Cycle, 325
Archaic Duet, 99, 311
As Poor Richard Says, 325
As Thousands Cheer, 326
Atavisms, 110, 317
Authentic Galliarde, 119
Authentic Pavanne, 119

B

Bacchanale, 316, 324
Ballad in a Popular Style, 58, 71, 323
Ballad of Molly Pitcher, The, 112
Bargain Counter, 152
Barker: A Play of Carnival Life in Three Acts, The, 22, 113
Berceuse–Copyright 1934, 45
Billy the Kid, 289, 330
Bird Spell, 111
Black Tambourine, 120
"Bonja Song" from *American Folk Suite*. See *American Folk Suite*
Bourrée, 45
Bridge, The, 19, 325

C

Cafe Chantant–Five A.M., 120
California Suite, 88
Cancion y Danza, 88
Candide, 91, 92, 320, 324, 326, 329
Case History No.—, 324; photo 264
Celebration, 51, 199, 318
Ceremonial Dance, 88, **202**, 333, 337
Ceremonials, 317
Chaconne: The Pilgrim's Progress, 112
Choreartium, 156
Chromatic Eccentricities, 324
Chronicle, 71, 311, 324
City Nocturne, 59, 72, 324
City Portrait, 289
Coach with the Six Insides, The, 317
Composition for a Fugitive Spot, 111
Conquest, 84, 316, 330
Corybantic, 26
"Costume," a Paragraph from "Information for Students, Bennington School of Dance at Mills College 1939," 88
Counterpoint No. 2, 43
Courante, Contagion, 88
Credo in Us, 119, **227**, 229, 256, 258, 316, 333, 336
Cry, The, 324
Cube, 99

D

Dance in the Early Morning, 50
Dance in Three Parts, 324
Dance in Two Parts: A Cry Rises in the Land, New Destinies, 59
Dance of Sport, 326
Dance of the Elevens, 92
Dances of Women, 320
Dances of Work, 326
Dance of Work and Play, 1, 15, 74, 75, 79, 80, **184–86**, 187, 335, 337; photo 185
Dance Prelude, 42
Dance Sonata, 1, 15, 17, 75, 79, 80, **186-87**, 261, 320, 335, 337
Dance Stanzas, 59
Dance to the People, 71, **156**, 335, 337
Dance Variations, 127, 335. See also *New Dance*
Dance with words, 111
Dance Americaine, 326
Danza, 88
Danza de la Muerte, 30, 65, 71, 157, **158-59**, 255, 321, 336, 337

Danzas Mexicanas, 84, 88, **202-3**, 306-9 *passim*, 312, 321, 324, 336, 337
Dark of the Moon, 320
Deaths and Entrances, 25, 117, 119, 199, 320, 321, 331
Decade: A Biography of Modern Dance 1930 to 1940, 1, 22, 104, 105, 106, 114, 117, **216-21**, 321, 330, 335, 337; designs 217, 218
Deep Song, 155
Diagonal, 111
Diagonal Line, 88
Dialogues, 322
Dilemma (Mabry), 112, 338
Dilemmas (Dudley), 49
Directions, 70, 80
Disinherited, The, 49
Dithyrambic, 42, 136
Diversion of Angels. See *Wilderness Stair*
Divertissements, 57
Drama of Motion, 320
Drive, 59
Dust Bowl Ballads, 323. See also *Two Dust Bowl Ballads*

E

Earth Primitive, 254
Earth Saga, 79, 80, **178**, 326, 336, 337; photo 178
Ekstasis, 59, 71, 198, 317. See also *Exstasis, Two Lyric Fragments*
Electra, 325
Elegy, 50; photo 262
Emperor Jones, 310
Encounter, 57, 69
Epilogue to Victory, 70
Es Mujer, 105, 112, 338
Evening, The, 111
Every Soul is a Circus, 101, 110, 199, 223, 225, 311, 316
Evocation, 324
Exhibition Piece, 45, 70
Exstasis, Two Lyric Fragments, 43. See also *Ekstasis*
Exultation, 79

F

Fables for Our Time, 326
Façade-Esposizione Italiana, 30, 65, 72, **159-60**, 266, 336, 337
Fanfare, 112, 338
Fantastic Symphony, 159
Fare Thee Well, 111
Fatherland, 49
Festive Rhythm, 73, 324; photo 72
Festive Rites, 71, **156-58**, 323, 335, 337; photo 157
Filling Station, 318
Fire Cycle, 50
First Heritage, 70
Fixations, One, Two and Three, 79
Flapper and the Quarterback, The, 327
Flickers, 117, 310, 324
Folksay, 120, 323
Folk Song, 45
Four Chromatic Eccentricities, 59
Four Little Salon Pieces, 58
Four Walls, 321
Four Walls Blues, 120
Frankie and Johnny, 323, 330
Frenetic Rhythms, 43, 324
From "The Swallow-Book" by Ernst Toller, 112, 338
Frontier, 59, 71, 131, 155, 253, 311, 319. See also *Perspectives*

G

Garden is Political, The, 99
Gay Promenade, 59
Glückliche Hand, Die 320
Go Down Death, 320
Golden Fleece, The, 319, 321
Green Land, The, 324
Greeting, 49
Guns and Castanets, 323
Gymnopedies, 326

H

Happy Hypocrite, The, 152, 203, 326
Harlequinade, 43, 59, 71
Harlequin for President, 57
Harmonica Breakdown, 112, 120, 317
His Best Gal, 325
Hoofer, The. See *Hoofer on a Fiver*
Hoofer on a Fiver, 111, 120
Horizons, 59, 132
House Divided, A, 324
How Long Brethren?, 329
Hunger, 58

I

Icaro, 320
I'd Rather Be Right, 321
Immediate Tragedy–Dance of Dedication, 1, 30, 63, 65, 70, 71, **154-56**, 196, 198, 316, 334, 336; drawing 155
Imperial Gesture, 59, 71, 317
Impresario: An Operatic Squabble, The, 22, 104, 113
Impressionism, 311
Impressions of a Dance Hall, 49
In a Quiet Space, 59
Inquest, 322, 331
Insubstantial Pageant–A Dance of Experience, 99, **204**, 259, 317, 334, 337
Integrales, 131
In the Clearing: Variations on a Theme, 70, 80, 120, 325
In Time of Armament, 112, **216**, 260, 320, 334, 337
Invention, 322
It's a Bargain at Any Price, 120, 122, 338

J

Jazz Study to "St. Louis Blues," 99
Johnny Got His Gun, 95

K

Kentucky Hill Tune, 99
Kinetic Pantomime, 43, 326
King and the Duke: A Melodramatic Farce from "Huckleberry Finn," The, 95, 96, 99, 325
Kiss Me, Kate, 26, 319
Kiss of Judas, The, 99, 311.

L

Lamentation, 42, 59, 71, 311, 318
Lament for Ignacio Sánchez Mejías, 25, 322
Letter to the World, 1, 18, 20, 22, 27, 30, 93, 94, 96, 98, 101, 105-9 *passim*, 114, 199, **208-14**, 223, 225, 256, 259, 260, 265, 290, 307, 308, 311, 316-18 *passim*, 320, 321, 330, 334, 337; photo 209
Liberty Song, 117
Liberty Tree–A Set of Four Dances, 99, **204**, 259, 261, 334, 337
Life Begins at 8:40, 320
Life of the Bee, 51, 130, 320
Light Plan Only, 99
Line and Plane, 79, 252
Line in Space, 79
"Loure" from *Suite*. See *Suite*
Lucrece, 318
Lynch Town, 105, 111
Lyric Jazz Study, 99
Lysistrata, 320

M

Machine Ballet, 324
Medieval Dance: The Kiss of Judas. See *The Kiss of Judas*
Mal de siècle, 323
Malinche, La, 322
Marching Song, 131. See also *Perspectives*
Memorial–To the Trivial, 43. See also *Memorials*
Memorials, 51, 323, 326
Merely a Beginning, 326
Metropolitan Daily, 319, 325, 330
Mexican Suite. See *Danzas Mexicanas*
"Mississippi Sketches" from "The River" by Pare Lorenz, 112, 338
Momentum, 70
Moor's Pavane, The, 322
Mountain Song, 99
Music Montage Using Two Victrolas, 99
My Fair Lady, 319
My Son, My Enemy, 317

N

Namesake, 321
Negro Spirituals, 328
"Never Sign a Letter Mrs." from "Etiquette" by Emily Post, 88
New Dance, 1, 30, 31, 47, 51, 59, 60, 61, 63, 71, 80, 92, **127-30**, 141, 142, 143, 144, 181, 218, 253, 256, 261, 284, 286, 308, 309, 310, 312, 313, 314, 317, 321, 324, 326, 335, 337; photos 59, 60, 127-29. See also *New Dance Trilogy*
New Dance Trilogy, 47, 53, 61, 92, 128, 129, 140, 141,

143, 181, 284, 290, 329. See also *New Dance; Theatre Piece; With My Red Fires*
Night Journey, 318
Night Suite, 112
"Nine Notations" from "Thirteen Ways of Looking at a Blackbird," 88
No Retreat, 70

O

Obsession, 70
Obsession of the Spiral, 50
Ode to Freedom, 79, 80, **176**, 336
Oklahoma, 318, 331
On My Mother's Side, 312, 324
Opening Dance, 1, 70, 71, **154**, 334, 337; drawing 154
Opus 51, 27, 74, 76, 79, 80, **188-91**, 312, 313, 317, 326, 336, 337; photos 188, 189
Opus for Three and Props, 72, **160**, 335, 336
Orestes, 320
Out of One Happening, 79, 80, **179**, 325, 336, 337

P

Panorama, 1, 14, 20, 27, 30, 46, 50, 51, 61, 63, 109, **131-37**, 197, 308, 311, 317, 321, 322, 329, 334, 337; design 133
Parade, 320
Passacaglia. See *Passacaglia in C minor*
Passacaglia in C minor, 1, 15, 17, 18, 30, 74, 75, 79, 80, **180-83**, 261, 307, 308, 310, 312, 313, 314, 317, 335; photos 180, 182.
Passacaglia and Fugue in C minor. See *Passacaglia in C minor*
Pattern for the Imperial Procession, 112, 338
Patricks Day Parade, 111
Pavane, 45
Pavane–Authentic, 79
Penitente, El, 1, 20, 22, 27, 30, 93, 98, 101, 105, 107, 109, 114, **205-8**, 223, 225, 256, 259, 260, 273, 307, 308, 310, 311, 314, 316, 318, 319, 321, 322, 330, 334, 337
Pentatonic Study, 111
People, Yes, The, 325
Performance, 322
Perspectives, 51, 131, 311. See also *Frontier* and *Marching Song*
Petrouchka, 320
Piazza Sketches–From a Mid-Western Suite, Alone; Together, 59. See also *Americana* (Van Tuyl)
Pilgrims Progress, The, 324
Pleasures of Counterpoint No. 2, 324
Pocahontas, 57, 58
Praeludium, 59
Prairie, 289
Prelude, 72, 324
Primitive Canticles, 43
Primitive Mysteries, 136, 207, 307, 318, 319, 328
Primitive Rhythm, 59
Primitive Studies, 88
Processional, 45
Promenade, 57
Public Condolences, 70
Public Rejoicings, 70
Punch and The Judy, 1, 22, 69, 104, 105, 107, 108, 110, 114, 117, 119, 120, 199, **221-25**, 256, 260, 307, 317, 318, 321, 323, 330, 334, 337

Q

Quest: A Choreographic Pantomime, 1, 27, 30, 53, 59, 61, 143, **147-52**, 306, 321, 329, 336, 337; photo 148

R

Race of Life, 80, 188, 312, 317
Ravage, 71, **156**, 324, 335, 337
Religious Medieval Study, 111
Renaissance Testimonials, 119, **227**, 324, 333, 336
Restless Song, 120, 122, 338
Rhythm II, 72
Ridicolosamente, 45
Road to Success, 59
Roberta, 321
Rodeo, 331
Roi Fait un Discours au Rythm d'une Courante, Le, 45
Rondo, 45
Romantic Dances, 58
Romantic Theme, 79, 80, 88, **177**, 324, 336, 337
Rosalinda, 322
Rudepoema, 43, 285
Run Little Chillun!, 320
Running Laughter, 120; photo 270
Rustica, 45

S

Sacre du Printemps, 318, 320, 328
Salutation, 59, 70, 72
Sarabande (Butler), 112, 338
Sarabande (Graham), 59, 202, 317
Sarabande (Holm), 324
Sarabande, Resentment, 88
Satyric Festival Song, 42, 59, 71
Scheherazade, 329
"Scherzo" from *Suite*. See *Suite*
School for Husbands, The, 320
School for Wives, The, 22, 104, 113
Seasons, The, 317
Sea Bourne, 325
Sea Gives Up Its Ghosts, The, 164
Seeds of Brightness, 119, **227**, 228, 229, 256, 334, 337
Serenade, 260
Shakers, The, 105, 110, 111, 278, 312, 320, 328
Short Story, 120
Showpiece, 69, 193, 222, 260, 318, 322
Sing for your Supper, 325
Sinister Resonance, 50, **127**, 334
Slaughter of the Innocents, 323
Soaring, 319
Sonata Pathetique, 319
Song for Soviet Youth Day, 324
Soundless Song, The, 322
Speaker, 58, 71, 323
Spirit of the Land Moves in the Blood, The, 88, **202**, 333
Spirit Possessed, 99. See also *Air Primitive*
Statement of Dissent, 80, 88, **177**, 178, 261, 310, 336, 337
Story of Mankind, The, 25, 324
Strangler, The, 26
Streetcar Named Desire, A, 321, 323
Studies in Americana, American Greeting, 79. See also *American Greetings*
Studies in Conflict, 51, 326
Study in Cerebralism: Abstract, 70
Study in Dissonance, 111
Suite, 120, **230**, 323, 334
Suite in B minor, 88,
Suspension, 318
Swallow-Book, The. See *From "The Swallow Book" by Ernst Toller*
Sylphides, Les, 329

T

Tell Me of the Living, 120
Theater Piece No. 2, 323
Theatre Piece, 53, 59, 60, 61 63, 70, 128, 129, 141, 142, 144, 284, 286, 316, 324; photo 61, 62. See also *New Dance Trilogy*
Themes from a Slavic People, 49
Theodolina, Queen of the Amazons, 119
They Too Are Exiles, 317
Three Dances of Judith, 70
Three Mazurkas, 43
Three Negro Poems, 49
Three-part Canon, 45
Three Sarabandes, 112. See also *Act of Faith, Pattern for the Imperial Procession, Sarabande*
Threnody, 70
Time is Money, 49
'Tis of Thee, 320
To a Green Mountain Boy, 120
Today's Stepchild, 112, 338
Totenmal, Das, 319
To the Dance, 70, 312
Traditions, 51, 317
Tragic Departure, 79
Tragic Exodus, 317, 319, 321
Trailbreaker-Kentucky, 112
Transformations of Medusa, The, 120, **228**, 229, 317, 334, 337
Transition (Desca), 58
Transitions (Graham), 43, 51, 317
Trend, 1, 14, 17, 18, 20, 23, 27, 30, 31, 63, 65, 68, 70, 72, 78, **161-73**, 253, 290, 307, 308, 319, 321, 324, 329, 335, 337; photo 161; design 167
Trickster Coyote, 112
Triumphant Figure, 70
Trojan Incident, 324

Two Dust Bowl Ballads, 120. See also *Dust Bowl Ballads*
Two Ecstatic Themes, 43, 320
Two Sarabandes, 50

V

Valse, La, 320
"Variations and Conclusion" from *New Dance*, 129, 141, 309, 312–14 *passim*; photo 60
Village I Knew, The, 323

W

Waltz, 70
War Is Beautiful, 159, 160, 323
War Lyrics, 326
Water Study, 320
We Are the Living: Premonition, Catastrophe, Renewal-Affirmation, 75, 79
Well Fed, 58
When Johnny Comes Marching Home, 128
Wilderness Stair, 26, 316
Willie the Weeper, 320
With My Red Fires, 1, 14, 20, 53, 57, 59, 60, 128, 129, **139–46**, 147, 148, 170, 181, 220, 284, 286, 306–8 *passim*, 310, 313, 314, 321, 324, 329, 335, 337; photos 141, 145. See also *New Dance Trilogy*
Wrestlers, The, 311

X

Xochitl, 326

Y

Yankee Bluebritches—A Green Mountain Dance, 112. See also *Yankee Bluebritches—A Vermont Fantasy*
Yankee Bluebritches—A Vermont Fantasy, 99, **204–5**, 210, 259, 320, 334, 337
Yankee Clipper, 69
Yankee Doodle Greets Columbus, 1492, 105, 338

Z

Zweispiel, 45

NAME INDEX

Page numbers in boldface denote major references. "Credits" refers to participation in Bennington productions. Consult the filmography, pp. 309-13, for additional information not included in the index, and see also Appendix C, "Bennington Credits," for summary listings.

A

Adair, Ellen, credits 45
Adair, Mary Standring, credits 161, 186
Adams, Maude, 42
Alexander, Ruth, 2, 305; credits 45
Alkire, Helen, credits 2, 161
Allen, Frederick Lewis, 344
Allen, Louise, 129; credits 139, 147
Alvarez, Anita, 136; credits 131, 191-92
Alvin Theatre, 159, 211
Amaya, Carmen, 211
Amster, Patricia, credits 139
American Ballet, 14
American Ballet Theater. *See* Ballet Theatre
American Dance Association, 69, 70, 158
American Dance Festival, 2, **25, 26, 34 n.45,** 129, 141, 143, 181, 182, 206, 260, 266. *See also* Connecticut College and Palmer Auditorium
American Dance Theater, xi, 182
American Pictures, 87
American School of the Dance, 34 n.46
Andrews, Mary Alice, credits 161
Appia, Adolphe, 17, 109, 223
Arbeau, Thoinot, credits 119
Archibald, Billy, 180, 188
Argentina, La, 7
Armando, E., 61, 139, 147
Aronson, Fannie, 2, 57, 110; credits 59, 112
Ashermann, Otto, credits 139, 147
Asquith, Ruby, credits 57, 69
Atchison, Nanette, credits 139
Atheneos, Cleo, 42, 231
Aubry, Jean, credits 156, 176

B

Babitz, Sol, 87
Babitz, Thelma, credits 191-92
Bach, Helen, 127
Bach, Johann Sebastian, 17, 75, 117, 144, 183, 230; credits 45, 50, 80, 88, 101, 113, 120, 180, 216, 230
Bacon, Ernst, credits 101
Bakst, Morris, credits 127
Balanchine, George, 15, 258, 260
Balcom, Lois, reviews 107, 112, 122, 123 n.4, 199, 221
Bales, William (Bill), 2, 20, 29, 37 n.145, 104, 105, 110, 112, 117, 150, 240, 241, 245, **315**; credits 71, 80, 111, 112, 120, 139, 147, 180, 188, 230; photo 60
Ballet Caravan, The, 14, 15, 31, 54, 57, 58, 64, 69, 99, 193, 198, 222, 251, 259, 260; credits 57, 69
Ballet Russe, 289
Ballet Theatre, 106, 143
Ballou, Esther Williamson. *See* Williamson, Esther
Ballwebber, Edith, 87
Balz, Patricia, credits 216
Barber, Samuel, credits 101
Barclift, Edgar, credits 139, 147
Barnard College, 8, 129
Barnitz, Dorothy, credits 156
Barrows, John, credits 113
Bartenieff, Irma. *See* Dombois-Bartenieff, Irma
Bartók, Bela, credits 45, 49, 79
Barzun, Jacques, 49
Barzun, Lucretia, credits, 59
Bauhaus, 265
Beals, Carol, credits, 161
Becker, John, credits, 113
Beebe, Elizabeth, 77; credits 177, 184, 186
Beethoven, Ludwig van, credits, 43
Beiswanger, Barbara Page, 73, 78, 154, 180. *See also* Page, Barbara; credits 180
Beiswanger, George W., 8, 10, 15, 17, 26, 28, 49, 75, 78, 81 n.1, 97, 106, **266, 315**; reviews and articles 98, 183, 186, 187, 189, 190, 194, 196, 229, **280-83**.
Belitt, Ben, 2, 19, 84-86, 88, 89, 96, 216, 243, **265**, 308, **315**; credits 88
Bellanca, Mirthe, credits 180, 188
Belles Artes (Mexico), 181
Benjamin, Stanton, credits 112
Bennett, Shirley, credits 178
Bennington Armory. *See* Vermont State Armory
Bennington College Commons Building. *See* Commons Building
Bennington College Theatre. *See* College Theatre
Bergamasco, Hugo, credits, 71, 131, 161
Berkshire Music Festival, 13, 24, 99
Bernstein, Sidney, 305
Bettis, Valerie, 167, 265
Biehle, Martha H., photo 38
Bird, Bonnie, 8, 10, 18, 133, 233, 234, 256, 258; credits 131
Bird, Dorothy, 41, 133, 231, 233-35, 237; credits 131; photo 38
Black Mountain College, xi, 30, 256, 257
Blake, William, 139, 140, 144, 146
Blecher, Miriam, credits 131
Blitzstein, Marc, credits 101
Blom, Eric, 113
Bloomer, Elizabeth A. (Betty), 2, 57, 159. *See*

also Ford, Betty; credits 159; photo 273
Bloomer, Ruth, 2, 26, 42, 49, 57; credits 45, 59, 70, 79
Boas, Franziska, 2, 17, 68, 86, 88, 238, 239, 241–43, 252, 255, **316**; credits 59, 79, 80, 87, 88, 161, 177, 184, 186, 188; photo 238
Boas, Franz, 255
Bockman, George, 2, 29, 94, 95, 129, 177, 237, 240, 241; credits 71, 80, 99, 127, 177, 180, 188; photos 60, 128, 129
Boepple, Paul, 78
Bohm, Jerome, reviews 134, 135
Boleslavsky, Richard, 254
Bollard, Katherine, credits, 186
Boone, Peggy, credits, 59
Boris, Ruthanna, 58; credits 57, 69
Bostock, Kenneth, credits 128
Bosworth, Francis, 78
Bottomly, Helen, credits 99, 120
Bouchard, Thomas, 57, 68, 167, 203, **305–7**, 308
Bowles, Paul, credits, 69, 101
Bradley, Mabel Warren, 344
Brady, Anita, credits, 139
Bredt, Prudence, credits, 131
Brenner, Muriel, credits, 113
Brenner, Muriel V., credits, 191
Brinnin, John Malcolm, 94, 95; credits 99, 111
Broadway, 25, 26, 98, 99, 113, 118
Brockway, Thomas (Tom), 6
Brooklyn Academy of Music, 211
Budapest String Quartet, 82, 87
Brooks, Jerry, credits, 127
Brown, credits, 58
Brown, Dora, credits, 59
Brownell, Sally, 236; credits 139, 147
Browning, Marjorie, credits 178
Bryan, Julien, 308
Bryan, Julien and Marian, 307
Bryan, Marian Knighton, 251. *See also* Knighton, Marian
Buchanan, Lynn, credits 139, 147
Burgess, Lillian, credits, 139
Burke, Owen, reviews, 174 n.20, 175 n.67
Burt, Karen, reviews 90, 92 n.18; credits 59, 88
Butler, Ethel, 18, 47, 83, 84, 86, 87, 95, 98, 119, 134, 194, 195, **202**, 240–42, 244–46, 256, **269**, 316; credits 88, 99, 101, 112, 114, 119, 131, 191, **202**, 208, 221; photos 87, 100 243
Butler, Gervaise, reviews 168, 173
Butler, John, 206, 211
Byrd, William, credits, 45

C

Caccialanza, Gisella, credits 57
Cage, John, 35 n.78, 87, 117, 132, **227–29**, 256–58, **316**; review 118; credits 87, 119, 227
Cage, Xenia, 348; credits 87
Caiserman, Nina, credits 159
Calafati, Nancy, credits 119, 227
Calder, Alexander (Sandy), 46, 47, 131–34; credits 131
Calla Travis School of Dance, 57
Campbell, David, 98; credits 99, 111, 112, 114, 120, 208, 221
Campbell, Dr. Douglas, 87
Campbell, Joseph, 228, **274**
Canton, William, credits 139, 147
Carleton College, 176
Carnegie Foundation, 11
Carnegie Hall, 195, 198
Carpenter, Edward, 140
Carpenter, John Alden, credits, 113
Carper, Betty, credits 139
Carr, Deborah. Theatre Dance Ensemble, 129
Carter, Elliott, Jr., 58; review 173; credits 57, 69
Cassidy, Rosalind, 18, 19, 82
Caturla, Alejandro, credits 50
Cave, Mary Frances, credits 186
Cazden, Norman, 181
Center Theatre, 169
Central High School of Needle Trades, 195, 230
Chamberlain, Richard, credits 112, 113
Chambonnières, Jacques Champion de, credits, 45, 113
Chanler, Theodore, credits, 101
Charise, Noel, credits, 127
Chavez, Carlos, credits 43, 70, 88, 112, 202
Cheeseman, Joan, credits 113, 120
Chellis, Pauline, credits 158, 188
Cheney, Sheldon, 79
Chicago School of Design, 35 n.78
Chilkowsky, Nadia, credits 131
Christensen, Harold, credits 57, 69
Christensen, Lew, 260; credits 57, 69
Church, Marjorie, reviews 54, 58, 151, 235; credits 59
Clarke, Henry. *See* Clarke, Henry Leland
Clarke, Henry Leland, **158–59**, **316**; credits 71 158
Cleveland Playhouse, 61
Clurman, Harold, 30
Cocteau, Jean, 96
Codd, Margaret, credits, 113
Code, Grant, review 191
Cohan, Robert, 206, 211
Cohen, Selma Jeanne, 128, 180, 219
College Theatre, 14, 18, 20, 93, 99, 104, 109, 113
Colman, John, credits 80, 176
Colorado College (summer dance program, Colorado Springs), 20, 25, 27, 105, 107, 117
Colorado State Teachers College, 36 n.90
Columbia University, 8, 9, 10, 11
Commons Building, photo 13
Concert Theatre, 223
Connecticut College, 2, 25, 26, 95, 257. *See also* American Dance Festival
Conrad, Sherman, reviews 100, 101, 102 n.15, 115 n.4, 207, 213, 220, 325
Copland, Aaron, credits 42, 216
Coppage, Keith, 167; credits 161, 184, 186
Corelli, Arcangelo, credits 50
Cornish, Nellie Centennial, 8, 256
Cornish School, 8, 49, 84, 86, 256, 258
Cosner, Sara Jean, credits 156, 180
Coss, John J., 11, 344
Coudy, Douglas, credits 69
Cowell, Henry, 8, 22, 50, 104, 113, 154–56, **316**; reviews 113, 222; credits 50, 59, 71, 73, 79, 87, 112, 113, 127, 154
Craig, Gordan, 22, 221–22, 224
Crane, Hart, 19
Crawford, credits 50
Creston, Paul, credits 120
Crowell, David, credits 113
Cuddeback, Caryl, credits 58, 161
Cumpson, Harry, credits 216
Cushing, Maxine (later Maxine Cushing Gray), 32, 189; reviews 75–76; credits 139, 188
Cunningham Dance Company, 256
Cunningham, Merce, 2, 8, 20, 25, 27, 29, 30, **84**, 86, 92, 98, 117, 120, 132, 205–7, 223–25, **227–29**, 249, 250, 255, **256–58**, 261, 308, **316, 317**; credits 87, 88, 101, 114, 119, 120, 205, 208, 221, 227, 228; photos 87, 257
Cunningham, Mercer. *See* Cunningham, Merce
Cunningham, Mercier. *See* Cunningham, Merce
Cunningham, Phyllis, credits 111

D

Dalcroze, Emile. *See* Jaques-Dalcroze, Emile.
Dalcroze School of Music, 78
Dana, Margery, review 37 n.138
Dance International 1900–1937, 155, 169
Dandrieu, Francois, credits 113
Dance, Guild, The, 69
Dance Notation Bureau, 141, 182
Dance Observer, The, 16, 28, 54, 118
Dance Repertory Theatre, 7, 11
Dancers' Association, The, 69
Dancers En Route, 255
Danieli, Fred, credits 69
Davenport, Molly, credits 216
Davis, Elizabeth Ann, credits 161
Davis, Evans, 217; credits 216
Davis, Evelyn, 42; credits 131
Davis, Evelyn School, 42

de Blasiis, Giovannina, credits 111
de Bry, Theodore, credits 57
Debussy, Claude, credits, 216
de Falla, Manuel, credits 43
de Gray, Julian, credits 50
de Mille, Agnes, 2, 7, 11, 31 34 n.34, **288, 289**
de Mondonville, J. C., credits 101
Denby, Edwin, reviews 16, 199, 208, 213, 224
Denecke, H., Jr., credits 131
Denishawn, xi, 8, 11, 28, 55, 76, 106, 118, 130, 141, 188, 210, 220, 284
de Remer, Dini, 42, 231–35, 237, 238, 240; credits 45; photo 38
Desca, Eva, 2, 57, 143; credits 58, 139; photo 60
Desenberg, Bertha Rhea, 305
Dewey, John, 6, 268, 281
Diaghilev, Serge, 283
Diamond, David, review 194–95
Diamond, Ruth, credits 58–59
Dickinson, Emily, 108, 109, 117, 208–10, 212, 213, 224, 265
Disston, Natalie, credits 113
Dixon, Joseph M., credits 113
Dobbins, Christine, credits 45
Doering, Jane, credits 69
Dollar, William, 54, 260; credits 57
Dombois-Bartenieff, Irma, 57
Douglas, Dorothea, credits 120
Dudley, Jane, 2, 22, 29, 37 n.145, 46, 49, 94, 105, 110, 118, 211, 213, 216, 260, **317**; credits 99, 111, 112, 114, 119, 120, 131, 191–92, 208, 221, 230; photo 100
Dudley, Hermine, credits 161
Dudley-Maslow-Bales Company, 26
Dudley-Maslow-Bales Trio, 117, 120
Dudley, Margaret, credits 59
Duke University, 26. *See also* American Dance Festival
Duncan, Anna, 6
Duncan, Isadora, 7, 26, 66, 79, 210, 281–83, 289, 290, 306, 307
Durand, Carolyn, 164, 239–41; credits 59, 161, 184, 186
Dyer, Carlos, credits 204

E

Earle, Elsie, C., credits 186
Edwards, Jonathan, 196, 198–99
Einert, Margaret, 78
Ellfeldt, Lois, credits 139
Ellis, Helen, credits 161
Elmhirst, Mrs. Leonard K's Committee, 48, 49
Elser, Marianne, credits 161
Elwell, Herbert, credits 113, 217
Engel, Lehman A., 259, **317**; credits 43, 51, 59, 71, 99, 111, 204
Erdman, Jean Marion, 2, 22, 25, 29, 69, 78, 94, 98, 105, 110, 117, 120, 150, 165–66, 194, **210, 211, 216**, 222, 224, **227–29**, 256, 260, **269, 317**; credits 70, 99, 101, 112, 114, 119, 120, 159, 191, 208, 216, 221, **227, 228**; photo 100

F

Fairchild, Blair, credits 99
Farnaby, Giles, credits 113
Fasch, J. F., credits, 45
Fearing, Kenneth, credits 58
Federal Dance Project (WPA) 8, 27, 30, 33 n.17, 34 n.34, 143
Federal Theatre Project (WPA), 78
Fergusson, Francis, 19, 20, 22, 24, 69, 96, 98, 100, 104, 113, 193, 198, **317**; credits 99, 113
Fergusson, Marion C., 245; credits 113
Findlay, Elsa, 6
Fine, Vivian, 2, 78, 80, 128, **188–89**, 241, **317**; credits 43, 51, 78, 80, 127, **188**, 217
Fisher, Nelle, 95; credits 99, 101, 208; photo 100
Flade, Tina (later Tina Flade Mooney), 14, 18, 35 n.78, 47, 49, **50–51**, 83, 234, **317, 318**; credits 50, 127; photo 262; drawing 46
Fleming, Betty, credits 45
Flier, Frieda, credits 101, 208; photo 101
Fokine, Mikhail, 283, 288, 289
Fonaroff, Nina, 2, 94, 105, 111, 112, 117, 120, 256; credits 99, 111, 112, 114, 119, 120, 191, 208, 221; photo 100
Foote, Horton, review 118–19
Ford, Betty (Mrs. Gerald R.), 273. *See also* Bloomer, Elizabeth
Forsythe, Reginald, credits 80
Forte, Jane, credits 176
46th Street Theatre, 223
Foster, Geronimo Baquerio, credits 112
Frampton, Eleanor, 2, 78; credits 188
Franklin, Elizabeth Jennings, 344
Frankenstein, Alfred, reviews 98, 203
Frees, Octavia, credits 112
Friedman, Madge, credits 114, 221
Funaroff, S., credits 49
Funston, Nancy, credits 131
Fruhauf, Aline, drawings 41, 46, 53, 74, 93, 103, 116

G

Gainer, Joan, 181
Garcia, Gloria, 2; credits 180, 216
Garrett, Harriet, credits 114, 221
Garrett, William, credits 139, 147
Gates, Alice, credits 59, 131
General Stark Theatre, 22, 104, 113
Gentile, Gerard, 57, 61, 68, 142, **166–67**; credits 71, 139, 147, 156, 158, 159, 160, 161
Gentry, Eve, 2, 64, 66, 120, **164–66, 271**, 305. *See also* Greenhood, Henrietta
Georgi, Yvonne, 7
Gerschefski, Edwin, credits 113
Gershek, S., credits 61, 71, 139, 147, 161
Gerson, Beatrice, credits 127, 128
Gibbons, Olando, credits 113
Gibbs, Angelica, article 209, 210
Gifford, Joseph. *See* Gornbein, Joseph
Gilbert, Ralph, 78, 241, 242, 259, 261, **318**; credits 78, 79, 87, 88, 99, 112, 191, 202, 204, 216
Gilfond, Henry, 31, 75, 195; reviews 158, 159, 160, 172, 176–79, 186, 190, 191
Gilfond, Edythe, 18, 77, **195**; credits 101, 112, 120, 191, 204, 205, 208
Gillette, Mary, credits 161, 178
Glass, Edward, 68, 69, 217, 241, 242; credits 70, 71, 80, 112, 161, 191, 216
Glassberg, Mildred, credits 131
Glinka, Mikhail Ivanovitch, credits 57
Gluck, C. W., credits 216
Godard, Benjamin, credits 57
Godwin, Dwight, 206
Golden Gate Exposition, 83
Goldenberg, M., credits 70
Goldman, Richard Franko, credits 113
Goldwater, Mary Anne, credits 131
Goode, Elizabeth, review 202
Goodman, Benny, 82, 87
Goodsitt, Minnie, credits 79
Gordon, Philip, credits 71, 139, 147
Gornbein, Joseph (later Joseph Gifford), 2, 98, 110; credits 111, 112, 216
Gottesleben, Elizabeth, credits 58, 59
Graham camp, 76
Graham, Georgia, 8
Graham, Martha, 1, 2, 6–8, 10–12, 14, 15, 17–20, 21–26, **27**, 28, 29, **30**, 31, 32, 41–43, 46–50, 54–57, 59, 63–66, 69, 74, 75, 77–79, 83–86, 88–91, 93–96, **98**, 104–6, **107**, 108–110, 117, 119, 131–36, 154–56, 166, 169, 179, **191–99**, 202, 204, 205–8, **208–14**, 216, **221–25**, 228, 229, 231, 233–35, 237, 240–42, 245, 246, 251, 253–56, 258–61, 265–67, 269, 273, **278–79, 288**, 290, 305–8, **318**, 344; credits 42, 51, 59, 68, 70, 71, 80, 89, 101, 114, 131, 154, 191–92, 205, 208, 221; photos 27, 38, 41, 93, 97, 100, 192, 195, 196, 259, 269, 272; films 310–12
Graham, Martha, Dance groups and Company, 6, 22, 49, 51, 75, 76, 80, 81 n.9, 84, 91, 93, 98, 101, 105, 107, 110, 113, 114, 117, 119, 120, 131, 191,

221, 250, 251, 256, 259, 269; photos 97, 100, 195
Graham, Martha. School, 250
Graham studio, 10, 193
Graham, Wanda, credits 80, 176, 177
Grant, Mary, credits 205
Gray, Charles Harold, 344
Gray, Harriette Ann, 2, 57; credits 71, 139, 147, 180, 188
Gray, Maxine Cushing. *See* Cushing, Maxine
Green, Gertrude, credits 112, 158
Green Mountain Festival, 22, 104, 110
Green Ray, 2, 78, **194-96**, 198, 241, **318**; credits 78, 80, 191
Greenhood, Henrietta (later Eve Gentry), 24, 117, 119, 120, 122, 246. *See also* Gentry, Eve; credits 120, 161-62, 184, 186
Gregory, Winifred, credits 178
Group Theatre, 30
Gruenberg, Louis, credits 49
Guest, Ann Hutchinson, 308. *See also* Hutchinson, Ann
Guild Theatre, 155, 181, 184, 187, 189, 211
Guion, David, credits 59
Guthrie, Woody, credits 120

H

Halffter, Ernest, credits 50
Hall, George, 211; credits 208
Halpern, Elizabeth, credits 120, 208; photo 100
Halprin, Anna Schuman, 2, **267**. *See also* Schuman, Ann; credits 80, 88, 176
Hamilton, Charles, credits 216
Handel, G. F., credits 43, 51, 101
Hanson, Maricaro, 176
Harker, James W., credits 112
Harper, Margot, credits 176
Harrigan and Hart, credits 111
Harris, Natalie, credits 159, 191
Harris, Roy, 99, 117, 128
Harris, Saralee, credits 186
Harrison, Lou, 18, 35 n.78; credits 87, 113
Hart, Foundation, 252
Hartford Park Department, Recreational Division, 69
Hartford Parks Marionette Theatre, 252
Hasburgh, Rabana, credits 57, 69
Hatfield, Donald, 86, 305
Hatfield, Ruth Sanders, 305
Haveman, Victor, 87
Hawkins, Alma, 2, 78
Hawkins, Erick, 2, 14, 20, 22, **24**, 26, 27, 29, 64, 69, 75, 78, 93, 98, 99, 105, 110, 119, 193-94, 197-98, **204-5**, 206-8, 210, 216, 222, 224, 225, 229, 244-46, 249, **259-61**, **318**; credits 57, 69, 99, 101, 112, 114, 191-92, 204, 205, 208, 216; photos 192, 195, 196, 259, 272
Hawkins, Frances, 14, 49, 81 n.9, 98, 199
Hays, Jeanne, credits 179
Hayes, Elizabeth, credits 178
H'Doubler, Margaret, 7, 33 n.9, 41, 42, 79, 251; photo 267
Heater, Mary, credits 69
Hecht, Molly, credits 158, 188
Heghinian, Marie, credits 45, 131
Heisey, Ruth Ann, credits 70
Hellebrandt, Beatrice, 17; credits 58, 59, 70
Herbert, credits 208, 221
Herring, Hubert, article 5
Hetzel, Helene, credits 139
Hill, Martha (later Mrs. Thurston Davies), 1, **6-7**, 8-15, 18-27, **28-30**, 34 n.34, 41, 42, 50, 54, 56, 85, 86, 89, 95, 96, 98-100, 104, 119, 232, 233, 235-46, 250-52, 254, 260, 261, 265, 266, 273, **277**, 308, **318-19**; credits 43, 58, 59, 70, 79, 88, 99, 112, 113; photos 38, 261, 273, 276
Hindemith, Paul, credits 58
Hinkson, Mary, 206
Hippodrome (New York), 142, 146, 149, 151, 169
Hirsh, Merle, credits 49, 131
Hitler, Adolf, 290
Holden, Frances Coleman, 344
Hollywood, 85, 98, 118
Holm, Hanya, 1, 2, 8, 10-12, 14, 15, 17-20, 23, 25, 26, **27**, 29-31, 41, 42, 45, 46, 49, 54-57, **59-60**, 63, 65, 66, 68-70, 73-75, 77, 84, 86, 88-91, 93, 94, 98, 105, 107, 110, 117, 119, **161-73**, **184-87**, 231, 235, 237, 239, 240-42, 244, 251, 253-55, 260, 261, **263**, 267, 271, **278-79**, 290, 305, 308, **319**, 344; credits 43, 59, 72, 79, 80, 89, 99, **161-62**, **184**, **186**; photos 17, 43, 67, 90, 185, 263; film 310
Holm, Hanya. Dance groups, 59, 60, 69, 73, 80, 91, 107, 161, 169, 184, 186, 305; photos *Frontispiece*, 43, 45, 64-72, 82, 161, 162, 263
Holm, Hanya. School of Dance, 60
Honegger, Arthur, credits 49
Horan, Robert, reviews 222-24
Horne, Frank, credits 49
Horner, Betty Jean, credits 111, 120
Horst, Betty, 79
Horst, Louis, 1, 2, 6, 8, 10-12, 15-17, 23, 25, 28, 29, 42, 49, 54, 66, 86, 94, 96, 98, 101, 110, 117, 119, 122, 131, 132, 155, 177, 186, 205, 207, 210, 228, 229, 232-46, 251, 252, **254**, 255-58, 261, 267, 269, 273, 277, **279**, 308, **319**, 344; review 88; credits 45, 51, 58, 59, 70, 71, 78, 79, 88, 101, 112, 113, 119, 120, 131, 191, 205, 208, 221, 228; photos 28, 38, 235, 268, 272; drawing 116
Horton, Lester, 2, 18, 84, 256
Howe, Eugene C., 140
Howe, Mary, credits 101
Howe, Mary Carlisle, 344
Howe, Molly, credits 99
Hoxsie, Ita, credits 113
Hudelson, Ben, credits 113
Hughes, Langston, credits 49
Humphrey, Doris, 1, 7, 8, 10-12, 14, 15, 17-19, 21-26, **27**, 30, 31, 36 n.90, n.107, 41-43, 47-50, 53-57, 59, 61, 63, 64, 69, 70, 74-77, 79, 80, 82, 84-86, 88-91, 93-96, 98, 104-7, 110, 116, 117, 122, **128**, 130, **140-46**, 149, 150-52, 165, 170, 176, **180-83**, 188, 202, **216-21**, 231, 233, 234, 236, 237, 240-42, 245, 251, 254-56, 260, 261, 265, 266, **278**, **284-87**, 290, 305, 306, 308, **319-20**, 344; credits 43, 51, 60, 61, 68, 70, 71, 80, 89, 111, 114, 127, 139, 180, 216; photos 24, 60, 111, 127, 128, 141, 145, 182, 248, 267, 272, 274, 285; drawing 103; films 309, 310, 312, 313
Humphrey, Doris. Dance group, 57, 80, 90, 91, 139, 147; photo 267
Humphrey, Doris. Studio, 42
Humphrey-Weidman, 2, 29, 31, 75, 94, 98, 106, 111, 119, 157, 181, 267, **278**, 305
Humphrey-Weidman. Dance groups and Company, 15, 22, 25, 51, 60, 61, 63, 70, 71, 76, 84, 105, 107, 110, 113, 114, 127, 128, 139, 149, 165, 180, 216, 218, 305; photo 182
Humphrey-Weidman Repertory Class (1941), 111, 245
Humphrey-Weidman Studio (18th St.), 27
Humphrey-Weidman Studio Theatre (16th St.), 22, 105, 112, 120, 143, 181, 183, 189, 203, 218, 219, 227, 228
Hunt, Ruth, 50, 127, 233; credits 50, 127
Hurok, Sol, 8
Hussey, Delia, 2, 42; credits 79
Hutchinson, Ann (later Ann Hutchinson Guest, Mrs. Ivor Guest), 2, **94-95**, 98, 211. *See also* Guest, Ann Hutchinson; photo 100

I

Ide, Letitia, 233; credits 51, 127
Imig, Katherine, credits 186
Imperial Society of Teachers of Dancing, 308
Ipcar, Melvene, credits 59
Isaacs, Edith, 21
Ito, Michio, 8
Ives, Burl, credits 120
Ives, Charles, credits 101
Ives, Ruth, credits 112, 113

J

Jackson, Edna Morse, 344
Jacob's Pillow, 7, 24, 25, 36 n.107, 55, 116
Jaffay, Marva, credits 161
James, Elisabeth, credits 113

Jaques-Dalcroze, Emile, 109
Jennings, Mrs. Frederic B., 5
Jester, Ralph, 85
Jewell, Margaret, credits 161
Johnson, Hazel, credits 119, 120, 227
Johnson, Hunter, 2, 96, 101, 117, 119, 205, **209-10**, 213, 259, 260, 320; credits 99, 101, 112, 204, 208, 216
Johnson, Virginia Hall, credits, 191-92
Joiner, Betty, 18, 35 n.71, 68, 78, 87, 168, 176; credits 71, 156, 158, 159, 160, 161, 176, 178, 179; drawings 63, 82
Jones, Barbara, 6, 37 n.146
Jones, Lewis Webster, **23**, 24, 25, 85
Jooss-Leeder School, 94, 95
Judson Dance Theater, xi
Juilliard School of Music (dance department), 2, 6, 26, 143, 181, 260
Junger, Esther (later Esther Junger Klempner), 2, 14, 63, **64**, 65, 68, 70, 72, **157-58**, 238, **272**, **320**; credits 71, 72, 156, 160; photos 157, 272
Jurist, 59

K

Kadinoff, Bernard, credits, 216
Kagan, Miriam, credits, 161, 184, 186
Kahn, Alex, 217; credits 216
Kahn, Victoria, credits 156
Kansas State Teachers College, 6
Kaschmann, Truda, 2, 57, 254; credits 58, 70, 79
Katz, Isabelle, credits 59
Kavan, Albia, credits 57, 69
Kaye, Joseph Arnold, 50; reviews 77, 144, 146, 176, 183, 187, 191, 197-98
Kaye, Nora, 143
Keeney, Wendell, credits 99
Kellogg School of Physical Education (Battle Creek, Michigan), 6, 9
Kepes, Georgy, 35 n.78
Kerr, Harrison, 2, 17, 75, 78, 168, 187, 241, **320**; credits 78, 80, 186
Kilpatrick, William Heard, 6
King, Eleanor, 2, 14, 75, 77, 79, **176-77**, 180, 240, **320**; credits 80, 176, 177
Kinsky, France, credits 139, 147, 180
Kirkpatrick, John, reviews, 96, 100, 101, 213
Kirkpatrick, Ralph, 20, 22, 104; credits 101, 113
Kirschner, Gussie, credits 131
Kirstein, Lincoln, 15, 20, 34 n.46, n.51, 47, 54, 57-58, 64, 69, 79, 94, 193, 258-60; reviews 75, 96, 97, 156, **196-97**; credits 57, 69
Klein, Erika, credits 61, 128
Klempner, Esther Junger. *See* Junger, Esther
Kloepper, Louise, 2, 14, 18, 19, 35 n.78, 75, 77, 79, 80, 84, 86-88, 91, 163, 164, 172, **178**, 237, 238, 240, 242, 261, **271**, 308, **320-21**; credits 59, 80, 88, 161-62, 177, 178; photos *Frontispiece*, 45, 64, 86
Kloepper, Louise, Group, photo 178
Knight, Helen, credits 58, 161
Knighton, Marian (Mrs. Julien), 2, 42. *See also* Bryan, Marian Knighton
Kobeleff, 6
Kodály, Zoltan, credits 42, 59, 71
Koenig, Rose, review 156
Kolodin, review 213
Koner, Pauline, 2, 8
Korvin, Ada, credits 127, 139, 147
Kosa, Gyorgy, credits 49
Krakovsky, Miriam, 129; credits 128, 139, 147
Kreutzberg, Harald, 7
Krevitsky, Nathan [Nik], 86; credits 112
Krokover, Rosalyn, 103; review 225
Kronstadt, Frances, credits 156
Krutch, Joseph Wood, 282
Kuch, Richard, 206

L

Laban, Rudolf von, 94-95
Lack, Lillian, credits 179
Lack, Pearl (later Pearl Lang), 105, 110, 216, 223. *See also* Lang, Pearl; credits 111, 114, 120, 221
Lambranzi, credits 59
Lane, Frederic, credits 139, 147
Lang, Pearl, 2, 206, 211. *See also* Lack, Pearl
Lanfer, Helen, credits 119, 120, 227, 230
Langbert, Edith, credits 131
Lapzeson, Noemi, 206
Larmanjat, credits 59, 120
Laskey, Charles, credits 57
Lathrop, Welland, 2, 49
Lauer, Eleanor, 2, 35 n.78, 69; credits 70, 79, 80, 179
Lauterer, Arch, 2, 10, 13, 17-20, 24, 25, 27, 29, 46, 49, 63, 69, 75, 77, 79, 80, 85, 86, 93, 95, 98, 99, 104, **107-10**, 117, 131, 132, 134, 142, 155, 166-68, 169, 173, 176, 197, 206, 207, 211-13, 218, **222-23**, 224, 241-45, 252, 254, 258, 260, 265, 308, **321**; credits 51, 79, 80, 88, 99, 101, 112, 131, 176, 177, 178, 179, 180, 184, 186, 188, 191, 205, 208, 216, 221, 222; designs 133, 167, 217, 218; drawings 154, 155
Lauterer, Helen Forrest (Mrs. Arch), 10
Lawrence, Pauline, 8, 35 n.71, 42, 78, 85, 106, 142, 148, 232-34, 236, 237, 240, 242, 260, **321**; credits 42, 43, 51, 61, 70, 80, 127, 139, 147, 180, 188, 216
Law, Andrew, credits 176
Lawton, Dorothy, 11, 344
Ledoux, Ruth, credits 161
Leigh, Robert Devore, 1, 5, **9-13**, 19, **21**, 23, 33 n.1, 250, 266, 277, **321**, 344; photo 21
Leigh, Mrs. Robert, 6
Leon, Paul, credits 139, 147
Leonard, Clair, 147, 236, **321**; credits 58, 61, 70, 147
Leonard, Warren, 7
Levy, Joan, 129, 234, 236, 305; credits 71, 127, 139, 147; photo 60
Lewis, Hildegarde, credits 161
Lewis, Monde Lux, credits 120
Lewisohn, Margaret S., 344
Liandre, Lil, credits 49, 131
Lidster, Miriam Bleamaster, 308
Lidy, Margaret, 238, 240; credits 70, 179
Lieberthal, Hortense, 86, 119, 237, 240, 242, 243, 246; credits 88, 113, 159, 178
Liebich, Sasha (later Mark Ryder), 105, 110, 223. *See also* Ryder, Mark; credits 114, 120, 221
Liebling, credits 57
Lillback, Elna, 131
Limón, José, 2, 14, 18, 19, 25, 29-31, 35, 63, **64**, 65, 68, 70, 72, 73 n.7, 80, **84**, 86-88, 92, 150, 151, 157, **158-59**, 174 n.15, 181, **202-3**, 233, 234, 236, 238, 242, 250, 253, 255, 256, 306, 308, **321-22**; credits 51, 71, 72, 80, 88, 127, 139, 147, 156, 158, 160, 202; photos 60, 128, 129, 272, 275
Limón, José. Dance Company, 25, 26, 182
Lincoln, Abraham, 193
Lincoln School, Teachers College, 7
Lindsay, Vachel, credits 101
Lippincott, Gertrude, 2, 69; credits 79, 176
Lisser Hall (Mills College), 87; photo 84
Liszt, Franz, credits 57
Litz, Katherine, 2, 94, 98, 129, 143, 144; credits 71, 80, 99, 127, 139, 147, 180, 188, 216; photos 60, 141
Livingston, Barbara, credits 114, 221
Lloyd, Margaret, **28**, 95, **322**; reviews and articles 54, 55, 60, 61, 75, 77, 84, 85, 96, 97, 100, 106, **107-10**, 112, 132, 135, 141-42, 143-44, 146, 148, 150, 151, 164, 168, 170, 177, 179, 181, 182-83, 184, 186, 187, 190, 198, 205-6, 207, 208, 210, 211, 213, 217-18, 219, 222, 230, 306
Lloyd, Norman, 2, 16, 17, 24, 42, 46, 49, 54, 57, 77, 78, 86, 89, 98, 110, 119, 120, 122, **131-32**, 135, 147, **154**, 158, 166, 168, 184, **186**, 232-46, 308, **322**, 344; credits 43, 45, 51, 60, 61, 68, 70, 71, 73, 78, 79, 80, 88, 112, 119, 131, 139, 147, 154, 158, 161, 176, 177, 184, 216, 227; photos 38, 264
Lloyd, Norman and Ruth, 42, 57, 69, 128
Lloyd, Ruth, 16, 49, 119, 132-33, 232, 233, 235-38, 240, 242, 243, **322**; credits 45, 60, 70, 78, 79, 112, 139, 147, 159, 177, 184; photo 38

Locke, Caroline, credits 161, 184, 186
Logan, Eileen, credits 156
London, Lorna, credits 69
London Contemporary Dance Theatre, 206
Lopatnikov, Nikolai, credits 42, 70, 80
Lord, Lois, credits 79
Lorenz, Pare, 178; credits 112
Lorenz, Yolanda, 237, 241; credits 70, 111, 186
Loring, Eugene, 260, **288, 289**, credits 57, 69
Louis, Murray, 169
Louther, William, 206
Love, Paul, 54, 69, 140, 142, 149; reviews 76, 151, 158, 160, 172
Lovejoy, Beatrice, credits 139, 186
Lubell, Naomi, 70; credits 131, 159
Lucas, Marjorie, review 91–92
Luening, Ethel, 119; credits 113
Luening, Otto, 16, 17, 19, 20, 24, 25, 98, 104, 119, **273, 322, 323**; credits 78, 101, 113, 205, 216
Lully, Jean-Baptiste, 113
Lunsford, Virginia, credits 113
Lunt-Fontanne Theatre, 206
Lynn, Fara, credits 58
Lyon, Annabelle, credits 57
Lyons, James, credits 158

M

Mabry, Iris, 2, 110; credits 111, 112, 114, 221
McBride, Robert G., 2, 25, 69, 119, **222**, 224, 260, 273, **323**; credits 69, 101, 114, 120, 158, 205
McCausland, Elizabeth, reviews, 207, 213
McCullough, John, 6
McDonagh, Don, 47, 134, 193, 205
McDonald, Frances, credits 139
McDonald, Gene, 206
MacDougall, Gregory, 92
McDougle, Ann, credits 101
MacEwan, Charlotte, credits 45
McKnight, Nancy, 42, 231, 233, 234, 236; credits 43, 58, 59, 61, 139, 147
MacLaughlin, Beatrice, credits, 99
MacLeish, Archibald, 202
McNally, Thomas, credits 59
MacNaughton, Anne, credits 139, 147
Mansfield Theatre, 206, 211
McPhee, Colin, credits 43, 216
Maginnis, Maria, 78, 110, 245; credits 180, 216
Malingreau, credits 99
Malipiero, credits 43
Malipiero, Francesco, credits 50
Malon, Ray, credits 113, 119, 120, 227
Mamorsky, Morris, 68, 69, 78, 157, 237, 238, 240, 241, 323; credits 71, 78, 80, 156, 180
Mann, Ethel (later Linda Mann Reed), 57, 78; credits 139, 180
Manning, Katherine, 18, 84, 86–88, 91, 92, 98, 234, 236, 240–42, 244; credits 71, 88, 99, 127, 139, 147, 180; photos 60, 91
Mansfield, Portia, 6, 8
Maracci, Carmelita, 75
Marchowsky, Marie, credits 49, 131, 191
Marcus, Reba, credits 101
Marie-Jeanne, 206; credits 69
Marsh, Lucile, article 33 n.18
Martel, Gene, 42, 231
Martin, John, 1, **8–10**, 11, 12, 15, 21, 28, 34 n.51, 47, 50, 51, 54, 70, 75, 78, 79, 93, 110, 168, 173, 181, 210, 211, 219, 232, 234, 236, 238, 239, **254, 266, 279, 323**, 344; reviews and articles 7, 9, 12, 29, 31, 41, 51, 59–60, 63, 66, 67–68, 72, 76–77, 95–97, 99, 106, 117, 118, 130, 134, 135, 141, 142, 144, 146–48, 150, 151, 155–56, 157–59, 162–64, 166–70, 172, 176–79, 182, 183, 186, 187, 190, 197, 207, 208, 212, 214, 219–20, 222, 224, **288–90**, 306; photos 253, 266, 275
Martin, John and Louise, 77
Martin, Keith, credits 57
Martin, Louise, 2, 49, 234, 236, 238, 252, **254, 323**; photos 239, 275
Marting, Alice, credits 139
Marvin, Elisabeth, credits 120
Maslow, Sophie, 29, 94, 117, 133, **323**; credits 49, 99, 101, 120, 131, 191–2, 208, 230; photo 100
Massine, Léonide, 156, 159
Matons, William, 150, 234, 236; credits 51, 58, 127, 139, 147; photo 128
Maxine Elliott Theatre, 223
Mazia, Marjorie, 2; credits 99, 101, 191, 208
Mecca Auditorium (New York City Center), 167, 168
Medtner, Nikolai, credits 43, 216
Mehlman, Lily, credits 49, 131
Melby, Ernest, 25
Mendelsohn, May, credits 178
Mendelssohn, Felix, 189
Meredith, Charles, credits 208
Meredith, Margaret, 210, 212, 213; credits 208
Mettler, Barbara, 2, 57; credits 59, 70
Milhaud, Darius, credits 112
Miller, Carl, credits 99, 112
Miller, Freda, D., 78, 242; credits 79, 88
Mills College, 1, 10, 14–16, 18–20, 22, 35 n.78, 36 n.90, 47, 59, 76, 82–89, 91, 203, 251, 255, 256, 265, 266, 305, 308. *See also* Lisser Hall
Milton, Paul R., article 33 n.14
Mishnun, Virginia, reviews **55–56**, 62 n.4, 144, 151, 172
Moholy-Nagy, 35 n.78
Molière. *See* Poquelin, Jean Baptiste
Mompou, Federico, credits 88, 99, 112
Monticello College, 78
Moomaw, Virginia 2
Mooney, Tina Flade. *See* Flade, Tina
Moore, Claudia, 2, 98, 110, 244, 245; credits 180, 216
Moore, Elizabeth, credits 159
Moore, Eloise, credits 139
Moore, Hanna, credits 57
Moore, Mary, credits 131
Morgan, Barbara, 78, 87, 167, 193, 206, **305–7**
Morgenthau, Mrs. Rita Wallace, 99
Morley, Thomas, credits 113
Moross, Jerome, 2, 42, 231, 233, **323**; credits 43, 51, 71, 156
Morris, Stephen, 129, 130
Moulton, Marion, credits 179
Mozart, Wolfgang Amadeus, 22, 104; credits 57, 69, 113
Muehl, Marjorie, credits 80, 179
Mulcahy, Alice M., credits 176
Mueller, John, 180
Mumford, Lewis, 280
Mundstock, Tosia, credits 59
Munson, Marjorie, credits 69
Munt, Maxine, credits 188
Murray, Ruth Love, 2, 35 n.78, 42; credits 45
Mussolini, Benito, 136

N

Nash, Jay B., 11, 344
Nast, Condé, 306
National Educational Television, 182
National Endowment for the Arts, 2
National Theatre, 25, 195, 223
Neighborhood Playhouse, 8, 99
New College, Columbia University, 9, 10, 42
New Dance Group, 46, 49
New Dance League, 14, 47, 49, 54, 57, 58, 69, 135
New Masses, 159, 195
New Music Quarterly Recordings, 78, 168
New School for Social Research, 8, 9
New York Public Library, 11, 12
New York State Theater (Lincoln Center), 182
New York Times Hall, 230
New York University, 6, 7, 10, 11, 25, 26
New York Wigman School of the Dance, The, 8, 10, 55, 59, 60. *See also* Wigman Schools
Nicholson, Kenyon, 22; credits 113
Nijinsky, Vaslav, 283
Nikolais, Alwin, 2, 57, 69, 70, 78, 86, 158, 165, 169, 249, 250, **252–55**, 308; credits 70, 79, 158; photo 253
Niles, Nath., credits 176
Noguchi, Isamu, 79, 131, 205; credits 114
Nora Bayes Theater, 143
Nordoff, Paul, credits 59, 70, 101
North, Alexander (Alex), 2, 49, 68, 79, 132, 160, 233, 234, **323, 324**; credits 58, 71, 72, **159**
Northwestern University, 36 n.90

Noverre, Jean- Georges, 288
Nowak, Lionel, 2, 203, 218, 242, **324**; credits 88, 101, 113, 202, 216
Nureyev, Rudolph, 206

O

Ochsner, Berta, credits 45
Ocko, Edna, reviews 138 n.33, 144
O'Donnell, May 29, 31, 42, 84, 133, 134, 232, 233, 235, 236, 240, 241, 268; credits 45, 131, 191–92; photos 38, 195, 268
O'Donnell, Mary P., 6
Ogborn, Jane, 49, 131, 232, 234; credits 51, 131; photo 38
Ohio Wesleyan University, 42
Oppenheimer, Pegge, credits 180
Orcutt, Edith, 129, 237, 240, 241; credits 58, 71, 127, 139, 147, 180; photos 60, 129
Oregon State College (Corvallis), 78, 308
Orlov, Carlotte, credits 186
Ornstein, Leo, credits 43
Osato, Teru, credits 112
Otto-Betz, Irma, 57
Owen, Janet, article 40

P

Page, Barbara, 2, 7, 28, 41, 42, **277–79**. *See also* Beiswanger, Barbara Page
Paine, Thomas, 193
Palmer Auditorium (Connecticut College), 25
Palmer, Joyce, credits 178
Palmer, Winthrop, article 152
Paneyko, Mirko, 166, 168; credits 161
Paramount Pictures, 85
Park, Edwin Avery, credits 113
Park, Rosemary, 25
Parker, Will, credits 113
Parmet, Ruth, credits 216
Parnas, credits 49
Pasquini, Bernardo, credits 113
Pavlova, Anna, 47
Payne, Victoria, credits 161
Pease, Esther, 2; reviews 88, 202
Peretti, V., credits 61, 70, 71, 131, 139, 147, 161
Perry, Charlotte, 8
Perry, Jane Lee, credits 139, 192
Perry-Mansfield (Steamboat Springs, Colorado), 8, 11
Philharmonic Hall, Lincoln Center, 181
Phillipe, I., credits 180
Piscator, Erwin, 95
Piston, Walter, credits 113
Plymouth Theatre, 223
Poglietti, Allessandro, credits 113
Poldowski, credits, 120
Pollins, Harvey, 2, 42, 68, 69, 78, 231, 234, 237, 239–41, **324**; credits 43, 59, 71, 78, 80, 88, 156, 161, 177, 178, 186
Poquelin, Jean Baptiste [pseud. Molière], 22, 104; credits 113
Porter, Quincy, 99; credits 101
Post, Emily, 89
Poulenc, Francis, credits 57
Powers, Maxwell, **324**; credits 111, 119, 216, 227
Prahl, Marie, credits 179
Priest, Helen, (later Helen Priest Rogers), 2, 20, 42, 78, 98, 244; credits 131, 192
Prokofiev, Serge, credits 45, 49, 50, 57, 58, 88
Purcell, Henry, credits 101

R

Rainbow Room, 117
Rameau, Jean Philippe, credits 45, 59, 113
Ramsey, Margaret, credits 156
Raphael, Miriam, credits 71
Ravel, Maurice, credits 45, 49, 50, 57, 59
Raye, Zelia, 308
Red Jacket of the Senecas, 193
Reddin, Josephine, credits 162
Reed, Linda Mann. *See* Mann, Ethel
Reese, Ida, credits 216
Reinhardt, Max, 24
Reitell, Elizabeth, credits 208
Reuschel, Nelly, 6
Richardson, Raith, credits 113
Riegger, Wallingford, 2, 23, 57, 63, 68, 72, 128–30, **141**, 147, **166–68**, 170, 186, 236, 239, **324**; credits 43, 51, 59, 60, 61, 71, 73, 78, 80, 112, **127**, **139**, **161**, 217; drawing 53; photo 274
Robinson, Earl, credits 112
Rockefeller Foundation, 2
Rockwell, Paul, credits 113
Rodion, Rima, credits 156
Roeder, Harriet, 2, 69, 98, 105, 110, 244, 245; credits 112, 162, 184, 186
Rogers, Helen Priest. *See* Priest, Helen
Roland, Norma, review 138 n.8
Rolfe, Edwin, credits 112
Rooker, Carmen, 2
Rosenblatt, Esther, 19
Rosenmüller, Johannes, credits 101
Ross, Bertram, 206
Ross, Bertram. Company, 206
Ross, Dorothy, credits 188
Roundabout Theatre Stage One, 182
Rudd, William H., credits 161
Rudhyar, Dane, 67, 169; credits 50, 51
Russell, Kaya, credits 139, 192
Russell, Theodore, credits 205
Russell, William, credits 87
Ryder, Mark, 2, 211, **268**. *See also* Liebich, Sasha
Ryder, Marian, credits 176

S

Sabin, Robert, reviews 205, 220, 222
Sachs, Curt, 78, 79, 183, 250; photo 274
St. Denis, Ruth, 7, **66–67**, 130, 169, 199
Sandburg, Carl, credits 120
Sandi, Louis, credits 112
Sarah Lawrence College, 42, 69, 250, 307
Sargent, Winthrop, credits 216
Saroyan, William, 21, 217
Satie, Erik, credits 99
Satlein, Pearl, credits 131, 159
Saurborn, Jeannette, credits 162
Savage, Silvine, credits 58
Scanlon, Elaine, credits 192
Scarlatti, Domenico, credits 57, 113
School of American Ballet, 14, 47, 49, 94, 256, 258, 260
Schlundt, Christena L., 11, 34 n.34
Schneider, Florence, credits 131
Schneider, Margery, credits 59, 70
Schoenberg, Arnold, credits 50
Schönberg, Bessie, 1, 10, 11, 18, 24, 29, 42, 70, 86, 98, 110, 119, 232, 233, 235, 237, 240, 242–46, 249, **250–52**, 254, **324**; credits 43, 58, 70, 79, 88, 99, 112; photos 38, 250, 251
Schubert, Franz, credits 57
Schuman, Ann (later Anna Halprin), 78, 86. *See also* Halprin, Anna Schuman
Schumann, Robert, credits 43
Schurman, Nona, 2, 86, 117, 122, 129, 217, 246, 305; credits 88, 120, 216; photo 270
Schwartz, Polly Ann, credits 179
Scott, Marion, 105; credits 114, 221
Scriabin, Alexander, credits 49, 50, 58, 216
Seckler, Beatrice, 129, 165, **267**; credits 80, 127, 139, 147, 180, 188, 216; photos 60, 129
Seelye, Mary-Averett, 2, 245; credits 111, 113
Sepmeier, Klara, credits 178
Seymour, Henry, 77, 86, 241–42; credits 79, 80, 88 191
Shankar, Uday, 7
Shapero, Lillian, 75, 78; credits 79
Shaw, Lloyd, 87
Shaw, Mildred Rea, credits 176
Shawn, Ted, 7, 24, 29, 55, 116, 152, 199, 260, 283
Shawn, Ted. Dance groups. 7, 13
Shawn, Ted. School for Men, 23
Shearer, Sybil L., 2, 29, 42, 234, 236, 240, 241, 250, **272**; credits 71, 80, 127, 139, 147, 180; photos 60, 270
Shebalin, V. Y., credits 49
Shelly, Mary Josephine, 1, **9**, 10–13, 15, 19, 20, 23–28, 36 n.90, 49, 66, 85, 98, 105, 117, 233, 251, 252, 260, 261, **266**, 277, **324**; credits 88; photos 38, 90, 261

Sherman, Lee, 240, 241; credits 71, 180, 188
Shoki, Sai, 79
Shostakovitch, Dmitri, credits 58, 72, 160
Shurr, Gertrude, 233, 234; credits 131, 191; photo 268
Silva, Nell, review 89, 90–91
Silverman, Selma, credits 139
Simon, Henry W., review 102 n.14
Sklar, George, 49
Slagle, Kathleen, credits 131
Sloan, Ruth, credits 71
Slonimsky, Nicolas, 166, 168, 169
Smith [pseud. of *Variety* critic], review 113
Smith, Cecil, review 97
Smith, Dorothy, credits 162
Smith, Moses, reviews 167–69
Sokolow, Anna, 2, 14, 29, 30, 54, 57, 63, **64**, 65, 66, 68, 70, 72, 79, 136, **159–60**, 194, 233, 234, 238, 255, **264**, 265, **325**; credits 49, 58, 71, 131, **159**, 160; photo 264
Sorell, Walter, 184
Sparling, Peter, 206
Spaulding, Barbara, credits 180
Spelman, Marva, credits 184, 186
Spellman College, 23
Sperber, Dorothy, article 102 102 n.1
Spreen, Hildegard L., credits 186
Stambaugh, Sidney, credits 113
Stanford University, 36 n.90
Stanislavsky, Konstantin, 254
Stanwood, Shirley, credits 113
Stapp, Philip, 78; credits 79, 101, 112
Starks, Mary, credits 176, 177
Steffes, Germaine, credits 156
Steiner, Ralph, 49
Stern, Ann, 129
Stern, Anne D., credits 188
Stevens, Houseley, Jr., 192, 197, 198; credits 192
Stevens, Wallace, 89; credits 88
Steward, Helen, credits 69
Stimer, David, credits 57, 69
Stockbridge Summer Theater, 13
Stodelle, Ernestine, article 207–8
Stokowski, Leopold, 24, 95, 180
Strand, Paul, 207
Strater, Margaret, 222, 316; credits 120, 159, 192
Straus, Joann, credits 119, 120, 227, 228
Strauss, credits 57
Strauss, Claire, credits 192
Stravinsky, Igor, credits 50
Struppa, Eleanor, credits 192
Stuart, Muriel, 2, 47, 49, 133–34; credits 131
Studio Theatre. *See* Humphrey–Weidman Studio Theatre.
Sunstein, Frances, credits 114, 221
Swan, Nathalie, 344
Sweetser, Emily, credits 113
Szymanowski, Karol, credits 101

T

Tafarella, H., credits 61, 70, 131, 139, 147, 161
Tamiris (Helen), 2, 7, 8, 11, 28, 34 n.34, 36 n.107, 65, 75, 86, 116, 117, 265
Tanner, Virginia, 2, 106, 110; credits 111
Tansman, Alexander, credits 43, 45
Tanzer, Mildred, credits 127, 128
Tarack, Gerald, 141
Tarnower, Lydia, credits 161
"T.B.W." [pseud. critic *Brooklyn Eagle*] review 47–48
Tcherepnin, credits 120
Teachers College, Columbia University, 6, 7, 9
Terry, Peter, credits 158
Terry, Sonny, credits 120
Terry, Sonny and Oh Red, credits 112
Terry, Walter, 28, 35 n.53, **62 n.17**, 140–41, 165, 210, 211, 219, 222, **265**, **325**; reviews 28, 58, 94, 98–100, 106, 117–18, 141, 144, 183, 191, 198–99, 207, 210, 212–13, 220, 224–25
Theatre Arts Magazine, 97
Theatre Dance Company Studio, 176, 177
Thomas, Marnie, 206
Thommen, Edward, 245; credits 113
Thompson, Betty Lynd, 2, 78, 305, 308
Thompson, Jeanne, credits 216
Thompson, Randall, 89
Tillich, Paul, 162
Toch, Ernst, credits 43, 59, 70, 71
Toller, Ernst, credits 112
Torré, credits 57
Tower Theatre, Flora Stone Mather College, 166
Tracht, Mary, credits 139
Trevor, Maxine, credits 131
Triuna Island, Institute for Arts in the Theatre, 54
Trofimov, Eva, credits 156
Trowbridge, Charlotte, 224; credits 112, 119, 120, 204, 221, 227, 228
Tucker, Gregory, 1, 2, 10, 11, 19, 20, 25, 42, 49, 78, 95, 99, 117, 199, 229, 232, 240, **325**, 344; credits 43, 70, 78, 80, 88, **99–100**, 120 **177**, **179**, **228**; photo 38
Tudor, Antony, 288
Twain, Mark, 100

U

University of California, 36 n.90
University of Chicago, 7, 9, 25, 42, 69, 87, 179
University of Maryland, 36 n.90, 96
University of Minnesota, 69
University of Oregon, 7, 9, 42, 250
University of Pennsylvania, 49
University of Wisconsin, 7, 42
Urner, Patricia, credits 180

V

Vail, Edith, credits 162
van Barneveld, Elizabeth, credits 159
van Gelder, Bernice, 2, 57, 163, 167; credits 139, 161–62
Van Tuyl, Marian, 2, 14, 19, 35 n.78, 42, 46, 57, 69, 75, 77, 79, 80, 84, 133, **179**, 240, **325**; credits 45, 59, 70, 80, 131, 179
Van Tuyl, Marian. Group, 69, 70
Van Vactor, David, credits 113
Van Vleet, Phyllis, credits 58, 59
Varèse, Edgard, 17, 63, 164–68, 172, 306; credits 73, 161
Venable, Lucy, 181, 182
Verdon, Florence, credits 131
Vermont State Armory, 14, 18, 20, 23, 61, 75, 79, 80, 93, 109, 132, 142, 146, 148, 167, 266
Vermont State Symphony Orchestra, 104, 110, 113
Verne, Lily, credits 71, 139, 147
Vernet, Horace, credits 57
Vestoff-Serova, 6
Vickery, Katherine, reviews 51, 136
Villa-Lobos, Heitor, credits 43
Vitak, Albertina, reviews 176, 179, 183, 186, 187, 191, 198
Vivaldi, Antonio, credits 43
von Schadow, J. G., credits, 57

W

Waine, Allen, credits 216
Wallman, Margarete, 55
Wardell, Bertha, 307
Warwick, Florence, 78; credits 59, 79, 162
Washington Irving High School, 149, 156, 203
Waters, Elizabeth, 163, 237, 238, 240, 241; credits 59, 161–62, 184, 186; photos *Frontispiece*, 65
Wayne University, 42
Weigt, Claire I., credits 186
Weisshaus, Imre, credits 42, 59, 71
Weidman, Charles, 1, 7, 8, 10–12, 14, 15, 18, 19, 21–26, **27**, 30, 31, 36n, 41–43, 47, 49, 50, 53, 55–57, 59, 63, 64, 66, 68–70, 74, 75, 77, 79, 84, 86, 88–94, 96, 98, 105, 106, 110, 116, 117, 128, **129**, 130, 143, 144, **147–52**, 159, 181, **188–91**, 202, 219–21, 231, 233, 234, 236, 237, 240–42, 245, 251, 254–56, 260, 265, **272**, **278**, 284–85, **287**, 305, 308, **325–26**, 344; credits 43, 51, 60, 61, 70, 71, 80, 89, 111, 114, 127, 139, **147**, 180, **188**, 216; drawing 74; photos 60, 85, 111, 127, 128, 131, 182, 188, 189, 248, 272, 287; films 309, 310, 312, 313

Weidman, Charles. Dance groups, 80, 90–92, 139, 147, 149, 188; photo 188
Weidman, Charles. Men's Workshop, 55
Welch, James, credits 158
Wellesley College, 10
Wellesz, Egon, credits 70
Wells, Mary Ann, 2, 86
Wells, Mary Ann. School of Dancing, Seattle, 86
Western Reserve University, 57, 61, 166
Weston, Dorothy, photo 257
Whicher, George, 209
White, Audrey, credits 69
White, Emily, credits 158
Whithorne, Emerson, credits 101
Whitney, Mary Elizabeth, credits 158
Whitney, William C. Foundation, 34 n.46, n.53
Wiesner, Theodora, 2, 49, 110, 119; credits 70, 79, 80, 119, 131, 179
Wigman, Mary, 7, 8, 18, 51, 55, 60, 254
Wigman Schools, 55. *See also* New York Wigman School of the Dance
Wilcox, Martha, 2; credits 162, 186
Wile, Mildred, 2, 86, 238, 240, 243, 244; credits 70, 79, 88, 158
Wilker, Drusa, 78; credits 79, 119
Williams, Jean, 57, 235, 236; credits 58, 59, 70
Williams, Zoe, 86, 256; credits 87, 88, 112, 120
Williamson, Esther (later Esther Ballou), 2, 35 n.78, 69, 78, 235-38, 240, 242, 243, 273, **326**; credits 49, 58, 59, 70, 78, 80, 158, 177, 178
Willman, Theresa, credits 139
Wilsey, Colin, credits 131
Wilson, Carolyn, credits 112
Wilson, Lucretia, 163, 237, 238; credits 73, 161–62; *Frontispiece*
Wilson, Samuel, review 97
Windsperger, Lothar, credits 111
Wise, John, 193
Wolf, Olga, credits 179
Wood, David, 206
Woodford, Charles Frances, 106, 113 n.12
Woodford, Charles Humphrey, Jr., photo 274
Woolley, Isabelle Baker, 344
Workers Dance Group, 47
Workers Dance League, 47
Works Progress Administration (WPA), 26
Wright, Frank Lloyd, 281

Y

Yaddo, 13
Yaddo Festival Committee, 99
Yale Puppeteers, 78
Youshkoff, J., credits 71, 131, 161
YMHA (92nd St., New York), 158, 204
YM-YWHA (92nd St., New York), 189, 203, 206
YWCA, Hartford, 57
YWCA, Minneapolis, 78

Z

Zellmer, David, 98; credits 114, 120, 208, 221
Ziegfeld Theatre, 206
Zook, Mildred, credits 139, 180
Zwilling, Mathilde, credits 120

A note on the production of this volume
Designed by Jack Schwartz and
produced by Cathy Carpenter,
with editorial direction from Michael Sims.
Composed in 10 pt. Press Roman on an
IBM Electronic 'Selectric' Composer
by Heilan Yvette Grimes
of Dot & Line Graphics, Lexington, Mass.
Printed on 70# Patina, an acid-free paper,
and bound by Halliday Lithograph, Inc.,
of Hanover , Massachusetts.